shooter's Bible ®

FRONT COVER

The young shooter being tutored by his proud father on the front cover of this year's edition is holding a Tikka M-65 Target rifle.

BACK COVER

The handgun pictured on the back cover is Llama's new M-82 model, a double action 9mm semiautomatic pistol. The lever action rifle shown below is a Winchester Deluxe Model 71 (caliber .348). It was manufactured in 1936, about the time Stoeger's 1938 catalog was published (see p. 10). We thank the gun's owner, Joseph Lue de Grof of Navy Arms, for the use of his prized possession.

NO. 79
1988 EDITION

EDITOR:
William S. Jarrett

FIREARMS CONSULTANTS:
Frank Ercolino, Jim Lagiss
Bill Meade, Vincent A. Pestilli,
and Robert A. Scanlon

COVER PHOTOGRAPHER:
Ray Wells

DESIGN AND PRODUCTION:
Publishers Graphics
Bethel, Connecticut

TYPOGRAPHY AND COMPOSITION:
Publishers Phototype International
Carlstadt, New Jersey

PUBLISHER:
Robert E. Weise

STOEGER PUBLISHING COMPANY

Published by Stoeger Publishing Company
55 Ruta Court
South Hackensack, New Jersey 07606

Library of Congress Catalog Card No.: 63-6200

International Standard Book No.: 0080-9365

Manufactured in the United States of America

Distributed to the book trade and to the sporting goods trade by Stoeger Industries, 55 Ruta Court, South Hackensack, New Jersey 07606

In Canada, distributed to the book trade and to the sporting goods trade by Stoeger Trading Company, 169 Idema Road, Markham, Ontario, L3R 1A9.

Contents

This 79th edition of Shooter's Bible is dedicated to the memory of Horace Smith and Daniel Baird Wesson, co-founders in 1852 of the famed manufacturer of firearms which still bears their names. Brief biographies of both men appear on the opposite page.

SMITH & WESSON: PARTNERS OF INVENTIVENESS

From the beginning of their long business relationship, Horace Smith and Daniel Baird Wesson shared a dream: the development of a repeating firearm. During their individual apprenticeships, they touched shoulders with such pioneers of the industry as Samuel Colt and Oliver Winchester, and in so doing made important contributions to the creation of the Walker Colt and the lever-action system that emerged as the Winchester rifle.

But their own fame came from the development of the first practical self-contained metallic cartridge in America and the revolver from which it was to be fired. While revolutionizing the arms industry, the two men built a profitable and rewarding business venture for themselves.

Horace Smith was born on October 28, 1808, in Cheshire, Massachusetts. At the age of four, he moved with his family to Springfield, where his father, a carpenter by trade, had accepted a job at the Springfield Armory complex. Horace began his apprenticeship in 1824 at the Armory, where he was later credited with having invented several types of gun-making machines, including one used for checkering hammers.

In 1842, after some 18 years at the Armory, Smith moved to Connecticut, where he worked for, among others, a manufacturer of percussion pepperbox pistols. During this same period, he was credited with the invention of an explosive bullet used to kill whales; and in 1850 he is known to have manufactured a recently invented magazine-loaded pistol. Then, in August of 1851, Smith was issued a patent for improvements he had made on a repeating rifle invented by Walter Hunt. The following year he moved to Worcester, Massachusetts, Daniel Wesson's hometown, and there the two men met probably for the first time. They formed their first business partnership in 1852, and it endured off and on for more than 20 years. Horace Smith died on

January 14, 1893, at the age of 84, leaving behind a legacy rich in the lore of America's firearms industry.

His longtime partner, Daniel Baird Wesson, was born on May 18, 1825, in Worcester. Wesson's older brother, Edwin, became famous as an excellent shot and maker of highly accurate target rifles, and it was his influence that undoubtedly kindled young Daniel's strong interest in guns. In fact, Daniel served his apprenticeship under Edwin, turning out Wesson target rifles. Other important influences in Wesson's career were Samuel Colt, on whose behalf the Wesson brothers manufactured 1,000 barrels for Colt's large pistol, and Captain Samuel Walker of the U.S. Army.

In the spring of 1848, Daniel and Edwin pulled up stakes and moved their gun shop to Hartford, Connecticut, and a few months later Daniel was released from his apprenticeship. But just as Wesson's career was about to blossom, his brother Edwin died suddenly. Daniel was forced to borrow heavily to keep the business going, but in the end the company was sold at public auction, whereupon Wesson joined the newly formed Massachusetts Arms Company under Thomas Warner.

Eventually, Daniel returned to Worcester in search of work, and there he met his future partner. By 1856, the firm of Smith & Wesson was firmly established in nearby Springfield and the future was theirs. Wesson devoted his time and energy to the company until his death on August 4, 1906. "No thing of importance will come about without effort," he had once written. Surely his life was an accurate reflection of that noble axiom.

[Editor's Note: The biographical material above has been excerpted from History of Smith & Wesson *by Roy G. Jinks (Beinfeld Publishing Inc., 1977).]*

FOREWORD

This year's production of *Shooter's Bible*—our 79th edition—is dedicated to Horace Smith and Daniel Wesson, co-founders in 1852 of the famous gun manufacturer that still proudly bears their names.

You'll notice a singular departure this year from our usual format: for the first time ever, we've added color to our pages! When we decided to reproduce several pages of Stoeger's 1938 catalog in this year's edition, it seemed only natural that we reprint them in a sepia tone in order to create the kind of nostalgic mood this feature article calls for. Turn to p. 10 and you'll understand better what we mean.

There's another interesting example of gun history starting on p. 64: Dr. Jim Casada's article on Thomas ("Mr. Sam") Samworth, the legendary editor and publisher of gun books, many of them now considered classics in their field. History buffs will also enjoy Jim Cobb's informative piece on L.C. Smith and his famous shotgun.

The modern era is equally well represented in the article section, starting off with a chapter taken from John Donnelly's new, one-of-a-kind book, *Handloader's Manual of Cartridge Conversions*. The author has used his considerable talents and computer wizardry to create more than 1000 conversions. Now that the computer age has solidly entered the shooter's world, we've added another piece by Ralph Quinn on *Computer Riflery*, a fascinating topic about which all shooters should at least be aware.

Our article section this year also includes pieces by Stan Trzoniec on *Small Game Hunting*, Don Lewis on *Shotgun Nomenclature*, and Toby Bridges on the *Modern Muzzleloader*.

As always, we've gathered together in the catalog section the latest information on guns, sights and scopes, ammo, reloading and books about the shooter's world. Among the new names we've added for 1988 are Uberti, Gamba, Merkel, Diarm, American Industries, Brno, B-Square, Excam, Hatfield and Hammerli.

We remain dedicated to providing you with the most accurate, up-to-date facts about your favorite subject. And, as this 79th edition goes *to bed*, we look forward to your comments, pro and con.

William S. Jarrett
Editor

Articles

Licensed by United States
Dept. of State Office of
Arms and Munitions Control
License No. 18

STOEGER'S
CATALOG AND HANDBOOK

ARMS AND AMMUNITION
AMERICAN AND IMPORTED

GUN ACCESSORIES AND REPAIR PARTS

CATALOG
No 30

A. F. STOEGER INC.
AMERICA'S GREAT GUN HOUSE
507 FIFTH AVENUE AT 42nd ST.
NEW YORK N.Y.

PRICE
50 CENTS

VANDERBILT 3-3507

CABLE STOEGER NEW YORK

FIFTY YEARS AGO IN SHOOTER'S BIBLE

Editor's Note: While browsing through a copy of A.F. Stoeger's 1938 catalog (which later evolved into what is now *Shooter's Bible*), it occurred to us that our readers might like to see what guns were available half a century ago——what they looked like, how much they cost, and so forth. We've selected a representative sampling of rifles from our old catalog as the first in what we suspect will become a recurring series in future editions of *Shooter's Bible*, including handguns, shotguns, and other firearms popular in the 1930's. The following pages are reprinted exactly as they appeared in our 1938 catalog. We hope you enjoy this nostalgic look at the past. And for those who insist that rifles haven't really changed much over the years, what follows should be a real eye opener!

WINCHESTER HIGH POWER BOLT ACTION RIFLES

MODEL 70
STANDARD GRADE

Model 70 Bolt Action Repeating Rifle—Standard Grade

For .22 Hornet, .250-3000 Savage, .270 Winchester, .30 Gov't '06, 7 m/m, Super Speed .257 Winchester Roberts, .375 H and H Magnum, Super Speed .220 Winchester Swift, or .300 H and H Magnum.

The highest development in bolt action sporting rifles in a series of calibers to cover a wide variety of big game hunting. Six shot repeater. Standard rifle has 24 inch round tapered Winchester Proof Steel barrel with integral ramp base and quick detachable sight cover .220 Winchester Swift and .300 H and H Magnum in 26 inch only. One piece stock of selected American black walnut with checkered pistol grip, checkered steel butt plate and finely formed semi-beavertail checkered forearm. Stock dimensions—measured from point blank line of sight—

Length of Pull .... 13½"
Drop at Comb .... 1⅝"
Drop at Heel .... 2⅝"

Speed lock. New design bolt stop operating independently of trigger. Fast handling bolt handle designed to clear any standard telescope sight. New fast-operating 3-position safety lock operating horizontally. Staggered box type magazine with hinged floor plate for easy unloading and cleaning. Lyman 31-W gold bead front sight on ramp and Winchester 22-G open sporting rear sight. Screw holes for telescope sight blocks. Solid frame only. Weight about 8 lbs.

Price $61.25

Model 70 Bolt Action Repeating Rifle With 20 Inch Round Barrel

For .22 Hornet, .250-3000 Savage, .270 Winchester, .30 Gov't '06, 7 m/m or Super Speed, .257 Winchester Roberts. Other specifications same as standard Model 70 rifle. Weight about 7½ lb.

Price $61.25

MODEL 70
STANDARD GRADE
WITH LYMAN WJS

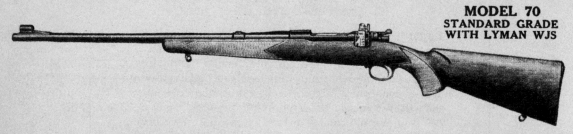

Model 70 Bolt Action Repeating Rifle With Lyman 48 WJS Receiver Sight

Rifle same as standard rifle described above except with Lyman 48 WJS Micrometer Wind Gauge Receiver Sight in place of Winchester 22-G open sporting rear sight.

Price $74.25

Model 70 Bolt Action Repeating Rifle With 20 Inch Round Barrel and Lyman 48 WJS Receiver Sight

Rifle same as Model 70 Rifle with 20 inch round barrel except Lyman 48 WJS Micrometer Wind Gauge Receiver Sight in place of Winchester 22-G open sporting rear sight.

Price $74.25

MODEL 70
STANDARD GRADE
WITH LYMAN 57

Model 70 Bolt Action Repeating Rifle With Lyman 57 W Receiver Sight

Rifle same as standard rifle described above except with Lyman 57 W Micrometer Wind Gauge Receiver Sight in place of Winchester 22-G open sporting rear sight.

Price $67.25

Model 70 Bolt Action Repeating Rifle With 20 Inch Round Barrel and Lyman 57 W Receiver Sight

Rifle same as Model 70 Rifle with 20 inch round barrel except Lyman 57 W Micrometer Wind Gauge Receiver Sight in place of Winchester 22-G open sporting rear sight.

Price $67.25

WINCHESTER LEVER ACTION RIFLES

MODEL 71
FOR BIG GAME HUNTING

The new Winchester Model 71 universal big-game rifle, with new 86 Golden Jubilee action and shooting the new Super Speed .348 Winchester cartridge, is the world's latest and greatest achievement in a sporting rifle of this handy, dependable and popular type. With its new modern high-efficiency hunting cartridge, developed exclusively for it and furnished with bullets in a choice of two weights, suited for any and all big game on the American continent. Besides important new ballistic superiority, this new Winchester has many other new advantages commending it to you for better success in bringing down big game. Together, your rifle and its cartridge will carry out every promise implied by the exceptional circumstances of their combined development and final production—the modern equivalent of the wonderfully efficient lever-action Winchester and cartridge which preceded them by a span of fifty years—the great Model 86 and black-powder .45-70. Here, in detail, are the facts concerning Model 71 which you wish to know:

Entirely new caliber, which is .348, with 150-gr. bullet giving 2920 f.s. muzzle velocity and 2840 f.p. muzzle energy; with 200-gr. bullet giving muzzle velocity of 2535 f.s. and muzzle energy of 2860 f.p. A new Winchester development with a special new Winchester Super Speed cartridge produced exclusively for this new rifle. The cartridge in both bullet weights being furnished with soft-point bullet, smokeless powder and Winchester Staynless non-corrosive, non-mercuric priming. For comparative ballistics see ballistics section.

SPECIFICATIONS

Caliber, Super Speed .348 Winchester. Barrel 20″ or 24″, round tapered; Gold bead front sight on ramp with removable cover; choice of peep or open rear sight, both quick-adjustable. Solid frame (not takedown). Lever action. Tubular magazine, four shots in magazine with one in chamber makes five-shot repeater. Shotgun butt-stock with pistol grip; semi-beavertail fore-end; pistol grip and fore-end checkered. Furnished with 1-inch N.R.A. leather gunsling attached by quick-detachable bow swivels. Weight about 8 lbs. Also furnished without checkering on stock and fore-end, without pistol-grip cap and without sling and swivels, at proportionate reduction in price.

Model 71 Rifle with Lyman No. 31W front sight and Winchester 22K sporting rear sight.......................................$57.75
Model 71 Rifle with Lyman No. 31W front sight and Winchester 98A peep sight, as illustrated............................. 57.75
Model 71 Rifle without checkering, gun sling and swivels with Winchester 22K sporting rear sight........................... 49.95
Model 71 Rifle without checkering, gun sling and swivels with Winchester 98A peep sight................................. 49.95

MODEL 94 CARBINE
SOLID FRAME

AMERICA'S FAVORITE DEER RIFLE

FOR .30 (.30-30) WINCHESTER OR .32 WIN. SPECIAL C. F. CARTRIDGES

Model 94 has been for over forty years one of the famous Winchester lever action arms. It is recommended in both calibers for deer and similar game.

The mechanism is simple, accurate and reliable. The breech bolt, operated by a finger lever, is locked by a vertical locking block, which shows on the top of the gun when closed and covers the whole rear of the breech bolt. The firing pin is positively withdrawn at the first opening motion, and the trigger locked until the parts are again in firing position. The magazine is filled while the gun is closed, through the spring cover at the side.

Model 94 Carbine is both calibers furnished to standard specifications only.

SPECIFICATIONS

BARREL—20 inch round with ramp front sight base.

STOCK—Straight grip carbine type stock and forearm. Steel carbine butt plate.

SIGHTS—Lyman gold bead front sight mounted on ramp with sight cover. Adjustable carbine rear.

MAGAZINE—Full Magazine. Holds six shots which, with one in the chamber, makes carbine a seven shot repeater.

WEIGHT—About 6¼ pounds.

Price $30.00

MODEL 65
SOLID FRAME

FOR SMALL AND MEDIUM SIZED GAME

SHOOTS .25-20 or .32 (.32-20) Winchester Center Fire Cartridges

An easy-to-carry, fast-handling, reliable rifle styled for quick, accurate shooting. In .32 popular for varmints treed by dogs and for deer at short range. In .25-20 very satisfactory for woodchucks or marmots, foxes, coyotes, bobcats, turkeys, sometimes geese—according to situation and shooting regulations. A real light-weight, with new specially designed N.R.A. type shotgun stock with pistol grip, and gracefully tapered 22-inch round barrel, having ramp front sight base. Stock and forearm of walnut. A development of the well-known Winchester Model 92—the choice of over a million hunters. Lighter trigger pull. New sights—Lyman Gold Bead 31W front; Winchester 22H Rocky Mountain adjustable rear. Half-magazines only—7 shots. One in the chamber makes this an eight-shot repeater. Weight about 6½ pounds. Solid frame only.

Price $39.75

WINCHESTER BOLT ACTION SMALL BORE .22 RIFLES
(WITH AND WITHOUT TELESCOPE)

MODEL 67
TAKEDOWN—SINGLE SHOT

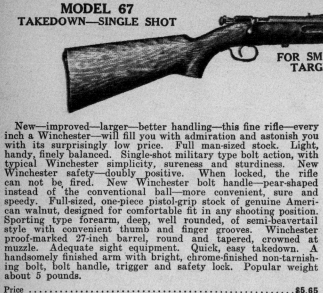

FOR SMALL GAME AND TARGET SHOOTING

Shoots .22 Short, .22 Long and .22 Long Rifle rim fire cartridges interchangeably. Regular or Super-Speed. Also chambered for .22 W.R.F. only

SPECIFICATIONS
1. 27-inch round, tapered Winchester proof-marked barrel—precision drilled, reamed and rifled for Winchester accuracy—crowned at muzzle.
2. Sporting rear sight with sliding elevator.
3. Sporting bead front sight—with bright, non-tarnishing alloy bead.
4. Military firing-pin safety lock—safe, sure. When locked the erect thumb lever tells instantly, standing up in line of vision.
5. Instantly removable bolt. No extra parts to drop or lose. Carry it in your pocket or pack, others can't use your rifle in your absence. At home, for same precaution lock it in a drawer.
6. New design bolt handle—pear-shaped, bright chrome finish. Fits hand better, works sure and fast.
7. Bolt is short and compact; aids accuracy, works faster, lessens vibration. Removed, gives free access for cleaning bore.
8. New safety firing pin never touches cartridge except when trigger is pulled.
9. Ejector automatic, positive, throws empty cartridge clear of rifle.
10. Man-sized stock of real walnut, with full pistol grip.
11. Deep, wide, semi-beavertail forearm, non-slip thumb-and-finger grooves.
12. Shotgun type non-skid composition butt plate.
13. Light yet steady, evenly balanced weight of about 5 pounds.
14. Take-down screw placed behind balance, out of the way of shooter's hand.

New—improved—larger—better handling—this fine rifle—every inch a Winchester—will fill you with admiration and astonish you with its surprisingly low price. Full man-sized stock. Light, handy, finely balanced. Single-shot military type bolt action, with typical Winchester simplicity, sureness and sturdiness. New Winchester safety—doubly positive. When locked, the rifle can not be fired. New Winchester bolt handle—pear-shaped instead of the conventional ball—more convenient, sure and speedy. Full-sized, one-piece pistol-grip stock of genuine American walnut, designed for comfortable fit in any shooting position. Sporting type forearm, deep, well rounded, of semi-beavertail style with convenient thumb and finger grooves. Winchester proof-marked 27-inch barrel, round and tapered, crowned at muzzle. Adequate sight equipment. Quick, easy takedown. A handsomely finished arm with bright, chrome-finished non-tarnishing bolt, bolt handle, trigger and safety lock. Popular weight about 5 pounds.

Price $5.65

MODEL 67 WITH TELESCOPE SIGHT
The Model 67 may be had with factory mounted telescope sight bases and either 2¾ X or 5 X Winchester telescope. Same scope illustrated on Model 677 on preceding page, but slightly higher mounts to clear iron sights.

Model 67, Complete with 2¾ X Scope, price $11.00
Model 67, Complete with 5 X Scope, price 12.50

MODEL 68
TAKEDOWN—SINGLE SHOT

FOR TARGET SHOOTING AND SMALL GAME

Shoots .22 Short, Long and Long Rifle Cartridges. Also chambered for .22 W.R.F. only.

Model 68 has all of the new features of the Model 67 and in addition is equipped with a combination of target sights unequalled in a rifle in this grade.

This new Winchester has a ramp-base front sight with sight cover and a unique peep rear sight with graduated click adjustments for both elevation and windage.

To adjust Model 68 rear sight—to raise sight, turn the notched disc to the right the necessary number of clicks. To adjust for windage, push the pointer to the right or left as required.

Model 68 is fitted with a positive extractor which withdraws the fired shell and throws it clear of the rifle.

Price $6.40

MODEL 68 WITH TELESCOPE SIGHT
The Model 68 may be had with factory mounted telescope sight bases and Winchester 5 X Scope only. See preceding page for type of scope shown on Model 677.

Model 68, Complete with 5 X Scope, price $13.25

MODEL 69 BOLT ACTION REPEATING RIFLE
BOX MAGAZINE—TAKE-DOWN

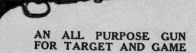

AN ALL PURPOSE GUN FOR TARGET AND GAME

SHOOTS .22 Short, .22 Long and .22 Long Rifle Rim Fire Cartridges

Rifle, 25" round tapered barrel, with crowned muzzle, sporting type walnut pistol grip stock, semi-beavertail fore-end, Winchester 97-A front sight fitted with ramp and sight cover and Winchester 96-B peep rear sight. New design pear shaped bolt handle. Composition butt plate $11.95

Rifle, as above, with Winchester 32-B Open Sight in place of 96-B peep rear sight $11.50
Extra 5-cartridge magazine 1.00
Extra 10-cartridge magazine 1.25

MODEL 69 WITH TELESCOPE SIGHT
The Model 69 may be had with factory mounted telescope sight bases and either 2¾ X or 5 X Winchester telescope. Same telescope as shown on Model 697 on preceding page, but slightly higher mounts to clear iron sights.

Model 69, Peep Sights, Complete with 2¾ X Telescope, price $17.30
Model 69, Peep Sights, Complete with 5 X Telescope, price 18.80
Model 69, Open Sights, Complete with 2¾ X Telescope, price 16.85
Model 69, Open Sights, Complete with 5 X Telescope, price 18.35

REMINGTON AUTOMATIC AND REPEATING RIFLES
REMINGTON .22 CAL. RIFLES WITH TELESCOPE

With Micrometer Click Mount
Especially Adapted to Remington .22 Caliber Rifles

This illustration shows the "Sportmaster"—Remington No. 341P Grade rifle with Weaver No. 344 telescope mounted. Note how telescope does not interfere with use of Remington peep sights. It is equally well adapted to the "Targetmaster" Model 41, "Speedmaster" Model 241, and "Fieldmaster" Model 121 Slide Action Repeater. Weight of telescope, about 10½ ounces; length, 12½ inches.

Weaver No. 344 Telescope, when ordered with rifles, extra.........**$8.25**

MODEL 341P WITH LYMAN EXPERT SCOPE, AS ILLUSTRATED $25.20

NOTE:—Rifles ordered with this Weaver scope will be drilled and tapped for it. The scope will be packed, detached, in the same carton with the rifle and may easily be attached by means of two thumb screws.

Weaver No. 344 Telescope, when ordered without rifles, extra......**$8.00**
Drilling and tapping, when scope is not ordered, extra.............**.25**

"SPEEDMASTER" Model 241
TAKE DOWN

For Small Game
For Plinking

SHOOTS .22 SHORT ONLY OR .22 LONG RIFLE ONLY, ORDINARY OR HI-SPEED

If YOU seek a light, graceful, fast-shooting, hard-hitting rifle for all 'round use—ridding the world of vermin pests, for "plinking" or for small game in season—the Model 241 Autoloader is "made to order" for you.

It fires as fast as you can work your trigger finger. It is operated by the recoil which ejects the empty cartridge, puts in a new one and cocks the action. Autoloading—but reliable.

Accuracy? All you'd expect of a Remington. Finest barrels, rifled the Remington way; good sighting equipment; careful fitting of parts and that silky smooth action to rattle out the shots without disturbing your aim. No other .22 repeater can give such results.

Convenience? Model 241 takes down in a jiffy and stores in suitcase or dufflebag; the breech block removes for cleaning without tools; you can buy ammunition for the Model 241 at any crossroad store.

Model 241SA is chambered for the regular or Hi-Speed .22 Short; the

Model 241LA for regular or high speed .22 Long Rifle cartridges. Not interchangeable. The magazine is in the stock and is easily loaded.

SPECIFICATIONS OF NO. 241 STANDARD GRADE

Hammerless, take-down, solid breech; 24 inch round, gracefully tapered barrel. Full-sized half pistol grip and semi-beavertail fore-end of genuine American walnut. Shotgun style steel butt plate, corrugated to prevent slipping. Chambered for .22 Short cartridge only or .22 Long Rifle cartridge only. Hi-Speed and regular. (When ordering specifically mention caliber wanted, either .22 Short or Long Rifle). .22 Short magazine holds 15 cartridges. .22 Long Rifle magazine holds 10 cartridges. Step adjustable sporting rear sight. White metal bead front sight. Length over-all 41½ inches. Length taken down 24 inches. Weight about 6 pounds.

No. 241SA or 241LA. "Standard" Grade **$31.45**
No. 241SC or 241LC. "Special" Grade 50.75
No. 241SD or 241LD. "Peerless" Grade 85.95
No. 241SE or 241LE. "Expert" Grade 122.25
No. 241SF or 241LF. "Premier" Grade 147.55

"FIELDMASTER" Model 121
TAKE DOWN

MOST MODERN SLIDE-ACTION .22 REPEATING RIFLE
Made for .22 Short, .22 Long, .22 Long Rifle or .22 Rem. Spec. Cartridges
• New Grooved Semi-Beavertail Fore-End • New Shotgun Style Butt Plate
• New Half-Pistol Grip Stock • Increased Magazine Capacity • Longer,
Heavier Barrel • Easy Takedown • Excellent Accuracy • Solid Safety
Breech

Always a step ahead in gun design. Remington offers the "FIELDMASTER" with its long, semi-beavertail fore-end, properly shaped pistol grip, and shotgun style butt plate. These features permit quick aiming, fast firing, and straight shooting from any position. The fore-end fits man or boy and is grooved to prevent slipping. The barrel is longer, heavier and more accurate. With magazine capacity greatly increased the "FIELD-MASTER" holds 20 Short, 15 Long or 14 Long rifle cartridges which may be used interchangeably without adjustment. Rifles especially chambered for the .22 Rem. Special Cartridge have a

12 shot magazine capacity. Its easy takedown feature is popular everywhere for it packs conveniently in a suitcase. A cross bolt safety available for either left or right handed shooters is easily operated with the trigger finger. The sights are white metal bead front and step adjustable rear. For all-round easy handling, light weight, straight and fast shooting the "FIELDMASTER" is in a class by itself.

SPECIFICATIONS

The "FIELDMASTER" Model 121A

"Standard" Grade. Takedown, hammerless, solid breech; 24-inch round barrel; American walnut pistol grip stock with shotgun style steel butt plate; grooved semi-beavertail fore-end; chambered for .22 Short, Long and Long Rifle cartridges which may be used interchangeably without adjustment. Magazine holds 20 Short, 15 Long or 14 Long Rifle Cartridges. Rear sight with adjustable step for elevation; white metal bead front sight; length taken down 27½ inches. Weight, about 6 pounds.

MODEL 121S—"Remington Special" Grade. Same as 121A, except it is chambered for .22 Rem. Special (.22 W.R.F.) cartridges only. Magazine holds 12 cartridges.

No. 121A "Standard" Grade **$24.95**
No. 121S "Remington Special" Grade 24.95
No. 121D "Peerless" Grade 79.45
No. 121E "Expert" Grade 115.75
No. 121F "Premier" Grade 141.00

REMINGTON BOLT ACTION RIFLES

THE "RANGEMASTER"

Weight about 12 lbs.

MODEL 37
CAL. .22

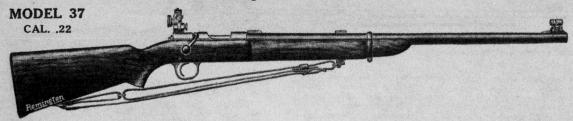

The Remington Model 37, is the latest development of a long awaited target rifle. It is the first real target rifle—complete with no extras further required to purchase, as the factory has seen to it that the shooter will get a rifle for the first time furnished with micrometer and globe sight, sling, and adjustable swivel. The following features stand out on this rifle.

(1) Heavy barrel, 28" rifled by a special Remington process, and carefully selected for extreme accuracy making it the most accurate ever produced. It is double counter-sunk at the muzzle for protection, and chambered so that loaded cartridges may be removed without leaving the bullet in the barrel. The barrel is full floating, and its accuracy is not affected by changes in temperature or sling tension.

(2) The new specially designed micrometer rear sight for the Model 37 with ¼ minute clicks for windage and elevation comes with a six hole eye piece permanently attached, and is mounted on a block similar to a telescope block, and can be instantly removed. Due to its rugged construction it can be replaced without changing the point of impact.

(3) Front Sight is the well known Redfield Globe sight and can be removed from the special matted ramp by turning locking nut. It includes a full set of inserts. The line of sight with either iron sights or telescope is identically the same, thus eliminating the necessity for a special cheek piece.

(4) The new Remington target stock especially designed for this new rifle comes with, full comb stock, pistol grip, semi-beaver tail fore-end, and sharp checkered steel butt plate.

(5) Great care has been given to the trigger pull. It is adjustable by a small set screw conveniently located in the trigger controlling the adjustment. The let-off is sharp and crisp without drag or creep. By holding the trigger all the way to the rear the bolt is easily removed for cleaning.

(6) Each rifle is supplied with a five shot magazine made with milled steel (not a stamping) feeding the cartridges smoothly and positively. Also, an additional dummy magazine with special loading platform for single loading which protects the bullet from shaving is supplied without extra charge.

(7) A unique feature of the Model 37 is the adjustable front swivel and Carney sling. This allows placing the swivel correctly for the shooter whether he has long or short arms.

Model 37, Complete **$69.95**

MODEL 30A AND 30R

For Big Game   Caliber U. S. 30/06 Springfield Only

Unsurpassed accuracy—the result of carefully selected barrels, bored and rifled to exact standards; superb balance and beauty of line—the outcome of traditional Remington engineering and craftsmanship; dependable, smooth working mechanism—due to Remington precision production and absolute synchronization of working parts.

OUTSTANDING FEATURES OF THE MODEL 30 RIFLE

When bolt is pulled back it is stopped by a bolt stop—not on the sear or trigger as in most other bolt action rifles. Detachable magazine bottom for cleaning. Safety is positive and conveniently located for quick operation. Durable American walnut stock and fore-end, both checkered. Floating barrel to give maximum accuracy. Barrel is not attached to fore-stock. Uplift of bolt permits proper fitting of telescope.

No. 30A—"Standard" Grade, 22-inch barrel **$56.95**
No. 30R—"Carbine," 20-inch barrel (not checkered) 51.95

SPECIFICATIONS 30A

No. 30A "Standard" Grade, 22-inch barrel; American walnut stock, half pistol grip and fore-end finely checkered. Rifle style steel butt plate, grooved to prevent slipping. Rifle cocks on opening movement of bolt. Top of receiver matted. Short, snappy, light, single trigger pull. Thumb-operated safety. Buckhorn adjustable rear sight with gold bead front sight. Receiver drilled and tapped for Lyman No. 48R micrometer windgauge sight. Magazine holds 5 cartridges. Length over all 42¾ inches. Weight, about 7¼ pounds.

SPECIFICATIONS 30R

No. 30R Carbine. Same as 30A "Standard" Grade except that barrel is 20 inches long. Stock furnished without checkering. Shotgun style steel butt plate. Weight, about 7 pounds.

⅞-inch Sling Strap (leather, Whelen type); with hooks, extra.....**$2.00**
⅞-inch Sling Strap (leather, Whelen type); with quick release swivels, extra 4.40

MODEL 30SL

For Big Game   MADE IN 30/06 SPRINGFIELD AND .257 REMINGTON-ROBERTS (.25 ROBERTS) CALIBERS WITH 24-INCH BARREL

Note the design of stock and fore-end of Model 30S embodying the best ideas of many of America's foremost sportsmen; the full pistol grip, capped; the double trigger pull of military type; the matted front sight ramp, with removable guard; the modern Lyman receiver sight; the steel butt plate; the handsome checkering and the facility with which telescope can be mounted and used.

See Stoeger's Peerless stocks and sporting telescopes for Model 30 Rifles.

SPECIFICATIONS 30S

Model 30S "Special" Grade; made in .30 Springfield '06, and .257 Remington-Roberts (.25 Roberts) calibers with 24-inch barrel. Carefully bored and rifled for extreme accuracy; special high comb stock of American walnut, checkered; long, full forestock; steel butt plate; Lyman No. 48 windgauge receiver full pistol grip with rubber cap; shotgun style sight; gold bead front sight mounted on a matted ramp with removable guard; double trigger pull of the military type (option of single pull); wide screw eyes for quick release swivels (option of regular screw eyes). Rifle cocks on opening movement of bolt. Top of receiver matted. Thumb-operated safety. Magazine holds 5 cartridges. Weight, about 8 pounds.

No. 30SL—"Special" Grade with Lyman No. 48 sight......................**$69.95**
No. 30SR—"Special" Grade with Redfield No. 102R receiver sight 61.90
No. 30SX—"Special" Grade without receiver sight but with step adjustable open rear sight on barrel 56.95
⅞-inch Sling Strap (leather, Whelen type); with hooks, extra................... 2.00
⅞-inch Sling Strap (leather, Whelen type); with quick release swivels, extra........ 4.40

©   **SEE INSIDE FRONT COVER "HOW TO ORDER"**

SAVAGE MODEL 99 HIGH POWER RIFLES

MODEL 99-H CARBINE

THE FAVORITE SADDLE RIFLE

CALIBERS: .30-30, .303 and .250-3000

Model 99-H Carbine—Solid Frame. 20-inch special medium weight barrel. Walnut carbine stock and forearm. Steel butt plate. Adjustable semi-buckhorn rear sight and bead front sight. Weight 6½ pounds. Matted trigger.

The Savage Carbine has been designed for men who require a compact, sturdy, well-balanced rifle, for use in the saddle or in thickly timbered country. A rifle that is light and fast in action, but which packs a blow with sufficient power for big game.

Note its clean-cut lines, not an extra ounce of weight anywhere, and it holds firm and steady. Its barrel is made of the same "Hi-Pressure" steel that goes into all other Savage Model 99 barrels and is rifled and chambered in accordance with the exact Savage standards. These features combine to make this rifle admirably suited for guides, trappers and sportsmen desiring a sturdy rifle for rough, exacting service at a low price.
Model 99-H Carbine—solid frame..........................$44.25

MODEL 99-R

THE IDEAL DEER RIFLE

CALIBERS: .250-3000 and .303 with 22 in. barrel. .300 with 24 in. barrel.

Model 99-R—Solid Frame. Tapered medium weight round barrel. Raised ramp front sight base. Special large stock and forearm of selected walnut, oil finish, corrugated steel butt plate of

shotgun design. Full pistol grip stock. Fine checkering on grip and forearm. Adjustable Semi-Buckhorn rear sight and gold bead front sight. Matted trigger. Weight about 7¼ pounds.

The Model 99-R has been designed to meet the demands of expert riflemen requiring a solid frame rifle of extreme accuracy. An ideal deer rifle.
Model 99-R, solid frame...............................$53.50

MODEL 99-RS

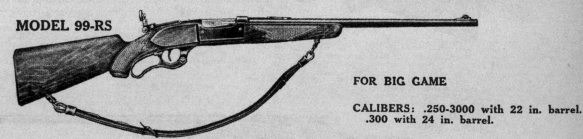

FOR BIG GAME

CALIBERS: .250-3000 with 22 in. barrel. .300 with 24 in. barrel.

Model 99-RS. Solid Frame. Same specifications as Model 99-R with following refinements: Lyman windgauge and elevation adjustment rear peep sight, Lyman folding leaf middle and gold bead front sight. Also equipped with ⅞ inch combined adjustable leather sling and carrying strap with quick release swivels and screw studs. Weight about 7½ pounds.

The Model 99-RS is the same rifle as the Model 99-R, with additional equipment consisting of special sights, with accurate windage and elevation adjustments and a sling strap, which is provided for ease in carrying and as an aid to steady holding.

Model 99-RS, solid frame...............................$64.00

MODEL 99-K

FOR BIG GAME

CALIBERS: .22 Hi-Power, .30-30, .303 and .250-3000 with 22 inch barrel. .300 with 24 inch barrel.

Model 99-K—Take-down. Same specifications as Model 99-G with following refinements: Selected American walnut stock and forearm—special fancy hand checkering on forearm, panels and

grip. Receiver and barrel artistically engraved. Action carefully fitted and stoned. Lyman rear peep sight, folding middle sight and gold bead front sight. Matted trigger.

The Model 99-K is our finest grade rifle and is a beautiful specimen of the gunmaker's art. The checkering and engraving are unusually attractive.
Model 99-K, Takedown $78.75

SAVAGE SMALL BORE .22 CALIBER RIFLES

MODEL 19
TARGET RIFLE

FOR TARGET SHOOTING & SMALL GAME

CALIBERS: .22 Long Rifle and .22 Hornet

Model 19—.22 caliber repeating bolt action rifle (new design). Caliber—.22 long rifle, rimfire, suitable for use with all "high-speed" and "regular" cartridges. Stock—one-piece, oil finished, walnut, pistol grip with beaver-tail forearm full 2 inches wide, checkered steel butt plate. Drop at heel 1⅞ inches, drop at comb 1⅝ inches, length 13½ inches, butt plate 1⅝ inches wide, 5⅛ inches long, over all length stock 32 inches. Barrel—heavy 25-inch barrel, 30½ inches over all sighting radius. Magazine—5-shot, curved, detachable; positive loading; a spring snap lock at rear functions easily and locks securely. Bolt action—2 locking lugs. New high-speed lock—the speed of the new lock is less than 2/1000 of a second. Open loading port—the large loading port will be appreciated whenever rifle is used in single shot firing. Sights—New design, No. 15 Savage aperture extension rear sight with click adjustments for elevation and windage. Drilled

for telescope sight blocks. Weight—about 8 pounds. Swivels—for 1¼-inch sling strap; front swivel 16½ inches forward of trigger.

Model 19-L—.22 long rifle. Standard rifle as above except with Lyman No. 48-Y micrometer rear sight and No. 17-A hooded front sight.

Model 19-H—.22 Hornet. Same sights, stock and barrel specifications as standard Model 19. Barrel is high-pressure smokeless steel. Loading port, magazine and bolt mechanism same as Model 23-D. Chambered for the sensational Hornet Cartridge. Barrel drilled for telescope sight blocks. The straight stock makes this the ideal arm to equip with telescope for target practice or precise small game and vermin shooting.

Model 19—target rifle, .22 long rifle $36.00
Model 19-L—target rifle, .22 long rifle 48.25
Model 19-H—target rifle, .22 Hornet 42.50

MODEL 23AA
GAME RIFLE

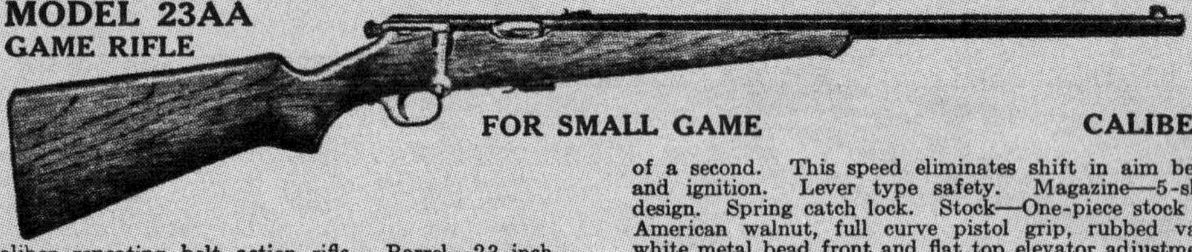

FOR SMALL GAME

CALIBER: .22 Long Rifle

Model 23AA—.22 caliber repeating bolt action rifle. Barrel—23-inch round, tapered. Chambered for .22 short, .22 long and .22 long rifle, regular or high speed cartridges. Action—polished bolt, double locking lugs. New high-speed lock—the speed of the new lock is less than 2-1000

of a second. This speed eliminates shift in aim between release of trigger and ignition. Lever type safety. Magazine—5-shot, detachable, curved design. Spring catch lock. Stock—One-piece stock and forearm of selected American walnut, full curve pistol grip, rubbed varnish finish. Sights—white metal bead front and flat top elevator adjustment rear sight. Receiver tapped for new No. 10 Savage aperture rear sight. Weight—about 6 pounds.

Model 23-AA—.22 caliber Sporter Rifle $21.50

MODEL 3
GAME RIFLE

FOR SMALL GAME

CALIBER: .22 Long Rifle

Model 3—.22 caliber bolt action single shot rifle, take-down. Barrel—26-inch round, tapered. Chambered for .22 short, long and .22 long rifle, regular or high-speed cartridges. Action—chromium plated bolt and trigger. Stock—one-piece full pistol grip stock and large forearm of selected walnut, finger grooves in forearm, steel butt plate 1⅜ x 4½ inches. Forearm 1⅜ inches wide at take-down screw, stock length 28¼ inches. Overall length 43½ inches. Sights—gold bead front sight and adjustable flat

top rear sight. Receiver drilled and tapped for No. 55 Lyman rear peep sight. Weight—about 4½ pounds.
Model 3—single shot bolt action rifle $5.65
Model 3-S—Specifications—Same as Model 3 Rifle shown above, except equipped with hooded front sight with 3 interchangeable inserts and receiver rear peep sight; with elevation and windage adjustments and sighting disc with three sizes of aperture openings—large, medium and small.
Price $6.40
Model 3-ST—Target—Same as 3-S, equipped with ⅞ inch sling strap and sling loops and studs.
Price $8.40

MODEL 4
GAME RIFLE

FOR SMALL GAME

CALIBER: .22 Long Rifle

Model 4—.22 caliber bolt action repeating rifle, take-down. Barrel—tapered, round, 24-inch, with crowned muzzle, for .22 long rifle, .22 long or .22 short, regular or high-speed cartridges, 5-shot detachable clip magazine. Action—all parts finely polished, self-cocking, bolt action with independent safety, chromium plated bolt and trigger. Stock—one-piece full pistol grip stock and large forearm of selected walnut, finger grooves in

forearm, steel butt plate. Sights—gold bead front and sporting rear with elevation adjustment. Receiver drilled and tapped for No. 55 Lyman receiver sight. Weight—about 5½ pounds.
Model 4—bolt action repeating rifle $11.00
Model 5—Same as Model 4, but with tubular magazine. Price.... 13.35
Model 4-S—Specifications—Same as Model 4 Rifle shown above, except equipped with hooded front sight with 3 interchangeable inserts and receiver rear peep sight; with elevation and windage adjustments and sighting disc with three sizes of aperture openings—large, medium and small.
Price $11.75
Extra Magazine .... .65
Model 5S—Same as Model 4S, but with tubular magazine. Price.. 14.10

MODEL 29

FOR SMALL GAME

CALIBER: .22 Long Rifle

Model 29—.22 caliber hammerless, slide forearm action repeating rifle. Caliber—chambered for .22 long rifle rim fire cartridges. Will also function and shoot without adjustment, .22 long or .22 short rim fire cartridges. Suitable for use with either high-speed or regular cartridges. Barrel—24 in. Octagon. Stock—Selected Walnut stock, full pistol grip checkered; extra long walnut forearm checkered. Magazine—Tubular, capacity 20 short, 17 long or 15 long rifle cartridges. Action—Takedown

Receiver, one-piece bolt easily removed for cleaning, short forearm stroke ejects and loads; positive operation. Push button type safety in rear of trigger guard. Sights—Adjustable flat top sporting rear sight; gold bead front sight. Stock tank drilled and tapped for all standard aperture Sights. Weight—About 5½ pounds
A "man's size" rifle—the extra long "man's size" checkered forearm gives this rifle perfect balance and permits the shooter to extend his left arm into a relaxed and easy shooting position.
Model 29—slide action repeating rifle $21.00
Model 29-S—Same as Model 29, but with Savage No. 30 rear peep sight and Savage No. 31 Folding middle sight $23.50

© **ORDER BLANK IN MIDDLE AND INDEX IN BACK OF CATALOG**

SAVAGE & STEVENS .22 CAL. RIFLES WITH 'SCOPES

The Savage and Stevens Arms Company have taken the lead in offering their most popular .22 Cal. rifles completely factory fitted and equipped with telescope mounts and sights. The telescopes used are of the well known Weaver design. The 3 power No. 10 'scope corresponding to the Weaver No. 329, while the 4 power No. 20 'scope with internal windage and elevation corresponds with the Weaver No. 344. The popular and well proven type "M" mounts are used thruout. Since full details of both the rifles and scopes will be found elsewhere in this catalog, we are presenting herewith only illustrations of the guns in question with a brief description together with price which includes complete outfit exactly as illustrated.

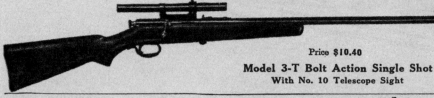

Price $10.40
Model 3-T Bolt Action Single Shot
With No. 10 Telescope Sight

.22 caliber short, long or long rifle; regular or high speed, 26 in. barrel; walnut stock; take-down. Length over all 43 inches. Gold bead front sight and adjustable flat top rear sight.

.22 caliber, short, long or long rifle, regular or high speed. 24 inch barrel, 5-shot clip magazine, walnut stock. Take-down. Gold bead front sight and sporting rear sight with elevation adjustment.

Price $19.00
Model 4-T Bolt Action Repeating Rifle
With No. 20 Telescope Sight

.22 caliber, short, long or long rifle, regular or high speed. 24 inch barrel. Tubular magazine. Capacity: 15 .22 long rifle, 17 .22 long or 21 .22 short cartridges. Oil finished walnut stock. Gold bead front and sporting rear sight with elevation and windage adjustments.

Price $21.35
Model 5-T Bolt Action Repeating Rifle
With No. 20 Telescope Sight

.22 long rifle, regular and high speed. 23 inch tapered barrel. 5-shot clip magazine. Bolt action, two locking lugs. Quick ignition, convenient safety, polished bolt. Oil finished walnut stock. White metal bead front and flat top elevation adjustment rear sight.

Price $29.50
Model 23-AA Sporter
With No. 20 Telescope Sight

Price $44.00
Model 23-D (.22 Hornet)
With No. 20 Telescope Sight

.22 Hornet caliber. 25 inch high-pressure smokeless steel barrel, 5-shot clip magazine. Bolt action, two locking lugs. Quick ignition, convenient safety, polished bolt. Oil finished walnut stock. White metal bead front and flat top elevation adjustment rear sight.

.22 caliber short, long or long rifle, regular or high speed. 24 inch barrel, bolt action, single shot. Pistol grip stock, forend with black tip, walnut finish. Gold bead front and sporting rear sight with elevation and windage adjustment.

Price $10.45
Stevens No. 53T Buckhorn Rifle
With No. 10 Telescope Sight

.22 caliber short, long or long rifle, regular or high-speed. 24 inch barrel, 5-shot detachable clip magazine. Bolt action. Pistol rip stock, forend with black tip, walnut finish. Gold bead front and sporting rear sight with elevation and windage adjustment.

Price $18.50
Stevens No. 56T Buckhorn Rifle
With No. 20 Telescope Sight

.22 caliber short, long or long rifle, regular or high speed. 24 inch barrel. Tubular magazine, capacity 15 .22 long rifle, 17 .22 long or 21 .22 short cartridges. Bolt action. Gold bead front and sporting rear sight with elevation and windage adjustments.

Price $20.50
Stevens No. 66T Buckhorn Rifle
With No. 20 Telescope Sight

A RIFLE EQUIPPED WITH A TELESCOPE MEANS BETTER SHOOTING

SPECIAL DE LUXE HORNET RIFLES

NO. 970 STOEGER HORNET

The new Stoeger Hornet Rifle is unquestionably the neatest regular Hornet Rifle on the market. The action employed has been especially designed for us for the Hornet Cartridge, and is not remodeled to suit the cartridge. The workmanship, design, material, style and balance are perfect.

The barrel is fitted with matted ramp front sight with sight protector, while the rear sight is of the English three leaf style, marked for 100, 200 and 300 yards. The stock is of Circassian walnut with cheek piece, about 13¼ inches long, with steel butt plate, steel pistol grip cap, genuine East Indian Buffalo Horn forend tip. Carefully checkered on forearm and pistol grips and fitted with first class swivels. Weight about 7¾ pounds.

The magazine opens downward on a hinge, permitting easy loading and unloading.

No. 970 Stoeger Hornet Rifle...........................$125.00
No. 971 Stoeger Hornet Rifle with special De Luxe Engraving.... 175.00

NO. 981 LUNA HORNET RIFLE

The Luna Target Rifle is the latest and finest precision rifle manufactured by Ernst Friederich Buechel, originator of the genuine "Tell" and "Luna" pistols. Only the very finest material, finish and workmanship. A rifle of truly phenomenal accuracy and built just right to have the proper "hang." Selected walnut stock with cheek piece. Full checkered, full pistol grip and forend. Falling block action. Micrometer wind gauge rear sight with disc as well as perfectly adjustable rear sight on barrel. Both sights are readily adjusted or entirely removed by means of a key which is supplied with each rifle. Ramp front sight with two interchangeable sights. Barrel length, 29 inches; weight about 8¼ pounds.

No. 980—Luna Rifle, chambered for .22 Long Rifle Cartridges.
Price $195.00
No. 981—Luna Rifle, chambered for the new Winchester .22 C.F. "Hornet" cartridge, fitted with Lyman No. 17A and Lyman No. 103 rear. The perfect and ideal Vermin gun. Price........ 195.00

NO. 3070 SCOTT MARTINI HORNET RIFLE

No. 3070—Scott Martini Rifle, built on the British Martini Action. This is the finest and most accurate rifle that can be manufactured. Furnished in various calibers such as .22 caliber, .32/20 caliber, etc. 26 inch barrel, fitted with B. S. A. No. 8 Peep Sight, also special folding leaf sights for 50, 100 and 200 yards; special ivory bead sight, with sight protector. Finest Circassian walnut stock; ivory tipped forearm, pistol grip and forearm neatly checkered. Sling swivels. Weight about 4 pounds.

On special order this rifle will be made up, at no extra charge, for the new .22 W. C. F. "Hornet" cartridge.

Price $195.00

NO. 956 PRECISION HORNET RIFLE

"PRECISION" .22 CALIBER HORNET RIFLE

> **IMPORTANT NOTICE**
> This model has been discontinued and is being replaced by a heavier five shot repeater. Details upon request.
> Approximate price will be about $50.00

No. 956—Light Precision Rifle, especially made for the new "Hornet" cartridge. This rifle has 24-inch barrel; weighs 4 pounds, 14 ounces and has an overall length of 41 inches. The stock is of fine dark walnut with fully checkered forearm and pistol grip. The bolt handle is of the large flat Mannlicher style, chromium plated. The rear sight is of the adjustable screw type and permits great accuracy. A well built and exceedingly neat gun, representing the best rifle of its type.

Price $18.50

MOSSBERG RIFLES AND TELESCOPIC SIGHTS

Model 43 with Mossberg No. 6 Scope Sight Attached
Model L43 New left hand model

FEATURES AND SPECIFICATIONS

Note low position of scope, due to removable section of peep sight and design of action. Target grade clip type repeater—designed for combination use of scope and metallic sights.

Heavy barrel, accurately rifled, 26 inch length, crowned muzzle chambered for 22 cal. long rifle, standard or high speed ammunition.

Long oil-finished walnut stock, designed for four-position use. Large beavertail forearm extending almost to trigger guard, full cheek piece, corrugated steel butt plate.

New Lyman No. 57M receiver peep sight and 17A Front made especially. See bottom of page for description.

Drilled and tapped for Mossberg scope mounts.

Grooved trigger, set at 3½ to 4½ pounds trigger pull. Has hardened steel insert or contact on hardened firing pin.

MODEL 43
MODEL L43

New type action with hardened cam-action speed lock. Can be worked either as repeater or single loader with scope in lowest possible position. Semi-hammerless, with thumb safety operating directly on trigger. Self-cocking on up stroke of lever.

New detachable swivels, with 4 aperture plate in fore-end of stock allowing selective location of front swivel for variation of arm lengths.

Barrel band at front end of stock.

Chrome plated bolt, lever and trigger.

Magazine capacity 7 long rifle cartridges.

Weight 8 pounds, length overall 44 inches.

Model 43	$19.95
Model 43 with scope, as illustrated	26.45
Model L43	24.35
Model L43 with scope	30.85

Model 46A
The New All-Purpose Recreation Rifle
Model 46AT fitted with target grade stock and heavy barrel. Weight 9 lbs.
Model L46A-LS Left hand model with Lyman Sights

First popular-priced repeater designed expressly for combination telescopic and metallic sights. When fitted with Mossberg No. 6 Mount and Scope, lever can be worked with scope down close to top of barrel. New No. 4 Micrometer Peep sight swings in under scope for peep sight shooting, and swings to side to allow scope to drop to line of metallic sights for scope shooting. Self-cocking, with visible optional safety. Chrome plated bolt, lever and trigger. Short hammer-fall to obtain speed lock. Straight line feed into chamber, taking all lengths of .22's. Magazine takes 15 long rifle, 18 long or 22 short cartridges. Receiver drilled and tapped for Mossberg Scope Mounts. Barrel 26 inches tapered.

Optional sight equipment on Models 46A and 35A:—New Lyman No. 57M with Mossberg 4A Selective Disc and special Lyman No. 17A Front sight. Price on each model $5.00 extra.

Genuine walnut stock, full beavertail, cheek piece detachable swivels, corrugated steel butt plate. Hooded ramp front and No. 4 "Micro-click" peep sights are standard equipment. Scope and Mount extra. Length 44½ inches. Weight 7½ pounds.

Model 46A	$13.85
Model 46AT	14.95
Model L46A-LS	22.75
Model 46A with scope, as illustrated	20.35

MODEL 45A
MODEL 45AC
MODEL L45A

Identically the same action as No. 46, with alterations in stock, barrel and sight equipment. Barrel 24 inches tapered. Walnut-finished stock with steel butt plate and detachable swivels. Hooded front ramp, No. 3 peep and new adjustable open rear sights as

standard equipment allows both open and peep sight shooting without any tools necessary to change from one to the other. Receiver drilled and tapped to take Mossberg Scope Mounts. Weight of mount and scope 1¼ pounds. A whale of a lot of gun for the money! Length 42½ inches. Weight 6¾ pounds.

Model 45A	$11.85
Model 25A—Similar to Model 45, but single shot. Lgth. 41 inches. Wgt. 4½ lbs.	5.90
Model 45AC—Same as 45A, but plain sights	11.25
Model L45A—Same as 45A, but left hand bolt	15.25

Model 35A
The New Popular-Priced Target Grade Single Shot
Model 35A-LS with Lyman Sights

First target grade single shot at a popular price. Same sight equipment as No. 46A Receiver drilled and tapped with Mossberg Scope Mounts. Target grade walnut stock with extra long beavertail, cheek piece, corrugated steel butt plate, and detachable swivels. Designed specifically for "4-position" shooting. Self-cocking visible safety. 26 inch heavy barrel, chambered

for .22 long rifle. Length 44½ inches. Weight 8¼ pounds.

Model 35A	$11.25
Model 35A with scope, as illustrated	17.75
Model 35A-LS—Same as 35A, but with Lyman sights	16.25

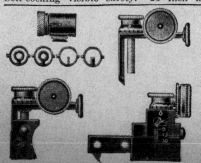

MOSSBERG-LYMAN SIGHTS

Lyman No. 57M Receiver Peep Sight. Micrometer click adjustments, with ¼ minute graduations equivalent to ¼" change in point of impact at 100 yards. Push-button lock releases elevation side so it can be either reversed or removed entirely, allowing ample room for use of MOSSBERG scope sights right down to top of receiver. Complete with 4-aperture selective peep disc, operated by turning outside case clockwise.

Regular equipment on Model 43. Optional on Models 35A and 46A. Extra cost.$4.00

Extra cost when ordered separately for Models 35A and 46A or old Models 35 and 46. Price................ 6.00

NO. 4 MICRO-CLICK PEEP

Micrometer adjustments, with clicks and double locks. Swinging feature allows scope to be used in *low* position. No. 4A selective disc gives choice of 4 apertures by turning outside rim. Complete sight available for other makes of rifles and No. 4A disc for other makes of peep sights.

Price complete...$2.00
Selective disc only. .95

GENUINE MAUSER SPORTING RIFLES

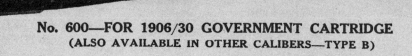

No. 600—FOR 1906/30 GOVERNMENT CARTRIDGE
(ALSO AVAILABLE IN OTHER CALIBERS—TYPE B)

No. 600. As illustrated; fine walnut stock with cheek-piece, hard rubber butt plate, checkered full pistol grip with metal cap. The barrel is 24 inches round, and fitted with front ramp sight with silver bead and sight protector; the rear sight is either of the three-leaf type or the tangent curve, as illustrated on opposite page. Weight about 7¼ pounds. Fitted with first-class sling swivels. Supplied in caliber .30-06 U. S., making the ideal sporting rifle for all American game, small and large.

No. 600, Cal. .30-06 U. S.—Price..........................$125.00

This same model may also be had in the following calibers:

                                            Price

No. 601, Cal. 7 x 57 m/m..........................$110.00
No. 602, Cal. 8 x 60 m/m.......................... 110.00
No. 603, Cal. 9 x 57 m/m.......................... 110.00
No. 607, Cal. 9.3 x 62 m/m........................ 125.00
No. 608, Cal. 10.75 x 68 m/m...................... 125.00

No. 605K CAL. .250-3000 SAVAGE CARTRIDGE
(ALSO AVAILABLE IN OTHER CALIBERS—TYPE B)

No. 604K, 605K, 606K. These rifles are essentially the same as the Model 600, but are particularly light, short rifles built on special short actions. The barrel is 20 inches, and the front sight ramp has a ring base which encircles the muzzle.

                                            Price

No. 604K, Cal. 6.5 x 54 m/m Mauser......................$125.00
No. 605K, Cal. 250-3000 Savage 125.00
No. 606K, Cal. 8 x 51 m/m.............................. 125.00

LEOPARD

CHOICE OF CALIBER

Mauser magazine sporting rifles are made in the bores shown in the ballistic tables below.

The light short rifles, caliber 6.5 m/m K (.256" short), 8 m/m K (.315 short) and .250-300 are to be considered special deer stalking rifles and are suitable for similar light game.

For heavier game we recommend caliber .30-06 U. S.; 7 m/m (.276); .280; 8 x 60 m/m (.315); .318; 9 m/m (.354) and 9.3 m/m (.366), the 7 m/m and .280 being preferred where stress is laid on a flat trajectory and long range shooting.

For heavy thick-skinned game, like rhino, elephant and dangerous animals of prey, our caliber 9.3 m/m (.366), 10.75 m/m (.423) and .404 Eley, especially the latter, are the most suitable.

Another important factor to be considered in the choice of the caliber is the facility of obtaining the cartridges from the trade in different countries. Mauser cartridges are available in big game hunting centers and are carried in stock by us in New York.

Illustration on left shows leopard killed in South West Africa with an original Mauser Sporting Rifle, caliber 8 m/m.

BALLISTICS OF THE MAUSER SPORTING RIFLES

Designation of rifle and cartridge	Mauser 6.5x 51 m/m	Mauser 8x 51 m/m	Mauser 7x 57 m/m	Mauser 8x 60 m/m	Mauser 9x 57 m/m	Mauser 9.3x 62 m/m	Mauser 10.75x 68 m/m	.250–3000 Savage	.280 Ross Rimless	.300 U.S. 1906	.318 W.R.	.404 Eley
Length of barrel of rifle..........inch	21.60	21.60	23.60	23.60	23.60	23.60	23.60	21.60	23.60	23.60	23.60	23.60
Length of barrel of carbine......inch	19.70	19.70	19.70	19.70	19.70					19.70		
Total length of rifle................inch	42.30	42.30	44.80	44.80	44.80	44.80	44.80	40.30	45.30	45	45	45
Total length of carbine............inch	40.35	40.35	40.85	40.80	40.80			40.30		41		
Weight of rifle.......................lb.	5.95	5.95	7.15	7.15	7.15	7.3	7.5	5.95	7.7	7.4	7.7	8.2
Weight of carbine...................lb.	5.85	5.85	6.85	6.82	6.85					6.85		
Weight of bullet...................grains	119	158	154	154	247	285	347	87	150	150	250	400
Weight of powder.................grains	33.2	38.6	50.1	52.5	46.3	54	64.8		53.5			82
Weight of cartridge...............grains	308	348	376	378	455	502	602	278	467	383	475	748
Length of cartridge................inch	2.68	2.68	3.07	3.15	3.03	3.29	3.23	2.52	3.449	3.331	3.523	3.504
Length of bullet....................inch	1.023	.887	1.22	1.063	1.102	1.181	1.044	.85	1.228	1.095	1.495	1.165
Muzzle velocity (Vo).............f. s.	2362	2380	2740	3000	2296	2296	2313	3080	2870	3000	2230	2160
Muzzle energy (Eo)...............f. lbs.	1468	1990	2567	3085	2885	3486	4123	1840	2710	2980	2700	4173
Height of trajectory at a range of. 100 yards: inch	.922	1.025	.657	0.63	1.025	.922	.922	.6	.70	.6	.98	.86
Height of trajectory at a range of. 200 yards: inch	4.40	4.65	2.52	2.45	4.60	4.40	4.55	2.4	2.59	2.4	4.13	3.9
Height of trajectory at a range of. 300 yards: inch	10.67	11.85	5.98	6.07	11.70	10.67	11.40	6.3	7.0	6.3	8.74	10

WALTHER .22 CAL. RIFLES AND CROSS BOWS

.22 CAL. OLYMPIC MATCH RIFLE

Interchangeable front sights supplied with rifle.

Price $250.00

SPECIFICATIONS:

Barrel Length: 65 cm. (26") Length of rifle: 115 cm. (45¼")
Barrel Diameter: 25 mm. (1") Weight: about 6 kg. ,13¼ lbs.)
Line of sight: 80 cm. (31½")

The Walther Olympic Match rifle constitutes a class in itself. It has been made as a result of experience gathered at National and International Championships throughout the world and meets the most stringent requirements such as are to be contended with in International competition.

The rifle is fitted with micrometer extension rear sight with lock. The full, checkered pistol grip has an indentation for the thumb of the right hand permitting an entirely natural position of the hand. The rifle is equipped with adjustable Schuetzen type butt plate. The full, beaver-tail forearm is covered with corrugated rubber to permit a perfect grip for off-hand shooting. The barrel, receiver and sights have a sand-blasted effect in order to eliminate disturbing light reflections. New style light military type trigger may be adjusted as low as 10 oz. without altering the resistance of the initial pull. The rifle, being intended only for match use is a single shot. Upon special order the rifle may also be had with set trigger. The travel of the firing pin is but 5 mm. which is *LESS* than 2/10" and represents the shortest travel on any rifle on the market. Each barrel used in this model is specially selected from thousands for the very highest degree of accuracy.

FOR TARGET SHOOTING AND SMALL GAME

.22 CALIBER AUTOMATIC AND TARGET RIFLE

AUTOMATIC—REPEATER—SINGLE SHOT

Rifle satisfies in every particular the wish expressed by leading sportsmen for a REAL MAN'S .22 caliber rifle. It is constructed according to specifications laid down by authorities on small bore rifles. It has been designed and built for use as a fine target rifle, or for use in the field. A special feature of this rifle is that it may be used as a single shot, repeater or

CHIEF ADVANTAGES OF THE NEW WALTHER

1. The rifle can be used as a single shot rifle, as a repeating rifle or as an automatic rifle as desired.
2. When using the rifle as an automatic or as a repeater, no part of the breech block moves toward the rear, and the shooter can not be injured by a defective cartridge.
3. The breech block can be lifted from the receiver from the rear, thereby giving easy and quick access to all parts of the lock and the barrel for cleaning purposes.
4. The regular stock magazine holds 5 cartridges, but extra

automatic rifle. The change is made in an instant, by simply lifting bolt handle. No tool required. The experience obtained in the manufacture of self loading arms during the past fifty years by the WALTHER ARMS factory guarantees the reliable functioning as well as the highest grade of workmanship, which is found on no other .22 caliber rifle.

magazines of 9 shot capacity can be furnished, at small additional charge.
5. This Model has folding safety on bolt head as used on many high power rifles.
6. The trigger has a uniform easy pull, which can be regulated to pull harder or easier.
7. The shooting of the rifle is of the highest order.
8. The rifle can be loaded or unloaded when the safety is on.

SPECIFICATIONS OF THE WALTHER PRECISION RIFLE

Automatic Repeater and Single Shot Rifle for target or sporting use, walnut stock.
Length of barrel, 24½ inches.
Length of rifle, 43 inches.
Weight of rifle, about 7 pounds.
Front sight pushed into sight base from side.
Sliding leaf sight has horizontally adjustable notch.

Stock is of first class walnut, grooved pistol grip checkered with fish-skin design, with heel plate and swivels.
Safety. Same as is generally placed on high power rifles.
Trigger. Has easy pull with point.
The lock parts and the barrel are black burnished.
The rifle can also be furnished with telescope at extra cost.
Price: Walther Precision Rifle .22 long rifle Caliber.............$87.50

EXTRAS	Price
Single Shot Adaptor	$1.50
Cheek piece on stock	4.00
Full Length Mannlicher Style Stock	15.00
Telescope Zeiss "Zielklein" 2¼X, including tunnel mount and testing	70.00
Telescope Oigee "Gnomet" 2½X, including tunnel mount and testing	50.00

	Price
Aperture rearsight	$8.50
Muzzle Protector	.60
5 Shot Magazine	1.50
9 Shot Magazine	3.00
Charges for special high grade engraving and horn fore-end cap	16.00

CROSS BOWS

STANDARD GRADE

TARGET GRADE

Made of selected walnut with double steel bow spring. Adjustable sights, hair trigger, and target style steel butt plate. This Cross-Bow is of heavy construction and requires the use of a special cocking lever which is supplied with it. Accurate up to 40 yards. Supplied with three special precision steel pointed darts. Weight, about 7 pounds.
Price $85.00
Extra Darts ....Each 1.00

Made of walnut with strong steel bow spring. Can be conveniently cocked by hand, and consequently ideal for boys of 12 to 16 years. Fitted with single trigger and cheek piece. Supplied with three steel tipped darts. Weight, about 3 pounds.
Price $27.50
Extra Darts ....Each .75

GENUINE MAUSER BIG GAME RIFLES

By virtue of the outstanding strength of the Genuine Mauser Action, it has been adapted or closely followed by almost every army in the world. This same virtue puts the Genuine Mauser Action rifle in a class by itself for the heaviest kinds of loads under the strain of which other actions would be ruined, to say nothing of the possible serious injury or even death to shooter in such a case. It may be said that all big game hunting is carried on either with this style rifle or the double barreled rifles such as described on page 139 of this catalog, but the great

majority of big game hunters use the Mauser Action because it allows a great number of shots, very seldom gets out of order, is easily repaired, and costs but a fraction of the price of the double rifle. It is interesting to note that almost without exception, all fine English magazine rifles for big game turned out by world famous makers employ only the Original Mauser Action, an undisputed attest to its supremacy. We take especial pleasure in offering the following big game rifles and are prepared to build any special rifle using the genuine Mauser action.

NOS. 627 AND 628
(TYPE A)

Models 627 and 628. These represent the heaviest big game rifles built by the Mauser Factory. They are built on the famous Mauser Magnum Actions, which are recognized the world over as by far the strongest action ever made, and one which assures positive safety and reliability even under excessive breech pressures. These rifles are especially made for use against the heaviest and most dangerous game, particularly however for tough skinned game such as elephant and rhinoceros.

Model 627, Cal. 10.75 x 68—Price........$175.00 Model 628, Cal. .404 Jeffery—Price.......$250.00
May also be had on special order in the following calibers:—
Model 628A, Cal. 280 Ross—Price........$250.00 Model 628B, Cal. .318 W. R. Express—Price.$250.00

NO. 626
(TYPE A)

No. 626. This rifle is considered by most seasoned hunters as the ideal game rifle for African and Indo-Chinese soft skinned big game. It is also just the rifle for Grizzly and Alaskan Brown Bear. The specifications of this rifle are the same as in model 625, except that the barrel is 25 inches and the weight about eight pounds.

Illustration shows floor plate open for cleaning and removal of cartridges. A convenient and valuable feature of all Mauser rifles.

No. 626 Cal. 9.3 x 62 m/m—Price........................$175.00

GENUINE MAUSER FACTORY MOUNTED TELESCOPES

When Mauser Rifles are desired with telescopes, we strongly urge that, whenever possible the genuine Original Mauser Mounts and factory mounting be taken, with all the advantages offered through the factories' superior experience and facilities for this work and in which they have always specialized.

All Mauser rifles with telescope are carefully shot in and targeted at 100, 200, and 300 meters. Due to the special receivers used on Original Mauser Telescopic Rifles, the Mauser Mount is not adapted to finished rifles not originally designed for 'scopes, and for such rifles we refer our customers to the special Stoeger Side Mount and Two Piece Mount illustrated and described in this catalog on pages 33 and 34.

When fitted by the Mauser factory, a special receiver with square top bridge is employed, into which a square notch is recessed for the rear base, thus avoiding the necessity of soldering or screwing on and assuring not only a great enhancement in appearance, but absolute rigidity and dependability. The front base is dovetailed into a lateral slot across the top of the receiver. As a result of this method, there is nothing to protrude when the 'scope is detached. The 'scope may be snapped onto the rifle with a single movement of one hand, and is equally simple to remove which is done by pressing the button on the right side of the bridge and lifting the rear part of the 'scope.

The windage is taken care of by means of an azmuth adjusting screw on the rear telescope support; the elevation is regulated by means of a dial on top of the telescope itself. Factory mounted 'scopes are zeroed for windage and the dial is marked for 100, 200, and 300 meters. Both mounts are tunnelled, thus permitting the simultaneous use of both telescopic and regulation sights.

The telescopes regularly furnished and recommended for all general hunting purposes by the Mauser Factory are the Hensoldt Dyalitan 4 X and the Zeiss Zielvier 4 X, although any other 'scope may be had. Because the Mauser Mounts are standard for 27 m/m ring diameter, such as the 'scopes mentioned, any other ring diameter means special work at an added cost.

Extra cost of any Original Mauser with mounts and telescope, including fitting to rifle and targetting at 100, 200, and 300 meters, employing Zeiss Zielvier 4 X or Hensoldt Dyalitan 4 X $100.00

Extra cost of any Original Mauser with mounts and telescope, including fitting to rifle and targetting at 100, 200, and 300 meters, employing any other telescope of 27 m/m ring diameter:— Cost of telescope selected plus........................$45.00

Extra cost of any Original Mauser with mounts and telescope, including fitting to rifle and targetting at 100, 200, and 300 meters, employing any telescope of any other ring diameter than 27 m/m :—Cost of telescope selected plus.....................$60.00

Elephant Shot with Original Mauser Sporting Rifle Cal. 10.75 x 68 m/m

© **ORDER BLANK IN MIDDLE AND INDEX IN BACK OF CATALOG**

ORIGINAL MAUSER .22 CALIBER TARGET RIFLE

In its main structural features the new action is very similar to the Mauser revolving cylinder breech mechanism Model '98 which is unexcelled as regards strength, reliability and simplicity. Cocking is effected both on opening and closing. A cam surface along which the bolt slides on opening the breech initiates the loosening of the cartridge case and assures easy ejection.

The striker and firing pin are one piece eliminating vibration and insuring shortest firing time, precision, and evenness of action. An adjustable double pull off is provided answering the most exacting requirements. The limitation of the backward movement of the bolt is no longer effected by the sear, but by means of a special bolt catch movably connected with receiver. Barrels of best special steel.

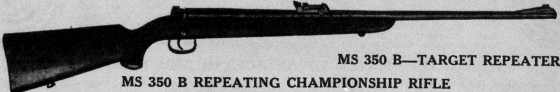

MS 350 B—TARGET REPEATER

MS 350 B REPEATING CHAMPIONSHIP RIFLE

Round barrel 26½" long. Action and barrel grooved for sight and telescope sight. Detachable and adjustable Micrometer or Tangent sight. The sight has a reversible leaf 1 7/16" wide. V cut for triangular foresight, U cut for bead and blade foresights. Windgauge adjusted by a graduated screw with locking pin. The foresights, driven in from front, are interchangeable, a triangular, bead and blade foresight being supplied. Bolt with wing safety. Trigger and trigger guard roughened. Selected walnut stock with vulcanite heelplate and pistol grip with vulcanite cap. Chequered fore-end and pistol grip. All metal parts durable black. Peepsight at extra cost.

Total length about 45½". Weight about 8 lbs., 6 ozs.

Shooting results of guaranteed excellence in accordance with the standards of the "Deutschen Versuchsanstalt für Handfeuerwaffen in Berlin-Wannsee."

This model is supplied with a magazine for 5 cartridges. A magazine taking 10 cartridges can be supplied at extra cost.
Price $88.00

ES 350 B SINGLE SHOT CHAMPIONSHIP RIFLE

Round barrel 26½" long. Action and barrel grooved for sight and telescope sight. Detachable and adjustable Micrometer or Tangent sight. The sight has a reversible leaf 1 7/16" wide. V cut for triangular foresight, U cut for bead and blade foresights. Windgauge adjusted by a graduated screw with locking pin. The foresights, driven in from front, are interchangeable, a triangular, bead and blade foresight being supplied. Bolt with wing safety. Trigger and trigger guard roughened. Selected walnut stock with vulcanite heelplate and pistol grip with vulcanite cap. Chequered fore-end and pistol grip. All metal parts durable black. Peepsight at extra cost.

Total length about 45½". Weight about 8 lbs.

Shooting results of guaranteed excellence in accordance with the standards of the "Deutschen Versuchsanstalt für Handfeuerwaffen in Berlin-Wannsee."
Price $78.00

MS 420 B REPEATER

Round barrel 26½" long. Interchangeable foresights, blade, triangular or bead inserted from front. Tangent sight 30 to 200 yards with windgauge, with reversible leaf, V or U cut. Bolt with wing safety action. Action grooved for telescope sight.

Walnut stock with vulcanite heelplate and chequered pistol grip. Sling rings. Barrel, action and parts durable black.

Total length about 45½". Weight about 8 pounds.

This model has a magazine for 5 cartridges. If required a magazine holding 10 cartridges can be supplied at extra.
Price $68.00

ES 340 B

The standard Small-bore Rifle for Rifle Clubs, with round barrel 26½" long, with interchangeable foresights inserted from front, tangent sight 30 to 200 yards with windgauge with reversible leaf, U cut for bead and blade foresight, V cut for triangular foresight. Bolt with wing safety action. Action grooved for telescope sight. Trigger and trigger guard roughened. Walnut stock with steel heelplate. Barrel, action and parts durable black. If required: stock with vulcanite heelplate and pistol grip chequered at extra cost. Total length 45½". Wgt. about 7¾ lbs.
Price $58.00

MM 410 B REPEATER

Round barrel 23½" long. Tangent sight 30 to 200 yards with windgauge, with reversible leaf, V and U cut. Interchangeable foresights, triangular, bead and blade, inserted from front. Bolt with wing safety action. Trigger and trigger guard roughened. Action grooved for telescope sight. Walnut stock with vulcanite heelplate and chequered pistol grip. Sling rings. All metal parts durable black. Total length about 42½". Weight about 6¼ lbs.

This model has a magazine for 5 cartridges. If required a magazine holding 10 cartridges can be supplied at extra cost.
Price $68.00

"SPORT-MODEL" (S. M. 34) CAL. .22 LONG RIFLE

The "Sport-model" is a single shot rifle, which in appearance and make-up resembles the Model '98 Military Rifle.

Length of barrel 26". Tangent sight 25 to 200 yards. Triangular foresight to push in from side. Full walnut stock.

Hand safety. Sling rings. Steel heelplate. Swivel hook on fore-end of stock for piling. Muzzle protector and cover. Adjustable sling on side of weapon.
Price $68.00

PEEP SIGHT

To permit of firing with any type of sight, all models can now be delivered with Peep sight (at an extra charge).

The Peep sight is mounted on the neck of the butt, the fitting being effected by means of a base let into the stock, and in which the Peep sight is inserted and screwed tight.

For elevation and lateral adjustment, the Peep sight is provided with a transverse support. The adjustment is effected by means of square bolt screws. The horizontal support is provided with marks for indicating the extent of the adjustment. When adjusting the point of impact it should be born in mind that a quarter turn of the screw displaces the point of impact at 50 metres range by about 1 cm to the left, right, up or down respectively, i. e., to approximately the width of a ring on the target. The majority of aiming devices, such as Peep sight discs, revolving diaphragms, telescopic Peep sights, etc., can be fitted on the Peep sight, in so far as the special threads permit.

Extra for Peep sight on any Model (not sold separately) $11.00

GENUINE MANNLICHER-SCHOENAUER RIFLES
FOR THE U. S. 1906 CARTRIDGE
ALSO

6.5 x 53 m/m; 7 x 57 m/m; 7 x 64 m/m; 8 x 56 m/m; 8 x 60 m/m;
9 x 56 m/m; 9.3 x 62 m/m; 9.5 x 57 m/m; 10.75 x 68 m/m

The Mannlicher-Schoenauer Hunting Rifle is a typical product of the Steyr Arms Factory, which for many decades has held a leading position in the manufacture of army rifles. Developed through the precision, durability and regularity brought on by the most critical requirements of military production, the Mannlicher-Schoenauer Hunting Rifle not only combines these qualities perfectly, but thanks its world wide reputation to its lightness, ease of handling, and Austrian good taste in appearance which combines utility and constructional correctness with external beauty, which accounts for the uniqueness of this arm.

AMONG THE SPECIAL ADVANTAGES OF THIS RIFLE ARE

1.—The light weight of the arm: 6 pounds and 9 ounces to 6 pounds and 13 ounces.

2.—The easy manipulation of the bolt on opening and closing, which when closed is completely and safely locked.

3.—The small dimensions of the magazine which is entirely within the stock and completely closed on the bottom, preventing the possibility of the entrance of dirt or dust.

4.—The use of the rotating cartridge platform upon which the cartridges are concentrated. This has the advantage over the usual so-called zig-zag position, that all possibility of jamming is eliminated.

5.—The high accuracy of the arm.

6.—The bolt as well as the magazine can be disassembled and assembled very quickly without the aid of any tools.

7.—The loaded rifle may be put on safe by turning the safety leaf to the field, whereupon the gun may neither be fired nor the bolt opened.

8.—Only first class, scientifically and practically tested material is used.

The MANNLICHER-SCHOENAUER CARBINE—5 shots (a sixth shot may be put in the barrel when the magazine is loaded); two leaf hunting sights for 100 and 200 yards. Ramp front sight adjustable laterally, single or double set trigger, full stock with pistol grip and cheek piece. Sling swivels, steel butt plate with trap with recess for two cartridges and cleaning rod.

	Price		Price
Cal. 30-06 U. S., 20 in. bbl.; ent. length 41 in. (carbine)	$135.00	Cal. 8 x 56 m/m, 20 in. bbl.; entire length 41 in.	$110.00
Cal. 6.5 x 53 m/m, 18 in. bbl.; entire length 39 in.	110.00	Cal. 9 x 56 m/m, 20 in. bbl.; entire length 41 in.	110.00
Cal. 7 x 57 m/m. 20 in. bbl.; entire length 41 in.	110.00	Cal. 9.5 x 57 m/m, 20 in. bbl.; entire length 41 in.	110.00

MANNLICHER-SCHOENAUER HIGH VELOCITY RIFLE with sporter half stock, single or double set trigger, steel butt plate with trap and specially built in magazine for take down cleaning rod and two cartridges. British style three leaf sight.
This model regularly available in the following calibers and specifications:

	Price		Price
Cal. .30-06 U. S., 24 in. bbl.; entire length 45 in.	$150.00	Cal. 8 x 60 m/m, 24 in. bbl.; entire length 45 in.	$150.00
Cal. 7 x 64 m/m, 24 in. bbl.; entire length 45 in.	150.00	Cal. 9.3 x 62, 24 in. bbl.; entire length 45 in.	150.00
Cal. 10.75 x 68 m/m, 24 in. bbl.; entire length 45 in.	$150.00		

TAKE DOWN MODEL

The magazine is taken out of the action. The spring pin in the fore-end of the stock on the right side is then taken out by depressing the milled part of its spring. The flatshaped catch in front of the trigger guard is then turned from left to right, which releases the action and the barrel and action can be detached from the stock.

When putting together proceed in the reverse order. This model is particularly handy for traveling, as it takes down to an overall length of about 32 inches and may be carried in an ordinary suitcase. The take down model is only made in the sporter half stock model, not in the carbine, and on special order only.

Extra cost $15.00

Upon special order and at an extra charge, the following special work can be carried out by the factory:—Time of delivery:—

Special orders for Mannlicher-Schoenauer Rifles require a delivery of approximately twelve weeks.

Extra long barrel, up to 23 inches, caliber 6.5 m/m	$15.00
Extra long barrel, up to 24 inches, caliber 8.2 m/m	15.00
Extra long barrel, up to 25 inches, caliber 9 m/m	15.00
Extra long barrel, up to 26 inches, caliber 9.5 m/m	15.00
Sight protector	1.00
Stock of specially selected pretty wood	20.00
Stock specifications differing from standard	15.00
Full stock in rifles which normally have half stock	10.00
Horn cap at the muzzle of sporter type	6.00

Telescope mount and shooting in, exclusive of cost of 'scope (see pages 35 and 36 and add cost of desired telescope).

Special testing or shooting in with foreign ammunition	$35.00
Extra for rib	35.00
Antinit without rib	30.00
Antinit with rib	45.00
Special folding peep sight	12.00
Takedown model extra	15.00
Extra light rifles (not for high speed rifles)	25.00

©   **A NEW GUN CARRIES A FACTORY GUARANTEE**

DETAILS OF MANNLICHER-SCHOENAUER RIFLES

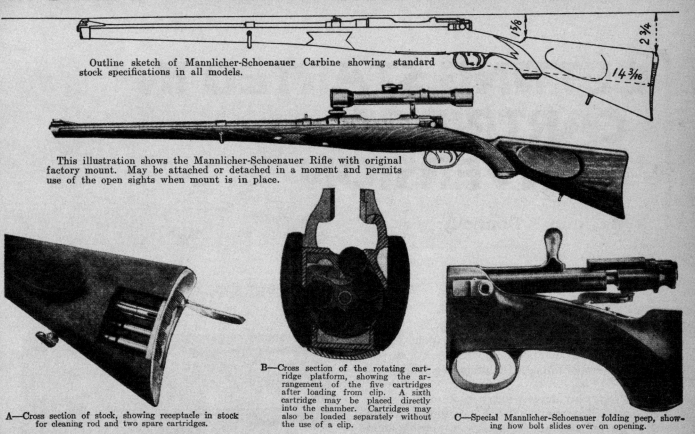

Outline sketch of Mannlicher-Schoenauer Carbine showing standard stock specifications in all models.

This illustration shows the Mannlicher-Schoenauer Rifle with original factory mount. May be attached or detached in a moment and permits use of the open sights when mount is in place.

A—Cross section of stock, showing receptacle in stock for cleaning rod and two spare cartridges.

B—Cross section of the rotating cartridge platform, showing the arrangement of the five cartridges after loading from clip. A sixth cartridge may be placed directly into the chamber. Cartridges may also be loaded separately without the use of a clip.

C—Special Mannlicher-Schoenauer folding peep, showing how bolt slides over on opening.

CONSTRUCTIVE BALLISTICS OF THE MANNLICHER-SCHOENAUER SPORTING RIFLES

Caliber	Cartridge	Powder Wt. Grains	Style of Bullet	Bullet Wt. Grains	Bullet length inches	Muzzle velocity ft. sec.	Muzzle energy ft. lbs.	Trajectory, Inches Height at Mid-Range 100 yds.	200 yds.	300 yds.
6.7		37	Soft-Nose ogival	157.5	1.2	2395	1990	.6″	3.2″	9″
6.7		38.5	S-Soft-Nose	123.5	1.24	2690	1980	.44″	2.45″	7″
8.2	Mannlicher-	43	Soft-Nose ogival	200.6	1.05	2225	2150	.79″	4″	11″
8.2	Schoenauer	48	S-Soft-Nose	170	1.1	2515	2418	.63″	2.9″	8.2″
9.0		48.5	Soft-Nose ogival	247	1.07	2160	2564	.85″	4.2″	11.5″
9.5		52.5	Soft-Nose ogival	271.6	1.04	2225	2980	.85″	4.4″	12.6″
30–06	Springfield	53	Brass-Point	180.5	1.24	2760	3000	.5″	2.3″	6.3″
7.0	7 x 64	51	Hollow-Point	173	1.25	2650	2700	.6″	2.6″	6.5″
8.0	8 x 60	54	Copper-Point-Torpedo	185	1.3	2775	3285	.4″	2.5″	6.07″

Original Mannlicher-Schoenauer Rifle Parts

Part No.	Name	Price	Part No.	Name	Price	Part No.	Name	Price	Part No.	Name	Price
*1	Barrel	$25.00	31	Scw. for mag. cart. stp.	.25	*46	Front pivot for car.	1.25	72	Front connect. screw	.50
2	Foresight	1.50	32/1	Hairtrigger plate	3.00	48	Back pivot for car.	.75	73	Frnt. con. scrw. washer	.25
*3	Foresight block	1.75	32/2	Set trigger	1.50	49	Trigger guard	3.00	74	Horn end for grip end	1.00
*5	Backsight base	2.00	32/3	Set trigger spring	1.50	50	Trigger guard screw	.35	75	Horn cap screw	.25
*6	Stand. sgt. for 1 leaf	1.25	32/4	Set trig. spg. screw	.35	51	Upper sling ring	1.00	76	Horn cap pin	.25
*7	Sight leaf	1.00	32/5	Set trig. reg. screw	.35	52	Upper sling band	1.00		Various Parts for the Sporter	
8	Sight leaf pin	.25	32/6	Set trigger pin	.25	53	Upper sling ring scrw.	.35		Half Stock	
14	Body	27.50	32/7	Hair trigger	1.50	54	Up. slng. rng. scrw. nut	.25	6a	Stand. sight for 1 leaf with wide notch.	1.75
15	Bolt catch	1.50	32/8	Hair trigger spring	.35	55	Lowel sling swivel	1.25	7a	Sgt. lf. with wide ntch.	1.00
16	Bolt catch spring	.25	32/9	Hair trigger pin	.25	56	Low. sling swiv. screw	.50	14/1	Grooved tang	1.75
17	Bolt catch pin	.25	32/10	Hair trigger catch	.50	57	Lower sling swivel connecting screw	.25	32	Single trigger	1.50
*18	Bolt	7.50	34	Sear lever	2.00	58	Butt plate		49/1	Trig. grd. for sing. trig.	5.00
18/1	Spring catch for firing pin nut	1.00	35	Pivot pin for sear lever	.25	59	Butt plate trap		49/2	Trigger guard catch	.75
19	Cocking piece	4.50	36	Sear	1.50	60	Butt plate trap spg.	3.50	49/3	Trig. guard ctch. lev.	.75
20	Safety catch	3.00	37	Sear pivot	.25	61	Butt plate trap spring screw		49/4	Trig. grd. catch. spg.	.25
21	Safety catch spring	.25	37/1	Trigger lever	2.00	63	Rub. lin. for butt plate	1.25	49/5	Trig. guard catch. pin	.25
22	Firing pin spring	1.00	37/2	Trigger lever pivot	.25	64	Screw	.35	49/6	Trig. guard lever pin	.25
23	Firing pin	3.50	37/3	Roller for trig. lever	.35	*65	Stock	40.00	69	Scrw. for spg. pin plate	.35
24	Firing pin nut	1.75	37/4	Roller pin	.25	66	Fore-end cap	1.75	71a	Rear connect. screw.	.35
25	Bolt head	3.50	38	Trigger spring	.50	67	Fore-end cap screw	.25	80a	Upper sling eye	2.50
*26	Ejector	1.50	*39	Cartridge carrier	4.00	68	Fore-end cap nut	.75	81a	Up. sling eye screw.	.50
27	Ejector screw	.25	*40	Cartridge carrier frame	4.00	69	Fore-end cap nut scrw.	.25	85	Spring pin	1.00
*28	Extractor	2.00	*41	Cart. car. cover plate	2.50	70	Screw sleeve	.25	86	Spring pin spring	1.25
*29	Mag. cartridge stop.	2.50	42	Cover plate catch	1.25	71	Rear connect. screw.	.50	87	Spring pin plate	.50
30	Spg. for mag. cart. stp.	.25	43	Fast. spg. for cov. plate	.25				88	Fore sight protector	1.00
			45	Cartridge carrier spg.	.50						

* Complete bolt assmb. 17.50
* Complete bolt head. 6.00

* Complete blued barrel with sgts. & swivel 30.00
* Complete stock.... 37.50

* Four piece collap. clng. rod for stock.... 3.50

Note: All Mannlicher-Schoenauer parts are interchangeable, but in ordering those parts marked with an asterick*, it is essential to state caliber.

GETTING STARTED IN CARTRIDGE CONVERSION

By John J. Donnelly

The following article is excerpted from John J. Donnelly's new book, *The Handloader's Manual of Cartridge Conversions* (Stoeger Publishing Co., 1987).

There's growing interest today in obsolete, foreign, metric, and wildcat ammunition. For reasons of economics and greater accuracy, we are also witnessing an increasing number of handloaders. These factors combined cannot survive for very long without spurring interest in handloading at all levels of expertise.

Whether experienced or not, handloaders should be aware of how the brass cartridge case evolved into its modern version. You have to go clear back to the Civil War, when most firearms in America featured either percussion or rimfire ignition. By the end of the war, the percussion firearm was already passing into history as bigger and better rimfire cartridges appeared on the market. Notable among these were the .56 caliber Spencer, the .54 Ballard, and the .52 Sharps & Hankins.

Following the Civil War, experiments with centerfire priming dealt a death blow to the large-bore rimfires.

These two cartridges date from the approximate time in history when cartridges were moving from inside priming to centerfire. On the left is a .56–56 Spencer. The one on the right is a .50–60 Peabody.

The U.S. Army tested several inside-primed cartridges and used the Benet inside cup primed round for several years before Colonel Hiram Berdan's exterior primer, invented in 1866, was adopted. This primer is still used in the military ammunition of many nations.

At the same time, the British were working on ammunition for the Snider conversion of the Enfield muzzleloading rifle. Under the direction of Colonel Edward Boxer, whose cartridge used a primer different from that of Berdan's, this model carried its own anvil. Berdan's primer, on the other hand, incorporated the anvil as part of the brass case in the center of the primer pocket, with two flashholes, one on either side of the anvil. Boxer's idea was subsequently adopted by U.S. ammunition producers, in part because it made the reloading of ammunition a much more practical matter.

John J. Donnelly was born in Chicago and grew up in New Hampshire. In 1972, a lifelong interest in firearms led Donnelly to become actively engaged in the mechanics of ammunition assembly. He formed his own custom ammunition and consulting firm, called Ballistek, in Lake Havasu City, Arizona, where he now lives and works. *The Handloader's Manual of Cartridge Conversion* is Donnelly's first book.

The cartridge shown on the left is an early rimfire version of the .50–70 Government. In the center is a Remington centerfire; and on the right is a .50–70 Government cartridge made in 1975 from Dixie Gun Works brass.

Brass Extrusion Labs, Ltd. (BELL) offers a complete line of rare and exotic cases, including the .577 Nitro Express shown here. Most cases are "Basic," meaning they must be formed and trimmed before use.

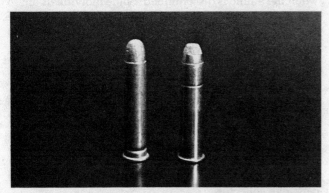

On the left is an early .45–70 cartridge utilizing inside priming (rimfire). On the right, a contemporary .45–70 manufactured by Winchester.

By the early 1870's, the march of American settlers westward was in full swing, and thus a good, available supply of reliable ammunition became a necessity. It soon became apparent that Berdan-primed ammunition was too difficult to reload out on the open plains, especially with screaming hordes of belligerent warriors dashing about. Moreover, not many of our frontier ancestors perceived much merit in lugging tons of ammo west in their Conestoga wagons. Enter the Boxer primer.

After adoption of the .45-70 Spring cartridge in 1873, inside primed ammunition was used for a few years, but eventually it was replaced by the Boxer-primed cartridge. Reloading apparatus soon became a part of every infantry company's supply kit, thus marking the advent of reloading in America.

Britain—and for that matter most of Europe—did not consider field reloading a necessary pastime for their troops, however, and adopted the cheaper Berdan primer for their metallics. Surprisingly few changes have taken place—in both cases and primers—since 1875. The materials in current use are vastly superior, of course, but their physical essence remains unchanged.

■ MODERN PRODUCTION

Modern brass cases are produced under exacting specifications. While each case manufacturer has his own recipe for brass, the basic formulas of copper and zinc have remained unchanged over the years. The exact ratio affects the forming characteristics and ultimate strength of the case considerably; hence, each manufacturer uses the blend he believes is most superior.

Cartridge cases begin life as flat sheets rolled into great long coils. These brass sheets are first heated, then rolled to exact, predetermined thicknesses. The sheets then pass through blanking presses, which punch out disks of proper diameter to avoid as much waste as possible. The disks then enter a carefully planned series of annealing, lubrication, and drawing processes.

A drawing die is little more than a polished hole in a tool steel plate. Poised above this hole is the male portion of the die, which is a highly polished tool steel finger. The outside diameter of this finger is slightly smaller than the female die's inside diameter. In use, a disk of annealed brass is centered above the female cavity; when the press cycles, the male portion enters the female cavity, pulling the brass with it.

After drawing, the disk, which resembles a small cup, passes into another draw die and the procedure is repeated. The second die set contains a female cavity with a smaller inside diameter and a male pin with a larger outside diameter. Drawing is performed several times until a long, cylindrical tube of brass with a solid bottom is produced. Somewhere along the line, a small nipple is added to one of the female dies at its base, thus forming the primer pocket and headstamp.

The tubes move next to another highly automated machine that plunge-cuts the rim diameter and the ex-

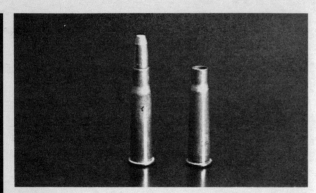

At left is an original Winchester .33 WCF cartridge. The case on the right is a .45–70 Government reformed to .33 WCF.

tractor groove. After turning, the flashhole is punched, followed by annealing, subsequent neck forming (if required), and final trimming to the required length.

Each step in this procedure is monitored by quality control instruments and personnel. The chances of a missed operation showing up at the end of the line are therefore quite slim. A finished round of ammunition without a flashhole connecting the primer to the powder would be dangerous indeed. During 20 years of handloading ammunition, the author has found one case—in a box of new, unprimed .38 Special brass—that did not sport a flashhole. This case is still around as a reminder that large manufacturers are not infallible, and that new cases should always be closely scrutinized before use.

It does not take 20 years on a Detroit assembly line to realize that the above procedure is complex and very expensive. Many modern machines of this type can take days to tool up, and the added expense of tool maintenance and constant upkeep can only be justified for extended runs producing millions upon millions of cases.

■ WHY THEY'RE GONE

In 1902, Winchester Repeating Arms introduced the .33 WCF cartridge and simultaneously announced the availability of its M86 lever rifles so chambered. This combo became very popular, mostly because the 200 grain factory bullet exited the muzzle at some 2200 fps, delivering slightly better than a ton of energy. In 1936, Winchester unveiled its much stronger M71 rifle, along with a new cartridge made to complement the stronger breech. This was the .348 WCF cartridge, whose 200 grain factory loading produced almost 1½ tons of energy at 2325 fps. Owners of the M86 quickly began trading for M71's and .33 WCF ammo sales plummeted. The cartridge was discontinued in 1941.

Although World War II certainly had some influence on this disappearance, the bottom line indicated that sales of .33 WCF ammo had dropped off in favor of the more powerful .348. Moreover, Winchester could not justify the set-up and tooling costs for the .33, and thus this once great cartridge became obsolete. A few years later, the .358 WCF appeared, causing the .348 to pass into oblivion as well.

A cartridge can become obsolete in other ways, too. In some instances, a manufacturer may conjure up a new cartridge and firearm, place it on the market, then discontinue its sale after only a year or so because of general lack of interest (an example of this would be the .38-45 Stevens). For whatever reason, a host of cartridges has been introduced and later been discontinued over the years. It follows that many firearms are also produced for these cartridges, but they do *not* evaporate when the ammo is discontinued. Some individuals opt to rechamber, rebarrel, rebore or commit some other act of violence upon these relics in an effort to remain on the firing line. This is unfortunate and should only be considered when every possibility of obtaining shootable ammo has been exhausted. It is interesting to note that by the time you read this, several more familiar cartridges may have disappeared, most notably the .38-40 and .44-40 Winchesters, the .358 WCF, .35 Rem., .32 Win. Spl., .303 Savage, .30-40 Krag, and .30 Rem. A point is reached where it is no longer profitable to manufacture these and other cartridges, and they must then pass inevitably into the realm of the custom loader and cartridge collector.

■ CASE NOMENCLATURE

Most reloaders are familiar with the basic terms that apply to cartridge brass, but let's review here the common types of existing cases and the manner in which they *headspace*. The "target" notation indicates that portion of the case that must position itself accurately against the mating chamber surface so as to establish the *headspace dimension*. The dimension from the target to the head is very critical, and a tolerance of plus-or minus- .001 must be held. The remaining distance—i.e., case length minus headspace—is critical only in the positive direction. That is, the dimension from the target to the mouth can be considerably shorter, but never longer. As an example of this chambering irregularity, consider the .38 Special cartridge in a .357 Magnum chamber.

The various names associated with cartridges, new and obsolete, are a result of every naming system imaginable. In an effort to shed more light on this subject, the cartridge names have been divided into the following groups. These groups, in turn, have been broken up into sub-groups for added clarity.

1. *Named for parent company*
   .17 Remington (.17 is the caliber, Remington is the designer)

CASE NOMENCLATURE

EXAMPLE: .308 WIN.

EXAMPLE: .38 SPL.

A – BODY   E – WEB   J – PRIMER POCKET
B – NECK   F – BASE   K – RIM
C – SHOULDER   G – HEAD   L – EXTRACTOR GROOVE
D – MOUTH   H – FLASH HOLE

.25-20 Winchester (.25 is the caliber, with 20 grains of black powder in the original load, produced by Winchester)

2. *Named for individual designer*
.257 Roberts

3. *Named for particular weapon*
.30 Carbine (.30 is the caliber; "Carbine" refers to the M1 military carbine)
.30-40 Krag (.30 is the caliber; 40 grains refers to black powder content; Krag refers to the rifle, a Krag-Jorgensen)

4. *Named for weapon action type*
.351 WSL (caliber is .35; WSL denotes "Winchester Self-loading")

5. *Named for issuing government*
.303 British (caliber is .303; British:British military)

6. *Named for relative performance*
.357 Magnum or .357 Maximum

7. *Named to describe case*
.32 Ballard Extra Long (implies that another car-

CASE MEASUREMENTS

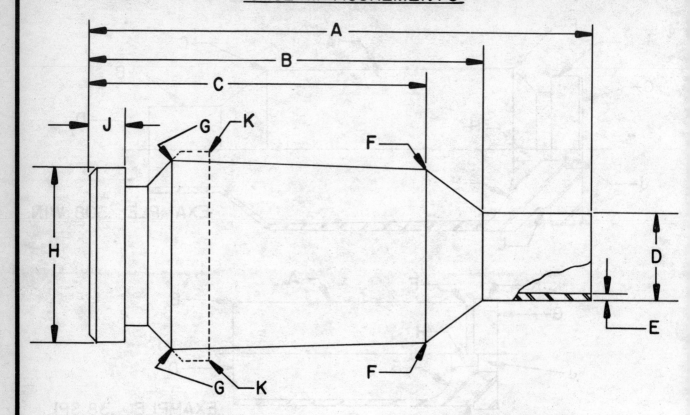

A – OVERALL LENGTH
B – LENGTH TO NECK
C – LENGTH TO SHOULDER
D – NECK OUTSIDE DIAMETER
E – NECK WALL THICKNESS
F – SHOULDER DIAMETER

G – BASE DIAMETER
H – RIM DIAMETER
J – RIM THICKNESS
K – BELT DIAMETER

tridge—i.e., the .32 Ballard Long—exists)
.40-50 Sharps Necked (caliber is .40; contains 50 grains black powder; produced by Sharps; implies existence of .40-50 Straight Sharps)

8. *Names associated with a date*
.38-50 Maynard 1882 (suggests that another version, earlier or later, exists)

9. *Named for ignition principle*
.38 Long Centerfire (implies that a rimfire version exists)
.58 Berdan Carbine (this case is Berdan primed or is used in a Berdan weapon)

10. *Wildcats*
7mm-08 (caliber is 7mm or .284; projectile is in a .308 case)

.243 Ackley Improved (a .243 Winchester case has increased powder capacity due to Ackley's improvement)

11. *Names selected at random*
.218 Bee, or .22 Hornet (in which "Bee" and "Hornet" are merely arbitrary terms)
.40-70 Peabody "What Cheer" (refers to a rifle range in Rhode Island known by that name)

12. *Metric*
7 × 57mm Mauser (caliber is 7mm or .284; case is 57mm or 2.244″ long)
6.5 × 57R (caliber is 6.5mm or .264; case is 57mm or 2.244″ long; "R" means rimmed)
8 × 57JS
8 × 57JR (same as above, except case is rimmed)

8 × 57R (same as above, except .323 dia. rimmed case)

8 × 57 (.323 diameter assumed rimless)

Note: "J" above denotes the German infantry cartridge, with its smaller diameter (.318) "JS" is slightly larger (.323).

If some of this nomenclature seems confusing, don't worry about it unnecessarily. The 12 major categories provided here are meant simply to illustrate how cartridges are named. Those who spend a great amount of time in and around handloading will soon become accustomed to these and other strange letters and symbols.

To illustrate further why it is so difficult to place each cartridge in its proper niche, let's examine some additional (but common) aberrations:

- The .218 Bee uses .224 diameter projectiles, as do the .220 Swift, .222 Remington, .223 Remington, and .225 Winchester.
- The 6.5 Remington Magnum uses .264 diameter bullets (which actually measure 6.70mm in diameter). Why isn't it called the 6.7 Remington Magnum? That's a good—but unanswerable—question.
- The .270 Winchester and .270 Weatherby both use .277 diameter bullets.
- The 7 × 57 Mauser cartridge (see above) uses a .284 diameter bullet and is actually 2.235" in length; to be consistent, the cartridge should be labeled: "7.2 × 56.8."
- The .303 Savage uses a .308 diameter bullet, while the .303 British uses a .311 diameter bullet.
- The .256 (6,5) Newton uses a .264 diameter bullet, which actually measures 6,7mm in diameter.
- In U.S. nomenclature, .40 can indicate anything from .403 diameter to .424, while .44 can mean anything from .422 to .450 in diameter.

Obviously, nothing can ever be assumed in cartridge nomenclature. These examples are only part of the mystery. Metric and British ammunition compound the confusion even further. Delving into cartridge nomenclature is much like the first day on a new job—it seems impossible that you could ever memorize everyone's name, but you do in time. Happily, the same applies to handloading.

This discussion of cartridge names requires one more clarification. In referring to the group called "Names at Random," this may be an accurate description in terms of "Bee" and "Hornet", but such is not always the case. Often the tags applied to such cartridges have a legitimate, if cloudy, validity, including the following:

A&M	—Atkinson & Marquart, Arizona gunsmiths
Ackley	—Paul O. Ackley, gunsmith and experimenter
AMP	—Auto Mag. Pistol
AR	—Auto Rim (rimmed version of automatic for use in revolvers)
Auto	—Implies use in a semi or full-automatic weapon
B&D	—Bain & Davis, gunsmiths
Barnes	—Frank C. Barnes, experimenter and writer
Belted	—Belted base case (i.e. 7mm Remington Magnum)
Bergmann	—Thedore Bergmann, weapon & ammunition designer
Borchardt	—Hugo Borchardt, weapon designer
BR	—Benchrest
Donaldson	—Harvey Donaldson, ammunition experimenter
DWM	—Deutsche Waffen und Munitionsfabriken
Everlasting	—Extra heavy walled cases (for longer life in reloading)
Express	—Magnum(-ish), special design
Flanged	—Rimmed (e.g., .30-30 WCF)
H&H	—Holland & Holland, British weapon manufacturers
Harvey	—Jim Harvey, Connecticut ammunition experimenter
Herrett	—Steve Herrett, stockmaker, experimenter
Johnson	—Melvin M. Johnson, marine weapon designer
Kilbourne	—Lyle Kilbourne, experimenter
Kynoch	—British ammunition manufacturer
Maynard	—Maynard Company, weapon manufacturer (circa 1882)
MAS	—Manufacture d' Arms de St. Etienne (French arsenal)
MMJ	—See Johnson
Newton	—Charles Newton, weapon designer & manufacturer (circa 1915)
Nitro Express	—Generally indicates smokeless powder is used
Norma	—A.B. Norma Projektilfabrik, Swedish munitions manufacturer
OKH	—Charles O'Neil, Elmer Keith, Don Hopkins

Page	—Warren Page, experimenter, shooter, writer
Peabody	—H.L. Peabody, weapon designer (Boston, Mass.)
PPC	—Pindell Palm Corporation
RCBS	—Fred Huntington, Huntington Die Specialties (founder of RCBS; also Rockchucker & Super RC)
Rigby	—J. Rigby & Co., English weapon manufacturer
Roberts	—Ned H. Roberts, ballistic experimenter (circa 1925)
Sharps	—Sharps Rifle Manufacturing Company (circa 1870)
Springfield	—Springfield Armory (Springfield, Mass.)
SS	—Single Shot
S&W	—Smith & Wesson
Vom Hofe	—E.A. Vom Hofe, Austrian weapon manufacturer
WCF	—Winchester Centerfire
Webley	—British Arms Manufacturer
Wesson	—Frank Wesson, weapon designer & manufacturer (circa 1870)
Whelen	—Col. Townsend Whelen, hunter, writer, experimenter
WSL	—Winchester Self-loading

When undertaking the fabrication of any cartridge for the first time, it is strongly recommended that you begin with a clean workbench and a note pad. First, select the appropriate starter case and sketch out a rough plan of attack. As each operation is performed, note your success or failure. Keep these notes as clear and concise as possible, including details of any lubrication applied or any extra cleaning or polishing required. Gradually, these notes will grow into a record that includes all the information required to produce that same ammunition again, months or years later, without repeating the negative results of the first attempt. Unfortunately, there is no standard form with which to record this work; all you need, actually, is a yellow legal pad on which you have carefully noted these points:

Original case	Trimming
Precleaning	F/L sizing
Annealing	Fireforming
Pre-trimming	Cleaning
Forming	Special notes
Lathe work (including tools)	Seating
	Crimping

You should also keep careful records on powder, primers, lengths and diameters, along with dates and other pertinent information.

■ CALIBER DETERMINATION

Imagine this scene at your local gunshop:

"I'd like some bullets for my gun," says the customer.

"Yes, sir," replies the owner, "and what caliber and bullet weight would you be interested in?"

"What do you mean?" exclaims the customer, assuming his needs must be obvious from the lever rifle he is holding.

"I mean," calmly explains the custom loader, "do you want bullets, or do you want loaded cartridges?"

"Bullets, cartridges, whatever you want to call 'em. I need them for this here rifle!"

The loader, who is beginning to get the picture, then asks, "What cartridge is your rifle chambered for, sir?"

"Damned if I know! Bought her this morning at a yard sale."

That may sound like an improbable scenario, but it has doubtless occurred many times at one gunshop or another all over the country. Too often, gun owners who seek ammo for their weapons do not have the slightest idea what cartridges are required. Granted, it is often possible to determine the chambering from markings on the weapon, but many weapons have been produced in this country and abroad for which ammo has long since disappeared. Such firearms must be rechambered, rebored or otherwise altered to accept more common ammo. In other instances, chambers are reworked to accept their owners' own "wildcat" designs. For whatever reason, it is often necessary to start with a firearm of unknown caliber and determine what cartridge can be safely used, a task best accomplished by using two rather simple gunsmithing techniques: *bore slugging* and *chamber casting*.

■ BORE SLUGGING

Slugging the bore of a firearm is a highly accurate method of determining what diameter bullet is required for that particular gun. Knowing the bullet diameter will, in turn, help finalize the cartridge dimensions.

To start this operation, select a lead bullet with a diameter slightly larger than the bore. To determine the bore diameter at the muzzle, use the inside diameter measuring fingers of a dial vernier caliper. Be certain that both fingers are contacting the larger diameter.

Next, select a bullet mold that will cast a slug slightly larger in diameter than the bore. If the bore measures, say, 0.446″, then any .45 caliber mold (0.451 to 0.458) will do the trick. A long rifle slug is easier to measure, by the way, than a shorter pistol bullet. Cast a couple of

CARTRIDGE HEADSPACE

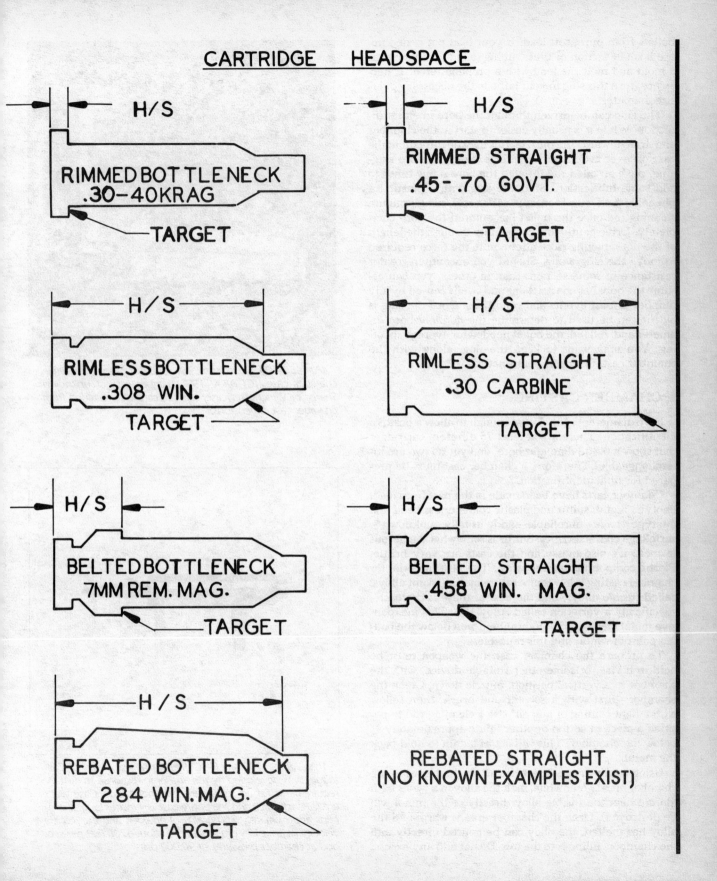

H/S

RIMMED BOTTLENECK
.30-40 KRAG

TARGET

H/S

RIMMED STRAIGHT
.45-.70 GOVT.

TARGET

H/S

RIMLESS BOTTLENECK
.308 WIN.

TARGET

H/S

RIMLESS STRAIGHT
.30 CARBINE

TARGET

H/S

BELTED BOTTLENECK
7MM REM. MAG.

TARGET

H/S

BELTED STRAIGHT
.458 WIN. MAG.

TARGET

H/S

REBATED BOTTLENECK
284 WIN. MAG.

TARGET

REBATED STRAIGHT
(NO KNOWN EXAMPLES EXIST)

bullets from pure, soft lead. If your lead pot is tied up, use a small section of brass tubing (oiled for release) as a mold and melt the lead with a propane torch. If necessary, turn this slug in your lathe to the necessary oversize diameter.

The slug can be driven through the bore in either direction. While it is usually easier to start in the chamber and drive towards the muzzle, this may be difficult in the case of lever action carbines, for example. Before slugging, push an oiled rag through the bore a few times to add some lubrication. Start the slug with a plastic (or phenolic) mallet and continue with a stiff, nonaluminum cleaning rod once the bullet has entered the bore completely. Drive gently and completely through the length of the bore, paying close attention to the force required to move the slug along. Should you encounter greater resistance in some sections than in others, you can assume the bore has constrictions and swells caused by any number of past events and conditions. Once the slug is out, it can be used to determine the *nominal* bore diameter and, indeed, the bullet needed for average shooting. You may want to keep the slug, along with the chamber cast, for future reference.

■ CHAMBER CASTING

Bore diameter is not always enough to allow a positive identification. There are at least 75 different cartridges that show a 0.308 diameter bore, and yet no two are interchangeable! Therefore, a chamber cast must be prepared for final identification.

Chamber casts have been made in the past from lead, linotype metal, sulfur and plastic compounds. Lead and linotype have unreliable—and usually unknown—shrinkage characteristics. Sulfur is somewhat dangerous to melt; it's also messy and the casts are very brittle. Plastic compounds tend to warp. The best material for chamber casting is low temperature melting point alloys, called *fusible* alloys, and the best of these is *cerrosafe*, specifically a variation called Alloy 158. This inexpensive metal melts at 158° Fahrenheit, well below the boiling point of water, and it is reusable.

To prepare the chamber cast, the weapon must be held in a vise, or some other suitable device, with the chamber in a vertical position, muzzle down. Clean the chamber—first with a solvent and brush, then follow with a light coating of gun oil. Use a cleaning rod to position a piece of cotton or other fabric approximately 1″ below the chamber. This will act as a dam to hold back the metal.

Using a hair dryer, direct hot air on the barrel in the chamber area. Meanwhile, melt the alloy in a water bath (do *not* heat the fusible alloy directly or the metal will be destroyed). Once the chamber area is warm and the alloy has melted, the alloy can be poured directly into the chamber, filling it to the top. Do not add any excess;

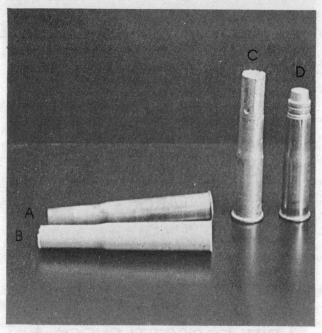

(A) .450-400 Nitro case; (B) .450-400 acrylic facsimile chamber case; (C) Alloy 158 chamber cast of unknown Sharps or Winchester case; and (D) cartridge resulting from chamber cast dimensions.

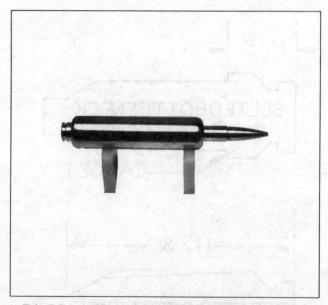

This 7,8 × 102mm HHC (Hemispherical Headed Cartridge) was developed by the author in response to military requirements for an 1800-yard sniper cartridge. Case walls are $^1/_{10}$-inch thick and the entire case is 4 inches long. It contains approximately 200 grains of powder, and the muzzle velocity (with a 190 grain bullet) is about 4200 feet per second at chamber pressures of 90,000 psi.

it will only have to be removed later. Wait about one hour until the cast has cooled to the ambient temperature. Most fusible alloys expand slightly as they cool. This expansion will disappear when the cast cools, but not before. Do not try to remove the cast before the hour is up; otherwise, you will damage the weapon and the cast.

Once cooled, the cast is easily tapped out with a cleaning rod. You now have an exact reproduction of the chamber and should be able to make an accurate identification.

Readers who are interested in delving further into the fascinating world of cartridge conversion are invited to study the author's recently published work on the subject, *The Handloader's Manual of Cartridge Conversions,* which includes full how to instructions and more than 900 conversions.

COMPUTER BALLISTICS: THE BRAVE NEW WORLD OF CARTRIDGE SELECTION

by Ralph F. Quinn

To all those millions of licensed hunters who pursue the 25 classified species of big game in the U.S. and Canada, the message is clear: *Move over, world, and make way for Computer Ballistics*. Careful study of standard ballistic tables may be adequate for practical big game hunting, but all fall considerably short of informing riflemen about *what they need to know* concerning the performance of their chosen calibers, particularly where long range hunting is involved. That's where the modern home computer enters the picture.

If you count yourself among those who feel that computers are best left to the experts, think again. If you can run a videocassette unit in your living room, or take a picture with an auto-focus camera, then you can run a computer program. All you have to do is turn on the unit, type "LOAD PROGRAM, RUN", and you are in ballistics business.

Any computer program is merely a set of instructions that tell a series of microchips how to solve a given problem. Knowing how to tackle the problem initially obviously requires in–depth knowledge; but with the external ballistics software that's available today, all the hunter-shooter need do is purchase a disc or cassette compatible with his home computer and go at it. Several publishers of scientific and engineering software offer such discs, among them Pab Software (P.O. Box 15397, Fort Wayne, Indiana 46885). The cost is modest—usually $25 for a floppy disc or tape.

▮ HUNTING THE COUES DEER

What will a computer program do for you? Let's suppose you need to know what rifle/cartridge is best to use for hunting Boone and Crockett class Coues deer in Arizona's Rincon Mountains. This diminutive whitetail of the Sonoran Desert is one of the toughest big game species known to the American Southwest. It has to be tough if it is to survive in that moonscape environment. Moreover, it's a difficult animal to spot and tougher still to approach. Ask any hunter who regularly persues *Odocoileus virginianus couesi*.

Typically, any rifleman in high mountain desert country is at a serious disadvantage from the start. The big bucks are well aware of the hunter's existence and they keep their distance accordingly. Knowing the exact range, therefore, is vital if the hunter is to take maximum advantage of his selected caliber. For one thing, thermal drafts surging upward can cause extreme bullet drift, not to mention such other adverse factors as the high altitude. In this case, a 7mm Magnum cartridge has been selected. And yet, a ballistics table indicates serious gaps with that choice, especially at intermediate and long ranges. Clearly, a more detailed ballistics table is needed to pinpoint shots on target at 200 yards and over.

> **Ralph Quinn has been writing articles and books and producing films on hunting and fishing for many years. His most recent film production featured the Coues deer on location in Arizona. The software program he developed on personal ballistics for hunting calibers, as described in this article, was generated on a Radio Shack Model 3 unit with two-disc drive.**

Running an external ballistics program on your home computer can be an uncomplicated process that saves time as well as money.

Table I (below) lists the exact trajectory printout for the 7mm 140 grain Sierra bullet in question. Note that the program is zeroed at 400 yards with a range increment of 50. To run a similar listing for a particular cartridge, an operator merely types in the interval desired and the range at which the rifle is to be zeroed. The computer then provides the information needed to make the first shot count, including total drop, maximum height above the line of sight, elevation, and wind deflection. There's no need to know complex formulas for momentum, energy, or coefficient calculations.

■ A DEFINITION OF TERMS

For readers who do not fully understand the terminology used in a ballistic essay, a brief definition of terms is in order. First, *external ballistics* is the detailed study of what happens to a bullet *after* it leaves the muzzle. The science of ballistics includes muzzle energy, velocity and trajectory, each of equal importance to the hunter in selecting and comparing the pros and cons of various cartridges. By comparing numbers beforehand,

the hunter is better able to make an intelligent decision about which caliber or cartridge to choose.

Muzzle energy is a measurement expressing foot pounds of impact. Most ballistic charts give energy figures at muzzle and at 200 yards, whereas computer programs are expressed from 0 to 1000 yards. Energy levels are important to the hunter, because they help determine how rapidly a load and bullet lose impact (i.e., killing power) in flight.

Velocity is the speed at which a bullet travels, measured in feet per second (fps). Again, most ballistic charts provide muzzle and 200-yard velocities, leaving large gaps in bullet performance. If you want to know the velocity of your favorite cartridge at 25-foot increments over 600 yards, your computer can deliver the answers immediately. This measurement is extremely important in cartridge and bullet weight selection.

Finally, *trajectory* is the curved path taken by the bullet from muzzle to target. It is the *degree* of curve that is important to the shooter-hunter, since bullet design and muzzle velocity are inseparable. Thus, energy, velocity and trajectory all combine to spell the difference

THIS IS DETAILED TRAJECTORY FOR ZEROING AT 400 YDS.   TABLE I

MUZZLE VELOCITY (FPS):	3200
RANGE (YARDS):	400
REMAINING VELOCITY (FPS):	2578
REMAINING ENERGY (FT-LBS):	2065
TIME OF FLIGHT (SEC):	.418
TOTAL DROP (INCHES):	31.5
MAX HEIGHT ABOVE SIGHT LINE (INCHES)	7.9
ELEVATION REQUIRED (MOA):	8.2
DEFLECTION FOR 10-MPH CROSSWIND (INCHES):	7.6

RANGE YARDS	VELOCITY FPS	BULLET PATH FROM SIGHT LINE MOA	BULLET PATH FROM SIGHT LINE INCHES	10-MPH WIND INCHES
50	3117	4.4	2.2	.1
100	3036	5	5	.4
150	2956	4.6	6.8	1
200	2878	3.9	7.7	1.8
250	2801	3	7.5	2.8
300	2725	2.1	6.2	4.2
350	2651	1.1	3.7	5.8
400	2578	0	0	7.6
450	2506	−1.1	−5	9.7
500	2435	−2.3	−11.3	12.1
550	2365	−3.5	−19.1	14.8
600	2296	−4.8	−28.6	17.9

Big game hunters find external programs valuable in pinpointing shots at long range. Knowing your kill area measurements beforehand can pay large dividends in the field.

between one shot kills, complete misses, or wounded game. To make this point more emphatically, note in Table I how trajectory is listed for 400-yard zeroing. Under the heading "Range/Yards", find the 400-yard listing. In the MOA (Minute of Angle) column, "zero" indicates the rifle is dead on at that distance. Under normal circumstances, a hunter typically zeroes his rifle at 100 yards, but he has no idea of where the bullet is or what it's doing at 400 or 500 yards. With a computer printout, however, it's a simple matter of reading the numbers. Referring again to Table I, if the shooter has only 50 yards to work with, he merely adjusts the scope 4.4 inches (see MOA column) above the line of sight to hit 400 yards point of aim. In other examples, at 450 yards the bullet drops only 5 inches from the line of sight, while at 500 yards the drop is 11.3 inches.

Does all this indicate that a 7mm Magnum is the best choice for a 500-yard rifle shot at a Coues deer? The final answer depends, of course, on the skill of the shooter and the circumstances surrounding the shot. The point is, the hunter now knows ahead of time that, all things

being equal, a 140 grain Sierra out of a 7mm Mag zeroed at 400 yards will land somewhere in the chest cavity area of a whitetail at 500 yards. It all depends on the shooter.

Equally important, wind drift at 500 yards is also indicated. In a 10-knot situation, the bullet will impact, left or right, within the same kill area. With the wind at 5 knots, the distance is reduced by one-half. To eliminate wind drift and bullet drop factors, the hunter should top his long distance piece with a 6-20 × variable scope designed to handle such information. Thus, by using a Ranging 1000 to establish distance, one-shot kills at 400 (or more) yards should become almost routine.

ONE-SHOT KILLS ON SMALL GAME

For another example of "computer riflery," let's head east about 1,800 miles, where a computer printout details the performance of varminter Charlie Keefus's pet cartridge—the .219 Zipper (a rimmed cartridge which

Portable range finders help big game and varmint hunters alike by providing accurate distances to the target.

With his chronograph, this ballistician averages out his 5-shot velocities and inserts the data into his computer program. The printouts supply detailed trajectories for point of aim distances.

uses a .224 bullet; it was introduced by Winchester in 1937 and is now obsolete)—for long-range, one-shot kills on woodchucks.

Traditional ballistics tables are wholly lacking in .219 performance, but with a computer printout similar to Table II (opposite page) the answers come quickly to the surface. As with most of his wildcat loads, Keefus records a 5-shot velocity check on his Ohler chronograph, averages the group, then notes the resulting velocity on the software program. The printout (Table II) provides range, remaining velocity and energy, total drop, maximum height above bore, and deflection in 10 mph wind. With the computer printout indicating the needed sight elevation for zero range, it becomes a simple matter of placing the reticule on one center and targeting a second bull—say 2.6 inches—above. The .224 bullet will strike dead on at 250 yards and will hit 9.3 inches low at 400 yards, well within the body height of an average groundhog.

Another useful piece of information available on an external ballistic program is *bullet momentum*. If you're a metallic silhouette shooter and you know the estab-

lished ranges for each target—ram, boar, chicken, and so on—it's easy to select the right bullet and caliber combination to generate enough foot pounds and momentum to drop the iron cutouts. Again, this information can be called up within seconds—just type in the necessary information and let your computer do the rest.

■ HELP FOR THE AVERAGE SHOOTER

If you don't claim to be a precision varminter or Olympic-class silhouette shooter, but just an average guy whose longest kill was on a whitetail mule deer at 125 yards, this external program is still worth its weight in gold. Beyond saving hundreds of dollars in reloading components and countless hours studying ballistic charts, you can now make informed decisions about which cartridges deliver the needed on-target energy to take down your favorite game animal.

"But," you protest, "I already know how my .35 Remington performs on deer. Why do I need a computer to tell me what I already know?"

```
MANUFACTURER    SAVAGE
TYPE FIREARM    SINGLE SHOT
SERIAL NO.      XXXX
```

219 ZIPPER IMP.

BALLISTIC COEFFICIENT: .227

GUN ALTITUDE (FT): 850

TABLE II

BULLET WEIGHT (GRS): 52

TEMPERATURE (DEG-F): 72

RANGE YARDS	REM VEL	REM ENERGY	TOTAL DROP	MOMEN-TUM	MAX HEIGHT	DEFL. IN 10MPH WIND
0	3650	1538	0	27.1	-1.5	0
50	3419	1350	.3	25.4	0	.2
100	3201	1183	1.4	23.7	0	1
150	2994	1035	3.4	22.2	.3	2.3
200	2796	902	6.3	20.7	1.1	4.2
250	2607	784	10.3	19.3	2.3	6.7
300	2425	679	15.6	18	3.9	10
350	2251	585	22.3	16.7	6	14
400	2084	501	30.9	15.4	8.7	19
450	1923	427	41.3	14.2	12.1	24.9
500	1772	363	54.3	13.1	16.5	32
550	1630	307	70.2	12.1	22	40.4
600	1497	259	89.3	11.1	28.8	50

CUT OUT FOR FIELD REFERENCE

FOR ZEROING AT 350 YDS

RANGE YARDS	FROM SIGHT LINE INS.
25	.1
50	1.6
75	2.8
100	3.9
125	4.7
150	5.4
175	5.7
200	5.9
225	5.7
250	5.2
275	4.5
300	3.4
325	1.9
350	0
375	-2.3
400	-5.1

THIS IS DETAILED TRAJECTORY FOR ZEROING AT 350 YDS.

MUZZLE VELOCITY (FPS):	3650
RANGE (YARDS):	350
REMAINING VELOCITY (FPS):	2251
REMAINING ENERGY (FT-LBS):	585
TIME OF FLIGHT (SEC):	.367
TOTAL DROP (INCHES);	22.3
MAX HEIGHT ABOVE SIGHT LINE (INCHES):	6
ELEVATION REQUIRED (MOA):	6.8
DEFLECTION FOR 10-MPH CROSSWIND (INCHES):	14

Varminters, such as this woodchuck shooter, find external programs valuable in targeting their favorite loads at long range.

From varmint cartridges to booming Bertha's, computer printouts supply detailed information for one-shot kills: (l. to r.) .22 Hornet; .223; .243 Win.; .308; 6.5 Rem.Mag.; .270 Win.; .300 Win.

Given the velocity of a 5-shot group, this computer shooter can print accurate data for favored loads at distances up to 1,000 yards.

For one thing, there are about a dozen .30 calibers which are adequate for deer—but which one of those is ideal for you is another story. Just because Uncle Harry knocked over a passel of timbered whitetails with his .32 Special, that doesn't make the cartridge right for deer-sized animals in the midwest, west or southwest areas. Show up in Arizona with a scoped .32 and chances are good you'll be outdistanced and undergunned.

Some 25 years ago, Parker Ackley published his *Handbook For Shooters and Reloaders*. In that work, he discussed at length how much energy was needed to kill game animals. The energy deemed adequate for deer, antelope and the like was, according to Ackley, about 1,200 foot pounds. That is, whether the average range at which this game is taken measures 40 or 400 yards, the bullet must generate 1,200 pounds of energy at point of impact, not at muzzle. By staying in the timber and

keeping your shots well within the killing range of the .32, you will find this caliber to be adequate.

But what about all the other .30 caliber possibilities? A quick printout from your favorite software program can clear the air in a hurry. Just type in the ballistic coefficient, the altitude at which the rifle will be used, the bullet weight, the average temperature expected during the hunt, and then read off the energy figures (see Table III below).

As with all shooting sports, the taking of big game with a particular load and rifle is largely a mental process. Knowing well in advance how a certain load will perform ballistically is a big help in scoring one-shot kills. Efficiency and practicality are hallmarks of the modern rifleman; by using a personal computer, even the average hunter can maximize both of these all-important categories. It's time to give it a try.

	MANUFACTURER	
98	TYPE FIREARM	
99	SERIAL NO.	
100		
101	7MM	140 GR SIERRA
102		
103	BALLISTIC COEFFICIENT: .49	
104		
105	GUN ALTITUDE (FT): 6100	
106		

TABLE III

BULLET WEIGHT (GRS): 140

TEMPERATURE (DEG-F): 55

RANGE YARDS	REM VEL	REM ENERGY	TOTAL DROP	MOMEN-TUM	MAX HEIGHT	DEFL. IN 10 MPH WIND
0	3200	3183	0	64	-1.5	0
100	3036	2865	1.8	60.7	0	.4
200	2878	2574	7.3	57.5	1.3	1.8
300	2725	2308	17	54.5	3.9	4.2
400	2578	2065	31.5	51.5	7.9	7.6
500	2435	1843	51	48.6	13.4	12.1
600	2296	1639	76.5	45.9	20.9	17.9
700	2163	1454	108.8	43.2	30.5	25.2
800	2034	1285	148.2	40.6	42.6	33.9
900	1908	1132	195.8	38.1	57.5	43.9
1000	1789	995	253.6	35.7	76.1	56.1

HUNTING SMALL GAME WITH AN AUTOLOADER

by Stanley Trzoniec

Until recently, it was fashionable among experienced hunters to look down at those novice gunners who used autoloading single shot rimfires in pursuit of woodchucks and other small game. But with wild game acreage shrinking constantly, the need to stalk close and shoot near appears to be on the upswing, especially in more urbanized sections of the country.

Moreover, today's trend toward modernization has prompted a need among hunters everywhere to try new guns as well as techniques. Such is the case with the autoloading twenty-two rimfire rifle, which until recently was considered by the sporting intelligentsia to be less than functional and dependent on ammunition of faultless quality. Bad hunters relied on these repeaters to compensate for their lack of skill at one-shot opportunities.

If one model has led the way in this mini-revolution, it might well be Remington's Model 552, an autoloading .22 rimfire that can chamber and shoot .22 shorts, longs and long rifles with ease. This gun first hit the market in 1957 under the name of the "552 Speedmaster." According to the company catalog, it looked and handled much like its big brother, the 740 centerfire rifle. After 1984, the streamlined Model 552 sported a deeper, more polished look that included an extensive fleur-de-lis checkering pattern complete with Remington's famous RKW finish.

This trio of popular rimfires includes (left to right): S&W Model 41, Remington 552 Speedmaster, and Weatherby Mark XXII.

Stanley Trzoniec is a veteran firearms writer and photographer who has long specialized in the reporting of all modern weapons. An accomplished handloader, he has written on this subject for virtually every major firearms journal. Currently Special Projects Editor of Guns Magazine, he is also the author of several books, including a major work on the .22 Rimfire to be published in early 1988.

Another Remington success story involves the plastic rifle known as Nylon 66. Introduced to the public in 1959, it was touted as one of the world's most reliable autoloaders. It proved itself early on by shooting over 100,000 rounds with no malfunctions in a record-breaking shootout that pitted expert marksman Tom Frye against 100,000 wooden blocks. Today, after undergoing a dozen variations in as many years, the Nylon 66 remains the autoloader most relied on by serious hunters, regardless of weather or other physical conditions.

Remington's Nylon 66 carries this tag on the butt. The knob that sticks out of the butt plate is for loading purposes. After loading, a quarter-turn locks it flush with the end of the stock.

▌ THE WEATHERBY MARK XXII

Another auto rimfire that has made a comeback recently is Weatherby's Mark XXII. Noted mostly for its classy styling and good looks, this gun is now made to fit the life-styles of those affluent American hunters who appreciate the creature comforts. Like the Remington, the Weatherby's tubular magazine has a carniverous ap-

It was off the market for several years, but the Mark XXII is back in style in both tubular and magazine form.

A close-up view of the Mark XXII reveals its clean lines and special mounting of the Weatherby scope. This gun can be fired in both single shot and semiautomatic modes.

This Browning .22 automatic is loaded through a slot on the buttstock. From here the ammo rides home in a tube to the receiver.

petite for ammo and an excellent ability for follow-up shots. Its single-shot option is an ideal choice for those who are enjoying their first forays into the bush and are especially safety-conscious.

All decked out in select claro walnut, the Weatherby glistens with quality. The stock is hand checkered, and its forend features fancy wood accents. A rubber butt pad is included so that the rifle can be propped against a tree without fear of its sliding off and discharging by accident. With Weatherby's own 7/8-inch-diameter scope mounted and sighted in at 50 yards, the Mark XXII can deliver under one-inch groups with ease.

BROWNING, RUGER AND MARLIN AUTOLOADERS

John Browning led off the parade toward blowback .22's in 1913 with his Model 43. It seems only fitting, therefore, that Browning's firm still carries automatic .22's in stock. Browning's ideas have been carried through in a neat take-down rifle that's just right for the backpacker or inland hunter. Presently available only in Grade I, this .22 auto measures slightly over 19 inches when broken down in two pieces. Having been in production for about 75 years now without major modifications, one must salute Mr. Browning once more for his foresight and inventive genius.

Next to Browning, many people rate William Ruger high on the list of innovative firearms designers. When Ruger's Model 10/22 was first introduced many years ago, it looked much like its companion piece, the .44 Magnum. Since then, the 10/22 has been improved greatly with a higher comb for scope mounting, hand checkering and sling swivels, making it a real "man's" weapon out in the field.

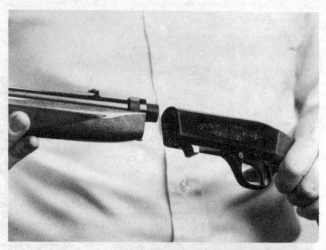

Backpackers will appreciate Browning's take-down design features (above). Note the under receiver operating lever. There is no outside bolt handle on this model.

For those who take their hunting quite seriously, Sturm, Ruger & Company recently made available a "Camo" multi-colored laminated stock, making it that much easier to blend into the woods. Scope mounts, in the form of bases that adapt to popular tip-off mounts, make this clip-fed auto an excellent value for *all* sportsmen.

No essay on rimfire autoloaders would be complete without mentioning Marlin, which has more than 3 million units sold to its credit in semiautomatics alone. Marlin's current listing shows six models, including the popular and inexpensive Model 60. With an action snuggled up in a walnut-finished hardwood stock, this gun with its 22-inch barrel remains the top choice of those

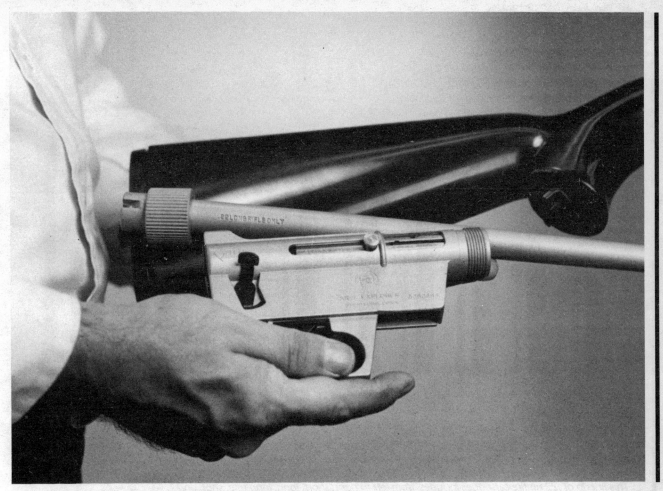

For survivalists, Charter Arms produces a semiautomatic (above) in which all of the parts shown (plus a magazine) fit in the buttstock in the rear.

who seek a hardworking, accurate rifle for small game hunting.

As for magazine-fed Marlin's, three models are available: Model 995, Model 70, and Model 70P (for *Papoose*). Model 70P, like the Browning semiautomatic .22, is a take-down gun and is sold with a bright red carrying case that even floats (for canoe day-trippers who want their cake and eat it too).

Other notable gun makers in this field include Heckler & Koch, which makes a slick Magnum autoloader; Savage, with its time-tested offerings; Charter Arms, which produces a survival rifle called the Explorer; and numerous other makes and model variations and imports.

SAFETY AND ACCURACY: PRIME PREREQUISITES

As with any semiautomatic weapon, the question of *safety* is paramount among users. First, you should al-ways assume that any automatic weapon is loaded when the bolt is closed. Some semis have been known to go off at the ranges too often to assume otherwise. Also, never shoot at flat rocks, the surfaces of water, or even straight down the side of a hill. Fast moving, light, 40 grain bullets have a nasty habit of ricocheting and can play havoc with these surfaces. Identify your target before the trigger is pulled. Know your backstop or land terrain (remembering that .22 rimfires can travel up to a mile). And unload the gun when you're finished.

Unfortunately, the diminutive .22 rimfire has an unwarranted reputation for inaccuracy in practical hunting situations. While automatic rimfires may tend to be slightly less accurate than some other guns, they are, on the whole, perfectly adequate and fully acceptable for use in small game hunting at moderate distances. Take, for example, Weatherby's Mark XXII. In a test firing against a famous make bolt action rifle, using Remington's Standard Velocity brand of rimfire fodder, the bolt

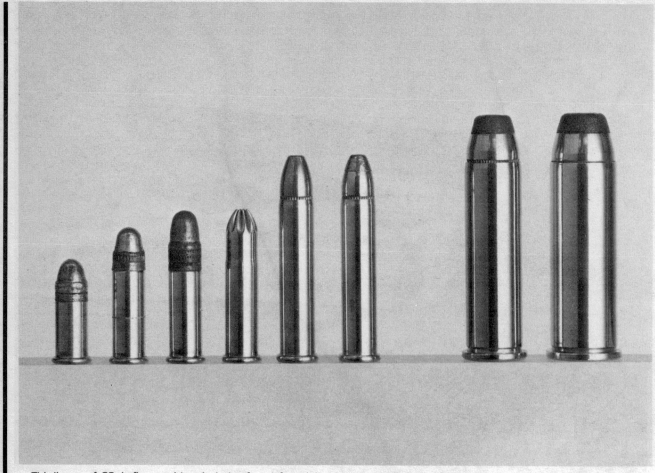

This lineup of .22 rimfire cartridges includes, from left to right: short, long, long rifle, shot, and Winchester Magnum Rimfire (WMR) in both hollow point and full metal jacketed form. The .357 and .44 Magnum centerfire cartridges are shown at right for comparison.

produced groups in the .600-inch range at a distance of 50 yards. The Weatherby, meanwhile, printed 5-shot groups that averaged .820 inches. Firing Federal's Silhouette brand, the same bolt action model formed neat 1.020-inch circles, which the Mark XXII surpassed with .910 inches. In any event, the difference in accuracy is not worth serious consideration under normal field conditions.

■ A QUESTION OF BALLISTICS

Accuracy aside, the question arises: What can you actually hunt with a .22 autoloader? Once you arrive at the 100-yard mark, the most vital statistic comes under the heading of *terminal ballistics*. A close look at factory ballistics tells the story, one which any good shooter should file away in his data bank for retrieval as he lines up a groundhog 100 yards distant.

Tubular magazines are easily loaded and locked down for safety.

Never underestimate the power of the .22 rimfire. These bars of soap show the relative power factors of (l. to r.) short, long, and long rifle cartridges.

Starting out at 1255 feet per second (fps), a high velocity long rifle registers 140 foot pounds of energy (fpe) at the muzzle. But one of the smallest .22 centerfire rounds, the .22 Hornet, utilizing a 45 grain bullet against the rimfire's 40-grainer, can hit 2,690 fps with 773 fpe. At 100 yards, the .22 long rifle peters out to 92 fpe, while the screaming Hornet still measures up to 417 fpe. The harsh fact is, one slip of the trigger can easily result in a miss or, worse still, a sorely wounded animal.

One effective way to ensure accuracy is to install a scope. Famous makers like Bushnell, Redfield, Burris and Leupold all cater to rimfire buffs. Their scopes come in 3/4-inch (by Redfield), 7/8-inch (Weatherby), or 1-inch (Leupold) tube diameters. Avoid the less expensive plastic lenses, which can lead to serious shooter eye fatigue, and opt for a quality scope. A super high quality scope, parallax-free at 50 yards, is your best bet. Thus, by keeping your ego and range down to 100 yards or less

(60 to 75 is ideal), rabbits, raccoons, woodchucks, possums, prairie dogs and squirrels should offer more than enough field opportunities to fill your larder. As in any hunting expedition, success very often comes from the hunter's knowledge of shooting positions, field conditions, and the game itself.

Once the game is in sight, assume a position that best guarantees a nice, steady shot. Don't ever assume that simply because you have an automatic rifle in your hands you can be lazy or sloppy with the first try. This is not only foolhardy, it's unsportsmanlike in the true sense of the word. Advantageous field conditions, such as wet ground, can often allow you to get closer without making a sound, as will solid rock or powdered snow. By carefully combining these elements, you can ensure the ongoing challenge of small game hunting.

Aside from a bit more care on the inside workings, maintaining a .22 rimfire is relatively easy. Just by

Kids flock to the .22 like ducks to water. Here the author teaches the fine art of hunting small game to his daughter, Randee.

An operating lever is included on the Remington 552 to shuck the first round into the chamber (but only after you've entered the hunting field).

cleaning the bore once a summer for test purposes can do the job. Simply because autoloading firearms have more moving parts than their bolt or wheel gun counterparts doesn't mean you must load them up with space-age, state-of-the-art lubricants, either. To the contrary, semiautos thrive best on minimum lubrication. In fact, less lube means less residue trapped in the innards of your gun. And too much debris inside all too often leads to malfunctions somewhere down the line.

In retrospect, it seems safe to say that semiautomatic rimfire arms have come of age. For all-day hunting, accuracy and dependability, you can't—and shouldn't— fight the temptation. Instead, open yourself to a new challenge. It just might bring back some happy, worthwhile memories.

UPGRADING THE MUZZLELOADERS FOR THE 1980'S

by Toby Bridges

Since the rebirth of the muzzleloading sports in the 1950's, nostalgia has played an important role in determining which models became popular—and which did not. Unless they followed along certain traditional muzzleloading lines, these rifles didn't remain on the market for very long. But times are changing all that. No longer is it necessary for muzzleloaders to own and shoot rifles that resemble something out of the distant past. Today's market is beginning to cater to an entirely new breed of black powder shooter—the modern muzzleloading hunter.

In a sense, this metamorphosis in muzzleloaders parallels what happened in archery during the 1960's, when the compound bow was introduced. At first, diehard bowhunters vowed they would never hunt with such gadgetry, and retail shop owners refused to handle this "high tech" equipment. And yet, despite this dismal start, it is now virtually impossible to find a retail archery outlet that does not handle bows of this design; in fact, most offer a wide variety of models. The compound bow has so dominated the archery market that it has be-

come increasingly difficult to find shops that handle any of the old recurves at all.

The reasons for this revolution in bowhunting are quite evident. For one thing, the modern technology behind this new bow appealed most to new, young bowhunters. The weapon's reduced draw weight and much faster arrow speed allowed the beginning bowhunter to become more proficient with less effort and in a shorter period of time.

Just as the lengthy archery season lured many modern hunters to take up bowhunting for big game, so the special muzzleloading or black powder big game seasons (which are now held in all but six or seven states) have induced many hunters to pick up a muzzleloader for the first time. The result: a brand new muzzleloading market, one that's geared to the demands of the modern hunter who has turned to muzzleloading because of the extended season and, in some instances, the bonus game that's allowed by certain special hunts.

As a result, given a choice between frontloaders with traditional styling and a more efficient modern version, a growing number of these new hunters will choose the latter. A rifle with good original lines will always have some appeal, of course, but when a muzzleloader is chosen primarily for hunting deer and other big game, the serious hunter will usually opt for a modern design, one that promises more reliability, efficiency, and accuracy. Several recently introduced models have, in fact, been designed especially for that same black powder hunter who demands something new and different. Because of this trend, three of today's muzzleloading hunter's rifles are so modern they don't even resemble muzzleloaders anymore.

Toby Bridges began hunting with muzzleloading guns in 1967 and has relied on them completely since 1976. His black powder hunts have rewarded him with literally dozens of big game trophies. Bridges is a veteran freelance writer and editor of articles and books, among them *Advanced Muzzleloader's Guide* (Stoeger Publishing Co., 1985) and most recently, *Custom Muzzleloading Rifles* (Stackpole, 1986).

While the longer barreled rifles of the traditional Kentucky/Pennsylvania type (above) can be a pleasure to shoot, they may also prove too unwieldy in dense cover or from elevated tree stands.

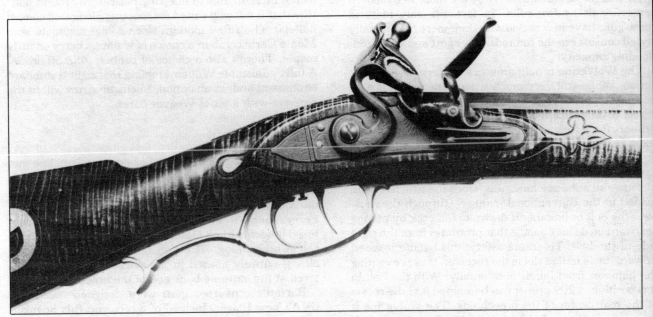

Flintlock rifles similar to this fine custom model made by Leroy Fleanor will always appeal to students of traditional styling. But serious muzzleloading hunters are turning to more effective modern designs.

Michigan Arms' in-line action Wolverine lends itself well to scope fitting.

THE WOLVERINE

At first glance, Michigan Arms' *Wolverine*, CVA's *Blazer*, and Modern Muzzleloading's *MK-1* rifles don't even look like frontloaders. They are more like modern centerfire or rimfire rifles. In fact, the only features these guns have in common with their more traditionally styled cousins are the ramrods they sport and their frontloading capacity.

The Wolverine is built around a modern, in-line type action. While still very much a percussion rifle, it does not rely on percussion caps of any kind for ignition. Instead, it uses exceptionally hot standard 209 shotshell primers for setting off the powder charge. Ignition is almost as fast as with a modern centerfire rifle, with equally positive results. The Wolverine's in-line action fires from the "open bolt" position, much like the action of some full auto-machine guns. Once the rifle has been loaded in the conventional manner—through the muzzle—the bolt or hammer is drawn to full cock by pulling rearward on a short handle that protrudes from the right side of the bolt. To ensure safety, this handle is eased upward into a milled slot in the receiver, thus preventing the hammer from falling accidentally. With the bolt in this position, a 209 primer can be slipped into the recess at the rear center of the breechplug. The Wolverine is then ready to fire—the shooter needs only to flip the bolt handle out of the safety notch, sight in on the target, and apply pressure to the adjustable Timney trigger.

The Wolverine's specifications include the following: an octagonal barrel measuring one inch in diameter and 26 inches in length; a bore rifled with deep .010 inch grooves; and a rate of twist equaling one turn in 66 inches (making this in-line rifle basically a "round ball" rifle that is not well suited for shooting elongated conical bullets). The rifle's modern stock comes complete with Monte Carlo comb in a choice of walnut, cherry or curly maple. There's also a choice of caliber: .45, .50 or .54. A fully adjustable Williams folding rear sight is standard equipment and, as an option, Michigan Arms will fit the receiver with a set of Weaver bases.

THE BLAZER

CVA's *Blazer* has a totally modern design. The gun isn't all that different actionwise, though, from a rare Civil War carbine produced by J.B. Barrett. Following the Confederate Army's successful raid on Harper's Ferry Arsenal in Virginia in 1859, Barrett fitted the captured breechloading Hall barrels with a combination receiver/breechplug. The gun featured a simple action almost entirely housed in the stock, and a nipple centered at the extreme back end of the breechplug.

Barrett's converted guns were designed much like CVA's new Blazer. Instead of a receiver, this Spanish-built, moderately priced hunting rifle features an octagon barrel with a 15/16 inch diameter; it is simply fitted with a breechplug into which a nipple is threaded at rear

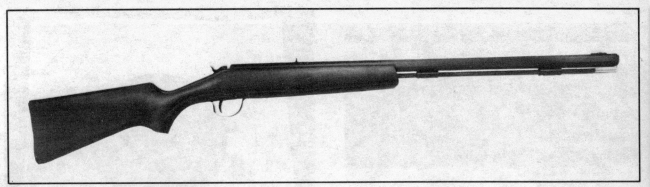

CVA's single-shot Blazer is a simple, economically priced modern muzzleloading design built expressly for today's black powder hunter.

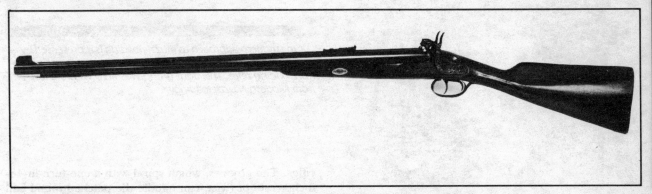

The adjustable rear sight of this CVA double Express rifle prints the side-by-side bores "on" at about 90 yards.

center. Only two parts of the Blazer's action are visible externally—the hammer and trigger. Everything else is housed in the modernistic hardwood stock, which closely resembles the stocks found on many .22 semiauto rifles. Fire from an exploding cap enters the rear of the Blazer's barrel without having to travel around corners in the flash channel. Ignition is fast and spontaneous. But when hefty powder charges are fired behind heavy conical-type bullets, blowback created by high pressures can cause real problems. Fortunately, CVA has selected rifling—with a twist rate of one turn in 66 inches—that is more suitable for shooting the patched round ball. With 60 or 70 grain charges of FFg, this .50 caliber front-loader develops more than enough power for dropping large game at reasonable distances without blowback, an important consideration.

■ THE MK-1

Perhaps the most advanced muzzleloading hunter's rifle ever offered is the unique, in-line *MK-1* produced by Modern Muzzleloading. Featuring two safeties and a receiver that forms an integral part of the barrel, it even outdoes most modern centerfire rifles. In addition to its conventional sliding safety (located along the right side of the receiver), the MK-1 comes equipped with a secondary safety on the hammer bolt itself. When threaded forward on the cocked bolt, it prevents the hammer from bottoming out on the nipple—even when the trigger is pulled. It takes only a second to thread the nut to the rear. The sliding safety alongside the receiver must then be in the forward position before the rifle will fire. This is a welcome feature for hunters who travel in rough terrain, as well as tree stand hunters who must hoist their rifles onto lofty platforms.

The MK-1's receiver and barrel are rigid, having been machined from the same piece of steel. Actually, the receiver is the rear portion of the barrel, reamed free of rifling and slightly enlarged to accommodate the bolt. The breechplug is threaded into the rear of the remaining rifled portion. To allow capping of the nipple, a large port is milled into the right side of the receiver. Another

One modern approach to muzzleloading is represented by these plastic sabots for shooting pistol slugs in larger bore frontloading rifles. This tight group was fired with the MK-1 from Modern Muzzleloading.

The author poses with a Tennessee wild boar he took with his very modern MK-1 muzzleloading rifle and hollow-pointed slugs.

milled cut can be found along the bottom of the receiver to allow for installation of the adjustable Timney trigger. To reduce muzzle and barrel heaviness, the gun's octagon barrel stock is turned round immediately ahead of the receiver section and tapered all the way to the muzzle. Shooters can choose between .50 or .54 caliber and among three barrel lengths: 24, 26 and 28 inches. The MK-1 comes fitted with a rubber recoil pad on an American walnut stock. An adjustable folding rear sight is standard equipment, with Weaver scope bases installed as an option. Studs for attaching a sling are also provided.

The barrel of the Modern Muzzleloading MK-1 is manufactured from the same kind of steel used in many high-grade, centerfire rifles. Although the grooves measure only .005 inch in depth, they are not produced simply by pulling a hardened button through a polished barrel blank, as with most mass-produced reproduction rifles. The grooves, which spiral with a one-turn-in-48-inches rate of twist, can handle the patched round ball and most of the muzzleloading conical bullets now on the market.

▌ OTHER NEW MAJOR CONTENDERS

While the three companies and their muzzleloaders described above represent the most advanced models among today's frontloading hunters' rifles, they are by no means the only new entries in this growing market.

For example, Navy Arms has made a stab at revitalizing interest in shooting and hunting with muzzleloaders of the so-called "mule ear" variety. These percussion rifles feature hammers that are positioned to swing on a horizontal arc instead of the customary vertical arc. The nipple threads directly into the wide flat of the octagonal barrel. Fire from the exploding percussion cap travels directly into the bore without having to wind around corners in the flash channel. Ignition is fast, positive, and ideal for the hunter who demands sure-fire performance. Navy Arms currently offers two models—a lightweight "mule ear" in .32, .36 and .45 caliber, and a heavier .50 caliber model for big game hunters.

Mowrey Gun Works currently produces an Ethan Allen muzzleloading rifle (c. 1850) in a variety of models for hunting everything from squirrels to elk. The firm's newest version features an exceptionally fast rate of

The action on this MK-1 muzzleloader incorporates two safeties. In addition to the sliding safety along the right side of the receiver, the nut-like arrangement at the rear of the bolt/hammer threads forward to prevent the hammer from striking the nipple.

Navy Arms offers a line of these dependable slideslappers, or "mule ear" percussion rifles, for hunters who demand spontaneous ignition.

Outwardly, Mowrey's new IN30 rifle displays an authentic Ethan Allen design circa 1850; it has, however, been fitted with a fast twist barrel designed especially for today's muzzleloading big game projectiles.

Mowrey's Ethan Allen action (above) is wholly contained within the rifle's steel receiver.

twist—one turn in 30 inches—and has shallow .005 inch deep grooves designed for shooting conical muzzleloading bullets (Mowrey's new Model IN30, in fact, holds the distinction of being the only rifle designed to shoot the conical bullet exclusively). The rifling is too fast for the patched round ball ahead of hunting powder charges; that same fast twist, however, stabilizes the big bullets and gives the rifle amazing accuracy.

One aspect of muzzleloading rifles that proves frustrating to many modern hunters is their single-shot capacity. While the multi-shot frontloader is hardly a new idea, not many have been produced in recent years. Trail Guns Armory has been importing (from Italy) a well-made, side-by-side percussion rifle in .58 × .58, .50 × .50, .58 × 12 gauge, and more recently .54 × .54 calibers. The Kodiak double rifle was, until recently, the only such reproduction gun available, but now CVA and Iver Johnson's Arms are offering double rifles of their own. CVA's model is fitted with twin .50 caliber barrels measuring 28 inches in length. By tapering the barrels their full length, CVA has reduced the weight of this side-by-side to slightly more than nine pounds. The grooves of its one-turn-in-48 inches rifling measure .006

Many of today's reproduction rifles feature moderately fast twist barrels for stabilizing the elongated conicals, such as the T/C Maxi-Ball shown here with a round ball of the same caliber.

The author is rocked back by a heavy charge of FFg behind a heavy conical bullet in one of Trail Guns Armory's .58 caliber side-by-side Kodiak rifles.

Iver Johnson's new over/under .50 caliber rifle (above) is one of several double rifles now on the market for black powder big game hunting enthusiasts.

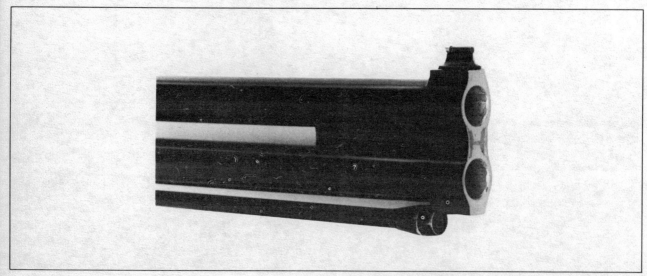

To keep the weight down, the barrels of this Iver Johnson double are turned round for about half their length, then rejoined at the muzzle.

inches and are designed to handle either the patched round ball or the conical bullet. The bores have been regulated so that shots converge at about 90 yards.

Iver Johnson's double rifle is of the stack-tubed variety. As novel as this may seem, the over/under percussion rifle has been around for quite a while. A few gun makers built such rifles as far back as the mid- to late 1800s. Iver Johnson's new .50 caliber double, however, offers something quite different: its barrels are octagonal at the breech end, measuring 15/16–inch across the flats. Near the forearm tip, the barrels are then turned all the way to the muzzle, where they are solidly bridged by a strong section of rib. This treatment keeps the weight of

the 26-inch barreled over/under close to 8.4 pounds. A hooked breech system allows separation of the barrels from the stock assembly for fast, effective cleaning (the breechplugs can also be easily removed for cleaning).

It may well be that these modern muzzleloaders with their contemporary styling will never completely replace the more traditional frontloading rifles—at least, not the way in which the compound bow has taken over from the recurve bow. But as more hunters turn to muzzleloading, for whatever reasons, it's a sure bet that more rifles will be introduced that closely resemble the modern types these shooters have become accustomed to carrying afield.

THE SAGA OF THOMAS "MR. SAM" SAMWORTH

by Dr. Jim Casada

To most gun lovers and hunting buffs, the name Thomas Samworth is hardly a household word. Yet "Mr. Sam," as he was affectionately referred to in his later years, ranks among the "greats" who have been associated with the exciting world of guns and shooting during the 20th century. In his own way, he did as much as anyone to promote a universal understanding of guns.

Abbie Johnson, a gun collector who became a close friend of "Mr. Sam," recalled his first meeting with Samworth. At the time, Johnson owned a Russian-made pistol about which he knew nothing beyond the fact that it was of Russian origin. Because of that, he had been unable to locate ammunition to fit the weapon. One day, while casually discussing the pistol with a friend, Johnson learned about a man who might be able to help him. His name was Thomas Samworth and he had recently moved to Dirleton Plantation, located a few miles outside of Georgetown, South Carolina (where Johnson lived). And so, a few days later, Johnson drove out to Dirleton, introduced himself to Samworth, and inquired if he knew anything about the Russian pistol. "Mr. Sam" took the gun in hand and, without further ado, led Johnson to a huge collection of glass jars—hundreds of them

in all—lining the shelves of his workroom. Each jar held dozens of shells of a certain type, and without hesitating Samworth picked out one of the jars and produced a handful of ammunition made specifically for the Russian pistol. He then proceeded to describe, in great detail, how and when the pistol was made.

According to Johnson and others who came to know Samworth intimately, there was precious little the man did not know about guns. As a prodigious editor and publisher of books and magazines about weaponry, Samworth wrought near miracles in publicizing the shooting sports and generally expanding man's knowledge and consciousness about guns and ammunition. It was, for example, his innovative genius that gave the National Rifle Association's house publication the title it bears to this day: *American Rifleman*. Later, as a one-man editor-publisher, he produced more than 50 volumes, many of them still recognized as standards in the field.

▌ THE EARLY YEARS

Born in Wilmington, Delaware, on October 25, 1888, "Mr. Sam" was the son of a frugal, hard working couple of limited means. While still a small boy, Samworth moved with his family to a farm near Pike Creek, a tiny rural community near Wilmington. There young Thomas reacted eagerly to the opportunities afforded by rural life. He hunted, fished, and trapped on the family's 89 acres, and to those carefree days of adolescence he later credited his life-long devotion to guns and the sporting life. His only real concern then was that he never had enough money to buy cartridges for his single-shot .22. His love of hunting was so strong, in fact, that

Dr. Jim Casada has been teaching and lecturing on history at Winthrop College in Rock Hill, South Carolina, for many years. An active writer on sports topics in his spare time, Casada contributes two weekly newspaper columns and is Editor-at-Large for *Sporting Classics* magazine. He is presently finishing up a book manuscript entitled *Africa's Great Hunters.*

This portrait of "Mr. Sam" was painted during his final years.

Samworth poses for the camera during his early twenties, sometime between 1910 and 1915.

he gladly gave up the usual temptations of youth, such as tobacco, so that he'd have enough money to buy ammunition. Perhaps therein lay the key to "Mr. Sam's" longevity (he died in his 93rd year). He was always convinced that hunting in the outdoors had kept him hardy, and that being a nonsmoker only enhanced his robust nature.

As with most self-made men, Samworth put his keen mind to good use in the school of practical experience. Keenly observant, his entire life became an unending process of self-education, especially where guns and wildlife were concerned. Always eager for new information, his eternal curiosity led him into a secondary career as a nature photographer. During Samworth's later years, visitors to Dirleton were urged—no, commanded—to look at his latest slides, many of them featuring the waterfowl found in that part of the country. He was equally proud of his gun collection and the six-foot stack of books he had published on various aspects of the shooter's world. No visitor could come away from Dirleton without sensing his host's great love of nature and outdoor life. In 1962, Samworth's love of the outdoors took a more practical form when he donated his beloved Dirleton Plantation to the State of South Carolina, so that, in his words, "Every boy has the chance I had to enjoy hunting." This lovely 600-acre Low Country estate has since provided South Carolinians with more than two decades of unsurpassed duck hunting.

Samworth (center) explores the South Carolina countryside with two state wildlife officials during one of "Mr. Sam's" frequent photographic forays.

Samworth's beloved home on Dirleton Plantation, near Georgetown, SC. Here he and a hired hand produced an entire publishing program, packing and shipping each book order by hand.

First Lieutenant Thomas G. Samworth, while stationed in Texas, somewhere near the Mexican border, in 1916.

■ A GENIUS AT WORK

After Samworth had grown into manhood, he served for a time in the Delaware National Guard, rising to the rank of second lieutenant. Thanks to that experience and his magical way with weapons, his 1916 enlistment in the U.S. Army came at the entry level of first lieutenant with the Second Pennsylvania Infantry. He was later reassigned to the Sixth U.S. Cavalry in Big Bend, Texas.

Despite a strong, personal desire for combat service, Samworth never made it from the arid, open spaces of Texas to the mud-filled trenches on the western front in France. He was, quite simply, too valuable as an expert in weapon design and production to be sent over as front line cannon fodder. His superiors, who were well aware of Samworth's exceptional skills in these areas, acted contrary to standard military procedure—that of giving every man the duties for which he was least well qualified—and assigned him to the munitions division of the giant DuPont Company.

There "Mr. Sam" quickly demonstrated his remarkable ingenuity by recommending a whole series of modifications in U.S. Army rifles and their loads. Among these were improved shell ejection systems and a more accurate calculation of how much powder was needed for each round. Quality control was much too slack, he felt, resulting in an inconsistent and wasteful use of firing power. Samworth was equally convinced that cleaner loads were the answer to the very serious problem of

mechanism fouling. Carbon build-up and jamming were, in his eyes, unacceptable in weapons designed for combat use where human lives were on the line. By the end of the war, he and DuPont had made positive steps toward improving this situation, and in so doing Samworth won respect among the military and munitions industry hierarchy as a small arms genius. DuPont was so convinced of his value, in fact, that they offered Samworth a job immediately upon his release from military duty. These were exciting times in the industry. Smokeless powder was being improved, and for a time Samworth continued to work on and refine rifle firing mechanisms along with determining precisely what charge worked best in various gun calibers.

In the end, though, Samworth was simply too much of an innovator and individualist to pursue a corporate or military career. Although he admired certain members of the DuPont family, others he found a major source of constant annoyance. Not surprisingly, given his well deserved reputation for saying what he felt, an explosion was forthcoming. Tired of having too many bosses telling him what to do, Samworth finally erupted in anger one day in 1921 and left the company for good.

▋ A GREAT PUBLISHER IS BORN

Soon after this rather abrupt parting of the ways, Samworth linked his fortunes with those of the still small and struggling National Rifle Association. It barely numbered 2,000 members at that time and its house publication was a magazine of mediocre quality, called *Arms and the Man*. As co-editor, Samworth soon convinced NRA's chairman, Sandy McNabb, that a much more lively and readable magazine was needed. Mc-Nabb accepted his proposal and Samworth began making the changes that eventually helped convert the NRA into an influential force on a national level.

One of his first changes was to rename the magazine, which henceforth became *American Rifleman*. Samworth proved to be every writer's dream of the ideal editor, a man who took infinite pains with their manuscripts and yet always took care not to intrude on their prose. With his intimate knowledge of the world of guns, moreover, he saved more than one good author from making potentially embarrassing mistakes. He also saw to it that his contributors were paid well and promptly, all of which led in time to a remarkably talented stable of writers for *American Rifleman*. Among them was Townsend Whelen, who went on to become one of the nation's most popular sporting writers of the 1930s and 1940s. Recognizing Whelen's talent and appeal, Samworth combined several of his articles into a book, which he published in 1927 under the title *Amateur Gunsmithing*. The book was not a major financial success, however, and NRA chairman McNabb decided not to support further undertakings of this nature.

At this point, Samworth decided to take matters into his own hands and enter the publishing business on his own. He left the NRA with the assurance that he had been in large measure responsible for fostering the organization's phenomenal growth. Surely he deserves a larger measure of credit for NRA's success than is usually accorded him.

As a book publisher, "Mr. Sam" found his true calling. Having established his Small-Arms Technical Publishing Company, he nurtured the fledgling business through the lean years of the Depression to real financial success. The titles produced under his imprint (see partial listing at the end of this article) are a lasting testament to his love of gun-related subjects and his incredible tenacity. The financial problems caused by the Depression alone would have overwhelmed a lesser man, yet this was only one of many problems Samworth faced and overcame.

Even as he began his efforts as an independent publisher, Samworth made another move which led to near disaster. Using money he had saved from selling firearm

Samworth, the editor, pauses during a proofreading chore at his Small-Arms Technical Publishing Company.

plans and ideas to DuPont, he bought 700 acres of land on the New River in Onslow County, North Carolina. Samworth liked the area for its rural character and natural beauty—a perfect setting for pursuing his publishing business and outdoor interests. Ordinarily, such a purchase made so close to the onset of hard economic times would have been a wise investment, but Samworth had failed to reckon with the unwelcome intrusion of the U.S. Marine Corps. To his everlasting dismay, the Marines decided that Samworth's tract would be ideal for training purposes. A protracted court battle ensued, with Samworth unfairly matched against the limitless resources of the government. It was a heartbreaking experience which ended, predictably, with Samworth being a loser in every sense. He received only $14,000 for the land—a third of what he had paid for it and perhaps a tenth of what it was worth by the time the case was settled. To make matters worse, the presiding judge added insult to injury by publicly chastising Samworth for his lack of patriotism.

THE TWILIGHT YEARS

Such an experience would have embittered most men, but "Mr. Sam" was made of stern stuff. Instead of giving up, he set about resurrecting his life, starting with the Small-Arms Technical Publishing Company. The business was now showing a steady and growing profit, and by 1941 Samworth had accumulated enough resources to buy the Exchange Plantation on the Pee Dee River in South Carolina. Five years later, he acquired his beloved Dirleton Plantation, where he spent the last 35 years of his life.

Between 1927, when the first book published under the Small-Arms Technical Publishing Company imprint appeared, and the late 1950s, when he eased into semi-retirement, "Mr. Sam" oversaw the publication of dozens of classic books on guns and hunting. Today these volumes are, almost without exception, collectors' items. Equally significant, the information they contain has kept its value and attests to the meticulous manner in which Samworth first obtained capable authors, then gently nurtured their efforts until they reached fruition in printed form. Among the many leading gun authorities who wrote for him were, in addition to Whelen, Elmer Keith, Charles Askins, John "Pondoro" Taylor, Edward C. Crossman, and the dean of .22 rifle experts, Charles Singer Landis. While often highly technical in nature, their works enjoyed excellent sales and were always authoritative, readable and definitive. At least two of the books, Taylor's *African Rifles & Cartridges* and Henry Edwards Davis' *The American Wild Turkey*, rank among the finest sporting books ever published in America.

Samworth stopped accepting new manuscripts in the

This sampling of books published by Samworth's company shows the depth and diversity of his publishing program.

Here "Mr. Sam" poses at Dirleton in his customary attire, complete with walking stick and favorite duck call.

early 1950s and began to wind up his publishing enterprise and ease into retirement. According to those who knew him well in his later years, Samworth became a personality not to be missed. A "man's man" of delightfully cantankerous eccentricity, "Mr. Sam" cut a formidable figure. One suspects that he secretly reveled in his assumed role of the aging Southern Squire. He offered his candid opinions on any topic one might choose, and he could wax eloquent for hours on guns and shooting authorities he had known, neither mincing words nor suffering fools gladly. His command of foul language was legendary, and woe unto him who became the target of "Mr. Sam's" verbal blasts. Still, beneath that gruff exterior lurked a gentle soul who was the essence of goodness. Anyone who really knew "Mr. Sam" adored the man and treasured his friendship.

In the final decade of his life, Samworth seldom hunted with guns, although cameras were another story. When he died on December 29, 1981, at the age of 93, he left behind much for which outdoorsmen in general and gun lovers in particular can be grateful. Every American who collects, uses, or simply enjoys guns should be aware of what this man accomplished. In short, "Mr. Sam" left his indelible marks on sporting posterity, and through the dozens of gun books for which he was primarily responsible this remarkable man still lives among us.

BOOKS PUBLISHED BY THOMAS SAMWORTH'S SMALL-ARMS TECHNICAL PUBLISHING COMPANY

Advanced Gunsmithing by Wayne F. Vickery. 1940.

African Rifles & Cartridges by John Taylor. 1948.

The American Wild Turkey by Henry E. Davis. 1949.

Automatic Pistol Marksmanship by William Reichenbach. 1937.

Big Game Hunting and Marksmanship by Kenneth F. Lee. 1941.

Big Game Rifles and Cartridges by Elmer Keith. 1936.

The Book of the Springfield by Edward C. Crossman. 1932. (Note: A new edition appeared in 1951, with Roy F. Dunlap providing supplementary text).

The Checkering and Carving of Gunstocks by Monty Kennedy. 1952.

Elementary Gunsmithing by Perry D. Frazer. 1938.

English Guns and Rifles by John Nigel George. 1947.

English Pistols and Revolvers by John Nigel George. 1938.

Firearm Blueing and Browning by R.H. Angier. 1936.

Firearm Design and Assembly (3 vols.) by Alvin Linden.

Gunsmithing by Roy F. Dunlap. 1950.

The Gunsmith's Manual (1945 reprint) by James P. Stelle (originally published in 1882).

Gunstock Finishing and Care by A. Donald Newell. 1949.

Handloading Ammunition by J. Randall Mattern. 1926.

Handloader's Manual by Earl Naramore. 1937.

Military and Sporting Rifle Shooting by Edward C. Crossman. 1932.

Modern American Pistols and Revolvers by Arthur C. Gould. 1946 (reprint of 1892 edition).

Modern American Rifles by Arthur C. Gould. 1945 (reprint of 1890 ed.).

Modern Gunsmithing by Clyde Baker. 1928 (2nd ed., 1933).

Modern Shotguns and Loads by Charles Askins. 1929.

Pistols and Revolvers and Their Use by Julian Hatcher. 1927.

Ordnance Went Up Front by Roy F. Dunlap. 1948.

Principles and Practices of Loading Ammunition by Earl Naramore. 1954.

Professional Gunsmithing by Walter J. Howe. 1946.

A Rifleman Went To War by Herbert W. McBride. 1935.

Shots Fired in Anger by John B. George. 1947.

Sixguns and Bullseyes by William Reichenbach. 1936.

Sixgun Cartridges and Loads by Elmer Keith. 1936.

Small Arms Design and Ballistics (2 vols.) by Townshend Whelen. 1945.

Small-bore Rifle Shooting by Edward C. Crossman. 1927.

Telescopic Rifle Sights by Townsend Whelen. 1936.

Textbook of Automatic Pistols by R.K. Wilson. 1944.

Textbook of Firearms Investigation by Julian Hatcher. 1935 (2-vol. edition pub. 1943).

Textbook of Pistols and Revolvers by Julian Hatcher. 1935.

.22 Caliber Rifle Shooting by Charles S. Landis. 1932.

.22 Caliber Varmint Rifles by Charles S. Landis. 1947.

Wilderness Hunting and Wildcraft by Townsend Whelen. 1927.

With British Snipers To The Reich by C. Shore. 1949.

The Woodchuck Hunter by Paul G. Estey. 1936.

Note: Since no comprehensive record of Samworth's publications exists, the author would welcome information from readers about other books "Mr. Sam" is known to have published.

AN INSIDE LOOK AT THE SHOTGUN

by Don Lewis

The most used firearm in America today is unquestionably the shotgun. Each year, people from all walks of life spend hundreds of hours afield or on competition ranges armed with their trusty scatterguns. With its expanding shot charge, the shotgun ought to be the easiest firearm to master; and yet poor shotgun shooters abound. Why this is so remains a mystery, but perhaps a review of simple basics, including gun nomenclature and common shooting errors, will enlighten the novice and provide new food for thought among those who think they've learned all there is to know about shotguns.

To begin, the shotgun dates back to the blunderbuss, which appeared in the early 1620's. Later, when military weaponry arrived on the scene with its ability to fire both single and multiple projectiles, the idea of using shot charges for hunting game as well quickly became reality.

Not to belabor the obvious, but a shotgun is vastly different from a rifle. The latter is equipped with sights and fires a single projectile that can be guided accurately over long distances. The shotgun is a short-range firearm that throws an expanding charge of pellets to compensate for its pointing errors. Thus, the shotgunner need not be as precise as the rifleman.

■ ADVENT OF THE CHOKE

The expanding shot charge is called a pattern, and its size and density is controlled by the constriction, or choke, in the muzzle and the size of shot used. In general, this choke constriction includes the following degrees: skeet, improved cylinder, modified, and full. Barrels with no choke at all throw patterns filled with large, doughnut-shaped gaps. The discovery of chokes came about shortly after the Civil War and was the creation of a waterfowl hunter named Fred Kimble of Illinois (an English gunmaker, W.R. Pape, having acquired a choke patent in 1886, also lays claim to this innovation). Kimble found that by placing a constriction in the muzzle of his black powder, single barrel shotgun he could achieve tighter, more accurate patterns. Moreover, he could now hit ducks and geese with his choked shotgun at ranges previously unheard of. Whereas Kimble's approach was doubtless borne of trial and error, the modern shotgun offers several degrees of choke designed expressly for certain types of shooting.

Skeet boring is quite close to improved cylinder (I/C) in that roughly 45 percent of its pattern forms a 30-inch circle at 40 yards. Modified choke offers a more even pattern of 55 percent, which explains why it serves the average hunter best. For years, full choke was supposed to put 70 percent of its pattern in the 30-inch circle, but many of today's full choke barrels do even better—especially with 12-gauge chambering.

A recently retired corporate executive, Don Lewis now spends most of his time testing and evaluating guns and scopes in his own well-equipped shop in Kittanning, Pennsylvania. In addition to contributing regularly to *Shooter's Bible*, Lewis writes about gun-related subjects for *Pennsylvania Game News*, *Pennsylvania Sportsman*, and other prominent periodicals in the field.

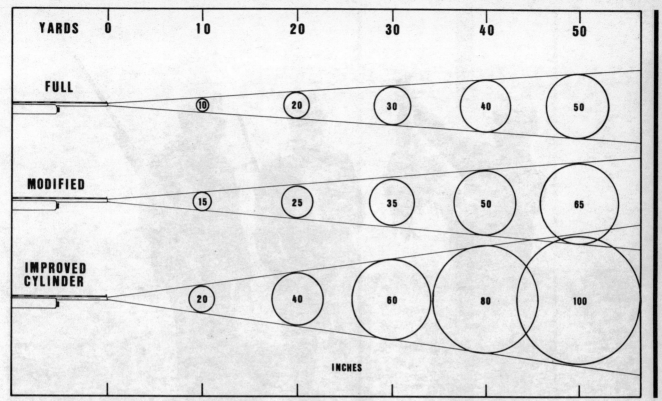

YARDS	0	10	20	30	40	50

FULL
(10) (20) (30) (40) (50)

MODIFIED
(15) (25) (35) (50) (65)

IMPROVED CYLINDER
(20) (40) (60) (80) (100)

INCHES

This drawing illustrates how choke constriction controls the spread of the pattern at 50 yards. Different gauges and barrel lengths will, of course, cause these pattern spreads to differ somewhat, but the results will remain the same in principle.

The purpose of this screw choke—called "Excentrix" (manufactured by Briley Mfg. Co., Houston, Texas)—is to correct or change the point of impact. The choke is machined with a restrictive diameter bored-in at an angle calculated to deflect the shot string, thereby changing the point of impact.

Choke is a complex matter that defies easy definition. For example, the stamping found on every shotgun barrel is not necessarily proof positive of the barrel's patterning ability. Large, heavy shot may require less choking than small shot, and too much choke is worse than too little. The proper amount of choke depends entirely on the distance involved. Since a vast majority of field shots—both in small game and jump shooting of waterfowl—are less than 35 yards, choke constriction that is tighter than modified usually works against the hunter. Thus, the rabbit and grouse hunter will perform better as a rule with improved cylinder.

ROLL OUT THE BARREL

A shotgun barrel is much more than a round piece of steel with a hole bored through it. In simple terms, the shotgun barrel consists of a shell head cut, chamber, forcing cone, straight bore, and choke. The shell head accepts the rim of the shot shell, while the chamber determines in part how well the barrel will pattern. The chamber is not merely a smooth, oversized part of the

A group of hunters (including the author at right) admires a goose that was bagged moments before with a long-barreled shotgun choked full.

barrel; it must be the correct size. An oversized barrel will cause head cracks and case swelling; and a chamber that is too small can prevent easy removal of fired cases.

For example, let's dissect a 20-gauge shotgun. The shell head rim cut will start out at roughly .766″ and taper slightly to a length of .080″. The chamber proper starts at the end of the rim cut with a diameter of .699″ and then tapers slightly at a rate of .005″ for each inch of chamber length. A 20-gauge with a 2 3/4″ chamber will therefore measure .699″ in diameter at the rim and taper to .685″. This slight chamber taper actually serves as an aid in case removal.

Some shotgun experts claim that a slight gain in pattern uniformity results when a chamber is purposely cut about 1/16″ short. This allows the case to unfold into the forcing cone, creating a tight seal that prevents gases from escaping around the wads (and thereby breaking the shot charge before it enters the forcing cone). The main drawbacks to shortening the chamber are higher chamber pressures and the possibility that small pieces of the case end will shred and adhere to the bore, thereby threatening pattern performance and creating barrel obstructions. Using modern plastic shot cup/wad columns, shot charges are largely unaffected by gas leakage.

Conversely, when a short shell is fired in a long chamber some pattern loss can be expected. When a 2 3/4″ case is unfolded (2 3/4″ representing the length of a fired case, not a loaded one), there still remains 1/4″ of unused chamber space. As the shot charge exits the case, it expands to full chamber size. At that point, gases may mix with the pellets and cause a breakup, or balling, and some pressure loss.

Shot deformation is the Achilles heel of the tight pat-

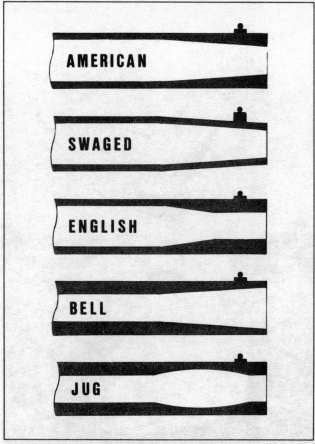

The five choke constrictions in this drawing are used to control the spread of the pattern.

tern. Deformed pellets become what are called "flyers" when they sail out of the main pattern, reducing the size of the pellet count and causing gaps in the pattern. The theory that pellets are deformed only in the choke area is false, though. Pellets are more often deformed in the forcing cone, which explains why better patterns are obtained with muzzleloader shotguns (which have no chamber or forcing cone) than with many up-to-date models. Steel shot, by the way, does not deform and will generally fly truer and form more uniform patterns.

Again, using the 20-gauge example, the forcing cone squeezes the shot from .685"—the end of the chamber measurement—to .615", which is the actual bore diameter of a 20-gauger. This abrupt squeezing process necessarily deforms a large number of pellets. Naturally, the longer the forcing cone, the less deformation. But long forcing cones are expensive to make, so most gun companies stay with the short cones. That isn't all bad, because it helps balance light shot charges and also contributes to the combustion of some powders. Eliminating the forcing cone and replacing it with a long, gradual ta-per to the true bore size would admittedly solve many pattern problems. But this would require expensive reamers and draw boring equipment, luxuries which few gunners could afford. A more reasonable approach would be to test the scattergun on a pattern board until the right shot/powder combination was found for a particular barrel.

DOUBLE BARRELS, PUMPS, AND LEVERS

The shotgun began as a single barrel model. Adding a second barrel was the product of either Italian or Spanish gunsmiths. The pump and semiautomatic are American innovations. The former dates back before the turn of the century, while the autoloader arrived a short time later. Early in the 1900's, the lever action shotgun gained some popularity, and now several firms offer bolt action models. Whatever type of action one uses is purely a matter of personal preference. Some small game hunters prefer the inexpensive single shot gun because it forces them to take more time. With just one shot to make, the hunter is forced to wait until the target stands at a point where the pattern can expand to its maximum diameter. Finally, the slide, or pump, action shotgun has remained a favorite over the years as well. And now, more and more shooters are switching to autoloaders.

Over the decades, the most popular shotgun has been the double barrel, whether side-by-side or over/under. With two barrels, there can be two choke borings, which makes the two-barrel model two guns in one. It is also more compact. One of the major drawbacks with the semiautomatic and pump models is the long receiver, or action. These guns also weigh as much as a full pound more than other models.

Among the repeating shotguns, the semiautomatic may have an edge in speed, but a good slide action shooter can give it a run for its money. In the end, it is the shooter's decision based on what he feels works best for him.

THE RIGHT GAUGE FOR YOU

Gauges run along much the same line. At first glance, it may appear that the 12-gauge, with its larger shot charge, ought to be the #1 choice among small game hunters. However, a growing number of shotgunners has begun to realize that there's more to a shotgun than its ability to throw super-heavy shot charges. Federal's Premium Magnum 12-gauge heavyweight carries a full two ounces of BB's, 2's, 4's and 6's. But a charge of one ounce is plenty for most types of small game shooting, a requirement that even the 28-gauge can meet.

The 3-inch 20-gauge shotgun, having reached the height of its popularity, has literally sounded the death

A rooster explodes suddenly from the underbrush and the action that follows is fast and furious. If the gun does not fit the hunter properly, he won't have much chance of bagging this elusive target.

knell for the famous 16-gauge. This is a sad commentary, for the 16-gauge can easily match the performance of the 3-inch 20, and it is about on a par with 12 ounces of shot from the larger 12-gauge. Moreover, where variety is desired shotshell reloading fans can do wonders with the 16.

The 34-inch 10-gauge Magnum case can consume a massive 22 ounces of shot and is meant primarily for use on waterfowl. Normal gun weights for this big shell weapon run over 10 pounds, making it much too heavy for normal field use.

The old 28-gauge, which is practically moribund among the hunting set, remains a far wiser choice nonetheless for the young hunter than does the .410 bore. The latter may have a more nostalgic past, but its small

4-ounce load in a 2 3/4″ case (and only 11/16-ounce in the 3-inch shell) yields thin patterns. This demands extremely precise shooting and actually puts the new hunter at a disadvantage. While the 28-gauge can handle one ounce of shot, it is designed more or less for a 3/4-ounce shot charge. It cannot be considered a top small game shell, and while it is definitely superior to the 3-inch .410 bore, it is still lacking in pattern density for all-round field shooting. Remember, a shot pellet cannot be guided. The hunter must depend on sheer numbers or density of the pattern to make a clean kill. Dense patterns are therefore vastly superior to thin ones. It's as simple as that.

For beginners, the wisest choice remains the 20-gauge. Recoil is less severe and shot charges go up to 12 ounces in the 3-inch Magnum load. It's not true that the hunter with a 20-gauge is undergunned. Many experienced shotgunners have gone into the field armed only with 20-gauge outfits without feeling undergunned.

▌ THE IMPORTANCE OF PROPER FIT

Shotgunning in the field is known as "reflex shooting." That means the action takes place in a matter of a few seconds. And because there's so little time to adjust the shotgun to the shooter's shoulder pocket, the shotgun must *fit*. If it doesn't, then the brand, model, or type of action will be of small consequence. The shotgun that doesn't fit the hunter becomes nothing more than excess baggage.

This problem of fit rests normally with the length of the stock. Not all hunters are built alike, which means that a 14 1/4″ stock cannot fit all shooters. The competitive shooter's success is especially dependent on a good fit. The stock must be the correct length for a comfortable mount, a good grip on the stock, and proper positioning of the cheek on the comb. The comb acts somewhat like a rear sight; it must fit the shooter's facial contour so as to place the shooting eye the correct distance above the rib.

Other stock dimensions—such as drop and pitch—also govern where the patterns will form. Comb and heel drop represent the vertical measurements (in inches) from an imaginary line running back from the top of the barrel to the top of the comb and heel of the stock at the recoil pad (see drawing A below). Shotguns made during the gaslight era had too much drop, causing the guns to shoot low and forcing the comb hard into the shooter's cheek.

Pitch is best described as the angle formed by the intersection of the line of bore to a line drawn at right angles to the heel and toe of the butt (see drawing B). Place a gun flat on its buttplate, with its action touching a wall. The distance (in inches) from the muzzle to the wall represents the amount of pitch (or tipdown). Pitch and drop both play a major role in the vertical control of the pattern.

Most U.S. manufacturers today produce the pistol grip-type stock. Some hunting outfits and most trap guns feature a Monte Carlo comb, which offers several ad-

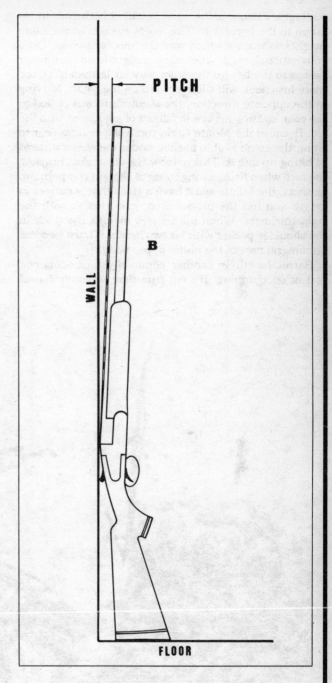

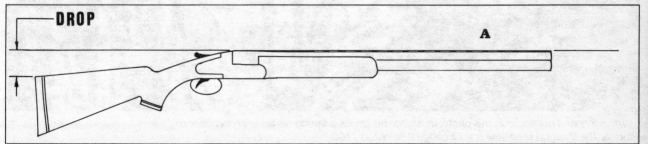

vantages. First, it is the same height at both ends in relation to the barrel rib. This keeps the eye at the same height, no matter which way the shooter swings. On a conventional stock, the more a right-handed shooter swings to the left (or the other way for lefthanders), the more his cheek will slide forward on the comb. Moving in the opposite direction, the shooter's face is pulled to the rear, causing his eye to fall out of alignment with the rib. Because the Monte Carlo comb slopes from rear to front, the comb is able to slide under the cheek instead of biting up into it. This reduces the chances of bruising the face when firing a long string of shots in competition. In short, the hunter must have a stock that is correct in length and has the proper drop, and a comb with the right thickness. When the shooter mounts the stock in the shoulder pocket with his two hands, it must become an integral part of the entire upper body.

Barrel length is another commonly misunderstood fact of shotgunning. It's not true that excessive barrel length increases velocity or makes the shot charge travel farther. In general, barrel length beyond 25 inches contributes nothing to velocity or distance. The long barrel is easier and smoother to swing than a short one, making it definitely advantageous for the waterfowler, dove hunter and trap shooter. The 26- or 28-inch barrel is more than adequate for field use involving all types of small game.

▌ IMPROVING THE PATTERN

With game habitat disappearing across the nation, a hunter will never learn to shoot efficiently simply by hunting. Much like the rifleman, the shotgunner must first print a lot of holes in paper. Range patterning and trap and skeet shooting will definitely enhance a hunter's success ratio. While the rifleman knows it takes range shooting to determine the accuracy potential of a rifle, many shotgunners assume that the scattergun im-

The successful hunter, as in this photo, must face his target, pivoting his body in one smooth motion. The shotgun used here is a 12 gauge Remington 1100.

BALLISTIC DATA ON LEAD SHOT

SPHERE OF DIAMETER .13 INCH
BALLISTIC COEFFICIENT: .0274

FOR FACTOR: 1.000
PROJECTILE WEIGHT (GRS):
3.24

No. 4 shot

RANGE YARDS	VELOCITY FT/SEC	ENERGY FT–LBS	T. OF F. SECOND	DROP INCHES	ELEV. 'MOA'	WIND DEF INCH/10MPH
0	1200	10	0	0	0	0
5	1093	9	.013	0	.6	.1
10	1004	7	.027	.1	1.4	.4
15	929	6	.043	.3	2.2	1
20	865	5	.06	.6	3.1	1.7
25	810	5	.078	1	4.1	2.7
30	761	4	.097	1.6	5.2	3.8
35	717	4	.117	2.2	6.4	5.2
40	676	3	.138	3.1	7.7	6.8
45	637	3	.161	4.1	9.2	8.6
50	600	3	.186	5.4	10.9	10.8

SPHERE OF DIAMETER .11 INCH
BALLISTIC COEFFICIENT: .0229

FORM FACTOR: 1.000
PROJECTILE WEIGHT (GRS):
1.94

No. 6 shot

RANGE YARDS	VELOCITY FT/SEC	ENERGY FT–LBS	T. OF F. SECOND	DROP INCHES	ELEV. 'MOA'	WIND DEF INCH/10MPH
0	1200	6	0	0	0	0
5	1074	5	.013	0	.7	.1
10	973	4	.028	.1	1.4	.5
15	890	3	.044	.3	2.3	1.1
20	821	3	.062	.6	3.2	2
25	762	3	.081	1.1	4.3	3.2
30	709	2	.101	1.7	5.6	4.6
35	661	2	.123	2.4	6.9	6.2
40	617	2	.146	3.4	8.4	8.1
45	575	1	.172	4.6	10.1	10.4
50	537	1	.199	6	12	12.9

SPHERE OF DIAMETER .095 INCH
BALLISTIC COEFFICIENT: .0198

FORM FACTOR: 1.000
PROJECTILE WEIGHT (GRS):
1.25

No. 7 1/2 shot

RANGE YARDS	VELOCITY FT/SEC	ENERGY FT–LBS	T. OF F. SECOND	DROP INCHES	ELEV. 'MOA'	WIND DEF INCH/10MPH
0	1200	4	0	0	0	0
5	1057	3	.013	0	.7	.1
10	945	2	.028	.1	1.4	.6
15	856	2	.045	.4	2.3	1.3
20	783	2	.063	.7	3.4	2.3
25	720	1	.083	1.1	4.6	3.7
30	664	1	.105	1.8	5.9	5.3
35	612	1	.129	2.6	7.4	7.2
40	565	1	.154	3.7	9.1	9.5
45	523	1	.182	5	11.1	12.2
50	483	1	.212	6.6	13.3	15.3

Heading home after a successful hunt.

pacts where it is pointed. Nothing could be farther from the truth.

It's a known fact that drop, comb height, butt pitch and rib height play major roles in determining where and how the pattern forms. It's logical to assume, therefore, that every shotgun should be test fired on the range in order to find out where it impacts in relation to where it is being pointed. There are several reasons why the shotgun doesn't impact where the shooter thinks he's pointing. Take the rib, for example. If it is off-center at the muzzle, the pattern will be left or right by as much as 6 inches. Such impact problems are common with two-barrel shotguns. A double or over/under will impact both barrels on the same spot only at one distance from the muzzle; but one barrel may shoot right, the other high. This may never come to light unless five or ten-shot strings are fired on a patterning board.

Incidentally, add-on choke devices can actually help create off-center patterns. In fact, the installation of a choke by the manufacturer, whether it be swaged in or cut with a reamer, can send the shot charge *away* from the point of aim. This makes it all the more essential that your shotgun be well tested before it is used, whether for hunting or competition.

For the hunter, best results usually come from a pattern that centers directly above the front sight at normal field shooting ranges. Knowing the pattern size, density and shot size are essential for the hunter if he is to achieve the most uniform pattern at those ranges.

Much can be learned about forward allowance—or lead—on the trap and skeet fields. Most shotshells are fired at moving targets from an angle. Whether it's a slight angle or a full crossing shot, the hunter's goal is to make his shot charge intercept the target at a given point. That means the muzzle must be in front of the angling target when the shot is fired. There is no cut-and-dried answer in determining the proper lead, although it can be worked out mathematically—assuming the hunter has the time to make such calculations. The only practical solution for shooters is to *keep the shotgun moving at all times*.

Learning to *face the target* is another important element in hunting. It's next to impossible to twist the shoulders and arms and fire accurately at the same time. But pivoting the body in one fluid motion from the hips up can turn a 90-degree shot into a slight angle or even straightaway shot. Shifting the feet and entire body in alignment with the target will definitely enhance your game bag content.

It all boils down to a few basics: Point the scattergun instead of aiming it; swing the body evenly, starting from the rear and following along the target's path; don't shoot until the muzzle flashes out in front; and keep the gun moving. Remember, good shots are made, not born. Know your shotgun intimately; fire it often between seasons; and when you pattern, keep careful records. You may never reach perfection, but you'll be far more successful.

THE LASTING LEGACY OF "L. C. SMITH"

by Jim Cobb

Many articles and at least one book have been written about the famous L.C. Smith shotgun, but there remains some confusion over the differences between those guns that were made before 1913 and after. That was the year when the Hunter Arms Company changed the grading and marking systems on all L.C. Smith guns following Hunter's acquisition of the L.C. Smith Gun Company in 1913.

Actually, the celebrated L.C. Smith guns were manufactured by four different companies. The name "L.C. Smith" may appear on these guns, but Smith himself had little, if anything, to do with the design and manufacture of the weapon that bears his name, Lyman Cornelius Smith. A native of upstate New York, he had married a wealthy woman and parlayed her capital into various business ventures. Smith first became involved in the gunmaking trade after his brother, Leroy, introduced him to the Baker brothers, W.H. and Ellis. The Bakers and Smiths formed a partnership in 1877 and began producing patent firearms under the name "W.H. Baker and Sons." The factory was located in Syracuse, New York, and there the two sets of brothers made dou-

Jim Cobb is a bird hunter, waterfowl shooter, and avid collector (and user) of fine American-made shotguns. The author of numerous articles on guns and hunting, including a regular feature for *North American Hunter*, he has been published in *Arms Gazette*, *Man At Arms*, *Sports Afield*, and many others. His book on Dan Lefever (*Lefever: Guns of Lasting Fame*) was published in 1986.

L.C. Smith catalog cover, 1884.

Lyman Cornelius Smith (1850–1910)

Alexander T. Brown (1854–1929)

The L.C. Smith gun factory in Syracuse, N.Y., which the company bought in 1881. Seven years later the company was sold to Hunter Arms.

ble barrel hammer guns and three barrel drillings. The partnership did not last long, for soon W.H. Baker and Leroy Smith left to form what became another famous gun maker: Ithaca Gun Company, of Ithaca, New York.

A few years later, L.C. Smith hired a genius in gun design, a man named Alexander T. Brown, who created a new double barrel hammer gun and later a hammerless model bearing the name "L.C. Smith." (Brown later invented a method for making rubber tires, which formed the beginnings of the Dunlop Tire company). The com-

This patented center draft lock was one of Alexander T. Brown's creations.

pany continued to produce these shotguns in the Syracuse plant in six different grades, which the company named "Quality" (i.e., "Quality 2", "Quality 3", etc.). More than 6,000 of these guns were produced from 1881 to 1888.

L.C. Smith sold his share of the company in 1888 to the Hunter brothers, who promptly moved the plant—lock, stock and barrel—to Fulton, New York. Lyman Cornelius then retired from the gun business and founded a typewriter company, which produced the famous Smith Corona machines. L.C. died in 1910 at the age of 60.

Meanwhile, the Hunters decided not to change the name of their gun; apparently the name "L.C. Smith" had become too closely identified with the world of fine sporting firearms. The only change the Hunters made was to drop the word "Quality" and add several new grades to the line. Beginning in 1892, their guns were referred to in numerical order, starting with 00 and proceeding to 0, 1, 2, 3, Pigeon, 4, A1, 5, A2, and A3. On top of the barrel, near the breech end of the gun, the words "Hunter Arms, Fulton, N.Y." were clearly printed. But "L.C. Smith" remained inscribed on the lock plates, and that is where the confusion arose. Gun enthusiasts, after examining the top rib, assumed that

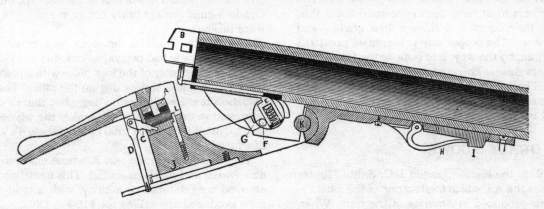

A Represents our Double Cross-locking Rotary bolt
B Extension of the Top Rib.
C Coupler.
D Lever and Post.
E Ejector, passing through the diameter, and operated by the rotation
      of Eccentric Joint Check.
F Eccentric Pin of Rotary Check.

G Receiving Slot in frame for Eccentric.
H Compensating Spring for Forend.
I Forend Lug attached to barrels.
J Bolt Spring.
K Hinge-pin or Roll, supported by solid metal of the frame.
L Trip, holding locking device open to receive extension until the gun
      is closed.

This sectional cut from the L.C. Smith catalog (c. 1887) shows the interior of the hammerless shotgun.

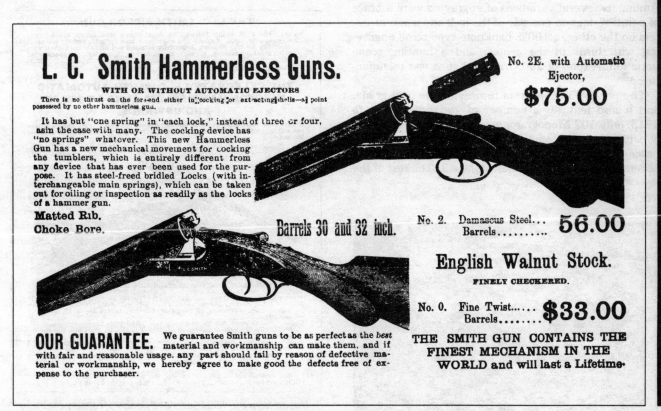

An ad from Percy's Gun and Fur House catalog (1878) shows L.C. Smith's Grades 2, 2E (with automatic ejector) and 0 guns, by far the most expensive items listed.

the gun was not an "L.C. Smith" and pass it by. The Hunter brothers must have been concerned about this, for in 1913 they decided to change their grading and marking system. The proper way to identify a pre-1913 L.C. Smith gun, by the way, is to remove the forend and break the gun down. The grade will be marked on the watertable. The number will appear as "1" or "2" and so on, and sometimes the letter "E" (for *auto ejector*) will lie adjacent to, or just below, the number.

▌ FROM GRADE 3 DOWN

Before 1913, the highest graded L.C. Smith-Hunter Arms gun was the A3, which made it one of the most expensive guns produced in America at the time. When Grade A3 was introduced, it was listed at $740, a price almost unheard of in 1898. It was gold inlayed and covered with scroll and fine banknote-style engraving. The motif on the side plates was usually a pointing dog; in most cases, it was a setter, which became the Hunter Arms trademark. At the breech end of the barrels were gold inlayed lightning streaks. Because a total of only 17 were manufactured, the A3 on today's market will probably fetch in excess of $5,000.

The next gun down the scale is Grade A2, which was quite similar to the A3 except that it lacked gold inlays. Among its several variations of engraving were a brace of pointing dogs on one side of the lock and a pair of setters on the other; a 100% banknote-type scroll engraving with birds in the center; and a hunting scene variation. A total of 200 Grade A2 guns was manufactured.

The pre-1913 Monogram represents the next grade, and it also features a number of variations. Prior to 1913, only 102 Monograms were manufactured. Grade 5, which later became the Crown Grade, featured a brace of pointer dogs engraved on the left lock and a pair of setters on the right, similar to the A3. The rest of the gun was decorated in oak leaf and scroll-type engraving. Grade 5 guns remain fairly common since 484 of them were produced.

L.C. Smith Grade 4, however, is a relatively rare piece. This grade had two variations, one an oval-shaped rosette in the center of the lock plate with a pointing dog on one side and a setting dog on the other. The second variation featured the same dogs, but there's a rosette engraved in the center, which makes the whole illustration seem off balance. A total of 301 Grade 4's was manufactured.

The next lower grade was 3, whose engravings were also varied and nicely executed. This model apparently enjoyed considerable popularity, with a total of 3,790 guns produced and selling for $100 in 1892.

Grade 2 was advertised as the "Knockout" grade. Its normal pattern of engraving depicts a woodcock on one side and a quail on the other, each enlarged within two circles. The popularity of this gun is evidenced by the fact that 12,887 units were produced.

The next grade—the Pigeon—sold for $150 in 1898 and is considered a relatively rare piece. It has a pigeon on one side of the lock and a clay pigeon (engraved with scrollwork) on the other. Only 1,214 Pigeon grades were

This ad from the 1887 Sears and Roebuck catalog emphasizes the high quality of L.C. Smith's guns. Note the absence of a Grade 4 model.

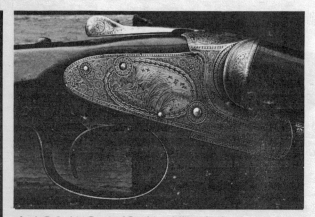

An L.C. Smith Grade A2 with a Miller single trigger.

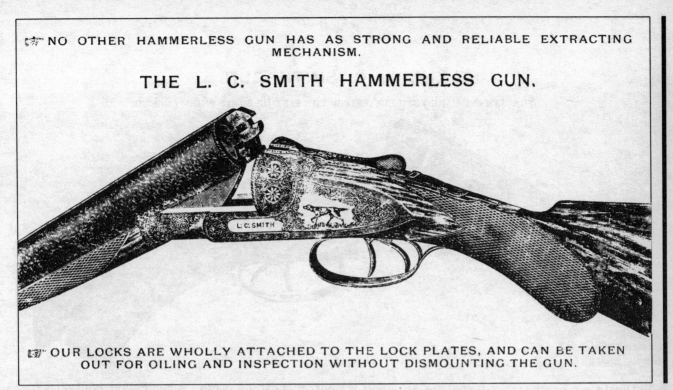

☞ NO OTHER HAMMERLESS GUN HAS AS STRONG AND RELIABLE EXTRACTING MECHANISM.

THE L. C. SMITH HAMMERLESS GUN.

☞ OUR LOCKS ARE WHOLLY ATTACHED TO THE LOCK PLATES, AND CAN BE TAKEN OUT FOR OILING AND INSPECTION WITHOUT DISMOUNTING THE GUN.

This page from L.C. Smith's 1887 catalog shows a Quality 6 gun priced at $300, the equivalent today of several thousands of dollars.

made. Grade 1, which features a rosette on the center of each lock, has 26-inch Damascus barrels. These were quite rare on guns made before 1920. It also has straight grip stocks and no-shock recoil pads. Hunter manufactured 10,221 of these guns.

Grade 0, which features engravings around the locks, sold for $47 in 1898. Production reached 29,360 units. Grade 00, the company's lowest grade hammerless, had no engravings at all on the locks. It was Hunter's biggest seller by far, with 117,264 pieces sold. The "00" sold for $37 in 1898; by comparison, the 1903 Sears and Roebuck catalog listed the Parker VH grade at $36.85, the Baker A grade at $37.10, the Ithaca grade 14 also at $37.10, the Winchester Model 1897 pump repeater at $17.82, and the Marlin 1898 at $16.25.

In 1913, the Hunter brothers decided to change the grading system of their guns to the now familiar names of Field, Ideal, Trap, Specialty, Eagle, Crown, Premiere, Monogram and Deluxe. These newly appointed guns were marked as such on the left rib: "Hunter Arms Co., maker, Fulton, New York, USA.", and on the right rib: "L.C. Smith" together with the grade name and arrows on each side.

The engravings were also changed dramatically. The Field gun replaced the 00 grade and was never engraved—it had only a flat, smooth surface that was nor-

mally case hardened. The Ideal grade bore a simple oak leaf sign with some scroll. The Specialty grade featured scrollwork and a quail on the left lock, with a flying duck on the right. The Trap grade was engraved with scenes of a man shooting trap on the left side and, on the right side, a man shooting in a field.

The next highest grade (Eagle) showed a flying eagle on either side of the lock. The Crown grade, which was much more distinctive and elegant, featured pointing dogs within an oval, heavy scroll engravings, intricate designs, and a crown on the tang opener. Since the Monogram, Premiere and Deluxe grades were all custom guns made to order, any kind of engraving style might be found. The Premiere and Deluxe models, which were inlayed with gold pointing dogs or flying birds, are truly magnificent works of art and are extremely valuable.

Unfortunately, the Hunter Arms Company went bankrupt in 1945, and as a result of the settlement the entire company and all of its assets were acquired by the Marlin Firearms Company of New Haven, Connecticut. Marlin produced approximately 57,000 "L.C. Smith" guns from 1945 until 1949. Then, on January 16, 1949, disaster struck. The entire top floor of the old Hunter Arms plant in Fulton caved in, destroying thousands of dollars worth of equipment. Since it was not economically feasible for Marlin to rebuild the plant, it was

THE L. C. SMITH GUN.

THE HAMMERS ARE ENTIRELY BELOW THE LINE OF SIGHT WHEN COCKED.

Top-Lever, double cross-bolted, the strongest fastener that can be made. It has Patent Joint check, Patent Shell Extractor, Patent Forend, Solid Head Plungers, Rebounding Locks, and all improvements known to the art of Gun Making.

☞ NO EXTRA CHARGE FOR OUR RUBBER BUTT PLATE. WE PUT THEM ON ALL GRADES OF THE SMITH GUN. ☜

A Quality 7 double barrel shotgun, c. 1887.

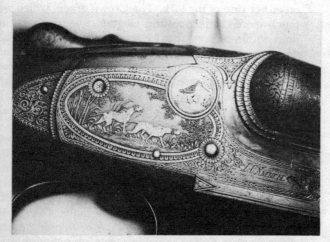
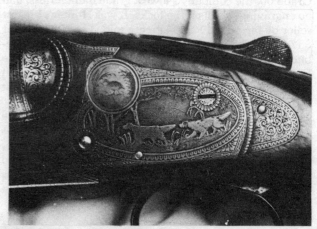

On this Grade A2 gun, note the unusual step side plates, which were found on early L.C. Smith guns. The woodcock and quail inside the circles were also used as the pattern for the company's Grade 2 guns.

closed down and the remaining useful parts transported to the New Haven factory. The L.C. Smith name thus lay dormant until 1968, when Marlin decided to reintroduce the old L.C. Smith gun. Production began in 1969 and soon about 2,000 Field grade guns—exact duplicates of those made by Hunter Arms—were produced.

■ MODERN TIMES

By the early 1970's, the economy made double gun production impractical, and so in 1971 the company was forced to discontinue manufacturing all Smith guns. The double barrel shotgun in America is now undergoing a revival, though, and it is possible that Marlin will elect to resume production. The cost will be high because of the handwork and handfitting required in the production of these guns.

Those who seek L.C. Smith shotguns today can probably find them with greater ease than they will a Parker or Lefever. Total production of Smith double barrel shotguns was approximately 445,000, which makes them far more common than Parkers, which number around 200,000, or Lefevers, which total only 75,000 or so. As for the going price of an L.C. Smith gun, the lower Field grade—and similar models in the old 00 and 0 grades—run anywhere from $350 to $450, depending on their condition. The Ideal model and Grade 2 cost around $600, whereas the older style grading guns command higher prices. Grade 3 runs about $700, but grades 4, 5, and higher are too rare to make even an educated guess at their prices. The Specialty grade fetches about $800 to $900; the Eagle is $900 to $1,000; and the Crown runs $1,500 to $1,800, all depending upon their condition. For guns in 20 gauge, you can expect to pay 50 to 75 percent more; these models are extremely rare and are actively sought by bird hunters for their delicate balance and light weight. In addition to 12, 16 and 20 gauge, Smith also made guns in 10 and .410. The latter commands about $2,600 even in the lowest Field grade.

Keep in mind that these prices are only estimates. They refer to guns made with fluid steel barrels (Damascus runs about 75 percent less) and those that are in excellent or original condition.

SHOOTER'S BIBLE CATALOG SECTION

Complete Illustrated Listing of Guns, Specifications & Accessories

HANDGUNS

RIFLES

SHOTGUNS

PARAMILITARY

BLACK POWDER

SCOPES & SIGHTS

AMMUNITION

BALLISTICS

RELOADING

Handguns

FOR ADDRESSES AND PHONE
NUMBERS OF MANUFACTURERS AND
DISTRIBUTORS INCLUDED IN THIS
SECTION, SEE *DIRECTORY OF
MANUFACTURERS AND SUPPLIERS*

ACTION ARMS PISTOLS

Crafted by the Swiss, this new double action handgun is available in two sizes and calibers (9mm and the new .41 Action Express). Can also be used cocked and locked.

AT-84

SPECIFICATIONS
Operation: Locked breech, inertial firing pin
Safety system: Thumb safety; cocked & locked or double action
Ammunition: 9mm or .41 Action Express
Sights: Front: fixed blade Rear: drift adjustable
Stock: Checkered Walnut
Finish: Blued Metal
Barrel length: 4.72″
Length-overall: 8.10″
Weight-Unloaded: 35.3 oz.
Magazines: 9mm-15 md./41 A.E.-10 md.
Price: $498.00

AT-84P

SPECIFICATIONS
Operation: Locked breech: inertial firing pin
Safety System: Thumb safety; cocked & locked or double action
Ammunition: 9mm or .41 Action Express
Sights: Front: fixed blade Rear: drift adjustable
Stock: Checkered Walnut
Finish: Blued Metal
Barrel length: 3.66″
Length-overall: 7.24″
Weight-Unloaded: 32.1 oz.
Magazines: 9mm-13 md./41 A.E.-8 md.
Price: $498.00

AMERICAN DERRINGER PISTOLS

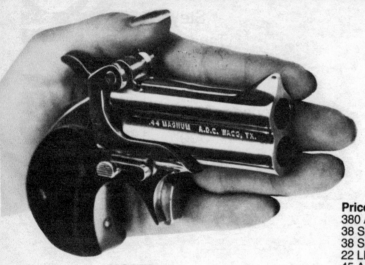

MODEL 1

This small, powerful pocket pistol is built from high tensile strength stainless steel. It can handle over 22 different rifle and pistol calibers, including the 44 Magnum cartridge. All guns are equipped with rosewood grips and come in a high polish or satin finish., Each also comes equipped with manually operated "Hammer-Block" safety.

SPECIFICATIONS
Calibers: 38 Super, 38 Special, 380 Auto, 9mm Luger, 32 Mag., 30-30 Win., 30 Luger, 223 Rem. Commercial Ammo, 22 LR, 22 Rimfire Mag., 22 Hornet, 45 Colt, 45 Auto, 45 Win. Mag., 45-70 (single shot) 44 Mag., 44-40 Win., 44 Special, 41 Mag., 410, 357 Maximum, 357 Magnum
Overall Length: 4.82″
Barrel length: 3″
Weight: 15 oz. (in 45 Auto cal.)
Action: Single action w/automatic barrel selection
Number of shots: 2

Prices:
380 Auto, 9mm Luger $172.50
38 Spec., 32 Mag. 187.50
38 Spec. shot shells, 38 Super, 32-20 . . . . 199.95
22 LR, 22 Mag. rimfire 218.00
45 Auto., 10mm Auto 218.00
357 Mag. 225.00
357 Max. 250.00
44 Spec., 44-40 Win., 45 Colt, 38-40 . . . . 275.00
45 Colt, 2½″ .410 Snake w/45 cal. rifled barrel 312.50
45 Win. Mag., 44 Mag., 41 Mag., 30-30 Win.,
   223 Rem., dual caliber Derringers 369.00

Also available:
Ultra Lightweight (7½ oz.) Model 7
Prices:
38 S&W $157.50
32 Mag., 32 S&W Long 172.50
38 Spec. 187.50
22 LR 187.50
44 Spec. 500.00
380 Auto 145.00

Light Weight (11 oz.) Double Derringer Model 11
Available in 38 Special $157.50

AMERICAN DERRINGER PISTOLS

MODEL 4 (Stainless Steel Double Derringer)

SPECIFICATIONS
Calibers: 3″ .410 or 45 Colt lower barrel
Overall length: 6″
Barrel length: 4.1″
Weight: 16½ oz.
Price. $350.00
Alaskan Survival Model with 45-70 upper barrel,
    3″ .410/45 Colt lower barrel 369.00

MODEL 3 (Stainless Steel Single Shot Derringer)

SPECIFICATIONS
Caliber: 38 Special
Overall length: 4.9″
Barrel length: 2½″
Weight: 8.5 oz.
Safety: Manual "Hammer-Block"
Grips: Rosewood
Price: $115.00

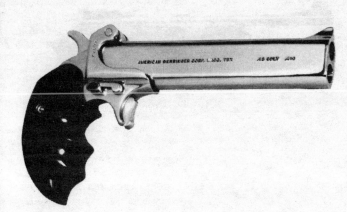

MODEL 6 (Stainless Steel Double Derringer)

SPECIFICATIONS
Calibers: .410 and 45 Colt
Overall length: 8.2″
Barrel length: 6″
Weight: 21 oz.
Finish: Satin or high polish stainless steel
Price: $369.00 ($350.00 in grey matte finish)

AMERICAN DERRINGER PISTOLS

SEMMERLING LM-4
VEST-POCKET .45

SPECIFICATIONS
Caliber: 45 ACP or 9mm
Action: Double action
Capacity: 5 rounds
Overall length: 5″
Price: Blue finish $1250.00
Stainless steel 1500.00

ANSCHUTZ PISTOL

EXEMPLAR
$359.00 ($385.00 MAGNUM)

SPECIFICATIONS
Caliber: 22 LR and 22 Magnum
Barrel length: 10″
Overall length: 17″
Weight: 3¹/₃ lbs.
Action: Match 64 left
Trigger: #5091—two stage adjustable
Safety: slide
Sights: hooded ramp post front; open notched rear; adj. for windage and elevation
Stock: European walnut
Capacity: 5 shot clip

ASTRA PISTOLS & REVOLVERS

357 MAGNUM

MODEL A-90

ASTRA 357 MAG. (shown above in 4″ barrel)

Potent, powerful and smooth as silk: the Astra 357. Chambered for the hot 357 Magnum cartridge, this large-frame revolver also handles the popular 38 Special, making it equally suitable for the serious target shooter and for the sportsman.

All forged steel and highly polished to a rich blue, the Astra 357 has a heavyweight barrel with integral rib and ejector shroud. The rear sight is click-adjustable for windage and elevation. The hammer is of the wide-spur target type, and the trigger is grooved. The grips are of checkered hardwood. The cylinder is recessed, and the gun utilizes a spring-loaded, floating firing pin for additional safety.

The internal lockwork of the Astra 357 is as finely fitted and finished as the exterior, giving it a smoothness second to none. There's even a four-stage adjustment to control spring tension on the hammer.

The Astra 357 is available with 3-inch, 4-inch, 6-inch and 8½-inch barrel. The 4-inch and longer-barreled models have square butts and are supplied with comfortable, hand-filling oversized grips. Length overall with 6-inch barrel is 11½ inches.

Barrel Length	Finish	Caliber	Weight	
3″	Blue	357 Mag.	36 oz.	$285.00
4″	Stainless	357 Mag.	36 oz.	330.00
4″ & 6″	Blue	357 Mag.	37 oz.	295.00
8½″	Blue	357 Mag.	44 oz.	305.00

ASTRA CONSTABLE 22 L.R. & 380 ACP

The Astra Constable is a double-action, all-steel, small-frame auto, so you can safely carry it fully loaded with a round in the chamber and the safety off. A single pull of the trigger then cocks and fires the pistol without the necessity of cocking the hammer manually, as is necessary with most autos. The thumb safety completely blocks the hammer and actually locks the firing pin in place until released. The barrel is rigidly mounted in the frame for greater accuracy and the gun features quick, no-tool takedown, integral non-glare rib on the slide, push-button magazine release and a round, non-snagging hammer spur. **Barrel length:** 3½″. **Weight:** 37 oz. (380 ACP) and 28 oz. (22 LR). **Capacity:** 10 rds. (22 LR) and 7 rds. (380 ACP).

22 LR Blue	$315.00
380 ACP Blue	295.00
22 LR Chrome	330.00
380 ACP Chrome Engraved	390.00
22 LR Blue Engraved	395.00
380 ACP Blue Engraved	375.00
22 LR Chrome Engraved	410.00
380 ACP A-60 (13 rds.)	375.00

ASTRA MODEL A-90

Double-action, semiautomatic pistol in 9mm Parabellum and 45 ACP.

Features include an advanced, smooth double-action mechanism, increased magazine capacity (15 rounds in 9mm, 9 rounds in 45 ACP), all-steel construction, compact size, loaded chamber indicator, combat-style trigger guard, optional right-side slide release. **Barrel length:** 3¾″. **Weight:** 36 oz. (37 oz. in 45 ACP). **Price: $425.00.**

ASTRA SPORT & SERVICE REVOLVERS MODELS 44 & 45

Designed around the popular lines of its forerunner, the Astra 357, this revolver features wide-spur target hammers and a four-position main spring adjustment device which allows for custom tuning of trigger pull. Includes oversized, beefed-up frame and target-style grips to provide balanced weight distribution and minimize recoil.

The revolvers, finished in deep astral blue, are available with 6-inch barrels which feature integral sight ribs and shrouds for the ejector rods. Grooved triggers, ramp front sights and fully adjustable rear sights are standard on all models.

	Barrel Length	Finish	Caliber	Price
Model 44	6″	Blue	44 Mag.	395.00
Model 45	6″	Blue	45 Colt	315.00

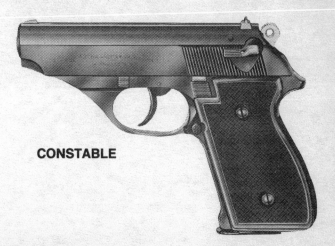

CONSTABLE

BEEMAN PISTOLS

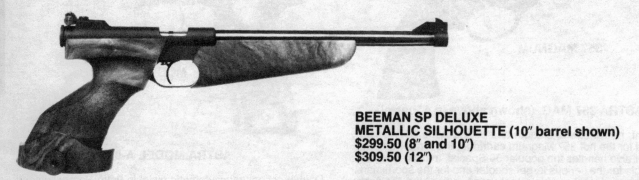

BEEMAN SP DELUXE
METALLIC SILHOUETTE (10″ barrel shown)
$299.50 (8″ and 10″)
$309.50 (12″)

SPECIFICATIONS
Caliber: 22 LR. **Capacity:** Single shot. **Barrel lengths:** 8″, 10″, 12″. **Grips:** Walnut target w/adjustable palm rest. **Sights:** Adjustable rear sight; receiver ground for scope mount.
Beeman SP Standard (not shown): Same as Deluxe model without detachable forearms and balance weight.
Price: $249.50 (8″ and 10″); **$259.00** (12″); **$279.50** (15″).

BEEMAN UNIQUE 2000-U
5-SHOT SEMIAUTOMATIC
$998.00 (right)
$1050.00 (left)

This improved version of the 823-U includes a reshaped grip, a redesigned firing mechanism, a faster falling hammer, and a dry firing mechanism that is easier to use. Trigger weight is only 3.5 oz. Features special light alloy frame and solid steel slide and shock absorber. Five vents reduce recoil; three removable vent screws adjust for jump control and velocity. Counter-weights available. **Caliber:** 22 Short. **Weight:** 2.7 lbs.

BEEMAN PISTOLS & REVOLVERS

BEEMAN/FAS 602
$936.25 (right); $973.75 (left)

This standard fire 22 LR semiautomatic pistol has a trigger pull of 1,050 gms. (2.3 lbs.) in two adjustable stages, thus enabling the best shot release. Grip well and magazine do not interfere with grip outline. **Sight radius:** 8½". **Weight:** 2.5 lbs. **Capacity:** 5 shots. Also available in 32 S&W wadcutter **(Model 603)**

BEEMAN/FAS 601 (not shown)

This semiautomatic rapid fire pistol has six gas vents to reduce muzzle jump and assure maximum stability while firing. Magazine inserts from top to eliminate interference with grip angle and magazine well. Trigger is adjustable and easily removed. **Caliber:** 22 Short. **Sight radius:** 9¼". **Weight:** 2.6 lbs. **Price: $942.50**

BEEMAN/KORTH
$1777–$3096

The metal parts of this revolver are hammer-forged steel super-hardened to high tensile strength. Cylinder gap of .002" eliminates stretching of the frame while firing, reduces flash, and increases velocity. **Caliber:** 357 Mag. or 22 LR w/interchangeable combo cylinders of 357 Mag./9mm Para or 22 LR/22 WMR. **Grips:** Walnut. **Barrel lengths:** 6" (Target); 3", 4", 6" (Combat).

BEEMAN/UNIQUE 69 TARGET PISTOL
$779.00 (right); $818.00 (left)

SPECIFICATIONS
Caliber: 22 LR. **Capacity:** 5-shot magazine. **Sight radius:** 8.7". **Weight:** 2.2 lbs. **Grips:** Adjustable, anatomically shaped. **Features:** Trigger adjusts for position and pull weight; several barrel counterweights available; dry firing device; meets all U.I.T. requirements.

BERETTA SMALL FRAME PISTOLS

MODEL 21
$210.00

A 22LR caliber double-action semiautomatic with 8-round capacity. A safe, dependable, accurate small-bore pistol for plinkers, campers, and competitive paper bull's-eye shooters.

SPECIFICATIONS
Caliber: 22LR double-action semiautomatic. **Magazine capacity:** 8 rounds. **Overall length:** 4.9″. **Barrel length:** 3.8″. **Weight:** 11.8 oz. **Sights:** Blade in front, V-notch in rear. **Grips:** Walnut. **Frame:** Special alloy.

MODEL 21

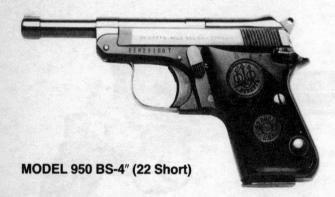

MODEL 950 BS-4″ (22 Short)

MODEL 71

A medium frame single action pistol for the casual shooter. It features a slanted grip for maximum comfort and a crisp, progressive trigger pull. Model 71 has a 6″ barrel, an 8-round magazine capacity, and an adjustable rear sight. Price upon request.

MODEL 950
Single Action Semiautomatic

SPECIFICATIONS
Calibers: 25 ACP and 22 Short. **Barrel length:** 2¹/₂″ in 25 cal.; 2¹/₂″ or 4″ in 22 cal. **Overall length:** 4¹/₂″. **Overall height:** 3.4″. **Safety:** External, thumb-operated. **Magazine:** 8 rounds (25 cal.); 6 rounds (22 Short). **Sights:** Blade front; V-notch rear. **Weight:** 10 oz. in 22 cal., 8 oz. in 25 cal.

Model 950 BS (22S cal. 7-shot or 25 cal. 9-shot). . . **$150.00**
    in nickel 170.00
    with 4″ barrel (22S only) 150.00
Model 950 EL (with gold engraving) 210.00

BERETTA PISTOLS

MODEL SB-92F (9mm)

This 9mm Parabellum semiautomatic pistol is specifically designed for use by law enforcement agencies. It has also been adopted as the official sidearm of the U.S. Army, Navy, Marine Corp, Air Force and Coast Guard. Its 15-round firepower combines with flawless reliability and safety to make it the ideal police and military sidearm. Its firing mechanism will handle thousands of rounds without malfunction. And the ambidextrous triple-safety mechanism features a passive firing pin blocking bar, a slide safety that acts as a decocking lever, plus a unique firing pin to insure that a falling hammer can never break safety and discharge accidentally.

SPECIFICATIONS
Caliber: 9mm Parabellum. **Overall length:** 8.54". **Height:** 5.4". **Barrel length:** 4.92". **Weight** (empty): 34 oz. **Magazine:** 15 rounds, removable floorplate. **Rear sight:** Fixed, driftable for windage. **Slide stop:** Holds slide open after last round, manually operable.

Model 92SB-F $595.00
(Wood grips $15.00 additional)

BERETTA PISTOLS MODEL 81 SERIES

Prices:
Model 84 Plastic	$460.00
Model 84 Wood	485.00
Model 84 Wood/Nickel	515.00
Model 85 Wood	365.00
Model 86 Wood	N.A.
Model 87 BB	415.00

MODEL 87BB

BERETTA MEDIUM FRAME PISTOLS

MODEL 84 BB

This pistol is pocket size with a large magazine capacity. The lockwork is of double-action type. The first shot (with hammer down, chamber loaded) can be fired by a double-action pull on the trigger without cocking the hammer manually.

The pistol also features a favorable grip angle for natural pointing, positive thumb safety (uniquely designed for both right- and left-handed operation), quick takedown (by means of special takedown button) and a conveniently located magazine release. Black plastic grips. Wood grips available at extra cost.

MODEL 84

SPECIFICATIONS
Caliber: 380 Auto (9mm Short). **Weight:** 1 lb. 7 oz. (approx.).
Barrel length: 3³/₄". (approx.) **Overall length:** 6¹/₂". (approx.)
Sights: Fixed front and rear. **Magazine capacity:** 13 rounds.
Height overall: 4¹/₄" (approx.).

Model 84 (with plastic grips). $495.00
Model 84 (with wood grips) 510.00
   in nickel 550.00

MODEL 85BB
$460.00

This double action semiautomatic pistol features walnut grips, blued steel slide, ambidextrous safety, and anodized alloy frame with a single line 8-round magazine.

SPECIFICATIONS
Caliber: 380 Auto. **Barrel length:** 3.82". **Weight** (empty): 21.8 oz. **Overall length:** 6.8". **Overall height:** 4.8". **Capacity:** 8 rounds. **Sights:** Blade integral with slide (front); Square notched bar, dovetailed to slide (rear).

Also available in nickel $500.00

MODEL 86
$400.00

Contains all the features of Model 85BB plus a safe, convenient tip-up barrel for direct chamber loading without working manual slide.

SPECIFICATIONS
Caliber: 380 Auto. **Barrel length:** 4.33". **Overall length:** 7.33". **Weight** (empty): 23 oz. **Overall height:** 4.8". **Capacity:** 8 rounds. **Grip:** Walnut or plastic.

With wood grips $480.00

BERNARDELLI PISTOLS

MODEL 80

Caliber: 22 LR, 10 Shot; 380 ACP, 7" Shot. **Barrel:** 3.54". **Overall length:** 6.45". **Weight:** 26.8 oz. **Stock:** Checkered plastic w/thumb rest (wrap around). **Sights:** Adjustable. **Features:** Hammer-blocking slide safety which locks firing pin to permit loading or clearing of chamber with safety engaged. Loaded round indicator, adjustable rear sight. White outline rear sight and white dot front sight. Dual recoil buffer springs. Serrated trigger. Inertia-type firing pin. Magazine follower interlock holds slide open after last round is fired.

Model 80 22 LR $215.00
          380 ACP 220.00

Also: Model 90 (not shown). Available in 22 LR and 32 ACP. $245.00.

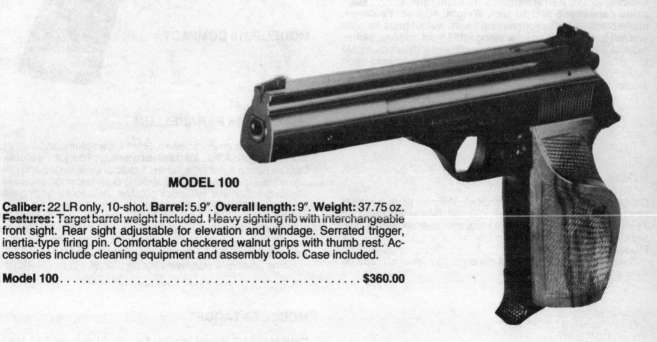

MODEL 100

Caliber: 22 LR only, 10-shot. **Barrel:** 5.9". **Overall length:** 9". **Weight:** 37.75 oz.
Features: Target barrel weight included. Heavy sighting rib with interchangeable front sight. Rear sight adjustable for elevation and windage. Serrated trigger, inertia-type firing pin. Comfortable checkered walnut grips with thumb rest. Accessories include cleaning equipment and assembly tools. Case included.

Model 100 . . . . $360.00

BERNARDELLI PISTOLS

MODEL P010 STANDARD

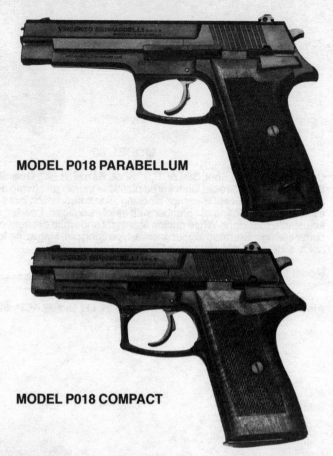

MODEL P018 PARABELLUM

MODEL P018 COMPACT

MODEL P010 STANDARD

Caliber: 22 LR. **Barrel length:** 5.9″. **Sight radius:** 7.5″. **Magazine capacity:** 5 and 10 shot. **Weight:** 40.5 oz. **Features:** matte black reflection-preventing finish; walnut grips for right and left hand shooters; interchangeable front and rear sights; external hammer with safety notch; pivoted trigger adjustable for pull weight and take-ups; external slide catch for hold-open device; manual safety; inertia safe firing pin.
Model P010 . . . . **$417.00**

MODEL U.S.A.

Calibers: 22 LR (10-shot magazine), 7,65mm (8-shot magazine) and 9mm short (7-shot magazine). **Barrel length:** 3.5″. **Features:** firing pin block; loaded chamber indicator; adj. sight; steel frame; plastic grips.
Model U.S.A. **$207.00**
    Same as above with walnut grips **263.00**

MODEL AMR

Calibers: 9mm short, 7,65mm, and 22 LR. **Barrel lengths:** 6″, 8″ and 10″. **Features:** adj. sight; plastic grips; anatomic adj. grips (left grip has thumb rest).
Model AMR **$228.00**
    Same as above with walnut grips **282.00**

MODEL P018 PARABELLUM

Caliber: 7,65mm Parabellum, 9mm Parabellum, and 9 × 21. **Barrel length:** 4.75″. **Magazine capacity:** 16 shot. **Features:** Double action automatic made of special steel forged and precision milled; manual safety locking both hammer, slide and trigger mechanism, half-cock position, auto-locking firing pin; blued or parkerized plastic grips.
Model P018 . . . . **$382.00**
    Same model with walnut grips **438.00**

Also available: **Model P018 Compact** (4″ barrel). . . . **397.00**
    Same as above with walnut grips **425.00**

MODEL 69 TARGET

Caliber: 22 LR **Barrel length:** 5.9″. **Sight radius:** 7.1″. **Magazine capacity:** 10 shot. **Features:** special steel receiver; wide walnut wrap-around grip (right and left hand); hand checkered; external hammer; rear sight adj. for windage and elevation; interchangeable front sights; hold-open device; manual safety; magazine safety; inertial safe firing pin.
Weight: 2.2 lbs.
Model 69 . . . . **$295.00**

BERSA AUTOMATIC PISTOLS

SINGLE ACTION

MODEL 383
$188.00

SPECIFICATIONS
Caliber: 380 Auto
Barrel length: 3½"
Capacity: 7 + 1 in chamber
Sights: Front blade sight integral on slide; rear sight square
notched adjustable for windage
Grips: Target-type nylon
Action: Blow back
Finish: Blue

MODEL 383

DOUBLE ACTION

MODEL 383 DA
$239.00

SPECIFICATIONS
Caliber: 380 Auto
Barrel length: 3½"
Action: Blow back
Sights: Front blade sight integral on slide; rear sight square
notched adjustable for windage
Capacity: 7 + 1 in chamber
Grips: Custom wood
Model 223 DA: Same specifications but in 22 LR. Magazine
capacity = 10 + 1. **$239.00**
Also available in Satin Nickel finish: **$279.00**

MODEL 383 DA

BERSA AUTOMATIC PISTOLS

MODEL 224 DA
$239.00

SPECIFICATIONS
Caliber: 22 LR
Barrel length: 4"
Action: Blow back
Sights: Front blade sight on barrel; rear sight square notched adjustable for windage
Capacity: 10 + 1 in chamber
Grips: Custom wood
Finish: Blue
Model 226 DA: Same specifications and price but with 6" barrel.

MODEL 226 DA
$239.00

Specifications same as **Model 224** but with 6" barrel.

MODEL 226 DA

BRNO PISTOLS

MODEL CZ 75
$599.00

This 9mm double action service pistol features an all-steel frame, 15-shot magazine, and two integral locking lugs on top of barrel which fit into matching recesses in the slide. When slide is pulled forward, the barrel is forced downward and unlocked from the slide stop pin (which fits through the slotted barrel tang.) A pivot type extractor is pinned on the right side of the slide behind the ejection port. Trigger pull is 9 lbs.

SPECIFICATIONS
Caliber: 9mm Parabellum. **Barrel length:** 4.7". **Overall length:** 8.1". **Height:** 5.4". **Weight:** 35 oz.

BROWNING AUTOMATIC PISTOLS

BUCK MARK .22 PISTOL
$176.95

Magazine capacity: 10 rounds. **Overall length:** 9¹/₂". **Barrel length:** 5¹/₂". **Height:** 5³/₈". **Weight:** 35 oz. **Grips:** Black molded. **Rear sights:** Screw adjusts for vertical correction; drift adjustable for windage.

Prices:
Standard	$176.95
Plus (w/contoured, laminated woodgrips)	208.95
Silhouette	299.95
Varmint	269.95

BUCK MARK SILHOUETTE

MODEL BDA-380.

MODEL BDA-380. A high-powered, double-action pistol with fixed sights in 380 caliber.

BDA-380 nickel . . . . **$458.50**   BDA-380 std. **$435.50**

SEMIAUTOMATIC PISTOL SPECIFICATIONS

	BUCK MARK 22	BDA-380 (DOUBLE ACTION)
Capacity of Magazine	10	13
Overall length	9¹/₂"	6³/₄"
Barrel Length	5¹/₂"	3¹³/₁₆"
Height	5³/₈"	4³/₄"
Weight (Empty)	32 oz.	23 oz.
Sight radius	8"	4¹⁵/₁₆"
Ammunition	22LR	380 Auto
Grips	Black, Molded	Walnut
Front Sights	¹/₈" wide	¹/₁₆" wide
Rear Sights	Screw adjustable for windage and elevation.	Square notch. Drift adjustable for windage.
Grades Available	Standard	Standard, Nickel

BROWNING AUTOMATIC PISTOLS

**9mm HI-POWER
SINGLE ACTION 9mm**

**DOUBLE ACTION 9mm
$493.95**

The Browning 9mm Parabellum, also known as the 9mm Browning Hi-Power, has a 14-cartridge capacity and weighs 2 pounds. The push-button magazine release permits swift, convenient withdrawal of the magazine.

The 9mm is available with either a fixed-blade front sight and a windage-adjustable rear sight or a non-glare rear sight, screw adjustable for both windage and elevation. The front sight is a 1/8-inch wide blade mounted on a ramp. The rear surface of the blade is serrated to prevent glare.

In addition to the manual safety, the firing mechanism includes an external hammer, making it easy to ascertain whether the pistol is cocked.

Prices:

Standard **$512.95**
Polished blue with adjustable sights **564.95**
Matte blue ambidextrous safety **474.95**

Also available: new 9mm double action pistol with fixed sights, standard matte finish. **$408.95.**

9MM SEMIAUTOMATIC PISTOL (SINGLE AND DOUBLE ACTION)

	SINGLE ACTION FIXED SIGHTS	SINGLE ACTION ADJUSTABLE SIGHTS	DOUBLE ACTION FIXED SIGHTS
Finish	Polished Blue, Matte, or Nickel	Polished Blue or Nickel	Matte
Capacity of Magazine	13	13	14
Overall Length	$7^3/_4''$	$7^3/_4''$	$7^3/_4''$
Barrel Length	$4^{21}/_{32}''$	$4^{21}/_{32}''$	$4^{21}/_{32}''$
Height	5''	5''	5''
Weight (Empty)	32 oz.	32 oz.	32 oz.
Sight Radius	$6^5/_{16}''$	$6^3/_8''$	$6^5/_{16}''$
Ammunition	9mm Luger, (Parabellum)	9mm Luger, (Parabellum)	9mm Luger, (Parabellum)
Grips	Checkered Walnut	Checkered Walnut	Polyamide
Front Sights	$1/_8''$	$1/_8''$ wide on ramp	$1/_8''$
Rear Sights	Drift adjustable for windage.	Screw adjustable for windage and elevation.	Drift adjustable for windage.

CHARTER ARMS REVOLVERS

BULLDOG 44 SPECIAL

SPECIFICATIONS
Caliber: 44 Special. **Type of action:** 5-shot, single- and double-action. **Barrel length:** 3″. **Overall length:** 7³/₄″. **Height:** 5″. **Weight:** 19 oz. **Grips:** Neoprene or American walnut hand-checkered bulldog grips. **Sights:** Patridge-type, ⁹/₆₄″ wide front; square-notched rear. **Finish:** High-luster Service Blue or Stainless Steel.

Also available: new 44SPL Bulldog Pug Model with 2¹/₂″ barrel and ramp front sight. **Overall length:** 7¹/₄″.

Prices:
Blue finish with pocket hammer (2¹/₂″) $216.60
Blue finish with Bulldog grips (3″) 216.60
Stainless Steel finish with Bulldog grips 260.23
with neoprene grips and pocket hammer 263.72

**BULLDOG 44
SPECIAL
5-SHOT**

357 MAGNUM REVOLVER
BULLDOG "TRACKER"

SPECIFICATIONS
Caliber: 357 Magnum. **Type of action:** 5-shot. **Barrel length:** 2¹/₂″. **Overall length:** 7¹/₂″ (2¹/₂ bbl.). **Height:** 5¹/₈″. **Weight:** 21 oz. **Grips:** Hand-checkered walnut, square butt design. **Sights:** Ramp front sight; adjustable square-notched rear; elevation reference lines; definite click indicator. **Finish:** Service blue.

Price:
Blue finish and Square Butt or Bulldog grips $214.00

**357 MAGNUM REVOLVER
BULLDOG "TRACKER"**

POLICE BULLDOG
6-SHOT REVOLVER

SPECIFICATIONS
Caliber: 38 Special and 32 H&R Magnum. **Type of action:** 6-shot single and double action. **Barrel length:** 4″. **Overall length:** 9″. **Height:** 5″. **Weight:** 20 to 23¹/₂ oz. **Grips:** square butt, American walnut hand-checkered. **Sights:** Full-length ramp front; square notch rear (adjustable rear sight on 32 H&R Mag.). **Finish:** High-luster service blue.
Price $217.17
Stainless steel 263.00

**POLICE BULLDOG
6-SHOT REVOLVER**

POLICE UNDERCOVER

SPECIFICATIONS
Caliber: 32 H&R Magnum and 38 Special. **Type of action:** 6-shot single and double action. **Barrel length:** 2″. **Height:** 4¹/₂″. **Weight:** 17¹/₂ oz. (2″ barrel) and 19 oz. (4″ barrel.) **Grips:** Checkered walnut panel. **Sights:** Patridge-type ramp front sight, square-notch rear sight. **Finish:** Blue.

Price $217.74
Stainless steel and checkered walnut panel 252.00

POLICE UNDERCOVER

CHARTER ARMS REVOLVERS

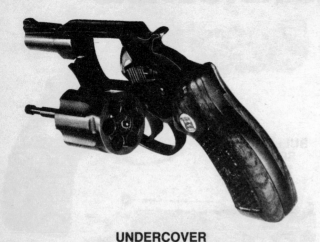

UNDERCOVER
32 S&W Long

SPECIFICATIONS
Caliber: 32 S&W Long. **Type of Action:** 6-shot, single- and double-action. **Barrel length:** 2". **Overall length:** 6¼". **Height:** 4⅛". **Weight:** 16 oz. **Grips:** Checkered walnut panel. **Sights:** Wide Patridge-type front; notch rear ⁹⁄₆₄". **Rifling:** One turn in 17", right hand twist. **Finish:** High-luster Service Blue.

Price:
Blue finish with regular grips $198.87

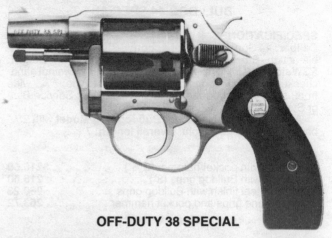

OFF-DUTY 38 SPECIAL

SPECIFICATIONS
Caliber: .38 Special. **Type of action:** 5-shot single- and double-action. **Barrel length:** 2". **Overall length:** 6¼". **Height:** 4¼". **Weight:** 16 oz. (mat-black), 17 oz. (stainless steel). **Grips:** Smooth walnut, checkered walnut, or neoprene. **Sights:** Patridge-type ramp front sight (with new "red dot" feature), square notch rear sight.

Prices:
Mat-black finish. $167.30
Stainless steel 230.42

UNDERCOVER 38 SPECIAL

SPECIFICATIONS
Caliber: 38 Special (Mid-Range & Standard). **Type of Action:** 5 shots, single- and double-action. **Barrel length:** 2" or 3". **Overall length:** 6¼" (2" bbl.), 8" (3" bbl.). **Height:** 4¼" (2" bbl.), 4¾" (3" bbl.). **Weight:** 16 oz. (2" bbl.), 17½ oz. (3" bbl.). **Grips:** American walnut hand-checkered. **Sights:** Patridge-type ramp front, square-notched rear. **Finish:** High-luster Service Blue or Stainless Steel.

Prices:
2" barrel blue finish with checkered panel grips $198.87
2" barrel stainless steel with checkered panel grips . . 252.00
3" barrel blue finish with checkered panel grips 198.87

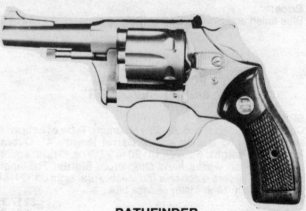

PATHFINDER
22 L.R.

SPECIFICATIONS
Caliber: 22 Magnum and 22 LR. **Type of action:** 6-shot, single and double action. **Barrel length:** 2", 3" or 6". **Overall length:** 7¾" (3" bbl.); 10⅝" (6" bbl.). **Height:** 4¾" (3" bbl.); 5" (6" bbl.). **Weight:** 20 oz. (3" bbl.); 22½ oz. (6" bbl.). **Grips:** Hand-checkered square butt or checkered walnut panel. **Sights:** Patridge-type ramp front sight; fully adjustable notch rear sight. **Finish:** High luster service blue.

Prices:
With 2" or 3" barrel $210.65
With 6" barrel 222.11
With 3" barrel in stainless steel. 255.20

COLT AUTOMATIC PISTOLS

COMBAT COMMANDER

The semiautomatic Combat Commander, available in 45 ACP, 38 Super or 9mm Luger, boasts an all-steel frame that supplies the pistol with an extra measure of heft and stability. This outstanding Colt also offers fixed square-notch rear and fixed blade front, lanyard-style hammer and thumb and grip safety.

Caliber	Weight	Overall Length	Magazine Rounds	Finish	Price
45 ACP	36 oz.	7⅞″	7	Blue	$539.95
38 Super	36½ oz.	7⅞″	9	Blue	544.95
9mm Luger	36½ oz.	7⅞″	9	Blue	544.95

COMBAT COMMANDER
4¼″ barrel only

LIGHTWEIGHT COMMANDER

This lightweight, shorter version of the Government Model offers increased ease of carrying with the firepower of the 45 ACP. The Lightweight Commander features alloy frame, fixed-style sights, grooved trigger, lanyard-style hammer and walnut stocks; also thumb and grip safety, and firing pin safety.

SPECIFICATIONS
Weight: 27 oz.
Barrel length: 4¼″
Overall length: 7⅞″
Magazine rounds: 7
Finish: Blue
Price: $537.50

LIGHTWEIGHT COMMANDER
4¼″ barrel only

GOLD CUP NATIONAL MATCH

SPECIFICATIONS
Caliber: 45 ACP
Capacity: 7 rounds
Barrel length: 5″
Weight: 38½ oz.
Overall length: 8⅜″
Sights: Undercut front; adjustable rear
Hammer: Serrated target hammer
Stock: Checkered walnut
Finish: Colt blue
Price: $699.95
Also available in stainless steel: **$749.95**; and bright stainless: $799.95.
Now available: COMBAT ELITE .45 ACP. Features 3 dot front and rear combat sights, extended grip safety.
Price: $659.95

GOLD CUP NATIONAL MATCH

COLT AUTOMATIC PISTOLS
MK IV SERIES 80

GOVERNMENT MODEL

GOVERNMENT MODEL 380 AUTOMATIC

This scaled-down version of the 1911 A1 Colt Government Model does not include a grip safety. It incorporates the use of a firing pin safety to provide for a safe method to carry a round in the chamber in a "cocked and locked" mode. This provides for a consistent trigger pull rather than the double-action style of a heavy first pull.

SPECIFICATIONS
Caliber: 380 ACP
Barrel length: 3.29″
Height: 4.4″
Weight (empty): 21.8 oz.
Overall length: 6.15″
Magazine capacity: 7 rounds
Sights: Fixed ramp blade in front; fixed square notch in rear
Grip: Composition stocks
Finish: Blue
Price: $349.95
Satin Nickel **389.95**
Coltguard **369.95**

GOVERNMENT MODEL

These full-size automatic pistols, available exclusively with 5-inch barrels, may be had in 45 ACP, 9mm Luger, 38 Super and 22 LR. The Government Model's special features included fixed military sights, grip and thumb safeties, grooved trigger, walnut stocks and Accurizor barrel and bushing.

Caliber	Weight	Overall Length	Magazine Rounds	Finish	Price
45 ACP	38 oz.	8³/₈″	7	Blue	$539.95
				Stainless	579.95
38 Super	39 oz.	8³/₈″	9	Blue	544.95
9mm Luger	39 oz.	8³/₈″	9	Nickel	599.95
				Blue	544.95

GOVERNMENT MODEL
380 AUTOMATIC

DELTA ELITE

The proven design and reliability of Colt's Government Model has been combined with the new powerful 10mm auto cartridge to produce a highly effective shooting system for hunting, law enforcement and personal protection. The velocity and energy of the 10mm cartridge make this pistol ideal for the serious handgun hunter and the law enforcement professional who insists on down-range stopping power. Price to be announced.

SPECIFICATIONS:
Caliber: 10mm
Type: 0 Frame, Semi-Automatic Pistol
Barrel length: 5″
Weight (empty): 39 oz.
Overall length: 8¹/₂″
Cylinder capacity: 7 rds.
Sights: 3 dot high profile front and rear combat sights
Sight radius: 6¹/₂″
Grip: Rubber combat stocks with Delta medallion
Safety: Trigger safety lock (thumb safety) is located on left hand side of receiver; grip safety is located on backstrap
Rifling: 6 groove, lefthand twist, one turn in 16″
Finish: Blue

COLT PISTOLS

COLT MUSTANG .380

This new backup automatic has four times the knockdown power of most 25 ACP automatics.

SPECIFICATIONS
Caliber: 380 ACP
Capacity: 5 rounds
Weight: 18.5 oz.
Overall length: 5.65″
Height: 3.9″
Price: $349.95 ($389.95 in nickel)
Also available: **MUSTANG POCKET LITE 380** with aluminum alloy receiver; 1/2″ shorter than standard 380; weighs only 12.5 oz.

COLT OFFICER'S ACP

SPECIFICATIONS
Caliber: 45 ACP
Barrel length: 3⅝″
Overall length: 7¼″
Weight: 34 oz.
Price: $519.95 (matte finish)
      579.95 (stainless steel)
      539.95 (lightweight, 3″ barrel)

COLT REVOLVERS

KING COBRA
357 MAGNUM

This new "snake" revolver features a solid barrel rib, full length ejector rod housing, red ramp front sight, white outline adjustable rear sight, and new "gripper" rubber combat grips. All stainless steel.

SPECIFICATIONS
Caliber: 357 Magnum
Barrel lengths: 2″, 4″, 6″
Weight: 42 oz.
Price: $399.95 (2″ price to be announced)

COLT REVOLVERS

PYTHON
357 MAGNUM (shown with 6″ barrel)

The Colt Python revolver, suitable for hunting, target shooting and police use, is chambered for the powerful 357 Magnum cartridge. Python features include ventilated rib, fast cocking, wide-spur hammer, trigger and grips, adjustable rear and ramp-type front sights, $1/8$″ wide.

SPECIFICATIONS
Caliber: 357 Mag.
Barrel length: $2^1/2$″, 4″, 6″, 8″ (357 Mag.)
Overall length: $11^1/4$″
Weight: $43^1/2$ oz.
Stock: Checkered walnut
Finish: Colt royal blue, stainless and bright steel (not in 8″)

Caliber	Barrel	Finish	Price
357 Mag.	$2^1/2$″, 4″, 6″, 8″	Blue	$699.95
357 Mag.	$2\ ^1/2$″, 4″, 6″	St.S.	799.95

Now available: **Python Ultimate Stainless Steel,** in $2^1/2$″, 4″ and 6″ barrels. **$819.95.**

PEACEKEEPER 357 MAGNUM

The Peacekeeper is a medium frame 357 Magnum with an adjustable white outline rear sight, a red insert ramp-style front sight, and round bottom rubber grip.

SPECIFICATIONS
Caliber: 357 Magnum
Capacity: 6 shots
Overall length: $9^1/8$″ (4″ barrel) and $11^1/8$″ (6″ barrel)
Barrel lengths: 4″ and 6″
Weight: 42 oz. (4″ barrel) and 46 oz. (6″ barrel)
Sights: Adjustable white outline (rear); red insert ramp style (front)
Finish: Nonreflective matte blue
Price: $329.95

COONAN ARMS

MODEL B 357 MAGNUM
$625.00

Caliber: 357 Magnum
Magazine capacity: 7 rounds
Barrel length: 5″
Overall length: 8.3″
Weight (empty): 42 oz.
Height: 5.6″
Sights: Ramp interchangeable (front); fixed, adjustable for windage only (rear)
Grips: Smooth black walnut
Safety features: Hammer lock; half-notch lock; grip lock; inertia firing pin

DAKOTA SINGLE ACTION REVOLVERS

MODEL 1873 (With Extra Cylinder)
$495.00

SPECIFICATIONS
Calibers: 22 LR, 22 Mag., 357 Mag., 45 Long Colt, 30 M1 Carbine, 38-40 cal., 32-20 cal., 44-40 cal. **Barrel lengths:** 3¹/₂″, 4³/₄″, 5¹/₂″, 7¹/₂″. **Finish:** Engraved models, blue or nickel. **Special feature:** Each gun is fitted with second caliber.

DAKOTA TARGET
$425.00

SPECIFICATIONS
Calibers: 45 Long Colt, 357 Magnum, 22 LR. **Barrel lengths:** 5¹/₂″ and 7¹/₂″. **Finish:** Polished blue. **Special features:** Case-hardened frame, one-piece walnut grips, brass back strap, ramp front blade target sight and adjustable rear sight.

MODEL 1875 "OUTLAW"
$395.00 ($470.00 nickel)

SPECIFICATIONS
Calibers: 45 Long Colt, 357 Magnum, 44-40 cal. **Barrel length:** 7¹/₂″. **Finish:** Blue. **Special features:** Case-hardened frame, walnut grips; an exact replica of Remington #3 revolver produced from 1875 to 1889. Factory Engraved Model: **$600.00**

DAKOTA BISLEY
$495.00

SPECIFICATIONS
Calibers: 44-40 cal., 45 Long Colt, 357 Mag. **Barrel lengths:** 5¹/₂″ and 7¹/₂″. Also available: **Dakota Bisley Engraved Model** with same barrel lengths and calibers **$680.00**

DAVIS PISTOLS

MODEL D-22 DERRINGER
$64.90

SPECIFICATIONS
Calibers: 25 Auto, 22 LR, 32 Auto, 22 Mag.
Barrel length: 2.4″
Overall length: 4″
Height: 2.8″
Weight: 9.5 oz.
Capacity: 2 shot
Grips: Laminated wood
Finish: Black teflon or chrome (32 Auto in chrome only)

MODEL P-32
$64.50

SPECIFICATIONS
Caliber: 32 Auto
Barrel length: 2.8″
Overall length: 5.4″
Height: 4″
Magazine capacity: 6 rounds
Weight (empty): 22 oz.
Grips: Laminated wood
Finish: Black teflon or chrome
Price: to be announced

DETONICS

COMBAT MASTER™ 45 ACP (Stainless Steel)

Caliber: 45 ACP, 6-shot clip; 451 Detonics Magnum, 6-shot clip. 38S and 9mm available on special order.
Barrel length: 3¹/₂″
Weight: 29 oz. (empty); **MK VII** 26 oz.
Overall length: 6³/₄″
Stock: Checkered walnut
Sights: Combat type, fixed; adj. sights available
Features: Self-adjusting cone barrel centering system, beveled magazine inlet, "full clip" indicator in base of magazine; throated barrel and polished feed ramp.
Price:
  MK I, matte stainless, fixed sights $671.95
  MK VI, polished stainless, adj. sights 755.95

**COMBAT MASTER
45 ACP**

SERVICEMASTER II
(not shown)

A new, shortened version of the Scoremaster, this model features coned barrel and recoil systems.

Caliber: 45 ACP
Barrel: 4¹/₄″
Weight: 39 oz.
Capacity: 7 (plus 1 chambered)
Sights: Millett (rear); interchangeable (front)
Price: $899.95

DETONICS

SCOREMASTER (Stainless Steel)

Caliber: 45 ACP, 7-shot clip; 451 Detonics Magnum, 7-shot clip
Barrel length: 5" or 6" heavyweight match barrel.
Weight: 42 oz. (5" barrel)
Overall length: 8³/₈" (5" barrel)
Stock: Pachmayr grips and M.S. housing
Sights: Low-Base Bomar Rear Sight
Features: Stainless steel construction; self-centering barrel system; patented Detonics recoil system; combat tuned; ambidextrous safety; extended grip safety; National Match tolerances: extended magazine release
Price: 45 ACP and 451 Detonics Magnum. $1095.00
    With 6" barrel 1112.00

THE JANUS SCOREMASTER

The Janus Scoremaster is two pistols in one: a stock 5" barrel and slide mounted front sight convertible (in five minutes with a ¹/₁₆" punch) into a 5¹/₂" comp gun with front sight mounted on the specialist comp.

SPECIFICATIONS
Caliber: 45 ACP.
Barrel length: 5.2" w/stock barrel; 5.6" w/comp. barrel
Overall length: 8³/₈" w/stock barrel; 10" w/comp. barrel
Weight: 42 oz. w/stock barrel; 46 oz. with comp. barrel
Sights: Adj. rear sight, Millet on slide, hand serrated; custom front sight on compensator
Capacity: 7 rounds plus 1 chambered
Rifling: 1 turn in 16"; left hand turn, 6 grooves
Finish: polished side of slide w/matte satin surfaces
Price: $1650.00
Note: Owners of Detonics **Scoremaster** models can have their guns retrofitted with the Janus compensated barrel unit. Old unit will be returned with both barrels (see Detonics address in Directory of Manufacturers). **Price: $600.00.**

F.I.E. HANDGUNS

DERRINGER D-86 SINGLE SHOT
$89.95 ($94.95 DELUXE)

SPECIFICATIONS
Caliber: 38 Special
Barrel length: 3"
Weight: 11 oz.
Sights: fixed
Safety: transfer bar
Finish: Dyna-chrome hard matte or bright blue
Grips: black nylon (Standard) and walnut (Deluxe)

TITAN 25 SEMIAUTOMATIC
$69.96

SPECIFICATIONS
Caliber: 25 ACP
Barrel length: 2¹/₂"
Weight: 12 oz.
Sights: ramp front, fixed rear
Hammer: serrated external
Grips: European walnut
Trigger lock: thumb operated
Also available in Dyna-Chrome **($74.95)** and gold trim **($89.95)**

TITAN TIGER DOUBLE ACTION REVOLVER
$144.95

SPECIFICATIONS
Caliber: 38 Special
Barrel length: 2" or 4"
Sights: ramp front, fixed rear
Grips: composite, checkered
Features: swing-out cylinder with thumb latch release

ARMINIUS REVOLVERS

SPECIFICATIONS
Calibers: 22S/L/LR, 22 WMR, 22 Combo w/interchangeable cylinders, 32 S&W Long, 38 Special, 357 Magnum
Barrel lengths: 2", 3", 4" and 6"
Sights: fixed or micro-adjustable
Weight: 26 oz. - 30 oz.
Capacity: 8 rds (22), 7 rds (32 S&W), 6 rds (all others)
Prices: $157.95 (22 LR and 32 S&W snub nose)
          131.95 (22 LR 4" and 6"; 32 S&W 6" blue)
          174.95 (22 Combo 6" blue)
          159.95 (38 Special 4" and 6")
          209.95 (357 Magnum 3", 4" and 6")

F.I.E. PISTOLS

MODEL TZ75
$374.95 (9mm)

SPECIFICATIONS
Caliber: 9mm double action
Capacity: 15 + 1
Barrel length: 4¹/₂″
Overall length: 8¹/₄″
Height: 5¹/₂″
Weight: 35 oz.
Sights: D/T ramp front (white insert); rear (white outline) adjustable for windage
Grips: European walnut, black rubber (optional)

Available in satin chrome: **$394.95**

MODEL A27BW "THE BEST"
25ACP SEMIAUTOMATIC
$139.95

Once known as the "Astra Cub" and later as the "Colt Junior," this classic is now known as "The Best" pistol.

SPECIFICATIONS
Capacity: 6 shots
Barrel length: 2¹/₂″
Overall length: 6³/₄″
Weight: 12 oz.
Stock: Checkered walnut
Sights: Fixed

MODEL TITAN II

SPECIFICATIONS
Caliber: 22LR, 32 ACP, 380 ACP
Barrel length: 3¹/₄″
Overall length: 6¹/₂″
Capacity: 10 + 1
Finish: Blue
Grip: European walnut
Sights: Integral tapered post front sight; windage adjustable rear sight
Weight: 25¹/₂ oz.

Prices
```
22LR  Blue . . . . . . . . . . . . . . . . . . . . . . . . . . . . $145.95
32ACP  Blue. . . . . . . . . . . . . . . . . . . . . . . . . . . . 154.95
       Chrome . . . . . . . . . . . . . . . . . . . . . . . . . . . 169.95
380ACP  Blue . . . . . . . . . . . . . . . . . . . . . . . . . . . 199.95
        Chrome . . . . . . . . . . . . . . . . . . . . . . . . . . 209.95
```

SUPER TITAN II (not shown)

SPECIFICATIONS
Weight: 28 oz.
Barrel length: 3¹/₄″
```
Super Titan II  (Cal. 32ACP) Blue . . . . . . . . . . . . . $194.95
Super Titan II  (Cal. 380ACP) Blue . . . . . . . . . . . . $234.95
```

FREEDOM ARMS

FA-BG-22LR

FA-L-22LR

FA-S-22LR

Model	22 LONG RIFLE REVOLVERS	Prices
FA-S-22LR	Stainless Steel Mini-Revolver with 1-inch contoured barrel, partial high gloss finish. Caliber 22 Long Rifle.	$113.25
FA-L-22LR	Stainless Steel Mini-Revolver with 1³/₄-inch contoured barrel, partial high gloss finish. Caliber 22 Long Rifle.	113.25
FA-BG-22LR	Stainless Steel Mini-Revolver with 3-inch tapered barrel, partial high gloss finish, custom oversized grips. Caliber 22 Long Rifle.	127.50

Above prices include soft zipper pouch and simulated ebony grips.

NEW 22 PERCUSSION REVOLVERS

FA-S-22P	Stainless Steel Percussion Mini-Revolver with 1-inch contoured barrel, partial high gloss finish.	$138.95
FA-L-22P	Stainless Steel Percussion Mini-Revolver with 1³/₄-inch contoured barrel, partial high gloss finish.	138.95
FA-BG-22P	Stainless Steel Percussion Mini-Revolver with 3-inch tapered barrel, partial high gloss finish, custom oversized grips.	153.25

All Percussion Revolver prices include the following: powder measure, bullet setting tool, twenty bullets, soft zipper pouch and simulated ebony grips.

22 WIN. MAGNUM REVOLVERS

FA-S-22M	Stainless Steel Mini-Revolver with 1-inch contoured barrel, partial high gloss finish.	$133.25
FA-L-22M	Stainless Steel Mini-Revolver with 1³/₄-inch contoured barrel, partial high gloss finish.	133.25
FA-BG-22M	Stainless Steel Mini-Revolver with 3-inch tapered barrel, partial high gloss finish and custom oversized grips.	147.60
FA-LRCYL	22 Long Rifle cylinder fitted to Magnum Revolver. (If Long Rifle cylinder is not ordered with new Magnum Revolver, gun must be returned to factory and a $10.00 fitting charge will be added.)	20.95

Prices include soft zipper pouch.

Model No.	454 CASULL	Price
FA-454AS	Adjustable sight 454 Casull, 4³/₄″, 6″, 7¹/₂″, 10″ or 12″ barrel, stainless steel, brush finish, impregnated hardwood grips.	$1060.00
FA-454FS	Same as above with fixed sight	960.00

HAMMERLI PISTOLS

MODEL 150 FREE PISTOL
$1665.00 ($1715.00 Left Hand)

SPECIFICATIONS
Caliber: 22 LR
Overall length: 17.2″
Weight: 45.6 oz.
Trigger action: Infinitely variable set trigger weight; cocking lever located on left of receiver; trigger length variable along weapon axis
Sights: Sight radius 14.8″; micrometer rear sight adj. for windage and elevation
Locking action: Martini-type locking action w/side-mounted locking lever
Barrel: Free floating, cold swaged precision barrel w/low axis relative to the hand
Ignition: Horizontal firing pin (hammerless) in line w/barrel axis; firing pin travel 0.15″
Grips: Selected walnut w/adj. hand rest for direct arm to barrel extension
MODEL 150L: Same as above but w/left hand adjustable grips

MODEL 152 ELECTRONIC PISTOL
$1825.00 ($1875.00 Left Hand)

SPECIFICATIONS:
Same as **Model 150** except trigger action is electronic. Features short lock time (1.7 milliseconds between trigger actuation and firing pin impact), light trigger pull, and extended battery life.

HAMMERLI PISTOLS

MODEL 208 TARGET PISTOL
$1389.00 ($1419.00 Left Hand)

SPECIFICATIONS:
Caliber: 22LR
Barrel length: 6″
Overall length: 10.2″
Weight: 37.3 oz. (w/accessories)
Capacity: 8 rounds
Sight radius: 8.3″
Sights: Micrometer rear sight w/notch width; standard front blade
DELUXE MODEL (Right Hand only): **$3250.00**

MODEL 215 TARGET PISTOL
$1095.00 ($1125.00 Left Hand)

SPECIFICATIONS
Same as **Model 208** except it has fewer "luxury" features. Also available: **MODEL 212 Hunter's Pistol** featuring safety catch, nonslip slide and optimal balance. **Price: $1359.00.**

MODEL 232 RAPID FIRE PISTOL
$1214.00 ($1244.00 Left Hand)

SPECIFICATIONS:
Caliber: 22 Short
Barrel length: 5.2″
Overall length: 10.5″
Weight: 44 oz.
Sight radius: 9.6″
Capacity: 5 rounds
Grips: Adjustable (add **$40** for wraparound grips)

IVER JOHNSON PISTOLS

380 PONY

All-steel, the 380 Pony is chambered for 380 ACP. The magazine holds six rounds. For maximum security, the pistol features an inertia firing pin, and the large thumb safety cams the hammer out of contact with the sear. The windage-adjustable rear sight is rounded on its outer dimensions so it won't snag on clothing. Grips are of solid walnut, and the backstrap is extra long to protect the shooter's hand.
Length: 6". **Height:** 4.3".

380 PONY AUTO PISTOL

Model	Grips	Finish	Cal.	Barrel	Sights	Price
PO380B	Walnut	Blue	.380	3.1 in.	Adjustable	**$260.00**
PO380M	Walnut	Military	.380	3.1 in.	Adjustable	260.00
PO380N	Walnut	Nickel	.380	3.1 in.	Adjustable	291.25

POCKET PISTOL
TP22 & TP25

These 22- and 25-caliber pocket pistols offer a maximum of convenience when carried. The 7-shot capacity, small size and light weight are enhanced by the hammer safety and fast-handling double-action design.
Barrel length: 3". **Overall length:** 5.5". **Weight:** 12 oz. (empty). **Grips:** Black plastic. **Finish:** Blue.

TP22 (22LR) $154.00
TP25 (25ACP) 154.00

DOUBLE ACTION 9mm AUTOMATIC
$300.00-$350.00

SPECIFICATIONS
Caliber: 9mm. **Barrel length:** 3". **Overall length:** 6½". **Weight:** 26 oz. **Sights:** Blade front; adjustable rear. **Finish:** Blue or matte blue. **Grip:** Smooth hardwood. **Magazine capacity:** 6 rounds.

IVER JOHNSON PISTOLS

TRAILSMAN MODEL TM22PB
(4½″ & 6″ barrel length)

SPECIFICATIONS
Caliber: 22 LR. **Weight:** 1 lb. 14 ozs. and 2 lbs. **Overall length:** 8.75″ and 10.25″. **Width:** 1.5″. **Height:** 4.5″. **Finish:** Blue steel. **Magazine capacity:** 10 rounds. **Stocks:** Composition checkered. **Sights:** Fixed target.

TM22PB $191.00
with hardwood stock and high polish finish. 215.00

KIMBER PISTOL

PREDATOR
$995.00 (Hunter Grade)
$1195.00 (Super Grade)

SPECIFICATIONS
Calibers: 221 Fireball, 223 Rem., 6mm TCU 6 × 45mm, 7mm TCU
Action: single shot bolt action
Stock: select French walnut w/ebony forend tip and grip cap (Super Grade); AA claro (Hunter Grade)

L.A.R. GRIZZLY

MARK I
GRIZZLY WIN MAG
$675.00

This semiautomatic pistol is a direct descendant of the tried and trusted 1911-type .45 automatic, but with the added advantage of increased caliber capacity.

SPECIFICATIONS
Calibers: 45 Win. Mag., 45 ACP, 357 Mag.
Barrel length: $6^1/2''$
Overall length: $10^1/2''$
Weight (empty): 48 oz.
Height: $5^3/4''$
Sights: Fixed, ramped blade (front); fully adjustable for elevation and windage (rear)
Magazine capacity: 7 rounds
Grips: Checkered rubber, nonslip, combat-type
Safeties: Grip depressor, manual thumb, slide-out-of-battery disconnect
Materials: Mil spec 4140 steel slide and receiver with non-corrosive, heat-treated, special alloy sttels for other parts

Same model in 357 Magnum **$699.00**
Also available: **Win Mag Compensator**. **60.00**

$6^1/2''$ BARREL

8" BARREL

10" BARREL

Also available: Grizzly Win Mag with 8" and 10" Barrels in 45 Win Mag, 357 Magnum, 45 ACP and 357/45 Grizzly Win Mag.
Model G-WM8 (8" barrel in 45 Win Mag, 45 ACP, or 357/45 Grizzly Win Mag **$1250.00**
Model G357M8 (8" barrel in 357 Magnum) **1275.00**
Model G-WM10 (10" barrel in 45 Win Mag, 45 ACP, or 357/45 Grizzly Win Mag **1313.00**
Model G357M10 (10" barrel in 357 Magnum) **1337.50**

LLAMA REVOLVERS

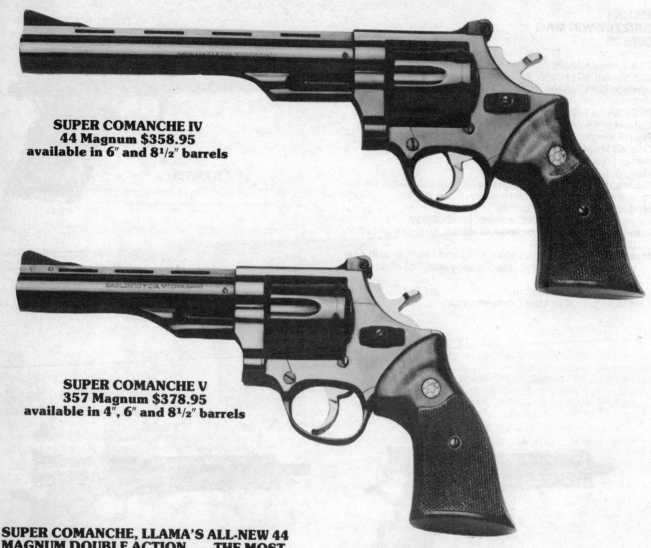

SUPER COMANCHE IV
44 Magnum $358.95
available in 6″ and 8¹/₂″ barrels

SUPER COMANCHE V
357 Magnum $378.95
available in 4″, 6″ and 8¹/₂″ barrels

SUPER COMANCHE, LLAMA'S ALL-NEW 44 MAGNUM DOUBLE ACTION . . . THE MOST RUGGED, ACCURATE REVOLVER BUILT

Three years of intensive product development and generations of prototypes evolved before final specifications were
set for this all-new Super Comanche. If ever a handgun was
conceived, designed and built to fit the exacting requirements of big-bore handgunners, this one is it.

Take the frame for example: it's massive. The most solid,
most rugged of any other double-action revolver. Its weight
and balance are such that the heavy recoil generated by the
powerful 44 Magnum cartridge is easily and comfortably
controlled, even when rapid firing in the double-action mode.
In the single-action mode, the broad, serrated hammer-spur
makes cocking easy and fast.

Instead of a single cylinder latch, the new Llama has two.
In addition to the conventional center pin at the rear of the
ratchet, there's a second latch up front which locks the crane
to the frame at the underside of the barrel ring. Using this
two-lock system, the cylinder and crane are locked in a more
positive manner that can be achieved using the common de-
tent/ball arrangement found on other revolvers.

Only coil springs are used throughout. Not only does this
provide added strength in a critical area, but the added rigidity raises the gun's accuracy potential as well. Also aiding
accuracy is the heavyweight barrel measuring .815 inch in
diameter. A matte-finish rib reduces glare and helps get on
target faster.

But building the strongest and most accurate revolver
were only two of the three basic goals Llama engineers set for
themselves; they also wanted to build the safest. To that end,
the hammer is mounted on an eccentric cam, the position of
which is controlled by the trigger. Only when the latter is
fully depressed can the firing pin contact the primer. Accidental discharge is virtually impossible.

LLAMA REVOLVERS

LLAMA "Super Comanche" 44 Magnum Revolver Specifications

CALIBER:	.44 Magnum	44 Magnum
BARREL LENGTH:	6"	8½"
NUMBER OF SHOTS:	6 shots	
FRAME:	Forged high tensile strength steel	
ACTION:	Double action	
TRIGGER:	Smooth extra wide	
HAMMER:	Wide spur, deep positive serrations	
SIGHTS:	Rear-click adjustable for windage and elevation, leaf serrated to cut down on glare. Front-ramped blade.	
SIGHT RADIUS:	8"	10⅜"
GRIPS:	Oversized target, walnut. Checkered	
WEIGHT:	3 lbs., 2 ozs.	3 lbs., 8 ozs.
OVER-ALL LENGTH:	11¾"	14½"
FINISH:	High polished, deep blue	
SAFETY FEATURE:	The hammer is mounted on an eccentric cam, the position of which is controlled by the trigger. Only when the latter is fully depressed can the firing pin contact the primer.	

LLAMA SUPER COMANCHE 357 MAGNUM REVOLVER

The 357 ammunition that is manufactured today is becoming more and more powerful. These hotter loads create additional recoil that causes undesirable battering of internal parts and excessive stretching of the frame. As a result, shooting accuracy as well as the average firing life of the traditional 357 has been decreased.

Llama engineers built this all new 357 on the big, brawny Super Comanche frame. This frame, forged for strength, absorbs the maximum amount of recoil, reduces muzzle jump, provides greater balance, control and accuracy, and a longer

firing life. For double added safety, Llama engineered an eccentric cam-hammer system that makes accidental discharge virtually impossible, and incorporated the "old reliable" triple lock crane cylinder support for additional locking strength.

And to satisfy those shooters who prefer a lighter, more compact gun, Llama engineers designed a second all-new 357, built on a medium weight frame, which also features the eccentric cam-hammer system, perfect balance and true accuracy.

Specifications

CALIBER:	357 Magnum		
BARREL LENGTH:	4"	6"	8½"
NUMBER OF SHOTS:	6 shots		
FRAME:	Forged high tensile strength steel		
ACTION:	Conventional double action		
TRIGGER:	Smooth extra wide		
HAMMER:	Wide spur, deep positive serrations		
SIGHTS:	Rear-click adjustable for windage and elevation, leaf serrated to cut down on glare. Front-ramped blade.		
SIGHT RADIUS:	6"	8"	10⅜"
GRIPS:	Oversized target, walnut. Checkered		
WEIGHT:	3 lbs.	3 lbs., 6 ozs.	3 lbs., 12 ozs.
OVER-ALL LENGTH:	9⅞"	11⅞"	14½"
FINISH:	High polished, deep blue		
SAFETY FEATURE:	The hammer is mounted on an eccentric cam, the position of which is controlled by the trigger. Only when the latter is fully depressed can the firing pin contact the primer.		

LLAMA REVOLVERS

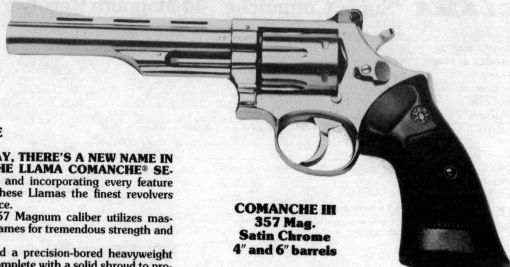

LLAMA COMANCHE

IN REVOLVERS TODAY, THERE'S A NEW NAME IN EXCELLENCE, IT'S THE LLAMA COMANCHE® SERIES. Designed for you and incorporating every feature worth having to make these Llamas the finest revolvers made today . . . at any price.

The sledgehammer 357 Magnum caliber utilizes massively forged solid-steel frames for tremendous strength and enduring reliability.

Up front, Llama added a precision-bored heavyweight barrel of target quality, complete with a solid shroud to protect the ejector rod, and a raised ventilated-rib that dissipates heat from the barrel to give you a clear, sharp sight image even when the action gets hot.

On the inside, everything is finely fitted and polished, for a double action that's slick and smooth, and a single-action trigger pull that's light, crisp and clean. Llama gave all Comanches a floating firing pin for greater safety and dependability.

357 Mag. Standard Blue 4″, 6″ **$271.95**
357 Mag. Satin Chrome 4″, 6″ **324.95**

**COMANCHE III
357 Mag.
Satin Chrome
4″ and 6″ barrels**

Specifications

CALIBERS:	357 Magnum
BARREL LENGTH:	4 and 6-inch
NUMBER OF SHOTS:	6 shots
FRAME:	Forged high hensile strength steel. Serrated front and back strap.
ACTION:	Double-action. Floating firing pin.
TRIGGER:	Wide grooved target trigger. Case-hardened.
HAMMER:	Wide spur target hammer with serrated gripping surface. Case-hardened.
SIGHTS:	Square notch rear sight with windage and elevation adjustments; serrated quick-draw front sight on ramp.
SIGHT RADIUS:	With 4-inch barrel—5³⁄₄″; with 6-inch barrel—7³⁄₄″.
GRIPS:	Oversized target, walnut. Checkered.
WEIGHT:	w/4″ bbl.—2 lbs., 4ozs. w/6″ bbl.—2 lbs., 7 ozs.
OVER-ALL LENGTH:	With 4-inch barrel—9¹⁄₄″; with 6-inch barrel—11″.
FINISH:	High-polished, deep blue. Deluxe models; satin chrome (.357 w/4″ & 6″ bbl.)
SAFETY FEATURE:	The hammer is mounted on an eccentric cam, the position of which is controlled by the trigger. Only when the latter is fully depressed can the firing pin contact the primer.

LLAMA AUTOMATIC PISTOLS

Llama's newest 9mm single action is a compact version of its 9mm semi-auto, a gun which over the years has earned the kind of trust that has made it the issued side arm of countless military and law enforcement agencies throughout the world

The small-frame Llama models, available in 22 LR and 380 Auto., are impressively compact handguns. All frames are precision machined of high strength steel, yet weigh a featherlight 23 ounces. A full complement of safeties . . . side lever, half-cock and grip . . . is incorporated.

Every small-frame Llama is complete with ventilated rib, wide-spur serrated target-type hammer and adjustable rear sight. NEW. Also available in 45 caliber automatic.

The large-frame Llama models, available in potent 45 ACP, are completely crafted of high strength steel.

**NEW 9mm PARABELLUM
STANDARD BLUE
$307.00**

LLAMA COMPACT 45

**LLAMA SMALL-FRAME
AUTOMATIC WITH
DEEP BLUE FINISH
22 Caliber and 380 Caliber
$261.00**

LLAMA AUTOMATIC PISTOLS

**LLAMA SMALL-FRAME
AUTOMATIC PISTOL IN
SATIN CHROME FINISH
22 and 380 Caliber
$327.00**

LLAMA Automatic Pistol Specifications

TYPE:	Small Frame Auto Pistols		Compact Frame Auto Pistols		Large Frame Auto Pistols
CALIBERS:	22 LR	380 Auto.	9mm Parabellum	45 Auto	45 Auto.
FRAME:	Precision machined form high strength steel. Serrated front strap, checkered (curved) backstrap.		Precision machined form high strength steel. Serrated front strap, checkered (curved) backstrap.		Precision machined from high strength steel. Plain front strap, checkered (curved) backstrap.
TRIGGER:	Serrated		Serrated		Serrated
HAMMER:	External. Wide spur, serrated.		External. Wide spur, serrated.		External. Wide spur, serrated.
OPERATION:	Straight blow-back.		Locked breech.		Locked breech.
LOADED CHAMBER INDICATOR:	No	Yes	No	No	Yes
SAFETIES:	Side lever thumb safety, grip safety.		Side lever thumb safety, grip safety.		Side lever thumb safety, grip safety.
GRIPS:	Modified thumbrest black plastic grips.		Genuine walnut on blue models. Genuine teakwood on satin chrome.		Genuine walnut on blue models. Genuine teakwood on satin chrome.
SIGHTS:	Square notch rear, and Patridge-type front, screw adjustable rear sight for windage		Square notch rear, and Patridge-type front, screw adjustable rear sight for windage.		Square notch rear, and Patridge-type front, screw adjustable rear sight for windage
SIGHT RADIUS:	$4^1/4''$		$6^1/4''$		$6^1/4''$
MAGAZINE CAPACITY:	8-shot	7-shot	9-shot	7-shot	7-shot
WEIGHT:	23 ounces		37 ounces	34 ounces	36 ounces
BARREL LENGTH:	$3^{11}/16''$		5''		5''
OVERALL LENGTH:	$6^1/2''$		$7^7/8''$		$8^1/2''$
HEIGHT:	$4^3/8''$		$5^7/16''$		$5^1/3''$
FINISH:	Std. models; High-polished, deep blue. Deluxe models; satin chrome (22, 380, 45)		Std. models; High-polished, deep blue. Deluxe models; satin chrome (22, 380, 45)		Std. models; High-polished, deep blue. Deluxe models; satin chrome (22, 380, 45)

LLAMA AUTOMATIC PISTOLS

Machined and polished to perfection. These truly magnificent firearms come complete with ventilated rib for maximum heat dissipation, wide-spur checkered target-type hammer, adjustable rear sight and genuine walnut grips.

In addition to High Polished Deep Blue, the following superb handguns are available in handsome Satin Chrome 22 LR, 380 Auto., 45 ACP.

**LLAMA LARGE-FRAME
AUTOMATIC PISTOL IN
SATIN CHROME FINISH**
45 Auto Caliber
$414.00

**LLAMA LARGE-FRAME
AUTOMATIC WITH
DEEP BLUE FINISH**
45 Auto Caliber
$307.00

LLAMA PISTOLS

MODEL M-82 (9mm)
$750.00

SPECIFICATIONS

Caliber: 9 mm. Parabellum
Magazine: 15 cartridges (15 + 1 shot)
Length overall: 8¼″
Height: 5⁵/₁₆″
Maximum width: 1³/₈″
Weight (Unloaded) steel: 39 oz.
Weight (Unloaded) Light Alloy: 31 oz.
Barrel length: 4¹/₂″
No. of barreling grooves: 6
Stocks: Plastic
Finish: Blued

After nearly a decade of research, development and testing, the new Llama M-82 is being offered to the gun buying public. Representing the state-of-the-art in double action, semiauto pistol design, this handgun offers a unique blend of highly innovative technical features, combined with the kind of ergonomic design and practical performance that are so important in day-to-day use. It's the kind demanded by military and law enforcement personnel, as well as by competitive combat shooters and otherwise knowledgeable handgunners.

Whatever criteria are used in judging a DA semiauto—whether accuracy, reliability, simplicity of design, looks, compactness, quality of fit, or finish—all are effectively combined in the M-82. The following features indicate why pistol experts are already hailing this new Llama as the world's finest production combat handgun.

1. MINIMAL BARREL/SLIDE DISPLACEMENT: As the slide moves rearward during the firing cycle, the lineal displacement required to unlock the action is but a fraction of that in other double action designs. This translates into less wear and tear on the mechanism, as well as allowing tighter tolerances. That, in turn, means greater accuracy, greater durability.

2. POSITIVE SAFETY MECHANISM: Even when at rest and with the safety disengaged, the hammer does not contact the firing pin, making this gun one of the safest handguns available today.

3. TWIN LUG LOCK-UP: Unlike other DA's, which rely on a single locking lug engagement in the ceiling of the slide, the M-82 has two lugs in the "three and nine o'clock" position. This unique system provides greater strength, greater rigidity. . . . and greater accuracy.

4. FULL-LENGTH GUIDE RAILS: For more positive, accurate alignment of barrel, slide and frame, the Llama's slide is engaged by guide rails the entire length of its movement (some autos allow as much as two inches of unsupported slide movement).

5. MAXIMUM FIREPOWER: The M-82's staggered magazine holds 15 rounds, plus one in the chamber. This potent firepower is made possible by an overall grip dimension small enough to fit comfortably in the average hand.

6. RECESSED BREECH FACE: Unlike other guns featuring flat breech faces, the Llama's is recessed, much like most modern high-powered rifles. This additional support in the critical case head area means greater safety.

7. AMBIDEXTROUS SAFETY: Allows the M-82 to be used with equal speed and convenience by both right- and left-handed shooters.

8. CHANGEABLE MAGAZINE RELEASE: Normally positioned on the left side of the grip for right-handed shooters, the clip release button on the M-82 can be changed easily to the other side for southpaw use.

9. ARTICULATED FIRING PIN: Another excellent Llama feature is its virtually unbreakable firing pin. In fact, it's guaranteed not to break—for life.

10. COMPACT SIZE: Despite its 16-shot capability, the M-82 is neither heavy nor bulky. Its overall dimensions are short—8¼″ in length, 5 ⁵/₆″ in height, and 1 ³/₈″ in extreme width. Empty weight is 39 ounces.

11. ENLARGED EJECTION PORT: To preclude any sort of ejection problems brought about by variation in loads or in slide velocity, the ejection port is slightly oversize.

12. MODULAR GRIP DESIGN: The hammer strut and main spring are housed in a separate sub-assembly which easily detaches from the frame for routine cleaning and maintenance.

13. INSTANT DISASSEMBLY: The M-82 can be field stripped in less than five seconds—without tools.

Desert Eagle

Angelo 370-2960

243-0819

Paul Call Tues 7pm

Pat Dave
Pete
6 Guns Gary

650°° Blue

Tri. 659-9600

674°° Blue
789°⁴⁵ 44" "
Nickel / 800°°

Stainless

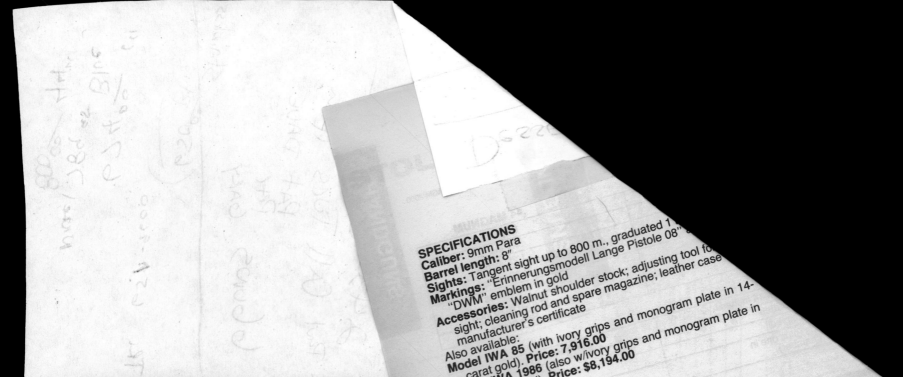

SPECIFICATIONS
Caliber: 9mm Para
Barrel length: 8″
Sights: Tangent sight up to 800 m., graduated 1
Markings: "Erinnerungsmodell Lange Pistole 08″
"DWM" emblem in gold
Accessories: Walnut shoulder stock; adjusting tool fo
sight; cleaning rod and spare magazine; leather case
manufacturer's certificate
Also available:
Model IWA 85 (with ivory grips and monogram plate in 14-
carat gold). **Price: 7,916.00**
IWA 1986 (also w/ivory grips and monogram plate in
Price: $8,194.00

SPECIFICATIONS
Caliber: 9mm Para
Barrel length: 8″
Sights: Tangent sight up to 800 m., graduated 1 to 8
Markings: "Erinnerungsmodell Lange Pistole 08" as well as "DWM" emblem in gold
Accessories: Walnut shoulder stock; adjusting tool for front sight; cleaning rod and spare magazine; leather case with manufacturer's certificate
Also available:
Model IWA 85 (with ivory grips and monogram plate in 14-carat gold). **Price: 7,916.00**
Model IWA 1986 (also w/ivory grips and monogram plate in 14-carat gold). **Price: $8,194.00**

LUGER "LANGE PISTOLE 08"
$7,325.00

STANDARD LUGER #2 (not shown)
9mm w/4″ or 6″ barrel. **Price: $3,283.00**

Model IWA 83 (with ivory grips and monogram plate in 14-carat gold. **Price: $7,122.00**

Model IWA 84 (with ivory grips and monogram plate in 14-carat gold). **Price: $8,392.00**

MOA MAXIMUM PISTOL

MAXIMUM

This new single shot pistol with its unique falling block action performs like a finely tuned rifle. The single piece receiver of chromoly steel is mated to a Douglas barrel for optimum accuracy and strength.

SPECIFICATIONS
Calibers: 22 Hornet to 358 Win.
Barrel lengths: 10″ and 14″
Weight: 3 lb. 13 oz. (10″); 4 lb. 3 oz. (14″)
Price: $499.00
Also available: **Maximum Carbine** w/18″ barrel: **$575.00**

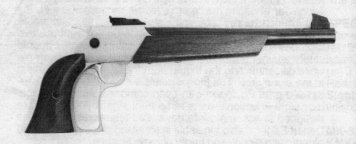

MAGNUM RESEARCH

DESERT EAGLE PISTOL
.357/.44 MAGNUM

SPECIFICATIONS	.357 MAGNUM	.44 MAGNUM
Length, with 6 inch barrel	10.6 inches	10.6 inches
Height	5.6 inches	5.7 inches
Width	1.25 inches	1.25 inches
Trigger reach	2.75 inches	2.75 inches
Sight radius (with 6 inch barrel)	8.5 inches	8.5 inches
Additional available barrels	14 inch	14 inch & 10 inch
Weight	See below	See below

Mechanical Features

	.357 MAGNUM	.44 MAGNUM
Bore rifling — Six rib	Polygonal: 1 turn in 14 inches	Polygonal: 1 turn in 18 inches
Method of operation	Gas operated	Gas operated
Method of locking	Rotating bolt	Rotating bolt
Magazine capacity	9 rounds (plus one in chamber)	8 rounds (plus one in chamber)

DESERT EAGLE — WEIGHT TABLES
.357 Magnum

Frame	Without Magazine		With Empty Magazine	
	6" Barrel	14" Barrel	6" Barrel	14" Barrel
	ounces	ounces	ounces	ounces
Aluninum	47.8	55.0	51.9	59.1
Steel	58.3	65.5	62.4	96.6
Stainless	58.3	65.5	62.4	69.6

.44 Magnum

Frame	Without Magazine		With Empty Magazine	
	6" Barrel	14" Barrel	6" Barrel	14" Barrel
	ounces	ounces	ounces	ounces
Aluminum	52.3	61.0	56.4	65.1
Steel	62.8	71.5	66.9	75.6
Stainless	62.8	71.5	66.9	75.6

.357 MAGNUM
$589.00
$789.00 w/14" barrel

The stopping power of the 44 Magnum is combined with the rapid fire capability of a semiauto in this gas-operated pistol. Manufactured by Israeli Military Industries (of Uzi and Galil weaponry fame), the Desert Eagle is supplied with a standard 6-inch barrel whose maximum effective range is 650 feet. Six and 14-inch barrels are optional and fully interchangeable without tools. Pistols feature rotating 3-lug bolt with positive lockup of the bolt. The ambidextrous safety provides double safety against accidental firing by immobilizing the firing pin while disconnecting the trigger from the hammer mechanism at the same time. The trigger guard is combat type for a two-handed grip. Equipped with open combat sights; adjustable rear sight is optional as is ramp front sights. All barrels are designed to accommodate dovetailed telescopic sights. The Desert Eagle is also available in stainless steel, polished and blued, satin nickel, and bright chrome finishes.

DESERT EAGLE
44 MAGNUM SEMIAUTO PISTOL
(Standard Parkerized finish)
$699.00 (w/6" barrel)
$908.00 w/14" barrel

NAVY ARMS
LUGER 22 AUTOMATIC PISTOLS

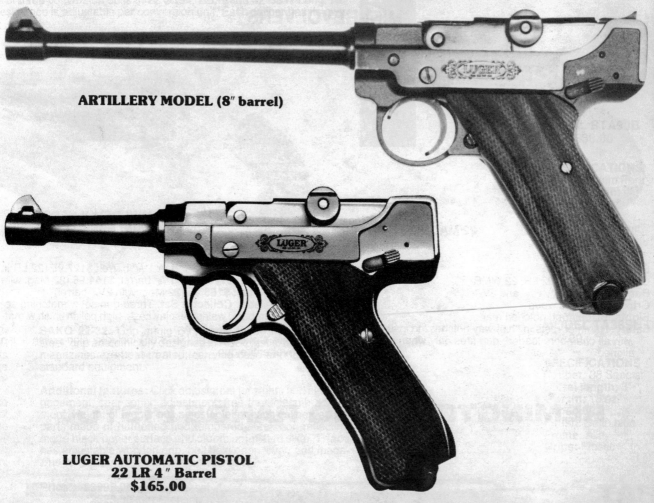

ARTILLERY MODEL (8″ barrel)

**LUGER AUTOMATIC PISTOL
22 LR 4″ Barrel
$165.00**

Chambered for the economical 22 LR, the newest Luger handles both standard and high-velocity cartridges interchangeably. The Luger features a one-piece, solidly forged and machined steel frame for total strength and accuracy, and all moving parts are engineered for steel-to-steel contact.

Also available: **War Model** $165.00
Naval Model. 165.00
Artillery Model 165.00

SPECIFICATIONS

MODELS:	Standard Luger	War	Naval	Artillery
CALIBER:	22 Long Rifle, standard or high velocity	same	same	same
MAGAZINE:	Ten-shot capacity clip-type magazine	same	same	same
BARREL LENGTH:	4″	same	6″	8″
SIGHTS:	Square blade front sight with square notch, stationary rear sight	same	adj. rear	same
SIGHT RADIUS:	8″	same	same	same
FRAME:	High tensile strength seal	same	same	same
GRIPS:	Genuine American black walnut, fully checkered	same	same	same
APPROX. WEIGHT:	1 lb. 13½ ozs.	same	3 lbs.	3¼ lbs.
OVERALL LENGTH:	8⅞″	same	11″	13″
SAFETY:	All models; Positive side lever safety, (Green Dot-Safe) (Red Dot-Fire)	same	same	same
FINISH:	Non-reflecting black	matte finish and blued	same	same

NORTH AMERICAN ARMS REVOLVERS
MINI-REVOLVERS

22 MAGNUM

**5-SHOT MINI-REVOLVERS
22 LR STAINLESS STEEL**

SPECIFICATIONS
Caliber: 22 Short, 22 LR, 22 WMR
Barrel length: 1¹/₈″, 1⁵/₈″ and 2¹/₂″
Grips: Laminated wood
Sights: Blade front, notched rear
Safety: Hammer rests in "half-way notches" to insure safety with all chambers loaded; gun fires only when cylinder is aligned

Prices: $125.95 (22 Short in 1¹/₈″ barrel; $127.95 (22 LR in 1⁵/₈″ barrel; $126.95 w/1¹/₈″ barrel; $144.95 (22 Mag. with 1⁵/₈″ barrel); $158.95 (22 Mag. with 2¹/₂″ barrel)
Also available: **Collector Set.** Three-gun set w/matching serial numbers, walnut display case, high polish finish w/matter contours. $545.00.
Deluxe Collector Set ($575.00) includes high polish finish over entire gun.

REMINGTON LONG RANGE PISTOL

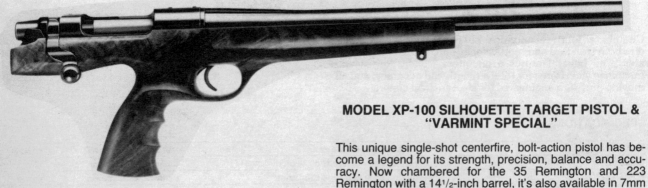

MODEL XP-100 SILHOUETTE TARGET PISTOL & "VARMINT SPECIAL"

This unique single-shot centerfire, bolt-action pistol has become a legend for its strength, precision, balance and accuracy. Now chambered for the 35 Remington and 223 Remington with a 14¹/₂-inch barrel, it's also available in 7mm BR Rem. Many consider this latter configuration to be the ideal factory-made metallic silhouette handgun for "unlimited" events.

All three "XP-100" handguns have one-piece DuPont "Zytel" nylon stocks with universal grips, two-position thumb safety switches, receivers drilled and tapped for scope mounts or receiver sights, and match-type grooved triggers.

Caliber: 35 Remington, 223 Remington, 7mm BR. **Barrel length:** 14¹/₂″. **Overall length:** 21¹/₄″. **Weight:** 4¹/₈ lbs. **Price:** $367.00 (7mm BR); $359.00 (223 Rem.); $380.00 (35 Rem.). Also available: **Custom Long Range** model. **Price: $887.00.**

ROSSI REVOLVERS

MODEL 68
$160.00 (3″ Barrel)
  165.00 (2″ Barrel)

SPECIFICATIONS
Caliber: 38 Special
Barrel length: 2″ and 3″
Overall length: 6½″ (2″ barrel); 7½″ (3″ barrel)
Weight: 21 oz. (2″ barrel); 23 oz. (3″ barrel)
Capacity: 5 rounds
Finish: Blue
Also available in nickel (3″ barrel only) **$170.00**

MODEL M951

Medium frame version with 6-round capacity.
Barrel length: 3″ and 4″
Overall length: 8″ and 9″
Weight: 27½ oz. and 30 oz.
Price: $213.00

MODEL 511 SPORTSMAN'S 22
$219.00

SPECIFICATIONS
Caliber: 22 LR
Barrel length: 4″
Overall length: 9″
Weight: 30 oz.
Capacity: 6 rounds
Finish: Stainless steel

MODEL M88
$195.00 (2″ barrel)

SPECIFICATIONS
Caliber: 38 Special
Barrel length: 2″, 3″
Capacity: 5 rounds, swing-out cylinder
Weight: 21 oz.
Sights: Ramp front, square notch rear adjustable for windage
Finish: Stainless steel
Model M88 in 3″ barrel **$190.00**

MODEL 851

Medium frame version with 6-round capacity
Barrel length: 3″ and 4″
Overall length: 8″ and 9″
Weight: 27½ oz. and 30 oz.
Price: $233.00

RUGER REVOLVERS

SPEED-SIX
Double Action, Round Butt
(Checkered Walnut Grip Panels)

The compact Speed-Six double action is of the same basic design, materials, and construction as the Police Service-Six revolver. Round butt-style frame is ideal when carrying comfort or compactness are important considerations.

SPECIFICATIONS
Capacity: Six shots. **Calibers:** 357 Magnum and 38 Special. **Barrels:** 2³/₄″, 4″; 5-groove rifling; 18³/₄″ right-hand twist. **Weight:** Approx. 2 lbs. (2³/₄″ barrel). **Overall length:** 7³/₄″ (2³/₄″ barrel). **Sights:** Fixed, non-adjustable. **Grips:** Checkered walnut; rubber grips available. **Finish:** Polished overall and blued; stainless steel models have brushed satin finish.

SPEED-SIX

Model	Caliber	Catalog Number	Barrel	Sights	Price
207	357 Mag.	SS-32	2³/₄″	Fixed	$292.00
207	357 Mag.	SS-32P***	2³/₄″	Fixed	292.00
207	357 Mag.	SS-34	4″	Fixed	292.00
208	38 Spec.	SS-82	2³/₄″	Fixed	292.00

***Checkered Rubber Grip with Finger Groove.

SPEED-SIX Stainless Steel

Model	Caliber	Catalog Number	Barrel	Sights	Price
737	357 Mag.	GS-32	2³/₄″	Fixed	$320.00
737	357 Mag.	GS-32P***	2³/₄″	Fixed	320.00
737	357 Mag.	GS-34	4″	Fixed	320.00
728	38 Spec.	GS-82	2³/₄″	Fixed	320.00

***Checkered Rubber Grip with Finger Groove.

REDHAWK DOUBLE-ACTION REVOLVER

There is no other revolver like the Ruger Redhawk. Knowledgeable sportsmen reaching for perfection in a big bore revolver will find that the Redhawk demonstrates its superiority at the target, whether silhouette shooting or hunting. Scope sight model shown above incorporates the patented Ruger integral Scope Mounting System with 1″ stainless steel Ruger scope rings.

Catalog Number	Caliber	Barrel Length	Overall Length	Approx. Weight (Ounces)	Price
RUGER REDHAWK REVOLVER					
KRH-415	41 Mag.	5¹/₂″	11″	52	447.50
KRH-41	41 Mag.	7¹/₂″	13″	52	447.50
KRH-41R*	41 Mag.	7¹/₂″	13″	52	447.50
KRH-445	44 Mag.	5¹/₂″	11″	52	447.50
KRH-44	44 Mag.	7¹/₂″	13″	52	447.50
KRH-44R*	44 Mag.	7¹/₂″	13″	52	482.50

*Scope model, with Integral Scope Mounts, 1″ Stainless Steel Ruger Scope rings.

NEW ALLOY STEEL REDHAWK

The popular Ruger Redhawk® double-action revolver is now available in an alloy steel model with blued finish in .41 Magnum and .44 Magnum calibers. The newest Redhawk, like the stainless steel model, is constructed of hardened chrome-moly and other alloy steels. The revolver is satin polished to a high lustre and finished in a rich blue.

Catalog Number	Caliber	Barrel Length	Overall Length	Approx. Weight (Ounces)	Price
RUGER REDHAWK REVOLVER					
RH-415	41 Mag.	5¹/₂″	11″	52	$397.00
RH-41	41 Mag.	7¹/₂″	13″	52	397.00
RH-41R*	41 Mag.	7¹/₂″	13″	52	430.00
RH-445	44 Mag.	5¹/₂″	11″	52	397.00
RH-44	44 Mag.	7¹/₂″	13″	52	397.00
RH-44R*	44 Mag.	7¹/₂″	13″	52	430.00

*Scope model, with Integral Scope Mounts, 1″ Ruger Scope rings.

A new **Super Redhawk** double action stainless steel revolver is also being introduced in 1986 featuring a heavy extended frame with 7¹/₂″ and 9¹/₂″ barrels. Cushioned grip panels will include Goncalo Alves wood grip panel inserts to provide comfortable, nonslip hold.

RUGER REVOLVERS

GP-100 357 MAGNUM

The first in an entirely new Ruger design series, the GP-100 is presented as a complete family of double action models in three basic frame sizes handling all popular caliber handgun ammunition, from 22 rimfire to 44 Magnum. The GP-100 is designed for the unlimited use of 357 Magnum ammunition in all factory loadings; it combines strength and reliability with accuracy and shooting comfort.

SPECIFICATIONS

BLUED FINISH GP-100 $340.00		STAINLESS STEEL GP-100 $370.00	
CALIBER	BARREL	CALIBER	BARREL
.357 Mag.	4″ Heavy	.357 Mag.	4″ Heavy
.357 Mag.	6″	.357 Mag.	6″
.357 Mag.	6″ Heavy	.357 Mag.	6″ Heavy

SERVICE-SIX DOUBLE ACTION REVOLVER

Ruger's Service-Six revolver incorporates the same construction and basic features found in the law enforcement double actions. Available in 357 Magnum and 38 Special with Goncalo Alves and rubber grips, blued or stainless steel.

SPECIFICATIONS

SERVICE-SIX $287.50

Model	Caliber	Catalog Number	Barrel	Sights
107	357 Mag.	SDA-32	2³/₄″	Fixed
107	357 Mag.	SDA-34	4″	Fixed
108	38 Spec.	SDA-84	4″	Fixed

SERVICE-SIX Stainless Steel $310.00

Model	Caliber	Catalog Number	Barrel	Sights
707	357 Mag.	GF-34	4″	Fixed
707	357 Mag.	GF-34P***	4″	Fixed
708	38 Spec.	GF-84	4″	Fixed
708	38 Spec.	GF-84P***	4″	Fixed

***Equipped with Checkered Rubber Grips.

RUGER REVOLVERS

NEW MODEL SINGLE-SIX REVOLVER

Caliber: 22 LR, 22 Short, 22 Long, 22 Win. Mag. Rimfire (fitted with WMR cylinder). **Barrel lengths:** 4⅝", 5½", 6½", 9½" (stainless steel model in 5½" and 6½" lengths only). **Weight** (approx.): 33 oz. (with 5½" barrel). **Sights:** Patridge-type ramp front sight; rear sight click adjustable for elevation and windage; protected by integral frame ribs. **Finish:** Blue or stainless steel. **Price: $220.75** ($278.00 in stainless steel).

NEW MODEL SINGLE-SIX SSM™ REVOLVER
$212.00

Caliber: 32 H&R Magnum; also handles 32 S&W and 32 S&W Long. **Barrel lengths:** 4⅝", 5½", 6½", 9½". **Weight** (approx.): 34 oz. with 6½" barrel.

NEW MODEL BISLEY BLACKHAWK REVOLVER
(not shown) $307.00

Calibers: 357 Mag., 41 Mag., 44 Mag., 45 Long Colt. **Barrel length:** 7½". **Weight** (approx.): 48 oz. **Sights:** Adjustable rear sight, ramp-style front sight. **Special features:** Unfluted cylinder rollmarked with classic foliate engraving pattern (or fluted cylinder without engraving); hammer is low with smoothly curved, deeply checkered wide spur positioned for easy cocking.

Also available in 22LR and 32 Mag. **Weight:** 41 oz. **Barrel length:** 6½". **Price: $258.00.**

MODEL BN-31
BLACKHAWK SINGLE-ACTION REVOLVER
(IN 30 CARBINE CALIBER) $247.75

Caliber: 30 Carbine. **Barrel length:** 7½"; 6-groove rifling; 20-inch twist. **Overall length:** 13⅛". **Weight:** 44 oz. **Springs:** Unbreakable music wire springs used throughout; no leaf springs. **Screws:** For security, Nylok® screws are used at all five locations that might be affected by recoil. **Sights:** Patridge-style, ramp front sight with ⅛" wide blade, matted to eliminate glare; rear sight adjustable for windage and elevation. **Ignition system:** Independent alloy steel firing pin, mounted in frame, transfer bar. **Frame:** Same cylinder frame as 44 Mag. Super Blackhawk. **Grips:** Genuine walnut. **Finish:** Polished, blued and anodized.

RUGER REVOLVERS

BLACKHAWK SINGLE-ACTION REVOLVER

SPECIFICATIONS
Caliber: 357 Magnum (interchangeable with 38 Special); 41 Magnum
Barrel lengths: 4⅝″ and 6½″
Frame: Chrome molybdenum steel with bridge reinforcement and rear-sight guard
Springs: Music wire springs throughout
Weight: 40 oz. with 4⅝″ barrel and 42 oz. with 6½″ barrel (in 357 Mag.); 38 oz. with 4⅝″ barrel and 40 oz. with 6½″ barrel (41 Mag.)
Sights: Patridge style, ramp front matted blade ⅛″ wide; rear sight click adjustable for windage and elevation
Grips: Genuine walnut
Finish: Polished and blued or stainless steel (357 Mag. only)

357 Magnum—4⅝″ barrel	$257.75
Stainless steel	317.50
357 Magnum—6½″ barrel	257.75
Stainless steel	317.50
38 Special (interchangeable)—4⅝″ barrel	270.00
38 Special (interchangeable)—6½″ barrel	270.00
Fitted with 9mm Parabellum extra cylinder; walnut panels	260.00
Note: convertible model not available in stainless steel	
41 Magnum—4⅝″ barrel	$257.75
41 Magnum—6½″ barrel	257.75
45 Long Colt—4⅝″ barrel	$257.75
45 Long Colt—7½″ barrel	257.75

SUPER BLACKHAWK SINGLE-ACTION REVOLVER

SPECIFICATIONS
Caliber: 44 Magnum; interchangeable with 44 Special
Barrel: 5½″, 7½″, 10½″
Frame: Chrome molybdenum steel with bridge reinforcement and rear sight guard
Springs: Music wire springs throughout
Weight: 48 oz. (7½″ bbl.) and 51 oz. (10½″ bbl.)
Sights: Patridge style, ramp front matted blade ⅛″ wide; rear sight click and adjustable for windage and elevation
Grip frame: Chrome molybdenum steel enlarged and contoured to minimize recoil effect

Trigger: Wide spur, low contour, sharply serrated for convenient cocking with minimum disturbance of grip
Overall length: 13⅜″
Finish: Stainless steel

S45N—5½″ barrel with steel grip frame	$297.50
KS47N—7½″ barrel with steel grip frame	325.00
KS411N—10½″ barrel with steel grip frame	325.00
S47N—7½″ barrel, with steel grip frame	297.50
S411N—10½″ barrel, with steel grip frame	297.50

RUGER 22 AUTOMATIC PISTOLS

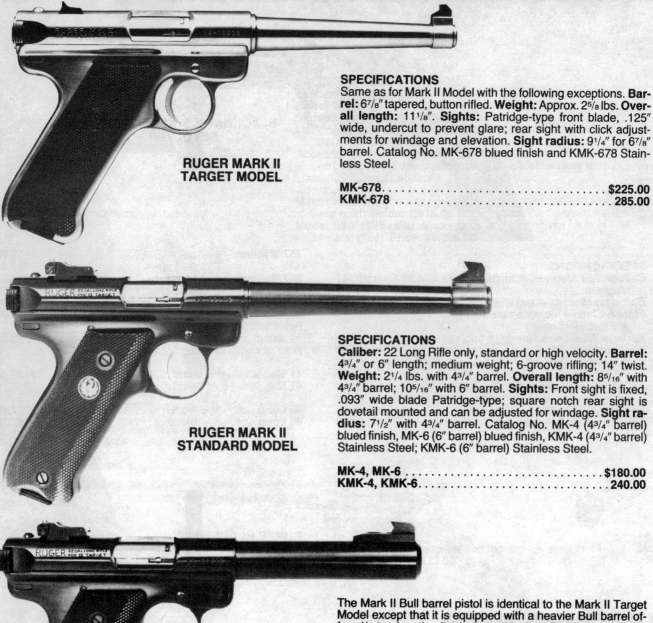

**RUGER MARK II
TARGET MODEL**

SPECIFICATIONS
Same as for Mark II Model with the following exceptions. **Barrel:** 6⅞" tapered, button rifled. **Weight:** Approx. 2⅝ lbs. **Overall length:** 11⅛". **Sights:** Patridge-type front blade, .125" wide, undercut to prevent glare; rear sight with click adjustments for windage and elevation. **Sight radius:** 9¼" for 6⅞" barrel. Catalog No. MK-678 blued finish and KMK-678 Stainless Steel.

MK-678. . . . .$225.00
KMK-678 . . . . 285.00

**RUGER MARK II
STANDARD MODEL**

SPECIFICATIONS
Caliber: 22 Long Rifle only, standard or high velocity. **Barrel:** 4¾" or 6" length; medium weight; 6-groove rifling; 14" twist. **Weight:** 2¼ lbs. with 4¾" barrel. **Overall length:** 8⁵/₁₆" with 4¾" barrel; 10⁵/₁₆" with 6" barrel. **Sights:** Front sight is fixed, .093" wide blade Patridge-type; square notch rear sight is dovetail mounted and can be adjusted for windage. **Sight radius:** 7½" with 4¾" barrel. Catalog No. MK-4 (4¾" barrel) blued finish, MK-6 (6" barrel) blued finish, KMK-4 (4¾" barrel) Stainless Steel; KMK-6 (6" barrel) Stainless Steel.

MK-4, MK-6 . . . .$180.00
KMK-4, KMK-6 . . . . 240.00

**RUGER MARK II
BULL BARREL MODEL**

The Mark II Bull barrel pistol is identical to the Mark II Target Model except that it is equipped with a heavier Bull barrel offered in two lengths, 5½ inches/10 inches. The Bull barrel configuration was developed to meet the needs of those shooters who prefer a greater concentration of weight at the muzzle. The longer barrel model meets all IHMSA regulations.

SPECIFICATIONS
Same as for Mark II model with the following exceptions: **Barrel:** 5½" or 10"; button rifled; shorter barrel untapered, longer barrel has slight taper. **Weight:** Approx. 2⁵/₇ lbs. with 5½" barrel; 3¼ lbs. with 10" barrel. **Sights:** Patridge-type front sight. Rear sight with click adjustments for windage and elevation. **Sight radius:** 7⅞" for 5½" barrel, 12⅜" for 10" barrel; blued finish. Catalog No. MK-512 5½" barrel and MK-10 10" barrel.

MK-512 and MK-10 Blued $225.00
KMK-512 and KMK-10 Stainless steel $285.00

SAKO OLYMPIC PISTOL

Three different pistols on the same frame. Take your choice of three conversion units in 22 Short, 22LR and 32 S&W Long. No need to adjust sights when you change caliber. Free travel resistance is adjustable per conversion unit. Each caliber has its own magazine. Carrying case and tool set standard equipment.

A choice of three conversion units for the frame of Sako's 22-32 and **Triace** conversion pistols in calibers 22 Short, 22 LR and 32 S&W Long. Each conversion unit is equipped with its own sights—no need to adjust the sights when you change the caliber. The free travel resistance is adjustable per conversion unit. Each caliber has its own magazines.

To change caliber, simply remove the magazine, release mounting screw, and pull the conversion unit forward. Mount the other unit and tighten the mounting screw, then insert the magazine of the caliber selected.

SAKO TRIACE: Grip angle 65°; frame made from investment casting steel; magazines of spring steel, lips flexible; standard equipment carrying case with tool set and cleaning set.

SAKO 22-32: Grip angle 60°; frame made from machined steel; grip anatomically designed in ABS plastic; hard wearing magazines are heat treated; carrying case and tool set are standard equipment.

Additional features: Click adjustment for sights and sear engagement; sear spring adjustment; free travel length adjustment; weight of trigger pull adjustable for each caliber; action parts made of hardened and tempered steel; non-reflecting matte black upper surface and chromium-plated slide. **Triace** has adjustable wooden grip, bolt hold open lever, and magazine for six cartridges on centerfire pistol.

Price: $3995.00 for 3 barrel set
2325.00 for pistol only

SAKO TRIACE

SPECIFICATIONS

International Standard		Rimfire	Centerfire
Caliber	22LR	22 Short	32 S&W Long
Barrel length	6 inches	6 inches	6 inches
Sight distance	8.25 inches	8.25-8.85 inches	8.25 inches
Capacity	5 rounds	5 rounds	6 rounds
Weight	46 oz.	44 oz.	48 oz.
Grip angle	65°	65°	65°

SAKO 22-32

SPECIFICATIONS

International Standard		Rimfire	Centerfire
Caliber	22LR	22 Short	32 S&W Long
Barrel length	6 inches	8.85 inches	6 inches
Sight distance	8.25 inches	8.85 inches	8.25 inches
Capacity	5 rounds	5 rounds	5 rounds
Weight	45.8 oz.	44 oz.	47.6 oz.
Grip angle	60°	60°	60°

SIG SAUER DOUBLE ACTION PISTOLS

MODEL 220 "EUROPEAN"

SPECIFICATIONS
Caliber: 38 Super, 9mm Parabellum, 45ACP
Capacity: 9 rounds (7 rounds in 45ACP)
Barrel length: 4.4″
Overall length: 8″
Weight: 26¹/₂ oz.
Finish: Blue
Price: $575.00
"AMERICAN" Model (in 45 ACP): **$625.00**

MODEL 225 (not shown)

SPECIFICATIONS
Caliber: 9mm Parabellum
Capacity: 8 rounds
Barrel length: 3.85″
Overall length: 7″
Weight: 26¹/₂ oz.
Finish: Blue
Price: $650.00

MODEL 226

SPECIFICATIONS
Caliber: 9mm Parabellum
Capacity: 15 rounds
Barrel length: 4.4″
Overall length: 7³/₄″
Weight: 30 oz.
Finish: Blue
Price: $675.00
Nickel: 745.00

MODEL 226

SINGLE ACTION MODEL P210 (not shown)

SPECIFICATIONS
Caliber: 9mm
Overall length: 8¹/₂″
Barrel length: 4.7″
Weight: 31.6 oz.
Capacity: 8 rounds
Price: $1,350.00

Also available: **MODEL P210-5:** $1,795.00
MODEL P210-6: 1,595.00

MODEL 230

SPECIFICATIONS
Caliber: 380ACP
Capacity: 7 rounds
Barrel length: 3.6″
Overall length: 6.6″
Weight: 16¹/₄ oz. (23 oz. in stainless steel)
Finish: Blue and stainless steel
Price: $450.00; in stainless steel: $525.00

SMITH & WESSON AUTO PISTOLS

MODEL 422
.22 SINGLE ACTION
$190.50 (Fixed Sight)
225.50 (Adjustable Sight)

Caliber: 22 LR
Capacity: 10 round (magazine furnished)
Barrel length: 4½" and 6"
Overall length: 7½" (4½" barrel) and 9" (6" barrel)
Weight: 22 oz. (4½" barrel) and 23 oz. (6" barrel)
Stock: plastic (field version) and checkered walnut w/S&W monogram (target version)
Front sight: serrated ramp w/.125" blade (field version); Patridge w/.125" blade (target version)
Rear sight: fixed sight w/.125" blade (field version): adjustable sight w/.125" blade (target version)
Hammer: .250" internal
Trigger: .312" serrated

22 CAL. AUTOMATIC PISTOL
Model No. 41
$519.00 Blue Only
(7³⁄₈" Barrel)

Caliber: 22 Long Rifle
Magazine capacity: 10 rounds
Barrel length: 5½" and 7³⁄₈"
Overall length: 12" with 7³⁄₈" barrel
Sight radius: 9⁵⁄₁₆" with 7³⁄₈" barrel
Weight: 43½ oz. with 7³⁄₈" barrel
Sights: Front, ⅛" Patridge undercut; rear, S&W micrometer click sight adjustable for windage and elevation
Stocks: Checkered walnut with modified thumb rest, equally adaptable to right- or left-handed shooters
Finish: S&W Bright Blue
Trigger: ³⁄₈" width, with S&W grooving and an adjustable trigger stop

38 MASTER
Model No. 52
$690.50 Bright Blue Only

Caliber: 38 S&W Special (for Mid-Range Wad Cutter only)
Magazine capacity: 5 rounds (2 five-round magazines furnished)
Barrel length: 5"
Overall length: 8⁵⁄₈"
Sight radius: 6¹⁵⁄₁₆"
Weight: 41 oz. with empty magazine
Sights: Front, ⅛" Patridge on ramp base; rear, new S&W micrometer click sight with wide ⁷⁄₈" sight slide
Stocks: Checkered walnut with S&W monograms
Finish: S&W Bright Blue with sandblast stippling around sighting area to break up light reflection
Trigger: ³⁄₈" width with S&W grooving and an adjustable trigger stop

SMITH & WESSON AUTO PISTOLS

9MM AUTOMATIC PISTOL
DOUBLE ACTION
Model 459
Blue $482.50–502.00

Caliber: 9mm Luger
Magazine capacity: Two 14-round magazines, furnished
Barrel length: 4″
Overall length: 7⁷/₁₆″
Weight: 28 oz.
Sights: Front, square ¹/₈″ serrated ramp; rear, square notch rear sight blade fully micrometer click adjustable
Stocks: Checkered high-impact molded nylon grips
Finish: Blue or nickel

9MM AUTOMATIC PISTOL
DOUBLE ACTION
Model 439
$443.00–463.00

Caliber: 9mm Luger
Magazine capacity: Two 8-round magazines, furnished
Barrel: 4″
Overall length: 7⁷/₁₆″
Weight: 30 oz.
Sights: Front, square ¹/₈″ serrated ramp; rear, square notch rear sight blade fully micrometer click adjustable
Stocks: Checkered walnut grips with S&W monograms
Finish: Blue

9MM AUTOMATIC PISTOL
DOUBLE ACTION
Model No. 469
$463.00

Caliber: 9mm Luger
Magazine capacity: Two 12-round magazines furnished
Barrel length: 3¹/₂″
Overall length: 6⁷/₈″
Weight: 26 oz.
Sights: Front, yellow ramp; rear, dovetail mounted square-notch white inline
Finish: Sandblasted blue

MODEL 639
Stainless Steel
$491.50–511.00

Caliber: 9mm Luger (Parabellum)
Capacity: 2 12-round magazines
Barrel length: 3¹/₂″
Overall length: 6¹³/₁₆″
Weight: 26 oz.
Finish: Non-glare blue

SMITH & WESSON AUTO PISTOLS

MODEL 645 AUTOMATIC

Caliber: 45 Auto
Action: Double action
Capacity: 8 rounds
Barrel length: 5″
Overall length: 8.7″
Weight: 37.6 oz.
Sights: Red ramp front, fixed rear (drift adjustable for windage)
Safety features: Manual with magazine interlock; internal firing pin safety
Finish: Stainless steel
Price: $578.50

MODEL 659
Stainless Steel
$534.50–556.00

Caliber: 9mm Luger (Parabellum)
Magazine capacity: 2 14-round magazines
Barrel length: 4″
Overall length: 7⁵/₈″
Weight: 39¹/₂ oz.
Finish: Satin

MODEL 669
STAINLESS STEEL
$507.50

Caliber: 9mm
Magazine capacity: 12-shot
Barrel length: 3¹/₂″
Overall length: 6¹³/₁₆″
Weight empty: 26 oz.
Sights: Serrated ramp w/red bar (front); fixed sight/white outline (rear)
Finish: Non-glare stainless

SMITH & WESSON

1953 22/32 KIT GUN
Model No. 34
$320.00 Blue

Caliber: 22 Long Rifle
Number of shots: 6
Barrel length: 2″, 4″
Overall length: 8″ with 4″ barrel and round butt
Weight: 22 1/4 oz. with 4″ barrel and round butt
Sights: Front, 1/10″ serrated ramp; rear, S&W micrometer click sight adjustable for windage and elevation
Stocks: Checked walnut Service with S&W monograms, round or square butt
Finish: S&W blue

STAINLESS STEEL MODELS
1977 22/32 KIT GUN
Model No. 63
$369.50 Stainless Steel

Caliber: 22 Long Rifle
Number of shots: 6
Barrel length: 4″
Weight: 24 1/2 oz. (empty)
Sights: 1/8″ red ramp front sight; rear sight is black stainless steel S&W micrometer click square-notch, adjustable for windage and elevation
Stocks: Square butt
Finish: Satin

MODEL 650 & 651 22 M.R.F.
$345.00 (4″ barrel)
$305.00 (3″ barrel)

Caliber: 22 Magnum Rim Fire (22 LR Auxiliary Cylinder optional) and 22 Winchester Rim Fire
Capacity: 6 shot cylinder
Barrel length: 3″ (Model 650); 4″ (Model 651)
Length overall: 7″ (Model 650); 8 5/8″ (Model 651)
Weight (empty): 23 1/2 oz. (Model 650); 24 1/2 oz. (Model 651)
Sights: Front: serrated ramp; rear: fixed square notch (Model 650); Model 651 has adjustable micrometer click sight
Stocks: Checkered walnut Service with S&W monograms; square butt (**Model 650** has round butt)
Finish: Stainless steel.

SMITH & WESSON

K-22 MASTERPIECE
Model No. 17

Caliber: 22 Long Rifle
Number of shots: 6
Barrel length: 4″, 6″, 8³/₈″
Overall length: 9⁵/₁₆″ (4″ barrel); 11¹/₈″ (6″ barrel); 13¹/₂″ (8³/₈″ barrel)
Weight loaded: 38¹/₂ oz. with 6″ barrel; 42¹/₂ oz. with 8³/₈″ barrel
Sights: Front, ¹/₈″ plain Patridge; rear, S&W micrometer click sight adjustable for windage and elevation
Stocks: Checkered walnut Service with S&W monograms
Finish: S&W blue
Prices: $325.50 (4″, 6″)
 391.00 (8³/₈″)

32 REGULATION POLICE
Model No. 31
$335.50 Blue Only

Caliber: 32 S&W Long
Number of shots: 6
Barrel length: 2″, 3″
Overall length: 8¹/₂″ with 4″ barrel
Weight: 18³/₄ oz. with 4″ barrel
Sights: Front, fixed, ¹/₁₀″ serrated ramp; rear square notch
Stocks: Checked walnut Service with S&W monograms
Finish: S&W blue

38 CHIEFS SPECIAL
Model 36
$285.50 Blue
$308.00 Nickel

Caliber: 38 S&W Special
Number of shots: 5
Barrel length: 2″ or 3″
Overall length: 6¹/₂″ with 2″ barrel and round butt
Weight: 19 oz. with 2″ barrel and round butt
Sights: Front, fixed, ¹/₁₀″ serrated ramp; rear square notch
Stocks: Checked walnut Service with S&W monograms, round or square butt
Finish: S&W blue or nickel
MODEL 37. Same as Model 36 except **Weight**-14 oz.
Price: $306.00 ($344.00 in nickel)

SMITH & WESSON

38 CHIEFS SPECIAL STAINLESS
Model No. 60
$345.00 Stainless Steel

Caliber: 38 S&W Special
Number of shots: 5
Barrel length: 2″
Overall length: 6½″
Weight: 19 oz.
Sights: Front fixed, ¹⁄₁₀″ serrated ramp; rear square notch
Stocks: Checked walnut Service with S&W monograms
Finish: Satin

38 BODYGUARD "AIRWEIGHT"
Model No. 38
$340.50 Blue
$382.00 Nickel

Caliber: 38 S&W Special
Number of shots: 5
Barrel length: 2″
Overall length: 6³⁄₈″
Weight: 14½ oz.
Sights: Front, fixed ¹⁄₁₀″ serrated ramp; rear square notch
Stocks: Checked walnut Service with S&W monograms
Finish: S&W blue or nickel

MODEL 49 .38 BODYGUARD
$303.50 (Blue)

Caliber: 38 S&W Special
Capacity: 5-shot cylinder
Barrel length: 2″
Overall length: 6¼″
Weight (empty): 20 oz.
Sights: Serrated ramp (front); fixed square notch (rear)
Finish: S&W blue

SMITH & WESSON REVOLVERS

MODEL 649 STAINLESS STEEL BODYGUARD
$360.00

Caliber: 38 Special
Capacity: 5 shots
Barrel length: 2"
Overall length: 6¼"
Sights: Serrated ramp front, fixed square notch rear
Weight: 20 oz.
Grips: round butt; checkered walnut service
Finish: Stainless steel

38 MILITARY & POLICE
Model No. 10
$287.50 Blue
$309.00 Nickel

Caliber: 38 S&W Special
Number of shots: 6
Barrel length: 2", 3" (also 3" heavy barrel), 4" (also 4" heavy barrel)
Weight: 30½ oz. with 4" barrel
Sights: Front, fixed ⅛" serrated ramp; rear square notch
Stocks: Checkered walnut Service with S&W monograms, round or square butt
Finish: S&W blue or nickel

38 MILITARY & POLICE STAINLESS
Model No. 64
$310.00

Caliber: 38 S&W Special
Number of Shots: 6
Barrel length: 4" heavy barrel, square butt; 3" heavy barrel, round butt; 2" regular barrel, round butt
Length overall: With 4" barrel, 9¼"; 7⅞", 3" barrel; 2" barrel, 6⅞"
Weight: With 4" barrel, 34 ounces; with 3" barrel, 30½ oz.; with 2" barrel, 28 oz.
Sights: Fixed, ⅛" serrated ramp front; square notch rear
Stocks: Checked walnut Service with S&W monograms
Finish: Satin
Ammunition: 38 S&W Special, 38 S&W Special Mid Range

SMITH & WESSON REVOLVERS

38 COMBAT MASTERPIECE
Model No. 15

Caliber: 38 S&W Special
Number of shots: 6
Barrel length: 2″, 4″, 6″, 8³/₈″
Overall length: 7¹/₄″ (2″ barrel); 9⁵/₁₆″ (4″ barrel); 11¹/₈″ (6″ barrel); 13¹/₂″ (8³/₈″ barrel)
Weight loaded: 34 oz. with 4″ barrel
Sights: Front, ¹/₈″ Baughman Quick Draw on plain ramp; rear, S&W micrometer click sight adjustable for windage and elevation
Stocks: Checkered walnut Service with S&W monograms
Finish: S&W blue or nickel
Prices: $330.50 (2″, 4″, 6″)
     340.50 (8³/₈″)
     354.00 (Nickel, 4″)

38 COMBAT MASTERPIECE REVOLVER
Model No. 67
$349.00 Stainless Steel

Caliber: 38 S&W Special
Number of shots: 6
Barrel length: 4″
Length overall: 9¹/₈″
Weight loaded: 34 oz.
Sights: Front: ¹/₈″ Rear: S&W Red Ramp on ramp base, S&W Micrometer Click Sights, adjustable for windage and elevation
Stocks: Checked walnut Service with S&W Monograms, square butt
Finish: Satin:
Trigger: S&W grooving with an adjustable trigger stop
Ammunition: 38 S&W Special, 38 S&W Special Mid Range

357 COMBAT MAGNUM REVOLVER
Model No. 66
$363.00–$405.50 Stainless Steel

Caliber: 357 Magnum (actual bullet dia. 38 S&W Spec.)
Number of shots: 6
Barrel length: 6″ or 4″ with square butt; 2¹/₂″ with round butt
Length overall: 9¹/₂″ with 4″ barrel; 7¹/₂″ with 2¹/₂″ barrel; 11³/₈″ with 6″ barrel
Weight: 35 ounces with 4″ barrel; 30¹/₂ oz. with 2¹/₂″ barrel; 39 oz. with 6″ barrel
Sights: Front: ¹/₈″. Rear: S&W Red Ramp on ramp base, S&W Micrometer Click Sight, adjustable for windage and elevation
Stocks: Checked Goncalo Alves target with square butt with S&W monograms
Finish: Satin
Trigger: S&W grooving with an adjustable trigger stop
Ammunition: 357 S&W Magnum, 38 S&W Special Hi-Speed, 38 S&W Special, 38 S&W Special Mid Range

SMITH & WESSON

"357" COMBAT MAGNUM
Model No. 19
$319.50–376.50 Bright Blue or Nickel

Caliber: 357 Magnum (actual bullet dia. 38 S&W Spec.)
Number of shots: 6
Barrel length: 2¹/₂", 4" and 6"
Overall length: 9¹/₂" with 4" barrel; 7¹/₂" with 2¹/₂" barrel; 11¹/₂" with 6" barrel
Weight: 35 oz. (2¹/₂" model weighs 31 oz.)
Sights: Front, ¹/₈" Baughman Quick Draw on 2¹/₂" or 4" barrel, ¹/₈" Patridge on 6" barrel; rear, S&W micrometer click sight adjustable for windage and elevation
Stocks: Checkered Goncalo Alves Target with S&W monograms
Finish: S&W bright blue or nickel

357 MILITARY & POLICE STAINLESS
HEAVY BARREL
Model No. 65
$310.00

Caliber: 357 Magnum and 38 S&W Special
Rounds: 6-shot cylinder capacity
Barrel length: 4" heavy barrel, square butt; 3" heavy barrel, round butt
Length overall: With 4" barrel, 9¹/₄"; with 3" barrel, 7⁵/₁₆"
Weight: With 4" barrel, 34 oz.; with 3" barrel, 31 oz.
Sights: Fixed, ¹/₈" serrated ramp front; square notch rear
Stocks: Checked walnut Service with S&W monograms, square butt
Finish: Satin

357 MILITARY & POLICE (HEAVY BARREL)
Model No. 13
$287.50 Blue

Caliber: 357 Magnum and 38 S&W Special
Rounds: 6-shot cylinder capacity
Barrel length: 3" and 4"
Overall length: 9¹/₄"
Weight: 34 oz.
Sights: Front, ¹/₈" serrated ramp; rear square notch
Stocks: Checkered walnut Service with S&W monograms, square butt (3" barrel has round butt)
Finish: S&W blue

SMITH & WESSON

MODEL 586
DISTINGUISHED COMBAT MAGNUM
$347.00–411.50

Caliber: 357 Magnum
Capacity: 6 shots
Barrel length: 4″, 6″, 8³/₈″
Overall length: 9³/₄″ with 4″ barrel; 11¹/₂″ with 6″ barrel; 13¹³/₁₆″ with 8³/₈″ barrel
Weight: 42 oz. with 4″ barrel; 46 oz. with 6″ barrel; 53 oz. with 8³/₈″ barrel
Sights: Front is S&W Red Ramp; rear is S&W Micrometer Click adjustable for windage and elevation; White outline notch. Option with 6″ barrel only—plain Patridge front with black outline notch
Stocks: Checkered Goncalo Alves with speedloader cutaway
Finish: S&W Blue or Nickel
Model 686: Same as Model 586 except finish is stainless steel, **$381.50–435.00.**

357 MAGNUM
Model No. 27
Bright Blue or Nickel
$389.50 (4″)
$364.00 (6″)
$390.50 (8³/₈″)

Caliber: 357 Magnum (actual bullet dia. 38 S&W Spec.)
Number of shots: 6
Barrel length: 4″, 6″ and 8³/₈″
Weight: 44 oz. with 4″ barrel; 45¹/₂ oz. with 6″; 49 oz. with 8³/₈″
Sights: Front, S&W Red Ramp (4″ barrel) and Patridge (6″ and 8³/₈″ barrels); rear, S&W micrometer click sight adjustable for windage and elevation
Stocks: Checkered walnut Service with S&W monograms
Frame: Finely checked top strap and barrel rib
Finish: S&W bright blue or nickel

41 MAGNUM
Model No. 57
$386.00 (4″ and 6″)
$400.00 (8³/₈″)

Caliber: 41 Magnum
Number of shots: 6
Barrel length: 4″, 6″ and 8³/₈″
Overall length: 11³/₈″ with 6″ barrel
Weight: 48 oz. with 6″ barrel
Sights: Front, ¹/₈″ S&W Red Ramp; rear, S&W micrometer click sight adjustable for windage and elevation; white outline notch
Stocks: Special oversize Target type of checkered Goncalo Alves, with S&W monograms
Hammer: Checked target type
Trigger: Grooved target type
Finish: S&W bright blue

SMITH & WESSON REVOLVERS

MODEL 657
STAINLESS STEEL
$431.00 (4″ and 6″)
$446.00 (8³/₈″)

Caliber: 41 Magnum
Magazine capacity: 6-shot cylinder
Barrel length: 4″, 6″, 8³/₈″
Overall length: 9⁵/₈″ (4″ barrel); 11³/₈″ (6″ barrel); 13¹⁵/₁₆″ (8³/₈″ barrel)
Weight empty: 44.2 oz. (4″ barrel); 48 oz. (6″ barrel); 52¹/₂ oz. (8³/₈″ barrel)
Sights: Serrated black ramp on ramp base (front); Blue S&W micrometer click sight adj. for windage and elevation (rear)
Finish: Satin

44 MAGNUM
Model No. 29
Bright Blue or Nickel
$425.50 (4″ and 6″)
$440.50 (8³/₈″)
$473.50 (10⁵/₈″)

Caliber: 44 Magnum
Number of shots: 6
Barrel length: 4″, 6″, 8³/₈″ and 10⁵/₈″ (blue only)
Overall length: 11⁷/₈″ with 6¹/₂″ barrel
Weight: 43 oz. with 4″ barrel; 47 oz. with 6″ barrel; 51¹/₂ oz. with 8³/₈″ barrel
Sights: Front, ¹/₈″ S&W Red Ramp; rear, S&W micrometer click sight adjustable for windage and elevation; white outline notch
Stocks: Special oversize target type of checked Goncalo Alves; with S&W monograms
Hammer: Checkered target type
Trigger: Grooved target type
Finish: S&W bright blue or nickel

MODEL 25
$386.50 (4″ and 6″)
$400.50 (8³/₈″)

Caliber: 45 Colt
Capacity: 6-shot cylinder
Barrel length: 4″, 6″, 8³/₈″
Overall length: 9⁹/₁₆″ (4″ barrel); 11³/₈″ (6″ barrel); 13⁷/₈″ (8³/₈″ barrel)
Weight (empty): 44 oz. (4″ barrel); 46 oz. (6″ barrel); 50 oz. (8³/₈″ barrel)
Sights: S&W red ramp on ramp base (front); S&W micrometer click sight w/white outline notch (rear), adj. for windage and elevation
Finish: S&W Bright blue or nickel

SPRINGFIELD ARMORY PISTOL

MODEL 1911-A1 STANDARD

An exact duplicate of the M1911-A1 pistol that served the U.S. armed forces for more than 70 years, this model has been precision manufactured from forged parts, including a forged frame, then hand assembled.

Calibers: 45 ACP and 9mm Parabellum
Weight: 35.62 oz.
Barrel length: 5.04″
Overall length: 8.59″
Trigger pull: 5 to 6.5 lbs.
Sight radius: 6.481″
Rifling: 45 ACP-right hand one-turn-in-sixteen, 6 groove; 9mm-left hand, one-turn-in-sixteen, 4 groove
Capacity: 45 ACP-7 in mag. 1 in chamber; 9mm-8 in mag. 1 in chamber

Model 1911-A1 . . . . $325.00
   Same model with parkerized finish 362.00
   Same model in kit form 356.00

STAR AUTOMATIC PISTOLS

STAR BKM & BM
9mm PARABELLUM

The Model BM offers all-steel construction, and the BKM offers a high strength, weight-saving duraluminum frame. An improved thumb safety locks both the slide and hammer with hammer cocked or uncocked; further, an automatic magazine safety locks the sear when the magazine is removed.

Overall length: 7.17″. **Barrel length:** 3.9″. **Magazine capacity:** 8 rounds. **Weight:** 34.06 oz. (BM); 25.59 oz. (BKM)

Model BM blue $330.00
Model BM chrome 345.00
Model BKM blue 330.00

STAR AUTOMATIC PISTOLS

STAR MODEL 30M
9mm PARA

The Model 30 features a staggered 15-round button release magazine, square notch rear sight (click-adjustable for windage) and square front sight (notched to diffuse light). Removable backstrap houses complete firing mechanism. All-steel frame (Model 30/PK = alloy frame).

Overall length: 8.07". **Height:** 5.32". **Barrel length:** 4.33" (Model 30PK = 3.86") **Weight:** 40.24 oz. (Model 30/Pk = 30.36 oz.)

Model 30M **$475.00**
Model 30/PK 475.00

STAR MODEL PD
45 ACP

Chambered for the sledgehammer 45 ACP, the PD is one of the smallest .45 caliber production pistols in the world.

Overall length: 7". **Barrel length:** 4". **Weight:** 25.5 oz. **Finish:** Blue. **Capacity:** 6 rounds.

45 ACP blue **$365.00**

STEYR PISTOLS

STEYR GB
Semi-Auto Pistol
$595.00

Caliber: 9mm Parabellum
Magazine capacity: 18 rounds
Action: Double; gas-delayed, blowback action
Barrel length: 5.4"
Overall length: 8.9"
Weight: 2.09 lbs. (empty)
Height: 5.7"
Sights: Fixed, open; notch rear, post front
Trigger pull: Approx. 4 lbs. (with hammer cocked); approx. 14 lbs. (with hammer uncocked)
Muzzle velocity: 1,184 fps
Safeties: Passive firing and hammer block safety, in cocked or uncocked hammer position.

TANARMI

MODEL BTA90B
$356.00

SPECIFICATIONS
Caliber: 9mm Para
Barrel length: 4″
Weight: 30 oz
Capacity: 12
Finish: Matte blue
Frame: Steel
Grips: Neoprene

MODEL TA76 REVOLVER
$65.00

SPECIFICATIONS
Caliber: 22LR
Barrel length: 4.75″
Capacity: 6
Finish: Satin blue
Frame: Alloy
Grips: Walnut

MODEL TA38SB DERRINGER
$88.00

SPECIFICATIONS
Caliber: 38 Special
Barrel length: 3″
Weight: 15 oz.
Capacity: 2
Finish: Satin blue
Frame: Alloy
Grips: Plastic

TARGA SEMIAUTOMATIC PISTOLS

MODEL GT26S
$92.00

SPECIFICATIONS
Caliber: 25ACP
Barrel length: 2¹/₂″
Capacity: 6
Finish: Satin blue
Frame: Steel
Grips: Walnut
Weight: 15 oz.

MODEL GT22T
$161.00

SPECIFICATIONS
Caliber: 22LR
Barrel length: 6″
Weight: 28 oz.
Capacity: 12
Frame: Steel
Finish: Satin blue
Grips: Walnut

TARGA SEMIAUTOMATIC PISTOLS

MODEL GT380XE
$191.00

SPECIFICATIONS
Caliber: 380ACP
Barrel length: 3.88″
Weight: 26 oz.
Capacity: 11
Finish: Satin blue
Frame: Steel
Grips: Walnut

TAURUS PISTOLS

MODEL PT 92

Caliber: 9mm Parabellum
Action: Semiautomatic double action
Hammer: Exposed
Barrel length: 4.92″
Overall length: 8.54″
Height: 5.39″
Width: 1.45″
Weight: (with empty magazine) 34 oz.
Rifling: R.H., 6 grooves
Front sight: Blade integral with slide
Rear sight: Notched bar dovetailed to slide
Safeties: (a) Ambidextrous manual safety locking trigger mechanism and slide in locked position; (b) half-cock position; (c) inertia operated firing pin; (d) chamber loaded indicator
Magazine: Staggered 15-shot capacity
Slide: Hold open upon firing last cartridge
Finish: Blue
Grips: Smooth Brazilian walnut

MODEL PT 92
$371.35

MODEL PT 99

Caliber: 9mm Parabellum
Action: Semiautomatic double action
Hammer: Exposed
Barrel length: 4.92″
Overall length: 8.54″
Height: 5.39″
Width: 1.45″
Weight: (with empty magazine) 34 oz.
Rifling: R.H., 6 grooves
Front sight: Blade Integral with slide
Rear sight: Micrometer click adjustable for elevation and windage
Safeties: (a) Ambidextrous manual safety locking trigger mechanism and slide in locked position; (b) half-cock position; (c) inertia operated firing pin; (d) chamber loaded indicator. **Magazine:** Staggered, 15-shot capacity
Slide: Hold open upon firing last cartridge
Finish: Blue
Grips: Smooth Brazilian walnut

MODEL PT 99
$397.85 (Blue)
411.16 (Satin)

TAURUS REVOLVERS

MODEL 73 (not shown)
$192.37 Blue
$209.43 Satin nickel

SPECIFICATIONS
Caliber: 32 Long
Capacity: 6 shot
Barrel length: 3″ heavy barrel
Weight: 20 oz.
Sights: Rear, square notch
Action: Double
Stock: Standard checkered
Finish: Blue or satin

MODEL 86 TARGET MASTER

SPECIFICATIONS
Caliber: 38 Special
Capacity: 6 shot
Barrel length: 6″
Weight: 34 oz.
Sights: Patridge-type front; micrometer click adjustable rear
   for windage and elevation
Action: Double
Stock: Checkered walnut target
Finish: Bright royal blue

Model 96 Target Scout: Same as Model 86 Target Master
   except 22 LR caliber. Blue.

MODEL 83 (not shown)
$196.25 Blue
$206.51 Satin

SPECIFICATIONS
Caliber: 38 Special
Action: Double
Number of shots: 6
Barrel length: 4″
Weight: 34½ oz.
Sights: Ramp, front; rear micrometer click adjustable for wind-
   age and elevation
Finish: Blue or satin
Stocks: Checkered walnut target

TARGET MASTER
$252.92

MODEL 80

SPECIFICATIONS
Caliber: 38 Special
Capacity: 6 shot
Barrel lengths: 3″, 4″
Weight: 33 oz.
Action: Double
Stock: Checkered walnut
Finish: Blue or satin

Model 80
$186.42 Blue
$197.81 Satin

MODEL 82

SPECIFICATIONS
Caliber: 38 Special
Capacity: 6 shot
Barrel lengths: 3″, 4″
Weight: 34 oz.
Action: Double
Stock: Checkered walnut
Finish: Blue or satin

Model 82
Heavy Barrel
$186.45 Blue
$197.81 Satin

TAURUS REVOLVERS

Model 65
$212.72 Blue
$223.64 Satin

SPECIFICATIONS
Caliber: 357 Magnum
Capacity: 6 shot
Barrel length: 3″, 4″
Weight: 34 oz.
Sights: Rear square notch; front ramp
Action: Double
Stock: Checkered walnut target
Finish: Royal blue or satin nickel

Model 66
$229.41 Blue
$239.69 Satin
$291.25 Stainless Steel

SPECIFICATIONS
Caliber: 357 Magnum; 38 Special
Capacity: 6 shot
Barrel length: 3″, 4″, 6″
Weight: 35 oz.
Sights: Serrated ramp front; rear micrometer click adjustable
for windage and elevation
Action: Double
Stock: Checkered walnut magna grips (3″); checkered walnut
target grips (4″ & 6″)
Finish: Royal blue or nickel

Model 85
$196.43 Blue
$210.70 Satin
$248.70 Stainless Steel

Caliber: 38 Special
Capacity: 5 shots
Barrel length: 2″ and 3″
Weight: 21 oz.
Sights: Notch rear sight, fixed sight
Action: Double
Stock: Brazilian checkered walnut
Finish: Blue, satin nickel or stainless steel

THOMPSON/CENTER

CONTENDER BULL BARREL

CONTENDER OCTAGON BARREL MODELS

This standard barrel is interchangeable with any model listed here. Available in 10-inch length, it is supplied with iron sights. Octagon barrel is available in 22 LR, 22 Win. Mag. No external choke in this model $325.00

CONTENDER SUPER "14"

CONTENDER SUPER "14" MODELS

Chambered in 12 calibers (22 LR, 222 Remington and 223 Remington, 6mm T.C.U., 6.5mm T.C.U., 7mm T.C.U., 30 Herrett, 30/30 Winchester, 357 Herrett, 357 Rem. Max., 35 Remington, and 44 Mag.), this gun is equipped with a 14-inch bull barrel, fully adjustable target rear sight and ramped front sight (Patridge-style). It offers a sight radius of 13½ inches, beavertail forend and grips designed by Steve Herrett. **Overall length:** 18¼". **Weight:** 3½ lbs. $335.00

CONTENDER BULL BARREL MODELS

This pistol with 10-inch barrel features fully adjustable Patridge-style iron sights.

Standard and Custom calibers available:
22 Long Rifle, 22 Hornet, 22 Win. Mag., 222 Rem., 223 Rem., 32 H&R Mag., 32/20 Win., 6.5mm T.C.U., 7mm T.C.U., 30/30 Win., 30 Herrett, 357 Herrett, 357 Mag., 41 Mag., 44 Mag., and 357 Rem. Max.
Bull Barrel (less internal choke) $325.00
Standard calibers available with internal choke:
.410, 45 Colt $330.00

ARMOUR ALLOY II CONTENDER

Armour Alloy II is a permanent, electroplated surface that will not separate from the base metal. It is harder than stainless steel and improves lubricity, causing actions to function smoother and enabling parts to move with less frictional drag. As a result, it provides 30% longer barrel life than stainless steel, reduces wear on moving parts, and shrugs off the effects of corrosion or erosion. It also reduces fouling to produce a more constant velocity shot after shot. All metal surfaces of this Contender Series, internal and external (excluding sights and springs) are finished in Armour Alloy II.
Calibers: 22 LR, 223 REM., 357 Magnum, 357 Rem. Max., 44 Magnum, 7mm TCU, 30/30 Win. 10" Bull Barrel Model); 45 Colt/.410 (Vent rib/Internal Choke Model); Super "14" Model same calibers as Bull Barrell except no 7mm TCU.
Prices:
Contender 10" Bull Barrel Model $395.00
Contender Vent Rib/Internal Choke Model 415.00
Contender Super "14" Model 405.00

CONTENDER VENTILATED RIB/INTERNAL CHOKE MODELS (not shown)

Featuring a raised ventilated (7/16-inch wide) rib, this Contender model is available in 45 Colt/.410 caliber. Its rear leaf sight folds down to provide an unobstructed sighting plane when the pistol is used with .410 ga. shot shells. A patented detachable choke (1⅞ inches long) screws into muzzle internally. **Barrel length:** 10 inches. $345.00

A. UBERTI REPLICA REVOLVERS

1873 STALLION QUICK DRAW SINGLE ACTION
$359.00

SPECIFICATIONS
Caliber: 22 LR, 22 Magnum (w/2 interchangeable cylinders)
Barrel length: 5 1/2 round (also avail. w/4 3/4" or 6 1/2" barrel)
Overall length: 10 3/4"
Weight: 2.42 lbs.
Sights: Fully adj. rear; ramp front
Capacity: 6 shots
Grip: One piece walnut
Frame: Stainless steel + all metal parts

Also available:
1873 Stallion Target Model (brass) $319.00
   Case hardened 339.00
   Stainless steel 379.00

1873 CATTLEMAN QUICK DRAW
$295.00 (Brass)
$319.00 (Steel)

SPECIFICATIONS
Caliber: 45 L.C., 44-40, 22LR, 22 Magnum, 38 Special
Barrel lengths: 4 3/4", 5 1/2", 7 1/2"; round tapered
Overall length: 10 3/4" (5 1/2" barrel)
Weight: 2.42 lbs.
Capacity: 6 shots
Grip: One piece walnut
Frame: Color case hardened steel

Also available in Stainless Steel: **$359.00**
Also available:
Cattleman S.A. Target (brass) $319.00
Steel 339.00
Stainless steel 379.00

1875 REMINGTON ARMY "OUTLAW"
$300.00

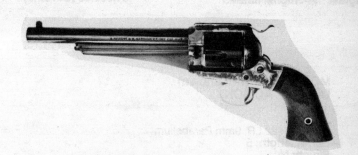

SPECIFICATIONS
Calibers: 357 Magnum, 45 Long Colt, 44–40
Barrel length: 7 1/2" round tapered
Overall length: 13 3/4"
Weight: 2.75 lbs.
Grips: Two-piece walnut
Frame: Color case hardened steel

Also available in nickel plate: **$340.00**

WALTHER PISTOLS

DOUBLE-ACTION AUTOMATIC PISTOLS

The Walther double-action system combines the principles of the double-action revolver with the advantages of the modern pistol . . . without the disadvantages inherent in either design.

Models PP and PPK/S differ only in the overall length of the barrel and slide. Both models offer the same features, including compact form, light weight, easy handling and absolute safety. Both models can be carried with a loaded chamber and closed hammer, but ready to fire either single- or double-action. Both models in calibers 32 ACP and 380 ACP are provided with a live round indicator pin to signal a loaded chamber. An automatic internal safety blocks the hammer to prevent accidental striking of the firing pin, except with a deliberate pull of the trigger. Sights are provided with white markings for high visibility in poor light. Rich Walther blue/black finish is standard and each pistol is complete with extra magazine with finger rest extension. Available in calibers 22 LR, 32 ACP and 380 ACP.

The Walther P-38 is a double-action, locked breech, semi-automatic pistol with an external hammer. Its compact form, light weight and easy handling are combined with the superb performance of the 9mm Luger Parabellum cartridge. The P-38 is equipped with both a manual and automatic safety, which allows it to be carried safely while the chamber is loaded. Available in calibers 9mm Luger Parabellum, 30 Luger and 22 LR with either a rugged non-reflective black finish or a polished blue finish.

SPECIFICATIONS
Overall length: Model PP 6.7″; PPK/S 6.1″; P-38 8½″; P-38 IV 8″; TPH 5⅜″
Height: Models PP, PPK/S 4.28″; P-38 5.39″; P-38 IV 5.39″; P-38K 5.39″
Weight: Model PP 23.5 oz; PPK/S 23 oz; P-38 28 oz.; P-38 IV (29 oz); TPH 14 oz.

MODEL PPK/S "AMERICAN"
7-shot Automatic

Caliber: 380 ACP
Barrel length: 3.27″
Finish: Walther blue
Price. $499.00
Stainless steel 499.00
Deluxe Engraved . . . . $1,550.00 (Blue); $1,700.00 (Silver); $1,600.00 (Chrome)

MODEL TPH DOUBLE ACTION

Considered by government agents and professional lawmen to be one of the cop undercover/back-up guns available. A scaled-down version of Walther's PP-PPK series chambered for .22 LR.

SPECIFICATIONS:
Barrel length: 2¼″. **Overall length:** 5⅜″. **Weight:** 14 oz.
Finish: stainless steel. **Price: $350.00.**

MODEL P-38 (not shown)
DOUBLE ACTION

Calibers: 22 LR, 9mm Parabellum
Barrel length: 5″
Finish: blue
Weight: 28 oz. (alloy); 34 oz. (steel)

Price:
22 Long Rifle $890.00
9mm Parabellum 800.00
Deluxe Engraved (9mm Para. only) . . . . . $1,750.00 (Blue)
2,050.00 (Gold)
1,950.00 (Silver)
1,850.00 (Chrome)
Now available: custom **all steel** classic (34 oz.) . . . 1100.00

WALTHER TARGET PISTOLS

WALTHER OSP
22 Short only

Walther match pistols are built to conform to ISU and NRA match target pistol regulations. The model GSP, caliber 22 LR is available with either 2.2 lb. (1000 gm) or 3.0 lbs. (1360 gm) trigger, and comes with 4¹/₂-inch barrel and special hand-fitting designed walnut stock. Sights consist of fixed front and adjustable rear sight. The GSP-C 32 S&W wadcutter center-fire pistol is factory tested with a 3.0 lb. trigger. The 22 LR conversion unit for the model GSP-C consists of an interchangeable barrel, a slide assembly and two magazines. **Weight:** 22-caliber model 44.8 oz.; 32 S&W 49.4 oz. **Overall length:** 11.8″. **Magazine capacity:** 5 shot.

Prices:

GSP—22 Long Rifle w/carrying case	$1200.00
GSP-C—32 S&W wadcutter w/carrying case	1375.00
22 LR conversion unit for GSP-C	725.00
22 Short conversion unit for GSP-C	750.00
32S&W wadcutter conversion unit for GSP-C	875.00
OSP Rapid Fire w/carrying case	1350.00

MODEL P-88 DA
$1040.00

Caliber: 9mm Para.
Capacity: 15 rds.
Barrel length: 4″
Overall length: 7³/₈″
Weight: 31¹/₂ oz.
Finish: Blue
Sights: Rear adj. for windage and elevation
Features: Internal safeties; ambidextrous de-cocking lever and magazine release button; lightweight alloy frame; loaded chamber indicator

WALTHER TARGET PISTOLS

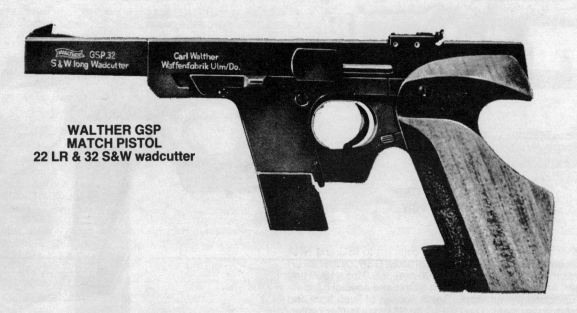

**WALTHER GSP
MATCH PISTOL
22 LR & 32 S&W wadcutter**

GSP JR. SEMIAUTOMATIC
$1200.00 (w/Carrying Case)

Caliber: 22 LR
Capacity: 5 rds.
Barrel length: 4¹/₂"
Overall length: 11.8"
Weight: 40.1 oz.

U.I.T.-BV
$1475.00

Caliber: 22 LR
Barrel length: 25¹/₂"
Overall length: 44³/₄"
Weight: 9 lbs.
Bolt action: Single shot; falling block

MODEL P-5 DA
$1040.00

Caliber: 9mm Para.
Capacity: 8 rds.
Barrel length: 3¹/₂"
Overall length: 7"
Weight: 28 oz.
Finish: Blue
Features: Four automatic built-in safety functions; lightweight alloy frame; supplied w/two magazines

DAN WESSON REVOLVERS

357 MAGNUM w/6" BARREL

357 MAGNUM REVOLVERS

Introduced in 1935, the 357 Magnum is still the top selling handgun caliber. It makes an excellent hunting sidearm, and many law enforcement agencies have adopted it as a duty caliber. Take your pick of Dan Wesson 357's; then, add to it's versatility with an additional barrel assembly option to alter it to your other needs.

SPECIFICATIONS
Action: Six-shot double and single action. **Ammunition:** 357 Magnum, 38 Special Hi-speed, 38 Special Mid-range. **Typical dimension:** 4" barrel revolver, 9¼" × 5¾". **Trigger:** Smooth, wide tang (³/₈") with overtravel adjustment. **Hammer:** Wide spur (³/₈") with short double-action travel. **Sights: Models 14 and 714,** ¹/₈" fixed serrated front; fixed rear integral with frame. **Models 15 and 715,** ¹/₈" serrated interchangeable front blade; red insert standard, yellow and white available; rear, standard white outline adjustable for windage and elevation; graduated click. 10", 12," 15" barrel assemblies have special front sights and instructions. **Rifling:** Six lands and grooves, right-hand twist, 1 turn in 18.75 inches (2¹/₂" thru 8" lengths); six lands & grooves, right-hand twist, 1 turn in 14 inches (10", 12", 15" lengths). **Note:** All 2¹/₂" guns shipped with undercover grips. 4" guns are shipped with service grips and the balance have oversized target grips.

Price:
Pistol Pac Models 14, 15, 714, 715 . . . . $418.20 to 814.50

MODEL	CALIBER	TYPE	BARREL LENGTHS & WEIGHT IN OUNCES							FINISH
			2½"	4"	6"	8"	10"	12"	15"	
14-2	.357 Magnum	Service	30	34	38	NA	NA	NA	NA	Satin Blue
14-2B	.357 Magnum	Service	30	34	38	NA	NA	NA	NA	Brite Blue
15-2	.357 Magnum	Target	32	36	40	44	50	54	59	Brite Blue
15-2V	.357 Magnum	Target	32	35	39	43	49	54	59	Brite Blue
15-2VH	.357 Magnum	Target	32	37	42	47	55	61	70	Brite Blue
714	.357 Magnum	Service	30	34	40	NA	NA	NA	NA	Satin Stainless Steel
715	.357 Magnum	Target	32	36	40	45	50	54	59	Satin Stainless Steel
715-V	.357 Magnum	Target	32	35	40	43	49	54	59	Satin Stainless Steel
715-VH	.357 Magnum	Target	32	37	42	49	55	61	70	Satin Stainless Steel

22 RIMFIRE and 22 MAGNUM REVOLVERS

Built on the same frames as the Dan Wesson 357 Magnum, these 22 rimfires offer the heft and balance of fine target revolvers. Affordable fun for the beginner or the expert.

SPECIFICATIONS
Action: Six-shot double and single action. **Ammunition:** Models 22 & 722, 22 Long Rifle; Models 22M & 722M, 22 Win. Mag. **Typical dimension:** 4" barrel revolver, 9¼" × 5¾". **Trigger:** Smooth, wide tang (³/₈") with overtravel adjustment. **Hammer:** Wide spur (³/₈") with short double-action travel. **Sights:** Front, ¹/₈" serrated, interchangeable blade; red insert standard, yellow and white available; rear, standard white outline adjustable for windage and elevation; graduated click. **Rifling:** Models 22 and 722, six lands and grooves, right-hand twist, 1 turn in 12 inches; Models 22M and 722M, six lands and grooves, right-hand twist, 1 turn in 16 inches. **Note:** All 2¹/₂" guns are shipped with undercover grips. 4" guns are shipped with service grips and the balance have oversized target grips.

Price:
Pistol Pac Models 22 and 722 . . . . $564.00 to $846.35

MODEL	CALIBER	TYPE	BARREL LENGTHS & WEIGHT IN OUNCES				FINISH
			2¼"	4"	6"	8"	
22	.22 L.R.	Target	36	40	44	49	Brite Blue
22-V	.22 L.R.	Target	36	40	44	49	Brite Blue
22-VH	.22 L.R.	Target	36	41	47	54	Brite Blue
22-M	.22 Win Mag	Target	36	40	44	49	Brite Blue
22M-V	.22 Win Mag	Target	36	40	44	49	Brite Blue
22M-VH	.22 Win Mag	Target	36	41	47	54	Brite Blue
722	.22 L.R.	Target	36	40	44	49	Satin Stainless Steel
722-V	.22 L.R.	Target	36	40	44	49	Satin Stainless Steel
722-VH	.22 L.R.	Target	36	41	47	54	Satin Stainless Steel
722M	.22 Win Mag	Target	36	40	44	49	Satin Stainless Steel
722M-V	.22 Win Mag	Target	36	40	44	49	Satin Stainless Steel
722M-VH	.22 Win Mag	Target	36	41	47	54	Satin Stainless Steel

DAN WESSON REVOLVERS

41 AND 44 MAGNUM REVOLVERS

The Dan Wesson 41 and 44 Magnum revolvers are available with a patented "Power Control" to reduce muzzle flip. Both the 41 and the 44 have a one-piece frame and patented gain bolt for maximum strength.

SPECIFICATIONS
Action: Six-shot double- and single-action. **Ammunition:** Models 41 and 741, 41 Magnum; Models 44 and 744, 44 Magnum and 44 Special. **Typical dimension:** 6″ barrel revolver, 12″ × 6.″ **Trigger:** Smooth, wide tang (3/8″) with overtravel adjustment. **Hammer:** Wide checkered spur with short double-action travel. **Sights:** Front, 1/8″ serrated interchangeable blade; red insert standard, yellow and white available; rear, standard white outline adjustable for windage and elevation; click graduated. **Rifling:** Eight lands and grooves, right-hand twist, 1 turn in 18.75 inches. **Note:** 4″, 6″, and 8″ 44 Magnum guns will be shipped with unported and Power Control barrels. 10″ 44 Magnum guns available only without Power Control. Only jacketed bullets should be used with the 44 Mag. Power Control or excessive leading will result.

Price:
Pistol Pac Model 41 . . . .$572.15–616.80
   Stainless Steel. .633.40–678.20
Pistol Pac Model 44 . . . . .649.10–695.25
   Stainless Steel. .747.15–795.45

MODEL 44-V
44 MAGNUM
w/8″ BARREL

MODEL	CALIBER	TYPE	BARREL LENGTHS & WEIGHT IN OUNCES				FINISH
			4″	6″	8″	10″*	
41-V	.41 Magnum	Target	48	53	58	64	Brite Blue
41-VH	.41 Magnum	Target	49	56	64	69	Brite Blue
44-V	.44 Magnum	Target	48	53	58	64	Brite Blue
44-VH	.44 Magnum	Target	49	56	64	69	Brite Blue
741-V	.41 Magnum	Target	48	53	58	64	Satin Stainless Steel
741-VH	.41 Magnum	Target	49	56	64	69	Satin Stainless Steel
744-V	.44 Magnum	Target	48	53	58	64	Satin Stainless Steel
744-VH	.44 Magnum	Target	49	56	64	69	Satin Stainless Steel

38 SPECIAL REVOLVER

For decades a favorite of security and law enforcement agencies, the 38 special still maintains it's reputation as a fine caliber for sportsmen and target shooters. Dan Wesson offers a choice of many barrel lengths in either the service or target configuration.

SPECIFICATIONS
Action: Six-shot double and single action. **Ammunition:** 38 Special Hi-speed, 38 Special Mid-range. **Typical dimension:** 4″ barrel revolver, 9¼″ × 5¾″. **Trigger:** Smooth, wide tang (3/8″) with overtravel adjustment. **Hammer:** Wide spur (3/8″) with short double travel. **Sights:** Models 8 and 708, 1/8″ fixed serrated front; fixed rear integral with frame. Models 9 and 709, 1/8″ serrated interchangeable front blade; red insert standard, yellow and white available; rear, standard white outline, adjustable for windage and elevation; graduated click. **Rifling:** Six lands and grooves, right-hand twist, 1 turn in 18.75 inches. **Note:** All 2½″ guns shipped with undercover grips. 4″ guns are shipped with service grips and the balance have oversized target grips.

Price: 38 Special Pistol Pacs $375.85–672.05
   Stainless Steel $430.65–744.30

MODEL	CALIBER	TYPE	BARREL LENGTHS & WEIGHT IN OUNCES				FINISH
			2½″	4″	6″	8″	
8-2	.38 Special	Service	30	34	38	N/A	Satin Blue
8-2B	.38 Special	Service	30	34	38	N/A	Brite Blue
9-2	.38 Special	Target	32	36	40	44	Brite Blue
9-2V	.38 Special	Target	32	35	39	43	Brite Blue
9-2VH	.38 Special	Target	32	37	42	47	Brite Blue
708	.38 Special	Service	30	34	38	N/A	Satin Stainless Steel
709	.38 Special	Target	32	36	40	44	Satin Stainless Steel
709-V	.38 Special	Target	32	35	39	43	Satin Stainless Steel
709-VH	.38 Special	Target	32	37	42	47	Satin Stainless Steel

DAN WESSON REVOLVERS

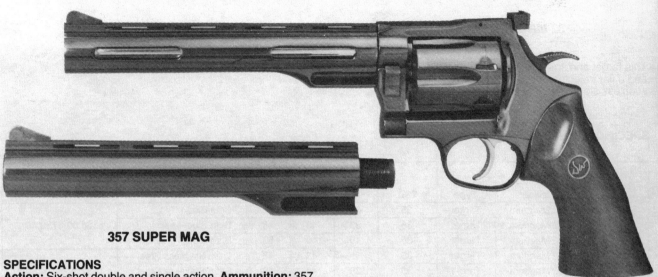

357 SUPER MAG

SPECIFICATIONS

Action: Six-shot double and single action. **Ammunition:** 357 Maximum. **Overall length:** 14.375″ with 8″ barrel. **Height:** 6.5″. **Trigger:** Clean let-off, wide tang with overtravel adjustment. **Hammer:** Wide spur with short double-action travel. **Sights:** ¹/₈″ serrated interchangeable front blade; red insert standard, yellow and white available; rear, new, interchangeable blade for wide or narrow notch sight picture; screwdriver adjustable for windage and elevation. **Rifling:** Six lands and grooves, right-hand twist, 1 in 18³/₄ inches.

SPECIFICATIONS

Model	Caliber	Type	Barrel lengths & Weight (oz.)			Finish	Price
			6″	8″	10″		
740-V	357 Max	Target	59.5	65	62	Brite blue	**$522.00–588.90**
740-VH	357 Max	Target	62	72	76	Brite blue	
740-V8S	357 Max	Target		64		Brite blue	

DAN WESSON ARMS PISTOL PAC OPTIONS

MODEL	CALIBER	TYPE	BARREL LENGTHS INCL.				Extra Grips	Addt'l. Sight Blades	Carry Case	Wrench & Gauge	Patch & Buckle
P-22	.22 L.R.	Target	2½	4	6	8	X	4	X	X	X
P-722	.22 L.R.	Target	2½	4	6	8	X	4	X	X	X
P-22M	.22 Win Mag	Target	2½	4	6	8	X	4	X	X	X
P-722M	.22 Win Mag	Target	2½	4	6	8	X	4	X	X	X
P-8-2	.38 Special	Service	2½	4	6	-	X	-	X	X	X
P-8-2B	.38 Special	Service	2½	4	6	-	X	-	X	X	X
P-9-2	.38 Special	Target	2½	4	6	8	X	4	X	X	X
P-708	.38 Special	Service	2½	4	6	-	X	-	X	X	X
P-709	.38 Special	Target	2½	4	6	8	X	4	X	X	X
P-14-2	.357 Magnum	Service	2½	4	6	-	X	-	X	X	X
P-14-2B	.357 Magnum	Service	2½	4	6	-	X	-	X	X	X
P-15-2	.357 Magnum	Target	2½	4	6	8	X	4	X	X	X
P-714	.357 Magnum	Service	2½	4	6	-	X	-	X	X	X
P-715	.357 Magnum	Target	2½	4	6	8	X	4	X	X	X
P-41	.41 Magnum	Target	-	-	6	8	X	2	X	X	X
P-741	.41 Magnum	Target	-	-	6	8	X	2	X	X	X
P-44*	.44 Magnum	Target	-	-	6	8	X	2	X	X	X
P-744*	.44 Magnum	Target	-	-	6	8	X	2	X	X	X

*Standard .44 pac includes a gun with 8″ unported barrel; an 8″ "POWER CONTROL" barrel; and two 6″ barrels—one unported and one "POWER CONTROL" with appropriate shroud.

DAN WESSON REVOLVERS

32 MAGNUM SIX SHOT

This target and small game gun offers a high muzzle velocity and a flat trajectory for better accuracy. Available in blue and stainless steel.

SPECIFICATIONS

Model	Caliber	Type	Barrel lengths & Weight in ounces				Finish	Prices
			2½″	4″	6″	8″		
32	.32 Magnum	Target	35	39	43	48	Brite Blue	
32V	.32 Magnum	Target	35	39	43	48	Brite Blue	$564.00-$738.40
32VH	.32 Magnum	Target	35	40	46	53	Brite Blue	
732	.32 Magnum	Target	35	39	43	48	Satin Stainless Steel	
732V	.32 Magnum	Target	35	39	43	48	Satin Stainless Steel	$632.10-$814.50
732VH	.32 Magnum	Target	35	40	46	53	Satin Stainless Steel	

45 COLT DOUBLE ACTION

Dan Wesson's interchangeable barrel design makes this model actually four guns in one. Its unique barrel shrouds stabilize the barrel for better control.

SPECIFICATIONS

Model No.	Barrel lengths	Finish	Price*
45	4″, 6″, 8″, 10″	Brite Blue	
45V	4″, 6″, 8″, 10″	Brite Blue	$285.85
45VH	4″, 6″, 8″, 10″	Brite Blue	
745	4″, 6″, 8″, 10″	Satin Stainless Steel	
745V	4″, 6″, 8″, 10″	Satin Stainless Steel	$285.85
745VH	4″, 6″, 8″, 10″	Satin Stainless Steel	

*Pistol Pacs: $649.10 ($795.45 in stainless steel)
Note: V = ventilated rib shroud; VH = ventilated heavy shroud.

HUNTER PAC

Offered in all magnum calibers with the following:
1. Complete gun in choice of caliber (22, 32, 357, 41, 44, 357 Supermag and 375 Supermag) with 8″ vent-heavy shroud.
2. 8″ vent shroud only, equipped with Burris scope mounts and scope (1½×-4× variable or fixed 2×).
3. Barrel changing tool and Dan Wesson emblem packed in attractive case.

Prices: $663.77 (32 Magnum w/2×) to $988.04 (357 Supermag Stainless w/1½×-4×)

Rifles

FOR ADDRESSES AND PHONE
NUMBERS OF MANUFACTURERS AND
DISTRIBUTORS INCLUDED IN THIS
SECTION, SEE *DIRECTORY OF
MANUFACTURERS AND SUPPLIERS*

ALPHA ARMS RIFLES

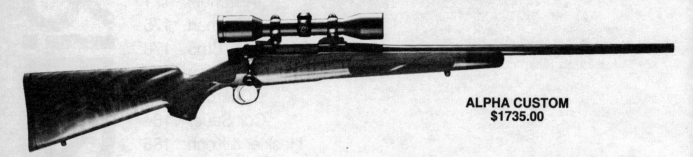

**ALPHA CUSTOM
$1735.00**

SPECIFICATIONS
Calibers: 222 Rem., 223 Rem. (Short Action; available in single shot only); 22-250 through 338-284 (Medium Action); 25-06 through 35 Whelen (Standard Action); Magnum Action available by special order only
Magazine capacity: Single shot in 222 and 223; 3 shots in standard calibers and most wildcats
Barrel length: 20″ to 24″ depending on caliber
Overall length: 40″ with 20″ barrel (short action)
Length of pull: 13 1/2″
Weight: 6 lbs.

Stock: Presentation grade California claro walnut; ribbon-style checkering pattern; hand-rubbed oil finish
Features: Left hand models available at no extra cost; custom inletted sling swivel studs standard; ebony forend tip standard; custom open sights; octagonal barrels available (integral quarter rib and express sights optional)
Also available: Alpha Grand Slam. Same specifications except weight = 6 1/2 lbs. Stock is combination fiberglass and wood. **Price: $1465.00.**

**ALPHA ALASKAN
$1735.00**

SPECIFICATIONS
Same as Alpha Grand Slam except barrel band type front sling swivel is soft soldered to barrel to prevent pinching with heavy recoiling calibers. Rear swivel stud is Talley-type inletted into stock.

**ALPHA JAGUAR
$995.00-$1595.00 (Grades 1,2,3,4)**

Calibers: up to .338 Win. Mag.
Weight: 7 1/2-9 lbs.
Action: Mauser type w/claw extractors, controlled feeding
Stock: Reinforced Alphawood w/pillar bedding
Also available: ALPHA BIG FIVE. Same specifications as Jaguar but in calibers from 338 Win. Mag through 458 Win. Mag. Includes barrel band sling swivel stud. **Price: $1795.00**

ANSCHUTZ RIFLES

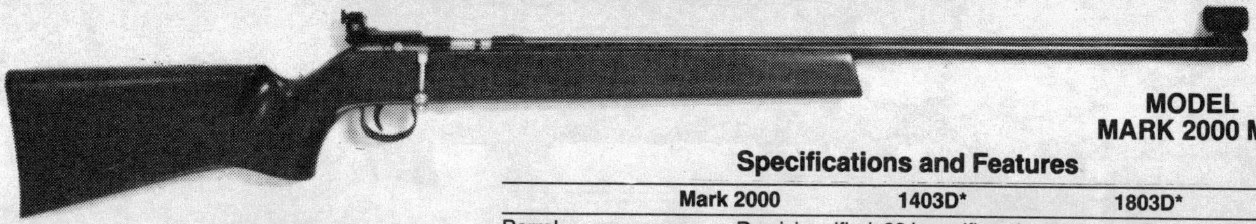

**MODEL
MARK 2000 MK**

**Match
Rifles**

Specifications and Features

	Mark 2000	1403D*	1803D*
Barrel	Precision rifled .22 long rifle only.		
Length	25¼" ¾" dia.	25¼" medium heavy ¹¹/₁₆" dia.	21½" ¾" dia.
Action	Single Shot. Large loading platform.		Match 54
Trigger	Factory set for crisp trigger pull 3 lbs.	1.1 lbs. Single stage, adjustable for weight of pull, take-up, over travel.	1 lb., 3.5 oz., 2 stage 5018 adjustable from 3½ oz. to 2 lbs.
Safety	Slide safety locks trigger.	Slide safety locks sear and bolt.	Wing type
Stock	Walnut finished hardwood.	Walnut finished hardwood. Cheek piece/Swivel Rail.	Walnut finish, cheek piece, stippled pistol grip and front stock.
Sights	Front-Insert type globesight. Rear (Micrometer click adjustments) available separately.	Takes Anschutz 6723 sights.	6727 Sight Set furnished with rifle.
Overall Length	43¼"	43¼"	42½"
Weight (avg.)	7½ lbs.	8.6 lbs. with sights	9 lbs. with sights

* Left hand rifles built to same specifications, except with left hand stock, cast off. Rate of Twist (R.H.) 1 turn in 16½" for 22 L.R.

Note: Prices listed on p. 173

**MODEL
64MS**

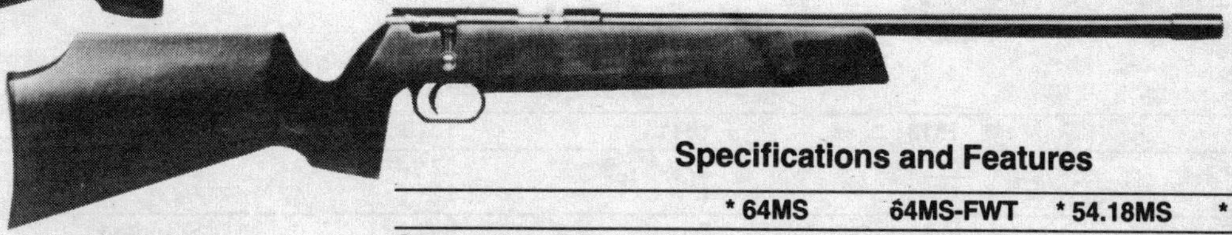

**MODEL
54.18MS**

**Metallic
Silhouette
Rifles**

Specifications and Features

	* 64MS	64MS-FWT	* 54.18MS	* 54.18MS-ED
Grooved for scope	•	•	•	•
Tapped for scope mount	•	•	•	•
Overall length	39.5"	39.5"	41"	52½"
Barrel length	21¼"	21¼"	22"	33½"
Length of pull	13½"	13½"	13¾"	13¾"
High cheek piece with Monte Carlo effect	•	•	•	•
Drop at Comb	1½"	1½"	1½"	1½"
Average weight	8 lbs.	6¼ lbs.	8 lbs. 6 oz.	8 lbs. 6 oz.
Trigger:	Two	Single	Two	Two
Stage	Model 5091	Model 5094	Model 5018	Model 5018
Factory adjusted weight	5.3 oz.	3.0 lbs.	3.9 oz.	3.9 oz.
Adjustable weight	4.9–7 oz.	2.2–4.4 lbs.	2.1–8.6 oz.	2.1–8.6 oz.
Safety	Slide	Slide	Slide	Slide

Prices for all models on this page are listed on p. 173.

* Left hand rifles are built to same specifications except with left hand stock cast off.

ANSCHUTZ RIFLES

MODEL 1813

MODEL 1811

MODEL 1807

MODEL 1808ED

International Match Rifles

Specifications and Features

	1813	1811	1810	1807	1808ED-Super
Barrel Length O/D	27¹/₄″ 1″	27¹/₄″ 1″	27¹/₄″ 1″	26″ ⁷/₈″	32¹/₂″ ⁷/₈″
Stock	Int'l.- Thumb Hole Adj. Palm Rest Adj. Hand Rest	Prone	Int'l.- Thumb Hole	Standard	Thumb Hole
Cheek Piece Butt Plate	Adj. Adj. Hook 10 Way Hook	Adj. Adj. 4 Way	Adj. Adj. Hook 10 Way Hook	Removable Adj. 4 Way	Adj. Adj. 4 Way
Recommended Sights	6720.6723	6720.6723	6720.6723	6720.6723	Grooved for Scope Mounts
Overall Length	45″-46″	45″-46″	45″-46″	43³/₄″-44¹/₂″	50¹/₂″
Overall Length to Hook	49.6″-51.2″		49.6″-51.2″		
Weight without sights (approx)	15.4 lbs.	11.9 lbs.	13.9 lbs.	10 lbs.	9¹/₄ lbs.
True Left—Hand Version	1813Left	1811Left	1810Left	1807Left	1808Left
Recommended Sights for Above Models	6720 *6720Left	6720 *6720Left	6720 *6720Left	6720 *6720Left	
Sling Swivel	w/adj. hand stop	w/adj. hand stop	w/adj.hand stop	w/adj. hand stop	

Prices for all models on this page are listed on p. 173.   *For left hand models.

ANSCHUTZ RIFLES

MODEL 1433D

MODEL 525

TARGET RIFLES

1808ED Super-Running Target **$1019.00**	1827B Biathlon w/sights **$1370.00**
1808ED Super L-Running Target **1185.00**	1827BT Biathlon w/sights **2685.00**

Without sights and sling swivel

1403D **$588.50**	1813 Super Match **1740.00**
1807 ISU Standard **1010.00**	1813L **1915.00**
1807 ISU Standard (Left) **1094.00**	64MS Silhouette 22 LR. **568.00**
2000MK w/out sights **329.50**	64MS Left **628.00**
1810 Super Match II **1576.00**	64MS FWT **568.00**
1810L Super Match II **1674.00**	54.18MS **957.00**
1811 Prone Match **1214.00**	54.18MSL **1052.00**
1811L **1347.00**	

SPORTER RIFLES (Custom, Classic & Mannlicher)

1416D 22LR **$464.00**	1418D 22LR Mannlicher **$664.00**
1416D Classic Left **531.50**	1518D 22M Mannlicher **669.00**
1516D 22 Magnum **504.50**	1422DCL 22 LR. **764.00**
1422D 22LR. **849.50**	1422DCL 22LR Meister Grade **875.00**
1422D 22LR Meister Grade. **930.00**	1522DCL 22M **780.00**
1522D 22M. **824.50**	1432DCL 22 H **849.00**
1432D 22H **909.00**	1532DCL 222R **849.00**
1532D 222 Remington **909.00**	525 22 LR Semiauto **349.50**
1532D 222R Classic **849.00**	

ANSCHUTZ RIFLES

THE ACHIEVER 22 LR
$299.00

SPECIFICATIONS
Barrel length: 19½"
Overall length: 35½"-36⅔"
Weight: 5 lbs.
Action: Mark 2000 type repeating
Trigger: #5066-two stage 2.6 lbs.
Safety: slide
Stock pull: 11⅞"-13"
Sights: hooded ramp front; rear marble folding leaf; adj. for windage and elevation
Capacity: 5 shot

THE KADETT 22 LR (not shown)
$265.00

SPECIFICATIONS
Barrel length: 22"
Overall length: 40"
Weight: 5½lbs.
Trigger: #5067-single stage
Safety: slide
Stock pull: 13¾"
Sights: hooded ramp front; Lyman folding rear; adj. for elevation
Action: Mark 2000 type repeating

SPECIFICATIONS

	Mark 2000	**1403D***	**1803D***
Barrel Length	25¼" ¾" dia.	Precision rifled .22 long rifle only 25" medium heavy ¹¹/₁₆" dia.	25½" ¾" dia.
Action	Match 2000	Match 64	Match 64
Trigger	Single stage. Factory set for crisp trigger pull 3 lbs.	1.1 lbs. Single stage, adjustable* for weight of pull, take-up over travel. #5093	#5091 2 stage adjustable* from 9.2 to 10.6 oz.
Safety	Slide safety locks trigger.	Slide safety locks sear and bolt.	Slide safety looks sear and bolt.
Stock	Walnut finished hardwood. Swivel rail.	Walnut finished hardwood. Cheek piece/ Swivel Rail. Stippling.	Blonde finish, adjustable cheek piece. stippled pistol grip and fore stock. Swivel rail.
Sights	Front: Insert type globe sight. Rear Micrometer with clock adjustments (available separately as S.S.#2, #3)	Takes Anschutz 6723 Sight Set (available separately.)	Takes Anschutz 6723 Sight Set (available separately.)
Overall Length	43¼"	43¼"	43¼"
Weight (avg.)	7½ lbs.	8.6 lbs. with sights	8.6 lbs.
Left Hand			1803D Left

1803D MATCH RIFLE

This medium weight rifle for intermediate and advanced Junior Match competition features the proven Match 64 action and a medium weight ¾" target barrel. No. 5093 trigger is 1.1 pound and adjustable. Target style cheek piece is also adjustable, as is rubber butt plate with two inserts. Styling includes honey-blonde European hardwood. I.S.U. target style stock with contrasting dark stippled checkering on deeply fluted thumb groove pistol grip and slide rail. **Price: $664.50 ($691.50 Left Hand Model)**

BEEMAN RIFLES

BEEMAN/WEIHRAUCH HW 60 SMALLBORE RIFLE
$460.00 (right)—$519.00 (left)

22 caliber LR, single shot. Improved bolt action. Adjustable match trigger with push button safety. Precision rifled barrel. Stippled forearm and pistol grip. Precision aperture sights, hooded front sight ramp. **Barrel length:** 26.8". **Overall length:** 45.7". **Weight:** 10.8 lbs.

BEEMAN/FWB 2000
From $897.76

22 caliber LR. Micrometer match aperture sights. Foresight with interchangeable inserts. Meets ISU standard rifle specifications. Short lock time. Precision match trigger adjustable for weight, release point, finger length, lateral position, or advanced electronic trigger. **Barrel length:** 22" and 26 1/4". **Overall length:** 39" and 43 3/4". **Weight:** 9 1/8 lbs. and 9 3/4 lbs. Left hand and electronic trigger versions available.

BEEMAN/FWB 2000
SUPER MATCH
$1295.00 Mech. Trigger $1595.00 Elect. Trigger

22 caliber LR. Developed from the highly successful design of the FWB 2000. Available with same outstanding mechanical trigger of the 2000 or the new electronic trigger. Anatomically correct thumbhole stock, accessory rails for moveable weights; adj. palm rest, adj. cheekpiece, adj. hooked buttplate; superb match sights. Left hand versions available.

BEEMAN/FWB 2600
$962.38 (right) — $1052.80 (left)

22 caliber LR. Designed as an identical small bore companion to the Beeman/FWB 600 Match air rifle. Super rigid stock made of laminated hardwood. Bull barrel free floats. Stock is cut low to permit complete ventilation around barrel. Match trigger has fingertip weight adjustment dial. Adjustable comb; match sights; single shot.

BEEMAN/KRICO RIFLES

Beeman/Krico rifles bring West German tradition to the world of varmint and big game hunting and target shooting in North America. Noted worldwide for their superb balance and handling, these rifles feature hammer forged, precision rifled barrels, exceptionally fine triggers, smoothly operating bolt actions, and interchangeable trigger modules. All models have cheekpieces and fine handcut checkering on the grips and forearms (except target models, which are stippled). All Beeman/Krico rifles are proofed at the factory for accuracy (at 100 meters, hunting rifles must group shots under 1.2 inches; target rifles are under .75 inches).

MODEL 400
$610.00

Classic German-style 22 Hornet varmint rifle. Beautifully designed for natural balance and easy handling. Detachable 5-shot magazine. Exceptional accuracy. Grooved for scopes. Smooth sliding bolt and crisp trigger action. **Overall length:** 43″. **Weight:** 6.8 lbs.

MODEL 420
$699.00 (scope not included)

22 Hornet varmint rifle with exceptionally sleek full stock. Has same features as Model 400, but with a double-set trigger for carefully aimed, precision shots. Detachable 5-shot magazine. The 22 Hornet caliber's light report and moderate power make it suitable for areas too populated for heavy cartridge use. **Overall length:** 38″. **Weight:** 6.5 lbs. Grooved for scopes.

MODEL 640 VARMINT
$935.00
(shown with optional Beeman scope)

Heavy barrel varmint rifle 222 Rem., 223 Rem., 22-250. Walnut stock has high, Monte Carlo comb, full cheekpiece, checkered grip with Wundhammer palm swell and rosewood forend tip and grip cap. **Heavy barrel length:** 23¾″ long; 4-shot magazine. **Overall length:** 43½″. **Weight:** 9.6 lbs.

MODEL 340
METALLIC SILHOUETTE RIFLE
$561.00

Heavy bull barrel adds extra control and steadiness. Tests produce 5-shot groups under ½″ ctc at 100 yards. Large, ¾″ diameter bolt knob for fast handling. 5-shot magazine. Double extractors. Match trigger adjusts from 14 to 28 oz. Franchi rubber buttplate. Stippled grip and forearm. Grooved for scopes. **Overall length:** 39½″. **Weight:** 7.5 lbs.

BEEMAN/KRICO RIFLES

MODEL 320 SPORTER
$518.00

Capacity: 5-shot magazine
Weight: 6¹/₂ lbs.
Features: Straight stock and full forearm; receiver ground for scope mounts

SPECIFICATIONS
Caliber: 22 LR
Overall length: 43″

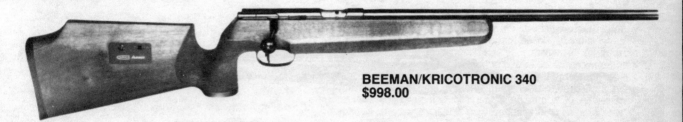

BEEMAN/KRICOTRONIC 340
$998.00

22 caliber LR. The only rifle with an operational electronic ignition system designed for conventional ammunition. The system eliminates the need for a firing pin, as ammunition is ignited by an electronic current. Lock time is virtually instantaneous. On-Off switch activates electronic system. Operates like a normal bolt action rifle. Stock design by Texas Silhouette Champion Mike Massey. Bull barrel.

MODEL 600/700
$985.00

SPECIFICATIONS
Calibers: 243 Rem., 308 Win., 270, 30-06
Overall length: 44″
Weight: 7 lbs.
Capacity: 3-shot magazine

Features: Drilled and tapped for scopes; double forward bolt lugs; silent safety; hammer swaged, chrome moly steel barrels
Model 620/720: Same specifications as 600/700 series except it features full stock style. **$899.00-$995.00**

MODEL 640 SUPER SNIPER
$1218.00

SPECIFICATIONS
Caliber: 308 Win. and 223 Rem.
Overall length: 44³/₄″
Weight: 9.4 lbs.
Capacity: 3-shot magazine

Features: Adjustable buttplate and cheekpiece; oversize bolt knob; match grade trigger w/trigger shoe; heavy barrel w/ military-style muzzle brake; drilled and tapped for scopes
Model 640: Standard sniper w/o adjustable cheekpiece. **$1015.00**

BRNO RIFLES

MODEL ZKK 600

MODEL ZKK 602

MODEL ZKK
SPECIFICATIONS

Model	Action Type	Cal.	Barrel Specifications			Overall Length	Weight	Magazine Capacity	Sighted In
			Length	Rifling Twist	#Lands				
ZKK 600	bolt	270 Win		1 in 10"	4			5	
		7×57	23.5 in	1 in 9"	4	44.0 in.	7 lbs. 2 oz.		110 yd.
		7×64		1 in 9"	4				
		30.06 Spring			4				
ZKK 601	bolt	223 Rem		1 in 12"	4			5	
		243 Win	23.5 in.	1 in 10"	4	43.0 in.	6 lbs. 13 oz.		110 yd.
		308 Win		1 in 12"	4				
ZKK 602	bolt	300 Win mag		1 in 10"	4			5	
		8×68		1 in 11"	4	45.5 in.	9 lb. 4 oz.		110 yd.
		375 H&H	25.0 in.	1 in 12"	4				
		458 Win mag		1 in 14"	4				

Prices:
Model ZKK 600 Standard $599.00
Model ZKK 601 Monte Carlo Stock 599.00
Model ZKK 602 Standard 639.00
Monte Carlo Stock 699.00

BROWNING LEVER ACTION RIFLES

MODEL 1885

MODEL 1885
$579.95

Calibers: 22-250; 223, 30-06, 270, 7mm Rem. Mag., 45-70 Govt. **Bolt system:** Falling block. **Barrel length:** 28″ (recessed muzzle). **Overall length:** 43¹/₂″. **Weight:** 8 lbs. 8 oz. **Action:** High wall type, single shot, lever action. **Sights:** Drilled and tapped for scope mounts; two-piece scope base available. **Hammer:** Exposed, serrated, three-position with inertia sear. **Stock and Forearm:** Select Walnut, straight grip stock and Schnabel forearm with cut checkering. Recoil pad standard.

BROWNING 92 (GRADE I)

Caliber: 357 Mag. **Action:** Lever operated with double verticle locks. Exposed 3 position hammer with half-cock position. Top ejection. **Receiver:** Forged and milled from high strength steel. **Barrel length:** 20″. Machined from forged, heat-treated billets of steel. Chambered and rifled for 357 Mag. and 44 Rem. Mag. caliber. Rifling twist 1 turn in 38″. **Sights:** Classic cloverleaf rear with notched elevation ramp. Steel post front. Sight radius 16⁵/₈″. **Trigger:** Gold plated. Trigger pull approximately 5¹/₂ lbs. **Magazine:** Tubular. Loading port in right side of receiver. Magazine capacity 11 rounds. **Stock and forearm:** Seasoned French walnut with high gloss finish. Straight grip stock and classic forearm style. Steel modified crescent butt plate.

Length of pull . . . . 12³/₄″
Drop at comb . . . . .2″
Drop at heel . . . . 2⁷/₈″
Overall length: 37¹/₂″. **Approximate weight:** 5¹/₂ lbs. **Receiver:** Hand-engraved scrollwork on both receiver sides.

Price $341.50

SPECIFICATIONS

Model	Calibers	Barrel Length	Sight Radius	Overall Length	Approximate Weight	Rate of Twist (R. Hand)
1886 Gr. I	45-70 Govt.	26″	22″	45″	9 lbs. 5 oz.	1 in 20″
1886 High Gr.	45-70 Govt.	26″	22″	45″	9 lbs. 5 oz.	1 in 20″
1885	.223 Rem.	28″	—	43¹/₂″	8 lbs. 13 oz.	1 in 12″
1885	22-250 Rem.	28″	—	43¹/₂″	8 lbs. 13 oz.	1 in 14″
1885	270 Win.	28″	—	43¹/₂″	8 lbs. 12 oz.	1 in 10″
1885	30-06 Sprg.	28″	—	43¹/₂″	8 lbs. 13 oz.	1 in 14″
1885	7mm Rem. Mag.	28″	—	43¹/₂″	8 lbs. 11 oz.	1 in 9¹/₂″
1885	45-70 Govt.	28″	21¹/₂″	43¹/₂″	8 lbs. 14 oz.	1 in 20″
'81 BLR	222 Rem.	20″	17³/₄″	39³/₄″	6 lbs. 15 oz.	1 in 14″
'81 BLR	223 Rem.	20″	17³/₄″	39³/₄″	6 lbs. 15 oz.	1 in 12″
'81 BLR	22-250 Rem.	20″	17³/₄″	39³/₄″	6 lbs. 15 oz.	1 in 14″
'81 BLR	243 Win.	20″	17³/₄″	39³/₄″	7 lbs. 2 oz.	1 in 10″
'81 BLR	257 Roberts	20″	17³/₄″	39³/₄″	7 lbs.	1 in 9¹/₂″
'81 BLR	7mm-08 Rem.	20″	17³/₄″	39³/₄″	7 lbs.	1 in 9¹/₂″
'81 BLR	308 Win.	20″	17³/₄″	39³/₄″	7 lbs.	1 in 12″
'81 BLR	258 Win.	20″	17³/₄″	39³/₄″	6 lbs. 14 oz.	1 in 12″
B-92	357 Magnum	20″	16⁵/₈″	37¹/₂″	6 lbs. 6 oz.	1 in 18³/₄″

BROWNING RIFLES

**MODEL 71
GRADE I CARBINE**

**MODEL 71
HIGH GRADE CARBINE**

SPECIFICATIONS

Caliber: 348 Win. **Barrel length:** 20″ (carbine) and 24″ (rifle). **Overall length:** 41″ (carbine) and 45″ (rifle). **Weight:** 8 lbs. (carbine) and 8 lbs. 2 oz. (rifle). **Sight radius:** 16³/₄″ (carbine) and 22″ (rifle). **Rate of twist:** (right hand): 1 in 12″. **Stock dimensions:** length of pull 13³/₈″; drop at comb 1⁷/₈″; drop at heel 2¹/₂″. **Stock and forearm:** Select walnut, full pistol grip stock with classic style forearm, straight metal buttplate.

Grade I has satin finish stock. High Grade has gloss finish with cut checkering. **Receiver and barrel:** round tapered barrels. Grade I blued on all metal surfaces. High Grade has blued barrel and hammer, gray steel receiver.

Grade I Carbine **$599.95**
High Grade Carbine and Rifle **979.95**

MODEL 81 BLR RIFLE

MODEL 81 BLR SPECIFICATIONS

Calibers: 222 Rem., 223 Rem. 22-250 Rem., 243 Win., 257 Roberts, 7mm-08 Rem., 308 Win. and 358 Win. **Approximate Weight:** 6 lbs. 15 oz. **Overall length:** 39³/₄″. **Action:** Lever action with rotating head, multiple lug breech bolt with recessed bolt face. Side ejection. **Barrel length:** 20″. Individually machined from forged, heat treated chrome-moly steel; crowned muzzle. **Rifling:** 243 Win., one turn in 10″; 308 and 358 Win., one turn in 12″. **Magazine:** Detachable, 4-round capacity. **Trigger:** Wide, grooved finger piece. Short crisp pull of 4¹/₂ pounds. Travels with lever. **Receiver:** Non-glare top. Drilled and tapped to accept most top scope mounts. Forged and milled steel. All parts are machine-finished and hand-fitted. Surface deeply polished. **Sights:** Low profile, square notch, screw adjustable rear sight. Gold bead on a hooded

raised ramp front sight. Sight radius: 17³/₄″. **Safety:** Exposed, 3-position hammer. Trigger disconnect system. Inertia firing pin. **Stock and forearm:** Select walnut with tough oil finish and sure-grip checkering, contoured for use with either open sights or scope. Straight grip stock. Deluxe recoil pad installed.
Length of pull . . . . 13³/₄″
Drop at comb . . . . 1³/₄″
Drop at heel . . . . 2³/₈″
Accessories: Extra magazines are available as well as sling swivel attachment for forearm bolt and butt-stock eyelet for sling mounting **$25.50**

Price (all calibers) **$449.95**

BROWNING RIFLES

MODEL BL-22 LEVER ACTION RIFLE: GRADE I

MODEL BL-22 LEVER ACTION RIFLE: GRADE II

MODEL BL-22 SPECIFICATIONS

Action: Short throw lever action. Lever travels through an arc of only 33 degrees and carries the trigger with it, preventing finger pinch between lever and trigger on the upward swing. The lever cycle ejects the fired shell, cocks the hammer and feeds a fresh round into the chamber. **Magazine:** Rifle is designed to handle 22 caliber ammunition *in any combination* from tubular magazine. Magazine capacity is 15 Long Rifles, 17 Longs and 22 Shorts. The positive magazine latch opens and closes easily from any position. **Safety:** A unique disconnect system prevents firing until the lever and breech are fully closed and pressure is released from and reapplied to the trigger. An inertia firing pin and an exposed hammer with a half-cock position are other safety features. **Receiver:** Forged and milled steel. Grooved. All parts are machine-finished and hand-fitted. **Trigger:** Clean and crisp without creep. Average pull 5 pounds. Trigger gold-plated on Grade II model. **Stock and forearm:** Forearm and straight grip butt stock are shaped from select, polished walnut. Hand checkered on Grade II model. Stock dimensions:

Length of Pull	13 1/2"
Drop at Comb	1 5/8"
Drop at Heel	2 1/4"

Sights: Precision, adjustable folding leaf rear sight. Raised bead front sight. **Scopes:** Grooved receiver will accept the Browning 22 riflescope (Model 1217) and two-piece ring mount (Model 9417) as well as most other groove or tip-off type mounts or receiver sights. **Engraving:** Grade II receiver and trigger guard are engraved with tasteful scroll designs. **Barrel length:** 20"; recessed muzzle. **Overall length:** 36 3/4". **Weight:** 5 pounds

Price:	Grade I	$277.95
	Grade II	317.95

MODEL A-BOLT 22 BOLT ACTION
$299.95

Caliber: 22 LR. **Barrel length:** 22". **Overall length:** 40 1/4". **Average weight:** 5 lbs. 9 oz. **Action:** Short throw bolt. Bolt cycles a round with 60° of bolt rotation. Firing pin acts as secondary extractor and ejector, snapping out fired rounds at prescribed speed. **Magazine:** Five and 15-shot magazine standard. Magazine/clip ejects with a push on magazine latch button. **Trigger:** Gold colored, screw adjustable. Pre-set at approx. 4 lbs. **Stock:** Laminated walnut, classic style with pistol grip. **Length of pull:** 13 3/4". **Drop at comb:** 3/4". **Drop at heel:** 1 1/2". **Sights:** Available with or without sights (add **$10** for sights). Ramp front and adjustable folding leaf rear on open sight model. **Scopes:** Grooved receiver for 22 mount. Drilled and tapped for full size scope mounts.

SPECIFICATIONS RIMFIRE RIFLES

Model	Caliber	Barrel Length	Sight Radius	Overall Length	Average Weight
A-Bolt 22	22 Long Rifle	22"	17 5/8"	40 1/4"	5 lbs. 9 oz.
22 Semi-Auto	22 Long Rifle	19 1/4"	16 1/4"	37"	4 lbs. 4 oz.
BL-22	22 Long Rifle, Longs, Shorts	20"	15 3/8"	36 3/4"	5 lbs.

BROWNING RIFLES

Standard Calibers (Grade I): $574.95
Magnum Calibers (Grade I): 634.95
North American Deer Issue: 3550.00

BAR SEMIAUTOMATIC RIFLE

SPECIFICATIONS

Model	Calibers	Barrel Length	Sight Radius*	Overall Length	Average Weight	Rate of Twist (Right Hand)
Standard	30-06 Sprg.	22″	17½″	43″	7 lbs. 6 oz.	1 in 10″
Standard	270 Win.	22″	17½″	43″	7 lbs. 9 oz.	1 in 10″
Standard	308 Win.	22″	17½″	43″	7 lbs. 9 oz.	1 in 12″
Standard	243 Win.	22″	17½″	43″	7 lbs. 10 oz.	1 in 10″
Magnum	7mm Rem. Mag.	24″	19½″	45″	8 lbs. 6 oz.	1 in 9½″
Magnum	300 Win. Mag.	24″	19½″	45″	8 lbs. 6 oz.	1 in 10″
Big Game Series Ltd. Edition	30-06 Sprg.	22″	17½″	43″	7 lbs. 6 oz.	1 in 10″

*Sights standard on Grade I only.

A-BOLT BOLT ACTION RIFLE

Calibers: 25-06 Rem., 270 Win., 280 Rem., 30-06 Sprg., 7mm Rem. Mag., 300 Win. Mag., 338 Win. Mag. **Action:** Short throw bolt of 60 degrees. Plunger-type ejector. **Magazine:** Detachable. Depress the magazine latch and the hinged floorplate swings down. The magazine can be removed from the floorplate for reloading or safety reasons. **Trigger:** Adjustable within the average range of 3 to 6 pounds. Also grooved to provide sure finger control. **Stock and forearm:** Stock is select grade American walnut cut to the lines of a classic sporter with a full pistol grip. Stock dimensions:

Length of Pull . . . . 13⅝″
Drop at Comb . . . . ¾″
Drop at Heel . . . . 1⅛″

Scopes: Closed. Clean tapered barrel. Receiver is drilled and tapped for a scope mount; or select **Hunter** model w/open sights. **Barrel length:** 24″. Hammer forged rifling where a precision machined mandrel is inserted into the bore. The mandrel is a reproduction of the rifling in reverse. As hammer forces are applied to the exterior of the barrel, the barrel is actually molded around the mandrel to produce flawless rifling and to guarantee a straight bore. Free floated. **Overall length:** 44¼″. **Weight:** 7 lbs. 8 oz. in Magnum; 6 lbs. 8 oz. in Short Action; 7 lbs. in Standard (Long Action).

Hunter	**$399.95**
Hunter w/open sights	449.95
Medallion	464.95
Left Hand Model	484.95
Stainless Stalker (no sights)	509.95
Camo Stalker (no sights)	424.95

Short Action A-Bolt available in 223 Rem., 22-250 Rem., 243 Win., 257 Roberts, 7mm-08 Rem., 308 Win.

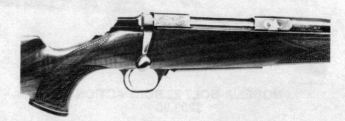

A-BOLT HIGH GRADE BOLT ACTION RIFLE
BIG HORN SHEEP LIMITED EDITION
$1365.00

Calibers: 270. Win. **Barrel length:** 22″. **Overall length:** 42¾″. **Approx. weight:** 6 lbs. 11 oz. **Stock:** High grade walnut profiled in classic style, embellished with cut skipline checkering with pearl border design. Rosewood forearm and grip caps. Brass spacers between stock and forearm and grip caps; also between recoil pad and stock. **Engraving:** Deep relief engraving on receiver, barrel, floorplate and trigger guard as setting for game species displayed in 24K gold. **Pronghorn Antelope Issue** (243 Win.): **$1240.00**

CHURCHILL RIFLES

The Churchill® bolt action centerfire rifles feature spoonbill shaped bolt handles and top grade European walnut stock with hand rubbed oil finish. Can be ordered with or without deluxe sights and are available in several calibers. The Regent is made from deluxe extra select European Walnut with 23-line hand cut checkering. Monte Carlo comb and cheekpiece included. The Highlander is made from standard grade European Walnut with hand cut checkering. The stock is a classic design with an oil finish.

Action: Bolt Action repeating
Receiver: Machined from solid block of forged high strength steel with hinged floorplate
Bolt: Machined forged steel with twin locking lugs and one large gas relief port
Barrel: Cold hammer forged steel
Safety: Positive non-slip thumb type on right side; locks trigger but allows bolt to be safely opened for unloading and inspection of the chamber
Stock: Select European Walnut with hand checkering and oil rubbed finish; swivel posts; recoil pad
Sights: Streamlined, contoured ramp; front gold bead; rear sight fully adjustable for windage and elevation

REGENT

SPECIFICATIONS

	Caliber	Overall length	Barrel length	Nominal weight	Magazine capacity	Price*
Highlander	.25-06 Rem.	42.5″	22″	7.5 lbs.	4 rds	$312.00
	.270 Win.	42.5″	22″	7.5 lbs.	4 rds	312.00
	.30-06 Spfd.	42.5″	22″	7.5 lbs.	4 rds	312.00
	7mm Rem. Mag.	44.5″	24″	8 lbs.	3 rds	312.00
Regent	.25-06 Rem.	42.5″	22″	7.5 lbs.	4 rds	514.00
	.270 Win.	42.5″	22″	7.5 lbs.	4 rds	514.00
	.30-06 Spfd.	42.5″	22″	7.5 lbs.	4 rds	514.00
	7mm Rem. Mag.	44.5″	24″	8 lbs.	3 rds	514.00

*Add $23.00 for sights

COLT SAUER HIGH POWER RIFLES

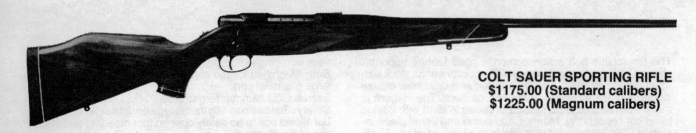

COLT SAUER SPORTING RIFLE
$1175.00 (Standard calibers)
$1225.00 (Magnum calibers)

Caliber: 25-06, 270, 30-06, 7mm Rem. Mag., 300 Win. Mag., 300 Weatherby Mag.
Capacity: 3 round with detachable magazines
Barrel length: 24″
Weight: Standard, 8 lb.; Mag., 8 lbs. 10 oz.
Overall length: 43³/₄″
Sights: Drilled and tapped for scope mounts
Action: Bolt action

Safety: Tang-type safety that mechanically locks the sear
Stock: American walnut, cast-off Monte Carlo design with cheekpiece; forend tip and pistol-grip cap are rosewood with white line spacers, hand-checkering and black recoil pad
Features: Unique barrel/receiver union, non-rotating bolt with 3 internal articulating locking lugs

COLT SAUER SHORT ACTION
$1175.00

Caliber: 243
Barrel length: 24″; Krupp Special Steel, hammer forged
Overall length: 43³/₄″
Stock: American walnut, Monte Carlo cheekpiece with rosewood forend tip and pistol grip cap
Weight (empty): 7 lbs. 8 oz.
Safety: Tang
Sights: Drilled and tapped for scope mounts

Magazine capacity: 3 rounds in detachable magazine
Finish: Colt Blue with polyurethane
Features: Features the same revolutionary non-rotating bolt with three large locking lugs. American walnut stock with high-gloss finish, 18-line-per-inch checkering, rosewood forend tip and grip cap, black recoil pad. Cocking indicator, loaded chamber indicator, and Safety-on bolt opening capability

COLT SAUER SAFARI
$1675.00

Caliber: 458 Win. Mag.
Capacity: 3 rounds with detachable magazines
Barrel length: 24″ round tapered
Weight: 10 lbs. without sights
Overall length: 44¹/₂″
Sights: Hooded ramp-style front; fully adjustable rear
Action: Bolt action

Safety: Tang type that mechanically locks the sear
Stock: Solid African bubinga wood, cast-off Monte Carlo design with cheekpiece, contrasting rosewood, forend tip and pistol-grip cap with white line spacers, and checkering on the forend and pistol grip
Features: Unique barrel/receiver union, non-rotating bolt with 3 internal articulating locking lugs

HECKLER & KOCH RIFLES

SEMIAUTOMATIC VARMINT RIFLES MODEL HK 300

The Model HK 300 features a European walnut checkered stock. All metal parts are finished in a high-luster custom blue. The receiver is fitted with special bases for HK 05 quick snap-on clamp mount with 1-inch rings that will fit all standard scopes. The positive locking action of the HK 05 provides for instant scope mounting with no change in zero, even after hundreds of repetitions. The rifle has a V-notch rear sight, adjustable for windage, and a front sight adjustable for elevation. Scope mounts are available as an additional accessory.

Caliber: 22 Winchester Magnum
Weight: 5.7 lbs.
Barrel length: 19.7″ (all-steel hammer forged, polygonal profile)
Overall length: 39.4″
Magazine: Box type; 5- and 15-round capacity
Sights: V-notch rear, adjustable for windage; post front, adjustable for elevation
Trigger: Single stage, 3½ lb. pull
Action: Straight blow-back inertia bolt
Stock: Top-grade European walnut, checkered pistol grip and forearm
Price: $426.00
HK-300 Package (includes 5-round magazine, B-Square mount and rings, Leupold 3×9 compact scope. . . 689.00

HEYM RIFLES

SAFETY MODEL 22S SHOTGUN/RIFLE
$1800.00

The Model 22S offers a special break-open action in which the cocking is accomplished by manually pushing forward a cocking slide located on the tang. For ultimate safety, the gun will automatically uncock by means of a built-in rocker weight if it is dropped or jostled about.
The Model 22S comes with single-set trigger, left-side barrel selector, arabesque engraving, walnut stock and an integral dovetail base for scope mounting.

SPECIFICATIONS
Shotgun barrels: 12 ga., 2¾″, 16 ga., 2¾″; 20 ga., 2¾″ and 3″. **Rifle barrels:** 22 Mag., 22 Hornet; 222 Rem.; 222 Rem. Mag.; 5.6 × 50 R Mag.; 6.5 × 57 R; 7 × 57 R; 243 Win. **Barrel length:** 24″. **Length of pull:** 14½″. **Overall length:** 40″.
Model 22SZ: Same as above, take-down model: . . $198.00 **additional**

MODEL 55BF O/U DOUBLE RIFLE (not shown)
$3950.00

This German-crafted shotgun/rifle combo features special corrosion-resistant chrome-molybdenum steel modified. Anson & Deeley action with standing sears. The barrels, of precision-forged Krupp Special Barrel Steel, are hand-polished and cold rust blued to a deep black satin finish. Oil-finished walnut stock comes with long pistol grip, German cheek-piece, slight hump back and handcut checkering. Leaf scroll is hand-engraved.

Interchangeable barrels are available:
Model 55BFW O/U Shotgun Rifle combo: $2250.00
Model 55BW O/U Rifle. 3250.00
Model 55FW O/U Shotgun w/ejectors 2250.00

SPECIFICATIONS
Shotgun barrels: 12 ga., 2¾″; 16 ga., 2¾″; 20 ga., 2¾″ and 3″. **Rifle barrels:** 5.6 × 50 R Mag; 6.5 × 57 R; 7 × 57 R; 7 × 65 R; 243 Win.; 308 Win.; 30-06 and others. **Barrel length:** 25″. **Length of pull:** 14½″. **Overlength length:** 42″. **Weight:** about 6¾ lbs.

HEYM RIFLES

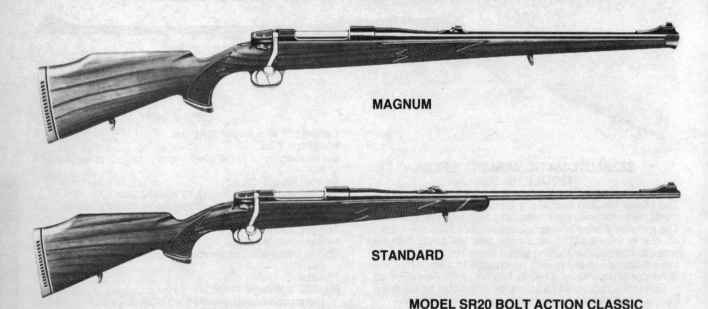

MAGNUM

STANDARD

MODEL SR20 BOLT ACTION CLASSIC

Features two rugged Mauser-type locking lugs. A special guide rail allows the bolt to operate smoothly through the full length of travel. All parts are interchangeable. The magazine holds five regular or three Magnum cartridges. A hinged floorplate with convenient latch makes unloading easy. **A full selection of a left-hand version is available.**

SPECIFICATIONS
Calibers: (Standard) 243 Win., 270 Win., 308 Win., 30-06; (Magnum) 7mm Rem. Mag., 300 Win. Mag., 375 H&H Mag., plus metric calibers.
Barrel length: 24″ (Standard) and 25″ (Magnum)
Length of pull: 14″
Weight: (Standard) 7 lb. 10 oz.; (Magnum) 8 lbs.
Stock: French walnut, hand checkering, Pachmayr Old English pad, oil finish, steel grip cap
Prices:
Model SR20 (Standard) $1125.00
   Left Hand version. 1290.00
Model SR20 (Magnum) 1150.00
   Left Hand version. 1340.00
Single set trigger for all models 75.00

MODEL SR20 CLASSIC

Features a hand-checkered, oil-finished stock, all-steel bottom metal with straddled floorplate and inside release, plus steel grip cap. Other specifications same as Model SR20.

Prices:
Model SR20 Classic Sporter $1125.00
Model SR20 Classic Magnum Sporter 1175.00
Model SR20 Classic Left Hand Sporter 1290.00
Model SR20 Classic Left Hand Magnum
   Sporter 1340.00
Custom open sights 350.00

HEYM RIFLES

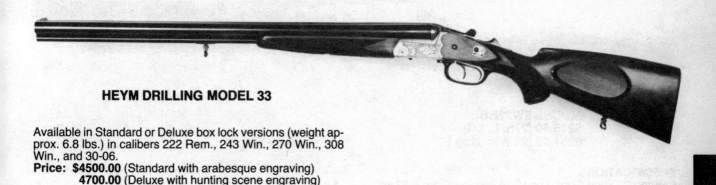

HEYM DRILLING MODEL 33

Available in Standard or Deluxe box lock versions (weight approx. 6.8 lbs.) in calibers 222 Rem., 243 Win., 270 Win., 308 Win., and 30-06.
Price: **$4500.00** (Standard with arabesque engraving)
            4700.00 (Deluxe with hunting scene engraving)

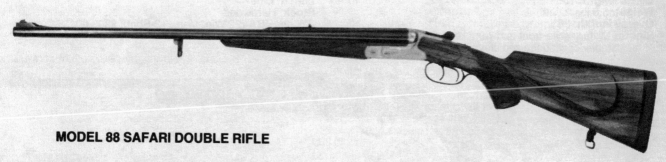

HEYM DRILLING MODEL 37

Available in same calibers as Model 33. Side lock models weigh approx. 8 lbs.
Price: **$6850.00** (Standard with border engraving)
            8200.00 (Deluxe with hunting scene engraving)

MODEL 88 SAFARI DOUBLE RIFLE

This German-built box lock model has a modified Anson & Deeley action with standing sears, plus Purdey-type double underlocking lugs and Greener extension with crossbolt. Actions are furnished with sliding safeties and cocking indicators on the top tang, nonbreakable coil springs, front single set triggers and steel trigger guards.

SPECIFICATIONS
Calibers: 375 H&H, 458 Winchester, 470 Nitro Express
Barrel length: 25″
Overall length: 42″

Weight: 10 lbs. (approx.)
Sights: Three leaf express sight with standing, shallow V-sight; large gold bead front sight

Prices:
Model 88 Safari in 375 H&H and 458 Win. **$7000.00**
            Same model in 470 Nitro Express 7600.00
Also available:
Model 88 B (Box lock w/ejectors in calibers 300 Win. Mag., 30-06, and 375 H&H Mag.) **$6800.00**
Model 88 B SS (Sidelock w/ejectors) 9900.00

IVER JOHNSON RIFLES

MODEL EW22HBL
$215.00 (22S, L, LR)
$231.00 (22 Win. Mag.)

SPECIFICATIONS
Caliber: 22 Short, Long, Long Rifle (also available in 22 Win. Mag.)
Barrel length: 18½"
Weight: 5¾ lbs.
Overall length: 36½"

Sights: Hooded ramp front; adjustable rear
Capacity: 21 Short, 17 Long, or 15 Long Rifle; can be mixed and loaded simultaneously; Magnum has 12-shot capacity
Finish: Blue
Stock: Hardwood

CARBINE MODEL EW22HBA
$183.00

SPECIFICATIONS
Caliber: 22LR
Barrel length: 18½"
Weight: 5.8 lbs.
Overall length: 38"
Sights: Military-style front and rear; rear sight is peep-type adjustable for windage and elevation

Capacity: 15 rounds
Finish: Blue
Stock: Hardwood
EW22MHBA (22 Win. Mag., 12-Shot): $303.00

L'IL CHAMP SINGLE SHOT
$89.00

SPECIFICATIONS
Caliber: 22 S, L & LR
Barrel length: 16¼"
Overall length: 32½"
Weight: 2 lbs. 11 oz.
Finish: Molded stock; nickel-plated bolt

K.D.F./VOERE RIFLES

VOERE TITAN
$899.00 (Standard)
949.00 (Magnum)

The Voere Titan is the same rifle as K.D.F.'s K-15 (or Klein-guenther) rifles of the past. The only difference is in the bedding. The Voere factory in West Germany uses a system in which a hardwood dowl pin is inserted into the stock to support the main tang screw. This allows the main screw to be tightened more firmly without putting pressure on the cross-grain of the stock itself. Features oil finished, hand checkered European walnut stock with recoil pad and quick disconnect sling swivels. **Calibers:** .243, 25-06, 7 × 57, 270, 308, and 30-06. **Magnum Calibers** include 7mm Rem., 257 Weath., 270 Weath., 308 Norma, 300 Win., and 300 Weath., and 375 H&H.

VOERE TITAN MENOR BOLT ACTION
$699.00 (without sights)

SPECIFICATIONS
Calibers: 222 Rem., 223 Rem. **Barrel length:** 23½". **Overall length:** 42". **Weight:** 6½ lbs. **Magazine capacity:** 4 rounds. Also available: **Titan Menor Match Single Shot** . . . $799.00

K.D.F. RIFLES

MODEL K-15 IMPROVED
$1200.00 ($1250.00 in Magnum)

SPECIFICATIONS

Caliber(s): 243; 25-06; 270; 7X57; 30-06; 308 Win.; 308 Norma; 300 Win. Mag.; 7mm Reg. Mag.; 375 H and H Mag, 270 Weatherby Mag.: 300 Weatherby Mag.; 257 Weatherby Mag. Other calibers available on special request. **Barrel length:** Standard, 24"; Magnum, 26". **Magazine capacity:** Standard, 4 cartridges; Magnum, 3 cartridges. **Trigger pull:** 13⁷/₈". **Overall length:** Standard, 44⁷/₈"; Magnum, 46⁷/₈". **Overall weight:** Approx. 8 lbs.

Shortest ignition time: Striker travels only 158-thousands of an inch. The extremely light striker is accelerated by a powerful striker spring . . . A patented two cocking cam design enables a very light and smooth cocking of the striker assembly . . . Two-piece firing pin.

Clip feature: Removable; can also be fed from top.

3 locking lugs: With large contact area . . . also Stellite locking insert.

60-Degree bolt lift only: For fast reloading.

Safety: Located on right-hand side . . . locking trigger and sear . . . Most convenient location.

Fine adjustable crisp trigger: 2¹/₂ lbs. to 7 lbs. . . . Two major moving parts only.

Stocks: American or European Walnut stocks with 1-inch recoil pad . . . Rosewood pistol grip cap . . . 20-line hand-checkering . . . Quick detachable swivels . . . Barrel is free floating . . . Oil finish . . . Available in right- or left-hand stocks . . . AAA grade stocks available. Monte Carlo style is standard. Classic, featherweight, thumbhole and competition style stocks available.

Receiver drilled and tapped for scope mounts:

Options: Iron sights . . . Set trigger . . . Recoil arrestor . . . KDF offers own bases to take 1" or 30mm rings.

Now available: .411 KDF Magnum Dangerous Game Rifle. Choice of iron sights or scope mounts and rings; also choice of finish. KDF recoil arrester included. Guaranteed to shoot 3 shots in ¹/₂" and 5 shots within 1" at 100 yards with proper loads. **Price: $1800.**

MODEL K-22 BOLT ACTION (22LR)
$325.00 (Standard)
475.00 (Deluxe)
525.00 (Magnum)

SPECIFICATIONS

Caliber: 22LR, 22 Mag.

Barrel length: 21.7"; chrome-Moly steel, 4 grooves, 4 lands

Action: two locking lugs w/large contact area 60° bolt lift

Overall length: 40"

Weight: 6.6 lbs.

Receiver: two rails for scope mounting; scope mounts available from K.D.F.

Stock: Beechwood, hand checkered, sling swivels, walnut stain, oil finish (Standard); European walnut, hand checkered, Rosewood forend; sling swivels, oil finish (Deluxe)

KIMBER RIFLES

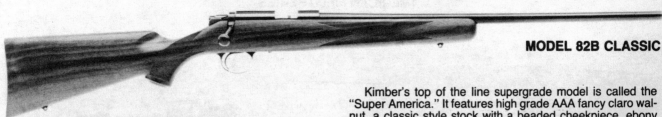

MODEL 82B CLASSIC

Kimber's top of the line supergrade model is called the "Super America." It features high grade AAA fancy claro walnut, a classic style stock with a beaded cheekpiece, ebony forend tip, 22 line per inch full coverage checkering, skeleton grip cap.

Prices (without sights):

Model 82 Classic, plain barrel **$750.00**
($795.00 in 22 Hornet and 22 WMR)
Model 82 Continental, plain barrel 850.00
($895.00 in 22 Hornet and 22 WMR)
Model 82 Custom Classic, plain barrel 995.00
($1040.00 in 22 Hornet and 22 WMR)
Additional feature: Iron sights fitted 55.00
Model 82 Super America 1150.00
($1195.00 in 22 WMR and 22 Hornet)
Model 82B Centennial 2950.00
Model 82B Super Continental 1465.00
($1510 in 22 WMR and 22 Hornet)

The Model 82 bolt-action sporter is available in calibers: 22 LR, 22 Hornet, .218 Bee & .25-20. The action is machined from solid steel and features a rear locking bolt with twin horizontally opposed locking lugs. The trigger is adjustable for pressure, overtravel and depth of sear engagement. The LR sporter is available with a 5- or 10-shot magazine; the Hornet a 3-shot flush fitting magazine; .218 & .25-20 are single shot. Special Kimber one-inch scope mount rings, machined from steel to fit the dovetailed receiver, are available in two heights. Also offered are open iron sights, hooded ramp front sight with bead and adjustable folding leaf rear sight.

Three stock styles are available: "Classic" style features a straight comb with no cheekpiece; "Cascade" style features a cheekpiece and Monte Carlo comb; and "Custom Classic" features fancy grade walnut, an ebony forend tip and Niedner-type butt plate.

MODEL 84 SPORTER (MINI-MAUSER)

The Kimber Model 84 bolt-action sporter is a small Mauser-style front-locking action designed for the .222 family of cartridges (.222 Rem., .223 Rem., .222 Rem. Mag., .221 Fireball, .17 Rem., 17 Mach IV, 5.6×50mm, 6×47, 6×45). It features a traditionally Mauser-type extractor claw, twin front locking lugs, a fully adjustable trigger and a steel-hinged floorplate and trigger guard. Magazine capacity is 5 rounds. The receiver is grooved to accept Kimber's one-inch steel scope mount rings.

Model 84 Classic, plain barrel **$885.00**
Model 84 Custom Classic, plain barrel 1130.00
Model 84 Super America 1285.00
Model 84 Continental (222 Rem. and 223 Rem. only) 985.00
Model 84 Super Continental (222 Rem. and 223 Rem. only) 1600.00

BIG GAME RIFLE

The design of this big bore centerfire bolt action sporting rifle draws on the famous breeching concepts of Paul Mauser. Its key features include the following: a receiver machined from solid chrome moly steel; integral bolt handle and bolt head; Mauser extractor; Model 70 override trigger design, 3-position safety, "inner collar" breeching concept for gas flow protection, ejector riding underneath left locking lug of bolt head; one-piece steel trigger guard and floor plate with positive locking of floorplate for heavy recoil protection; Model 84 style bolt stop.

Chambered for 270 Win., 280 Rem., 7mm Rem. Mag., 30-06, 338 Win. Mag., 300 Win. Mag. and 375 H&H Mag. Available in late summer of 1987 in Classic, Custom Classic and Super America models.

Prices:
Classic . . . . **$985.00** ($1185.00 in 375 H&H)
Custom Classic . . . . 1230.00 ($1430 in 375 H&H)
Super America . . . . 1385.00 ($1585 in 375 H&H

MARK X RIFLES

AMERICAN FIELD SERIES

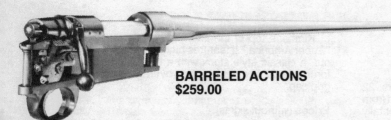

**BARRELED ACTIONS
$259.00**

Hand-fitted with premium hammer-forged barrels created from corrosion resistant chrome vanadium steel. Each barreled action is carefully proofed and marked under close government control, ready to drop into the stock of your choice.

Calibers: 22-250, 243, 25-06, 270, 7×57, 7mm Rem. Mag., 300 Win. Mag., 308, 30-06. **Barrel length:** 24". **Weight:** 5½ lbs. (5¾ lbs. in 22-250, 243, and 25-06). **Rifling twist:** 10 (14 in 22-250 and 9.5 in 7×57).

Also available in 375 H&H Mag. and 458 Win. Mag. Same barrel length but different weights 6 lbs. (375 H&H Mag.) and 5.75 lbs. (458 Win. Mag.). **Rifling twist:** 12 (375 H&H Mag.) and 14 (458 Win. Mag.). **Price: $339.00**

MAUSER SYSTEM ACTIONS
$199.00

Type A: 7×57mm to 30-06. Standard magazine (3⅜") and bolt face (.470"). **$199.00**
Type B: 22-250 to 308. Short magazine (2⅞"); standard bolt face. **$199.00**
Type C: 7mm Rem. Mag. to 458 Win. Mag. Standard magazine and Magnum bolt face (.532"). **$199.00**
Also available:
Type D: 300 Win. Mag. to 375 H&H. Magnum magazine (3¹¹/₁₆") and Magnum bolt face. **Price: $229.00**
Single Shot Action: $179.00
Mini-Mark X (.17 to .223): **$189.00**

AMERICAN FIELD SPORTING RIFLE SERIES
$499.00

Features forged and machined Mauser System actions . . . Hammer-forged, chrome-vanadium steel barrels . . . Drilled and tapped for scope mounts and receiver sights . . . Hooded ramp front and fully adjustable rear sight . . . All-steel button release magazine floor plate . . . Detachable sling swivels . . . Silent sliding thumb safety . . . Prime European walnut stocks . . . Sculpted, low-profile cheekpiece . . . Rubber recoil butt plate . . . Steel grip cap.

Calibers: 22-250, 243 Win., 25-06, 270 Win., 7×57, 308 Win., 30-06, 7mm Rem. Mag., 300 Win. Mag. **Barrel length:** 24". **Overall length:** 44". **Weight:** 7 lbs. **Capacity:** 5 rounds.

MINIATURE ACTION MARK X
$499.00

The miniature Mark X mauser system rifle features the proven mauser action scaled down to handle the high velocity .223 caliber
SPECIFICATIONS:
Caliber: 223
Capacity: 5 rounds
Barrel length: 20"
Overall length: 39¾"
Weight: 6.35 lbs.
Twist: 1 turn in 10"

MARLIN LEVER ACTION CARBINES

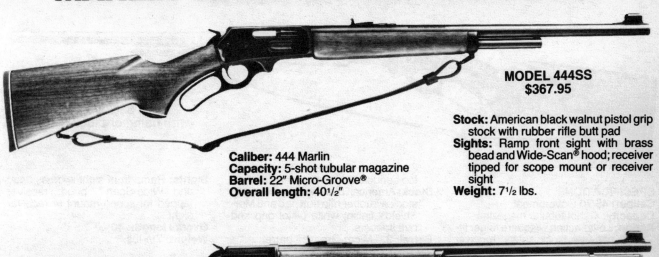

MODEL 444SS
$367.95

Caliber: 444 Marlin
Capacity: 5-shot tubular magazine
Barrel: 22" Micro-Groove®
Overall length: 40½"

Stock: American black walnut pistol grip stock with rubber rifle butt pad
Sights: Ramp front sight with brass bead and Wide-Scan® hood; receiver tipped for scope mount or receiver sight
Weight: 7½ lbs.

MARLIN GOLDEN 39A
$303.95

The Marlin lever-action 22 is the oldest (since 1891) shoulder gun still being manufactured.
Solid Receiver Top. You can easily mount a scope on your Marlin 39 by screwing on the machined scope adapter base provided. The screw-on base is a neater, more versatile method of mounting a scope on a 22 sporting rifle. The solid top receiver and scope adapter base provide a maximum in eye relief adjustment. If you prefer iron sights, you'll find the 39 receiver clean, flat and sandblasted to prevent glare.

Exclusive brass magazine tube.
Micro-Groove® Barrel. Marlin's famous rifling system of multi-grooving has consistently produced fine accuracy because the system grips the bullet more securely, minimizes distortion, and provides a better gas seal.

And the Model 39 maximizes accuracy with the heaviest barrels available on any lever-action 22.

SPECIFICATIONS
Caliber: 22 Short, Long and Long Rifle
Capacity: Tubular magazine holds 26 Short, 21 Long and 19 Long Rifle Cartridges
Action: Lever action; solid top receiver; side ejection; one-step takedown; deeply blued metal surfaces; re-

ceiver top sandblasted to prevent glare
Stock: Two-piece genuine American black walnut with fluted comb; full pistol grip and forend; blued-steel forend cap; sling swivels; grip cap; white butt plate and pistol-grip spacers; tough Mar-Shield® finish
Barrel: 24" with Micro-Groove® rifling (16 grooves)
Sights: Adjustable folding semi-buckhorn rear, ramp front sight with new Wide-Scan™ hood; solid top receiver tapped for scope mount or receiver sight; scope adapter base; offset hammer spur for scope use—works right or left
Overall length: 40"
Weight: About 6½ lbs.

MARLIN GOLDEN 39M
$303.95 (scope not included)

SPECIFICATIONS
Caliber: 22 Short, Long and Long Rifle
Capacity: Tubular magazine holds 21 Short, 16 Long or 15 Long Rifle cartridges
Action: Lever action with square finger lever; solid top receiver; side ejection; one-step takedown; deeply

blued-metal surfaces; receiver top sandblasted to prevent glare
Stock: Two-piece straight-grip genuine American black walnut with full forend; blued steel forend cap; sling swivels; white butt plate spacer; tough Mar-Shield® finish
Barrel: 20" with Micro-Groove® rifling (16 grooves)

Sights: Adjustable folding semi-buckhorn rear, ramp front sight and new Wide-Scan™ hood; solid top receiver tapped for scope mount or receiver sight; scope adapter base; offset hammer spur for scope use—works right or left
Overall length: 36"
Weight: About 6 lbs.

MARLIN LEVER ACTION CARBINES

MARLIN 1895SS
$367.95
(with hammer block safety)

SPECIFICATIONS
Caliber: 45/70 Government
Capacity: 4-shot tubular magazine
Action: Lever action w/square finger lever; hammer block safety; receiver top sandblasted to prevent glare
Stock: American black walnut pistol grip stock w/rubber rifle butt pad and Mar-Shield® finish; white pistol grip and butt spacers
Barrel: 22″ Micro-Groove® barrel

Sights: Ramp front sight w/brass bead and Wide-Scan™ hood; receiver tapped for scope mount or receiver sight
Overall length: 40½″
Weight: 7½ lbs.

MARLIN 1894S
$340.95
(with hammer block safety)

SPECIFICATIONS
Caliber : 44 Rem. Mag., 44 Special
Capacity: 10-shot tubular magazine
Action: Lever action w/square finger lever; hammer block safety

Stock: American black walnut stock w/ Mar-Shield™ finish; blued steel for-end cap
Barrel: 20″ Micro-Groove® barrel
Sights: Ramp front sight w/brass bead and Wide-Scan® hood; solid top receiver tapped for scope mount or receiver sight
Overall length: 37½″
Weight: 6 lbs.

MARLIN 1894CS 357 MAGNUM
$340.95

SPECIFICATIONS
Caliber: 357 Magnum, 38 Special
Capacity: 9-shot tubular magazine
Action: Lever action w/square finger lever; hammer block safety; side ejection; solid top receiver; deeply blued metal surfaces; receiver top sandblasted to prevent glare
Stock: Straight-grip two-piece genuine American black walnut with white butt plate spacer; tough Mar-Shield® finish.
Barrel: 18½″ long with modified Micro-Groove® rifling (12 grooves)

Sights: Adjustable semi-buckhorn folding rear, bead front; solid top receiver tapped for scope mount or receiver sight; offset hammer spur for scope use—adjustable for right- or left-hand use
Overall length: 36″
Weight: 6 lbs.

MARLIN LEVER ACTION CARBINES

MARLIN 336CS
(with hammer block safety)
$313.95 (scope not included)

SPECIFICATIONS
Caliber: 30/30 Win., 35 Rem.
Capacity: 6-shot tubular magazine
Action: Lever action w/hammer block safety; deeply blued metal surfaces; receiver top sandblasted to prevent glare
Stock: American black walnut pistol grip stock w/fluted comb and Mar-Shield® finish; deeply blued metal surfaces
Barrel: 20″ Micro-Groove® barrel
Sights: Adjustable folding semi-buckhorn rear; ramp front sight w/brass bead and removable Wide-Scan™ hood; tapped for receiver sight and scope mount; offset hammer spur for scope use (works right or left)
Overall length: 38¹/₂″
Weight: 7 lbs.

MARLIN 336TS
(with hammer block safety)
$313.95

SPECIFICATIONS
Caliber: 30/30 Win.
Capacity: 6-shot tubular magazine
Action: Lever action w/hammer block safety; deeply blued metal surfaces; receiver top sandblasted to prevent glare
Stock: American black walnut pistol grip stock w/fluted comb and Mar-Shield® finish; deeply blued metal surfaces
Sights: Adjustable folding semi-buckhorn rear; ramp front sight w/brass bead and removable Wide-Scan™ hood; tapped for receiver sight and scope mount; offset hammer spur for scope use (works right or left)
Barrel: 18¹/₂″ Micro-Groove® barrel
Overall length: 37″
Weight: 6¹/₂ lbs.

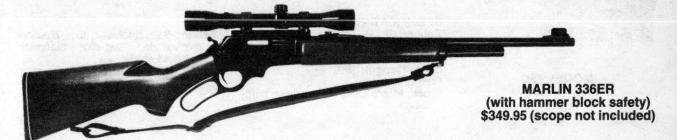

MARLIN 336ER
(with hammer block safety)
$349.95 (scope not included)

SPECIFICATIONS
Caliber: 356 Win.
Capacity: 5-shot tubular magazine
Action: Lever action w/hammer block safety; deeply blued metal surfaces; receiver top sandblasted to prevent glare
Stock: American black walnut pistol grip stock w/fluted comb and Mar-Shield® finish; deeply blued metal surfaces
Sights: Adjustable folding semi-buckhorn rear; ramp front sight w/brass bead and removable Wide-Scan™ hood; tapped for receiver sight and scope mount; offset hammer spur for scope use (works right or left)
Barrel: 20″ Micro-Groove® barrel
Overall length: 38¹/₂″
Weight: Approx. 6¹/₄ lbs.

RIFLES

MARLIN RIFLES

MODEL 30AS
$261.95

SPECIFICATIONS
Caliber : 30/30
Capacity: 6-shot tubular magazine
Action: Lever action w/hammer block safety; solid top receiver w/side ejection
Stock: Walnut finish hardwood stock w/ pistol grip

Sights: Tapped for scope mount and receiver sight; also available in combination w/4x, 32mm, 1″ scope
Barrel: 20″ Micro-Groove® barrel
Overall length: 38¼″
Weight: Approx. 7 lbs.

MARLIN 60
$111.95 (scope not included)

SPECIFICATIONS
Caliber: 22 Long Rifle
Capacity: 17-shot tubular magazine with patented closure system
Barrel length: 22″
Weight: 5½ lbs.
Overall length: 40½″
Sights: Ramp front sight; adjustable open rear, receiver grooved for tip-off scope mount

Action: Semiautomatic; side ejection; manual and automatic "last-shot" hold-open devices; receiver top has serrated, non-glare finish; cross-bolt safety
Stock: One-piece walnut-finished hardwood Monte Carlo stock with full pistol grip (shown here with Glenfield 200C, 4X scope)

MODEL 75C
$111.95

SPECIFICATIONS
Caliber: 22 LR
Capacity: 13-shot tubular magazine
Barrel length: 18″
Overall length: 36½″
Weight: 5 lbs.
Stock: Monte Carlo walnut finish hardwood

Action: Semiautomatic; side ejection; manual and "last-shot" automatic bolt hold-opens
Sights: Adjustable open rear; ramp front sight

MARLIN RIFLES

MODEL 25M
$126.95

SPECIFICATIONS

Caliber: 22 Win. Mag Rimfire (not interchangeable with any other 22 cartridge)
Capacity: 7-shot clip magazine
Stock: one-piece walnut-finished hardwood Monte Carlo with full pistol grip and sling swivels

Barrel length: 22″ with Micro-Groove rifling
Overall length: 41″
Weight: 6 lbs
Sights: adj. open rear, ramp front sight. Receiver grooved for tip-off scope mount

MODEL 25 MB MIDGET MAGNUM
$133.95 (w/scope)

SPECIFICATIONS

Same specifications as Model 25M except **barrel length** (16¼″), **overall length** (35¼″) and **weight:** (4¾ lbs.).

MARLIN 780
$152.95

MARLIN 781
$159.95

SPECIFICATIONS (MODEL 780)

Caliber: 22 Short, Long or Long Rifle
Capacity: Clip magazine holds 7 Short, Long or Long Rifle cartridges
Action: Bolt action; serrated, anti-glare receiver top; positive thumb safety; red cocking indicator
Stock: Monte Carlo genuine American black walnut with full pistol grip; checkering on pistol grip and underside of forend; white butt plate spacer; tough Mar-Shield® finish
Barrel: 22″ with Micro-Groove® rifling (16 grooves)
Sights: Adjustable folding semi-buckhorn rear; ramp front with Wide-Scan™ with hood; receiver grooved for tip-off scope mount
Overall length: 41″
Weight: About 5½ lbs.
Marlin 781: Specifications same as Marlin 780, except with tubular magazine that holds 25 Short, 19 Long or 17 Long Rifle cartridges. **Weight:** About 6 lbs.

MARLIN RIFLES

MODEL 9 CAMP CARBINE
$280.95

SPECIFICATIONS
Caliber: 9mm
Capacity: 12-shot clip (20-shot magazine available)
Action: Semi-automatic. Manual bolt hold-open. Garand-type safety, magazine safety, loaded chamber indicator. Solid-top, machined steel receiver is sandblasted to prevent glare, and is drilled and tapped for scope mounting.
Stock: Walnut finished hardwood with pistol grip; tough Mar-Shield™ finish; rubber rifle butt pad.
Barrel length: 16½" with Micro-Groove® rifling.
Sights: Adjustable rear, ramp front sight with brass bead; Wide-Scan™ hood. Receiver drilled and tapped for scope mount.
Overall length: 35½"
Weight: 6¾ lbs.

MODEL 45
$280.95

SPECIFICATIONS
Caliber: 45 Auto
Capacity: 7-shot clip
Barrel length: 16½"
Overall length: 35½"
Weight (approx.): 6.75 lbs.

Stock: Walnut finished hardwood with pistol grip; rubber rifle butt pad
Sights: Adjustable open rear; ramp front sight with brass bead; Wide-Scan hood

MARLIN 15Y "LITTLE BUCKAROO™"
Single Shot 22 Beginner's Rifle
$106.95 (scope not included)

SPECIFICATIONS
Caliber: 22 Short, Long or Long Rifle
Capacity: Single shot
Action: Bolt action; easy-load feed throat; thumb safety; red cocking indicator
Stock: One-piece walnut finish hardwood Monte Carlo with full pistol grip; tough Mar-Shield® finish
Barrel length: 16¼" (16 grooves)
Sights: Adjustable open rear; ramp front sight; free 4 × 15 scope included
Overall length: 33¼"
Weight: 4¼ lbs.

MARLIN RIFLES

MARLIN 70
$111.95 (scope not included)

SPECIFICATIONS
Caliber: 22 Long Rifle
Capacity: Chrome-plated 7-shot clip magazine
Barrel length: 18″
Weight: 5 lbs.
Overall length: 36½″
Sights: Adjustable open rear; ramp front sight; receiver grooved for tip-off scope mount

Action: Semiautomatic; side ejection; bolt hold-open device; receiver top has serrated, non-glare finish; cross-bolt safety
Stock: One-piece walnut finished hardwood Monte Carlo stock with full pistol grip

MODEL 70P "PAPOOSE"
$144.95 (scope included)

SPECIFICATIONS
Caliber: 22LR
Barrel length: 16¼″
Overall length: 35¼″
Weight: 3.75 lbs.
Capacity: 7-shot clip
Sights: Adjustable open rear; ramp front

Stock: Walnut-finished hardwood with full pistol grip
Action: Semiautomatic; side ejection; manual bolt hold-open; cross-bolt safety

MARLIN 22 RIFLES

MARLIN 783 MAGNUM
$174.95

SPECIFICATIONS
Caliber: 22 Win. Magnum Rimfire (not interchangeable with any other 22 cartridge)
Capacity: 12-shot tubular magazine with patented closure system
Action: Bolt action; serrated, anti-glare receiver top; positive thumb safety; red cocking indicator

Stock: Monte Carlo genuine American black walnut with full pistol grip; checkering on pistol grip and underside of forend; white butt plate spacer; swivel studs; tough Mar-Shield® finish
Barrel: 22″ with Micro-Groove® rifling (20 grooves)
Sights: Adjustable folding semi-buck-

horn rear; ramp front with Wide-Scan™ hood; receiver grooved for tip-off scope mount
Overall length: 41″
Weight: About 6 lbs.
Marlin 782 Magnum: $168.95
Specifications: Same as 783 Magnum, except with 7-shot clip magazine.

MARLIN 990
$158.95

SPECIFICATIONS
Caliber: 22 Long Rifle
Action: Semiautomatic
Capacity: 17-shot tubular magazine
Barrel: 22″ with Micro-Groove® rifling (16 grooves)
Stock: Monte Carlo genuine American

black walnut with fluted comb and full pistol grip; checkering on pistol grip and forend; tough Mar-Shield® finish
Sights: Adjustable folding semi-buck-horn rear; ramp front sight with brass bead, Wide-Scan™ hood

Overall length: 40³/₄″
Weight: About 5¹/₂ lbs.
Features: Receiver grooved tip-off scope; manual and automatic "last-shot" bolt hold-open devices; cross-bolt safety

MARLIN 995
$148.95

SPECIFICATIONS
Caliber: 22 Long Rifle
Action: Semiautomatic
Capacity: 7-shot clip magazine
Barrel: 18″ with Micro-Groove® rifling (16 grooves)
Stock: Monte Carlo genuine American

black walnut with full pistol grip; checkering on pistol grip and forend
Sights: Adjustable folding semi-buck-horn rear; ramp front sight with brass bead, Wide-Scan™ hood
Overall length: 36³/₄″

Weight: About 5¹/₂ lbs.
Features: Receiver grooved for tip-off scope mount; bolt hold-open device; cross-bolt safety

MAUSER RIFLES

MODEL 66 S
$2200.00

Calibers: 243 Win., 270 Win., 30-06, and 308 Win.
Barrel length: 24"
Weight: 7¼ lbs.
Also available:
Model 66 S Ultra (21" barrel)
Model 66 S (Magnum version in calibers 7mm Rem. Mag., 300 Win. Mag.). **Barrel length:** 26". **Weight:** 9¼ lbs.
Model 66 S Big Game Rifle (26" barrel) in 375 H&H Mag. and 458 Win. Mag.

This short action repeater rifle is internationally known for its outstanding handling qualities. The interchangeable barrel system allows the shooter to own one rifle with several extra barrels in different calibers. Includes special detachable sights, adjustable for windage and elevation, selected walnut stock, oiled and polished, fitted with Pachmayr recoil pad. Double trigger.

MODEL 66 SM
$2200.00

Calibers: 243 Win., 270 Win., 30-06, and 308 Win.
Barrel length: 24"
Weight: 7¼ lbs.
Also available:
Model 66 SM Ultra (21" barrel) in 30-06. Same model in Magnum (7mm Rem. Mag., 300 Win. Mag.) with 26" barrel.

Features detachable sights, adjustable for windage and elevation, oiled walnut stock with anatomical royal grip, forend with Mauser nose, Mauser safety, and Mauser-set trigger with cocking lever on tang.

MODEL 77 BOLT ACTION RIFLE
$1331.00

Caliber: 243 Win., 308 Win., 270 Win. **Barrel length:** 24"
Also available:
Model 77 Ultra (30-06 only; 20" barrel) 1394.50
Model 77 Sportsman (243 Win. and 308 Win. only) 1754.00

Includes detachable sights adjustable for windage, selected walnut stock, oiled, with rubber recoil pad, silent safety, Mauser-set trigger with cocking lever on tang, steel detachable box magazine.

MODEL 83
STANDARD SPORTING RIFLE
$2594.00

Features include cylinder locking action, three locking lugs in the rear of the action, single shot, patented silent safety with fail safe button, match trigger adjustable from outside, anatomical match stock of selected walnut with adjustable comb and butt plate. UIT Standard rifle. **Caliber:** 308 Win. **Barrel length:** 26"
Also available: **Match Rifle** (10-shot) $2766.00
Also available: **UIT Free Rifle** 2771.00

MOSSBERG CENTERFIRE RIFLES

MODEL 1500 MOUNTAINEER GRADE I
Calibers: 223 Rem., 7mm Mag.

MODEL 1700LS CLASSIC HUNTER
Bolt Action

Available in 30-06, 270 Win., and 243 Win. Features removable 5-round steel magazine with floorplate. All Smith & Wesson bolt-action rifles use select American walnut on stock and forend; ventilated rubber recoil pad (on Magnum models only) and non-slip hard butt plate for other calibers. Receivers are machined from single block of steel; barrels are proof-tested, cold hammer-forged steel. Positive, non-slip thumb-type safety on right side locks trigger but permits bolt to be opened for safe inspection and unloading.

MODEL 1500 CENTERFIRE RIFLES

CALIBERS		223	22-250	243	270	308	30-06	7MM MAG	300 WIN. MAG	338 WIN. MAG	Pull	Drop at Comb	Drop at Monte Carlo	Drop at Heel	Length overall	Magazine Capacity	Approx. Weight
RIFLING TWIST		1:12 R.H.	1:14 R.H.	1:10 R.H.	1:10 R.H.	1:12 R.H.	1:10 R.H.	1:9.5 R.H.	1:10 R.H.	1:10 R.H.							
MODEL 1500 GRADE 1	with or without Sights	●		●	●		●	●			13½"	1¾"		2¼"	42"	5/6	7 lbs. 10-oz.
MODEL 1500 GRADE II	with or without Sights	●	●	●	●	●	●	●	●	●	13½"	1¾"		2¼"	42"	5/6	7 lbs. 10-oz.
MODEL 1500 VARMINT without Sights	Blue	●	●			●					13½"	¾"	9/16"	1⅜"	44"	5/6	9 lbs. 5-oz.
	Parkerized	●				●											
MODEL 1550	with or without Sights			●	●		●				13½"	1¾"		2¼"	42"	5/6	7 lbs. 8-oz.
MODEL 1700 L/S without Sights				●	●		●				13¾"	⅞"		1½"	42½"	5	7 lbs.

NOTE: Models 1500 and 1700LS were formerly produced and distributed by Smith & Wesson. Contact O.F. Mossberg & Sons, Inc., for current suggested retail prices.

PARKER-HALE RIFLES

MODEL M81 CLASSIC
$699.95

SPECIFICATIONS
Calibers: 22/250, 243 Win., 6mm Rem., 270 Win., 308 Win., 30-06, 300 Win. Mag., 7mm Rem. Mag.
Barrel length: 24″
Overall length: 44¹/₂″
Capacity: 4 rounds
Weight: 7.75 lbs.
Length of pull: 13¹/₂″

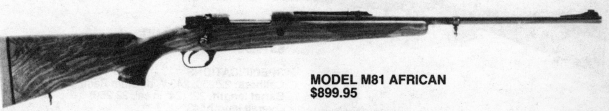

MODEL M81 AFRICAN
$899.95

SPECIFICATIONS
Calibers: 300 H&H, 308 Norma Mag., 375 H&H, 9.3 × 62.
Barrel length: 24″
Overall length: 44¹/₂″
Weight: 7.75 lbs.
Stock: Hand-checkered walnut
Features: All-steel trigger guard, adjustable trigger, barrel band front swivel, African express rear sight, hand-engraved receiver

MODEL 1100 LIGHTWEIGHT
$529.95

SPECIFICATIONS
Calibers: 22/250, 243 Win., 6mm Rem., 270 Win., 308 Win.
Barrel length: 22″
Overall length: 43″
Weight: 6¹/₂ lbs.
Capacity: 4 rounds
Length of pull: 13¹/₂″
Model 1100M African Magnum (375 H&H and 458 Win. Mag. only): **Barrel length:** 24″. **Overall length:** 46″. **Weight:** 9¹/₂ lbs. **Price:** $769.95.

PARKER-HALE RIFLES

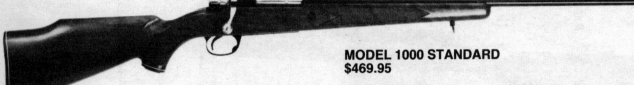

MODEL 1000 STANDARD
$469.95

SPECIFICATIONS
Calibers: 22/250, 243 Win., 6mm Rem., 270 Win., 308 Win.
Barrel length: 22″ (24″ in cal. 22/250)
Overall length: 43″
Weight: 7¼ lbs.
Capacity: 4 rounds
Length of pull: 13½″

MODEL 2100 MIDLAND
$319.95

SPECIFICATIONS
Calibers: 22/250, 243 Win., 6mm Rem., 270 Win., 308 Win.
Barrel length: 22″ (24″ in cal. 22/250)
Overall length: 43″
Weight: 7 lbs.
Capacity: 4 rounds
Length of pull: 13½″

MODEL 1200 SUPER
$599.95

SPECIFICATIONS
Calibers: 22/250, 243 Win., 6mm Rem., 270 Win., 308 Win.
Barrel length: 24″
Overall length: 44½″
Weight: 7½ lbs.
Capacity: 4 rounds
Length of pull: 13½″
Model 1200M Super Magnum (300 Win. Mag., 308 Norma
   Mag., and 7mm Rem. Mag. only): Same specifications as
   Model 1200 Super but capacity is 3 rounds. **Price: $599.95.**
Model 1200C Super Clip (243 Win., 6mm Rem., 270 Win.,
   308 Win. only): Same specifications as Model 1200 Super
   but weighs 7¾ lbs. **Price: $629.95.** Also available in 300
   Win. Mag. and 7mm Rem. Mag. (3 rounds only).
Model 1200V Super Varmint (22/250, 6mm Rem., 243 Win.,
   25/06 only): Same specifications as Model 1200 Super but
   weighs 9 lbs. **Price: $599.95.**

PARKER-HALE TARGET RIFLES

MODEL M87
$1099.95

This all-round high precision long range target rifle is available in several calibers suitable for silhouette or practical rifle competition and varmint shooting. The bolt is designed for smooth and rapid operation. The handle is tipped with a large diameter ball and allows ample clearance for aperture or telescopic sights. Integral dovetails on the action body provide positive scope mounting with Parker-Hale "Roll-Off" mounts.

SPECIFICATIONS
Calibers: 308 Win., 243 Win., 30-06 Springfield, 300 Win. Mag. (others on request) **Weight:** 10 lbs. (empty) **Barrel length:** 26" **Overall length:** 45" **Sights:** None fitted; action body dovetailed for Parker-Hale "Roll-Off" Scope mounts

MODEL M84 MK11 CANBERRA (not shown)
$1199.95 (7.62mm × 51 NATO)

Receiver is specifically designed for maximum rigidity with the framework of the rifle and a solid flat base with heavily reinforced flat top side. Action is securely fixed to the stock by two ¹/₄" socket head screws.

SPECIFICATIONS
Caliber: 7.62 × 51 NATO **Barrel length:** 27¹/₂" **Overall length:** 48" **Weight:** 11¹/₂ lbs. (w/sights & handstop) **Rifle twist:** 1 in 14" (1 in 10 and 1 in 12 made to order) **Capacity:** Single shot **Trigger pull weight:** 3¹/₂ lbs.

Also available: **MODEL M84 MK11 BISLEY.**
Same as "Canberra" but is produced in an alternative stock style (one for right handed shooters and one for left handers).

PERUGINI-VISINI RIFLES

BOXLOCK EXPRESS

OVER/UNDER EXPRESS

BOXLOCK EXPRESS
$4400.00

Features Anson & Deeley boxlock ejector with monobloc barrels. Standard open sights include a quarter rib with shallow "V" rear and ramp front sight. Standard action finish is border line engraving with casehardening in colors. Also available: **BOXLOCK MAGNUM EXPRESS** (see chart). **$8100.00**

OVER/UNDER EXPRESS
$6100.00

Over/Under boxlock ejector with monobloc barrels, quarter rib and ramp front sight. Action fences, borders and hinge pin area engraved. English style pistol grip stock and cheekpiece. Set front trigger available.

SIDELOCK SUPER EXPRESS
$13,100.00

Holland & Holland pattern sidelock ejector with chopper lump barrels. Quarter rib with multi-leaf express sights. Hand detachable locks and hinged front trigger. English style pistol grip stock and cheekpiece with H&H type steel grip cap with trap and spare-firing pins. Can be furnished with extra set of 20 gauge shotgun barrels. Standard action finish is border line engraving with either casehardening or coin finish. H&H pattern scroll engraving or choice of engraving available on order.

SPECIFICATIONS

	BOXLOCK EXPRESS	MAGNUM EXPRESS	OVER/UNDER	SIDELOCK SUPER EXPRESS
CALIBERS AVAILABLE:				
9.3×74R, .444 Mar	●			
.270 Win., .375 H&H, .458 Win.		●		
7mm Rem., 7×65R, 9.3×74R., 270 Win., .284 Win., .338 Win., .375 H&H, .458 Win.			●	
7mm Rem., 7×65R, 9.3×74R, .270 Win., .300 H&H, .338 Win., .375 H&H, .458 Win., 470 Nitro				●
BARRELS				
Satin Rust blue finish	●	●	●	●
Monobloc barrels	●	●	●	
Chopper Lump barrels				●
Lengths available: 23.6 or 24.8 in.	●	●		
Lengths available: 24 in.			●	
Lengths available: 22 or 24.8 in.				●
SIGHTS				
Quarter rib with shallow "V" rear and ramp front	●	●	●	●
Multiple leaf express sights				●
Swarovski-Kahles scope in claw mounts (opt.)	●	●	●	●
ACTION:				
Anson & Deeley, box lock	●	●		
Over/Under, boxlock			●	
Holland & Holland pattern sidelock				●
Automatic ejectors	●	●	●	●
Double triggers	●	●	●	●
Casehardened in colors (std.)	●	●	●	●
Coin finish (opt.)	●	●	●	●
Several optional engraving styles	●	●	●	●
STOCK & FOREARM:				
Hand rubbed oil finish		●		●
Satin finish	●		●	
English style pistol girp & cheekpiece	●	●	●	●
Recoil pad, 1/2-inch thick	●	●	●	●
Steel grip cap, H&H type with trap & spare strikers				●
Classic (splinter) forearm (std.)	●	●	●	●
Beavertail forearm (opt.)	●	●	●	●
Stock dimensions from open sight line: 1½"×2¼"×14⅛"	●			
WEIGHTS: (Depending on caliber and barrel length)				
7 lb. 8 oz. to 8 lb.	●			
8 lb. to 9 lb.		●	●	●
Over 9 lb. in heavy magnum calibers		●	●	●

PERUGINI-VISINI RIFLES

SINGLE SHOT EAGLE RIFLE
$5255.00

SPECIFICATIONS
Calibers: 17 Rem., 222, 22/250, 243, 270, 30-06, 7mm Rem. Mag., 300 Win. Mag., plus metric cartridges from 5,6 × 50R to 10,3 × 60R
Action: Anson & Deeley type
Trigger: Adj. set trigger

Stock: European select walnut; oil finished; hand checkered
Ejector: Normal, with wide ejector/cartridge contact surface
Locking device: Special patented type, on inclined planes with over-dimensioned latch

BOLT ACTION PROFESSIONAL CARBINE
$4250.00

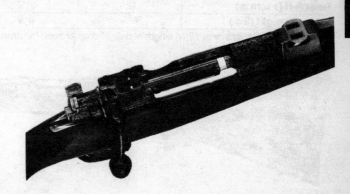

SPECIFICATIONS
Calibers: All current European and American calibers, from 222 Rem. up to 458 Win. Mag.
Action: F.N. type (or Mauser 98 K)
Barrel: Böhler steel
Trigger: Single trigger with adj. release/set trigger
Magazine: Classic, 3-shot; button release magazine floor plate
Safety: Sliding tang safety
Stock: European select walnut; oil finish, hand checkered
Sights: Ramp mounted front sight w/folding hood; folding leaves on rib (zeroed in at 50-100 m)
Finishing: Extra deep blue; checkered bolt knob and shaped belt handle; pistol grip can house spare front sight; hand-detachable sling swivels; English-style heel plate

DOUBLE RIFLE EXPRESS
$20,360

SPECIFICATIONS
Calibers: 9,3 × 74R, 375 H&H Mag., 458 Win. Mag.
Receiver: Carved from solid block of special steel
Barrels: Böhler steel; demibloc barrels
Locking device: Double Purdey style
Action: H&H type, hand detachable sidelocks internally gold plated; main spring fitted back to avoid weakening the receiver
Ejectors: Automatic ejectors with wide ejector/cartridge con-

tact surface, H&H type
Sights: Gold bead on ramp front; folding leaves rear on rib
Stock: High grade European select walnut briar; fine hand checkering
Finishing: Fine signed engraving; pistol grip can house a spare front sight; inserted firing pin carrier sleeve; extra long receiver tang; oil finished walnut; English-style heel plate

REMINGTON BOLT ACTION RIFLES

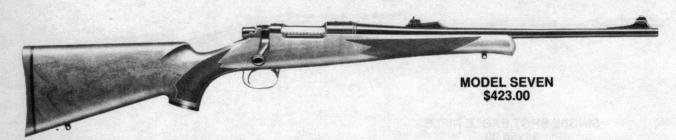

**MODEL SEVEN
$423.00**

Every Model Seven is built to the accuracy standards of our famous Model 700 and is individually test fired to prove it. Its 18½" Remington special steel barrel is free-floating out to a single pressure point at the forend tip. And there is ordnance-quality steel in everything from its fully enclosed bolt and ex-tractor system to its steel trigger guard and floor plate. Ramp front and fully adjustable rear sights, sling swivel studs are standard. Also available with Kevlar Reinforced Fiberglass Stock in 243 Win., 7mm-08 Rem., and 308 Win. **Price: $580.00.**

	223 Rem.	243 Win.	7mm-08 Rem.	6mm Rem.	308 Win.
Clip mag. capacity	5	4	4	4	4
Barrel length	18½"	18½"	18½"	18½"	18½"
Overall length	37½"	37½"	37½"	37½"	37½"
Twist R-H (1 turn in)	12"	9⅛"	9¼"	9⅛"	10"
Average weight (lbs.)	6¼	6¼	6¼	6¼	6¼

Standard Stock Dimensions: 13½" length of pull, 1" drop at heel, ⅝" drop at comb (measured from centerline of bore).

**MODEL 700 ADL DELUXE
$367.00 ($385.00 in 7mm Reg. Mag.)**

MODEL 700 ADL DELUXE Calibers: 22-250 Rem., 243 Win., 25-06 Rem., 270 Win., 30-06, 308 Win., 7mm Rem. Mag

**MODEL 700 CLASSIC (LIMITED EDITION)
$421.00**

Calibers: 338 Win. Mag.
Capacity: Same as Model 700 BDL
Barrel: 24"
Bolt: Jeweled with shrouded firing pin
Receiver: Drilled and tapped for scope mounts; fixed maga-zine with or without hinged floor plate
Stock: Cut-checkered select American walnut with quick de-tachable sling swivels installed; recoil pad standard equip-ment on Magnum rifles; installed at extra charge on others

REMINGTON BOLT ACTION RIFLES

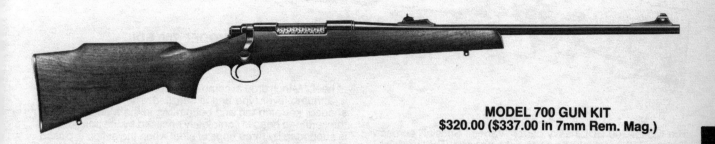

MODEL 700 GUN KIT
$320.00 ($337.00 in 7mm Rem. Mag.)

The Model 700 Gun Kit includes the Model 700 ADL barreled action (long and short), blind magazine (no floor plate), factory iron sights, and receiver drilled and tapped for scope mounts. The walnut stock with sling swivel studs and butt plate is furnished ready for final shaping, sanding and finishing. Stock inletting for the barreled action is completed to accurate di- mensions requiring no additional internal inletting or cutting. The kit package also includes an owner's manual with complete instructions on how to finish the stock and three checkering pattern templates. Choice of cartridges for which the barreled actions are chambered include the 243 Win., 270 Win., 30-06, 308 Win. and 7mm Rem. Mag.

MODEL 700 MOUNTAIN RIFLE
$432.00

A special lightweight version of the Remington Model 700 bolt action centerfire rifle. **Calibers:** 270 Win., 280 Rem., 30-06. **Weight:** 6³/₄ lbs. **Barrel length:** 22″. **Stock:** Straight-line comb with cheekpiece; satin stock finish.

MODEL 700 CUSTOM MOUNTAIN RIFLE
**Showing left side of synthetic
stock reinforced with Kevlar**

REMINGTON BOLT ACTION RIFLES

MODEL 700 BDL
HEAVY BARREL VARMINT SPECIAL
$453.00

The Model 700 BDL heavy barrel "Varmint Special" comes equipped with a 24-inch heavy target-type barrel. The "Varmint Special" is available in a wide range of popular high-velocity, varmint calibers, which include the 222 Rem., 223 Rem., 22-250 Rem., 308 Win., 6mm Rem., 243 Win., 25-06 Rem., and 7mm-08 Rem. The "Varmint Special" was designed for maximum-range precision shooting, suitable for chucks, foxes and other varmints.

Features include: hinged floor plate; quick release, swivels and strap; crisp trigger pull; American walnut stock, Monte Carlo style with cheekpiece; positive cut skip-line checkering on grip and all three sides of forend, grip cap with white line spacer and butt plate; DuPont developed RK-W wood finish. Stock dimensions are: 13³/₈-inch length of pull; 1³/₈ inch drop

at heel; ¹/₂-inch drop at comb (from open sight line). The safety is a thumb-lever type and is serrated. The bolt knob is oval shaped, serrated top and bottom. As in the Model 700 BDL, the cartridge head is completely encased by the bolt face and is supported by three rings of steel when the action is closed. The model is a very popular choice for metallic silhouette shooting.

Calibers	Clip Mag. Cap.	Overall Length	Av. Wt. Lbs.	Twist R-H 1 turn in
22-250 Remington	4	43¹/₂"	9	14
222 Remington	5	43¹/₂"	9	14
223 Remington	5	43¹/₂"	9	12
243 Winchester	4	43¹/₂"	9	9¹/₈
308 Winchester	4	43¹/₂"	8³/₄	10
7mm-08 Remington	4	43¹/₂"	8³/₄	9¹/₄
6mm Remington	4	43¹/₂"	9	9¹/₈

Also available: **MODEL 700 BDL SHORT ACTION LEFT HAND** in 243 Win., 270 Win., 30-06, 308 Win., and 7mm Rem. Mag. **Price: $438.00; Deluxe Model $471.00 ($488.00** in 7mm Rem. Mag.).

MODEL 700 SAFARI GRADE in 375 H&H Mag., 458 Win. Mag., and 8mm Rem. Mag. (Classic and Monte Carlo Style). **Price: 787.00**

MODEL 700 SPECIFICATIONS

Calibers	Mag. Cap.	Barrel Length[1]	"Mountain Rifle"*	"Limited Classic"	Varmint Special	ADL, BDL & "Custom"	Twist R-H 1 turn in
17 Rem.	5	24"	—	—	—	43¹/₂"/7¹/₄	9"
222 Rem.	5	24"	—	—	43¹/₂"/9	3¹/₂"/7¹/₄	14"
22-250 Rem.	4	24"	—	—	43¹/₂"/9	43¹/₂"/7¹/₂	14"
223 Rem.	5	24"	—	—	43¹/₂"/9	43¹/₂"/7¹/₄	12"
6mm Rem.*	4	22"	—	—	43¹/₂"/9	41¹/₂"/7¹/₄	9¹/₈"
243 Win.	4	22"	—	—	43¹/₂"/9	41¹/₂"/7¹/₄	9¹/₈"
25-06 Rem.	4	24"	—	—	—	41¹/₂"/7¹/₄	10"
270 Win.	4	22"	42¹/₂"/6³/₄	—	—	41¹/₂"/7¹/₄	10"
280 Rem.	4	22"	42¹/₂"/6³/₄	—	—	—	—
7mm-08 Rem.	4	22"	—	—	43¹/₂"/9	41¹/₂"/7¹/₄	9¹/₄"
30-06 & 30-06 "Accelerator"	4	22"	42¹/₂"/6³/₄	—	—	41¹/₂"/7¹/₄	10"
308 Win. & 308 "Accelerator"	4	22"	—	—	43¹/₂"/9	41¹/₂"/7¹/₄	10" 12"
7mm Rem. Mag.[2]	3	24"	—	—	—	44¹/₂"/7³/₄	9¹/₄"
300 Win. Mag.[2]	3	24"	—	—	—	44¹/₂"/7³/₄	10"
338 Win. Mag.[2]	4	24"	—	44¹/₂"/7⁷/₄	—	—	10"
Safari Grade*							
8mm Rem. Mag.	3	24"	—	—	—	44¹/₂"/10	10"
375 H&H Mag.[2]	3	24"	—	—	—	44¹/₂"/9	12"
458 Win. Mag.[2]	3	24"	—	—	—	44¹/₂"/9	14"

[1]"Varmint Special" equipped only with a 24" barrel.   [2]Recoil pad included.

REMINGTON BOLT ACTION RIFLES

MODEL 700 "RS"

MODEL 700 SYNTHETIC STOCKS

In answer to the demand for the lighter weight, strength and stability of synthetic stocks, Remington has introduced two new versions of its Model 700 centerfire rifle, as well as one version of its Model Seven. **Model 700 "RS"** introduces a new synthetic stock material called "Rynite", a DuPont thermoplastic resin with 35 percent glass reinforcement. This material provides more strength, stiffness and stability under a wide

range of temperature and humidity conditions. This model includes the "Mountain Rifle" stock style featuring a straight comb and cheekpiece with Monte Carlo. A black, solid rubber recoil pad and pistol grip cap (with the "RA" logo) offer a smooth, uncluttered profile. Model 700 "RS" is available with a 22" barrel in right hand, long action with hinged floor plate in 270 Win., 280 Rem. and 30-06. **Price: $533.00**

MODEL SEVEN "FS"

Model 700 "FS" features a fiberglass stock reinforced with DuPont "Kevlar" aramid fiber for extra strength. The stock is shaped in the classic style with straight comb, no cheekpiece or Monte Carlo, and a black, old English style rubber recoil pad. The action has a blind magazine without floor plate. Model 700 "FS" is available in both long and short and right and left hand actions. Right hand actions are chambered for 243 Win., 308 Win. and 7mm Rem. Mag. Left hand actions are available in 270 Win., 30-06 and 7mm Rem. Mag. **Price: $600.00 ($620.00 in 7mm Rem. Mag.).**
Model Seven "FS" is available in 243 Win., 7mm-08 Rem. and 308 Win. **Price: $580.00.**

SYNTHETIC STOCK RIFLES

Calibers	Mag. capacity	Barrel length	Overall length	Avg. Wt.	Twist R-H 1 turn in
Model 700 RS Rynite Stock BDL					
270 Win.	4	22"	42$\frac{1}{2}$	7$\frac{1}{4}$	10"
280 Rem.	4	22"	42$\frac{1}{2}$	7$\frac{1}{4}$	9$\frac{1}{4}$"
30-06	4	22"	42$\frac{1}{2}$	7$\frac{1}{4}$"	10"
Model 700 FS Fiberglass Stock ADL					
243 Win.	4	22"	41$\frac{5}{8}$	6$\frac{1}{4}$	9$\frac{1}{8}$"
270 Win.	4	22"	42$\frac{1}{2}$	6$\frac{1}{4}$	10"
30-06	4	22"	42$\frac{1}{2}$	6$\frac{1}{4}$	10"
308 Win.	4	22"	41$\frac{5}{8}$	6$\frac{1}{4}$	10"
7mm Rem. Mag.	3	24"	44$\frac{1}{2}$	6$\frac{3}{4}$	10"
Model Seven FS Fiberglass Stock					
243 Win.	4	18$\frac{1}{2}$"	37$\frac{1}{2}$	5$\frac{1}{4}$	9$\frac{1}{8}$"
7mm-08 Rem.	4	18$\frac{1}{2}$"	37$\frac{1}{2}$	5$\frac{1}{4}$	9$\frac{1}{4}$"
308 Win.	4	18$\frac{1}{2}$"	37$\frac{1}{2}$	5$\frac{1}{4}$	10"

REMINGTON SPORTSMAN RIFLES

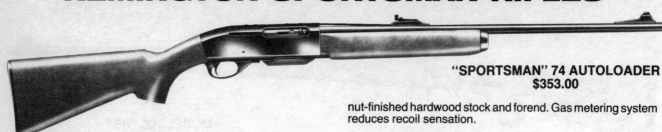

"SPORTSMAN" 74 AUTOLOADER
$353.00

The popularly priced "Sportsman" 74 autoloading centerfire rifle is chambered for the 30-06 Springfield cartridge. The gun offers quick, extra-shot performance, superb balance and exceptional accuracy. The bolt has massive locking lugs, similar to those of bolt-action rifles. Other features include removable 4-shot clip magazine, receiver drilled and tapped for scope mounts, detachable ramp front sight and step rear sight, wal-

nut-finished hardwood stock and forend. Gas metering system reduces recoil sensation.

Caliber: 30-06 Springfield
Capacity: 4-shot clip magazine
Barrel length: 22"
Overall length: 42"
Weight: 7½ lbs.
Length of pull: 13⅜"
Drop at heel: 2⅛"
Drop at comb: 1¹¹/₁₆"

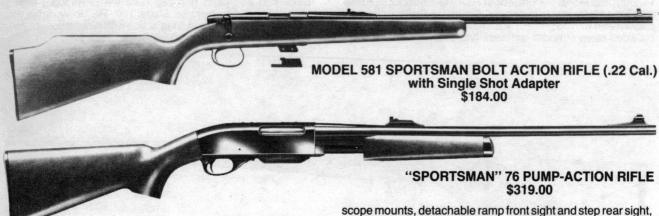

MODEL 581 SPORTSMAN BOLT ACTION RIFLE (.22 Cal.)
with Single Shot Adapter
$184.00

"SPORTSMAN" 76 PUMP-ACTION RIFLE
$319.00

scope mounts, detachable ramp front sight and step rear sight, walnut finished hardwood stock and forend.

The popularly priced "Sportsman" 76 pump-action centerfire rifle is chambered for the hard-hitting 30-06 Springfield cartridge. It gives you fast second-shot performance without your eyes leaving the target. Smooth double-action bars slide faster, with little effort. The bolt has massive locking lugs, similar to those of bolt-action rifles. Other features include removable 4-shot clip magazine, receiver drilled and tapped for

Caliber: 30-06 Springfield
Capacity: 4-shot clip magazine
Barrel length: 22"
Overall length: 42"
Weight: 7½ lbs.
Length of pull: 13⅜"
Drop at heel: 2⅛"
Drop at comb: 1¹¹/₁₆"

BIG GAME REPEATING RIFLES
"SPORTSMAN" 78 BOLT ACTION
$300.00

The popularly priced "Sportsman" 78 bolt-action centerfire rifle is chambered for the 243 Win., 308 Win., 270 Win. and 30-06 Springfield. It features the same rugged Remington action, bolt and barrel long recognized for their strength and accuracy by hunters and bench rest shooters alike. The straight comb, walnut-finished hardwood stock has classic lines and a rounded forend. Sights are fully adjustable and the receiver is drilled and tapped for easy scope mounting.

Caliber: 270 Win., 30-06 Springfield and now 243 Win., 308 Win.
Capacity: 4-shot clip magazine
Barrel length: 22"
Overall length: 42½"
Weight: 7 lbs.
Length of pull: 13⅜"
Drop at heel: 1" (from centerline of bore)
Drop at comb: ⁹/₁₆" (from centerline of bore)

REMINGTON CENTERFIRE RIFLES

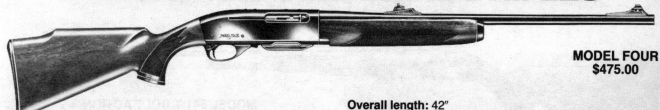

MODEL FOUR
$475.00

Calibers: 243 Win., 270 Win., 30-06 and 280 Win. (7mm Exp. Rem.)
Capacity: 5-shot in all calibers (4 in the magazine, 1 in the chamber); extra 4-shot magazine available
Action: Gas operated; receiver drilled and tapped for scope mounts; positive safety switch
Barrel length: 22″
Weight: 7¹/₂ lbs.

Overall length: 42″
Sights: Blade ramp front; adjustable sliding ramp rear
Stock: Checkered American walnut; Monte Carle stock with full cheekpiece; pistol grip; flared and checkered forend
Length of pull: 13¹⁵/₁₆″
Drop at heel: 2¹/₂″
Drop at comb: 1¹¹/₁₆″; with Monte Carlo, 1¹³/₁₆″
Model Four special order: D Peerless and F Premier Grades (both engraved) and F Premier Grade (engraved with gold inlay): **$2291.00-$7079.00**

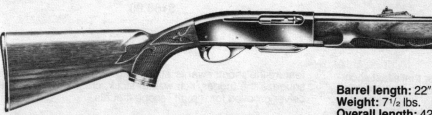

MODEL SIX
$439.00

Calibers: 6mm Rem., 243 Win., 270 Win., 30-06
Capacity: 5-shot capacity in all six calibers (4 in the removable clip, 1 in the chamber)
Action: Pump action
Barrel length: 22″
Weight: 7¹/₂ lbs.

Overall length: 42″
Sights: Blade ramp front sight; adjustable sliding ramp rear
Stock: Cut-checkered American walnut Monte Carlo stock with full cheekpiece; flared forend has full wraparound positive-cut checkering
Length of pull: 13¹⁵/₁₆″
Drop at heel: 2¹/₂″
Drop at comb: 13¹¹/₁₆″; with Monte Carlo, 1¹³/₁₆″
Model Six special order: D Peerless and F Premier Grades (both engraved) and F Premier Grade (engraved with gold inlay): **$2291.00-$7079.00**

MODEL 7400
$421.00

Calibers: 6mm Rem., 243 Win., 270 Win., 280 Rem., 30-06 and 308 Win.
Capacity: 5 centerfire cartridges (4 in the magazine, 1 in the chamber); extra 4-shot magazine available
Action: Gas operated; receiver drilled and tapped for scope mounts

Barrel length: 22″
Weight: 7¹/₂ lbs.
Overall length: 42″
Sights: Standard blade ramp front; sliding ramp rear
Stock: Checkered American walnut stock and forend; curved pistol grip
Length of pull: 13³/₈″
Drop at heel: 2¹/₄″
Drop at comb: 1¹³/₁₆″

MODEL 7600
$383.00

Calibers: 243 Win., 270 Win., 30-06 308 Win. and 30-06 Carbine
Capacity: 5-shot capacity in all six calibers (4 in the removable magazine, 1 in the chamber)
Action: Pump action

Barrel length: 22″ (18¹/₂″ in 30-06 Carbine)
Weight: 7¹/₂ lbs.
Overall length: 42″
Sights: Standard blade ramp front sight; sliding ramp rear, both removable
Stock: Checkered American walnut
Length of pull: 13³/₈″
Drop at heel: 2¹/₈″
Drop at comb: 1¹¹/₁₆″

REMINGTON RIMFIRE RIFLES

MODEL 541-T BOLT ACTION
$333.00

RIMFIRE RIFLES

Model	Action	Barrel Length	Overall Length	Average Weight (lbs.)	Magazine Capacity
541-T*	Bolt	24"	42½"	5⅞	5 Shot Clip*
522-A "Speedmaster"	Auto	21"	40"	5¾	15 Long Rifle
522 BDL Deluxe "Speedmaster"	Auto	21"	40"	5¾	15 Long Rifle
572-A "Fieldmaster"	Pump	21"	40"	5½	15 Long Rifle
572 BDL Deluxe "Fieldmaster"	Pump	21"	40"	5½	15 Long Rifle
Nylon 66 BD Black Diamond	Auto	19⅝"	38½"	4	14 Long Rifle
Nylon 66 MB Hohawk Brown	Auto	19⅝"	38½"	4	14 Long Rifle

Extra 5-shot or 10-shot clip available at extra cost.

MODEL 552 A SPEEDMASTER
$168.00

Here's the Remington 22-caliber autoloader that's fast shooting, accurate, nicely balanced—the rifle you'll want for small game hunting, controlling crop-destroying and marauding pests, or for just plain fun-shooting. The Model 552 has every feature the shooter wants, such as 20 shots as fast as you can squeeze the trigger, rich walnut stock, cross-bolt safety, receiver grooved for "tip-off" scope mounts.

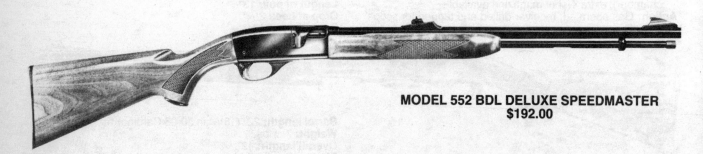

MODEL 552 BDL DELUXE SPEEDMASTER
$192.00

A deluxe model with all the tried and proven dependable mechanical features on the inside, plus special design and appearance extras on the outside. The 552 BDL sports tasteful Remington custom-impressed checkering on both stock and forend. Tough DuPont RK-W lifetime finish brings out the lustrous beauty of the walnut while protecting it. Sights are ramp-style in front and rugged big-game type fully adjustable in rear.

REMINGTON RIMFIRE RIFLES

**MODEL 572 A
FIELDMASTER
$176.00**

For the shooter who likes a pump-action 22-caliber rifle the "Fieldmaster" Model 572 A is best. Exclusive cartridge-feeding design prevents jamming, permits easy single loading. By simply removing the inner magazine tube, parent or instructor can convert the Model 572 into a single-shot rifle for the beginning shooter; when shooter is experienced, magazine tube can be put back again to make the Model 572 a repeater.

**MODEL 572 BDL DELUXE FIELDMASTER
$203.00**

MODEL 572 DELUXE

Features of this rifle with big-game feel and appearance are: DuPont's beautiful, tough RK-W finish; centerfire-rifle-type rear sight fully adjustable for both vertical and horizontal sight alignment; big-game style ramp front sight; handsome Remington impressed checkering on both stock and forend.

Action: Pump repeater
Caliber: 22 Short, Long and Long Rifle rimfire
Capacity: Tubular magazine holds 20 Short, 17 Long, 15 Long Rifle cartridges

Stock and forend: Model A, walnut finished hardwood; Model BDL, American walnut with tough DuPont RK-W lustrous finish and fine-line custom checkering
Sights: Model A, adjustable rear, bead front; Model BDL, fully adjustable rear, ramp front; screw removable
Safety: Positive cross bolt
Receiver: Grooved for "tip-off" scope mounts
Overall length: 40″
Barrel length: 21″
Average weight: 5½ lbs.

REMINGTON RIMFIRE RIFLES

NYLON 66 • MOHAWK BROWN
$124.00

The Nylon 66 Autoloading rifle is chambered for 22 Long Rifle cartridges. Tubular magazine thru butt stock holds 14 Long Rifle cartridges. Remington's Nylon 66 receiver parts, stock and barrel are interlocked with steel and structural nylon. There's no need for lubrication because friction-free parts glide on greaseless bearings of nylon. Barrel made of Rem-

ington proof steel. Stock is made of DuPont "Zytel" nylon, a new gunstock material. Resembles wood, weighs less than wood, outwears, outlasts wood. Stock features fine-line non-slip checkering, white diamond inlays and white line spacers at grip cap, butt plate and forend tip and has a lifetime warranty. Receiver is grooved for "tip-off" scope mounts.

NYLON 66 BLACK DIAMOND
$124.00

	NYLON 66 MOHAWK BROWN	NYLON 66 "BLACK DIAMOND"
Action	Autoloading	Autoloading
Caliber	22 Long Rifle Rimfire	22 Long Rifle Rimfire
Capacity	Tubular magazine thru butt stock holds 14 Long Rifle cartridges	Tubular magazine thru butt stock Holds 14 Long Rifle cartridges
Stock	DuPont "ZYTEL" nylon, checkered grip & forend with white diamond inlays, white line spacers on butt plate, grip cap & forend; black forend tip	DuPont "ZYTEL" nylon, checkered grip & forend with white diamond inlays, white line spacers on butt plate, grip & forend; sling strip and swivels installed: **$15.00**
Sights	Rear sight adjustable for windage and range; blade front, common sight line for iron sights and scope	Rear sight adjustable for windage and range; blade front, common sight line for iron sights and scope
Safety	Top-of-grip, positive	Top-of-grip, positive
Receiver	Grooved for "tip-off" scope mounts, double extractors	Grooved for "tip-off" scope mounts; double extractors; chrome-plated receiver and barrel
Overall length	38½"	38½"
Weight	4 lbs.	4 lbs.

REMINGTON TARGET RIFLES

**MODEL 40-XR
Rimfire Position Rifle
$720.00**

Stock designed with deep forend for more comfortable shooting in all positions. Butt plate vertically adjustable. Exclusive loading platform provides straight line feeding with no shaved bullets. Crisp, wide, adjustable match trigger. Meets all International Shooting Union standard rifle specifications.

Action: Bolt action, single shot
Caliber: 22 Long Rifle rimfire
Capacity: Single loading
Sights: Optional at extra cost. Williams Receiver No. FPTK and Redfield Globe front match sight
Safety: Positive serrated thumb safety
Receiver: Drilled and tapped for receiver sight
Barrel: 24″ medium weight target barrel countersunk at muzzle. Drilled and tapped for target scope blocks. Fitted with front sight base
Bolt: Artillery style with lock-up at rear. 6 locking lugs, double extractors
Trigger: Adjustable from 2 to 4 lbs.
Stock: Position style with Monte Carlo, cheekpiece and thumb groove; 5-way adjustable butt plate and full length guide rail
Overall length: 42¹/₂″
Average weight: 9¹/₄ lbs.

Also available: **MODEL 40-XR CUSTOM SPORTER** (22 cal.). Grade I **$1131.00.** Grade II **$2056.00** Grade III **$3267.00** Grade IV **$5067.00**

**MODEL 40-XC
National Match Course Rifle
$971.00**

Chambered solely for the 7.62mm NATO cartridge, this match rifle was designed to meet the needs of competitive shooters firing the national match courses. Position-style stock, five-shot repeater with top-loading magazine, anti-bind bolt and receiver and in the bright stainless steel barrel. Meets all International Shooting Union Army Rifle specifications. Weighs about 11 lbs.

Action: Bolt-action, single shot
Caliber: 22 Long Rifle rimfire
Capacity: Single loading
Sights: Optional at extra cost. Williams Receiver No. FPTK and Redfield Globe front match sight
Safety: Positive thumb safety
Length of pull: 13¹/₂″
Receiver: Drilled and tapped for receiver sight or target scope blocks
Barrel: 24″ heavy barrel
Bolt: Heavy, oversized locking lugs and double extractors
Trigger: Adjustable from 2 to 4 lbs.
Stock: Position style with front swivel block on forend guide rail
Overall length: 43¹/₂″
Average weight: 11 lbs.

REMINGTON TARGET RIFLES

MODEL 40-XB "RANGEMASTER"
Centerfire Rifle
$896.00

Barrels, in either standard or heavy weight, are unblued steel. Comb-grooved for easy bolt removal. Mershon White Line non-slip rubber butt plate supplied.

Action: Bolt—single shot in either standard or heavy barrel versions; repeater in heavy barrel only; receiver bedded to stock; barrel is free floating
Calibers: Single-shot, 222 Rem., 22-250 Rem., 6mm Rem., 243 Win., 7.62mm NATO (308 Win.), 30-06, 30-338 (30-7mm Mag.), 300 Win. Mag., 25-06 Rem., 7mm Rem. Mag.
Sights: No sights supplied; target scope blocks installed
Safety: Positive thumb operated
Receiver: Drilled and tapped for scope block and receiver sights
Barrel: Drilled and tapped for scope block and front target iron sight; muzzle diameter S2—approx. $3/4$", H2—approx. $7/8$"; unblued stainless steel only, $27^{1}/4$" long
Trigger: Adjustable from 2 to 4 lbs. pull; special 2-oz. trigger available at extra cost; single shot models only
Stock: American walnut; adjustable front swivel block on rail; rubber non-slip butt plate
Overall length: Approx. $45^{3}/4$"
Average weight: S2—$9^{1}/4$ lbs.; H2—$11^{1}/4$ lbs.

Also available: **Model 40-XB Kevlar. Barrel length** $27^{1}/4$"; **Overall length** $45\ ^{3}/4$"; **Weight** $9^{3}/4$ lbs. **Price: $1045.00.**

MODEL 40XB-BR
Bench Rest Centerfire Rifle
$945.00

Built with all the features of the extremely accurate Model 40-XB-CF but modified to give the competitive bench rest shooter a standardized rifle that provides the inherent accurracy advantages of a short, heavy, extremely stiff barrel. Wider, squared off forend gives a more stable rest on sandbags or other supports and meets weight limitations for the sporter and light-varmint classes of National Bench Rest Shooters Association competition.

Action: Bolt, single shot only
Calibers: 222 Rem., 22 Bench Rest Rem., 7.62 NATO (308 Win.), 6mm Bench Rest Rem., 223 Rem., 6x47
Sights: Supplied with target scope blocks
Safety: Positive thumb operated
Receiver: Drilled and tapped for target scope blocks
Barrel: Unblued stainless steel only; 20" barrel for Light Varmint Class; 24" barrel for Heavy Varmint Class.
Trigger: Adjustable from $1^{1}/2$ to $3^{1}/2$ lbs.; special 2-oz. trigger available at extra cost
Stock: Selected American walnut; length of pull—12"
Overall length: 38" with 20" barrel; 44" with 24" barrel
Average weight: Light Varmint Class (20" barrel) $9^{1}/4$ lbs.; Heavy Varmint Class (24" barrel) 11 lbs.

ROSSI RIFLES

Photographs not available from manufacturer at time of publication.

PUMP-ACTION GALLERY GUNS
MODEL M62SA
$175.00

Caliber: 22 LR
Capacity: 13 rds.
Barrel length: 23″
Overall length: 39¼″
Weight: 5½″ lbs.
Finish: Blue
Model M62SA w/Nickel finish. $189.00
Model 59 22 Magnum 215.00

MODEL M62SAC
$175.00

Caliber: 22 LR
Capacity: 12 rds.
Barrel length: 16½″
Overall length: 32¾″
Weight: 4¼″
Finish: Blue
Model M62SAC w/Nickel finish $189.00
Model M62SAC w/Octagon Barrel. 199.00

PUMA LEVER ACTION CARBINES
MODEL M92 SRS
$245.00

Caliber: 38 Special or 357 Magnum
Capacity: 7 rounds
Barrel length: 16″
Overall length: 33″
Weight: 5 lbs.
Finish: Blue

MODEL M92 SRC
$225.00

Caliber: 38 Special or 357 Magnum
Capacity: 10 rounds.
Barrel length: 20″
Overall length: 37″
Weight: 5¾″
Also available in 44/40 caliber **(Price: $260.00)** and 44 Magnum **(Price: $270.00)**

RUGER CARBINES

RUGER MINI-14

Materials: Heat-treated chrome molybdenum and other alloy steels as well as music wire coil springs are used throughout the mechanism to ensure reliability under field-operating conditions. **Safety:** The safety blocks both the hammer and sear. The slide can be cycled when the safety is on. The safety is mounted in the front of the trigger guard so that it may be set to Fire position without removing finger from trigger guard. **Firing pin:** The firing pin is retracted mechanically during the first part of the unlocking of the bolt. The rifle can only be fired when the bolt is safely locked. **Stock:** One-piece American hardwood reinforced with steel liner at stressed areas. Handguard and forearm separated by air space from barrel to promote cooling under rapid-fire conditions. **Field stripping:** The Carbine can be field stripped to its eight (8) basic sub-assemblies in a matter of seconds and without use of special tools.

MINI-14 SPECIFICATIONS
Caliber: 223 (5.56mm). **Length:** 37¼". **Weight:** 6 lbs. 4 oz. **Magazine:** 5-round, detachable box magazine. 20-shot and 30-shot magazines available. **Barrel length:** 18½".

Mini-14/5 Blued $405.50
Mini-14/5F Blued (folding stock) $483.50
K-Mini-14/5 Stainless Steel 447.00
K-MINI-14/5F (Stainless steel, folding stock) 514.50
Scopes not included

MINI-14 RANCH RIFLE

Caliber: 223 (5.56mm) or 7.62 × 39. **Length:** 37¼". **Weight:** 6 lbs. 8 oz. **Magazine:** 10-shot and 20-shot magazines available. **Barrel length:** 18¼".

Mini-14/5R Blued $437.00
K-Mini-14/5R Stainless Steel 478.50
K-Mini-14/5RF Stainless Steel (folding stock) 541.00

RUGER CARBINES

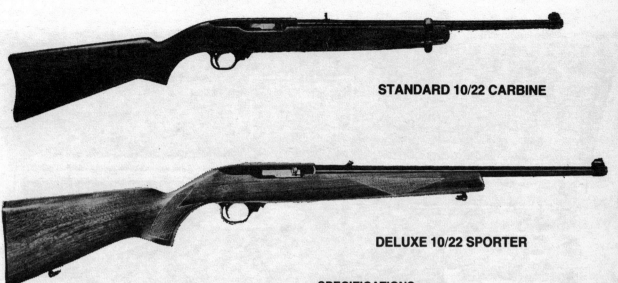

STANDARD 10/22 CARBINE

DELUXE 10/22 SPORTER

MODEL 10/22 CARBINE
22 LONG RIFLE CALIBER

Identical in size, balance and style to the Ruger 44 Magnum Carbine and nearly the same in weight, the 10/22 is a companion to its high-power counterpart. Construction of the 10/22 Carbine is rugged and follows the Ruger design practice of building a firearm from integrated sub-assemblies. For example, the trigger housing assembly contains the entire ignition system, which employs a high-speed, swinging hammer to ensure the shortest possible lock time. The barrel is assembled to the receiver by a unique dual-screw dovetail system that provides unusual rigidity and strength—and accounts, in part, for the exceptional accuracy of the 10/22.

SPECIFICATIONS
Caliber: 22 Long Rifle, high-speed or standard-velocity loads. **Barrel:** 18 1/2" long; barrel is assembled to the receiver by unique dual-screw dovetail mounting for added strength and rigidity. **Weight:** 5 lbs. **Overall length:** 37". **Sights:** 1/16" gold bead front sight; single folding leaf rear sight, adjustable for elevation; receiver drilled and tapped for scope blocks or tip-off mount adapter. **Magazine:** 10-shot capacity, exclusive Ruger rotary design; fits flush into stock. **Trigger:** Curved finger surface, 3/8" wide. **Safety:** Sliding cross-button type; safety locks both sear and hammer and cannot be put in safe position unless gun is cocked. **Stocks:** 10/22 R Standard Carbine is walnut; 10/22 RB is birch; 10/22 SP Deluxe Sporter is American walnut. **Finish:** Polished all over and blued or anodized.

Model 10/22-R Standard (walnut stock) $196.00
Model 10/22-RB Standard (birch stock) 176.00
Model 10/22-DSP Deluxe Sporter 222.00

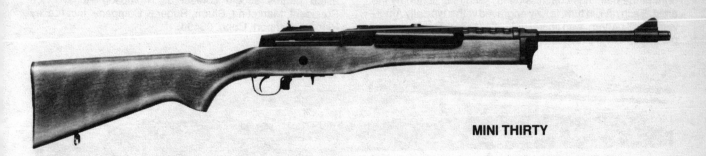

MINI THIRTY

This modified version of the Ruger Ranch rifle is chambered for the 7.62 × 39mm Russian service cartridge (used in the SKS carbine and AKM rifle). Designed for use with telescopic sights, it features a low, compact scope mounting for greater accuracy and carrying ease. **Barrel length:** 18 1/2". **Overall length:** 37 1/4". **Weight:** 7 lbs. 3 oz. (empty). **Magazine capacity:** 5 shots. **Rifling:** 6 grooves, right hand twist, one turn in 10". **Finish:** polished and blued overall. **Price:** $420.00

RUGER RIFLES
NO. 1 NORTH AMERICAN PRESENTATION

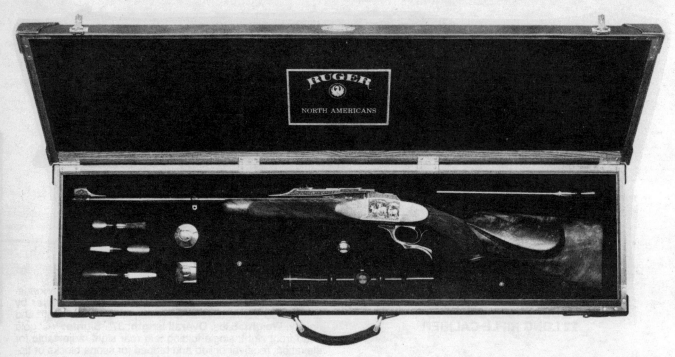

This unique series of presentation engraved and custom cased Ruger No. 1 single-shot rifles is reminiscent of the finest leather cased English guns of a century ago. Inspired by the works of a group of leading American wildlife artists, the Ruger *North Americans* will consist of a series of 21 Ruger No. 1 rifles, each depicting in fine engraving and deeply sculptured inlaid gold a major North American big-game animal, and will be chambered in a caliber appropriate to the game shown.

The first No. 1 rifle in the series will depict the Rocky Mountain bighorn sheep as rendered by Arizona artist Gary Swanson, one of the most popular wildlife artists today. Ech rifle in the series will be accompanied by a one-of-a-kind full color print of the paintings commissioned, each one signed by the artist. Each rifle, in turn, is fully engraved with a typically American scroll pattern, with liberal gold inlay lining. The Ruger eagle trademark is inlayed in gold on the underside of the lever,

and the grip cap bears a three-dimensional rendering in gold inlay of the bighorn sheep head.

The trunk-style Huey case is covered in heavy cowhide and lined in plush burgundy ultrasuede. A Leupold M86/6X Compact scope with engraved scope mounts and rings is fitted in the case, along with an assortment of gun care products. The beautifully figured wood used in the presentation stock of Northern California English Walnut. The pistol grip and forend are finely checkered 28 lines to the inch, and the butt is checkered and provided with a gracefully carved cheekpiece.

Price for the Ruger *North Americans* bighorn sheep presentation rifle is $45,000 (Federal excise tax included). Interested parties should contact J. Thompson Ruger, Vice President, Marketing, Sturm, Ruger & Company, Inc. (Lacey Place, Southport, Conn. 06490).

RUGER SINGLE-SHOT RIFLES

The following illustrations show the variations currently offered in the Ruger No. 1 Single-Shot Rifle Series. Ruger No. 1 rifles come fitted with selected American walnut stocks. Pistol grip and forearm are hand-checkered to a borderless design. **Price for any listed model is $575.00** (except No. 1 International Model).

NO. 1 LIGHT SPORTER

Calibers: 243 Win.; 30/06; 270 Win., 7 × 57mm. **Barrel length:** 22". **Sight:** Adjustable folding-leaf rear sight mounted on quarter rib with ramp front sight base and dovetail-type gold bead front sight; open. **Weight:** 7¼ lbs.

NO. 1 MEDIUM SPORTER

Calibers: 7mm Rem. Mag.; 300 Win. Mag.; 45/70; 338 Win. Mag. **Barrel length:** 26" (22" in 45/70). **Sights:** (same as above). **Weight:** 8 lbs. (7¼ lbs. in 45/70).

NO. 1 STANDARD RIFLE

Calibers: 22/250; 243 Win.; 6mm Rem.; 25/06; 270 Win.; 30/06; 7mm Rem. Mag.; 220 Swift; 338 Mag.; 280; 223; 257 Roberts, 270 Weatherby, 300 Mag., 300 Weatherby. **Barrel:** 26". **Sights:** Ruger steel tip-off scope rings, 1". **Weight:** 8 lbs.

NO. 1 SPECIAL VARMINTER

Calibers: 22/250; 25/06; 220 Swift; 223; 6mm. **Barrel length;** 24". **Sights:** Ruger steel blocks and tip-off scope rings, 1". **Weight:** 9 lbs.

RUGER RIFLES

NO. 1 TROPICAL RIFLE

Calibers: 375 H&H Mag.; 458 Win. Mag. **Barrel length:** 24″ (heavy). **Sights:** Adjustable folding-leaf rear sight mounted on quarter rib with ramp front sight base and dovetail-type gold bead front sight; open. **Weight:** 8¼ lbs. for 375; 9 lbs. for 458.

NO. 1 INTERNATIONAL (MODEL 1-RSI)
With Mannlicher Style Forearm

SPECIFICATIONS
Caliber: 243 Win., 30-06, 270 Win., and 7×57mm. **Barrel length:** 20″ (lightweight). **Overall length:** 36½″. **Weight:** 7¼ lbs. **Sights:** Adjustable folding leaf rear sight mounted on quarter rib with ramp front sight base and dovetail-type gold bead front sight.
Price **$595.00**

BOLT ACTION RIFLES

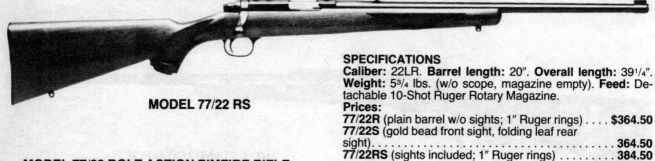

MODEL 77/22 RS

SPECIFICATIONS
Caliber: 22LR. **Barrel length:** 20″. **Overall length:** 39¼″. **Weight:** 5¾ lbs. (w/o scope, magazine empty). **Feed:** Detachable 10-Shot Ruger Rotary Magazine.
Prices:
77/22R (plain barrel w/o sights; 1″ Ruger rings) **$364.50**
77/22S (gold bead front sight, folding leaf rear sight) **364.50**
77/22RS (sights included; 1″ Ruger rings) **384.50**

MODEL 77/22 BOLT ACTION RIMFIRE RIFLE

The Ruger 22-caliber rimfire 77/22 bolt-action rifle offers the sportsman quality and value. It represents a blend of characteristics long associated with the famous Ruger M-77 rifle and the internationally popular Ruger 10/22 semiautomatic rimfire rifle. It has been built especially to function with the patented Ruger 10-Shot Rotary Magazine concept. The magazine throat, retaining lips, and ramps that guide the cartridge into the chamber are solid alloy steel that resists bending or deforming.

The bolt assembly is built to military rifle standards of quality, but it has been modified to function with the 22 rimfire cartridge. Accordingly, the front part of the bolt is nonrotating and the locking lugs have been moved back to the middle of the action. The rear part of the bolt rotates and cams like that of the Ruger M-77 rifle, and it is connected to the nonrotating forward part of the bolt by a sturdy joint.

The new 77/22 weighs just under six pounds and provides the smallbore shooter with a compact, featherweight arm that delivers performance and reliability. The heavy-duty receiver incorporates the integral scope bases of the patented Ruger Scope Mounting System, with 1-inch Ruger scope rings. A new 3-position safety offers a new dimension in security. With safety in its "lock" position, a dead bolt is cammed forward, locking the bolt handle down. In this position the action is locked closed and the handle cannot be raised.

A simplified bolt stop fits flush with the left side of the receiver and permits the bolt to be withdrawn from receiver merely by pressing down tightly. The new bolt locking system ensures positive lock-up by two large locking lugs on rotating part of bolt. A nonadjustable trigger mechanism is set for medium weight trigger pull. This mechanism includes a single strong coil spring for both sear recovery and trigger return. Lock time is 2.7 milliseconds.

All metal surfaces are finished in a deep, lustrous blue with nonglare surfaces on top of receiver. Stock is selected straight-grain American walnut, hand checkered with an attractive and durable polyurethane finish.

RUGER BOLT ACTION RIFLES

MODEL M-77RS

Integral Base Receiver, Ruger steel 1″ rings, open sights. **Calibers:** (Magnum action) 270, 7 × 57mm, 30-06 (with 22″ barrels), 25-06, 7mm Rem. Mag., 300 Win. Mag., 338 Win. Mag. (with 24″ barrels); and (Short Stroke action) 243, 308 (with 22″ barrels). **Weight:** Approx. 7 lbs.

Price **$498.00**

MODEL M-77RL ULTRA LIGHT

New 6-pound big game rifle in both long- and short-action versions, with Integral Base Receiver and 1″ Ruger scope rings. Luxury detailing throughout. **Calibers:** (Magnum action) 270, 30-06, 257 (all with 20″ barrels); and (Short Stroke action) 22-250, 243, .250-3000, 308 (with 22″ barrels). **Weight:** Approx. 6 lbs.

Price **$478.00**

MODEL M-77 ULTRA LIGHT

This big game bolt action rifle encompasses the traditional features that have made the Ruger M-77 one of the most popular centerfire rifles in the world. It includes a sliding top tang safety, a one-piece bolt with Mauser-type extractor and diagonal front mounting system. American walnut stock is hand checkered in a sharp diamond pattern. A rubber recoil pad, pistol grip cap and studs for mounting quick detachable sling swivels are standard. **Calibers:** 270, 30-06 (Magnum action); 243 and 308 (short stroke action). **Barrel length:** 18¹/₂″. **Overall length:** 38⁷/₈″. **Weight:** 6 lbs. (empty). **Sights:** Open. **Price: $474.00**

RUGER BOLT ACTION RIFLES

MODEL M-77RSI INTERNATIONAL

Mannlicher-type stock, Integral Base Receiver, open sights, Ruger 1″ steel rings. **Calibers:** (Short Stroke action) 22-250, 250-3000, 243, 270, 30-06, and 308 (all with 18½″ barrels). **Weight:** Approx. 7 lbs.

Price **$504.00**

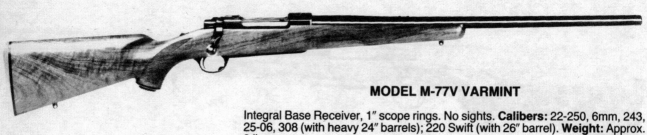

MODEL M-77V VARMINT

Integral Base Receiver, 1″ scope rings. No sights. **Calibers:** 22-250, 6mm, 243, 25-06, 308 (with heavy 24″ barrels); 220 Swift (with 26″ barrel). **Weight:** Approx. 9 lbs.

Price **$462.00**

MODEL M-77R (not shown)

Integral Base Receiver, 1″ scope rings. No sights. **Calibers:** (Magnum action) 270, 7 × 57mm, 257 Roberts, 280 Rem., 30-06 (all with 22″ barrels); 25-06, 7mm Rem. Mag., 300 Win. Mag., 338 Win. Mag. (all with 24″ barrels); and (Short Stroke action) 22-250, 6mm, 243, 308 (all with 22″ barrels); 220 Swift (with 24″ barrel). **Weight:** Approx. 7 lbs.

Price **$440.00**

MODEL M-77RS TROPICAL (not shown)

Integral Base Receiver (Magnum action only). Equipped with open sights and Ruger steel rings. **Caliber:** 458 Win. Mag. only. Steel trigger guard and floor plate. **Weight:** Approx. 8.75 lbs.

Price: **600.00**

SAKO FIBERCLASS RIFLES

NEW ALL WEATHER FIBERGLASS-STOCKED CENTERFIRE RIFLE

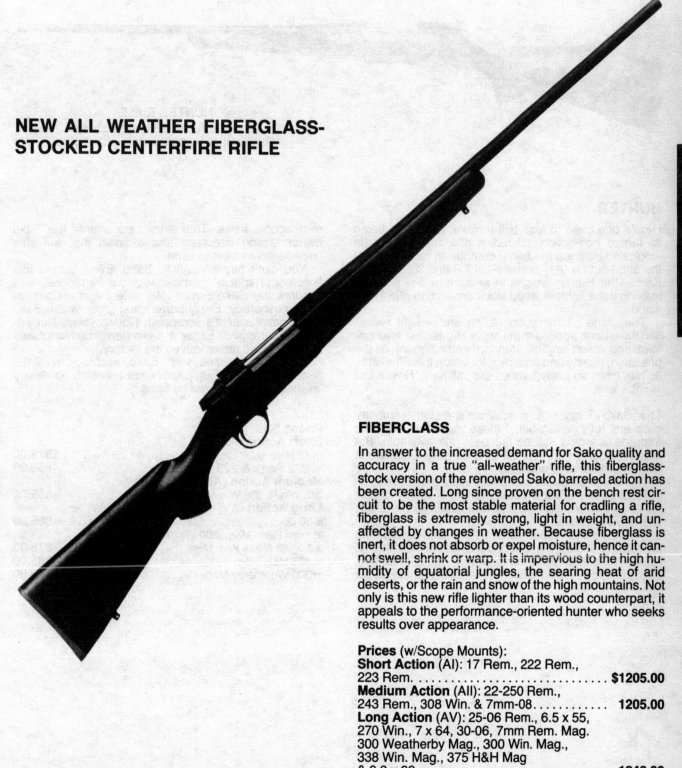

FIBERCLASS

In answer to the increased demand for Sako quality and accuracy in a true "all-weather" rifle, this fiberglass-stock version of the renowned Sako barreled action has been created. Long since proven on the bench rest circuit to be the most stable material for cradling a rifle, fiberglass is extremely strong, light in weight, and unaffected by changes in weather. Because fiberglass is inert, it does not absorb or expel moisture, hence it cannot swell, shrink or warp. It is impervious to the high humidity of equatorial jungles, the searing heat of arid deserts, or the rain and snow of the high mountains. Not only is this new rifle lighter than its wood counterpart, it appeals to the performance-oriented hunter who seeks results over appearance.

Prices (w/Scope Mounts):
Short Action (AI): 17 Rem., 222 Rem.,
223 Rem. **$1205.00**
Medium Action (AII): 22-250 Rem.,
243 Rem., 308 Win. & 7mm-08 . . . . 1205.00
Long Action (AV): 25-06 Rem., 6.5 x 55,
270 Win., 7 x 64, 30-06, 7mm Rem. Mag.
300 Weatherby Mag., 300 Win. Mag.,
338 Win. Mag., 375 H&H Mag
& 9.3 x 62 . . . . 1240.00

SAKO RIFLES

HUNTER RIFLE
lacquer finish without sights;
also available in oil finish with sights

HUNTER

Here's one case of less being more. Sako has taken its famed bolt-action, centerfire rifle, redesigned the stock and trimmed the barrel contour. In fact, in any of the short action (A1) calibers—.17 Rem., .222 or .223 Rem.—the Hunter weighs in at a mere 5³/₄ pounds, making it the lightest wood stock production rifle in the world.

The same cosmetic upgrading and weight reduction have been applied to the entire Hunter line in all calibers and action lengths, standard and magnum. All the precision, quality and accuracy for which this Finnish rifle has been so justly famous are still here. Now it just weighs less.

The Sako Trigger is a rifleman's delight—smooth, crisp and fully adjustable. If these were the only Sako features, it would still be the best rifle available. But the real quality that sets Sako apart from all others is its truly outstanding accuracy.

While many factors can affect a rifle's accuracy, 90 percent of any rifle's accuracy potential lies in its barrel. And the creation of superbly accurate barrels is where Sako excels.

The care that Sako takes in the cold-hammering processing of each barrel is unparalleled in the industry. As an example, after each barrel blank is drilled, it is diamond-lapped and then optically checked for microscopic flaws. This extra care affords the Sako owner lasting accuracy and a finish that will stay "new" season after season.

You can't buy an unfired Sako. Every gun is test fired using special overloaded proof cartridges. This ensures the Sako owner total safety and uncompromising accuracy. Every barrel must group within Sako specifications or it's scrapped. Not recycled. Not adjusted. Scrapped. Either a Sako barrel delivers Sako accuracy, or it never leaves the factory.

And hand-in-hand with Sako accuracy is Sako beauty. Genuine European walnut stocks, flawlessly finished and checkered by hand.

Prices

Short Action (AI)
in 17 Rem. **$875.00**
in 222 Rem. & 223 Rem. **855.00**
Medium Action (AII) in 22-250 Rem.,
243 Win. & 308 Win. **855.00**
Long Action (AV) in 25-06 Rem., 270 Win.
& 30-06 . . . . **865.00**
in 7mm Rem. Mag., 300 Win. Mag.
9.3 × 62 & 338 Win. Mag. **875.00**
in 375 H&H Mag. **885.00**
in 300 Weatherby Mag. **895.00**

SAKO CARBINES

SAKO CARBINE

Sako's Carbines combine the handiness and carrying qualities of the traditional, lever action "deer rifle" with the power of modern, high-performance cartridges. An abbreviated 18½-inch barrel trims the overall weight of the Carbine to just over 40 inches in the long (or AV) action calibers, and 39½" in the medium (or All) action calibers. Weight is a highly portable 7 and 6½ pounds, respectively (except in the .338 and .375 H&H calibers, which tip the scale at 7½ pounds).

As is appropriate for a rifle of this type, the Carbine is furnished with an excellent set of open sights; the rear is fully adjustable for windage and elevation, while the front is a non-glare serrated ramp with protective hood.

The Carbine is available in a choice of stocks: the traditional wood stock of European walnut done in a contemporary Monte Carlo style with a choice of hand-rubbed oil or gloss lacquer finish. Either way, hand-cut checkering is standard. The Mannlicher-style full-stock Carbine wears Sako's exclusive two-piece forearm, which joins beneath the barrel band. This independent forward section of the forearm eliminates the bedding problems normally associated with the full forestock. A blued steel muzzle cap puts the finishing touches on this European-styled Carbine.

For the hunter whose primary concerns are ruggedness and practicality, there's the Fiberclass Carbine. Stocked in the same distinctive black fiberglass stock as Sako's famed Fiberclass Rifle model, the Carbine offers the same advantages but in a shorter, lighter configuration. The Fiberclass Carbines in .338 and .375 H&H have become favorites with Alaskan guides, bush pilots, and all those who work or travel regularly in big bear country.

Prices:
Sako Carbine w/Scope Mounts in 22-250 Rem., 243 Rem., 308 Win. & 7mm-08 (Medium Action) **$855.00**
in 25-06 Rem., 6.5×55, 270 Win., 7×64 & 30-06 (Long Action) **865.00**
in 7mm Rem. Mag., 300 Win. Mag., 338 Win. Mag., 375 H&H Mag., & 9.3×62 (Long Action). **875.00**

Sako Fiberclass Carbine w/Scope Mounts in 25-06, 270 Win., & 30-06 (Long Action). **$1205.00**
in 7mm Rem. Mag., 300 Win. Mag. 338 Win. Mag. & 375 H&H Mag. (Long Action) **1240.00**

Sako Mannlicher-Style Carbine w/Scope Mounts in 222 Rem. (Short Action) **$957.00**
in 243 Win., & 308 Win. (Medium Action) **957.00**
in 270 Win., & 30-06 (Long Action). **957.00**
in 338 Win. Mag. & 375 H&H Mag. (Long Action). . . . **990.00**

SAKO MANNLICHER-STYLE CARBINE

SAKO RIFLES

LAMINATED STOCK MODELS

In response to the growing number of hunters and shooters who seek the strength and stability that a fiberglass stock provides, coupled with the warmth and feel of real wood, Sako introduces its Laminated Stock models.

Machined from blanks comprised of 36 individual layers of 1/16-inch hardwood veneers that are resin-bonded under extreme pressure, these stocks are virtually inert. Each layer of hardwood has been vacuum-impregnated with a permanent brown dye. The bisecting of various layers of veneers in the shaping of the stock results in a contour-line appearance similar to a piece of slab-sawed walnut. Because all Sako Laminated Stocks are of real wood, each one is unique, with its own shading, color and grain.

These stocks satisfy those whose sensibilities demand a rifle of wood and steel, but who also want state-of-the-art performance and practicality. Sako's Laminated Stock provides both, further establishing it among the most progressive manufacturers of sporting rifles—and the *only* one to offer hunters and shooters their choice of walnut, fiberglass or laminated stocks in 18 calibers (10 in Left Handed models), from .17 Remington to .375 H&H.

Prices:

Laminated w/Scope Mounts in 17 Rem., 222 Rem. (Short Action) and 22-250, 243 Rem., 308 Win. and 7mm-08 (Medium Action) **$980.00**
in 25-06 Rem., 6.5×55, 270 Win., 7×64 & 30-06 (Long Action) **980.00**
in 7mm Rem. Mag., 300 Win. Mag. & 338 Win. Mag. (Long Action) **990.00**
in 375 H&H Mag. (Long Action) **999.00**
Laminated Left-Handed w/Scope Mounts in 25-06, 6.5×55, 270 Win., 7×64, 30-06 (Long Action) **1000.00**
in 7mm Rem. Mag., 300 Win. Mag., 338 Win. Mag., & 9.3×62 (Long Action) **1020.00**
in 375 H&H Mag. (Long Action) **1030.00**

LEFT HANDED MODELS

Sako's new Left Handed models are based on mirror images of the right-handed models enjoyed by Sako owners for many years, with handle, extractor and ejection port all located on the port side. Naturally, the stock is also reversed, with the cheekpiece on the opposite side and the palm swell on the port side of the grip.

Otherwise, these guns are identical to the right-hand models. That means hammer-forged barrels, one-piece bolts with integral locking lugs and handles, integral scope mount tails, three-way adjustable triggers, Mauser-type inertia ejections, and one-piece steel trigger guard/magazine frames.

Sako's Left Handed rifles are available in all Long Action models. The Hunter Grade carries a durable, hand-rubbed oil finish with generous-size panels of hand-cut checkering, a presentation-style recoil pad, scope mounts, and sling swivel studs installed. The Deluxe model is distinguished by its rosewood forend tip and grip cap, its skip-line checkering and gloss lacquer finish atop a select-grade of highly figured European walnut. The metal work carries a deep, mirro-like blue that looks more like black chrome. Laminated and Fiberclass Long Action models are also available for lefthanders.

Prices:

Hunter Lightweight: w/Scope Mounts in 25-06, 6.5×55, 270 Win., 7×64 & 30-06 . . . . **$960.00**
in 7mm Rem. Mag., 300 Win. Mag., 338 Win. Mag., 9.3×62 & 375 H&H Mag. **973.00**

Deluxe w/Scope Mounts in 25-06, 6.5×55, 270 Win. Mag. 7×64, & 30-06 . . . . **$1288.00**
in 7mm Rem. Mag., 300 Win. Mag., 338 Win. Mag. & 9.3×62 . . . . **1325.00**
in 375 H&H Mag. **1375.00**

Fiberclass w/Scope Mounts in 25-06, 6.5×55, 270 Win., 7×64 & 30-06 . . . . **$1045.00**
in 7mm Rem., Mag., 300 Win. Mag., 338 Win. Mag & 9.3×62 . . . . **1055.00**
in 375 H&H Mag **1066.00**

Note: for **Laminated Left-Handed** models, see following page.

SAKO CUSTOM RIFLES

SAFARI GRADE

Crafted in the tradition of the classic British express rifles, Safari Grade is truly a professional's rifle. Every feature has been carefully thought out and executed with one goal in mind: functionality. The magazine is extended, allowing four belted magnums to be stored inside (instead of the usual three). The steel floorplate straddles the front of the trigger guard bow for added strength and security.

An express-style quarter rib provides a rigid, non-glare base for the rear sight, which consists of a fixed blade and one auxiliary fold-down. The front swivel is carried by a contoured barrel band to keep the stud away from the off-hand under the recoil of big calibers. The front sight assembly is also a barrel-band type for maximum strength. The blade sits on a non-glare ramp and is protected by a steel hood.

The Safari's barreled action carries a subtle semi-matte blue, which lends an understated elegance to this eminently practical rifle. The functional, classic-style stock is of European walnut selected especially for its strength with respect to grain orientation as well as for color and figure. A rosewood forend tip, a steel grip cap, an elegant, beaded cheekpiece and presentation-style recoil pad complete the stock embellishments.

Calibers: 300 Win. Mag., 338 Win. Mag & 375 H&H Mag. See also **Specifications Table**.
Price: $2245.00

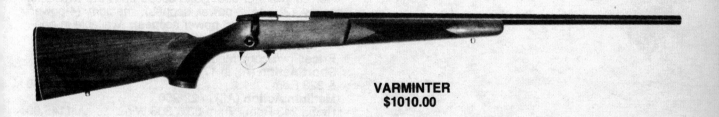

VARMINTER
$1010.00

The Sako Varminter is specifically designed with a prone-type stock for shooting from the ground or bench. The forend is extra wide to provide added steadiness when rested on sandbags or makeshift field rests.

Calibers: 222 Rem. & 223 Rem. (Short Action); 22-250, 243 Rem. & 308 Win. (Medium Action). Will also be available in the near future in 6mm PPC and 22 PPC. **Price: $1085.00**

SAKO RIFLES

DELUXE SHORT ACTION

DELUXE

All the fine-touch features you expect of the deluxe grade Sako are here—beautifully grained French Walnut, superbly done high-gloss finish, hand-cut checkering, deep rich bluing and rosewood forend tip and grip cap. And of course the accuracy, reliability and superior field performance for which Sako is so justly famous are still here too. It's all here—it just weighs less than it used to. Think of it as more for less.

In addition, the scope mounting system on these Sakos is among the strongest in the world. Instead of using separate bases, a tapered dovetail is milled right into the receiver, to which the scope rings are mounted. A beautiful system that's been proven by over 20 years of use. Sako scope rings are available in *low* (2½ to 3-power scopes), *medium* (4-power scopes) and *high* (6-power scopes). Available in one-inch only.

Prices (w/Scope Mounts)
Short Action (AI) in 17 Rem., 222 Rem.
& 223 Rem. **$1145.00**
Medium Action (AII) in 22-250
Rem., 243 Rem., 7mm-08 & 308 Win. 1145.00
Long Action (AV) in 25-06 Rem.,
270 Win., 30-06 . . . . 1145.00
in 7 mm Rem. Mag., 300 Win. Mag.,
338 Win. Mag., 9.3 × 62, 375 H&H Mag. 1160.00
in 300 Weatherby Mag. 1170.00

SAKO SUPER DELUXE $2245.00

Sako offers the Super Deluxe to the most discriminating gun buyer. This one-of-a-kind beauty is available on special order.

SAKO RIFLES

SAKO Rifle Specifications
The Closest To "Custom" in a Production Rifle

	Model	Action*	Dimensions: Total length (in)	Dimensions: Barrel length (in)	Dimensions: Weight (lbs)	Caliber/Rate of Twist: 17 Rem / 10"; 222 Rem / 14"; 223 Rem / 12"	Caliber/Rate of Twist: 22-250 Rem / 14"; 243 Win / 10"; 7 mm-08 / 9½"; 308 Win / 12"	Caliber/Rate of Twist: 25-06 Rem / 10"; 6.5 x 5.5 / 10"; 270 Win / 10"; 7 x 64 / 10"; 30-06 / 10"	Caliber/Rate of Twist: 7mm / Rem Mag. / 9½"; 300 Win Mag / 10	Caliber/Rate of Twist: 338 Win Mag / 10"; 9.3 x 62 / 14"; 375 H&H Mag / 12"	Stock Finish: Lacquered	Stock Finish: Oiled	Sights: Without sights	Sights: Open sights	Sights: Base for telescopic sight mounts	Magaz.: Magazine capacity	Butt plate: Rubber	Butt plate: Hard
RIFLES	HUNTER	A I	41½	21¼	5¾	• • •					•	•	•		•	6	•	
		A II	42½	21¾	6¾		• • • • 1) 1) 1)				•	•	•	•	•	5	•	
		A V	44	22	7¼			• • • • •			•	•	•	•	•	5	•	
		A V	44	22	7¼				• •		•	•	•	•	•	3	•	
		A V	44	22	7½					• • •	•	•	•	•	•	3	•	
	DELUXE	A I	41½	21¼	5¾	• • •					•	•	•		•	6	•	
		A II	42½	21¾	6¾		• • • •				•	•	•	•	•	5	•	
		A V	44	22	7¼			• • • • •			•	•	•	•	•	5	•	
		A V	44	22	7¼				• •		•	•	•	•	•	3	•	
		A V	44	22	7½					• • •	•	•	•	•	•	3	•	
	SUPERDELUXE	A I	41½	21¼	6¼	• • •					•	•	•	•	•	6	•	
		A II	42½	21¾	7		• • • •				•	•	•	•	•	5	•	
		A V	43½	22	7½			• • • • •			•	•	•	•	•	5	•	
		A V	43½	22	7½				• •		•	•	•	•	•	3	•	
		A V	43½	22	7¾					• • •	•	•	•	•	•	3	•	
	FIBERCLASS & LAMINATED	A II	42½	21¾	7		• • • •				•	•	•	•	•	5	•	
		A V	43½	22	7¼			• • • • •			L		•		•	5	•	
		A V	43½	22	7¼				• •		L		•		•	3	•	
		A V	43½	22	7½					• • •	L		•		•	3	•	
CARBINES	CARBINE	A II	39½	18½	6¾		• •1) •1) •1)					•		•	•	5	•	
		A V	40½	18½	7¼			• • • • •				•		•	•	5	•	
		A V	40½	18½	7¼				• •			•		•	•	3	•	
		A V	40½	18½	7¾					• • •		•		•	•	3	•	
	MANNLICHER-STYLE	A II	39½	18½	6½		• •1) •1) •1)					•		•	•	5	•	
		A V	40½	18½	7			• • • • •			L	•		•	•	5	•	
		A V	40½	18½	7				• •		L	•		•	•	3	•	
		A V	40½	18½	7½					• • •	L	•		•	•	3	•	
	FIBERCLASS	A V	40½	18½	7¼			• • • • •			L			•	•	5	•	
		A V	40½	18½	7¼				• •		L			•	•	3	•	
		A V	40½	18½	7½					• • •	L			•	•	3	•	
CUSTOM	SAFARI	A V	43	22	8¼					• • •		•		•	•	4	•	
	TARGET	A I	42¾	22¾	10	•3)						•	•		•2)	6	•	
		A II	45	25¼	10		• • 3)4)					•	•		•2)	5	•	
	VARMINT	A I	42¾	22¾	8½	• • •						•	•		•	6		•
		A II	43¼	22¾	8½		• • • •					•	•		•	5		•

All models can be supplied with stainless steel barrels to special order. 1) Available with detachable magazine to special order. 2) Diopter sight mounting set available as an accessory. 3) Available without magazine to special order. 4) Target 308 Win supplied with detachable magazine. Standard delivery includes two 5-round magazines.
L = Fiberglass stock, fully mat-checkered. All calibers available with stainless steel barrel, without open sights on special order.

*Actions are also known as A I = Short A II = Medium A III = Long
A IV =
A V =

RIFLES

SAKO ACTIONS

Only by building a rifle around a Sako action do shooters enjoy the choice of three different lengths, each scaled to a specific family of cartridges. The A1 (Short) action is miniaturized in every respect to match the .222 family, which includes everything from .17 Remington to .222 Remington Magnum. The A11 (Medium) action is scaled to the medium-length cartridges of standard (30-06) bolt face—.22-250, .243, 7mm-08, .308 or similar length cartridges. The AV (Long) action is offered in either standard or Magnum bolt face and accommodates cartridges up to 3.65 inches in overall length, including rounds like the .300 Weatherby and .375 H&H Magnum. For lefthanders, only Long Action is offered in either standard or magnum bolt face. All actions are furnished in-the-white only.

AI-1 (SHORT ACTION)
CALIBERS:
17 Rem.
222 Rem.
222 Rem. Mag.
223 Rem.
$366.00

AII-1 (MEDIUM ACTION)
CALIBERS:
22-250 Rem. (AII-3)
243 Win.
308 Win.
7 mm – 08
$366.00

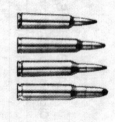

AV-4 (LONG ACTION)
CALIBERS:
25-06 Rem. (AV-1)
6.55 x 55
270 Win. (AV-1)
7 x 64
30-06 (AV-1)
7mm Rem. Mag.
300 Win. Mag.
338 Win. Mag.
9.3 x 62
375 H&H Mag.
$366.00

SAUER RIFLES

Maker of fine rifles and shotguns since 1751, the J.P. Sauer & Sohn Company of West Germany announces its Sauer 90 Bolt Action Rifle series in Short, Medium and Magnum, each available in numerous calibers. The Sauer 90 is also available in two configurations—Standard and Deluxe. The latter includes features of the Standard model as well as the following: premium European walnut stock, engine turned bolt, and gold-plated trigger. Prices furnished on request.

MODEL S-90 MEDIUM

MODEL S-90 STUTZEN

MODEL S-90 JUNIOR

SAUER RIFLES
SAUR 90

	JUNIOR	MEDIUM	MAGNUM	SAFARI	STUTZEN JR.	STUTZEN
Calibers	22 Rem., 22-250 Rem., 243 Win., 308 Win.	270 Win. 30-06 6.5 × 57 7 × 64 9.3 × 62	6.5 × 68 7mm Rem. Mag., 300 Win. Mag., 300 Weath. Mag. 375 H&H 8 × 685 9.3 × 64 Brenneke	458 Win. Mag.	222 Rem., 22-250 Rem., 243 Win., 308 Win.	6.5 × 57 270 Win., 7 × 64 30-06 9.3 × 62
Barrel length	22.4″	22.4″	26″	23.6″	20″	20″
Overall length	42.5″	43.3″	46.5″	44.8″	40″	41″
Weight	7.3 lbs.	7.5 lbs.	7.7 lbs.	10.6 lbs.	7.5 lbs.	7.7 lbs.

SAUER RIFLES

MODEL S-90 MAGNUM

MODEL 200

This new bolt action rifle can change calibers in minutes simply by changing barrels. A unique bolt-to-barrel lock-up system does not require that the barrel be threaded into the receiver. See also table below.

SPECIFICATIONS
Caliber: 243 Win., 270 Win., 25-06, 30-06, 308 Win. (short action in 243 Win. and 308 Win. only). **Barrel length:** 23.6″. **Length of pull:** 14.4″. **Weight:** 6.6 lbs. (L series) and 7.7 lbs. (S series).

Model 200 Features

	Standard	Deluxe	Deluxe E
Drilled and tapped for open sights	●	●	●
Drilled and tapped for scope mounts	●	●	●
Quick-release sling swivel	●	●	●
Conventional trigger (single set trigger optional)	●	●	●
Standard walnut stocks	●		
Deluxe stocks of walnut heartwood		●	
Deluxe stocks of select figured walnut			●
Rubber recoil pad	●		
Ventilated rubber recoil pad		●	●
Jewelled bolt		●	●
Engraved receiver (steel S series only)			●
Optional: Engraved barrel (steel S series only)			●

Optional Features

	Standard	Deluxe	Deluxe E
Set trigger (conventional trigger combined with single set trigger mechanism)	●	●	●
Open sights	●	●	●
Scope mounts	●	●	●
Premium quality stocks	●	●	
Monte-Carlo style buttstock (only suitable in combination with scopes)	●	●	●
Left-hand buttstock	●	●	●

SAVAGE CENTERFIRE RIFLES

MODEL 110 BOLT-ACTION
CENTERFIRE RIFLES
STANDARD AND MAGNUM CALIBERS

The Savage 100 Series features solid lockup, positive gas protection, precise head space, precision rifled barrels, and select walnut Monte Carlo stocks.

MODEL 110-E

MODEL 110-E
$325.00 ($309.00 w/o sights)
Calibers: 223, 22-250, 243 Win., 30-06, 270 Win., 7mm Rem. Mag.

A specially designed version of the 110 bolt action rifle featuring a free floating barrel, satin blue receiver (to reduce light reflections), and Wundhammer swell pistol grip. Internal box holds 4 rounds plus one in the chamber. Stock is select walnut with high Monte Carlo.

SPECIFICATIONS
Barrel length: 22" (24" Magnum). **Overall length:** 43" (45" Magnum). **Pull:** 13¹/₂". **Drop at comb:** 1⁵/₈". **Drop at heel:** 2¹/₄". **Weight:** 7 lbs. **Capacity:** 5. **Rate of twist:** 1 turn in 9¹/₂· (7mm Rem. Mag.); 1 turn in 10" (243, 30-06, 270); 1 turn in 12" (308); 1 turn in 14" (223, 22-250)

MODEL 110-K (not shown)
$399.00

SPECIFICATIONS

Calibers: 243, 270, 30-06, 338 Win. Mag. **Barrel length:** 22" (24" Magnum). **Overall length:** 43¹/₂" (45¹/₂" Magnum). **Pull:** 13¹/₂". **Drop at comb:** 1⁵/₈". **Drop at heel:** 2¹/₄". **Weight:** 7 lbs. **Capacity:** 5 (4 in Magnum). **Rate of twist:** 1 turn in 9¹/₂" (7mm Rem. Mag.); 1 turn in 10" (243, 270, 30-06, 338). **Features:** tapped for top mounted scope; free floating chrome moly barrel; top tang safety; multi-colored laminated hardwood Monte Carlo stock. **Sights:** Bead on removable ramp (front); removable, adjustable (rear).

SAVAGE CENTERFIRE RIFLES

MODEL 99-C LEVER ACTION
$525.00

Clip magazine allows for the chambering of pointed, high velocity big bore cartridges. **Action:** Hammerless, lever action, cocking indicator, top tang safety. **Magazine:** Detachable clip; holds 4 rounds plus one in the chamber. **Stock:** Select walnut with high Monte Carlo and deep fluted comb. Cut checkered stock and fore-end with swivel studs. Recoil pad and pistol grip cap. **Sights:** Detachable hooded ramp front sight, bead front sight on removable ramp adjustable rear sight. Tapped for top mount scopes. **Barrel length:** 22″ **Overall length:** 42³/₄″. **Weight:** 7 lbs. **Calibers:** .243 Win, .308 Win.

BOLT ACTION MODEL 110-DL (left hand)
$489.00
Calibers right/left hand; 223 30-06 Sprg., 270 Win., 7mm Rem. Mag. & 243 Mag.
MODEL 110-D (right-hand)
$409.00

SPECIFICATIONS
Barrel length: 22″ (24″ Magnum). **Overall length:** 43″ (45″ Magnum). **Pull:** 13¹/₂″; drop at comb: 1⁵/₈″; drop at heel: 2¹/₄″. **Weight:** 7-7³/₄ lbs. **Capacity:** 5 (4 in Magnum). **Rate of twist:** 1 turn in 9¹/₂″ (7mm Rem. Mag.); 1 turn in 10″ (243, 30-06, 270); 1 turn in 14″ (223).

MODEL 110-V

BOLT ACTION MODEL 110-V
$439.00
Calibers: 223, 22-250

SPECIFICATIONS
Barrel length: 25″. **Overall length:** 47″. **Stock length:** 13¹/₂″. **Drop at comb:** ⁹/₁₆″. **Drop at heel:** ⁹/₁₆″. **Weight:** 9 lbs. **Capacity:** 5 (1 in chamber).

SAVAGE/STEVENS 22 RIFLES

STEVENS MODEL 987 AUTOLOADER
22 Long Rifle with 1541 4X Scope and Mount
$119.00 (scope not included)

The Model 987-T has top tang safety and 15-shot capacity tubular magazine. Autoloading is with 22 long rifle only. Trigger must be pulled and released for each shot. Monte Carlo stock is walnut-finished hardwood.

SPECIFICATIONS
Barrel length: 20″. **Overall length:** 40½″. **Weight:** 6 lbs. **Action:** Semiautomatic. **Safety:** Top tang. **Stock:** Monte Carlo; walnut finished hardwood. **Rate of twist:** 1 turn in 16″. **Sights:** Sporting (front); open (rear). **Magazine type:** Tubular. **Capacity:** 16. **Features:** Grooved for scope; butt plate hard rubber.

STEVENS 72 CRACKSHOT
22 Long, Short and Long Rifle
$165.00

This unique falling block action is a pleasure to handle, shoot or simply admire. It offers balance, smooth functioning and safety. This popular 22 rifle is truly in the great Stevens tradition. It features an octagonal barrel, case-hardened frame, walnut stock and forend with oil finish.

SPECIFICATIONS
Barrel length: 22″. **Overall length:** 37″. **Weight:** 4½ lbs. **Sights:** Sporting (front); open (rear). **Safety:** Visible hammer, manual cocking. **Stock:** Walnut. **Rate of twist:** 1 turn in 16″. **Stock:** Walnut. **Capacity:** 1. **Features:** Falling block, butt plate hard rubber.

RIFLES

SOVEREIGN RIFLES

"LITTLE JOE" 22 SINGLE SHOT
$96.95

SPECIFICATIONS
Caliber: 22LR or 22 WRM
Barrel length: 18½"
Overall length: 35"
Weight: 3¾ lbs.
Sights: Adj. rear; hooded ramp front
Stock: Walnut finished hardwood "Classic" style
Operation: Bolt action w/cocking piece

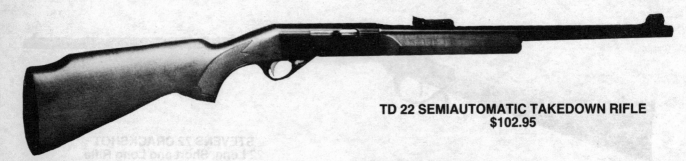

TD 22 SEMIAUTOMATIC TAKEDOWN RIFLE
$102.95

SPECIFICATIONS
Caliber: 22LR (HV)
Barrel length: 21"
Overall length: 41"
Weight: 6½ lbs.
Sights: Fully adj. rear; hooded ramp front; receiver grooved
for scope mounting
Capacity: 10 round clip
Stock: Walnut finished hardwood
Finish: Polished blue

STEYR-MANNLICHER RIFLES

MODEL MARKSMAN
(Shown with synthetic stock and optional Kahles ZF69 scope)

Features: Parkerized finish; choice of interchangeable single- or double-set triggers; detachable 5-shot rotary straight-line feed magazine of "Makrolon"; 10-shot magazine optional; heavy-duty receiver drilled and tapped for scope mounting.

Marksman:
Cycolac half stock.	$1050.00
Walnut half stock	1247.00
SSG Scope Mount	125.00

SPECIFICATIONS
Calibers: 243 Win., 308 Win. (7.62 × 51)
Barrel length: 26″
Weight: 8.6 lbs. (9.9 lbs. with Kahles scope)
Overall length: 44.5″
Stock: Choice of synthetic half stock of ABS "Cycolac" or walnut; removable spacers in butt section adjusts length of pull from 12³⁄₄″ to 14″
Sights: Hooded blade front; folding rear leaf sight

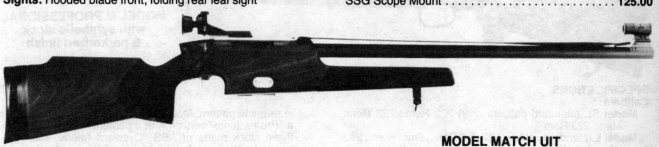

MODEL MATCH UIT

Match UIT:
Walnut half stock	$2192.00

Also available: **Model SSGT-II** w/26″ barrel; .308 caliber.
Price: $1183.00.

Features 26″ heavy barrel, 10-shot box magazine, match bolt, Walther target peep sights, mirage cover, and adjustable rail in forend to adjust sling travel. **Weight:** 11 lbs. **Calibers:** 308 Win. and 234 Win.

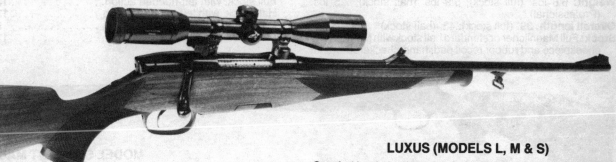

SPECIFICATIONS
Calibers: Model L (standard calibers) 22-250 Rem., 6mm Rem., 243 Win., 308 Win.
  Model L (optional metric calibers) 5.6 × 57
  Model M (standard calibers) 25-06 Rem., 270 Win., 7 × 57, 7 × 64, 30-06
  Model M (optional metric calibers) 6.5 × 55, 6.5 × 57, 7.5 × 55, 9.3 × 62
  Model S 300 Win. Mag., 7mm Rem. Mag. (barrel length: 26″)
Barrel length: 20″ (full stock); 23.6″ (half stock)
Weight: 6.8 lbs. (full stock); 6.9 lbs. (half stock)
Overall length: 39″ (full stock); 43″ (half stock)

LUXUS (MODELS L, M & S)

Stock: Hand-checkered walnut with Monte Carlo cheekpiece; either full Mannlicher or half stock; European hand-rubbed oil finish or high-gloss lacquer finish
Sights: Ramp front adjustable for elevation; open U-notch rear adjustable for windage
Features: Single combination trigger (becomes hair trigger when moved forward before firing); detachable 3-shot steel straight-line feed magazine (6-shot optional). 6 rear locking lugs; drilled and tapped for scope mounts

Prices:
Full stock (in **Model L & M** calibers)	$1458.00
Half stock (in **Model L & M** calibers)	1387.00
Half stock (in **Model S** calibers)	1525.00

STEYR-MANNLICHER RIFLES

MODEL L
shown with full stock
and double triggers

MODEL M
shown with half stock
and single trigger

MODEL M PROFESSIONAL
with synthetic stock
& parkerized finish

SPECIFICATIONS

Calibers:
Model SL (standard calibers only) 222 Rem., 222 Rem. Mag., 223 Rem.
Model L (standard calibers) 22-250 Rem., 6mm Rem., 243 Win., 308 Win.
Model L (optional metric caliber) 5.6×57
Model M (standard calibers) 25-06 Rem., 270 Win., 7×57, 7×64, 30-06 Spr.
Model M (optional metric calibers) 6.5×55, 6.5×57, 7.5×55, 8×57JS, 9.3×62
Barrel length: 20″ (full stock); 23.6″ (half stock)
Weight: 6.8 lbs. (full stock); 6.9 lbs. (half stock); 7.5 lbs. (Professional)
Overall length: 39″ (full stock); 43″ (half stock)
Stock: Full Mannlicher or standard half stock with Monte Carlo cheekpiece and rubber recoil pad; hand-checkered walnut

in skip-line pattern; Model M with half stock is available in a "Professional" version with a parkerized finish and synthetic stock made of ABS "Cycolac" (made with right-handed action only); left-handed action available in full stock and half stock.
Features: Choice of fine-crafted single- or double-set triggers. Detachable 5-shot rotary magazine of "Makrolon"; 6 rear locking lugs; drilled and tapped for scope mounting.

Model L Full stock	**$1120.00**
Model M Half stock	1040.00
Full stock, with left-handed action	1340.00
Half stock, with left-handed action	1278.00
Professional, with iron sights	935.00
Model SL	1120.00

MODEL S AND S/T MAGNUM

SPECIFICATIONS

Calibers:
Model S 257 Weatherby Mag., 264 Win. Mag., 300 Win. Mag., 7mm Rem. Mag., 300 H&H Mag., 375 H&H Mag.
Model S (Optional calibers) 6.5×68
Model S/T (Heavy barrel) 375 H&H Mag., 458 Win. Mag.
Model S/T (Optional caliber) 9.3×64
Barrel length: 26″ Model S/T (with 26″ heavy barrel)
Weight: 8.4 lbs. (Model S); 9.02 lbs. (Model S/T); add .66 lbs. for butt mag. opt.
Overall length: 45″

Stock: Half stock with Monte Carlo cheekpiece and rubber recoil pad; hand-checkered walnut in skip-line pattern; available with optional spare magazine inletted in butt stock.
Features: Choice of fine-crafted single- or double-set triggers; detachable 4-shot rotary magazine of "Makrolon"; 6 rear locking lugs; drilled and tapped for scope mounting.

Model S	**$1324.00**
Model S/T with opt. butt magazine	1405.00

THOMPSON/CENTER RIFLES

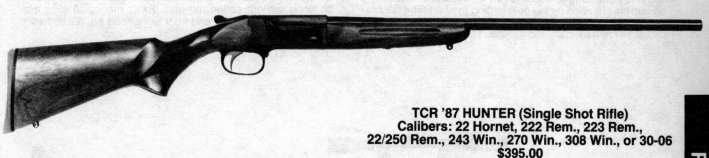

TCR '87 HUNTER (Single Shot Rifle)
Calibers: 22 Hornet, 222 Rem., 223 Rem., 22/250 Rem., 243 Win., 270 Win., 308 Win., or 30-06
$395.00

Barrels quickly interchange from one caliber to the next

Chambered for eight popular hunting cartridges, this superbly accurate sports rifle offers the simplicity and strength of a break-open design coupled with the unique feature of interchangeable barrels. Triggers function double set or single stage. A positive lock cross-bolt safety offers maximum security. Wood is hand-selected American black walnut from the Thompson/Center mill. All barrels are equipped with iron sights, removable for scope mounting.

SPECIFICATIONS
Barrel length: 23″ (Standard) and 25⅞″ (Silhouette/Varmint). **Overall length:** 39½″ (Standard) and 43⅜″ (Silhouette/Varmint). **Weight:** 6 lbs. 14 oz. (Standard) and 7 lbs. 8 oz. (Silhouette/Varmint).

THE CONTENDER CARBINE
$370.00

Available in 10 calibers: 22 LR, 22 Hornet, 222 Rem., 223 Rem., 7mm T.C.U., 7 × 30 Waters, 30/30 Win., 35 Rem., 44 Mag. and 357 Rem. Max. Barrels are 21″ long and are interchangeable, with adjustable iron sights and tapped and drilled for scope mounts. Accessory rifle barrels are **$160.00**. .410 ga. shotgun barrel (3″ shotshell): **$180.00**.

TIKKA RIFLES

Tikka Bolt Action Rifles combine aesthetic beauty, good balance and hard, rugged construction for bolt-action shooting. The barrels are rifled by the cold forging method. The double lugged chrome-moly bolt rides smoother and easier on double rails for efficient ejection and locking. The select grain walnut stock and palm-swelled grip are enhanced by the hand-cut checkering on both grip and forestock. Trigger adjustment can be done without action removal. Extra magazine clips are available. Sling swivels and front sight hood are packed with each gun.

M55 DELUXE

M55 STANDARD

MODEL M55
$575.00 (Standard)

SPECIFICATIONS
Calibers: 222 Rem., 223 Rem., 22-250 Rem., 243 Win., 308 Win. (6mm Rem. and 17 Rem. available in Standard and Deluxe models only)
Barrel length: 23.2″ (24.8″ in Sporter and Heavy Barrel models)
Overall length: 42.8″ (44″ in Sporter and Heavy Barrel models)
Weight: 7.25 lbs. (8.8 lbs. in Heavy Barrel; 9 lbs. in Sporter)

Prices (subject to change)
Standard $330.00
Deluxe 360.00
Trapper 330.00
Continental 375.00
Sporter 400.00
  with sights 420.00

TIKKA RIFLES

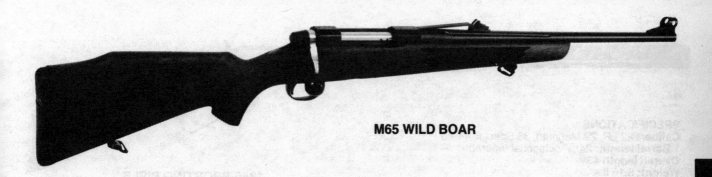

M65 WILD BOAR

M65 SPORTER MASTER

M65 SPORTER

MODEL M65
$610.00 (Standard)
650.00 (Magnum)

SPECIFICATIONS
Calibers: 25-06, 270 Win., 308 Win., 338 Win. Mag., 30-06, 7mm Rem. Mag., 9, 3 × 62, 300 Win. Mag. (Sporter and Heavy Barrel models in 270 Win., 308 Win., and 30-06 only)
Barrel length: 22.4″ (24.8″ in Sporter and Heavy Barrel models)
Overall length: 43.2″ (44″ in Sporter; 44.8″ in Heavy Barrel)
Weight: 7.5 lbs. (9.9 lbs. in Sporter and Heavy Barrel models)

Prices (subject to change)
Standard	$330.00
Deluxe	360.00
Sporter	405.00
with sights	425.00
Trapper (w/o sights)	330.00
with sights	350.00
Continental	375.00
Wild Boar	320.00

A. UBERTI RIFLES & CARBINES

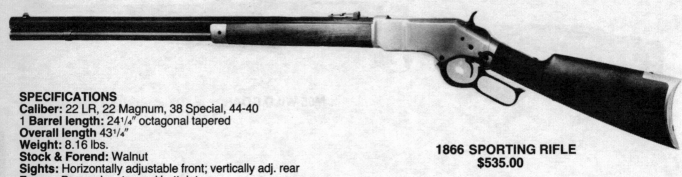

SPECIFICATIONS
Caliber: 22 LR, 22 Magnum, 38 Special, 44-40
1 Barrel length: 24¼" octagonal tapered
Overall length 43¼"
Weight: 8.16 lbs.
Stock & Forend: Walnut
Sights: Horizontally adjustable front; vertically adj. rear
Frame: Brass elevator and buttplate

1866 SPORTING RIFLE
$535.00

SPECIFICATIONS
Calibers: 22 LR, 22 Magnum, 38 Special, 44-40
Barrel length: 19" round tapered
Overall lenght: 38¼"
Weight: 7.38 lbs.
Sights: Fixed
Also available:
1873 Rifle w/24¼" barrel (43¼" overall). . . . **$659.00**

1873 CARBINE
$629.00

SPECIFICATIONS
Caliber: 44 Magnum (44-40 convert.)
Barrel length: 18" round
Overall length: 34"
Weight: 4.41 lbs.
Stock: Walnut w/brass buttplate
Also available:
Buckhorn S.A. Buntline & Target w/23" overall length . . .
   $355.00

BUCKHORN REVOLVING CARBINE

$429.00

WALTHER TARGET RIFLES

Photographs not available from manufacturer at time of publication.

U.I.T. MATCH
$1325.00

Caliber: 22 LR
Bolt action: Single shot
Barrel length: 25^1/$_2$″
Overall length: 44^3/$_4$″
Weight: 13 lbs.

KK/MS SILHOUETTE
$1050.00

Caliber: 22 LR
Bolt action: Single shot
Barrel length: 25^1/$_2$″
Overall length: 44^3/$_4$″
Weight: 8^3/$_4$ lbs

RUNNING BOAR
$1100.00

Caliber 22 LR
Bolt action: Single shot
Barrel length: 23^1/$_2$″
Overall length: 42″
Weight: 10^1/$_4$ lbs.

MODEL GX-1
$1900.00

Caliber: 22 LR
Bolt action: Single shot
Barrel length: 25^1/$_2$″
Overall length: 46″
Weight: 16^1/$_2$″

WEATHERBY RIFLES

MARK V LAZERMARK

With its intricately carved stock pattern, this Mark V model captures the beauty of Old World craftsmanship using today's most modern technology—laser.

224 and 22-250 Varmintmaster (24″ barrel)	**$1019.00**
240, 257, 270, 7mm & 300 W.M. and 30-06 (24″ barrel)	1105.00
378 W.M.	1281.00
340 W.M.	1127.00
460 W.M. (includes customized action, custom stock, integral muzzle brake)	1421.00

WEATHERBY RIFLES

MARK V DELUXE RIFLE

SPECIFICATIONS (see also table below)

224 Weatherby Mag., 22/250 Varmintmaster	**$971.00**
240, 257, 270, 7mm, 300 W.M., 30-06	**991.00** (24″ barrel);
	$987.00 (26″ barrel)
340 Weatherby Mag. only	**1011.00**
378 Weatherby Mag. only	**1165.00**
460 Weatherby Mag. only	**1305.00**

MARK V RIFLE SPECIFICATIONS

CALIBER	.224	.22/250	.240	.257	.270	7mm	.30-06	.300	.340	.378	.460
Model	Right hand 24″ or 26″ bbl. Left hand model not available.		Right or left hand 24″ bbl. Right hand 26″ bbl. Left hand 26″ bbl. **available in .300 cal. only**						Right or left hand 26″ bbl. only.	Right or left hand 26″ bbl. only.	Right or left hand 26″ bbl. only.
**Weight w/o sights	6¹/₂ lbs.		7¹/₄ lbs.						8¹/₂ lbs.		10¹/₂ lbs.
Overall length	43¹/₄″ or 45¹/₄″ dependent on barrel length		44¹/₂″ or 46¹/₂″ dependent on barrel length						46¹/₂″		
Capacity	5 shots; 4 in mag.; 1 in chamber	4 shots: 3 in mag.; 1 in chamber	6 shots: 4 in mag.; 1 in chamber	4 shots: 3 in magazine; 1 in chamber			5 shots: 4 in mag.; 1 in chamber	4 shots: 3 in magazine; 1 in chamber	3 shots: 2 in magazine; 1 in chamber		
Barrel	24″ standard or 26″ semi-target		24″ standard or 26″ #2 contour						26″ #2 contour	26″ #3 contour	26″ #4* contour
Rifling	1-14″ twist		1-9″ twist	1-10″ twist						1-12″ twist	1-16″ twist
Sights	Scope or iron sights extra										
Stocks: Deluxe	American walnut, individually hand-bedded to assure precision accuracy. High lustre, durable stock finish. Quick detachable sling swivels. Basket weave checkering. Monte Carlo style with cheek piece, especially designed for both scope and iron sighted rifles. Length of pull 13¹/₂″.									French walnut. Lgth Pull: 13⁷/₈″	
Lazermark	American walnut, individually hand-bedded to assure precision accuracy. High lustre, durable stock finish. Quick detachable sling swivels. Laser carving on forearm, pistol grip and under cheek piece. Monte Carlo style with cheek piece, especially designed for both scope and iron sighted rifles. Length of pull 13¹/₂″.									French walnut. Lgth Pull: 13⁷/₈″	
Fibermark	Not available		Molded fiberglass, individually hand bedded to assure precision accuracy. Non-glare, black, wrinkle finish. Quick detachable sling swivels. Monte Carlo style with cheek piece, especially designed for both scope and iron sighted rifles. Length of pull 13¹/₂″.						Not available.		
Action	Drop dimensions from bore centerline: Mark V— Comb: ³/₄″ Monte Carlo: ¹/₂″ Heel: 1¹/₂″ Varmintmaster— Comb: ⁹/₁₆″ Monte Carlo: ¹/₄″ Heel:1¹/₈										
	A scaled-down version of the popular Mark V action, with 6 precision locking lugs in place of 9.		Featuring the Mark V, world's strongest and safest action. The nine locking lugs have almost double the shear area of the lugs found on conventional bolt rifles. The cartridge case head is completely enclosed in the bolt and barrel. .460 action includes hand honing, bolt knob fully checkered, bolt and follower damascened, custom engraved floor plate.								
Safety	Forward moving release accessible and positive										

WEATHERBY RIFLES

MARK V FIBERMARK

The Fibermark's hand-molded fiberglass stock is impervious to climatic changes. It shoots with constant accuracy no matter what the weather—from desert heat to mountain snow. The stock is finished with a non-glare black wrinkle finish for a positive grip, even in wet, humid weather. Available in right-hand only, 24" or 26" barrels. **Weight:** 7¹/₄ lbs. (24") and 8 lbs. (26"). Additional specifications listed on page 246.

240, 257, 270, 7mm & 300 W.M. and 30-06 . . . . . **$1123.00**
24" barrel; add $20 for 26" barrel
340 W.M. 1143.00

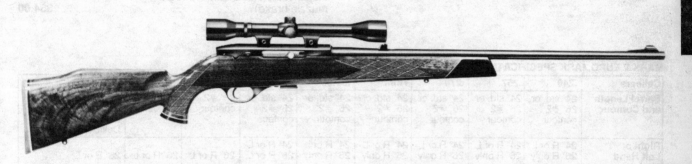

MARK XXII DELUXE 22 SEMIAUTOMATIC

Although lighter and handier than Weatherby's big game rifle, this .22 semiautomatic boasts the same pointing characteristics and basic stock design. It is also the only .22 which allows hunters to choose single shot or semiautomatic fire. The Mark XXII is available in both clip and tubular models. The tubular model has a 15 shot capacity; the clip model comes with a 10 shot magazine. Folding leaf rear iron sights adjustable for windage and elevation and ramp front sights are standard. The receiver is precision-grooved for dovetailed scope mounts. Other features include non-skid rubber butt pad, Monte Carlo stock, and rosewood forend tip. Specifications are listed below.

Price. $454.00

MARK XXII .22 AUTOMATIC SPECIFICATIONS

Action	Semi-automatic with single shot selector
Caliber	.22 long rifle cartridges only
Barrel	24", special steel, contoured barrel
Overall length	42¹/₄"
Magazine	Clip model—comes with 10-shot magazine. Extra 5 or 10-shot magazines available. Tubular model—15-shot capacity.
Stock	Select walnut, hand-checkered, Monte Carlo stock with cheek piece, Rosewood fore-end tip and pistol grip cap with diamond inlay. Non-skid rubber butt pad. Length of pull 13¹/₂".
Sights	Adjustable folding rear sight; ramp front sight.
Safety	Shotgun type tang safety.
Weight	Approx. 6 lbs. without scope.
Trigger	Crip, clean precision trigger pull.
Mounts	Receiver is precision-grooved for dovetail scope mounts.

WEATHERBY RIFLES

WEATHERBY EUROMARK

The principal features of this Mark V model include a hand-rubbed, satin oil finish Claro walnut stock and non-glare special process blue matte barreled action. Left hand models are available. Specifications are listed below.

22-250, 243, 25-06, 270, 7mm. Rem.	**$1040.00**
340 Win. Mag.	1060.00
.378 Win. Mag. (right/left hand)	1214.00
.460 Win. Mag. (right/left hand; includes custom stock, customized action, integral muzzle brake)	1354.00

MARK V EUROMARK SPECIFICATIONS

Calibers	.240	.257	.270	7mm	.30-06	.300	.340	.378	.460
Barrel Length and Contour	24″ std. or 26″ #2 contour	24″ std. or 26″ #2 contour	24″ std. or 26″ #2 contour	24″ std. or 26″ #2 contour	24″ std. or 26″ #2 contour	24″ std. or 26″ #2 contour	26″ #2 contour	26″ #3 contour	26″ #4 contour Pendleton Dekicker standard.
Right or Left Hand Model	24″ R or L 26″ R only	24″ R or L 26″ R only	24″ R or L 26″ R only	24″ R or L 26″ R only	24″ R or L 26″ R only	24″ R or L 26″ R only	26″ R or L	26″ R or L	26″ R or L
Approx. Weight without Sights	7¼ lbs.	7¼ lbs.	7¼ lbs.	7¼ lbs.	7¼ lbs.	7¼ lbs.	8½ lbs.	8½ lbs.	10½ lbs.
Overall Length	44½″ or 46½″	44½″ or 46½″	44½″ or 46½″	44½″ or 46½″	44½″ or 46½″	44½″ or 46½″	46½″	46½″	46½″
Magazine Cap.	4	3	3	3	4	3	3	2	2
Rifling	1-9″ twist	1-10″ twist	1-10″ twist	1-10″ twist	1-10″ twist	1-10″ twist	1-10″ twist	1-12″ twist	1-16″ twist
Stock	Made of American walnut. Individually hand-bedded to assure precision accuracy. High lustre, durable finish. Quick detachable sling swivels. Basket weave hand checkering. Monte Carlo style with cheek piece, especially designed for both scope and iron sighted rifles. Length of pull is 13½″. Drop dimensions from bore centerline are comb: ¾″, Monte Carlo: ½″, heel: 1½″								Made of European walnut. Extended tail of checkering on pistol drip. Length of pull is 13⅞″
Action	The Mark V has the world's strongest and safest action. The nine locking lugs have almost double the shear area of lugs found on conventional bolt action rifles. The cartridge case head is completely enclosed in the bolt and barrel.								Hand-honed action. Fully checkered bolt knob. Damascened bolt and follower. Custom engraved floor plate.
Safety	Forward moving release is accessible and positive.								
Sights	Scope or iron sights are extra.								
Mounts	Receiver drilled and tapped for all standard scope mounts.								

WEATHERBY RIFLES

VANGUARD VGX
Shown with Weatherby Supreme 3-9/XX44S Variable Scope on Buehler mount
$600.00 (without sights)

VANGUARD VGX SPECIFICATIONS (available in right-hand models only)

Calibers	.22-250 Rem.	.22-250 Rem.	.243 Win.	.25-06 Rem.	270 Win.	7mm Rem. Mag.	.30-06	.300 Win. Mag.
Barrel Length	24"	24"	24"	24"	24"	24"	24"	24"
Barrel Contour	No. 3	No. 2	No. 2	No. 2	No. 2	No. 2	No.2	No.2
Approx. Weight	8lb.8oz.	7lb.12oz.	7lb.14oz.	7lb.14oz.	7lb.14oz.	7lb.14oz.	7lb.14oz.	7x
Overall Length	44"*	44"*	44"*	44½"	44½"	44½"	44½"	44½"
Magazine Cap.	5 rnds.	5 rnds.	5 rnds.	5 rnds.	5 rnds.	3 rnds.	5 rnds.	3 rnds.
Rifling	1–14"	1–14"	1–10"	1–10"	1–10"	1–10"	1–10"	1–10"
Sights	Scope or iron sights available at extra cost							
Stock	American walnut, 13½" pull, custom checkering, recoil pad, high lustre finish; rosewood tip and cap.							
Action	Vanguard action of the improved Mauser type.							
Safety	Side operated, forward moving release, accessible and positive.							
Mounts	Van guard action accepts same bases as Mark V action.							

*.22–250 and .243 action is ½" shorter than the standard action.

VANGUARD VGS

The VGS offers the same performance and workmanship as the VGX. The hand-bedded, hammer-forged barrel guarantees accuracy of a 1½" or less 3-shot group at 100 yards.

Price (without sights) **$467.00**

VANGUARD VGS SPECIFICATIONS
(available in right-hand models only)

Calibers	.22-250 Rem.	.22-250 Rem.	.243 Win.	.25-06 Rem.	270 Win.	7mm Rem. Mag.	.30-06	.300 Win. Mag.
Barrel length	24"	24"	24"	24"	24"	24"	24"	24"
Barrel Contour	No. 3	No. 2	No. 2	No. 2	No. 2	No. 2	No. 2	No. 2
Approx. Weight	8lb. 8oz.	7lb. 12oz.	7lb. 12oz.	7lb. 14oz.	7lb. 14oz.	7lb. 14oz.	7lb. 14oz.	7lb. 14oz.
Overall Length	44"*	44"*	44"*	44½"	44½"	44½"	44½"	44½"
Magazine Cap.	5 rnds.	5 rnds.	5 rnds.	5 rnds.	5 rnds.	3 rnds.	5 rnds.	3 rnds.
Rifling	1-14"	1-14'in	1-10"	1-10"	1-10"	1-10"	1-10"	1-10"
Sights	Scope or iorn sights available at extra cost							
Stock	American walnut, 13½" pull, hand checkered, satin finish, butt pad. (Recoil pad on magnum models.)							
Action	Vanguard action of the improved Mauser type.							
Safety	Side operated, forward moving release, accessible and positive.							
Mounts	Vanguard action accepts samebases as Mark V action.							

*.22–250 and .243 action is ½" shorter than the standard action.

RIFLES

WEATHERBY RIFLES

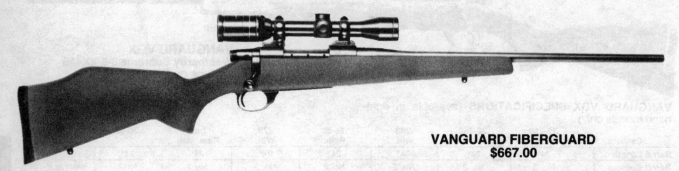

VANGUARD FIBERGUARD
$667.00

The Fiberguard rifle weighs less than 6½ lbs. and features a 20″ barrel. Its fiberglass stock eliminates warping and swelling. See Specifications table below.

VANGUARD VGL (not shown)

This rugged but lightweight version of the VGS weighs only 6½ pounds. It features smooth, dependable action with recessed bolt face and enclosed bolt sleeve. The shorter 20-inch barrel is streamlined from breech to muzzle. See Specifications table below.

Price: (without sights) $467.00

VANGUARD VGL AND FIBERGUARD SPECIFICATIONS
Vanguard rifles available in right hand models only

Calibers	223 Rem.	243 Win.	270 Win.	7mm Rem. Mag.	30-06	308 Win.
Barrel Length	20″	20″	20″	20″	20″	20″
Barrel Contour	No.1	No.1	No.1	No.1	No.1	No.1
Approx. Weight	6lb. 8oz.	6lb. 8oz.	6lb. 10oz.	6lb. 10oz.	6lb. 10oz.	6lb. 8oz.
Overall Length	*40 in.	*40 in.	40½ in.	40½ in.	40½ in.	*40 in.
Magazine Cap	6 rnds.	5 rnds.	5 rnds.	3 rnds.	5 rnds.	5 rnds.
Rifling	1-12″	1-10″	1-10″	1-10″	1-10″	1-10″
Sights	Scope or iron sights available at extra cost.					
Stock	Fiberglass hand molded stock with non-glare, forest green wrinkle finish, 13½″ pull, black butt pad. (Recoil pad on 7mm Rem. Mag.)					
Action	Vanguard action of the improved Mauser type. *Short action is ½″ shorter than the standard action.					
Safety	Side operated, forward moving release, accessible and positive.					
Mounts	Vanguard action accepts same bases as Mark V action.					

WHITWORTH SPORTING RIFLES
SAFARI GRADE EXPRESS MANNLICHER-STYLE CARBINES

MANNLICHER-STYLE CARBINES
$675.00

Available in five popular sporting **calibers:** 243 Win., 270 Win., 7 × 57mm Mauser, 308 Win., and 30-06. **Barrel length:** 20". **Overall length:** 40". **Weight:** 7 lbs. **Capacity:** 5 rounds.

EXPRESS RIFLES
$650.00

Features three safety-lug bolt design for added strength and security . . . Hand-rubbed European walnut stocks with sculpted continental-style cheekpiece . . . Custom three-leaf Express sight . . . Ramp mounted front sight with detachable hood . . . Three-point adjustable trigger . . . Premium hammer-forged chrome-vanadium steel barrels . . . Premium milled-steel Mauser System Action.

Calibers: 375 H&H Magnum and 458 Win. Mag. **Barrel length:** 24". **Overall length:** 44.75". **Weight:** 8¼ lbs. (375 H&H Mag.) and 8½ lbs. (458 Win. Mag.)

WINCHESTER BOLT ACTION RIFLES

MODEL 70 LIGHTWEIGHT RIFLE
$382.00

Available in **calibers:** 22-250 Rem., 223 Rem., 243 Win., 270 Win., 308 Win. and 30-06 Springfield. **Barrel length:** 22" (hammer forged barrel). **Weight:** 6½ lbs. **Stock:** Classic straight stock with satin finish and point pattern cut checkering. Furnished with sling swivel studs.

WINCHESTER BOLT ACTION RIFLES

MODEL 70XTR FEATHERWEIGHT
$444.00

Model 70 XTR Featherweight hunting rifles minimize weight for easy handling and carrying. A new Model 70 European Featherweight in 6.5×55mm Swedish Mauser is being offered for the first time in the U.S. Barrel and receiver have integral recoil lug machined from chrome molybdenum steel. Bolt body and locking lugs are machined from a single steel bar. Thermoplastic bedding mates the receiver recoil lug and the stock for maximum strength and accuracy. Bolt features a jeweled finish and knurled bolt handle. Three-position safety. Receivers drilled and tapped for scope mounting. One-piece walnut stocks are hand-worked and finished with genuine cut checkering.

Also available: **Model 70 XTR WIN-CAM FEATHER-WEIGHT** in 270 Win. and 30-06. **Weight:** 6³/₄ lbs. Camouflage stock. **Price: $464.00.**

MODEL 70XTR FEATHERWEIGHT SPECIFICATIONS

Model	Caliber	Magazine Capacity(a)	Barrel Length	Overall Length	Nominal Length of Pull	Nominal Drop at Comb	Nominal Drop at Heel	Nominal Weight (lbs.)	Rate of Twist (R.H.) 1 Turn in
70 XTR Featherweight	270 Win.	5	22″	42¹/₂″	13¹/₂″	9/16″	7/8″	6³/₄″	10″
Long Action	30-06	5	22″	42¹/₂″	13¹/₂″	9/16″	7/8″	6³/₄″	10″
70 XTR Featherweight	243 Win.	5	22″	42″	13¹/₂″	9/16″	7/8″	6¹/₂	10″
Short Action	308 Win.	5	22″	42″	13¹/₂″	9/16″	7/8″	6¹/₂	12″

(a) For additional capacity, add one round in chamber when ready to fire.

MODEL 70 WINLITE
$618.00

The fiberglass stock on this new model sets high standards for lightness, strength, and accuracy. Receiver bedding stability is assured with the use of thermoplastic and by fitting the barreled action individually to the stock. Critical inletted areas are molded into the stock, and the action bed and forend are reinforced Kevlar/Graphite for strength and rigidity. Special bedding pads are easily removed for "free-floating" the barrel if desired. Despite a dramatic weight reduction, there is no increase in the recoil sensation since the fiberglass material compresses during recoil, becoming a total recoil absorption device.

SPECIFICATIONS

Caliber:	270 Win.	30-06 Spfd.	7mm Rem. Mag.	338 Win. Mag.	280 Rem.	300 Win. Mag.
Mag. Cap.:	4*	4*	3*	3*	4	3
Barrel Length:	22″	22″	24″	24″	22″	24″
Overall Length:	42¹/₂″	42¹/₂″	44¹/₂″	44¹/₂″	42¹/₂″	44¹/₂″
Length of Pull:	13¹/₂″	13¹/₂″	13¹/₂″	13¹/₂″	13¹/₂″	13¹/₂″
**Drop at Comb:	9/16″	9/16″	9/16″	9/16″	9/16″	9/16″
**Drop at Heel:	1/2″	1/2″	1/2″	1/2″	1/2″	1/2″
Weight (lbs.)	6¹/₂″	6¹/₂″	7¹/₂″	7¹/₂″	6¹/₄-6¹/₂	6¹/₄-7
Rate of Twist:	10″	10″	9¹/₂″	10″	10″	10″

*For additional capacity, add one round in chamber when ready to fire.
**Drops are measured from centerline of bore.

WINCHESTER BOLT ACTION RIFLES

WINCHESTER RANGER®
BOLT ACTION CENTERFIRE RIFLE
$312.00

The Ranger Bolt Action Rifle comes with an American hardwood stock, a wear-resistant satin walnut finish, ramp bead-post front sight, steel barrel, three-position safety and engine-turned, anti-bind bolt. The receiver is drilled and tapped for scope mounting; accuracy is enhanced by thermoplastic bedding of the receiver. Barrel and receiver are brushed and blued.

SPECIFICATIONS

Model	Caliber	Magazine Capacity(a)	Barrel Length	Overall Length	Nominal Length of Pull	Nominal Drop at Comb	Nominal Drop at Heel	Nominal Weight (lbs.)	Rate of Twist (R.H.) 1 Turn in
Ranger	270 Win.	4	22″	42½″	13½″	1⅝″	2⅛″	7⅛	10″
Bolt Action Rifle Standard Action	30-06 Springfield	4	22″	42½″	13½″	1⅝″	2⅛″	7⅛	10″

(a) For additional capacity, add one round in chamber when ready to fire.

WINCHESTER RANGER®
YOUTH BOLT ACTION CARBINE
$320.00

This carbine offers dependable bolt action performance combined with a scaled-down design to fit the younger, smaller shooter. It features anti-bind bolt design, jeweled bolt, three-position safety, contoured recoil pad, ramped bead front sight, semi-buckhorn folding leaf rear sight, and sling swivels. Receiver is drilled and tapped for scope mounting. Stock is of American hardwood with protective satin walnut finish. Pistol grip, length of pull, overall length, and comb are all tailored to youth dimensions (see table).

SPECIFICATIONS

Model	Caliber	Magazine Capacity(a)	Barrel Length	Overall Length	Nominal Length of Pull	Nominal Drop at Comb	Nominal Drop at Heel	Nominal Weight (lbs.)	Rate of Twist (R.H.) 1 Turn in
Ranger Youth Short Action Rifle	243 Win.	4	20″	39″	12½″	1⁷⁄₁₆″	1¾″	5¾	10″

(a) For additional capacity, add one round in chamber when ready to fire.

RIFLES

WINCHESTER BOLT ACTION RIFLES

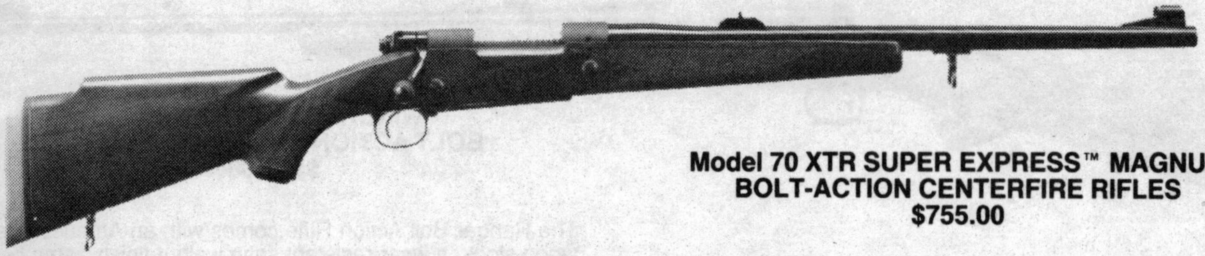

Model 70 XTR SUPER EXPRESS™ MAGNUM BOLT-ACTION CENTERFIRE RIFLES $755.00

Go after the biggest game in true Sporter style with these new Model 70 XTR Super Express Magnum rifles. Their high performance and dependability stem from the proven Model 70 African™ . . . now improved and upgraded with XTR styling and convenience features. This big game pair of rifles boasts all the Sporter Magnum features in 375 H&H and 458 Winchester Magnum calibers. The crisply styled Sporter stock design has the same innovative cheekpiece for shooter comfort, but is reinforced with two steel crossbolts for added strength.

The forward sling swivel is mounted directly on the rifle barrel for improved carrying balance and strength. Magazine capacity is three Magnum cartridges.

The new Monte Carlo stock with sculpted cheekpiece on Model 70 XTR Sporter Magnum and Super Express Magnum rifles is shown in the photo above.

XTR elegance checkering is custom-patterned at 18 lines per inch; wraps around forend for improved handling, gripping and appearance.

Also available: **MODEL 70XTR 50th ANNIVERSARY EDITION** in 300 Win. Mag. **Barrel length:** 24″. **Weight:** 7 lbs. **Price: $939.00** (w/sights).

SPECIFICATIONS FOR MODEL 70XTR **PRICES: $428.00** (w/o sights). **$755.00 SUPER EXPRESS MAGNUM** (w/sights)

Model	Order Symbol No.	Caliber	Magazine Capacity (A)	Barrel Length	Overall Length	Nominal Length Of Pull	Nominal Drop At: Comb	Heel	MC	Nominal Weight (Lbs.)	Rate Of Twist (R.H.) 1 Turn In	Sights
70XTR Long Action	G7063MXTR	270 Win.	5	24	44 1/2	13 1/2	9/16	1 5/16	3/4	7 3/4	10	Rifle
	G7063MSXTR	270 Win.	5	24	44 1/2	13 1/2	9/16	1 5/16	3/4	7 3/4	10	—
	G7064MXTR	30-06 Spgfld.	5	24	44 1/2	13 1/2	9/16	1 5/16	3/4	7 3/4	10	Rifle
	G7064MSXTR	30-06 Spgfld.	5	24	44 1/2	13 1/2	9/16	1 5/16	3/4	7 3/4	10	—
70XTR Short Action	G7060MSXTR	308 Win.	5	24″	44″	13 1/2″	9/16″	1 5/16″	3/4″	7 3/4	12″	—
70XTR Sporter Magnum Long Action	G7045MSXTR	264 Win. Mag.	3	24	44 1/2	13 1/2	9/16	1 5/16	3/4	7 3/4	9	—
	G7066MXTR	7mm Rem. Mag.	3	24	44 1/2	13 1/2	9/16	1 5/16	3/4	7 3/4	9 1/2	Rifle
	G7066MSXTR	7mm Rem. Mag.	3	24	44 1/2	13 1/2	9/16	1 5/16	3/4	7 3/4	9 1/2	—
	G7036MXTR	300 Win. Mag.	3	24	44 1/2	13 1/2	9/16	1 5/16	3/4	7 3/4	10	Rifle
	G7036MSXTR	300 Win. Mag.	3	24	44 1/2	13 1/2	9/16	1 5/16	3/4	7 3/4	10	—
	G70300W	300 Weatherby	3	24	44 1/2	13 1/2	9/16	1 5/16	3/4	7 3/4	10	—
		Mag.	3	24	44 1/2	13 1/2	9/16	1 5/16	3/4	7 3/4	10	—
	G7035MXTR	338 Win. Mag.	3	24	44 1/2	13 1/2	9/16	1 5/16	3/4	7 3/4	10	Rifle
	*G7035MSXTR	338 Win. Mag.	3	24	44 1/2	13 1/2	9/16	1 5/16	3/4	7 3/4	10	—
70XTR Sporter Varmint Short Action	G7015MSXTR	22-250 Rem.	5	24″	44″	13 1/2″	9/16″	1 5/16″	3/4″	7 3/4	14″	—
	G7023MSXTR	223 Rem.	5	24	44	13 1/2	9/16	1 5/16	3/4	7 3/4	12	—
	G7012MSXTR	243 Win.	5	24	44	13 1/2	9/16	1 5/16	3/4	7 3/4	10	—
70XTR Super Express Magnum Standard Action	G7037XXTR	375 H&H Mag.	3	24″	44″ 1/2	13 1/2″	9/16″	1 5/16″	3/4″	8 1/2	12″	Rifle
	G7055XXTR	458 Win. Mag.	3	22	42 1/2	13 1/2	9/16	1 5/16	3/4	8 1/2	14	Rifle

Drops are measured from center line of bore. (A) For additional capacity, add one round in chamber when ready to fire. MC-Monte Carlo stock.

WINCHESTER LEVER ACTION CARBINES & RIFLES

Model 94™ Side Eject™ Lever Action Centerfire carbines have been developed and refined through almost a century of sporting use and technological advancement. The new angled ejection system throws the spent cartridge away from the shooter's line of vision and does not interfere with top-mounted scopes. It features an improved, stabilized trigger mechanism with controlled pre-travel and short, crisp let-off.

Receivers are of forged steel. Chromium molybdenum barrels assure long-lasting strength. Chamber and rifling are cold-forged in a single operation for precise alignment and accuracy. The receiver is ported for angled ejection and scopes can be top-mounted.

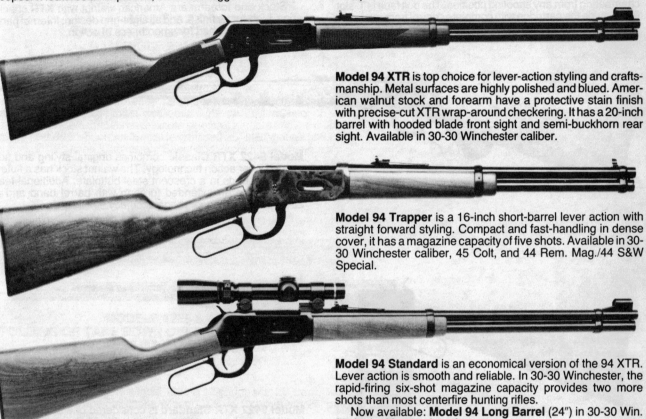

Model 94 XTR is top choice for lever-action styling and craftsmanship. Metal surfaces are highly polished and blued. American walnut stock and forearm have a protective stain finish with precise-cut XTR wrap-around checkering. It has a 20-inch barrel with hooded blade front sight and semi-buckhorn rear sight. Available in 30-30 Winchester caliber.

Model 94 Trapper is a 16-inch short-barrel lever action with straight forward styling. Compact and fast-handling in dense cover, it has a magazine capacity of five shots. Available in 30-30 Winchester caliber, 45 Colt, and 44 Rem. Mag./44 S&W Special.

Model 94 Standard is an economical version of the 94 XTR. Lever action is smooth and reliable. In 30-30 Winchester, the rapid-firing six-shot magazine capacity provides two more shots than most centerfire hunting rifles.

Now available: **Model 94 Long Barrel** (24″) in 30-30 Win. (7 shot) with extra long forearm.

MODEL 94 SIDE EJECT SPECIFICATIONS

Model	Caliber	Magazine Capacity (A)	Barrel Length	Overall Length	Nominal Length of Pull	Nominal Drop at Comb	Nominal Drop at Heel	Nominal Drop at M.C.	Nominal Weight (Lbs.)	Rate of Twist (R.H.) 1 Turn In	Sights	Price
94XTR Rifle	30-30 Win.	6	20″	37³/₄″	13″	1¹/₈″	1⁷/₈″	—	6¹/₂	12″	Rifle	$285.00
94 Standard Rifle	30-30 Win.	6	20	37³/₄	13	1¹/₈	1⁷/₈	—	6¹/₂	12	Rifle	261.00
94 Deluxe	30-30 Win.	6	20	37³/₄	13	1¹/₈	1⁷/₈	—	6¹/₂	12	Rifle	426.00
94 XTR Rifle	7-30 Waters	7	24	41³/₄	13	1¹/₈	1⁷/₈	—	7	12″	Rifle	305.00
94 Rifle	30-30 Win.	7	24	41³/₄	13	1¹/₈	1⁷/₈	—	7	12	Rifle	275.00
94 Trapper	30-30 Win.	5	16″	33³/₄″	13″	1¹/₈″	1⁷/₈″	—	6¹/₈	12″	Rifle	275.00
	45 Colt	9	16	33³/₄	13	1¹/₈	1⁷/₈	—	6	38	Rifle	261.00
	44 Rem. Mag./ 44 S&W Sp.	9	16	33³/₄	13	1¹/₈	1⁷/₈	—	6	38	Rifle	281.00
94 Big Bore	307 Win.	6	20″	37³/₄″	13″	1¹/₈″	1⁷/₈″	—	6¹/₂	12″	Rifle	282.00
Ranger	30-30 Win.	6	20″	37³/₄″	13″	1¹/₈″	1⁷/₈″	—	6¹/₂	12″	Rifle	229.00
	30-30	6	20	37³/₄	13	1¹/₈	1⁷/₈	—	6¹/₂	12	R/S	262.00

Drops are measured from center line of bore. (A) For additional capacity, add one round in chamber when ready to fire.
MC-Monte Carlo stock. R/S-Rifle sights and optional 4 × 32mm Bushnell® Sportview℠ scope with mounts.

WINCHESTER LEVER ACTION RIFLES

MODEL 9422 XTR
LEVER-ACTION RIMFIRE RIFLES

These Model 9422 XTR rimfire rifles combine classic 94 styling and handling in ultra-modern lever action 22s of superb craftsmanship. Handling and shooting characteristics are superior because of their carbine-like size.

Positive lever action and bolt design ensure feeding and chambering from any shooting position. The bolt face is T-slotted to guide the cartridge with complete control from magazine to chamber. A color-coded magazine follower shows when the brass magazine tube is empty. Receivers are grooved for scope mounting. Other functional features include exposed hammer with half-cock safety, hooded bead front sight, semi-buckhorn rear sight and side ejection of spent cartridges.

Stock and forearm are American walnut with XTR checkering, high-luster finish, and straight-grip design. Internal parts are carefully finished for smoothness of action.

Model 9422 XTR Classic combines original styling and advanced lever action technology. The walnut stock has a fluted comb and ends in a crescent steel buttplate. Additional features include an extended forearm with barrel band and a 22½" barrel for longer range accuracy.

Model 9422 XTR Magnum gives exceptional accuracy at longer ranges than conventional 22 rifles. It is designed specifically for the 22 Winchester Magnum Rimfire cartridge and holds 11 cartridges.

Model 9422 XTR Standard is considered one of the world's finest production sporting arms. It holds 21 Short, 17 Long or 15 Long Rifle cartridges.

Also available: **Win-Cam Magnum** featuring laminated non-glare, green-shaded stock and forearm. American hardwood stock is bonded to withstand all weather and climates.

SPECIFICATIONS

Model	Caliber	Magazine Capacity	Barrel Length	Overall Length	Nominal Length of Pull	Nominal Drop at Comb	Nominal Drop at Heel	Nominal Weight (lbs.)	Rate of Twist (R.H.) 1 Turn in	Price
9422 XTR Standard	22	21S, 17L, 15LR	20½"	37⅛"	13½"	1¾"	2½"	6¼	16"	
Magnum	22 WMR	11	20½"	37⅛"	13½"	1¾"	2½"	6¼	16"	$301.00
9422 XTR Classic										
Standard	22	21S, 17L, 15LR	22½"	39⅛"	13½"	1¾"	2½"	6½	16"	
Magnum	22 WMR	11	22½"	39⅛"	13½"	1¾"	2½"	6½	16"	$301.00

S-Short   L-Long   LR-Long Rifle   WMR-Winchester Magnum Rimfire

WINCHESTER LEVER ACTION RIFLES

**MODEL 94 SIDE EJECT™
STANDARD BIG BORE CARBINE
$282.00**

Winchester's powerful .307 hunting caliber combined with maximum lever action power and angled ejection provides hunters with improved performance and economy.

SPECIFICATIONS

Model	Caliber	Magazine Capacity(a)	Barrel Length	Overall Length	Nominal Length of Pull	Nominal Drop at Comb	Nominal Drop at Heel	Nominal Drop at MC	Nominal Weight (lbs.)	Rate of Twist (R.H.) 1 Turn in	Sights
94 Angle Eject Standard Big Bore	307 Win.	6	20″	38 1/8″	13 1/4″	1 3/4″	2 1/2″	1 1/2″	6 1/2	12″	—
70 Lightweight Long Action	270 Win.	5	22″	42 1/2″	13 1/2″	9/16″	7/8″	—	6 1/4	10″	—
	270 Win.	5	22	42 1/2	13 1/2	9/16	7/8	—	6 1/4	10	—
	30-06 Spgfld.	5	22	42 1/2	13 1/2	9/16	7/8	—	6 1/4	10	—
	30-06 Spgfld.	5	22	42 1/2	13 1/2	9/16	7/8	—	6 1/4	10	—
70 Lightweight Short Action	22-250 Rem.	5	22″	42″	13 1/2″	9/16″	7/8″	—	6	14″	—
	223 Rem.	6	22	42	13 1/2	9/16	7/8	—	6	12	—
	243 Win.	5	22	42	13 1/2	9/16	7/8	—	6	10	—
	308 Win.	5	22	42	13 1/2	9/16	7/8	—	6	12	—

*Limited production and/or availability.

**MODEL 94 WIN-TUFF RIFLE (20″ Barrel)
$402.00**

Includes all features and specifications of standard Model 94 plus tough laminated hardwood styled for the brush-gunning hunter who wants good concealment and a carbine that can stand up to all kinds of weather.

RIFLES

WINSLOW RIFLES

SPECIFICATIONS

Stock: Choice of two stock models. **The Plainsmaster** offers pinpoint accuracy in open country with full curl pistol grip and flat forearm. **The Bushmaster** offers lighter weight for bush country; slender pistol with palm swell; beavertail forend for light hand comfort. Both styles are of hand-rubbed black walnut. Length of pull—13½ inches; plainsmaster ⅜ inch castoff; Bushmaster ³⁄₁₆ inch castoff; all rifles are drilled and tapped to incorporate the use of telescopic sights; rifles with receiver or open sights are available on special order; all rifles are equipped with quick detachable sling swivel studs and white-line recoil pad. All Winslow stocks incorporate a slight castoff to deflect recoil, minimizing flinch and muzzle jump. **Magazine:** Staggered box type, four shot. (Blind in the stock has no floor plate). **Action:** Mauser Mark x Action. **Overall length:** 43″ (Standard Model); 45″ (Magnum); all Winslow rifles have company name and serial number and grade engraved on the action and caliber engraved on barrel. **Barrel:** Douglas barrel premium grade, chrome moly-type steel; all barrels, 20 caliber through 35 caliber, have six lands and grooves; barrels larger than 35 caliber have eight lands and grooves. All barrels are finished to (.2 to .4) micro inches inside the lands and grooves. **Total weight** (without scope): 7 to 7½ lbs. with 24″ barrel in standard calibers 243, 308, 270, etc; 8 to 9 lbs. with 26″ barrel in Magnum calibers 264 Win., 300 Wby., 458 Win., etc. Winslow rifles are made in the following calibers:

Standard cartridges: 22-250, 243 Win., 244 Rem., 257 Roberts, 308 Win., 30-06, 280 Rem., 270 Win., 25-06, 284 Win., 358 Win., and 7mm (7 × 57).

Magnum cartridges: 300 Weatherby, 300 Win., 338 Win., 358 Norma, 375 H.H., 458 Win., 257 Weatherby, 264 Win., 270 Weatherby, 7mm Weatherby, 7mm Rem., 300 H.H., 308 Norma.

Left-handed models available in most calibers.

WINSLOW BASIC RIFLE

The Basic Rifle, available in the Bushmaster stock, features one ivory diamond inlay in a rosewood grip cap and ivory trademark in bottom of forearm. Grace 'A' walnut jeweled bolt and follower **$1265.00.** Plainsmaster stock **$100.00** extra. **Left-hand** model **$1375.00**

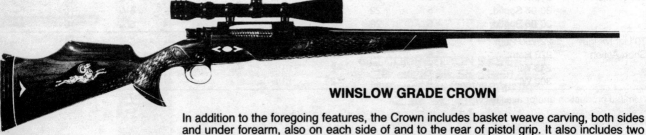

WINSLOW GRADE CROWN

In addition to the foregoing features, the Crown includes basket weave carving, both sides and under forearm, also on each side of and to the rear of pistol grip. It also includes two eight-point ivory and ebony inlays, one on each side of the magazine box, two large triangle ivory and ebony inlays, one on each side of the buttstock. **Price upon request.**

WINSLOW VARMINT

This 17 caliber is available in the Bushmaster stock and the Plainsmaster stock, which is a miniature of the original high roll-over cheekpiece and a round leading edge on the forearm, modified spoon billed pistol grip. Available in 17/222, 17/222 Mag. 17/233, 222 Rem. and 223. Regent grade shown. **Price upon request.**

shotguns

FOR ADDRESSES AND PHONE
NUMBERS OF MANUFACTURERS AND
DISTRIBUTORS INCLUDED IN THIS
SECTION, *SEE DIRECTORY OF
MANUFACTURERS AND SUPPLIERS*

ARMSPORT SHOTGUNS

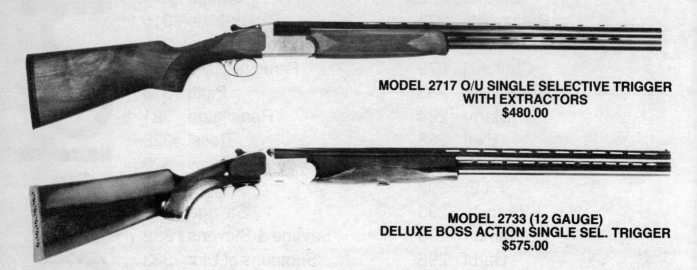

MODEL 2717 O/U SINGLE SELECTIVE TRIGGER WITH EXTRACTORS
$480.00

MODEL 2733 (12 GAUGE)
DELUXE BOSS ACTION SINGLE SEL. TRIGGER
$575.00

This is a superbly designed, handsomely engraved over-and-under shotgun with ventilated rib. The single selective trigger allows you to fire either barrel at will. It has exceptionally fine hand-picked walnut stock and forend, hand-crafted and fitted for generations of fine shooting. Gloss or oil finish. 12 gauge. 28-inch barrels choked Mod. and Full (Extractors). 3-inch Mag. shells.

Also available in:
Model 2719 20 Ga. 26" O/U 3" Mag. Imp. & Mod. . . **$480.00**
Model 2720 .410 Ga. 26" O/U 3" Mag. Imp. & Mod. non-selective trigger **540.00**
Model 2735 20 Ga. 26" O/U 3" Mag. Imp. & Mod. Deluxe Boss Action **575.00**

MODEL 2741 (12 GAUGE)
DELUXE BOSS ACTION O/U SINGLE SEL. TRIGGER
w/ AUTO EJECTORS
$675.00

Beautifully designed boss action over/under shotguns with both top and lateral vent ribs. Swell pistol grip and flare forend. Gloss or oil-finished stock. Chambered for 3-inch Magnum shells with chemically engraved silver finished receiver. 12 gauge with 28-inch barrels. Mod. and full chokes.

Also available in:
Model 2727 12 Ga. 28" Barrel O/U 3" Mag. Mod. & Full **$550.00**
Model 2729 20 Ga. 26" Barrel 3" Mag. Imp. & Mod. **550.00**
Model 2743 20 Ga. 26" Barrel 3" Mag. Imp. & Mod. Deluxe Boss Action **675.00**

ARMSPORT SHOTGUNS

"CONGRESS" COMBO SERIES

Both shotgun and rifle barrels of these "Turkey" guns are mated to shoot groups as close to perfect as possible. The fine grained palm swell full pistol grip rollover cheekpiece, walnut stock and forend are all hand checkered. Both 12 and 20 gauge top shotgun barrels are chambered to accept 3" magnum shells. The Double Trigger Model 2782 is available in 12 gauge over .222. The Deluxe Single Selective Trigger models are available in both 12 and 20 gauge over either .222, .243 or .270.

MODEL 2782 Combination Double Trigger
12 gauge/222 . . . . $ 950.00
MODEL 2783 Deluxe 12 gauge/222 w/lateral rib. . . 1350.00
MODEL 2784 Deluxe 12 gauge/243 w/lateral rib. . . 1350.00
MODEL 2785 Deluxe 12 gauge/270 w/lateral rib. . . 1350.00
MODEL 2786 Deluxe 20 gauge/222 w/lateral rib. . . 1350.00
MODEL 2787 Deluxe 20 gauge/243 w/lateral rib. . . 1350.00
MODEL 2788 Deluxe 20 gauge/270 w/lateral rib. . . 1350.00

COMBINATION O/U TURKEY GUN
MODEL 2782 (12 GAUGE)
$950.00

Armsport's over/under shotgun/rifle combination turkey gun is manufactured by one of Italy's finest gun factories. This 12 gauge, 3" mag. shotgun with .222 caliber rifle features chrome-lined barrels with an extra wide upper vent rib. The frame is built from a special solid steel block and has tempered antique silver finish or basic blue, both beautifully engraved. Its high luster walnut palm swell pistol grip and stock are gracefully made with schnabel forend, both checkered for sure grip. Fitted with rubber recoil pad.

Also available:
Model 2783 Deluxe w/lateral rib $1350.00
Models 2784 thru 2788 . . . . 1350.00

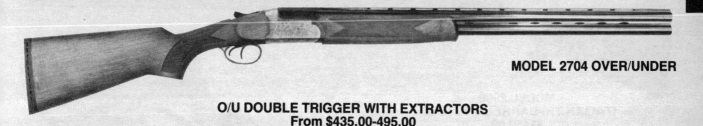

MODEL 2704 OVER/UNDER

O/U DOUBLE TRIGGER WITH EXTRACTORS
From $435.00-495.00

The Armsport over/unders with double triggers are lightweight, well balanced and are chambered for 3" Mag. shells. The special grade steel barrels are chrome lined, with both an upper vent rib and lateral vent rib. The fine grain walnut stock has a palm swell pistol grip and both the stock and schnabel-type forend have a deep, sure-grip checkering. The beautifully engraved antique silver receiver is engineered from the finest gun steel. The double trigger instantly allows the shooter his barrel choice.

Available in:
Model 2702 12 Ga. 28" O/U 3" Mag. 2 Trig. Ext. Mod & Full
Model 2704 20 Ga. 26" O/U 3" Mag. 2 Trig. Ext. Imp. & Mod
Model 2705 .410 Ga. 26" O/U 3" Mag. 2 Trig. Ext. Imp. & Mod
Model 2706 Commander O/U 3" Mag. 2 Trig. Ext. 12 ga. 20"

ARMSPORT SHOTGUNS

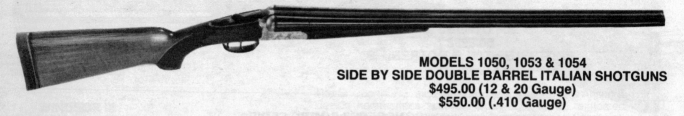

MODELS 1050, 1053 & 1054
SIDE BY SIDE DOUBLE BARREL ITALIAN SHOTGUNS
$495.00 (12 & 20 Gauge)
$550.00 (.410 Gauge)

Chambered for 3" magnum with hard chrome-lined barrels, these shotguns feature center ribs, fluorescent front sights, Italian box lock actions and gloss finish stocks and forends. Also antique silver finish receivers engraved with bird scenes.

Model 1050 is 12 gauge with 28" barrel with Modified & Full choke. Model 1053 is 20 gauge with 26" barrel with Imp. & Modified choke. Model 1054 is .410 gauge with 26" barrel with Imp. & Modified choke.

MODEL 2700
10 GAUGE OVER & UNDER GOOSEGUN
$735.00 ($795.00 Deluxe)

This 10 gauge 3½" "Fowler" Magnum Boss type action O/U Goosegun has two bottom locking lugs on its OM8 steel barrels attached to an antiqued silver finished action. Three Canada geese scenes are engraved on the two sides and bottom of the receiver. The hard chrome lined barrels have an extra wide 12mm top vent rib with a fluorescent front sight and a brass mid-bead sight. Both the 32" barrels choked full and the 38" barrels choked Imp. and Mod. will shoot steel BB's effectively. The walnut stock with rubber recoil pad and matching forend are hand checkered.

MODEL 2900
ITALIAN TRI-BARREL SHOTGUN
$1450.00

The only three-barrel shotgun being manufactured, Model 2900 features 28" barrels (12 gauge) lined and chambered for 3" magnum shells choked improved, modified and full. The front trigger fires the top two barrels and the rear trigger fires the bottom barrel. Made on a boss type action from special steel, the shotgun frame has two bottom locking lugs. The select grain walnut palm swell pistol grip stock and forend has a rubber recoil pad, high gloss finish and checkering.

ARMSPORT SHOTGUNS

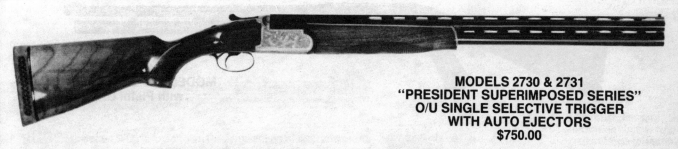

MODELS 2730 & 2731
"PRESIDENT SUPERIMPOSED SERIES"
O/U SINGLE SELECTIVE TRIGGER
WITH AUTO EJECTORS
$750.00

Milled from special high strength steel, these shotguns feature engraved antique silver finished boss type receiver fitted to special steel barrels with jewelled engine turned barrel lugs and hand checkered walnut stock with rubber recoil pad, palm swell full pistol grip and matching checkered semi-Schnaubel forend. Also, extra wide 12mm top vent rib with front fluorescent sight and brass mid-bead sight, plus lateral vent rib. All President models have single selective triggers and are chambered 3″ magnum. Barrel lengths are 26″ in 20 gauge and 27″ in 12 gauge. Chokes are Skeet and Skeet 6 Interchangeable.

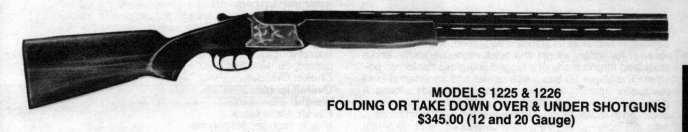

MODELS 1225 & 1226
FOLDING OR TAKE DOWN OVER & UNDER SHOTGUNS
$345.00 (12 and 20 Gauge)

Chambered for 3″ magnum shells. Can shoot steel shot. Top vent rib with front and mid-bead sights. Lateral vent rib. Engraved antique finish receiver. Walnut palm swell pistol grip stock. Schnabel-type forend. Cut checkering on stock and forend. Two triggers. Model 1225 is 12 gauge with 28″ barrel with Modified and Full choke. Model 1226 is 20 gauge with 26″ barrel and Imp. and Modified choke.

MODELS 1125, 1126 & 1127
TAKE DOWN SINGLE BARREL SHOTGUNS
$95.00

Machined from solid block of gun steel drop forging. Features a bottom lever take down opening action and a complete iron cross removable forend. Barrels are chambered for 3″ magnum shells with hard chrome lined barrels and bores for steel shot use. High gloss walnut finish stock and forend are checkered. Models 1125 and 1126 are 12 gauge with 28″ barrels (Model 1125 has Modified choke; Model 1126 is Full). Model 1127 is 20 gauge with 26″ barrel in Modified choke.

BENELLI SHOTGUN

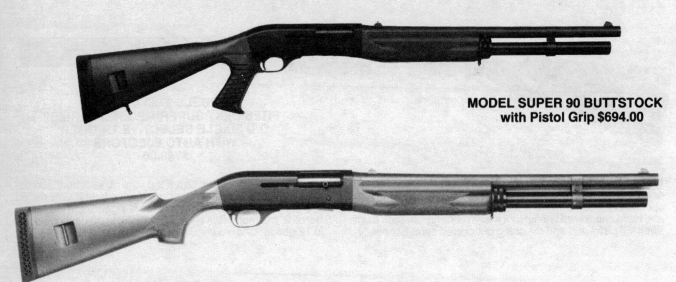

MODEL SUPER 90 BUTTSTOCK
with Pistol Grip $694.00

MODEL SUPER 90
$613.00

This 12 gauge auto-loader functions on a rotating bolt system that minimizes recoil and maximizes accuracy. It features an adjustable rear sight as standard equipment, a one piece alloy receiver for lighter weight and quick maneuverability, and a stock and forend made of a rugged fiberglass reinforced polymer. The Super 90 has a free carrier and an external shell release for lightning-like ammo changes or speedy reloads. A pistol grip stock is available as an accessory and the grip is enclosed in molded rubber to insulate the hand from recoil. Also available w/26" Vent rib (I/C) and 28" vent rib (Full): **$659.00**

SPECIFICATIONS
Gauge: 12
Chamber: 3"
Mag. capacity: 7
Barrel length: 19¾" (accessory field barrels avail. in 26" Improved, 28" Modified & 30" Full)
Choke: Cylinder
Overall length: 39¾"
Weight: 7 lbs. 4 oz.
Finish: Matte black
Stock: High impact polymer
Sights: Post front; fixed buckhorn rear drift adjustable

BERETTA SHOTGUNS

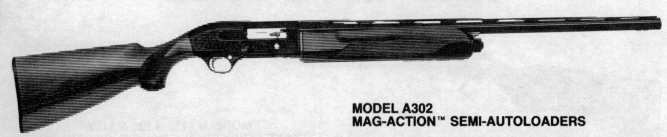

MODEL A302
MAG-ACTION™ SEMI-AUTOLOADERS

Beretta technology at its finest—one tough, machined action handles both 2¾- and 3-inch Magnum chambered barrels, easily interchanged on the same gun without any special tools or adjustment. Fully interchangeable barrels give maximum field flexibility and fast barrel changes, so you can mix up your bag of game at whim. And the A302's magazine cut-off lever lets you load automatically, or hand-chamber different loads for different game.

On its fast-swinging frame, Beretta designs state-of-the-field features into all A302's; hard-chrome-lined, nickel-chrome-moly steel barrels shrug off barrel-punishing steel shot and mag load forces; receivers are forged and machined from solid blocks of lightweight, top-quality alloy; gas-operated action with no washers, no rings, supremely reliable yet simple for field stripping; very low recoil; plus every safety feature possible in a shotgun, topped off with the rich touch of Beretta quality.

BERETTA SHOTGUNS

MODEL A303 SEMIAUTOMATIC
$545.00

This unique autoloader features flush-mounted, screw-in choke tubes, and a magazine cut off that allows shooters to hand-feed a lighter or heavier load into the breech without emptying the magazine.

SPECIFICATIONS
Gauge: 12 (3″ Magnum chamber)
Barrel lengths: 24″ 26″ 28″, 30″, 32″
Chokes: F, MC (24″, 30″ and 32″ barrels)
       IC, F, MC (26″ barrel)
       M, IM, F, MC (28″ barrel)

Gauge: 12 (2³/₄″ Chamber)
Barrel lengths: 24″ 26″ 28″, 30″
Chokes: IC, C (24″ barrel)
       M, IM, F, MC (28″ barrel)

Gauge: 20 (2³/₄″ or 3″ Magnum)
Barrel lengths: 26″ and 28″
Chokes: IC, M, MC (26″ barrel)
       M, IM, F, MC (28″ barrels)

A303 SLUG
Gauge: 12 (2³/₄″ Chamber)
Barrel lengths: 22″ and 24″
Choke: Slug (C)

A303 SLUG
Gauge: 20 (2³/₄″ chamber)
Barrel lengths: 22″
Chokes: Slug (C)
Weight: 7 lbs. (12 gauge) and 6 lbs. (20 gauge)*
Safety: Cross bolt
Action: Locked breech, gas operated
Sight: Vent. rib w/front metal bead
Stock length: 14⁷/₈″ length of pull
Capacity: Plugged to 2 rounds

MODEL A303 COMPETITION TRAP (not shown)
$575.00

The Beretta A303 Trap is the competition version of the proven A303 semiautomatic. Its gas-operated system lessens recoil; other features include wide floating vent rib with flourescent front and mid-rib bead sights, plus Monte Carlo stock fitted with American trap pad. The A303 also comes with hand-checkered stock and forend of select European walnut, plus gold-plated trigger.

SPECIFICATIONS
Gauge: 12
Barrel lengths: 30″ and 32″ (M,IM,F,MC)
Sight: Ventilated rib with flourescent front bead, metal middle bead

Action: Semiautomatic, locked breech, gas operated
Safety: Cross bolt
Ejector: Auto
Trigger: Gold plated
Stock: Select European walnut
Weight: 8 lbs.
Butt plate: Special trap recoil pad
Chamber: 2³/₄″

Also available: **MODEL A303 SKEET** (26″/12 or 20 gauge)

BERETTA SHOTGUNS

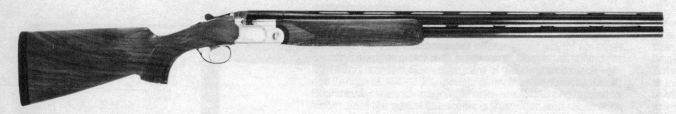

SERIES 682X COMPETITION TRAP O/U

Available in Competition Mono, Over/under or Mono Trap-O/U Combo Set, the 12-gauge 682X trap guns boast premium grade hand-checkered walnut stock and forend with International or Monte Carlo left- or right-hand stock and choice of 3 stock dimensions.

Features: Adjustable gold-plated, single selective sliding trigger for precise length of pull fit; fluorescent competition front sight; step-up top rib; Bruniton non-reflective black matte finish; low profile improved boxlock action; manual safety with barrel selector; 2³/₄" chambers; auto ejector; competition recoil pad butt plate; light hand-engraving; stock with silver oval for initials; silver inscription inlaid on trigger guard; handsome fitted case. **Weight:** Approx. 8 lbs.

Barrel length/Choke	Price
30" or 32" Imp. Mod./Full	$1960.00
30" or 32" Multi-choke	2030.00
(Mono) 32" or 34" Full	1820.00
(Mono) 32" or 34" Multi-choke	2100.00
Combo.—30" or 32" Imp. Mod./Full 32" or 34" Full (Mono)	2520.00
Comb.—30" or 32" Multi-choke 32" or 34" Multi-choke (Mono)	2660.00

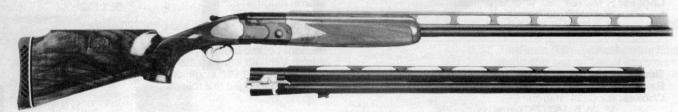

682X COMPETITION W/MONO AND COMBO O/U BARRELS

682 COMPETITION SKEET O/U
26" or 28" SK/SK $1960.00
4-Barrel Set (28") $4760.00
12, 20, 28, .410 Gauge

This skeet gun sports hand-checkered premium walnut stock, forged and hardened receiver, manual safety with trigger selector, auto ejector, stock with silver oval for initials, silver inlaid on trigger guard. Price includes fitted case.
Action: Low profile hard chrome-plated boxlock
Trigger: Hand-engraved, gold-plated single selective
Barrels: 26" or 28" rust blued barrels iwth 2³/₄" chambers
Stock Dimensions: Length of pull 14³/₈"; drop at comb 1¹/₄"; drop at heel 2¹/₈"
Sights: Fluorescent competition front and center bead sights
Weight: Approx. 8 lbs.

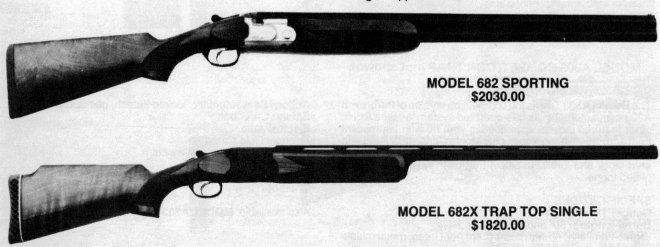

MODEL 682 SPORTING
$2030.00

MODEL 682X TRAP TOP SINGLE
$1820.00

BERETTA SHOTGUNS

A302 MULTI-CHOKE

MODEL A302
MAG-ACTION SYSTEM
MODEL A302 SEMI-AUTO SHOTGUN
(ONE COMPLETE ACTION WILL HANDLE
2³/₄″ OR 3″ INTERCHANGEABLE BARRELS)

Gauge	Chamber	Barrel Length	Choke	Price
12	(2³/₄″)	26″	Improved Cyl.	$480.00
12	(2³/₄″)	22″	Slug	480.00
12	(3″ Mag.)	28″	Modified	480.00
12	(3″ Mag.)	30″	Full	480.00
20	(2³/₄″)	26″	Improved Cyl.	480.00
20	(3″ Mag.)	28″	Modified	480.00

MODELS 626/627 SIDE-BY-SIDE FIELD SHOTGUNS

These good-looking field models feature low profile solid box-lock design, hand-fitted stocks and forends of handsome European walnut with deep diamond hand-checkering, tang-mounted safety/barrel selectors, single-selective trigger, metal bead sight and knurled rib. 12 gauge barrels are chambered 2³/₄″; 20 gauge barrels, 3″ Mag. **Model 626** has bright chrome finish, full hand-engraving. **Model 627** boasts hand-engraved side plates.

Model 627EL $1995.00
12 ga. 28″ Mod./Full
12 ga. 26″ Imp. Cyl./Mod.

Model 626 $995.00
12 ga. 26″ Imp. Cyl./Mod.
12 ga. 28″ Mod./Full (Straight Stock)
20 ga. 26″ Imp. Cyl./Mod. (Straight Stock)

Model 627EELL $3500.00
12 ga. 28″ Mod./Full (w/ or w/o Straight Stock)
12 ga. 26″ Imp. Cyl./Mod. (w/ or w/o Straight Stock)

SHOTGUNS

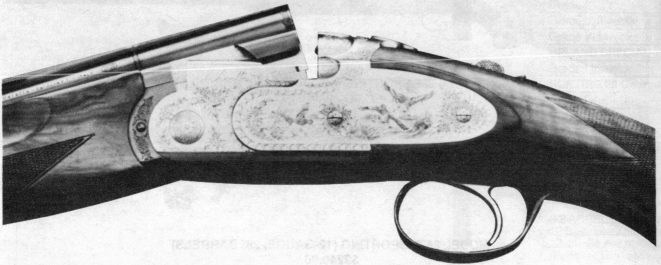

BERETTA SHOTGUNS

MODEL 686 FIELD GRADE
OVER/UNDER 12, 20 & 28 GAUGE
$925.00
MULTICHOKE 12 & 20 GAUGE
$1035.00

Barrels/chokes: 26″ with Imp. Cyl./Mod.; 28″ with Mod./Full. Multi-chokes also available. Vent. rib with metal bead sight
Action: Low profile, high-security box lock
Trigger: Selective single trigger, auto safety
Extractors: Auto ejectors
Stock: Choice European walnut, hand-checkered and hand-finished with a tough gloss finish
Weight: 7 lbs. 2 oz.

MODEL 687EL FIELD GRADE
O/U 12 & 20 GAUGE
$2400.00

The **687EL** features strong box-lock action handsomely tooled with floral hand-engraved decorative side plates, finest quality walnut stock accented with silver monogram plate, selective auto ejectors and fitted case. Also available: **Model 687EELL**, featuring a special premium walnut, custom-fitted stock and exquisitely engraved side-plate, game-scene motifs. **Price: $3600.00** (with case). Available also in 30″ M/F.

Barrels/chokes: 26″ with Imp. Cyl./Mod.; 28″ with Mod./Full.
Action: Low profile imp. box lock
Trigger: Single selective with manual safety
Extractors: Auto ejectors
Weight: 7 lbs. 2 oz.

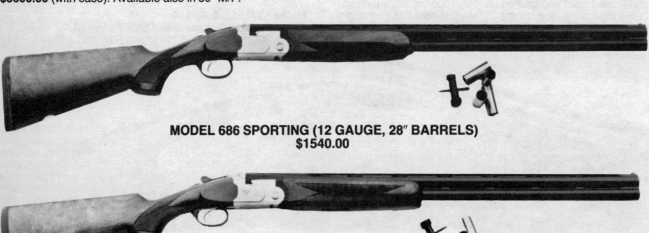

MODEL 686 SPORTING (12 GAUGE, 28″ BARRELS)
$1540.00

MODEL 687L SPORTING (12-GAUGE, 28″ BARRELS)
$2240.00

BERNARDELLI SHOTGUNS

Bernardelli shotguns are the creation of the Italian firm of Vincenzo Bernardelli, known for its fine quality firearms and commitment to excellence for more than a century. Most of the long arms featured below can be built with a variety of options, customized for the discriminating sportsman. With the exceptions indicated for each gun respectively, options include choice of barrel lengths and chokes; pistol or straight English grip stock; single selective or non-selective trigger; long tang trigger guard; checkered butt; beavertail forend; hand-cut rib; automatic safety; custom stock dimensions; standard or English recoil pad; extra set of barrels; choice of luggage gun case.

ELIO SIDE-BY-SIDE

ELIO SIDE-BY-SIDE
$1175.00
With Ejectors $1135.00

For gunners who prefer a lightweight 12 gauge double, the Elio weighs about 6¼ pounds and is designed around the Anson-Deeley action with Purdey locks. Intricate English rosette and scroll engraving and a coin finished receiver, fine hand-checkered European walnut stock, hinged front trigger on double trigger models.

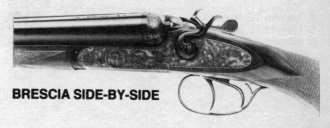

BRESCIA SIDE-BY-SIDE

BRESCIA SIDE-BY-SIDE
$1350.00

Available in 12, 16, or 20 gauge, the Brescia side-by-side features Greener or Purdey locks, small engravings, hardened marbled mounting, chrome-lined barrels, finely grained stock.

SLUG LUSSO DELUXE

SLUG SIDE-BY-SIDE
$946.00 ($993.00 w/single trigger)
SLUG LUSSO DELUXE
$1413.00 ($1460.00 w/single trigger)

Especially designed to pattern well with slugs and buckshot, this 12 gauge side-by-side has Anson & Deeley action, Purdey-type locks, reinforced breech, richly engraved hunting scene on white-finish receiver, automatic ejectors, rear adjustable sight with overturning leafs, cheekpiece, double triggers. Deluxe model has fully engraved sideplates.

HEMINGWAY SIDE-BY-SIDE
$1460.00 (not shown)
With Single Non-selective Trigger $1530.00

An elegant and light 12 gauge side-by-side suitable for upland bird hunting, the Hemingway features 23½-inch barrels without monobloc, right bore open and left one slightly Improved Cylinder, automatic ejectors, special rib with white bead front sight, hinged front trigger, woodcock hunting scenes engraved, long-type trigger guard and forend, hand-checkered walnut woods, metal shield for intials. Special steel frame and barrels. **Weight:** 6¼ lbs.

BERNARDELLI SHOTGUNS

S. UBERTO F.S.
$993.00
S. UBERTO F.S. WITH EJECTORS
$1093.00

The S. Uberto F.S. side-by-side offers shotgunners Anson & Deeley hammerless action, Purdey-style locks, reinforced breech, fine relief engravings with hunting scenes, finest walnut checkered stock and forend, right trigger folding. Available in 12 and 20 gauge.

S. UBERTO F.S. WITH EJECTORS

S. Uberto 1 w/modest engraving, marbled mounting **$792.00**
S. Uberto 1E/ejectors 893.00
S. Uberto 1E w/ejectors and single trigger 839.00
S. Uberto 2 E w/ejectors 937.00

ORIONE OVER/UNDER
$1097.00

Handsome and rugged, this Orione 12 gauge over/under sports double Purdey-type locks, ventilated rib, finely checkered pistol grip or English-style walnut stock, automatic ejectors.

Orione S with light engravings **$1128.00**
Orione L w/side reinforced breech, fine engravings, best-quality walnut 1235.00
Orione E w/side reinforced breech, exquisite engravings, best quality walnut 1346.00

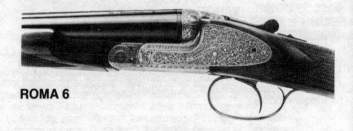

ROMA 6

ROMA 6
$1238.00
ROMA 6E WITH EJECTORS
$1338.00

Available in 12, or 20 gauge, the Roma 6 is Bernardelli's premier boxlock and a most popular model. This side-by-side shotgun features Anson & Deeley action with Purdey-style locks, sideplated and coin-finished receiver with elaborate scroll engraving covering 100% of the action, precision-bored barrels made of superior chromium steel, double triggers with front hinged trigger, hand-selected European walnut stock and forend with fine, hand-cut checkering.

Roma 3 w/modest engraving, marbled mounting . . . **$859.00**
Roma 3E w/ejectors 959.00
Roma 4 w/reinforced breech, fine English engravings, right trigger folding 1006.00
Roma 4E w/ejectors 1106.00

BERNARDELLI SHOTGUNS

HOLLAND LUSSO

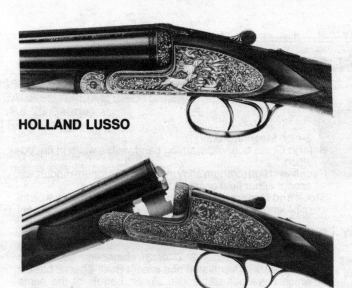

HOLLAND V.B.

HOLLAND LUSSO
$6643.00
HOLLAND V.B.
$5486.00
HOLLAND LISCIO (not shown)
$4763.00

These 12 gauge Holland & Holland style sidelock side-by-sides feature sidelocks with double safety levers, reinforced breech, three round Purdey locks, automatic ejectors, right trigger folding, striker retaining plates, best-quality walnut stock and finely chiselled high-grade engravings. The three shotguns differ only in the amount and intricacy of engravings.

MODEL 115 L OVER/UNDER (not shown)
$3170.00

The Model 115 L 12 gauge over/under features inclined plane lockings, ventilated bridged rib, checkered pistol grip walnut stock and forend, rich hand engravings on breech and all other metal parts, automatic ejector, single non-selective or selective trigger. Model 115 differs in its blued receiver with light hand engraving; Models 115 E and S differ from the 115 L only in the style and amount of engraving. Also available in Trap, Skeet, Pigeon or Monotrap/Combination.

Model 115	$1542.00
Model 115 E	3907.00
Model 115 S	1751.00
Model 115 Trap	1681.00

MODEL 120 O/U SHOTGUN/RIFLE COMBINATION
$1563.00

The Model 120 combination rifle/shotgun offers auto ejectors that can be changed into normal extractors by a patented device; set trigger, strong hinge pin, cross-bolt on the lumps, cheekpiece with walnut stock. Shotgun barrel in 12 gauge. Rifle barrel available in calibers 5.6×50R Mag., 5.6×57R, 6.5×55, 6.5×57R, 7×57R, 7×65R, 8×57JRS, 9.3×74R, 222 Rem., 243 Win., 308 Win., 30-06. Supplied on request with scope and interchangeable 12 gauge shotgun barrels.

MODEL 190 OVER/UNDER
$701.00 ($1054.00 fully engraved)

High-quality hunting over/under shotgun with special steel integral frame, strong cross hinge pin and locks on the lumps, automatic ejectors, ventilated rib, special steel barrels with chrome-plated bores, richly engraved frame, hand-checkered selected walnut stock and forend. Available with double trigger or single selective trigger, 12 gauge, 2³/₄" or 3" Magnum chambers. **Weight:** 6³/₄ pounds.

BROWNING AUTOMATIC SHOTGUNS

B-80 GAS-OPERATED
SEMI-AUTOMATIC SHOTGUN

Browning's rugged 12-gauge Superlight B-80 with 26-inch barrel weighs only 6 pounds 8 ounces and gives the upland hunter everything he could ask for in a gas-operated shotgun. The Superlight B-80 is the perfect combination of light weight and reliable firepower. The 12- and 20-gauge Hunting models feature a reliable 10-seal gas system for optimum performance and a choice of interchangeable 2¾- or 3-inch barrels with chrome-lined bores that shrug off the wearing effect of steel shot.

SPECIFICATIONS
Trigger: Crisp and positive
Chamber: Both 12- and 20-gauge barrels with 2¾" chambers will accept 2¾" standard and 2¾" Magnum loads; models with 3-inch Magnum chambers will function properly with 3-inch Magnums only

Safety: Cross bolt; red warning band visible when in fire position
Receiver: High strength alloy in light and Magnum models will accept either field or Magnum barrel
Stock and forearm: Walnut skillfully cut-checkered; full pistol grip; length of pull 14¼"; drop at comb 1⅝"; drop at heel 2½"; a field recoil pad is fitted
Gauge: 12 and 20 gauge
Barrels: 12 and 20 gauge interchangeable spare barrels available with either 2¾" or 3" chambers; barrels are equipped with ventilated ribs except Buck Special barrels which have adjustable rifle sights; barrels of the same gauge are interchangeable
Magazine capacity: Three 2¾" or 3" loads; or two 2¾" or 3" loads with the magazine plug installed; each gun comes with the magazine plug in place

Prices
Light 12 Invector, and Magnum 20 gauge, V.R. **$561.95**
Extra barrels $125.00–198.00

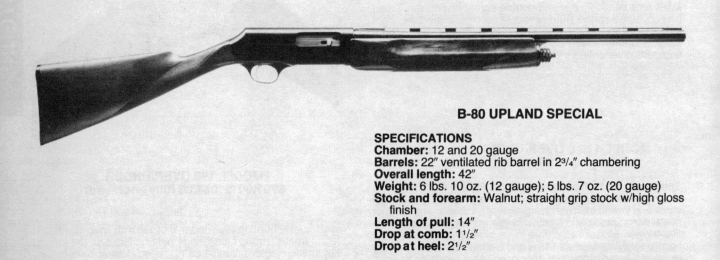

B-80 UPLAND SPECIAL

SPECIFICATIONS
Chamber: 12 and 20 gauge
Barrels: 22" ventilated rib barrel in 2¾" chambering
Overall length: 42"
Weight: 6 lbs. 10 oz. (12 gauge); 5 lbs. 7 oz. (20 gauge)
Stock and forearm: Walnut; straight grip stock w/high gloss finish
Length of pull: 14"
Drop at comb: 1½"
Drop at heel: 2½"

B-80 Upland Special **$561.95**

BROWNING AUTOMATIC SHOTGUNS

"SWEET SIXTEEN" AUTO-5

AUTO-5

The Browning Auto-5 Shotgun is offered in an unusually wide variety of models and specifications. The Browning 12-gauge 3-inch Magnum accepts up to and including the 3-inch, 1⅞ ounce, 12-gauge Magnum load, which contains only ⅛ ounce of shot less than the maximum 3½-inch 10-gauge load. The 2¾-inch Magnums and 2¾-inch high velocity shells may be used with equal pattern efficiency. Standard features include a special shock absorber and a hunting-style recoil pad. The Auto-5 is also available with the Invector screw-in choke system.

Browning also offers the 20 gauge in a 3-inch Magnum model. This powerful, light heavyweight offers maximum versatility to 20-gauge advocates. It handles the 20-gauge, 2¾-inch high velocity and Magnums, but it literally thrives on the 3-inch, 1¼-ounce load which delivers real 12-gauge performance in a 20-gauge package.

The 12-gauge Auto-5, chambered for regular 2¾-inch shells, handles all 12-gauge, 2¾-inch shells, from the very lightest 1 ounce field load to the heavy 1½-ounce Magnums. The Browning 20-gauge Auto-5 is lightweight and a top performer for the upland hunter. Yet, with 2¾-inch high velocity or 2¾-inch Magnums, it does a fine job in the duck blind.

24-inch barrels are available as an accessory.

Hunting Models:

Light 12, Sweet 16 and Light 20 gauge, Invector . . . **$632.95**
3" Magnum 12 and Magnum 20 gauge, Invector **643.95**
Limited issue, 12 gauge, 28" barrels, Modified choke, exquisite engraving, individually serial-numbered.
Classic edition, 5000 issued **1260.00**
Gold Classic edition, 500 issued **6500.00**
3" Magnum 12 and Magnum 20 gauge, Invector **604.95**
Light 12 Ventilated Rib **602.95**

BT-99 BROWNING TRAP SPECIAL

SPECIFICATIONS
Receiver: Machined steel, tastefully hand-engraved and richly blued
Barrel: Choice of 32" or 34" lengths; choke choice of Full, Improved Modified or Modified; chambered for 12 gauge, 2¾" shells only
Trigger: Gold-plated, crisp, positive, pull approximately 3½ lbs.
Stock and forearm: Select French walnut, hand-rubbed finish, sharp 20-line hand-checkering; Monte Carlo or conventional stock available; full pistol grip; length of pull 14⅜";

drop at comb 1⅜"; drop at heel 2"; full beavertail forearm
Safety: No manual safety, a feature preferred by trap shooters
Sights: Ivory front and center sight beads
Rib: High post, ventilated, full floating, matted, 11/32" wide
Recoil pad: Deluxe, contoured trap style
Weight: 8 lbs. with 32" barrel; 8 lbs. 3 oz. with 34" barrel
Automatic ejection: Fired shell ejected automatically on opening action, unfired shell elevated from chamber for convenient removal
Grade I Competition Invector (32" or 34" barrel) . . **$920.00**
($895.00 Non Invector)

BROWNING SHOTGUNS

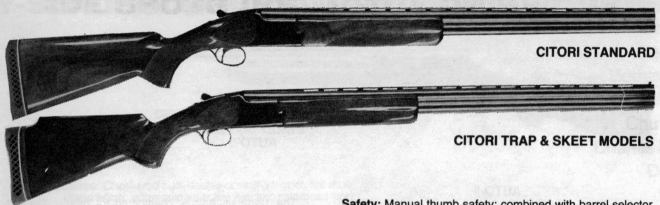

CITORI STANDARD

CITORI TRAP & SKEET MODELS

FIELD GRADE
Gauge: 12, 16, 20, 28 and .410 gauge
Barrels: 24″, 26″, 28″, or 30″ in 12 gauge; 28″ in 16 gauge; 24″, 26″, or 28″ in 20 gauge; ventilated rib with matted sighting plane; medium raised German nickel-silver sight bead; 26″ or 28″ in 28 gauge; 26″ or 28″ in .410 gauge
Overall length: All gauges 41″ with 24″ barrels; 43″ with 26″ barrels; 45″ with 28″ barrels; 47″ with 30″ barrels
Chokes: Mod.-Full, Invector in 30″ barrels; choice of Invector, Mod.-Full or Imp. Cyl.-Mod. in 28″ and 26″ barrels
Trigger: Single selective; gold-plated, fast and crisp
Chamber: All 20-gauge Field models and all 12-gauge Field models accept all 3″ Magnum loads as well as 2³/₄″ loads; 16 and 28-gauge accepts 2³/₄″ loads; .410-gauge accepts 2¹/₂″, 3″, or 3″ Mag. loads

Safety: Manual thumb safety; combined with barrel selector mechanism
Automatic ejectors: Fired shells thrown out of gun; unfired shells are elevated for easy removal
Approximate Weight:

	12 gauge	16 gauge	20 gauge
24″ barrels	6 lbs. 9 oz.		5 lbs. 12 oz.
26″ barrels	7 lbs. 9 oz.		6 lbs. 11 oz.
28″ barrels	7 lbs. 11 oz.	7 lbs	6 lbs. 13 oz.
30″ barrels	7 lbs. 13 oz		

Stock and forearm: Dense walnut; skillfully checkered; full pistol grip; hunting Beavertail forearm; field-type recoil pad installed on 12 gauge models

	12 gauge	20 gauge
Length of pull	14¹/₄″	14¹/₄″
Drop at comb	1⁵/₈″	1¹/₂″
Drop at heel	2¹/₂″	2³/₈″

HUNTING, SUPERLIGHT, UPLAND SPECIAL & SPORTER MODELS*

MAGNUM 12 and 20 GAUGE	Price
Grade I Invector	$ 902.00
Grade I	862.00
Grade III Invector	1220.00
Grade VI Invector	1790.00
SUPERLIGHT 12 AND 20 GAUGE	
Grade I Invector	928.00
Grade I	892.00
Grade III Invector	1220.00
Grade VI Invector	1790.00
UPLAND SPECIAL 12 AND 20 GAUGE	
Grade I Invector	928.00
HUNTING 28 Gauge and .410 Bore	
Grade I	892.00
Grade III	1342.00
Grade VI	1895.00
SUPERLIGHT 28 Gauge and .410 Bore	
Grade I	892.00
Grade III	1342.00
Grade VI	1895.00

TRAP MODELS (High Post Target Rib)	
Standard 12 Gauge	
Grade I Invector	$1010.00
Grade I	965.00
Grade III	1342.00
Grade VI Invector	1895.00
SKEET MODELS (High Post Target Rib)	
Standard 12 and 20 Gauge	
Grade I Invector	998.00
Grade I	966.00
Grade III	1342.00
Grade VI	1895.00
Standard 28 Gauge and .410 Bore	
Grade I	1010.00
Grade III	1342.00
Grade VI	1895.00

*NOTE : All Invector model Citori's are available in the High Grades.

4-BARREL SKEET SET
12 Gauge with one removable forearm and four sets of barrels, 12, 20, 28 and .410 gauges, high post target rib.
(Furnished with fitted luggage case for gun and extra barrels)

Grade 1	3235.00
Grade III	3550.00
Grade VI	4035.00

BROWNING SHOTGUNS

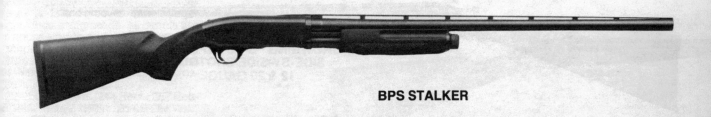

BPS PUMP SHOTGUN 12 GAUGE

Gauge: 12 and 20 gauge
Barrels: Choice of 22″, 26″, 28″, 30″ or 32″ lengths with high-post ventilated rib; Hunting model has German nickel sight bead
Action: Pump action with double-action bars; bottom loading and ejection; serrated slide release located at rear of trigger guard
Choke: Invector only
Trigger: Crisp and positive; let-off at 4½ lbs.
Chamber: 3″ chamber in Hunting models accepts all 2¾″, 2¾″ Magnum and 3″ Magnum shells; target models 2¾″ shells only

BPS STALKER

Safety: Convenient knurled-thumb, top-receiver safety; slide forward to shoot
Approximate weight: 7 lbs. 12 oz. with 28″ barrel
Overall length: 42¾″ with 22″ barrel; 46¾″ with 26″ barrel; 48¾″ with 28″ barrel; 50¾″ with 30″ barrel
Stock and forearm: Select walnut, weather-resistant finish, sharp 18-line checkering; full pistol grip; semi-beavertail forearm with finger grooves; length of pull 14¼″; drop at comb 1½″; drop at heel 2½″

Grade I, Hunting with Invector, 12 and 20 ga.,
V.R. $412.50
Grade I, Upland Special, 22 ″ barrel with Invector,
12 and 20 ga., V.R. 412.50
Extra barrels available . . . $120.00-177.00 (Buck Special)
Invector Stalker, 12 ga. only................... 399.50

BPS YOUTH & LADIES MODEL

SPECIFICATIONS
Chamber: 20 gauge only
Barrels: 22″ invector w/ventilated rib; interchangeable within gauge
Overall length: 41¾″
Weight (approx.): 6 lbs. 11 oz.
Stock and forearm: Straight grip stock of select walnut in durable gloss finish
Length of pull: 13¼″
Drop at comb: 1½″
Drop at heel: 2½″

BPS Youth & Ladies Model $412.50

BROWNING SHOTGUNS

BROWNING "B-SS" SPORTER SIDE-BY-SIDE SHOTGUN 12 & 20 GAUGE

The Browning Side-by-Side has a "mechanical" trigger which differs from the "inertia" trigger found on many two-barreled guns in that the recoil of the first shot is not used to set up the mechanism for the second shot. The first pull of the trigger fires the right barrel. The next pull fires the left barrel. The positive linkage of the B-SS mechanical trigger prevents doubling (both barrels firing at the same instant) or balking. The chromed trigger lets off crisply at about 4 1/2 pounds.

SPECIFICATIONS

Barrels: Choice of 26", 28" or 30" barrels; solid rib with matted top; sight bead is German nickel-silver

Choke: 30" barrels choked Full or Modified and Full; 28" barrel model choked Modified and Full; 26" barrels choked Modified and Full, or Improved Cylinder and Modified

Chamber: 2 3/4", 2 3/4" Mag. and 3" Mag. shells; Sidelock version accepts only 2 3/4" and 2 3/4" Mag.

Automatic safety: Goes "on safe" when breech is opened and remains there until manually moved to "off safe"

Automatic ejectors: Fired shells are thrown out of gun; unfired shells are elevated for easy removal

Weight: Approx. 7 lbs. 7 oz. with 30" barrels; approx. 7 lbs. 3 oz. with 26" barrels; approx. 7 lbs. 5 oz. with 28" barrels.

Sidelock—6 lbs. 11 oz. with 28" barrel; 6 lbs. 9 oz. with 26" barrel

Overall length: 43" with 26" barrels; 45" with 28" barrels; 47" with 30" barrels

Stock and forearm: French walnut, hand-rubbed finish, sharp 18-line hand-checkering; full pistol grip; full grip beavertail forearm; length of pull 14 1/4"; drop at comb 1 5/8"; drop at heel 2 1/2"

Grade I Standard with Barrel Selector . . . . $ 775.00
Grade I Sporter with Barrel Selector 775.00
Sidelock w/26" or 28 " barrels 2000.00

MODEL A-500 12 GAUGE SEMIAUTOMATIC

Designed and built in Belgium, the A-500 employs a short recoil system with a strong four-lug bolt design. There is no gas system to collect powder residues or grime, and no pistons, ports or cylinders to clean. Only one extractor is needed to pull the shell from the chamber. The stock has no drilled holes to accommodate action springs, making it that much stronger (especially where it bolts against the receiver).

SPECIFICATIONS

Barrel lengths: 26", 28" and 30"
Overall lengths: 45 1/2", 47 1/2" and 49 1/2"

Weight: 7 lbs. 3 oz. (26" barrel); 7 lbs. 5 oz. (28" barrel) and 7 lbs. 7 oz. (30" barrel)

Chamber: 3"

Choke: Invector

Stock dimensions: length of pull 14 1/4"; drop at comb 1 1/2"; drop at heel 2 1/2"

Safety: cross bolt, right or left hand

Action: short recoil operated with four lug rotary bolt

Barrel/receiver finish: deep high polish blued finish; receiver lightly engraved with scroll pattern

Model A-500 . . . . $552.00
   Extra barrels 194.95

CHURCHILL SHOTGUNS

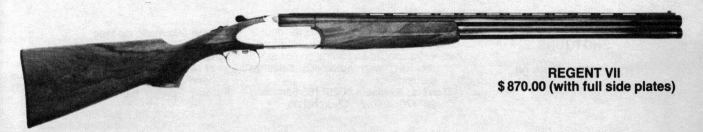

REGENT VII
$ 870.00 (with full side plates)

The Regent Grade over/under shotguns feature ventilated rib, single selective trigger, automatic safety, selective automatic ejectors and 2³/₄-inch (70 mm) chambers.

Barrels: 27″ long; chrome molybdenum steel with silver braised monobloc; insides of barrels are fully chromed; wide ventilated rib
Gauge/chokes: 12 and 20 gauge with ICT (interchangeable choke tubes) in Imp. Cyl./Mod./Full
Action: Forged nickel-chrome steel heat-treated for hardness before and after machining; engraved hunting scene in antique silver finish
Locks: Double bottom lock, made up of two smooth-fitting lugs, formed by an

ingenious sliding bolt that inserts into special slots in the lugs
Trigger: Single-selective trigger working off an inertia block; selection of the barrel is done by moving the safety button; the recoil of the first shot moves the block from one sear to the other to set up the second shot
Ejectors: Selective automatic
Stock: Fashioned from extra select fancy walnut in a genuine oil-rubbed finish with pistol grip; precise 22 line hand-checkering

REGENT GRADE COMPETITION SHOTGUNS

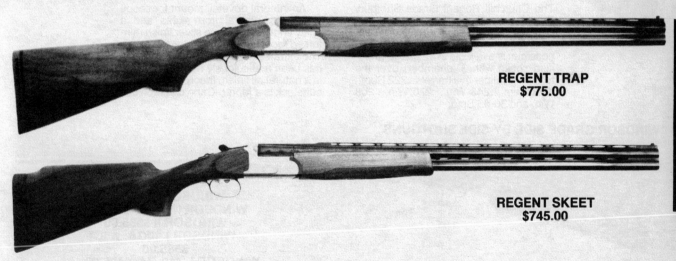

REGENT TRAP
$775.00

REGENT SKEET
$745.00

These competition shotguns feature selective automatic ejectors, chrome bores, single-selective triggers, safety and wide ventilated ribs. The Regent Trap model, in 12 gauge, has ventilated side ribs and is furnished with Monte Carlo stock and Supercushion recoil pad. The Regent Skeet is available in both 12 and 20 gauge.

MODEL	Gauge	Chamber	Barrel Length	Chokes	Overall Length	Length of Pull	Drop at Comb	Drop at Heel	Nominal Weight
GP7802 TRAP	12	2.75″	30″	IM & F	47.25″	14.5″	1.36″	1.5″	8 lbs.
GP7829 SKEET	12	2.75″	26″	SK & SK	43.94″	14.5″	1.5″	2.36″	7 lbs.
GP7853 SKEET	20	2.75″	26″	SK & SK	43.94″	14.5″	1.5″	2.36″	7 lbs.

CHURCHILL SHOTGUNS

REGENT GRADE SIDE-BY-SIDE SHOTGUNS

REGENT VI $765.00

Action: Regent VI Genuine double safety side lock, antique silver with extra special engraving on scalloped receiver; with automatic selective ejectors
Barrels: Available in 25″ (63.5cm) and 28″ (70cm) only; Churchill rib

Safety: Automatic top tang
Triggers: Double
Stock: Genuine oil-finish English stock of extra select European walnut, hand-checkered butt
Forend: Splinter; hand-checkered

Churchill Regent Grade side-by-side shotguns follow the long tradition of craftsmanship established by the finest English gunmakers. These guns combine classic historical design and detailed execution with elegant finishing.

Model	Right Hand	Gauge	Barrel	Chamber	Choke
Regent VI	GE6709	12	28″	2.75″	M&F
	GE6768	12	25″	2.75″	IC&M
	GE6806	12	27″	2.75″	ICT
	GE6857	12	25″	2.75″	ICT

The Churchill Regent Grade Shotgun/ Rifle Combination is the ultimate in performance and classic design for the over/under enthusiast. The multi-purpose gun is available in 12 gauge (Modified choke with 3″ chamber) over the following caliber rifle barrels: .222 Rem., .223 Rem., .243 Win., .270 Win., .308 Win. and 30-06 Spfd.

REGENT GRADE SHOTGUN/ RIFLE COMBINATION $720.00

An integral dovetail mount for scope mounting, integral iron sights and a finely engraved antique silver finish reinforced receiver are all standard features. The extra-select European walnut stock has been meticulously hand-checkered in a natural oil finish. Incorporated in the buttstock is a Monte-Carlo cheekpiece.

WINDSOR GRADE SIDE-BY-SIDE SHOTGUNS

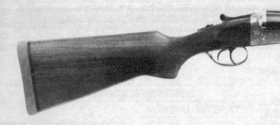

WINDSOR I $390.00
WINDSOR I 10 GA. $520.00
WINDSOR II $535.00
WINDSOR I 10GA. w/ICT $585.00
WINDSOR I .410 GA. $405.00

Perfect balance, elegance of line, richness of beautiful woods and careful fitting of metal to wood are the essence of Churchill shotguns.

Windsor I side-by-side shotguns are available in all gauges from 10 to .410 and in a wide range of barrels and chokes.

Windsor II side-by-side shotguns, with automatic selective ejectors, are available in 12 and 20 gauges only with optional interchangeable chokes (ICT).

Model	Gauge	Barrel Length	Chamber	Chokes
Windsor I (only)	10	32″	3½″	F&F
	16	28″	2³/₄″	M&F
	20 (youth)	24″	3″	M&F
	28	26″	3″	SKI&2, M&F
	.410	26″	3″	M&F
Windsor I & II	12	30″ or 32″	3″	F&F
	12	28″ or 30″	3″	M&F
	12, 20	26″	3″	IC&M
	20	28″	3″	M&F
Windsor II (only)	12	27″ or 30″	3″	ICT

CHURCHILL SHOTGUNS

WINDSOR GRADE OVER/UNDER SHOTGUNS

**WINDSOR III
OVER/UNDER**

**WINDSOR III $495.00
(with extractors)
With ICT Barrels $605.00
WINDSOR IV $575.00
(with automatic ejectors)
With ICT Barrels $685.00
WINDSOR III .410GA. $560.00**

Barrels: Chrome molybdenum steel with silver braised monobloc; insides of barrels are fully chromed; ventilated rib

Action: Forged nickel-chrome steel heat-treated for hardness before and after machining; richly engraved game scenes on antique silver finish

Locks: Double bottom lock made up of two smooth fitting lugs that is formed by an ingenious sliding bolt which inserts into special slots in the lugs

Trigger: Single selective trigger working off an inertia block. Selection of the barrel is done by moving the safety button; the recoil of the first shot moves the block from one sear to the other to set up the second shot

Stock: Made of select European walnut with oil finish; checkered; pistol grip

Model	Gauge	Barrel Length	Chokes
Windsor III & IV	12	30″	F&F, M&F
	12, 20	28″	M&F
	12, 20	26″	IC&M
	12, 20	27″	IC/M/F
	12	30″	M/F/XF
	.410	24″ or 26″	F&F
Windsor IV (only)	12, 20	26″	SK&SK

MONARCH OVER/UNDER

The Churchill Monarch over/under shotguns feature a high-lustre blued receiver, gold plated single selective trigger, ventilated rib, and European walnut stock with checkering and a protective polyurethane finish. Double bottom lock, made up of two smooth fitting lugs, is formed by an ingenious sliding bolt which inserts into special slots in the lugs.

Model	Gauge	Barrel Length	Chamber	Chokes	Nominal Weight	Price
GP8124	12	28	3	M&F	7 lbs. 7 oz.	$365.00
GP8140	12	26	3	IC&M	7 lbs. 6 oz.	365.00
GP8167	20	28	3	M&F	6 lbs. 8 oz.	365.00
GP8183	20	26	3	IC&M	6 lbs. 6 oz.	365.00
Double Trigger Models						
GP8221	12	28	3	M&F	7 lbs. 7 oz.	342.00
GP8248	12	26	3	IC & M	7 lbs. 6 oz.	342.00
GP8264	20	28	3	M&F	6 lbs. 8 oz.	342.00
GP8280	20	26	3	IC&M	6 lbs. 6 oz.	342.00

CHURCHILL SHOTGUNS

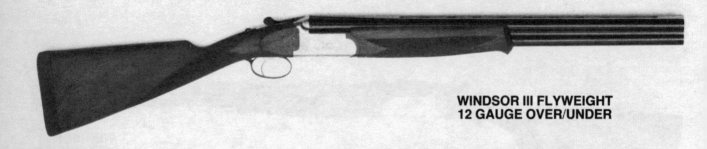

**WINDSOR III FLYWEIGHT
12 GAUGE OVER/UNDER**

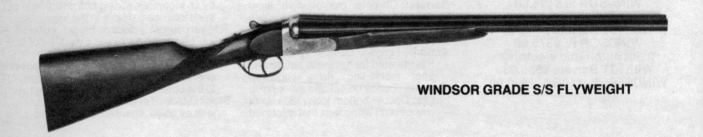

WINDSOR GRADE S/S FLYWEIGHT

FLYWEIGHT SHOTGUNS

Churchill Flyweight shotguns are right for ultra-responsive, fast-handling upland game hunting. The English-style straight grip buttstock and 23-inch or 25-inch barrels contribute to the line's fast and sure handling characteristics.

Churchill Flyweights are available with either Interchangeable Choke Tubes (ICT) or traditional chokes, in a wide range of side by sides, over/unders. They incorporate all the standard features found in the traditional line of Churchill shotguns.

SPECIFICATIONS WINDSOR FLYWEIGHT

	MODEL	GAUGE	BARREL in/cm	CHAMBER in/mm	CHOKE US/UK	Continental	NOMINAL WEIGHT lb-oz/kg	PRICE
SIDE BY SIDE	WINDSOR I	12	25/63.5	2³/₄/70	IC&M	1/4 & 1/2	7-0/3.18	$415.00
	WINDSOR I	16	25/63.5	2³/₄/70	IC&M	1/4 & 1/2	7-0/3.18	415.00
	WINDSOR I	20	23/58	3/76.2	IC&M	1/4 & 1/2	6-8/2.95	415.00
	WINDSOR I	28	23/58	3/76.2	IC&M	1/4 & 1/2	6-6/2.9	431.00
	WINDSOR I	410	23/58	3/76.2	F&F	1/1 & 1/1	5-12/2.61	431.00
OVER/UNDER	WINDSOR III	12	25/63.5	2³/₄/70	IC&M	1/4 & 1/2	6-10/3.01	$495.00
	WINDSOR III	12	25/63.5	2³/₄/70	ICT*		6-12/3.07	605.00
	WINDSOR III	20	23/58	3/76.2	IC&M	1/4 & 1/2	5-12/2.61	495.00
	WINDSOR III	20	23/58	3/76.2	ICT*		6-0/2.73	605.00
	WINDSOR III	410	23/58	3/76.2	F&F	1/1 & 1/1	6-0/2.73	560.00
	WINDSOR IV	12	25/63.5	2³/₄/70	IC&M	1/4 & 1/2	6-13/3.1	575.00
	WINDSOR IV	12	25/63.5	2³/₄/70	ICT*		6-15/3.15	745.00
	WINDSOR IV	20	23/58	3/76.2	IC&M	1/4 & 1/2	6-3/2.81	575.00
	WINDSOR IV	20	23/58	3/76.2	ICT*		6-0/2.73	745.00
	WINDSOR IV	410	23/58	3/76.2	F&F	1/1 & 1/1	6-4/2.84	685.00

CHARLES DALY SHOTGUNS

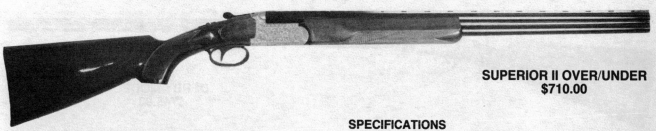

SUPERIOR II OVER/UNDER
$710.00

The Superior II Over/Under is a rugged shotgun that boasts a beautifully engraved silver receiver, single selective trigger, checkered pistol grip stock and forearm with recoil pad, ventilated rib, high-gloss wood finish with blued barrels. Selective auto ejectors.

SPECIFICATIONS

Gauge	Barrel Length	Chokes
12 Magnum	30″	Mod./Full
12, 20	28″	Mod./Full
12, 20	26″	Imp. Cyl./Mod.
12, 20	26″	Skeet

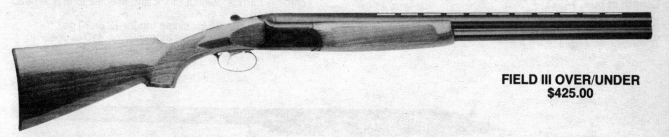

FIELD III OVER/UNDER
$425.00

This field grade over/under offers the same fine features as the other Charles Daly shotguns: excellent construction with a sound marriage of metal to wood. Checkered pistol grip and forearm, straight stock with high-gloss finish, 26- or 28-inch barrels with ventilated rib and single selective trigger. Non-selective extractors.

SPECIFICATIONS

Gauge	Barrel Length	Chokes
12 or 20	28″	Mod./Full
12 or 20	26″	Imp. Cyl./Mod.

GAS AUTOMATIC
From $365.00

The Charles Daly gas automatic features Invector Choke System with wrench; 12 gauge model available with 27-inch barrels; 12 gauge Magnum comes with 30-inch barrels. Ventilated rib.

Also available is a 12 gauge slug gun model with a 20″ barrel and a "Super Field" model with a 23″ barrel and Invector Choke System. The "Multi-XII" model (12 gauge only) features vent. rib w/Invector choke and fires 2¾″or 3″ magnum shells interchangeably.

OVER/UNDER DIAMOND TRAP AND SKEET (not shown)
$1030.00

12 gauge Trap gun features 30-inch ventilated rib barrel choked Improved Modified/Full, Monte Carlo stock with non-slip recoil pad, extra strong reinforced receiver, selective trigger and shell ejector.

12 gauge Skeet version is available with 26-inch barrels choked Skeet/Skeet, competition ventilated rib, oil-finished stock with non-slip recoil pad, selective trigger, separate shell ejectors.

DIARM SIDE-BY-SIDE SHOTGUNS

DERBY MODEL
$745.00

SPECIFICATIONS
Gauge: 12, 20, 28 or .410
Chamber: 3″
Barrel length: 25″ or 28″ (12 ga. IC/M or M/F); 25″ (20, 28 or .410 ga. IC/M)
Length of pull: 14⅛″
Drop at comb: 1⅜″
Drop at heel: 2⅜″
Weight: 7 lb. 1 oz. (12 ga.); 6 lbs. 4 oz. (20, 28 & .410 ga.)

Features: Checkered butt; double or single trigger; flat rib w/ matte finish; automatic selective ejector; gold bead front sight; English straight stock; manual thumb safety; precision made functioning side locks w/English style hand engraving on side plates; one-piece steel forged receiver; chrome barrels; walnut stock and splinter forend w/hand checkering
Additional **$50** charge for single trigger 12 or 20 ga.
Additional **$120.00** for single trigger 28 or .410 gauge.

WATERFOWL SPECIAL
$560.00

SPECIFICATIONS
Gauge: 10
Chamber: 3½″
Barrel length: 32″ (Full/Full)
Length of pull: 14⁵/₁₆″
Drop at comb: 1⅜″
Drop at heel: 2⅜″
Weight: 10 lbs. 13 oz.

Features: Fitted rubber recoil pad; double triggers; flat rib; precision made box locks w/engraved English style scroll work on side plates; one-piece steel forged receiver; Parkerized barrels and receiver; chrome barrels; manual thumb safety; dull finish walnut stock and beavertail forend w/hand checkering; sling swivels; camouflaged sling; specially designed for hunting large birds and other game

TURKEY SPECIAL
$595.00

Same specifications as **Waterfowl Special** except barrel length (26″) w/choke tubes.

DIARM SIDE-BY SIDE SHOTGUNS

AYA MODEL 2
$1650.00

SPECIFICATIONS

Gauge: 12, 20, 28 or .410 (and combination gauges)
Barrel length: 26″ or 28″ (12 or 20 ga. w/IC/M or M/F; 26″ (28 or .410 ga. w/IC/M)
Length of pull: 14¹/₄″
Drop at comb: 1¹/₂″
Drop at heel: 2¹/₂″
Weight: 7 lbs. (12 ga.); 6 lbs. 3 oz. (20 and .410 ga.); 6 lbs. (28 ga.)
Features: Checkered butt; double or single selective triggers; English concave rib; automatic selective ejectors; high grade hand-fitted and finished side locks w/scroll style hand engraving on side plates; one-piece steel forged receiver plates; automatic safety; walnut stock and splinter forend with hand checkering; English straight stock; hand rubbed oil finish wood; silver front bead; gas escape valves

12 or 20 gauge w/Single Trigger	$1805.00
28 or .410 w/Double Trigger	1795.00
28 or .410 w/Single Trigger	1950.00
2 barrel sets w/Double Trigger	2440.00
2 barrel sets w/Single Trigger	2595.00

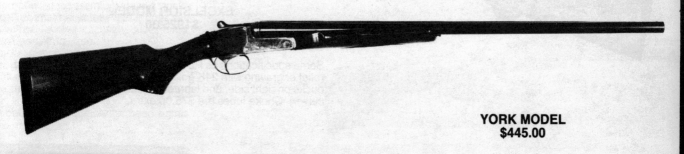

YORK MODEL
$445.00

SPECIFICATIONS

Gauge: 12, 20, 28 or .410
Chamber: 3″
Barrel length: 28″ (12 ga. w/M/F) or 25″ (12 ga. w/IC/M) or 25″ (20, 28 or .410 ga. w/IC/M)
Length of pull: 14¹/₈″
Drop at comb: 1³/₈″
Drop at heel: 2³/₈″

Weight: 7 lbs. 1 oz. (12 ga.); 6 lbs. 4 oz. (20, 28 and .410 gs.)
Features: Fitted recoil pad; flat matte rib; extractors; double triggers; precision made box locks; one-piece steel forged receiver; chrome barrels; manual thumb safety; walnut stock and beavertail forend w/hand checkering; pistol grip stock; gloss finished wood; gold front sight bead; independent floating firing pin

DIARM OVER-AND-UNDER SHOTGUNS

WATERFOWL SPECIAL
$650.00

SPECIFICATIONS
Gauge: 12
Chamber: 3"
Barrel length: 28"
Length of pull: 14 1/8"
Drop at comb: 1 3/8"
Drop at heel: 2 3/8"

Weight: 7 lbs. 1 oz.
Features: Fitted recoil pad; 1/4" vent rib; precision made box locks w/Parkerized finish side plates and barrels; one-piece steel forged receiver; monobloc chrome barrels; locking cross bolt; manual thumb safety; hand checkered dull finish walnut pistol grip stock and forend; camouflaged sling

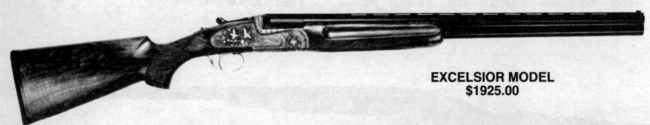

EXCELSIOR MODEL
$1925.00

Same specifications as Royal Model but with exquisite raised relief engraving with 24K gold plating (pheasants on left side, ducks on right side, and labrador retriever on underside of receiver). Choke tubes are $75.00 extra.

MODEL FS 200
$835.00

SPECIFICATIONS
Gauge: 12
Chamber: 2 3/4"
Barrel length: 28" or 32"
Choke: Skeet/Skeet or IM/F
Length of pull: 14 5/16"
Drop at comb: 1 3/8"
Drop at heel: 1 1/2"

Weight: 7 lbs. 11 oz.
Features: Fitted recoil pad; single selective trigger; automatic selective ejectors; chrome finish frame; 3/8" vent rib w/matte finish; swollen right palm pistol grip stock; central rib eliminated to improve wind resistance and optimize cooling of both barrels

DIARM OVER-AND-UNDER SHOTGUNS

SILVER MODEL
$545.00

SPECIFICATIONS
Gauge: 12 or 20
Chamber: 3"
Barrel length: 26" or 28"
Choke: Mod/Full or IC/Mod
Ejector: Automatic selective ejectors
Trigger: Single selective trigger
Length of pull: 14 1/8"
Drop at comb: 1 3/8"
Drop at heel: 2 3/8"
Weight: 7 lbs. 1 oz. (12 ga.)

Features: Precision made box locks w/brushed silver finish side plates: one-piece steel forged receiver; monobloc chrome barrels; locking cross bolt; manual thumb safety; hand checkered walnut pistol grip stock and forend; fitted recoil pad; 1/4" vent rib w/matte finish
Also available:
SILVER I (same as above but w/o automatic selective ejectors): **$449.00**
SILVER II (same as standard model but w/choke tubes): **$620.00**

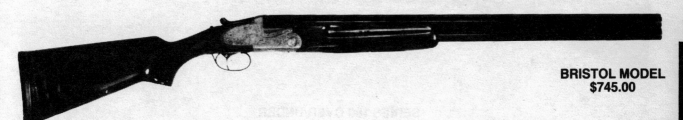

BRISTOL MODEL
$745.00

SPECIFICATIONS
Gauge: 12 or 20
Chamber: 3"
Barrel length: 24", 26" or 28"
Choke: IC/Mod, Mod/Full or Choke tubes ($50 additional)
Length of pull: 14 1/8"
Drop at comb: 1 3/8"
Drop at heel: 2 3/8"
Weight: 7 lbs. 1 oz.

Features: Fitted recoil pad; 1/4" vent rib w/matte finish; automatic selective ejector; single selective trigger; old silver finish frame; gold front sight bead; gold color trigger; precision made box locks w/engraved hunting scene on false die plates; one-piece steel forged receiver; monobloc chrome barrels; locking cross bolt; manual thumb safety; precision wood to metal fit; walnut stock and forend with hand checkering

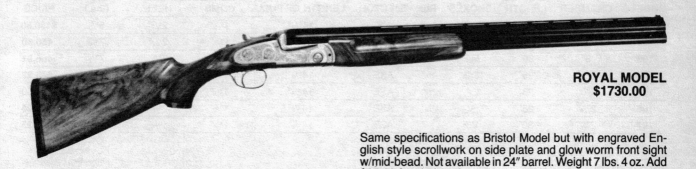

ROYAL MODEL
$1730.00

Same specifications as Bristol Model but with engraved English style scrollwork on side plate and glow worm front sight w/mid-bead. Not available in 24" barrel. Weight 7 lbs. 4 oz. Add $65.00 for choke tubes.

EXEL SHOTGUNS

MODEL 102

MODEL 101

SERIES 100 OVER/UNDER

Lightweight, well-balanced, and superb handling aptly describe these 12 gauge over/under shotguns. They feature single selective trigger system, selective auto ejectors, action machined from a solid block of special steel, hand-checkered European walnut stock with full pistol grip and tulip forend, black finish (except Model 105—Old Silver). **Models 105** and **106** are supplied with five choke tubes: Cyl., Imp. Cyl., Mod., Imp. Mod., Full. **Model 107, Trap:** upper barrel choked Full; lower barrel supplied with three choke tubes—Full, Imp. Mod., Mod.

MODELS	CHAMBER	BARREL LENGTH	CHOKES	RIB	EJECTOR	STOCK DIMENSIONS			AVERAGE WEIGHT (lbs.)	PRICE
						LENGTH OF PULL	NOMINAL DROP AT			
							COMB	HEEL		
101	2³/₄″	26″	IC/M	1/4″	NE	14³/₈″	1¹/₂″	2¹/₂″	6⁷/₈	$450.80
102	2³/₄″	28″	IC/IM	1/4″	NE	14³/₈″	1¹/₂″	2¹/₂″	7¹/₈	450.80
103	3″	30″	M/F	1/4″	NE	14³/₈″	1¹/₂″	2¹/₂″	7⁷/₈	466.91
104	2³/₄″	28″	IC/IM	1/4″	ASE	14³/₈″	1¹/₂″	2¹/₂″	7¹/₈	543.29
105	2³/₄″	28″	V	1/4″	ASE	14³/₈″	1¹/₂″	2¹/₂″	7³/₈	644.00
106	2³/₄″	28″	V	1/2″	ASE	14³/₈″	1¹/₂″	2¹/₈″	7³/₈	845.25
107	2³/₄″	30″	V/F	1/2″	ASE	14¹/₂″	1¹/₄″	1³/₄″	7³/₄	845.25

EXEL SHOTGUNS

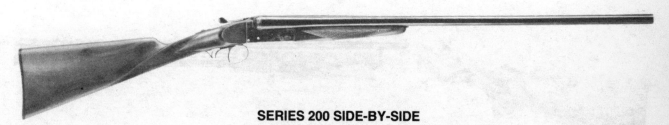

SERIES 200 SIDE-BY-SIDE

These classic double-barreled shotguns feature American or European-style stocks and forearms hand-checkered of European walnut; double triggers. **Stock dimensions:** Length of pull, 14³/₈″-14³/₄″; drop at comb, 1¹/₂″; drop at heel, 2¹/₂″. 20 gauge available in all models as listed below with 26- or 28-inch barrels in various choke combinations (does not apply to Model 51). Other choke combinations for other gauges available upon request. **Model 51** is folding shotgun, 6¹/₂″ × 26″.

MODELS	GAUGE	CHAMBER	BARREL LENGTH	CHOKES	RIB	EJECTOR	FRAME FINISH	STOCK	FOREND	AVERAGE WEIGHT (lbs.)	PRICE
51	410	3″	26″	M/F	—	NE	M	HPG	SP	4	$ 215.00
201	12	2³/₄″	28″	M/F	HMR	NE	M	SES	SP	7	428.91
202	12	2³/₄″	26″	IC/M	HMR	NE	M	SES	SP	7	428.91
203	20	3″	27″	M/F	HMR	NE	M	SES	SP	6¹/₂	428.91
203A	20	3″	26″	IC/M	HMR	NE	M	SES	SP	6¹/₂	428.91
281	28	2³/₄″	26″	M/F	HMR	NE	M	SES	SBV	6¹/₄	471.79
281A	28	2³/₄″	26″	IC/M	HMR	NE	M	SES	SBV	6¹/₄	471.79
240	410	3″	26″	F/M	HMR	NE	M	SES	SBV	5³/₄	471.79
240A	410	3″	26″	IC/M	HMR	NE	M	SES	SBV	5³/₄	471.79
207A	12	2³/₄″	28″	M/F	HMR	ASE	M	SES	SP	7	835.69
208A	12	2³/₄″	28″	M/F	OP	ASE	OP	OP	OP	7	925.23
209A	12	2³/₄″	26″	IC/M	OP	ASE	OP	OP	OP	7	925.33
210A	20	3″	27″	M/F	OP	ASE	OP	OP	OP	6¹/₂	925.33
211	12	2³/₄″	28″	M/F	OP	ASE	OP	OP	OP	6³/₄	3100.00
212	12	2³/₄″	26″	IC/M	OP	ASE	OP	OP	OP	6¹/₂	3100.00
213	20	3	27″	M/F	OP	ASE	OP	OP	OP	6¹/₂	3100.00

EXPLANATION OF SYMBOLS
Chokes: IC (Improved Cylinder); M (Modified); IM (Improved Modified); F (Full Choke); V (Variable Screw-in Interchangeable Chokes)
Ejectors: NE (Non-Ejector); ASE (Automatic Selective Ejectors)
Triggers: OP (Optional); SST (Selective Single Trigger); TSST (Twin Selective Single Trigger); NSST (Non-Selective Single Trigger); H (Outside Hammers)
Frame Finish: B (Black); OS (Old Silver); M (Marbled case hardened); OP (Optional)
Stocks: FPG (Full pistol grip); HPG (Half pistol grip); SES (Straight english style)
Forend: BV (Beavertail forend); SP (Splinter forend); OP (Optional); T (Tulip); TP (Tapered); SBV (Semi-beavertail forend)
Rib: HMR (High matted rib)

EXEL SHOTGUNS

SERIES 300 OVER/UNDER

Single and twin selective trigger systems and strong action highlight these sturdy, lightweight, reliable shotguns. Selective auto ejectors. Engraved receiver, hand-checkered European walnut stock and forend, full pistol grip. All Series 300 barrels and metal parts are finished in the "rustless" Black Chrome process. **Model 306A** avail. with extra interchangeable 12 gauge barrel set (no factory fitting): **$225.00. Model 306T,** Turkey Gun, supplied with special non-glare Black Chrome matte finish barrels, dull oil finished stock, sling swivels and four choke tubes: Full, Full, Imp. Cyl. and Mod. Other tubes available.

MODELS	GAUGE	CHAMBER	BARREL LENGTH	CHOKES	RIB	TRIGGERS	FOREND	LENGTH OF PULL	NOMINAL DROP AT COMB	NOMINAL DROP AT HEEL	AVERAGE WEIGHT (lbs.)	PRICE
303	12	2³/₄"	28"	IC/IM	¹/₅"	TSST	T	14³/₈"	1³/₈"	2¹/₂"	6¹/₂	622.71
304	12	2³/₄"	28"	M/F	¹/₅"	TSST	T	14³/₈"	1³/₈"	2¹/₂"	6¹/₂	622.71
305	12	2³/₄"	28"	(V)IC/IM	¹/₅"	TSST/SST	T	14³/₈"	1³/₈"	2¹/₂"	7	710.71
305A	20	3"	26"	(V)IC/IM	¹/₅"	SST	T	14³/₈"	1³/₈"	2¹/₂"	7	710.71
306	12	3"	28"	(V)M/F	¹/₅"	TSST	T	14³/₈"	1³/₈"	2¹/₂"	7	710.71
306A	20	3"	26"	(V)M/F	¹/₅"	SST	T	14³/₈"	1³/₈"	2¹/₂"	7	710.71
306T	12	3"	26"	V	¹/₅"	SST	TP	14³/₈"	1³/₈"	2¹/₂"	6¹/₂	710.71
307*	12	2³/₄"	28"	V/IC	¹/₂"	SST	BV	14³/₈"	1¹/₂"	1⁵/₈"	8	668.31
308*	12	2³/₄"	28"	V/IC	¹/₂"	SST	BV	14³/₈"	1¹/₂"	1⁵/₈"	8	668.31
309**	12	2³/₄"	29"	M/F	¹/₂"	SST	BV	14³/₈"	1¹/₂"	1⁵/₈"	7¹/₂	726.49
310**	12	2³/₄"	29"	IM/F	¹/₂"	SST	BV	14³/₈"	1¹/₂"	1⁵/₈"	7¹/₂	726.49

EXPLANATION OF SYMBOLS
Chokes: IC (Improved Cylinder); M (Modified); IM (Improved Modified); F (Full Choke); V (Variable Screw-in Interchangeable Chokes)
Ejectors: NE (Non-Ejector); ASE (Automatic Selective Ejectors)
Triggers: OP (Optional); SST (Selective Single Trigger); TSST (Twin Selective Single Trigger); NSST (Non-Selective Single Trigger); H (Oustide Hammers)
Frame Finish: B (Black); OS (Old Silver); M (Marbled case hardened); OP (Optional)
Stocks: FPG (Full pistol grip); HPG (Half pistol grip); SES (Straight english style)
Forend: BV (Beavertail forend); SP (Splinter forend); OP (Optional); T (Tulip); TP (Tapered); SBV (Semi-beavertail forend)
Rib: HMR (High matted rib)
*Trap Competition
**Super Trap or Super Skeet

EXEL SHOTGUNS

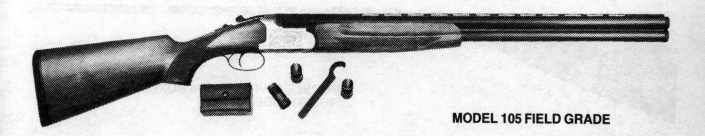

MODEL 105 FIELD GRADE

Gauge: 12 with 2³/₄" chambers
Barrels: 28" built on monobloc system, machined and threaded for screw-in choke tubes; flat ventilated rib
Chokes: 5 interchangeable tubes supplied—Cyl. (0); Imp. Cyl. (3); Mod. (5); Imp. Mod. (7); Full (10)
Trigger: Single selective, inertia type

Stock: Straight-grained walnut with diamond-checkered pistol grip and forend; fitted with solid rubber recoil pad; drop at comb, 1¹/₂"; drop at heel, 2¹/₂"; length of pull, 14³/₈".
Receiver: Silver, engraved with fine-line scroll of British design
Weight: 7+ lbs.
Price: $650.00 (with ejectors)

MODEL 106 SKEET GRADE

Gauge: 12 with 2³/₄" chambers
Barrels: 28" with ventilated rib
Chokes: 5 interchangeable choke tubes supplied—Cyl. (0); Imp. Cyl. (3); Mod. (5); Imp. Mod. (7); and Full (10)

Trigger: Single selective trigger
Safety: Automatic
Stock: European walnut with hand-checkering on pistol grip
Finish: Blued barrels and engraved receiver
Price: $845.00

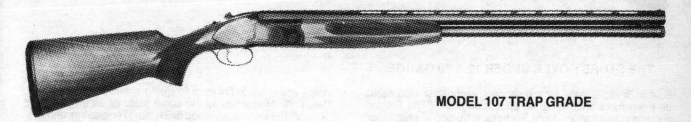

MODEL 107 TRAP GRADE

Gauge: 12 with 2³/₄" chambers
Barrels: 30" with ventilated rib
Chokes: 3 interchangeable choke tubes supplied—Mod. (5); Imp. Mod. (7); and Full (10)

Trigger: Single selective
Safety: Manual
Stock: European walnut with hand-checkered pistol grip
Finish: Blued barrels and engraved receiver
Price: $845.00

FERLIB SHOTGUNS

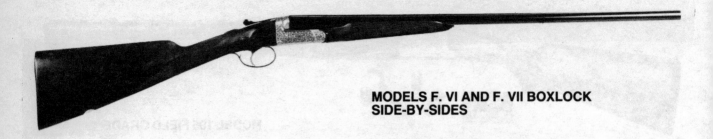

MODELS F. VI AND F. VII BOXLOCK SIDE-BY-SIDES

Hand-crafted by the small European artisan firm of the same name, Ferlib shotguns are high-quality, hand-fitted side-by-sides. With Anson & Deeley boxlock design, all Ferlib doubles are available in 12, 16, 20 and 28 gauge and .410 bore, with automatic ejectors, double triggers with front trigger hinged (non-selective single trigger is optional), hand-rubbed oil-finished straight grip stock with classic forearm (beavertail optional). Dovetail lump barrels have soft-luster blued finish; top rib is concave with file-cut matting. **Barrel length:** 25″-28″. **Stock dimensions:** Length of pull, 14½″; drop at comb, 1½″; drop at heel, 2¼. **Weight:** 12 ga., 6 lbs. 8 oz.–6 lbs. 14 oz.; 16 ga., 6 lbs. 4 oz.–6 lbs. 10 oz.; 20 ga., 5 lbs. 14 oz.–6 lbs. 4 oz.; 28 ga. and .410, 5 lbs. 6 oz.–5 lbs. 11 oz.

Model F. VI w/scalloped frame, border-line engraving, case-hardened colors, select walnut stock **$3500.00**
Model F. VII w/scalloped frame, full-coverage English scroll engraving, coin finish, select walnut stock **4500.00**
Model F. VII w/sideplates **5400.00**
Model F. VII/SC w/scalloped frame, game scene with either bulino engraved or gold inlayed birds and scroll accents with coin finish, special walnut stock with extra figure and color **5750.00**
Model F. VII/SC sideplated with either scroll or game scene engraving (w/either bulino or gold inlayed birds and coin finish), special walnut stock, extra figure and color on game scene version **6750.00**

F.I.E. SHOTGUNS

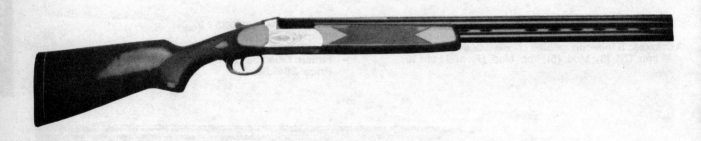

THE STURDY OVER/UNDER 12 & 20 GAUGE

Built in Brescia, Italy, for the shooting enthusiast who wants an over-under shotgun at an affordable price, "The Sturdy" accommodates all 2¾″ and 3″ shells, including 3″ Magnums. Other features include chrome lined 28″ barrels, modified and full chokes, ventilated rib, brass bead front sight, automatic safety, checkered European walnut stock and forend, and crossbolt locking system. The receiver is finished in brushed chrome engraved with game scenes.

In addition, the "Deluxe Sturdy" features a single selective trigger, screw-in choke tubes (full, modified, I.C., I.M., and cyl-inder), epoxy wood finish, auto ejectors, and scroll engraving. The "Priti" Model has all the same features as the standard "Sturdy" but with epoxy wood finish, scroll engraving, and rubber recoil pad.

Prices:
The Sturdy O/U $349.95
The Sturdy Deluxe 499.95
The Priti O/U 429.95

FRANCHI AUTOLOADING SHOTGUNS

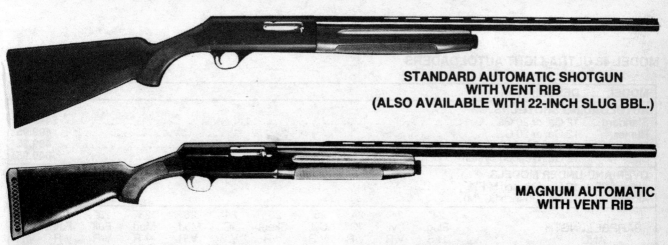

**STANDARD AUTOMATIC SHOTGUN
WITH VENT RIB
(ALSO AVAILABLE WITH 22-INCH SLUG BBL.)**

**MAGNUM AUTOMATIC
WITH VENT RIB**

SPECIFICATIONS
Gauges: 12 and 20; standard models chambered for all 2¾" shells; Magnum models chambered for all 3" shells

Barrels: Standard models 24", 26" and 28" long; standard 12 gauge only, 30"; Magnum 12 gauge, 32"; Magnum 20 gauge, 28"

Chokes: Standard models; Cylinder, Improved Cylinder, Modified and Full; Magnum models, Full

Safeties: Lateral push-button safety; removal of two lateral pins, located through the receiver permits the trigger-safety lifter mechanism to be removed as a single unit

Stocks: Stock and forend with fully machine-cut checkered pistol grip and foregrip; magnum models equipped with factory-fitted recoil pad (optional on other 12-gauge models)

Weights: Standard 12 gauge, 6 lbs. 4 oz.; Standard 20 gauge, 5 lbs. 2 oz.; Magnum 12 gauge, 8 lbs. 4 oz., 20 gauge Magnum, 6 lbs.

Overall length: 47½" with 28" barrel

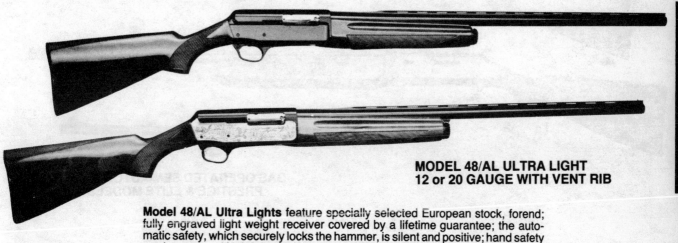

**MODEL 48/AL ULTRA LIGHT
12 or 20 GAUGE WITH VENT RIB**

Model 48/AL Ultra Lights feature specially selected European stock, forend; fully engraved light weight receiver covered by a lifetime guarantee; the automatic safety, which securely locks the hammer, is silent and positive; hand safety can be reversed for left-handed shooters; chrome-lined barrel for light weight and maximum strength; checkered pistol grip; reliable recoil action requiring no maintenance and no cleaning. Chambered for 2¾ shells.

SPECIFICATIONS
Gauge: 12, 12 ga. Magnum, 20

Barrel lengths (and chokes): 24" (slug w/rifled sights; cylinder bore; improved cylinder); 26" (cylinder bore; improved cylinder; modified); 28" (full & modified); 30" (full); 32" (full)

Mechanism: Recoil

Chamber: 2¾" (3" in 12 ga. Magnum)

Overall length: 47⅞" (w/28" barrel)

Weight: 6 lbs. 4 oz. (12 ga); 5 lbs. 2 oz. (20 ga)

Capacity: 5 shots

Safety: Lateral push button safety

Stock: Stock and forearm have machine cut diamond checkering (Magnum models equipped w/recoil pads)

Price: $499.95

FRANCHI AUTOLOADING SHOTGUNS

MODEL 48 ULTRA-LIGHT AUTOLOADERS

MODEL	DESCRIPTION									PRICE
AUTOLOADING SHOTGUNS										
Standard	12 Ga. or 20 Ga.									$449.95
Hunter	12 Ga. or 20 Ga.									499.95
Magnum	12 Ga., 3 in.									499.95
Spas-12	12 Ga. Weapon System									649.95
OVER-AND-UNDER MODELS										
Alcione 28	12 Ga. (28-inch M/F)									$749.95
Alcione 26	12 Ga. (26-inch I.C./M)									749.95

BARREL LENGTH AND CHOKE SELECTION		24" Slug. R/S	24" Cyl. V/R	24" IC V/R	26" Cyl. V/R	26" Skeet V/R	24" IC V/R	26" Mod. V/R	28" Mod. V/R	28" Full V/R	30" Full V/R	32" Full V/R
	12 Gauge	X	X	X	X	X	X	X	X	X	X	X
	20 Gauge	X	X	X	X	X	X	X	X	X	X	

R/S = Rifle sights   V/R = Vent. rib

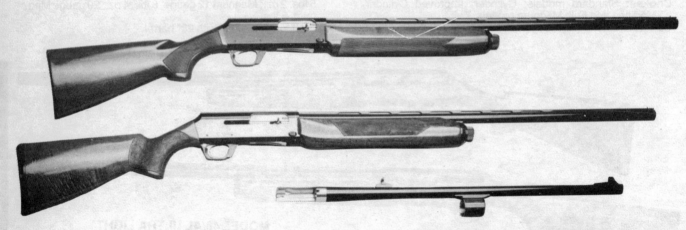

GAS OPERATED SEMIAUTOMATICS
PRESTIGE & ELITE MODELS

SPECIFICATIONS
Gauge: 12 (2¾" chamber)
Mechanism: Gas operated semiautomatic
Magazine capacity: 5
Barrel lengths (and chokes): 24" (slug barrel w/rifles sights); 26" (Modified, Improved cylinder); 28" (Full/Modified); 30" (Full)
Overall length: 50"
Weight: 7 lbs. 6 oz.
Features: Double cocking slide (dual rails); chrome plated sleeve; stainless steel piston; patented magazine discon-

nect system; gold plated trigger
Finish: Hand rubbed satin finish; grip holding checkering
Note: Elite Model features hand filed ventilated rib (7mm wide to reduce glare); red phosphorescent front sight; European walnut stock and forend; oil finish w/hand patterned checkering on forend and pistol grip stock; engraved receiver illustrates shooting scenes
Prices: $524.95 (Prestige)
$549.95 (Elite)

GAMBA SHOTGUNS

GRIFONE OVER-AND-UNDER
$935.00

SPECIFICATIONS
Gauge: 12
Barrel length: 28″ or 26³/₄″
Rib: Ventilated rib
Trigger: Double or single
Ejectors: Automatic
Mechanism: Boxlock

Locking: Lower locking bolt
Forend: Standard parrot-beak style
Weight: 7.05 lbs.
Chokes: Mod. Full and Imp. Cyl./Imp. Modified (4/2)
Engraving: Floral design and game scenes

MODEL 2100 RIOT GUN
$715.00

SPECIFICATIONS
Gauge: 12
Barrel length: 19¹/₂″
Sights: Super elevated line of sight on the frame; barrel w/o rib; brass bead on muzzle
Magazine capacity: Slide action 8-shot capacity

Receiver: Made from high tensile light alloy; bright black finish w/special treatment to prevent scratches
Stock: Black painted wood stock
Forend: Made from nylon (or wood on request)
Weight: 6.62 lbs.

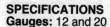

PRINCIPESSA SIDE-BY-SIDE
$1500.00

SPECIFICATIONS
Gauges: 12 and 20
Barrel length: 28″ or 26³/₄″ (20 ga.)
Chokes: Modified full or Imp. Cycl./Imp. Modified (4/2)
Rib: Plain
Trigger: Double or single trigger by request
Ejectors: Automatic
Mechanism: Boxlock

Stock: Stright English
Forend: Standard
Weight: 6.62 lbs. (12 ga.) or 6.18 lbs. (20 ga.)
Action: Made from special heat-treated chrome-nickel-molybdenum steel; case hardened finish (or color case hardened by request)

GAMBA SHOTGUNS

OXFORD 90 SIDE-BY-SIDE
$2065.00

SPECIFICATIONS
Gauge: 12
Barrel lengths: 27$\frac{1}{2}$″ or 26$\frac{3}{4}$″
Chokes: Mod. Full or Imp. Cyl./Imp. Modified (4/2)
Rib: Plain
Trigger: Double or single
Mechanism: Boxlock
Locking: Purdey system
Weight: 6.84 lbs. or 5.96 lbs.
Forend: Standard
Stock: Straight English or pistol grip

GARBI SIDELOCK SHOTGUNS

MODEL 100 SIDELOCK
$2450.00

Like this Model 100 shotgun, all Spanish-made Garbi models featured here are Holland & Holland pattern sidelock ejector guns with chopper lump (demibloc) barrels. They are built to English gun standards with regard to design, weight, balance and proportions, and all have the characteristic "feel" associated with the best London guns. All of the models offer fine 24-line hand-checkering, with outstanding quality wood-to-metal and metal-to-metal fit. The Model 100 is available in 12, 16, 20 and 28 gauge and sports Purdey-style fine scroll and rosette engraving, partly done by machine.

MODELS 101, 102 AND 103A (not shown)
$3600.00

Available in 12, 16, 20, and 28 gauge, the sidelocks are hand-crafted with hand-engraved receiver and select walnut straight grip stock.

SPECIFICATIONS
Barrels: 25″ to 30″ in 12 ga.; 25″ to 28″ in 16, 20 and 28 ga.; high-luster blued finish; smooth concave rib (optional Churchill or level, file-cut rib)
Action: Holland & Holland pattern sidelock; automatic ejec-

tors; double triggers with front trigger hinged; case-hardened
Stock/forend: Straight grip stock with checkered butt (optional pistol grip); hand-rubbed oil finish; classic (splinter) forend (optional beavertail)
Weight: 12 ga. game, 6 lbs. 8 oz. to 6 lbs. 12 oz.; 12 ga. pigeon or wildfowl, 7 lbs.–7lbs. 8 oz.; 16 ga., 6 lbs. 4 oz. to 6 lbs. 10 oz.; 20 ga., 5 lbs. 15 oz.–6 lbs. 4 oz.; 28 ga., 5 lbs. 6 oz.–5 lbs. 10 oz.

GOROSABEL SHOTGUNS

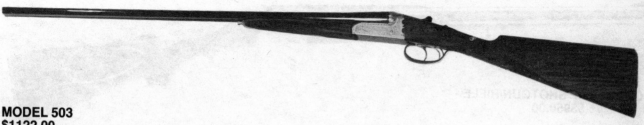

MODEL 503
$1122.00

SPECIFICATIONS
Gauge: 12, 16, 20, 28, .410
Action: Anson & Deeley style boxlock
Barrel lengths: 26", 27", 28"; all standard chokes and combinations
Stock: Select European walnut, English or pistol grip, silver or beavertail forend, hand checkering
Features: Best boxlock with scalloped frame and scroll engraving; automatic ejectors standard

SILVERPOINT
$1194.00

SPECIFICATIONS
Gauge: 12(2³/₄" or 3"); 20(2³/₄" or 3")
Action: Holland & Holland style sidelock
Barrel lengths: 26", 27", or 28"; all standard chokes and combinations
Stock: Select European walnut, English or pistol grip, silver or beavertail forend, hand checkering
Features: Holland style large scroll engraving

BLACKPOINT (not shown)
$1602.00

SPECIFICATIONS
Gauge: 16
Action: Holland & Holland style sidelock
Barrel lengths: 26", 27", 28"; all standard chokes and combinations
Stock: Select European walnut, English or pistol grip, silver or beavertail forend, hand checkering
Features: Purdey style fine scroll and rose engraving

Also available:

MODEL 501 BOXLOCK
$774.00 ($817.00 w/ejectors)

MODEL 502 BOXLOCK
$910.00 ($1040.00 w/ejectors)

MODEL 504 SIDELOCK
$816.00 ($982.00 w/ejectors)

HEYM COMBINATION GUNS

MODEL 55 BF SHOTGUN/RIFLE
$3950.00

This German-crafted shotgun/rifle combo features special corrosion-resistant chrome-molybdenum steel modified. Anson & Deeley action with standing sears. The barrels, of precision-forged Krupp Special Barrel Steel, are hand-polished and cold rust blued to a deep black satin finish. Oil-finished walnut stock comes with long pistol grip, German cheek-piece, slight hump back and handcut checkering. Leaf scroll is hand-engraved.

SPECIFICATIONS
Shotgun barrels: 12 ga., 2³/₄"; 16 ga., 2³/₄"; 20 ga., 2³/₄" and 3". **Rifle barrels:** 5.6 × 50 R Mag; 6.5 × 57 R; 7 × 57 R; 7 × 65 R; 243 Win.; 308 Win.; 30-06 and others. **Barrel length:** 25". **Length of pull:** 14¹/₂". **Overlength length:** 42". **Weight:** about 6³/₄ lbs.

SAFETY MODEL 22S $1800.00

The Model 22S offers a special break-open action in which the cocking is accomplished by manually pushing forward a cocking slide located on the tang. For ultimate safety, the gun will automatically uncock by means of a built-in rocker weight if it is dropped or jostled about.
The Model 22S comes with single-set trigger, left-side barrel selector, arabesque engraving, walnut stock and an integral dovetail base for scope mounting.

SPECIFICATIONS
Shotgun barrels: 16 ga., 2³/₄"; 20 ga., 2³/₄" and 3". **Rifle barrels:** 22 Mag., 22 Hornet; 222 Rem.; 222 Rem. Mag.; 5.6 × 50 R Mag.; 6.5 × 57 R; 7 × 57 R; 243 Win. **Barrel length:** 24". **Length of pull:** 14¹/₂". **Overall length:** 40". **Weight:** About 5¹/₂ lbs.

KRIEGHOFF SHOTGUNS

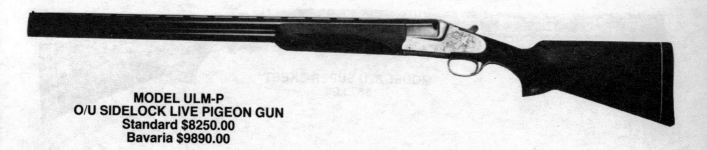

MODEL ULM-P
O/U SIDELOCK LIVE PIGEON GUN
Standard $8250.00
Bavaria $9890.00

SPECIFICATIONS
Gauge: 12
Chamber: 2³/₄"
Barrel: 28" or 30" long; tapered, ventilated rib
Choke: Top, Full; bottom, Imp. Mod.
Trigger action: Single trigger, non-selective bottom-top; hand-detachable sidelocks with coil springs; optional re-

lease trigger
Stock: Selected fancy English walnut, oil finish; length, 14³/₈"; drop at comb, 1³/₈"; optional custom-made stock
Forearm: Semi-beavertail
Engraving: Light scrollwork; optional engravings available
Weight: Approx. 8 lbs.

MODEL 82 SUPER GAME $579.00

Expertly made in Spain, the Laurona Model 82 over/unders feature automatic ejectors that combine mechanical extraction with spring ejection, twin single triggers, monobloc-constructed chrome-lined barrels treated with anti-rust black chrome finish and ventilated rib, artistically engraved, rust-resistant old-silver receiver, and automatic safety. **Gauge:** 12.

Barrel length: 28". **Chamber:** 2³/₄". **Chokes:** Mod./Full or Imp. Cyl./Imp. Mod. **Stock/forend:** Checkered tulip forend and pistol grip stock of walnut with plastic recoil pad. **Stock dimensions:** Length of pull, 14³/₈"; drop at comb, 1³/₈"; drop at heel, 2¹/₂". **Weight:** Approx. 7 lbs.

LAURONA OVER/UNDER SHOTGUNS

MODEL 82U SUPER SKEET
$673.00

MODEL 82 SUPER TRAP $638.00
(shown with optional Supreme engraving)

MODEL 82 TRAP AND PIGEON OVER/UNDERS

The Model 82 Trap and Pigeon over/unders offer the same fine features as the Game guns, except for non-selective single trigger, wider (8mm–13mm) ventilated rib, 28" or 29" barrels, automatic or non-automatic safety. **Stock:** On the 82 Trap Combination—pistol grip type with rubber recoil pad; 82 Trap Competition features walnut first-grade oil-finished Monte Carlo stock with special trap rubber recoil pad, imitation leather (optional pistol grip); 82 Super Trap and Pigeon guns boast special grade, oil-finished Monte Carlo stock with trap competition Pachmayr black rubber recoil pad, imitation leather (optional pistol grip). **Chokes:** Imp. Mod./Full or Mod./Full (Trap); Imp. Cyl./Imp. Mod. or Mod./Full (Pigeon). **Weight:** Approx. 7 1/4–8 lbs.

Other Model 82 Trap and Pigeon versions available:

Model 82 Trap Combination	$566.00
Model 82 Trap Competition	625.00
Model 82 Pigeon Competition	636.00
Model 82 Super Pigeon	638.00

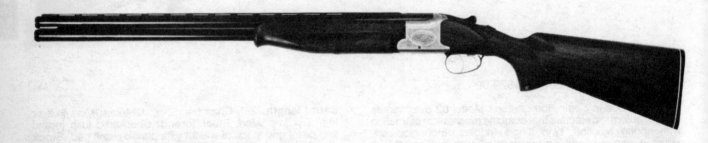

MODEL 83M MULTI-CHOKE $529.00

With chrome lining and black chrome outer finish on both the barrels and the interchangeable chokes, this Laurona Model 83 over/under offers hunters rust-resistant durability and versatility. **Gauge:** 12 or 20. **Chokes:** Choice of Full, Imp. Mod., Mod., Imp. Cyl.; two chokes supplied with purchase. **Barrel length:** 28" (12 ga.); 26" (20 ga.); with wide ventilated rib.

Chambers: 2 3/4" or 3". **Stock:** Full pistol grip walnut stock with tulip forend, both handsomely checkered. **Stock dimensions:** Length of pull, 14 3/8"; drop at comb, 1 3/8"; drop at heel, 2 1/2". **Weight:** 6 lbs. 10 oz. (20 ga.); 7 lbs. (12 ga.); **Other features:** Twin single triggers, automatic selective ejectors, beautifully engraved old-silver receiver.

LAURONA OVER/UNDER SHOTGUNS

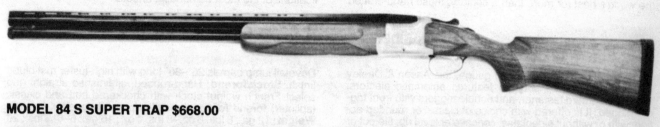

MODEL 84 S SUPER TRAP $668.00

Available in 12 gauge, the Model 84 S Super Trap features 29-inch chrome-lined and black-chrome finished barrels of monobloc construction with wide ventilated rib, single selective trigger and automatic selective ejectors. **Chokes:** Imp. Mod./ Full or Mod./Full. **Chambers:** 2³/₄″. **Stock/forend:** Walnut with full pistol grip and beavertail forend, both checkered. **Stock dimensions:** Length of pull, 14³/₈″; drop at comb, 1⁷/₁₆″; drop at heel, 1⁵/₈″. **Weight:** 7 lbs. 12 oz. (approx.).

MODEL 85 SUPER'S

Like the Model 82, the Model 85 Super over/unders come in a variety of styles to meet every gunner's needs. Available in Multi-choke design, all the Model 85's sport automatic selective ejectors, single selective trigger, exquisite engraving on anti-rust old-silver receiver, full pistol grip walnut stock (length of pull, 14 ³/₈″), checkered tulip or beavertail forend, chrome-lined barrels of monobloc construction with anti-rust black chrome finish and ventilated rib.

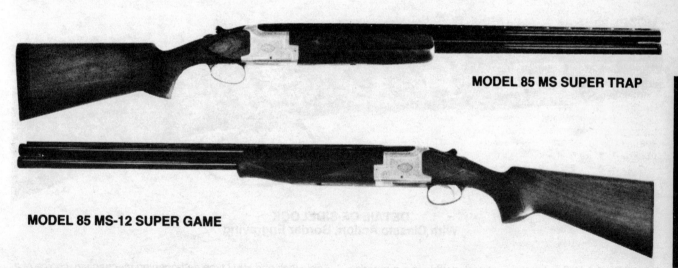

MODEL 85 MS SUPER TRAP

MODEL 85 MS-12 SUPER GAME

SPECIFICATIONS

Model	Gauge	Chamber	Barrel Length	Chokes	Drop at Comb	Drop at Heel	Weight	Price
85MS-12 Super Game	12	2³/₄″ or 3″	28″	Multi.	1³/₈″	2¹/₂″	7 lbs.	$579.00
85MS-20 Super Game	20	2³/₄″ or 3″	26″	Multi.	1³/₈″	2¹/₂″	6 lbs. 10 oz.	579.00
85MS Super Trap	12	2³/₄″	29″	Multi./F	1⁷/₁₆″	1⁵/₈″	7 lbs. 12 oz.	688.00
85MS Super Pigeon	12	2³/₄″	28″	Multi./F	1⁷/₁₆″	1⁵/₈″	7 lbs. 4 oz.	683.00
85S Super Skeet	12	2³/₄″	28″	Skeet/Skeet	1³/₈″	2¹/₂″	7 lbs. 1 oz.	673.00
85MS Spec. Sporting	12	2³/₄″	28″	Multi./F	1³/₈″	2¹/₂″	7 lbs. 4 oz.	582.00

LEBEAU-COURALLY SHOTGUNS

For generations, Lebeau-Courally has enjoyed the distinction of supplying guns to the royal houses of Europe. Rated among the world's best for more than a century, these hand-crafted shotguns are available with an extensive selection of intricate engraving patterns, and can be tailored to the custom specifications of the most demanding shooter.

BOXLOCK SIDE-BY-SIDE (not shown) $10,200.00

Available in 12, 16, 20, and 28 gauge, this Anson & Deeley boxlock side-by-side shotgun features automatic ejectors, Purdey-type third fastener, and double triggers with front trigger hinged. It is offered with choice of classic or rounded action, with or without sideplates, concave or level rib, file-cut or smooth, and choice of numerous engraving patterns. **Barrels:** Dovetail lump barrels 26"–30" long with high-luster rust blued finish. **Stock/forend:** Hand-rubbed, oil-finished straight grip select French walnut stock with checkered butt and classic (splinter) forend (optional pistol grip and beavertail forend). **Weight:** 12 ga., 6 lbs. 6 oz.–8 lbs. 4 oz.; 16 ga., 6–6½ lbs.; 20 ga., 5½ lbs.–6 lbs. 4 oz.; 28 ga., 5 lbs. 4 oz.-6 lbs.

**H&H SIDELOCK SHOTGUN
$20,600.00**

DETAIL OF SIDELOCK
With Classic Action, Border Engraving

This Holland & Holland pattern sidelock double is a gunner's dream—with automatic ejectors, chopper lump barrels of Walhreyne compressed steel, choice of classic or rounded action, concave or level rib, file-cut or smooth, double triggers with front trigger hinged (non-selective single trigger optional), coin finish or casehardened in colors, optional hand-detachable lock and H&H type self-opening mechanism, choice of a wide variety of engravings. **Barrel length:** 26"–30". **Gauges:** 12, 16, 20, and 28. **Stock/forend:** Best-quality French walnut stock with straight grip (pistol grip optional) and checkered butt; classic (splinter) forend (beavertail available). **Weight:** Same as Boxlock Side-by-Side.

MARLIN SHOTGUNS

MARLIN MODEL 55
GOOSE GUN
$194.95

High-flying ducks and geese are the Goose Gun's specialty. The Marlin Goose Gun has an extra-long 36-inch full-choked barrel and Magnum capability, making it the perfect choice for tough shots at wary waterfowl. It also features a quick-loading 2-shot clip magazine, a convenient leather carrying strap and a quality ventilated recoil pad.

SPECIFICATIONS
Gauge: 12; 2¾" Magnum, 3" Magnum or 2¾" regular shells
Choke: Full

Capacity: 2-shot clip magazine
Action: Bolt action; positive thumb safety; red cocking indicator
Stock: Walnut-finish hardwood with pistol grip and ventilated recoil pad; swivels and leather carrying strap; tough Mar-Shield® finish
Barrel length: 36"
Sights: Bead front sight and U-groove rear sight
Overall length: 56¾"
Weight: About 8 lbs.

MERKEL OVER & UNDER SHOTGUNS

Merkel over-and-unders were the first hunting guns with barrels arranged one above the other, and they have since proved to be able competitors of the side-by-side gun. Merkel superiority lies in the following details:
• The high, narrow forend protects the shooter's hand from the barrel in hot or cold climates.
• The forend is narrow and therefore lies snugly in the hand to permit easy and positive swinging.

• The slim barrel line provides an unobstructed field of view and thus permits rapid aiming and shooting.
• The over-and-under barrel arrangement reduces recoil error; the recoil merely pushes the muzzle up vertically.

For details and prices on available Merkel options, contact Armes de Chasse (see Directory of Manufacturers & Suppliers).

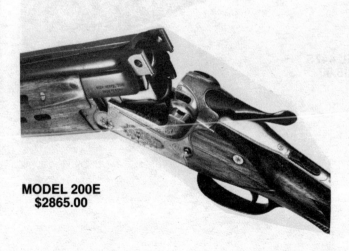

MODEL 200E
$2865.00

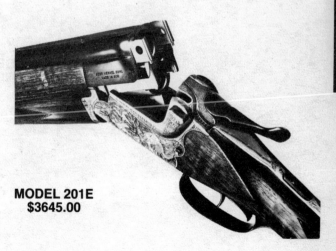

MODEL 201E
$3645.00

MERKEL SIDE-BY-SIDE SHOTGUNS

MODEL 47S
$3080.00

MODEL 247S
$3790.00

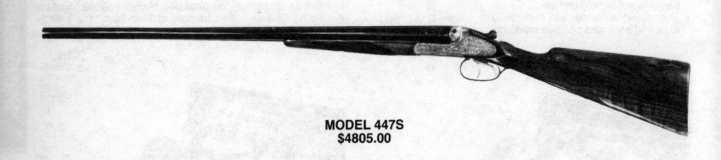

MODEL 447S
$4805.00

MERKEL SHOTGUNS

MODEL 203E
$7335.00

MODEL 303E
$11,600.00

MODEL 47E
$1225.00

MODEL 122E
$2360.00

MOSSBERG AUTOLOADING SHOTGUNS

The Model 712 Autoloader is designed to shoot any 12 gauge hunting load—from the lightest 2³/₄-inch field one-ounce load to the heaviest 3-inch magnums. *Features:* 5-shot capacity (4 with 3-inch magnums), unique gas regulating system, solid "steel-to-steel" lockup of bolt and barrel extension, high- strength lightweight alloy receiver, ambidextrous safety at top rear of receiver, dual shell latches, self-adjusting action bars, walnut-finished stock with checkering and recoil pad, internal ACCU-CHOKE II choke tubes that sit flush with the muzzle.

MODEL 712 AUTOLOADER—PLAIN BARREL
$333.95 SLUGSTER
$314.95 FIXED CHOKE (not shown)

MODEL 712—PLAIN BARREL
Slugster: 12 gauge with 24″ barrel, Cylinder choke, rifle sights.
Fixed Choke Model: 12 gauge with 28″ barrel, Mod. choke.

MODEL 712—VENT RIB
$352.95 ACCU-CHOKE II
$332.95 FIXED CHOKE (not shown)

MODEL 712—VENT RIB BARREL
ACCU-CHOKE II: 12 gauge with 24″ or 28″ barrel; Junior model also available with short 13″ buttstock.
Fixed Choke Model: 12 gauge with 28″ barrel, Mod. choke; or 30″ barrel, Full choke.

MODEL 712 12 GAUGE COMBO PACKS

Combo. X410: Includes 28″ vent rib barrel, Mod. choke, bead sight plus 24″ Slugster barrel with rifle sight. **$402.95.**
Combo. X450: 28″ vent rib ACCU-CHOKE II barrel with bead sight plus 24″ Slugster barrel with rifle sight. **$421.95.**

MOSSBERG PUMP SHOTGUNS

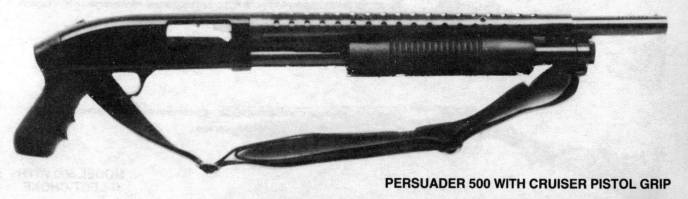

PERSUADER 500 WITH CRUISER PISTOL GRIP

12 GAUGE 8-SHOT PERSUADER (20″ Barrel)

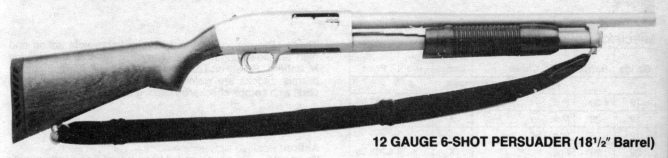

12 GAUGE 6-SHOT PERSUADER (18¹/₂″ Barrel)

6-SHOT CYLINDER BORE, BLUED

12 and 20 gauge, wood stock	$251.95
w/Rifle sight (12 ga. only)	270.95
Speed Feed stock (12 ga. only)	283.95
w/Rifle sight	303.95
Cruiser in 12, 20 & .410 ga.	251.95
Mini-Combos, 12 and 20 ga.	258.95
with Accu-II	278.95
Maxi-Combo, 12 and 20 ga.	281.95
with Speed Feed	313.95

Note: Some models available in Parkerized or Camo finish (12 ga., Cyl. Bore only)

8-SHOT CYLINDER BORE, BLUED, 20″ BARREL

Wood Stock, bead sight	$267.95
with rifle sight	287.95
Speed Feed, bead sight	299.95
Blued Mini-Combos	274.95
Speed Feed	307.95

Note: Some models available in Parkerized or Camo Finish

MODEL 500 SLIDE-ACTION LAW ENFORCEMENT "PERSUADER"

These slide-action shotguns are available in 6- or 8-shot versions, chambered for both 2³/₄-inch and 3-inch shells.

Six-shot models have 18¹/₂-inch barrel, overall length of 37³/₄ inches and a weight of 6¹/₄ pounds with full buttstock. (Also available in 20 gauge and .410 bore.)

Eight-shot models have 20-inch barrels, overall length of 39³/₄ inches and weigh 6³/₄ pounds with full buttstock.

Both 6- and 8-shot models are available in choice of blued, parkerized or nickel metal finish; satin or oiled walnut wood finish. Lightweight aluminum alloy receiver with steel locking bolt into barrel extension affords solid "steel-to-steel" lockup. Heavy-duty rubber recoil pads come on all full stock models; sling swivels on all models. Optional pistol grip and other accessories.

MOSSBERG PUMP SHOTGUNS

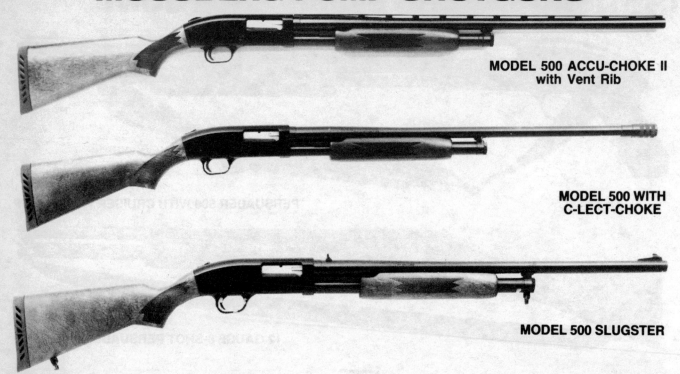

MODEL 500 ACCU-CHOKE II with Vent Rib

MODEL 500 WITH C-LECT-CHOKE

MODEL 500 SLUGSTER

SPECIFICATIONS

Gauge	Barrel	Choke	Plain Barrel	Vent. Rib	Price
FIXED CHOKE MODELS					
12	30″	Full	X	X	$247.95
12	28″	Modified	X	X	(plain)
12	26″	Imp. Cyl.		X	
20	28″	Full	X	X	$269.95
20	28″	Modified	X	X	(vent rib)
.410	26″	Full	X	X	
12	38″	Full	X		264.95
SLUGSTER MODELS with rifle sights—Receiver Drilled & Tapped					
12	18½″	Cylinder	X		
12	24″	Cylinder	X		265.95
20	24″	Cylinder	X		
C-LECT-CHOKE MODELS					
12	28″	C-LECT	X	X	$257.95
20	28″	C-LECT		X	279.95
ACCU-CHOKE MODELS					
12	28″	ACCU II	X	X	$267.95
12	20″	ACCU II		X	
12	24″	ACCU II		X	(plain)
20	24″	ACCU II	X		$288.95
20	24″	ACCU II		X	(vent rib)
20	24″	ACCU II Jr. Model		X	

These slide-action 500 models offer lightweight action and high tensile-strength alloys. They also feature the famous Mossberg "Safety on Top" and a full range of interchangeable barrels. Stocks are walnut-finished birch with rubber recoil pads with combs checkered pistol grip and forend.

MODEL 500 SPECIFICATIONS

Action: Positive slide-action
Barrel: 12 or 20 gauge and .410 bore with free-floating vent. rib; ACCU-CHOKE II interchangeable choke tubes; chambered for 2¾″ standard and Magnum and 3″ Magnum shells
Receiver: Aluminum alloy, deep blue/black finish; ordnance steel bolt locks in barrel extension for solid "steel-to-steel" lockup
Capacity: 6-shot (one less when using 3″ Magnum shells); plug for 3-shot capacity included
Safety: Top tang, thumb-operated; disconnecting trigger
Stock/forend: Walnut-finished American hardwood with checkering; rubber recoil pad
Standard stock dimensions: 14″ length of pull; 2½″ drop at heel; 1½″ drop at comb
Sights: Metal bead front
Overall length: 48″ with 28″ barrel
Weight: 12 ga. 7½ lbs.; 20 ga. 6¾ lbs.; .410 bore 6½ lbs.; Slugster 6¾ lbs.; Magnums 8½ lbs. (weight varies slightly due to wood density)

MOSSBERG PUMP SHOTGUNS

MODEL 500 CAMO/SPEEDFEED

MODEL 500 CAMO/SPEEDFEED

Same general specifications as standard Model 500, except all camo models have Speedfeed stock and synthetic forend, sling swivels, camo web strap, receiver drilled and tapped for scope mounting. **Price:** 30″ vent rib barrel with Full choke **$316.95;** 24″ vent rib ACCU II Turkey **$336.95;** 24″ Slugster **$313.95.**

MODEL 500 REGAL SERIES

MODEL 500 REGAL SERIES

"Custom" version of standard Model 500. Satin-finished select walnut sports 18-line/inch cut checkering on pistol grip and underside of forend, contoured rubber recoil pad, gold trigger and inlaid medallion on receiver.

Available in following models:
12 and 20 gauge, 28″ barrel, Modified: **$285.95**
12 and 20 gauge, 24″ and 28″ Accu-II: **$304.95**
12 and 20 gauge, 24″ and 28″, Acfcu-Mod (1 Modified tube and wrench only): **$292.95**
Combos (1 extra barrel): $324.95 (344.95 w/Accu-II)
Combos w/Accu-Mod only: **$329.95**

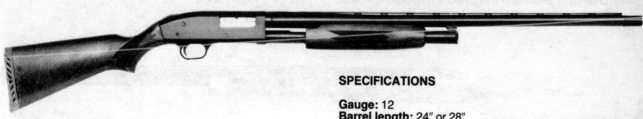

MODEL 500 ACCU-STEEL
$283.95

SPECIFICATIONS

Gauge: 12
Barrel length: 24″ or 28″
Sight: Bead
Features: Accu-Steel choke tube for BB's #1 and #2 steel shot; checkered walnut finished wood stock w/ventilated recoil pad

Also available:

Model 500 Accu-Steel w/Synthetic field/Camo **$298.95**
Model 500 Accu-Steel w/Speed Feed/Camo **332.95**

NAVY ARMS SHOTGUNS

MODEL 96
$634.00

Five fully interchangeable chokes make the Model 96 Over/ Under a versatile shotgun, useful for all types of upland and waterfowl hunting as well as target shooting. Italian made, this 12-gauge gun features 28-inch chrome-lined barrels with 3- inch chambers, ejectors, double ventilated rib construction, an engraved hard chrome reciver, European walnut stock with checkered wrist and forend and gold-plated single trigger. Chokes: Full; Imp. Cyl./ Mod.; Mod.; Imp. Cyl./Skeet; Cyl.

| MODEL 83 W/EXTRACTORS 12 and 20 GAUGE $398.00 | MODEL 93 W/EXTRACTORS 12 and 20 GAUGE $475.00 |

The Model 83/93 Bird Hunter is a quality field grade over/under available in 12 or 20 gauge. Manufactured in Italy, it features 28-inch chrome-lined barrels with 3-inch chambers; double vent rib construction, European walnut stock, hand-checkered wrist and forend, chrome engraved receiver and gold-plated triggers. Both gauges available in Mod./Full or Imp. Cyl./ Mod. chokes.

MODEL 100/150 FIELD HUNTER
MODEL 100 W/EXTRACTORS $475.00
MODEL 150 W/EJECTORS $574.00

Manufactured in Italy, this side-by-side field gun is available in 12 or 20 gauge. It features 28-inch chrome-lined barrels with 3-inch chambers, European walnut stock, checkering at wrist and forend, engraved and chromed receiver, gold-plated triggers. Choked Imp. Cyl./Mod. or Mod./Full. **Weight:** 6¹/₂ lbs. (20 ga.); 7 lbs. (12 ga.).

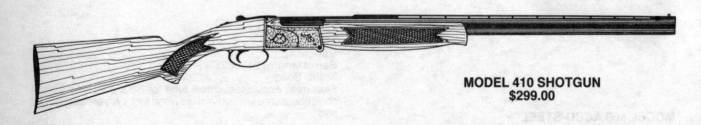

MODEL 410 SHOTGUN
$299.00

The Model 410 Italian-made over/under shotgun features European walnut stock checkered at the wrist and forend, 26-inch chrome-lined barrels with 3-inch chambers, ventilated rib barrel and an engraved, hard chrome receiver. **Chokes:** Full/Full or Skeet/Skeet. **Weight:** 6¹/₄ lbs.

OLIN/WINCHESTER SHOTGUNS

The **OLIN/WINCHESTER** Classic Doubles listed below are elegant, expertly crafted and feature Winchoke® versatility with the original Winchoke® interchangeable choke tube system. All 12- and 20-gauge field guns have 3-inch chambers; 28-gauge models have 2¾″. All Target guns (Trap and Skeet) have 2¾″ chambers, except the .410 bore which has 2½″. Stocks are either semi-pistol or pistol grip style. All Field and Competition models are furnished with handsome trunk-style gun case.

COMPETITION MODELS

MODEL	GAUGE	CHOKE	BARREL LENGTH	NOMINAL WEIGHT (lbs.)	PRICE
TRAP GUNS					
Diamond Grade					
Over and Under					
Trap—Standard	12	WT4	30″	8¾	1860.00
Trap—Monte Carlo	12	WT4	30″	8¾	1860.00
Trap—Standard	12	WT4	32″	9	1860.00
Trap—Monte Carlo	12	WT4	32″	9	1860.00
Diamond Grade					
Single Barrel					
Trap—Standard	12	WT4	34″	8¾	2145.00
Trap—Monte Carlo	12	WT4	34″	8¾	2145.00
Diamond Grade					
Combination Sets					
Trap—O/U Standard	12	WT4	30″	9	2940.00
Trap—SB Standard	12	WT4	34″	8¾	2940.00
Trap—O/U Monte Carlo	12	WT4	30″	9	2940.00
Trap—SB Monte Carlo	12	WT4	34″	8¾	2940.00
Trap—O/U Standard	12	WT4	32″	9¾	2940.00
Trap—SB Standard	12	WT4	34″	8¾″	2940.00
Trap—O/U Monte Carlo	12	WT4	32″	9	2940.00
Trap—SB Monte Carlo	12	WT4	34″	8¾	2940.00
Trap—O/U Standard	12	WT4	30″	9	2940.00
Trap—SB Standard	12	WT4	32″	8½	2940.00
Trap—O/U Monte Carlo	12	WT4	30″	9	2940.00
Trap—SB Monte Carlo	12	WT4	32″	8½	2940.00
Presentation Grade O/U Trap	12	IM/F	30″	8½	3945.00
SKEET GUNS					
Diamond Grade					
Over and Under					
Skeet Gun	12	S/S	27½″	7¼	1915.00
Skeet Gun	20	S/S	27½″	6½	1915.00
Skeet Gun	28	S/S	27½″	6½	1915.00
Skeet Gun	410	S/S	27½″	6⅔	1915.00
4-Barrel Skeet Set	12/20/ 28/.410	S/S	27½″	7½	5095.00
Presentation Grade Skeet	12	S/S	27″	7¾	3945.00

CHOKES
IC = Improved Cylinder
M = Modified
IM = Improved Modified
F = Full
S = Skeet
W4 = Winchokes 1 each.
    Full, Modified, Improved Cylinder and Skeet plus wrench.
W6 = Winchokes 1 each.

OLIN/WINCHESTER SHOTGUNS

DIAMOND GRADE "OVER SINGLE" TRAP

DIAMOND GRADE OVER/UNDER TRAP

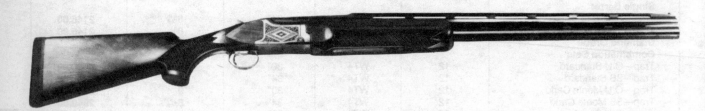

DIAMOND GRADE FOUR-BARREL SET

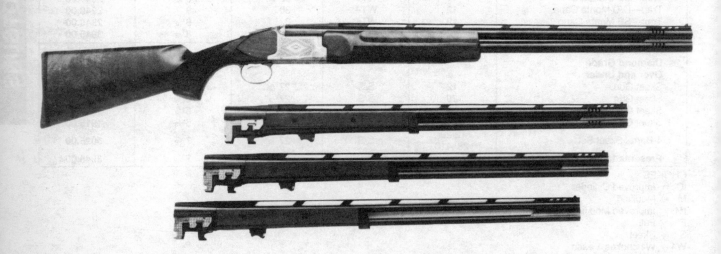

OLIN/WINCHESTER SHOTGUNS

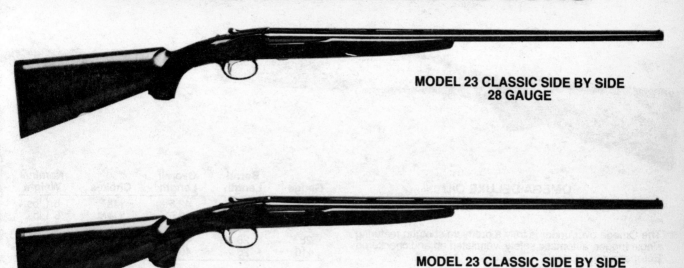

**MODEL 23 CLASSIC SIDE BY SIDE
28 GAUGE**

**MODEL 23 CLASSIC SIDE BY SIDE
410 GAUGE**

SPECIFICATIONS FIELD MODELS

MODEL	SYMBOL	GAUGE	CHOKE	BARREL LENGTH	OVERALL LENGTH	LENGTH OF PULL	DROP AT COMB	DROP AT HEEL	DROP AT MC	NOMINAL WEIGHT (lbs.)	PRICE
OVER AND UNDER											
Model 101											
Field Special	GEX27FWI	12	W3F	27″	43⁷/₈″	14¹/₄″	1¹/₂″	2¹/₄″	—	7	$1075.00
Lightweight-Winchoke	GLW27FW	12	W6	27″	43³/₄″	14¹/₈″	1¹/₂″	2¹/₄″	—	7	1400.00
Lightweight-Winchoke	GLW57FW	20	W4	27″	43³/₄″	14¹/₈″	1¹/₂″	2¹/₄″	—	6¹/₂	1400.00
Waterfowl-Winchoke	G101WF	12	WT4	30″	46⁷/₈″	14¹/₄″	1¹/₂″	2¹/₄″	—	7³/₄	1570.00
Pigeon Grade											
Lightweight-Winchoke	GPL27FWI	12	W6	27″	43³/₄″	14¹/₈″	1¹/₂″	2¹/₄″	—	7	1915.00
Lightweight-Winchoke	GPL57FWI	20	W4	27″	43³/₄″	14¹/₈″	1¹/₂″	2¹/₄″	—	6¹/₂	1915.00
Featherweight	GPF25E	12	IC/IM	25¹/₂″	42¹/₄″	14¹/₈″	1¹/₂″	2¹/₄″	—	6³/₄	1580.00
Featherweight	GPF55E	20	IC/M	25¹/₂″	42¹/₄″	14¹/₈″	1¹/₂″	2¹/₄″	—	6¹/₄	1580.00
Special Editions (Limited Availability)											
Super Pigeon	GPL27SPI	12	W6	27″	43³/₄″	14¹/₈″	1¹/₂″	2¹/₄″	—	7¹/₂	4590.00
Winchester Quail Special*	GPF25EWINQ†	12	W6	25¹/₂″	42¹/₄″	14¹/₈″	1¹/₂″	2¹/₄″	—	6³/₄	2080.00

ADDITIONAL SPECIFICATIONS

CHAMBERS
All field guns have 3″ chambers to allow use of both 2³/₄″ and 3″ shotshells. 28 gauge chambered 2³/₄″.

CHOKE SPECIFICATIONS
IC = Improved Cylinder
M = Modified
IM = Improved Modified
F = Full
W4 = Winchokes 1 each.
  Full, Modified, Improved Cylinder and Skeet plus wrench.
W6 = Winchokes 1 each.
  Full, Extra Full, Modified, Improved Modified, Improved Cylinder and Skeet plus wrench.

GUN CASES
All Olin/Winchester guns are supplied with handsome trunk style gun cases.

NOTES
All shotguns equipped with front and mid white sight beads.
†Straight English stock.
All other field stocks are either semi-pistol or pistol grip style.
—Rifle Caliber
*Also available in 28 gauge and .410 gauge **($2200.00)**

OMEGA SHOTGUNS

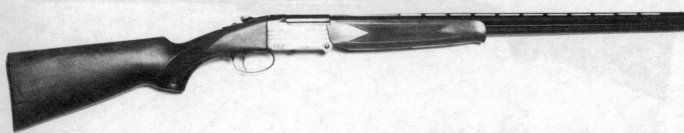

OMEGA DELUXE O/U
$315.00

The Omega over/under is truly a premium shotgun featuring single trigger, automatic safety, ventilated rib and checkered European walnut stock.

Gauge	Barrel Length	Overall Length	Chokes	Nominal Weight
20	28	42.5"	M&F	6.1 lbs.
20	26	40.5"	IC&M	6.1 lbs.
28	26	40.5"	IC&M	6.1 lbs.
28	26	40.5"	M&F	6.1 lbs.
.410	26	40.5"	F&F	5.5 lbs.

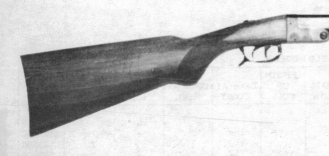

OMEGA DELUXE SIDE-BY-SIDE
$225.00
STANDARD
$202.00-240.00

Omega side-by-side shotguns are available in two models, both with double triggers and non-automatic safety. The Standard model has a checkered beechwood stock and semi-pistol grip. The Deluxe model has a checkered European walnut stock and low barrel rib. Both models come in .410 gauge with 26-inch barrels and Full/Full chokes. **Overall length:** 40½". **Weight:** 5½ lbs.

SINGLE BARREL SHOTGUNS
$89.00

The Omega single barrel shotguns feature a rebounding hammer system for safe and reliable shooting as well as an automatic ejector and Indonesian walnut stock. The top lever breaks to either side to accommodate a right or left hand shooter.

Also available: **Omega Deluxe Single Barrel** model with checkered walnut stock, top lever break, fully blued receiver, ventilated rib.

Gauge	Chamber (inches)	Barrel Length (inches)	Choke US/UK	Nominal Weight (lbs/oz.)
12	2¾	30/76	Full	6
12	2¾	28/70	Full	5-8
12	2¾	28/70	Modified	5-8
12	2¾	26/66	Imp. Cyl.	5-8
20	3	28/70	Full	5-8
20	3	28/70	Modified	5-8
20	3	26/66	Imp. Cyl.	5-6
410	3	26/66	Full	5

PARKER-HALE SHOTGUNS

Now available in the U.S., Parker-Hale side-by-side shotguns have long been favorites in Great Britain. Superbly crafted by the Spanish gunmaking firm of Ignacio Ugartechea, the "600" Series doubles are available in field grade boxlock models and "best" grade sidelock versions. Field grade models are offered in either extractor and ejector configurations. All models boast stocks of hand-checkered walnut finished with hand-rubbed oil, actions and parts machined from ordnance steel, standard auto safety, forged barrels, deep lustrous bluing and English scroll design engraving. **American** (A) models: Single non-selective trigger, pistol girp, beavertail forend, butt plate, raised matted rib. **English** (E) models: Double triggers, straight grip, splinter forend, checkered butt, concave rib; XXV models have Churchill-type rib. **Chokes:** Imp. Cyl./Mod.; Mod./Full. **Weight:** 12 ga., 6³/₄-7 lbs.; 20 ga. 5³/₄ lbs.-6 lbs.; 28 and .410 ga., 5¹/₄-5¹/₂ lbs. 3″ chambers on 20 and .410 ga.; 2³/₄ chambers on others.

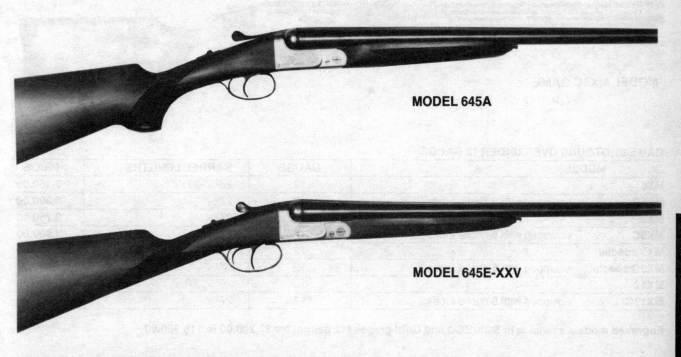

MODEL 645A

MODEL 645E-XXV

PARKER-HALE SIDE-BY-SIDE SHOTGUNS

Model	Gauges	Action	Barrel Length	Price
640E (English)	12, 16, 20	Boxlock	26″, 28″	$ 449.95
640E (English)	28, .410	Boxlock	27″	549.95
640A (American)	12, 16, 20	Boxlock	26″, 28″	599.95
645E (English)	12, 16, 20	Boxlock	26″, 28″	619.95
645E (English)	28, .410	Boxlock	27″	699.95
645A (American)	12, 16, 20	Boxlock	26″, 28″	729.95
645E-XXV (English)	12, 16, 20	Boxlock	25″	649.95
645E-XXV (English)	28, .410	Boxlock	25″	729.95
670E (English)	12, 16, 20	Sidelock	26″, 28″	2450.00
670E (English)	28, .410	Sidelock	27″	2600.00
680E-XXV (English)	12, 16, 20	Sidelock	25″	2350.00
680E-XXV (English)	28, .410	Sidelock	25″	2500.00

PERAZZI SHOTGUNS

For the past 20 years or so, Perazzi has concentrated solely on manufacturing competition shotguns for the world market. Today the name has become synonymous with excellence in competitive shooting. The heart of the Perazzi line is the classic over/under, whose barrels are soldered into a monobloc that holds the shell extractors. At the sides are the two locking lugs that link the barrels to the action, which is machined from a solid block of forged steel. Barrels come with flat, step or raised ventilated rib. The walnut forend, finely checkered, is available with schnabel, beavertail or English styling, and the walnut stock can be of standard, Monte Carlo, Skeet or English design. Double or single non-selective or selective triggers. Sideplates and receiver are masterfully engraved and transform these guns into veritable works of art.

MODEL MX3C GAME

GAME SHOTGUNS OVER/UNDER 12 GAUGE

MODEL		GAUGE	BARREL LENGTHS	PRICE
MX5		12	26³/₈"-27⁵/₈"	3,150.00
MX5C	equipped with 5 choke tubes	12	27⁵/₈"	3,300.00
MX3		12	27⁵/₈"	3,750.00
MX3C	equipped with 5 choke tubes	12	27⁵/₈"	3,900.00
MX3 special		12	27⁵/₈"	4,400.00
MX3C special	equipped with 5 choke tubes	12	27⁵/₈"	4,550.00
MX12		12	26³/₈"-27⁵/₈"	4,550.00
MX12C	equipped with 5 choke tubes	12	27⁵/₈"	4,700.00

Engraved models available in SC3, SCO and Gold grades (12 gauge) for $7,200.00 to $15,350.00

GAME SHOTGUNS OVER/UNDER 12 GAUGE

MODEL			GAUGE	BARREL LENGTHS	PRICE
MX20	SC3		20-28-410	26"	8,000.00
MX20C	SC3		20	26"	8,150.00
MX20	SCO		20-28-410	26"	13,150.00
MX20C	SCO		20	26"	13,300.00
SCO			20-28-410	26"-27⁵/₈"	15,350.00
MX20	gold		20-28-410	26"	15,200.00
MX20C	gold		20	26"	15,350.00
SCO	gold		20-28-410	26"-27⁵/₈"	17,100.00
SCO		SIDEPLATES	20-28-410	26"-27⁵/₈"	18,850.00
SCO	gold	SIDEPLATES	20-28-410	26-27⁵/₈"	21,650.00
EXTRA			20-28-410	26"-27⁵/₈"	37,150.00

PERAZZI SHOTGUNS

MODEL MX3 SKEET

AMERICAN SKEET SHOTGUNS OVER AND UNDER 4 GAUGE SETS

MODEL		GAUGE	BARREL LENGTHS	PRICE
MX3		12-20-28-410	27⅝″	8,500.00
MX3	special	12-20-28-410	27⅝″	10,200.00
MX3L		12-20-28-410	27⅝″	10,200.00
MIRAGEspecial		12-20-28-410	27⅝″	11,200.00
MX3S	SC3	12-20-28-410	27⅝″	14,900.00
MX3	SCO	12-20-28-410	27⅝″	18,250.00
MX3S	SCO	12-20-28-410	27⅝″	20,250.00
MX3	gold	12-20-28-410	27⅝″	19,900.00
MX3S	gold	12-20-28-410	27⅝″	22,300.00

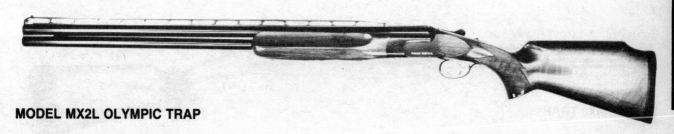

MODEL MX2L OLYMPIC TRAP

AMERICAN TRAP SHOTGUNS COMBO SETS

MODEL		GAUGE	BARREL LENGTHS	PRICE
MX3	COMBO*	12		5,000.00
MX3L	COMBO*	12		6,500.00
MX3 special	COMBO*	12	single barrel 32″-34″	5,800.00
MX8 special	COMBO* adjustable selective trigger	12	O/U BBL 29½″-31½″	6,900.00
GRAND AMERICA special COMBO* adjustable selective trigger		12		6,900.00
DB81 special	COMBO*	12		6,900.00

PERAZZI SHOTGUNS

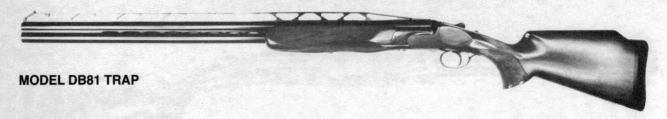

MODEL DB81 TRAP

OLYMPIC & AMERICAN TRAP, SKEET & SPORTING OVER AND UNDERS

MODEL		GAUGE	BARREL LENGTHS	PRICE
MX3		12	27⅝"-29½"-31½"	3,750.00
MX3B		12	27⅝"-29½"-31½"	3,750.00
MX3C	equipped with 5 choke tubes	12	27⅝"	3,900.00
MX3	special adjustable selective trigger	12	27⅝"-29½"-31½"	4,400.00
MX3C	special with 5 chokes-adjustable, selective trigger	12	27⅝"	4,550.00
MIRAGE*		12	27⅝"-29½"-31½"	4,550.00
MX8		12	27⅝"-29½"-31½"	4,550.00
MX8	special	12	27⅝"-29½"-31½"	4,550.00
DB81		12	29½"-31½"	4,800.00
MX1		12	27⅝"	4,800.00
MX1B		12	27⅝"	4,800.00
MX2		12	29½"	4,800.00
MX2L		12	29½"	4,800.00
MX3L		12	27⅝"-29½"-31½"	4,550.00
MX3BL		12	27⅝"-29½"-31½"	4,550.00
MX3CL	equipped with 5 choke tubes	12	27⅝"	4,700.00

Engraved models available in SC3, SCO and Gold Grades (12 Gauge) for $7200.00 to $15,200.00

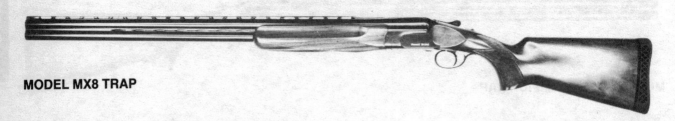

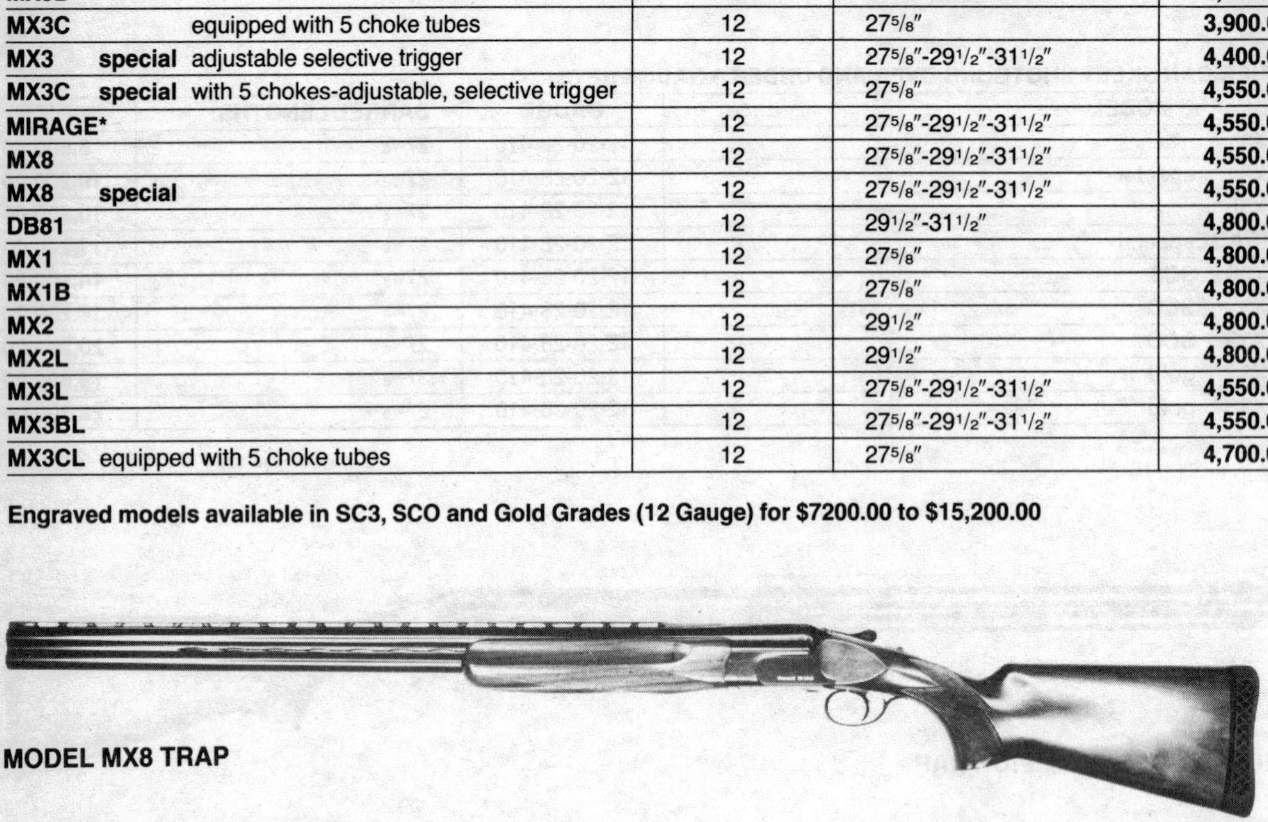

MODEL MX8 TRAP

AMERICAN TRAP SINGLE BARREL SHOTGUNS

MODEL		GAUGE	BARREL LENGTHS	PRICE
MX3	*	12	32"-34"	3,550.00
MX3 special*	adjustable selective trigger	12	32"-34"	4,150.00
TM1 special*	adjustable trigger	12	32"-34"	3,680.00
TMX special*	adjustable trigger	12	32"-34"	3,680.00
MX3L	*	12	32"-34"	4,350.00
MX8 special*	adjustable selective trigger	12	32"-34"	4,900.00
GRAND AMERICA special*	adjustable selective trigger	12	32"-34"	4,900.00

Engraved models available in SC3, SCO and Gold Grades from $6850.00 to $12,700.00

PERUGINI-VISINI SHOTGUNS

SIDE-BY-SIDE LIBERTY
$5255.00

SPECIFICATIONS
Calibers: 12, 20, 28, .410
Chamber: 2³/₄" and 3"
Stock: Straight English type; European select walnut; oil finish; fine hand checkering
Locking device: Double Purdey type lock
Action: Anson & Deeley type
Receiver: Special steel
Ejectors: Automatic ejectors w/wide ejector-cartridge contact surface
Finishing: Fine engraving; hinged front trigger; inserted firing-pin carrier sleeve
Features (optional): Extra set of barrels; choice of barrel length; special engravings; rubber English-style heel plate

SIDE-BY-SIDE CLASSIC
$10,970.00

Specifications same as "Liberty" model, except action is H&H type w/hand-detachable sidelocks internally gold-plated. Calibers are 12 and 20 only.

PIOTTI SHOTGUNS

One of Italy's top gunmakers, Piotti limits its production to a small number of hand-crafted, best-quality double-barreled shotguns whose shaping, checkering, stock, action and barrel work meets or allegedly exceeds the standards achieved in London prior to WWII. The Italian engravings are the finest ever and are becoming recognized as an art form in themselves.

All of the sidelock models exhibit the same overall design, materials and standards of workmanship; they differ only in the quality of the wood, shaping and sculpturing of the action, type of engraving and gold inlay work and other details. The Model Piuma differs from the other shotguns only in its Anson & Deeley boxlock design.

SPECIFICATIONS
Gauges: 10, 12, 16, 20, 28, .410
Chokes: As ordered
Barrels: 12 ga., 25" to 30"; other gauges, 25" to 28"; chopper lump (demi-bloc) barrels with soft-luster blued finish; level, file-cut rib or optional concave or ventilated rib
Action: Boxlock, Anson & Deeley; Sidelock, Holland & Holland pattern; both have automatic ejectors, double triggers with front trigger hinged (non-selective single trigger optional), coin finish or optional color case-hardening
Stock: Hand-rubbed oil finish (or optional satin luster) on straight grip stock with checkered butt (pistol grip optional)
Forend: Classic (splinter); optional beavertail
Weight: Ranges from 4 lbs. 15 oz. (.410 ga.) to 8 lbs. (12 ga.)

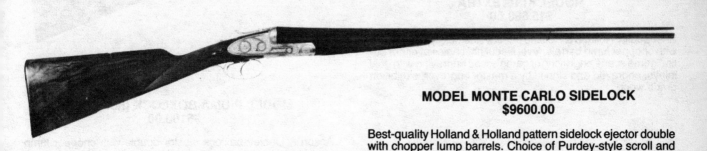

MODEL MONTE CARLO SIDELOCK
$9600.00

Best-quality Holland & Holland pattern sidelock ejector double with chopper lump barrels. Choice of Purdey-style scroll and rosette or Holland & Holland-style large scroll engraving.

PIOTTI SHOTGUNS

MODEL KING NO. 1 SIDELOCK
$11,800.00

Best-quality Holland & Holland pattern sidelock ejector double with chopper lump barrels, level file-cut rib, very fine, full coverage scroll engraving with small floral bouquets, gold crown in top lever, name in gold, and gold crest in forearm, finely figured wood.

MODEL LUNIK SIDELOCK
$12,500.00

Best-quality Holland & Holland pattern sidelock ejector double with chopper lump (demi-bloc) barrels, level, filecut rib, Renaissance-style, large scroll engraving in relief, gold crown in top lever, gold name, and gold crest in forearm, finely figured wood.

MODEL KING EXTRA
$15,600.00

Best-quality Holland & Holland pattern sidelock ejector double with chopper lump barrels, level filecut rib, choice of either bulino game scene engraving or game scene engraving with gold inlays, engraved and signed by a master engraver, exhibition grade wood.

MODEL PIUMA BOXLOCK (not shown)
$5100.00

Anson & Deeley boxlock ejector double with chopper lump (demi-bloc) barrels, and scalloped frame. Very attractive scroll and rosette engraving is standard. A number of optional engraving patterns including game scene and gold inlays are available at additional cost.

REMINGTON PUMP SHOTGUNS

MODEL 870 "TC" TRAP (12 GAUGE ONLY)
$520.00 ($533.00 with Monte Carlo Stock)

The 870 "TC" is a single-shot trap gun that features a unique gas-assisted recoil-reducing system, REM Choke and a high step-up ventilated rib. **Stock:** Redesigned stock and forend with cut-checkering and a satin finish; length of pull 14³/₈"; drop at heel 1⁷/₈"; drop at comb 1³/₈". **Weight:** 8¹/₂ lbs. **Barrel length:** 30".

MODEL 870 · 20 GAUGE LIGHTWEIGHT
$400.00

This is the pump action designed for the upland game hunter who wants enough power to stop fast flying game birds but light enough to be comfortable for all-day hunting. The 20-gauge Lightweight handles all 20-gauge 2³/₄-inch shells. **Stock:** American walnut stock and forend. **Barrel length:** 26" and 28". **Average weight:** 6 lbs.

MODEL 870 "YOUTH" GUN
20 GAUGE LIGHTWEIGHT
$400.00

The Model 870 "Youth" Gun brings Remington's pump action perfection to a whole new range of shooters. The Model 870 shotgun has been specially designed for youths and smaller-sized adults. It's a 20-gauge lightweight with a 1-inch shorter stock and 5-inch shorter barrel. Yet it is still all 870, complete with REM Choke and ventilated rib barrel. **Barrel length:** 21". **Stock Dimensions:** Length of pull 12¹/₂" (including recoil pad); drop at heel; 2¹/₂" drop at comb 1⁵/₈". **Overall length:** 40". **Average Weight:** 6 lbs. **Choke:** Mod. and Imp. Cyl.

REMINGTON PUMP SHOTGUNS

MODEL 870 WINGMASTER 12 GAUGE
$413.00 ($453.00 Left Hand)

This new restyled 870 "Wingmaster" pump has cut checkering on its satin finished American walnut stock and forend for confident handling, even in wet weather. An ivory bead "Bradley" type front sight is included. Rifle is available with 26", 28" and 30" barrel with REM Choke and handles 3" and 2¾" shells interchangeably. **Overall length:** 46½" (26" barrel), 48½" (28" barrel), 50½" (30" barrel). **Weight:** 7¼ lbs.
Also available: **Wingmaster Deer Gun** with Imp. Cyl. and rifle sights, 12 gauge only. **Barrel length:** 20" **Price: $367.00** Left hand model: **$407.00.**

MODEL 870 FIELD GRADE
$393.00

Receiver made from ordnance-quality steel. Barrel extension locks in the breech block to assure constant headspace. Cross-bolt safety switch. Vibra-horned metal finish, chrome-plate bolt. Metal bead front sight. **Gauge:** 20, 28 and .410. **Chamber:** 3". **Stock:** American walnut stock and forend have deep, sure checkering; fluted comb; wood protected by Du Pont's RK-W finish; distinctive white spacers at recoil pad and grip cap; length of pull 14"; drop at heel 2½"; drop at comb 1⅝"; 3-shot plug furnished. 28 gauge and .410 guns have butt plates, not recoil pads. **Weight** (approx): 20 gauge, 6½ lbs.; 28 gauge and .410, 6¼ lbs.

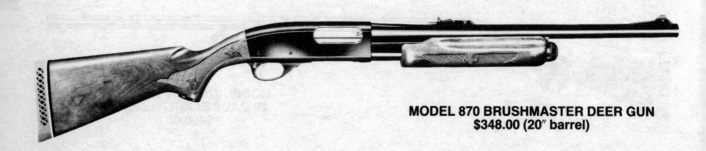

MODEL 870 BRUSHMASTER DEER GUN
$348.00 (20" barrel)

The Model 870 Brushmaster is made to handle rifled slugs and buck shot. With 20-inch barrel, 3-inch chamber, and fully adjustable rifle-type sights. Stock fitted with rubber recoil pad and white-line spacer. Also available in standard model, but with lacquer finish, no checkering, recoil pad, grip cap; special handy short forend. **Choke:** Imp. Cyl. **Weight:** 6¼ lbs.

REMINGTON PUMP SHOTGUNS

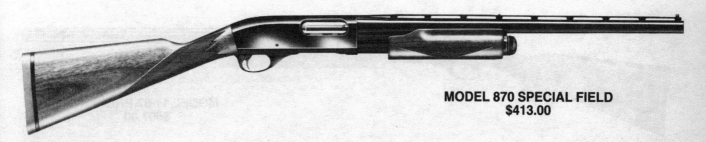

MODEL 870 SPECIAL FIELD
$413.00

The new Model 870 "Special Field" shotgun combines the traditional, straight-stock styling of years past with features never before available on a Remington pump. Its 21-inch vent rib barrel, slimmed and shortened forend, straight, cut-checkered stock offers upland hunters a quick, fast-pointing shotgun. The

"Special Field" is chambered for 3-inch shells and will also handle all 2³/₄-inch shells interchangeably. Barrels will not interchange with standard 870 barrels. **Overall length:** 41¹/₂". **Weight:** 7 lbs. (12 ga.); 6 lbs. (20 ga.).

MODEL 870 SPECIAL PURPOSE DEER GUN
$438.00

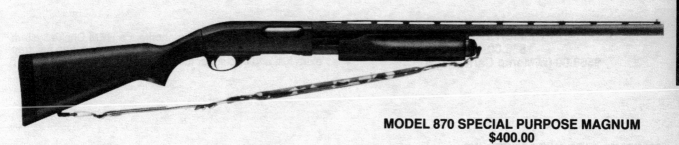

MODEL 870 SPECIAL PURPOSE MAGNUM
$400.00

Available in 12 gauge Magnum with 3-inch Mag. chamber, the Model 870 SP (Special Purpose) Magnum pump gun has been designed with waterfowlers and turkey hunters in mind. For concealment, all metal surfaces have been finished in nonglare, non-reflective Parkerized black. And all wood surfaces have been given a dull, non-reflective oil finish with a slightly rough feel for firmer grip. For ease of carrying, the SP Mag. Pump comes factory-equipped with a camo-patterned padded sling, attached at both ends by quick-detachable sling swivels. More than 2 inches wide at the shoulder, the sling is made of

durable Du Pont nylon "Cordura." **Barrel:** 26" or 30" chrome-lined barrel bore; ventilated rib. **Choke:** Full. **Stock:** Supplied with dark-colored recoil pad and black line spacers. **Overall length:** 46¹/₂" with 26" barrel; 50¹/₂" with 30" barrel. **Weight:** Approx. 7¹/₄ lbs.

Also available: **SPECIAL PURPOSE DEER GUN** (12 gauge) with rifle sights, recoil pad, Imp. Cyl. **Barrel length:** 20". **Overall length:** 40¹/₂." **Average weight:** 7 lbs. **Price: $355.00.**

REMINGTON SHOTGUNS

MODEL 11-87 PREMIER

**MODEL 11-87 PREMIER
$507.00**

The new Remington Model 11-87 "Premier" with REM Choke offers the dependability of a pump along with the easy shootability of an autoloader, the magnum power of a waterfowl gun, and the light handling of an upland gun. This new shotgun's standout attraction to the practical shooter is its ability to handle a broad variety of 12-gauge ammunition interchangeably. Switching from light, 2¾" field loads to heavy 3" magnums is simply a matter of inserting different shotgun shells. A new, patented pressure compensating gas system accomplishes this without the need for adjustments. An additional bonus to shooters is a 50 percent increase in overall performance endurance, revealed by extensive testing. Among the factors contributing to this high level of dependability and durability are:

• Extractor 30 percent thicker
• A redesigned, more durable firing pin retractor spring
• Heat treated pistol and piston seal
• Corrosion and rust resistant stainless steel magazine tube

The standard version of the 11-87 "Premier" shotgun is available with three ventilated rib barrel lengths—26,28 and 30—all with REM Choke. A left hand, mirror image version is available in 28" only. The Stock is satin finish with new cut checkering (20 lines per inch) featuring a "floating diamond" motif. Also, there's a solid brown presentation type butt pad and a grip cap with Remington's new "RA" logo. Forend has same satin finish and checkering pattern. Barrel and receiver include Bradley-type white-faced front sight and metal bead on barrel.

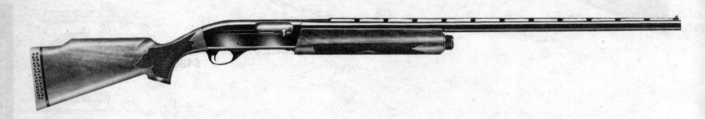

MODEL 11-87 PREMIER TARGET GRADES
$555.00
$568.00 (w/Monte Carlo Stock)

A 30" trap barrel offers trap shooters a REM Choke system with three interchangeable choke constrictions: trap full, trap extra full, and trap super full.

MODEL 11-87 PREMIER SHOTGUNS

Gauge	Barrel Length & Choke	Overall length	Avg. Wt. (lbs.)
12	30" REM Choke	50½	8⅜
	28" REM Choke	48¼	8¼
	28" REM Choke	48¼	8¼
	26" REM Choke	46	8⅛

*New for 1987. Each has a quickly accessible cross-bolt safety.

EXTRA BARRELS. 11-87 barrels are not interchangeable with the Remington Model 1100. Also, target barrels are designed for optimal performance with target loads and therefore are not pressure compensated. These guns, will, however, be pressure compensating and shoot all 12-gauge loads when equipped with an 11-87 Premier field barrel.

REMINGTON SHOTGUNS

MODEL 11-87 PREMIER SKEET 12 GAUGE
$547.00

This model features American walnut wood and distinctive cut checkering with satin finish, plus new two-piece butt plate. REM Choke system includes option of two skeet chokes—skeet and improved skeet. Trap and skeet guns are designed for 12-gauge target loads and are set to handle 2³/₄″ shells only.

MODEL 11-87 SPECIAL PURPOSE MAGNUM
$500.00

Features nonreflective wood and metal finish for all types of hunting where concealment is critical. Exposed metal surfaces of both barrel and receiver are Parkerized; bolt and carrier have non-glare blackened coloring. Barrel lengths: 26″ and 30″. Chamber: 3″. Choke: REM Choke.

MODEL 11-87 SPECIAL PURPOSE DEER GUN
$480.00

Features same finish as other SP models plus a padded, camostyle carrying sling of Cordura nylon with Q.D. sling swivels. Barrel is 21″ with rifle sights and slug choke (handles all 2³/₄″ and 3″ rifled slug and buckshot loads as well as high velocity field and magnum loads; does not function with light 2³/₄″ field loads).

REMINGTON AUTOLOADING SHOTGUNS

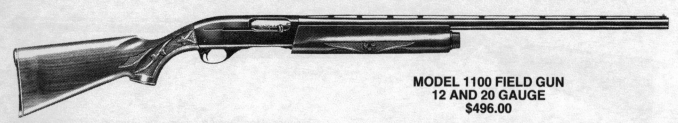

MODEL 1100 FIELD GUN
12 AND 20 GAUGE
$496.00

The Remington Model 1100 is a 5-shot gas-operated auto-loading shotgun with a gas metering system designed to reduce recoil effect. This design enables the shooter to use all 2³/₄-inch standard velocity "Express" and 2³/₄-inch Magnum loads without any gun adjustments. Barrels, within gauge and versions, are interchangeable. The 1100 is made in gauges of 12, 20, 28 and .410. All 12 and 20 gauge versions include REM Choke; interchangeable choke tubes in 26", 28" and 30" (12 gauge only) barrels. The solid-steel receiver features decorative scroll work. Stocks come with fine-line checkering in a

fleur-de-lis design combined with American walnut and a scratch-resistant finish. Features include white-diamond inlay in pistol-grip cap, white-line spacers, full beavertail forend, fluted-comb cuts, chrome-plated bolt and metal bead front sight. Made in U.S.A.

HIGH GRADE:
Model 1100 D Tournament with vent. rib barrel . . $2290.00
Model 1100 F Premier vent. rib barrel 4720.00
Model 1100 F Premier with gold inlay 7080.00

MODEL 1100 3" MAGNUM
12 & LIGHTWEIGHT-20 GAUGES
$507.00

Designed for 3-inch and 2³/₄-inch Magnum shells; accepts and functions with any 1100 standard 2³/₄-inch chambered barrel. Available in 12 gauge 30-inch or 28-inch plain or ventilated rib, and 28-inch in 20 gauge, plain or ventilated rib barrels. **Stock**

dimensions: 14" long including pad; 1¹/₂" drop at comb; furnished with recoil pad. **Weight:** About 8 lbs., 12 ga.; 6³/₄ lbs., 20 ga.

MODEL 1100 DEER GUN
12 & LIGHTWEIGHT-20 GAUGES
$463.00

Features 2-inch (12 gauge) and 20-inch (LT-20 gauge) barrels, Improved Cylinder choke. Rifle sights adjustable for windage and elevation. Recoil pad. Choked for both rifled slugs and

buck shot. **Weight:** 12 gauge, 7¹/₄ lbs.; 20 gauge, 6¹/₂ lbs. **Overall length:** 41" (12 gauge), 40" (LT-20 gauge).

MODEL 1100 SPECIAL FIELD (12 Gauge)
$507.00

The Model 1100 "Special Field" shotgun combines traditional, straight-stock styling with its 21-inch vent rib barrel and slimmed and shortened forend, which offer upland hunters a quick, fast-pointing shotgun. Non-engraved receiver; non-Magnum extra barrels are interchangeable with standard

Model 1100 barrels. **Overall length:** 41". **Stock dimensions:** Length of pull 14¹/₈"; drop at comb 1¹/₂"; drop at heel 2¹/₂". **Choke:** REM Choke system. **Weight:** 7¹/₄ lbs. (12 ga.); 6¹/₂ lbs. (20 ga.).

REMINGTON AUTOLOADING SHOTGUNS

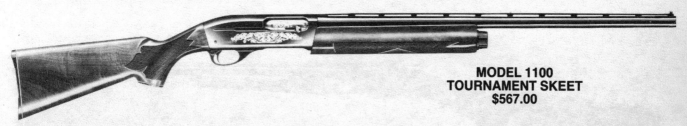

MODEL 1100
TOURNAMENT SKEET
$567.00

The world's winningest skeet gun, with high-grade positive cut-checkering on selected American walnut stock and forend. The LT-20 and 28 gauge Model 1100 Tournament Skeet guns have a higher vent rib to match the sight picture of the 12-gauge model. A true "matched set," with all the reliability, su-perb balance, and low recoil sensation that make it the choice of over 50% of the entrants in the world skeet shooting championships. Available in LT-20 and 28 gauges. **Barrel length:** 26″. **Choke:** REM Choke. **Weight:** 6¾ lbs. (20 ga.), 6½ lbs. (28 ga.).

MODEL 1100
TOURNAMENT SKEET SMALL GAUGE
$580.00

Quality and economy, American walnut stock and forend; and receiver engraving identical to that of the higher grade models distinguish this SA Grade Model 1100 auto Skeet gun. Avail-able in 28 ga., and .410 bore. **Stock dimensions:** Length of pull 14″; drop at heel 2½″; drop at comb 1½″. **Barrel length:** 25″ **Choke:** Skeet.

MODEL 1100 LT-20 YOUTH GUN • LIGHTWEIGHT
20 GAUGE ONLY
$505.00

The Model 1100 LT-20 Youth Gun autoloading shotgun features a shorter barrel (21″) and stock. **Overall length:** 39½″. **Weight:** 6½ lbs.

MODEL 1100 • 28 & .410 GAUGES
$504.00

The Remington Model 1100 Autoloading shotguns in 28 and .410 gauges are scaled-down models of the 12-gauge version. Built on their own receivers and frames, these small gauge shotguns are available in full (.410 only) and modified chokes with either plain or ventilated rib barrels.

SPECIFICATIONS
Type: Gas-operated. **Capacity:** 5-shot capacity with 28 ga. shells; 4-shot capacity with 3″ .410 ga. shells; 3-shot plug fur-nished. **Barrel:** 25″ barrel of special Remington ordnance steel; extra barrels interchangeable within gauge. **Chamber:** 3″ in .410, 2¾″ in 28 ga. **Safety:** Convenient cross-bolt type. **Receiver:** Made from solid steel, top matted, scroll work on bolt and both sides of receiver. **Stock dimensions:** Walnut; 14″ long; 2½″ drop at heel; 1½″ drop at comb. **Average weight:** 6½ lbs. (28 ga.) 7 lbs. (.410).

ROSSI SHOTGUNS

THE OVERLAND

OVERLAND DOUBLE. Available in a .410 bore and 12 or 20 gauge for both standard 2¾-inch shells or 3-inch Magnum. The 12 and 20 gauges are offered in the Coach Gun version with abbreviated 20-inch barrels with Improved and Modified chokes. All models feature a raised rib with matted sight surface, hardwood stocks, rounded semi-pistol grips, blued hammers, triggers and locking lever.

Gauge	Barrel Length	Choke	Price
12	20″	IC&M	**$295.00**
12	28″	M&F	295.00
20	20″, 26″	IC&M	295.00
.410 bore	26″	F&F	**300.00**

THE SQUIRE

SQUIRE DOUBLE. Available in .410 bore or 12 or 20 gauge, the Squire has 3-inch chambers to handle the full range of shotgun loads. Features double triggers, raised matted rib, beavertail forend and pistol grip. Twin underlugs mesh with synchronized sliding bolts for double-safe solid lockup.

Gauge	Barrel Length	Choke	Price
12	20″	IC&M	**$315.00**
12	28″	M&F	315.00
20	26″	IC&M	315.00
.410 bore	26″	F&F	**320.00**

ROTTWEIL SHOTGUNS

ROTTWEIL INTERNATIONAL TRAP
$2295.00

SPECIFICATIONS
Gauge: 12
Action: Boxlock
Barrel: 30″ Imp. Mod. & Full
Weight: 8 lbs.
Overall length: 48½″

Stock: European walnut, hand-checkered
Sights: Metal bead front
Features: Inertia-type trigger, interchangeable for any system; frame and lock milled from solid-steel block; retracting firing pins are spring mounted; all coil springs; selective single trigger; action engraved; extra barrels available

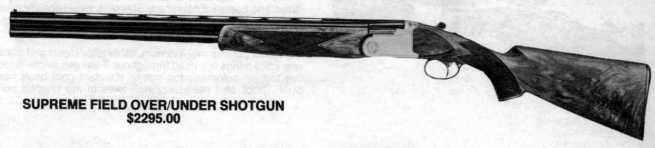

SUPREME FIELD OVER/UNDER SHOTGUN
$2295.00

SPECIFICATIONS
Gauge: 12 ga.
Action: Boxlock
Barrel: 28″ (Mod. & Full, Imp. Cyl. & Imp. Mod., Live Pigeon Mod. & Full), vent rib.
Weight: 7¼ lbs.

Overall length: 47″
Stock: European walnut, hand-checkered and rubbed
Sight: Metal bead front
Features: Removable single trigger assembly with button selector; retracting spring mounted firing pins; engraved action; extra barrels available

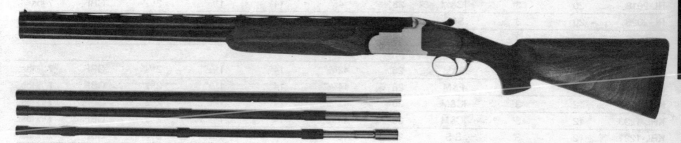

ROTTWEIL AMERICAN SKEET
$2395.00

SPECIFICATIONS
Gauge: 12 ga.
Action: Boxlock
Barrel: 27″ Skeet and Skeet choke, vent rib
Weight: 7½ lbs.
Overall length: 44½″

Stock: Selected European walnut, hand-checkered, modified forend
Sights: Plastic front housed in metallic sleeve with additional center bead
Features: Interchangeable inertia-type trigger group; receiver milled from solid block of special gun steel; retracting firing pins are spring mounted; all coil springs; first shotgun specially designed for tube sets

RUGER SHOTGUNS

RUGER RED LABEL OVER/UNDER 20 GAUGE
$798.00

WITH STAINLESS STEEL RECEIVER 12 GAUGE
$798.00

American walnut with hand-cut checkering. Pistol grip cap and rubber recoil pad are standard and all wood surfaces are polished and beautifully finished. Stainless steel receiver available on 12 gauge version; 20 gauge is satin polished and blued.

Hardened chrome molybdenum, other alloy steels and music wire coil springs are used throughout. Features single-selective trigger, automatic top safety, standard gold bead front sight. Stock and semi-beavertail forearm are shaped from

SPECIFICATIONS
RUGER OVER & UNDER SHOTGUN SPECIFICATIONS

Catalog Number	Gauge	Chamber	Choke	Barrel Length	Overall Length	Length of Pull	Drop at Comb	Drop at Heel	Sights	Weight
RL 2008	20	3″	F&M	28″	45″	14″	1½″	2½″	GBF	7 lbs.
RL-2016	20	3″	IC&M	26″	43″	14″	1½″	2½″	GBF	7 lbs.
RL-2018	20	3″	IC&M	28″	45″	14″	1½″	2½″	GBF	7 lbs.
RL-2026	20	3″	S&S	26″	43″	14″	1½″	2½″	GBF	7 lbs.
RL-2028	20	3″	S&S	28″	45″	14″	1½″	2½″	GBF	7 lbs.
Stainless Steel										
KRL-1232	12	3″	F&M	26″	42⅞″	14″	1½″	2½″	GBF	7½ lbs.
KRL-1235	12	3″	F&M	28″	44⅞″	14″	1½″	2½″	GBF	7½ lbs.
KRL-1230	12	3″	IC&M	26″	42⅞″	14″	1½″	2½″	GBF	7½ lbs.
KRL-1233	12	3″	IC&M	28″	44⅞″	14″	1½″	2½″	GBF	7½ lbs.
KRL-1231	12	3″	S/S	26″	42⅞″	14″	1½″	2½″	GBF	7½ lbs.
KRL-1234	12	3″	S/S	28″	44⅞″	14″	1½″	2½″	GBF	7½ lbs.

F-Full, M-Modified, IC-Improved Cylinder, S-Skeet, GBF-Gold Bead Front Sight

SAVAGE RIFLE/SHOTGUNS

SAVAGE MODEL 24-V COMBINATION RIFLE/SHOTGUN

Available in 222/20; 223/20; 30-30/20. Match a 20-gauge shotgun with any of five popular centerfire calibers. Frame is color case hardened and barrel is a deep, lustrous blue and tapped, ready for scope mounting. Two-way top opening lever.
Price. **$309.00**

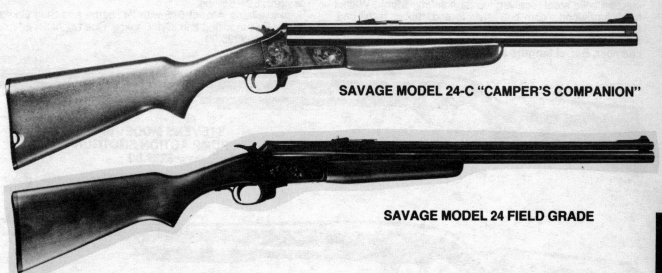

SAVAGE MODEL 24-C "CAMPER'S COMPANION"

SAVAGE MODEL 24 FIELD GRADE

SHOTGUNS

24-C Campers Companion Combination: 22 long rifle/20 gauge. At 5³/₄ pounds, it's a pound lighter and five inches shorter than other 24's. When stored in special case, it measures just 5 inches × 22 in. The case has handles for carrying, thongs for tying to pack or saddle. Recess in stock holds extra shells.
Price. **$239.00**

24 Field Grade Combinations: 22 long rifle/20 or .410 gauge; 22 Magnum/20. A combination gun at a field grade price makes this model an ideal first gun. It combines the ever popular 22 cartridge with either of two popular shotgun gauges. Walnut-finished hardwood stock and forend are coated with sturdy electro-cote. Barrel alignment band.
Price. **$209.00**

SPECIFICATIONS

Caliber and gauge	24V			24		
	222 20	223 20	30-30 20	22 L.R. 20	22 L.R. 410	22 Mag. 20
Barrel length 24" Full and Choke	●	●	●	●	●	●
Shotgun chambered for	2³/₄" & 3"			2³/₄" & 3"	2¹/₂" & 3"	2³/₄"
Length — Overall	40"			40"		
Length — Taken down	24"			24"		
Length — Pull	14"			14"		
Drop at — Comb	2"			2"		
Drop at — Monte Carlo	1³/₄"			2³/₄"		
Drop at — Heel	2⁵/₈"			2⁵/₈"		
Average weight (lbs.)	7			6¹/₂		

Rate of Twist (R.H.): 1 turn in 12" for 30-30 and .357 Rem. Mg.
1 turn in 14" for 222, 22 Hornet and 223
1 turn in 16" for 22 Mag. and 22 L.R.

SAVAGE & STEVENS PUMP SHOTGUNS

STEVENS MODEL 67 PUMP SHOTGUN
$229.00

A trim-looking, smooth-functioning pump shotgun economically priced. **Action:** Hammerless, pump action, with side ejection solid steel receiver; top tang safety. **Stock:** Walnut finish hardwood, "corn cob" style forend; rubber recoil pad. **Barrel:** All chambered for 2³/₄" or 3" shells in 12, 20 gauges and .410 bore. **Magazine:** Tubular, 4 shots plus one in the chamber. **Barrel lengths and chokes:** 12 gauge, 28" Mod.;

12 gauge 30" Full; 20 gauge 28" Mod.; .410 bore, 26" Full. **Overall length:** 45" (.410); 47" (20); 47⁵/₈" (12). **Approx. weight:** 6¹/₄–6³/₄ lbs.
Also available: **Model 675** with 24" barrel and Slug Choke Tube. Full, modified Imp. Cyl. Chokes. Open sight set adapts to vent rib. **$295.00**

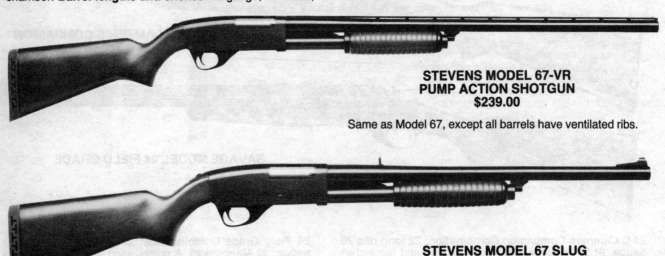

STEVENS MODEL 67-VR PUMP ACTION SHOTGUN
$239.00

Same as Model 67, except all barrels have ventilated ribs.

STEVENS MODEL 67 SLUG
$245.00

Rifle slug version of the Model 67 Pump Action Shotgun, in 12 gauge. **Stock:** Walnut finish hardwood buttstock and forend.

Magazine: 4 shot tubular. **Sights:** Ramp front with folding-leaf rear sight. **Barrel length:** 21" Cylinder bore. **Overall length:** 41". **Approx. weight:** 6¹/₂ lbs.

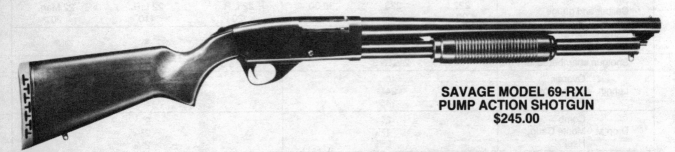

SAVAGE MODEL 69-RXL PUMP ACTION SHOTGUN
$245.00

Compact, smooth-functioning law enforcement version of the Model 67 pump shotgun. **Stock:** Tung oil-finished hardwood stock and forend; ventilated rubber recoil pad; studs for QD sling loops attached. **Magazine:** Tubular, 7 shots, plus one in

the chamber. **Barrel length:** 18¹/₄" Cylinder bore. **Overall length:** 39". **Gauge:** 12. **Chamber:** 2³/₄" and 3" shells. **Approx. weight:** 6³/₄ lbs. Also available in Stevens Model 311-R (cyl./cyl.): **$309.00.**

SHOTGUNS OF ULM

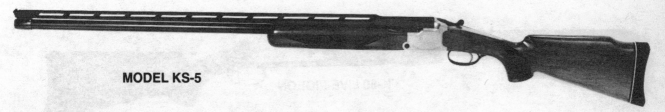

MODEL KS-5

The KS-5 is a single barrel trap gun with a ventilated, tapered step rib, case-hardened receiver and satin grey finished in electroless nickel. It features an adjustable point of impact by means of different optional fronthangers. Screw-in chokes are optional. Trigger is adjustable externally for poundage.

SPECIFICATIONS
Gauge:12
Chamber: 2³/₄″
Barrel length: 32″ or 34″
Choke: full; optional screw-in chokes
Rib: Tapered step; ventilated
Trigger: weight of pull adjust
Receiver: case-hardened; satin grey finished in electroless nickel
Forearm: beavertail
Grade: standard
Weight: approximately 8.6-8.8 lbs.
Case: aluminum
Price: $2350.00 (with full choke and case)
      2575.00 (with screw-in choke and case)
Screw-in choke barrels: $1200
Regular barrels: $975.00
Engraved models: $3550.00 and up

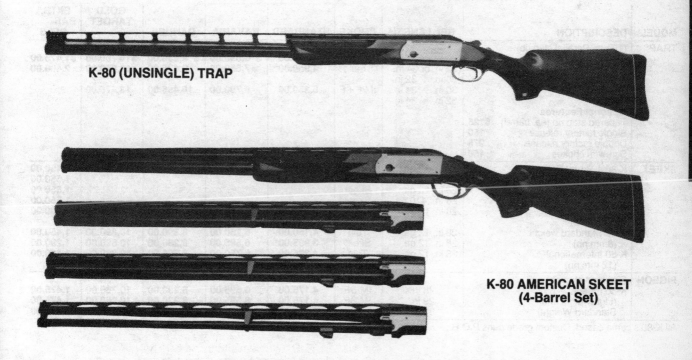

K-80 (UNSINGLE) TRAP

K-80 AMERICAN SKEET
(4-Barrel Set)

SHOTGUNS OF ULM

K-80 LIVE PIGEON

MODEL K-80 TRAP, SKEET AND LIVE PIGEON

Barrels: Made of Boehler steel; free-floating bottom barrel with adjustable point of impact; standard rib is ventilated tapered step; Trap, Skeet, Live Pigeon and International barrels all interchangeable
Receivers: Hard satin-nickel finish; case hardened; blue finish available as special order
Triggers: Wide profile, single selective, position adjustable

Ejectors: Selective automatic
Sights: Strong metal front sight with insert and metal center bead
Stocks: Hand-checkered and epoxy-finished select walnut stock and forearm; silver soldered metal-to-metal assemblies; quick-detachable palm swell stocks available in five different styles and dimensions

PRICES:

MODEL	DESCRIPTION		BBL LENGTH	CHOKE	STANDARD	BAVARIA	DANUBE	GOLD TARGET	EXTRA BARRELS
TRAP	(12mm, Parallel step rib)								
	K-80 Over & Under		30 in. or 32 in.	IM/F	$4,175.00	$ 6,595.00	$ 8,230.00	$10,760.00	$1,475.00
	K-80 Unsingle		32 in. or 34 in.	Full	4,950.00	7,550.00	9,125.00	11,650.00	2,400.00
	K-80 Combo		30 in. + 32 in.		6,350.00	8,790.00	10,495.00	13,475.00	
			30 in. + 34 in.	IM/F + F					
			32 in. + 34 in.						
	Optional Features								
	Tapered step rib (ea. barrel)	$125							
	Single factory release	150							
	Double factory release	275							
	Screw-in chokes	150							
SKEET	K-80 4-Barrel Set		28 in. 12 ga.	Tula	8,450.00	10,995.00	12,595.00	15,995.00	1,450.00
	(8mm rib)		28 in. 20 ga.	Skeet					1,550.00
			28 in. 28 ga.	Skeet					1,550.00
			28 in. .410 ga.	Skeet					1,550.00
	K-80 Lightweight		28 in. 12 ga.	Skeet	3,895.00	6,745.00	8,100.00	10,450.00	1,290.00
	(8 mm rib)								
	K-80 Standard weight		28 in. 12 ga.	Tula	4,150.00	6,750.00	8,390.00	10,890.00	1,450.00
	(8mm rib)		28 in. 12 ga.	Skeet	3,995.00	6,595.00	8,230.00	10,890.00	1,290.00
	K-80 International		28 in. 12 ga.	Tula	4,295.00	6,750.00	8,390.00	10,890.00	1,450.00
	(12 mm rib)								
PIGEON	(Tapered step rib)								
	K-80 Pigeon		28 in.	IM/SF	4,175.00	6,595.00	8,230.00	10,760.00	1,475.00
	(Lightweight and		29 in.	IM/SF	4,175.00	6,595.00	8,230.00	10,760.00	1,475.00
	Standard Weight)		30 in.	IM/SF	4,175.00	6,595.00	8,230.00	10,760.00	1,475.00

All K-80's come cased. Custom grade guns P.O.R.

SOVEREIGN SHOTGUNS

SIDE BY SIDE
$377.95

SPECIFICATIONS

Gauge: 12 (3″ chamber)
Barrel length: 28″
Choke: Mod./full
Weight: 6 lbs.
Stock: Walnut w/checkered pistol grip and forearm

Length of pull: 14½″
Drop at comb: 1½″
Drop at heel: 2″
Safety: Automatic
Receiver: Chrome engraved; monobloc construction

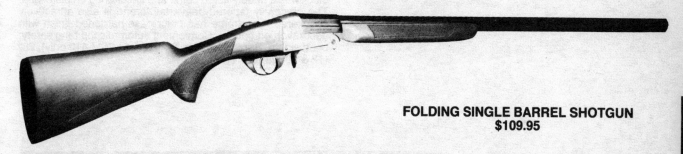

FOLDING SINGLE BARREL SHOTGUN
$109.95

SPECIFICATIONS

Gauge: 12, 16, 20 and .410 (3″ chamber)
Barrel length: 28″ (12, 16 and 20 ga.); 26″ (.410 ga.)
Weight: 6 lbs.
Choke: 12 and 20 ga. full/modified; 16 and .410 ga. full only

Stock: Walnut finished hardwood; chrome plated chamber and bore
Receiver: chrome engraved
Safety: Tang operated; automatic reset

OVER AND UNDER SHOTGUN
$320.95

SPECIFICATIONS

Gauge: 12 or 20 (2¾″ chamber)
Barrel length: 28″
Choke: Modified/full
Weight: 7 lbs. (12 ga.); 6¾ lbs. (20 ga.)
Stock: Walnut stock w/checkered pistol grip and forearm

Safety: Automatic
Receiver: Chrome engraved; monobloc construction
Length of pull: 14⅝″
Drop at comb: 1⅜″
Drop at heel: 2¼″

SHOTGUNS

STEVENS & FOX SHOTGUNS

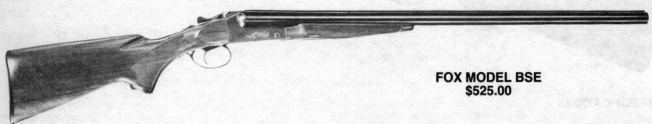

FOX MODEL BSE
$525.00

Fox B-SE. Gauges: 12, 20 and .410. Automatic ejectors are standard equipment on the Fox B-SE. Other fine gun features are the single trigger and ventilated rib. The B-SE has the lines found only in a double gun, enriched with materials and finishes typical of expensive custom guns. Its selected walnut stock has a deeply fluted comb and checkering on pistol grip. The gracefully tapered beavertail forend is also attractively checkered. The frame has color case-hardened finish with decoration on bottom. Convenient automatic top tang safety; bead sights. **Barrel lengths:** 24″ (12 ga.) 26″ (.410 only), 28″ (12 & 20 .ga), 30″ (12 ga. only).

STEVENS MODEL 311
$309.00

Model 311 double-barreled side-by-side shotgun features ventilated rib and lightweight barrels. **Action:** Break action, hammerless, with coil mainsprings, and double triggers. **Stock:** Walnut finish hardwood buttstock and forend; impressed checkering. **Gauges:** 3″ chambering for 12, 20 gauges and .410 bore. **Barrels and chokes:** 12 and 20 gauge, 26″ Imp. Cyl./Mod.; 28″ Mod./Full; 30″ Mod./Full (12 gauge only); .410 bore, 26″ Full/Full. **Overall length:** 41³/₄″–45³/₄″. **Approx. weight:** 7¹/₂ lbs. Automatic top tang safety, bead sight.

Also available: **Model 311R** designed for law enforcement use. **Barrel length:** 18¹/₄″. **Weight:** 6³/₄ lbs.

STOEGER SHOTGUNS

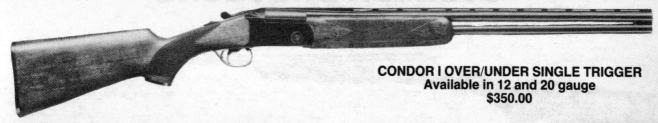

CONDOR I OVER/UNDER SINGLE TRIGGER
Available in 12 and 20 gauge
$350.00

The **STOEGER OVER/UNDER SINGLE TRIGGER** is a workhorse of a shotgun, designed for maximum dependability in heavy field use. The super-safe lock-up system makes use of a sliding underlug, the best system for over/under shotguns. A massive monobloc joins the barrel in a solid one-piece assembly at the breech end. Reliability is assured, thanks to the mechanical extraction system. Upon opening the breech, the spent shells are partially lifted from the chamber, allowing easy removal by hand. Stoeger barrels are of chrome-moly steel with micro-polished bores to give tight, consistent patterns.

They are specifically formulated for use with steel shot where Federal migratory bird regulations require. Atop the barrel is a sighting rib with an anti-glare surface. The buttstock and forend are of durable hardwood, hand-checkered and finished with an oil-based formula that takes dents and scratches in stride.

The Stoeger over/under shotgun is available in 12 or 20 gauge with 26-inch barrels choked Imp. Cyl./Mod. with 3-inch chambers; 12 or 20 gauge with 28-inch barrels choked Mod./Full, 3-inch chambers.

COACH GUN
Available in 12 and 20 gauge
$231.00

The **STOEGER CLASSIC SIDE-BY-SIDE COACH GUN** sports a 20-inch barrel. Lightning fast, it is the perfect shotgun for hunting upland game in dense brush or close quarters. This endurance-tested workhorse of a gun is designed from the ground up to give you years of trouble-free service. Two massive underlugs provide a super-safe, vise-tight locking system for lasting strength and durability. The mechanical extraction of spent shells and double-trigger mechanism assure reliability. The automatic safety is actuated whenever the action is

opened, whether or not the gun has been fired. The polish and blue is deep and rich, and the solid sighting rib is matte-finished for glare-free sighting. Chrome-moly steel barrels with micro-polished bores give dense, consistent patterns. The classic stock and forend are of durable hardwood . . . oil finished, hand-rubbed and hand-checkered.

Improved Cylinder/Modified choking and its short barrel make the Stoeger coach gun the ideal choice for hunting in close quarters, security and police work. 3-inch chambers.

UPLANDER SIDE-BY-SIDE
Available in 12, 20, 28 and .410 gauge
$238.00

The **STOEGER SIDE-BY-SIDE** is a rugged shotgun, endurance-tested and designed to give years of trouble-free service. A vise-tight, super-safe locking system is provided by two massive underlugs for lasting strength and durability. Two design features which make the Stoeger a standout for reliability are its positive mechanical extraction of spent shells and its traditional double-trigger mechanism. The safety is automatic

in that every time the action is opened, whether the gun has been fired or not, the safety is actuated. The polish and blue is deep and rich. The solid sighting rib carries a machined-in matte finish for glare-free sighting. Barrels are of chrome-moly steel with micro-polished bores to give dense, consistent patterns. The stock and forend are of classic design in durable hardwood . . . oil finished, hand-rubbed and hand-checkered.

STOEGER SHOTGUNS

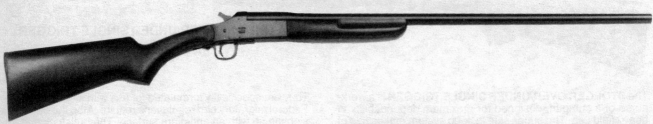

SINGLE BARREL
$88.00

Stoeger's new entry-level single barrel shotgun features a unique locking system. By pulling rearward on the trigger guard, the underlug engagement is released, thus opening the action. Single mechanical extraction makes for convenient removal of spent shells. For ease of operation and maximum safety, this single barrel shotgun is equipped with an exposed hammer, which must be cocked manually. A half-cocked setting on the hammer provides the safety mode.

The buttstock and semi-beavertail forearm are of durable Brazilian hardwood. Stoeger's new single barrel shotgun is available in 12, 20 gauge, and .410 bore.

Stoeger Shotgun Specifications

Model	Gauge	Chokes	Chamber	Barrel Length	Length of Pull	Drop at Comb	Drop at Heel	Approx. Average Weight	Safety	Extractors
Single Barrel	12	M, F, IC	2-3/4"	28"	14-1/2"	1-1/2"	2-1/2"	5-1/8 lbs.	Manual	Yes
	20	M, F, IC	3"	28"	14-1/2"	1-1/2"	2-1/2"	5-1/8 lbs.	Manual	Yes
	.410	M, F, IC	3"	28"	14-1/2"	1-1/2"	2-1/2"	5-1/8 lbs.	Manual	Yes
Side-by-Side	12	M/F, IC/M	3"	28"/26"	14-1/2"	1-1/2"	2-1/2"	7 lbs.	Automatic	Yes
	20	M/F, IC/M	3"	28"/26"	14-1/2"	1-1/2"	2-1/2"	6-3/4 lbs.	Automatic	Yes
	28	IC/M	2-3/4"	26"	14-1/2"	1-1/2"	2-1/2"	6-3/4 lbs.	Automatic	Yes
	.410	F/F, IC/M	3"	26"	14-1/2"	1-1/2"	2-1/2"	6-3/4 lbs.	Automatic	Yes
Over/Under	12	M/F, IC/M	3"	28"/26"	14-1/2"	1-1/2"	2-1/2"	7 lbs.	Manual	Yes
	20	M/F, IC/M	3"	28"/26"	14-1/2"	1-1/2"	2-1/2"	6-3/4 lbs.	Manual	Yes
Coach Gun	12	IC/M	3"	20"	14-1/2"	1-1/2"	2-1/2"	6-1/2 lbs.	Automatic	Yes
	20	IC/M	3"	20"	14-1/2"	1-1/2"	2-1/2"	6-1/2 lbs.	Automatic	Yes

TIKKA SHOTGUNS

TIKKA MO7
SHOTGUN/RIFLE COMBINATION
$1070.00

The Tikka MO7 Shotgun/Rifle combination features dovetails for attaching a telescopic sight, a single trigger with instant selector between the shotgun and rifle barrels, a ventilated rib, and a walnut stock with a palm-swell in the pistol grip.

Gauge/Caliber: 12/.222 Rem.
Overall length: Approx. 40²/₃″
Shotgun barrel length: Approx. 25″
Rifle barrel length: Approx. 22³/₄″
Weight: Approx. 7 lbs.

VALMET SHOTGUNS

AMERICAN SERIES

The American series 412 S models feature low-luster American walnut wood with streamlined tapers and high-quality checkering. The forearm is re-shaped, and has a new latch mechanism to accommodate different dimensions in extra barrel sets. And extra angle pieces and extenders are available to add to the butt plate. Convenient screw placement in the butt makes changes easy and permits the same gun to be made to fit almost anyone. Overall weight has been reduced by about 8 oz.

412 S FIELD SERIES
$874.00

The heart of the Valmet line, these O/U shotguns feature free interchangeability of barrels, stocks, and forearms into the 412 S series in all gauges. Also features simple barrel positioning adjustment, two-piece firing pin, monobloc locking shield for extra strength in protecting barrel shift, positive and automatic extraction models, top auto safety, trigger-located barrel selector barrel indicators, and standard stock with recoil pad.

SPECIFICATIONS

Gauge	Chamber	Barrel length	Average weight	Chokes
12	3″	24″	7¼ lbs.	IC/IC/M
12	3″	26″	7¼ lbs.	IC/M/IM
12	3″	28″	7½ lbs.	M/IM/F
12	3″	30″	7½ lbs.	M/IM/F
20	3″	28″	7¼ lbs.	IC/M/F

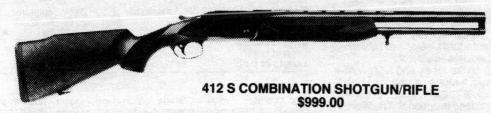

412 S COMBINATION SHOTGUN/RIFLE
$999.00

All of the fine quality features of the 412 S Series apply to these models as well. The 12 gauge 24-inch long barrel is chambered for 3-inch shells in all models. Monte Carlo stock with recoil pad. **Overall length:** 40″. **Weight:** 8 lbs.

Combination Shotgun/Rifle Specifications

Caliber	Barrel length	Chamber	Choke
222	24″	3″	Imp. Mod.
308	24″	3″	Imp. Mod.
30.06	24″	3″	Imp. Mod.
9.3 × 74R	24″	3″	Imp. Mod.

VALMET SHOTGUNS

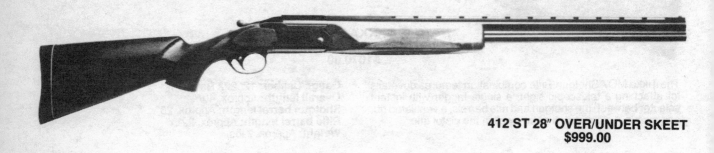

412 ST 28" OVER/UNDER SKEET
$999.00

412 ST 32" MONO TRAP
$999.00

412 ST TARGET SERIES

The 412 ST Target Series offers a wide selection of over/under designs plus two Mono Trap guns. Standard features include pre-drilled stocks for insertion of a recoil reducer; quick-change stock bolt and key to allow conversion from Trap to Skeet and back; American semi-fancy walnut stock and bea-vertail forend with deep checkering and checkered finger groove; recessed forend release to aid in hot weather shoot-ing; two wood finishes—low-gloss satin or high-gloss luster; barrels and receivers are either standard blue or satin chrome finish; barrel interchangeability; automatic ejectors.

Trap models have screw-in choke tubes and high venti-lated rib; rib is stepped and tapered, featuring a luminous bead at the end of the barrel. The "middle" bead remains polished metal, although a small luminous bead is optional. Traditional Monte Carlo stock has wide comb, double palm swell and Pachmayr recoil pad.

SPECIFICATIONS

	Trap	Skeet
Barrel length:	32" and 34" Mono Barrel 30" and 32" Over/Under	26" and 28" Over/Under
Choke:	M/IM/F	SK/SK
Gauge:	12 (2¾" chamber)	12 (2¾" chamber) 20 (3" chamber)
Weight:	9 lbs.	8 lbs.
Drop at comb:	1½"	1⅜"
Drop at heel:	1⅜"	2"
Length of pull:	14⁵⁄₁₆"	14⁵⁄₁₆"

Also available: **Premium Grade** featuring gold trigger, stock wrist checkering, matte nickel receiver, pre-drilled stock (1" dia.), matte blue locking bolt and lever, semi-fancy American walnut stock and forearm. **Price: $1199.00.**

VENTURA SHOTGUNS

VICTRX MODEL

Gauge: 12 ga. (2³/₄″); 20 ga. (3″); 28 ga. (2³/₄″); .410 ga. (3″)
Action: Anson and Deely boxlock with triple locks
Barrel lengths: 26″ and 28″
Stock: French walnut, hand-checkered, English straight or pistol grip stock with slender beavertail forend
Features: Single-selective trigger or double triggers; automatic ejectors. Options on these fine Italian guns include leather trunk case, wood cleaning rods, and brass snap caps
Weight: 12 ga. 6¹/₂ lbs. to .410 ga. 5¹/₂ lbs.
Price: . . . . $844.00 to $996.00

VICTRX EXTRA LUSSO MODEL

Gauge: 12 ga. (2³/₄″); 20 ga. (3″); 28 ga. (2³/₄″); .410 ga. (3″)
Action: Anson and Deeley boxlock with triple locks
Barrel lengths: 26″ and 28″
Stock: Select figured French walnut, hand-checkered, English straight or pistol grip stock with slender beavertail forend
Features: Single-selective trigger or double triggers; automatic ejectors; full floral engraving. Options on these fine Italian guns include five flush screw-in chokes, leather trunk case, wood cleaning rods, and brass snap caps
Weight: 12 ga. 6¹/₂ lbs. to .410 ga. 5¹/₂ lbs.
Price: . . . . $1148.00 to $1248.00

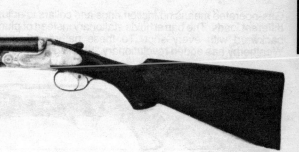

VENTURA REGIS MODEL

Gauge: 12 ga. (2³/₄″); 20 ga. (3″); 28 ga. (2³/₄″); .410 ga. (3″)
Action: H&H sidelock with intercepting safeties and triple locks
Barrel lengths: 26″ and 28″
Stock: Select figured French walnut, hand-checkered English straight or pistol grip stock with slender beavertail forend
Weight: 12 ga. 6¹/₂ lbs., to .410 ga., 5 lbs.
Features: Single selective trigger or double triggers, automatic ejectors; floral engraving. Options on these fine Italian guns include two sets of barrels, leather trunk case, wood cleaning rods and brass snap caps
Weight: 12 ga. 6¹/₂ lbs., to .410 ga. 5¹/₂ lbs.
Price: . . . . $1648.00 to $1796.00

WEATHERBY SHOTGUNS

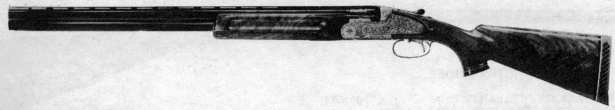

ATHENA OVER/UNDER

Receiver: The Athena receiver houses a strong, reliable box-lock action, yet it features side lock-type plates to carry through the fine floral engraving. The hinge pivots are made of a special high strength steel alloy. The locking system employs the time-tested Greener cross-bolt design. **Single selective trigger:** It is mechanically rather than recoil operated. This provides a fully automatic switchover, allowing the second barrel to be fired on a subsequent trigger pull, even in the event of a misfire. A flick of the trigger finger and the selector lever, located just in front of the trigger, is all the way to the left enabling you to fire the lower barrel first, or to the right for the upper barrel. The Athena trigger is selective as well. **Barrels:** The breech block is hand-fitted to the receiver, providing closest possible tolerances. Every Athena is equipped with a matted, ventilated rib and bead front sight. **Selective automatic ejec-**

tors: The Athena contains ejectors that are fully automatic both in selection and action. **Slide safety:** The safety is the traditional slide type located conveniently on the upper tang on top of the pistol grip. **Stock:** Each stock is carved from specially selected Claro walnut, with fine line hand-checkering and high luster finish. Trap model has Monte Carlo stock only. **Weight:** 12 ga. Field, 8 lbs.; 20 ga. Field, 7 lbs.; Trap, 8½ lbs.

Prices:
12 & 20 ga. Field	$1590.00
12 ga. Trap	1611.00
12 & 20 ga. Skeet	1601.00

MODEL 82 AUTOMATIC IMC (12 Ga.)
$550.00
BUCKMASTER AUTO SLUG $550.00

EIGHTY-TWO AUTOMATIC

Gas-operated means no friction rings and collars to adjust for different loads. The barrel holds stationary instead of plunging backward with every shot. To these natural advantages, Weatherby has added revolutionary "Floating Piston" action.

In the Weatherby Eighty-two, the piston "floats" freely on the magazine tube completely independent of every other part of the action. Nothing to get out of alignment. Nothing to cause drag or friction. **Weight:** 7½ lbs.

MODEL 92 PUMP IMC (12 Ga.)
$400.00
BUCKMASTER PUMP SLUG GUN $400.00

NINETY-TWO PUMP

The super-fast slide action operates on double rails for precision and reliability. No twists, no binds, no hang-ups. To remove a loaded round, push the gold-plated forearm release

lever to its forward position. Now the forearm is unlocked and the action can be opened. Both 82 and 92 models have front bead sights. Buckmaster Slug has rifle sight. **Weight:** 7½ lbs.

WEATHERBY SHOTGUNS

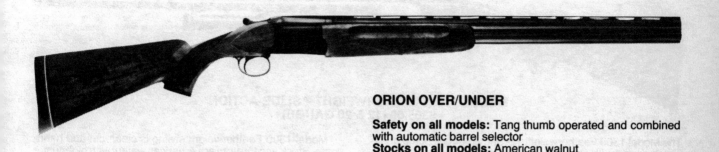

ORION OVER/UNDER

Safety on all models: Tang thumb operated and combined with automatic barrel selector
Stocks on all models: American walnut

ORION OVER/UNDER

For greater versatility, the Orion incorporates the integral multi-choke (IMC) system. Available in Extra-full, Full, Modified, Improved Modified, Improved Cylinder and Skeet, the choke tubes fit flush with the muzzle without detracting from the beauty of the gun. Three tubes are furnished with each gun. The precision hand-fitted monobloc and receiver are machined from high-strength steel with a highly polished finish. The box-lock design uses the Greener cross-bolt locking system and special sears maintain hammer engagement. Pistol grip stock and forearm are carved of Claro walnut with hand-checkered diamond inlay pattern and high-gloss finish.

Chrome moly steel barrels, and the receiver, are deeply blued. The Orion also features selective automatic ejectors, single selective trigger, front bead sight and ventilated rib. The Trap model boasts a curved trap-style recoil pad and is available with Monte Carlo stock only. **Weight:** 12 ga. Field, 7½ lbs.; 20 ga. Field, 7½ lbs.; Trap, 8 lbs.

Prices
Field Grade, 12 or 20 ga. **$1000.00**
Skeet Grade, 12 or 20 ga. 1011.00
Trap Grade, 12 ga. only 1051.00

ATHENA and ORION Over/Under Shotgun Specifications

Fixed choke models (except 12 GA. and 20 GA.)

Model	Chamber	Bbl Length	Chokes	Overall Length	Length of Pull	Comb	Drop at: Heel	**MC	Bead Sights	*Approx. Weight
Skeet/Skeet	3"	26"	S/S	43¼"	14¼"	1½"	2½"		White Fr, Mid Br	6½-7½ lb.
IMC Multi-Choke Field Models (12 GA. and 20 GA.)										
Field	3"	26"	M/IC/Sk	43¼"	14¼"	1½"	2½"		Brilliant Front	6½-7½ lb.
Field	3"	28"	F/M/IC	45¼"	14¼"	1½"	2½"		Brilliant Front	6½-7½ lb.
Field (12 GA. only)	3"	30"	F/M/F	47¼"	14¼"	1½"	2½"		Brilliant Front	7½-8 lb.
IMC Multi-Choke Trap Models (12 GA. only)										
Trap	2¾"	30"	F/M/IM	47½"	14⅜"	1⅜"	2⅛"	1¾"	White Fr, Mid Br	8-8½ lb.
Trap	2¾"	32"	F/M/IM	49½"	14⅜"	1⅜"	2⅛"	1¾"	White Fr, Mid Br	8-8½ lb.

**TRAP STOCKS AVAILABLE ONLY WITH MONTE CARLO.

Three tubes shown are furnished with IMC models. An Extra Full tube is also available as a separate item.

*Weight varies due to wood density.

WINCHESTER SHOTGUNS

MODEL 1300 FEATHERWEIGHT™ SLIDE-ACTION
$305.00 (12 & 20 GAUGE)

The Model 1300 Featherweight 12- and 20-gauge pump guns are designed with shorter 22-inch barrels for upland shooting and small, quick game. At 6³/₈ pounds, both are light-carrying, easy-swinging and lightning fast.

Their perfected slide action is one of the fastest, surest ever made. Twin-action slide bars prevent binding. The action permits ultra-fast follow-up shots. The front-locking rotating bolt locks the bolt into barrel with maximum strength and security. The ventilated rib barrel is chromium molybdenum steel, hot-formed for high strength.

Both 12- and 20-gauge versions handle 3-inch Magnum, 2³/₄-inch Magnum, and 2³/₄-inch standard shotshells interchangeably. Their 22-inch barrel is specially adapted for the Winchoke system, and each comes equipped with Full, Modified and Improved Cylinder Winchoke tubes and wrench. The Winchoke system and 3″ Magnum capability give these new shotguns the versatility for most upland game—and great potential as utility guns.

Model 1300 Featherweight styling is clean-cut and hand-some. Stock and forearm are American walnut with high-luster finish. Deep cut-checkering on pistol grip and traditional ribbing on the short, contoured forearm. Receivers are roll-engraved. Metal surfaces are highly polished and blued. Other features include cross-bolt safety with red indicator and metal front bead sight.

The 20-gauge Model 1300 Featherweight makes short work of upland birds. Equipped with serrated butt plate. The 12-gauge version delivers maximum versatility and performance for rabbits and small, fast game. The short barrel makes shotgun hunting for small game quick and responsive while the Winchoke system maximizes utility value. Equipped with rubber recoil pad. **Chamber:** 3″. **Barrel length:** 22″. **Overall length:** 42⁵/₈″. **Weight:** 6³/₈ lbs.
Also available: **Model 1300 XTR** with 28″ barrel. **Weight:** 7¹/₄ lbs. **Price: $350.00.**

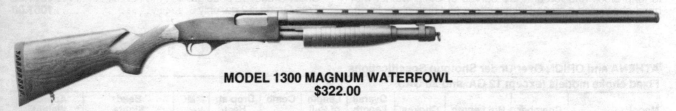

MODEL 1300 MAGNUM WATERFOWL
$322.00

The Model 1300 Magnum Waterfowl pump is designed specifically for hunting ducks and geese. It features a 30-inch ventilated rib barrel with the Winchoke System of interchangeable choke tubes (Extra Full, Full and Modified). Stock and forearm are of American walnut with a low-luster protective finish. All exterior metal surfaces have a special non-glare matte finish

to aid in hunter concealment. Other features include metal front bead sight, cross-bolt safety, rubber recoil pad and sling swivels. **Chamber:** 3″ Mag. **Overall length:** 50⁵/₈″. **Stock dimensions:** Length of pull, 14″; drop at comb, 1¹/₂″; drop at heel, 2¹/₂″; **Weight:** 7 lbs.

MODEL 1300 TURKEY SHOTGUN
WITH WINCHOKE®, V.R. (not shown)
$322.00

Available in 12 gauge only, the Model 1300 Turkey gun comes equipped with a 22-inch ventilated rib barrel, which includes the Winchester Winchoke system with Extra Full, Full and Modified choke tubes and wrench. Its walnut stock and forearm have a special low-luster protective finish; the receiver, barrel and all exterior metal surfaces feature a non-glare matte finish. The receiver is roll engraved. The pistol grip has deep-cut checkering; the contoured forearm is ribbed for sure gripping and has been modified for positioning and comfort. Other features include cross-bolt safety with red indicator blocks and metal bead sights. The 1300 Turkey Gun handles 3″ magnum,

2³/₄″ Magnum and 2³/₄″ standard shotshells interchangeably. **Chamber:** 3″ Mag., 5-shot capacity. **Overall length:** 42⁵/₈″. **Stock dimensions:** Length of pull, 14″; drop at comb, 1¹/₂″; drop at heel, 2¹/₂″. **Weight:** 6³/₈″.

Also available: **Turkey Win-Cam Camouflage** model w/vent ribs: **$399.00.**
Combo Pac Win-Cam Camouflage with extra barrel (12 ga. 30″ waterfowl w/12 ga. 22″ upland game); stock laminated w/ Win-Cam camouflage green and all metal parts with low reflecting matte finish. **Price: $412.00**

Manufacturer does not furnish suggested retail prices; above figures are estimated average prices.

WINCHESTER SECURITY SHOTGUNS

This trio of tough 12-gauge shotguns provides backup strength for security and police work as well as all-around utility. The action is one of the fastest second-shot pumps made. It features a front-locking rotating bolt for strength and secure, single-unit lock-up into the barrel. Twin-action slide bars prevent binding.

All three guns are chambered for 3-inch shotshells. They handle 3-inch Magnum, 2³/₄-inch Magnum and standard 2³/₄-inch shotshells interchangeably. They have cross-bolt safety, walnut-finished hardwood stock and forearm, black rubber butt pad and plain 18-inch barrel with Cylinder Bore choke. All are ultra-reliable and easy to handle.

Special chrome finishes on Police and Marine guns are actually triple-plated: first with copper for adherence, then with nickel for rust protection, and finally with chrome for a hard finish. This triple-plating assures durability and quality. Both guns have a forend cap with swivel to accommodate sling.

DEFENDER
$221.00

Also available: **DEFENDER COMBO** with pistol grip and extra hunting barrel. **$248.00 ($267.00 with vent. rib)**

Security Defender™ is ideal for home security use. The compact 35⁵/₈-inch overall length handles and stores easily. The Defender has a deep blued finish on metal surfaces and features a traditional ribbed forearm for sure pumping grip. It has a metal bead front sight. The magazine holds eight 12-gauge 2³/₄-inch shells. New version offers shotshell capacity of five 2³/₄" shells with optional metal bead front sight or rifle type (front and rear). **$214.00** (metal bead) and **$228.00** (rifle).

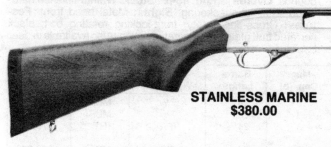

STAINLESS MARINE
$380.00

Security Police™ is designed for police and security force work. It features an 18-inch ordnance stainless steel barrel and a satin chrome finish on all external metal parts. The distinctive satin chrome finish diffuses light and resists corrosion. The magazine has a capacity of six 2³/₄-inch shotshells, plus one shell in the chamber. Optional metal bead front sight or rifle-type front and rear sights. **Price: $380.00.**

Also available: **Stainless Marine** model. Same specifications as Stainless Police model w/o satin finish.

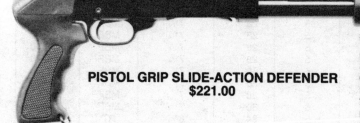

PISTOL GRIP SLIDE-ACTION DEFENDER
$221.00

Winchester Security shotguns offer the same features and performance at lower cost with a new high-strength pistol grip and forearm. The pistol grip features finger grooves and checkering for sure, fast handling. The shorter forearm is ribbed for positive grip and pumpability. Both pistol grip and forearm are high-impact-resistant ABS plastic with non-glare matte black finish. The Pistol Grip series is lighter in weight, compact, easily stored and fast handling.

Model	Order Symbol No.	Gauge	Chamber	Shotshell Capacity (A)	Choke	Barrel Length	Overall Length	Length Of Pull	Nominal Drop At Comb	Nominal Drop At Heel	Nominal Weight Lbs.	Sights
Defender	G1203DM2B	NEW—12	3" Mag.	5	Cyl. B.	18"	38⁵/₈"	14"	1³/₈"	2³/₄"	6¹/₄	MBF
	G1203DM2R	NEW—12	3" Mag.	5	Cyl. B.	18	38⁵/₈	14	1³/₈	2³/₄	6¹/₄	RT
	G1203DM1	12	3" Mag.	8*	Cyl. B.	18	38⁵/₈	14	1³/₈	2³/₄	6³/₄	MBF
Defender— Pistol Grip	G1203DM1PG	12	3" Mag.	8*	Cyl. B.	18"	28⁵/₈"	—	—	—	5¹/₂	MBF
Marine	G120321SR	12	3" Mag.	7*	Cyl. B.	18"	38⁵/₈"	14"	1³/₈"	2³/₄"	7	RT

(A) Includes one round in chamber when ready to fire. *One less for 3" shells. Cyl. B.-Cylinder Bore. MBF-Metal bead front. RT-Rifle type front and rear.

Manufacturer does not furnish suggested retail prices; above figures are estimated average prices.

WINCHESTER SHOTGUNS

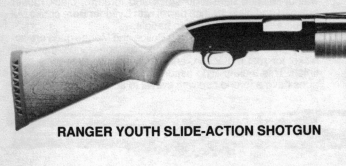

RANGER YOUTH SLIDE-ACTION SHOTGUN

Gauge: 20 gauge only; 3″ chamber; 5-shot magazine. **Barrel:** 22″ plain barrel; Winchoke (Full, Modified, Improved Cylinder). **Weight:** 6½ lbs. **Length:** 41⅝″. **Stock:** Walnut-finished hardwood with ribbed forend. **Sights:** Metal bead front. **Features:** Cross-bolt safety; black rubber butt pad; twin-action slide bars; front-locking rotating bolt; removable segmented magazine plug to limit shotshell capacity for training purposes; discount certificate for full-size adult stock. Also available in plain barrel w/Mod. choke.

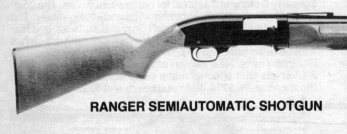

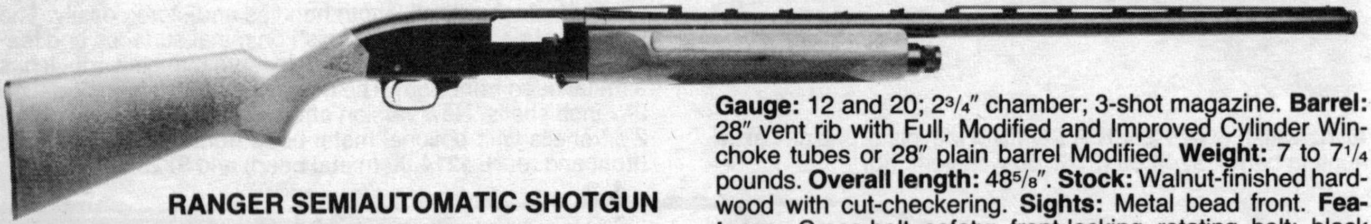

RANGER SEMIAUTOMATIC SHOTGUN

Gauge: 12 and 20; 2¾″ chamber; 3-shot magazine. **Barrel:** 28″ vent rib with Full, Modified and Improved Cylinder Winchoke tubes or 28″ plain barrel Modified. **Weight:** 7 to 7¼ pounds. **Overall length:** 48⅝″. **Stock:** Walnut-finished hardwood with cut-checkering. **Sights:** Metal bead front. **Features:** Cross-bolt safety; front-locking rotating bolt; black serrated butt plate, gas-operated action. Also available in deer barrel.

Winchester® Ranger® Semi-Automatic Shotguns

Model	Order Symbol No.	Gauge	Chamber	Mag. Cap. (b)	Barrel Length	Nominal Wgt. (lbs.)	Sights	Price
Winchoke (W3) VR	G14185R	12	2¾″	3	28″	7¼	MBF	$279.00
Winchoke (W3) VR	G14187R	20	2¾″	3	28″	7¼	MBF	279.00
Deer Barrel	G14110R	12	2¾″	3	24½″	6¾	RT	279.00
Deer Combination:	G141RC							
Deer Barrel		12	2¾″	3	24½″	6¾	RT	313.00
Winchoke (W3) VR		12	2¾″	3	28″	7¼	MBF	313.00

Winchester® Ranger® Slide Action Shotguns

Model	Order Symbol No.	Gauge	Chamber	Mag. Cap. (b)	Barrel Length	Nominal Wgt. (lbs.)	Sights	Price
Winchoke (W3) VR	G120385R	12	3″	5	28″	7¼	MBF	246.00
Winchoke (W3) VR	G120387R	20	3″	5	28″	7¼	MBF	246.00
VR Barrel Mod.	G120353R	12	3″	5	28″	7¼	MBF	229.00
VR Barrel Mod.	G120373R	20	3″	5	28″	7¼	MBF	229.00
VR Barrel Full	G120351R	12	3″	5	30″	7½	MBF	229.00
Plain Barrel Mod.	G120303R	12	3″	5	28″	7	MBF	211.00
Plain Barrel Mod.	G120323R	20	3″	5	28″	7	MBF	211.00
Plain Barrel Full	G120341R	12	3″	5	30″	7¼	MBF	211.00
Deer Barrel	G120310R	12	3″	5	24⅛″	6¾	RT	234.00
Deer Barrel	G120320R	20	3″	5	24⅛″	6¾	RT	234.00
Deer Combination:	G1203RC							
Deer Barrel		12	3″	5	24⅛″	6¾	RT	282.00
Winchoke (W3) VR		12	3″	5	28″	7¼	MBF	282.00
Deer Combination:	G120320RC							
Deer Barrel		20	3″	5	24⅛″	6¾	RT	282.00
Winchoke (W3) VR		20	3″	5	28″	7¼	MBF	282.00

Winchester® Ranger® Youth Slide Action Shotgun

Model	Order Symbol No.	Gauge	Chamber	Mag. Cap. (b)	Barrel Length	Nominal Wgt. (lbs.)	Sights	Price
Winchoke (W3) VR	G120330R	20	3″	5	22″	6¼	MBF	$253.00
Plain Barrel Mod.	G120333R	20	3″	5	22″	6⅛	MBF	218.00

Manufacturer does not furnish suggested retail prices; above figures are estimated average prices.

ANGELO ZOLI SHOTGUNS

Z43 STANDARD O/U SHOTGUN
$461.00

Gauges: 12 or 20. **Barrel lengths:** 26″, 28″ and 30″. Chambered for 3″. **Chokes:** F/M, M/IC. **Features:** Chrome-lined barrels, ventilated lateral ribs, standard extractors, single non-selective trigger, chromium-plated steel action, Browning-type locking with under locking bolt, walnut stock and forearm, glossy finish, automatic safety. **Weight:** Approx. 6¾-8 lbs.

Also available:
Model Z43 Special 12 gauge w/Multichoke **$611.00**
Model Z43 Deluxe w/vent. ribs, auto ejectors, engravings, removable stock . . . . **$786.00** ($871.00 w/Multichoke).

PRESENTATION O/U FIELD SHOTGUN
$907.00
$986.00 w/Multichoke

12 gauge only. **Barrel lengths:** 26″, 28″ and 30″. Chambered for 3″. **Chokes:** F/M, M/IC and Multichoke system (F, IM, M, IC, SK-w/Key). **Features:** Ventilated rib, chrome-lined barrels, automatic ejectors, single selective trigger, full side plate, selected walnut stock, full pistol grip. **Weight:** Approx. 8 lbs.

CAESAR SIDE-BY-SIDE
$1441.00

Entirely hand-made. 410 gauge only. **Barrel length:** 28″. Chambered for 3″. **Choke:** Full/Mod. **Features:** Chrome-lined barrels, automatic ejectors; exclusive Zoli single selective trigger, box lock, fancy walnut stock, English straight grip, splinter forearm, hand-checkered. Case extra. **Weight:** Approx. 5½ lbs.

CLASSIC SIDE-BY-SIDE
$746.00
$831.00 w/Multichoke

12 gauge only. **Barrel lengths:** 26″, 28″ and 30″. **Chokes:** F/M, M/IC and Multichoke system (F, IM, M, IC, SK-w/Key). **Features:** Chrome-lined barrels, single selective trigger, automatic ejectors, box lock. Case extra. **Weight:** Approx. 7½ lbs.

ANGELO ZOLI SHOTGUNS

AIRONE COMBO RIFLE/SHOTGUN
$840.00

12 ga. × 308 Win. or 12 ga. × 30-06. Monobloc system. **Features:** German-imported rifle barrel, front trigger fitted with adjustable double-set device, fine metal front and rear sights, short side-plate action, chrome-lined barrel, pistol grip, checkered walnut stock and forearm. **Weight:** Approx. 8 lbs.

CONDOR COMBO RIFLE/SHOTGUN
$775.00

12 ga. × 308 Win. or 12 ga. × 30-06. Monobloc system. German-imported rifle barrel, front trigger fitted with adjustable double-set device, front and rear iron sights, short side-plate action, pistol grip, checkered walnut stock and forearm. **Weight:** Approx. 8 lbs.

LEOPARD EXPRESS (not shown)
$1671.00

7 × 65R, 30-06, 375 H & H. Double set triggers, auto ejectors, engravings and hand checkered walnut stock. **Weight:** 8 lbs.

ST. GEORGE O/U COMPETITION TRAP COMBO (not shown)
$1732.00

12 gauge. **Barrel lengths:** 30″ and 32″. Chambered 2³/₄″. **Features:** High ventilated rib, non-chrome-lined barrels, two sights, automatic safety, automatic ejectors, double underlugs, wide locking bolt, single selective trigger, quick interchangable walnut stock (wrench included), oil finish, pistol grip, recoil pad, competition forearm. Case extra. **Weight:** Approx. 8 lbs. Comes with extra set of over and under trap barrels. Multichoke system (F, IM, M, IC, SK-w/Key). Also available: **ST. GEORGE TRAP** **$1124.00**

ST. GEORGE O/U COMPETITION SKEET (not shown)
$1124.00

Same general specifications as St. George Trap, except 26- and 28-inch barrels choked SK/SK. Single selective trigger. **Weight:** Approx. 7 lbs.

Paramilitary

FOR ADDRESSES AND PHONE
NUMBERS OF MANUFACTURERS AND
DISTRIBUTORS INCLUDED IN THIS
SECTION, SEE *DIRECTORY OF
MANUFACTURERS AND SUPPLIERS*

AMERICAN CARBINE

CALICO M•100 CARBINE
$299.95

Caliber: 22 LR
Barrel length: 16.1″
Overall length: 29.8″ (stock folded); 35.8″ (stock extended)
Weight: 5.7 lbs. (loaded); magazine w/100 rds 24 oz.
Height: 7.3″ (max.)
Magazine capacity: 100 rds.

Safety: ambidextrous, trigger and hammer block
Sights: post, adj. for elevation (front); notch, adj. for windage (rear)
Sight radius: 12.2″
Also available: **Calico M•100P Pistol 22 LR: $49.95**

AUTO-ORDNANCE

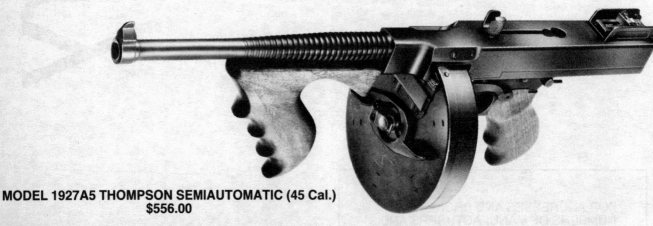

MODEL 1927A5 THOMPSON SEMIAUTOMATIC (45 Cal.)
$556.00

Featuring lightweight alloys for maximum shooting balance, this .45 semiautomatic pistol has an overall length of 26″ and is supplied with a 30-round magazine. Modeled after the famous Model 1928 but without the detachable buttstock, it is precision rifled; its 13″ barrel complements the gun's overall fine detail. It accepts all accessories common to the 1927A-1.

AUTO-ORDNANCE

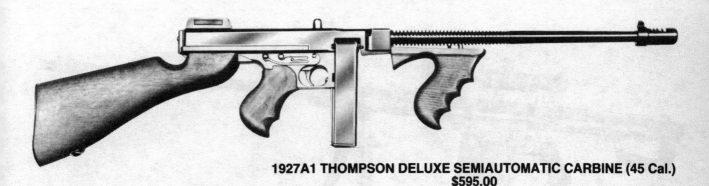

1927A1 THOMPSON DELUXE SEMIAUTOMATIC CARBINE (45 Cal.)
$595.00

The frame and receiver of this classic are durably manufactured from solid milled steel. It features finger-grooved vertical foregrip, a 16″ finned barrel, and an adjustable rear sight and compensator.

Model 1927A-1C Lightweight. $567.00

THOMPSON M1 SEMIAUTOMATIC CARBINE (45 Cal.)
$565.00

1911 A1 THOMPSON GOVERNMENT MODEL (45 Cal.)
$339.95

Considered by many to be the best and most popular automatic pistol in the world, this Model 1911 is now available in two other calibers as well—9mm and 38 Super. All parts are interchangeable with all other Government 1911 pistols. Constructed of durable 4140 steel, the frame and slide are finished in deep blue; each radius features a non-glare finish and both grips are enhanced by a special medallion.

1911A1 Government Model in 9mm or 38 Super . . $374.95

BARRETT SEMIAUTOMATIC RIFLES

BARRETT MODEL 82A1
$6895.00

Barrett's Model 82A1 (military configuration) features 4140 steel Match Grade barrel; high efficiency, low signature muzzle brake, two magazines; airtight and watertight fitted hard case.

SPECIFICATIONS
Caliber: 50 BMG (12.7mm)
Operation: Recoil, semiautomatic
Barrel length: 33″
Overall length: 61″
Capacity: 11 round detachable box magazine
Weight: 32.5 lbs.
Muzzle velocity: 2,848 fps
Sights: Leupold MI Ultra 10X telescope and rings w/iron sight backup

BERETTA SEMIAUTOMATIC RIFLES

BERETTA AR-70 SEMIAUTOMATIC RIFLE
$770.00

Optimum firepower and rugged dependability characterize this Beretta semiautomatic 223-caliber centerfire rifle. Special features include simple, fast take-down with no special tools needed. Far fewer component parts than similar centerfires. Every inch is crafted from the toughest materials in modern arsenal technology for all-weather, year-round use in any terrain. Comes with 8- and 30-round magazines, three-piece cleaning kit and military-style carrying strap.

SPECIFICATIONS
Action: Medium. **Barrel length:** 17.72″. **Magazine:** 8 or 30 rounds. **Sights:** Diopter sighting device adjustable for windage and elevation. **Finish:** Military-like exterior of antiabrasive, corrosion-free epoxy resins. **Weight:** 8.31 lbs.

COLT SEMIAUTOMATIC RIFLES

AR-15 A2 SPORTER II
$729.95 Sporter
769.95 Carbine

Designed from the famous Colt M-16 military rifle, the Colt AR-15 A2 is lightweight, with simple maintenance, easy handling and extreme accuracy. Semiautomatic 223 (5.56 mm) with 5-round magazine capacity. Features forward bolt assist, stiffer barrel with 1 turn in 7" rifling twist, strong nylon ribbed round handguard, buttstock and pistol grip, improved heat deflector and muzzle compensator. Front sight post adjustable for el-evation. Quick flip rear sight assembly with short-range and long-range tangs, adjustable for windage. **Weight:** 7½ lbs. **Overall length:** 39". **Barrel length:** 20". Prices include two 5-round magazines plus cleaning kit and nylon sling.

Carbine. Weight: 5.8 lbs. **Barrel length:** 16". **Overall length:** 35" w/buttstock extended; 32" closed.

AR-15A2 HBAR
$829.95

The new Colt AR-15A2 HBAR is a "heavier barrelled" version of the AR-15A2 Sporter II, with the larger diameter barrel extending from the muzzle to the receiver to give stability and added stiffness. It features the new target style rear sight recently adopted by the U.S. Military on their new M16A2, which is fully adjustable for windage and elevation out to 800 meters and is capable of fine adjustment at the longer ranges. This model also has a cartridge case deflector for lefthanded shooters. Weight is approximately 8 lbs.

DELTA H-BAR AR-15A2 RIFLE
$1299.95

This rifle has been selectively chosen and equipped with a 3 x 9 variable rubber armored scope, leather sling, shoulder stock cheekpiece, cleaning kit and carrying case.

Caliber: 223 Rem. **Barrel length:** 20". **Weight:** 8 lbs. **Price w/o above accessories:** $829.95

EMF SEMIAUTOMATIC CARBINES

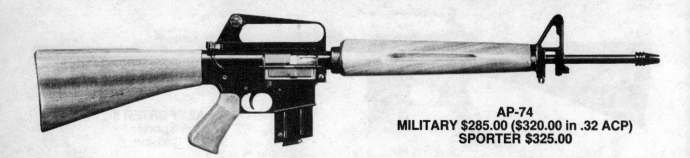

AP-74
MILITARY $285.00 ($320.00 in .32 ACP)
SPORTER $325.00

An outstanding copy of the U.S. Army Colt M-16 rifle, the AP-74 is extremely durable and dependable. Available with original military-type stock or in the sporter model with finely finished wood stock. In 22 Long Rifle or 32 ACP caliber. Military model available in 22 LR only; "dressed" with Cyclops scope, military mounts, Colt bayonet, sling and bipod.

SPECIFICATIONS
Magazine capacity: 15 rounds. **Barrel length:** 20″ w/flash reducer. **Overall length:** 38″. **Weight:** 6¾ lbs. **Front sight:** Protected pin. **Rear sight:** Selective protected peep, with apertures for long and close ranges. **Stock:** Strong, lightweight plastic; ventilated snap-out forend; fixed buttstock.

AP74 COMMANDO MODEL
w/WOOD STOCK
$335.00

AP74 ASSAULT MODEL
WITH FOLDING STOCK
22 LONG RIFLE ONLY
$325.00

Also available:
Paratrooper Carbine: $325.00
wood w/folding stock: $335.00

FABRIQUE NATIONALE RIFLES

LIGHT AUTOMATIC 7.62 NATO (308 MATCH)
$1258.00

This 308 Win. Match gas-operated semiautomatic has a rifled bore with 4 lands and grooves, plus right-hand twist, one turn in 12 inches. The rear sight is adjustable from 200 to 600 yards in 100 yard increments. Sight radius is 21³/₄ inches. Synthetic stock with ventilated forend. **Weight** (without magazine): 9 lbs.

7 oz. **Overall length:** 44¹/₂″. **Barrel length:** 21″ (24¹/₂″ with flash hider).

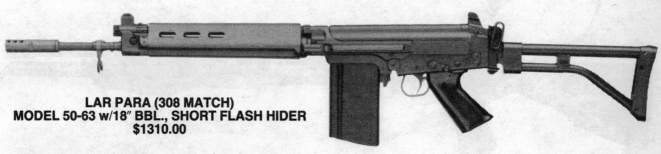

LAR PARA (308 MATCH)
MODEL 50-63 w/18″ BBL., SHORT FLASH HIDER
$1310.00

HEAVY BARREL MODEL 50.42 W/WOOD STOCK & METAL BIPOD (NOT SHOWN) $1654.00
WITH SYNTHETIC STOCK $1497.00 (Model 50.41)

FNC SEMIAUTOMATIC 223 REM.
PARATROOPER $782.00
STANDARD (not shown) $749.00

The FNC is a short, relatively light weapon with a fully locked mechanism functioning by an adjustable gas flow, plus smooth recoil and high accuracy. It is remarkably rugged, impervious to any adverse weather conditions and field strips effortlessly.

SPECIFICATIONS
Caliber: 223 Rem. (5.56mm). **Capacity:** 30-round magazine.
Action: Gas-operated, semiautomatic. **Barrel length:** 18″.
Weight: 9.6 lbs. with magazine. **Rifling:** 6 lands and grooves with right-hand twist, 1 turn in 12″. **Overall length:** 40″; 30″ with butt folded.

PARAMILITARY

FRANCHI

PARA RIMFIRE RIFLE
$279.95

This takedown semiautomatic rifle comes in its own contour-fitted carrying case, which features steel reinforced corners, latches and hinges. Rifle has an artillery type rear sight, hooded front sight, interior and exterior threaded muzzle, skel- eton buttstock. Other features include oil finished walnut forend, matte black receiver finish, O.D. web sling and disassembly tool.

SPAS-12 ASSAULT/POLICE SHOTGUN SYSTEM
$649.95

A slide action or gas operated semiautomatic shotgun featuring dual firing system, using all types of 2³/₄" shotshells. Offers maintenance-free parkerized finish, lightweight alloy receiver, anti-corrosive chrome-lined steel barrel and folding stock, plus nylon/resin pistol grip and forearm.

SPECIFICATIONS
Ammunition: 12 Ga. (2³/₄")
Choke: Cylinder bore
Capacity: 9 (8 plus 1 in chamber)
Barrel length: 21¹/₂"
Length w/stock folded: 31³/₄"
Length w/stock extended: 41"
Weight: 9.6 lbs.
Finish: Matte black

GALIL SEMIAUTOMATIC RIFLES

**MODEL 308 ARM 7.62 mm (.308 WIN.)
SEMIAUTOMATIC RIFLE**

Based on the battle-proven 5.56 mm (223) semiautomatic, the 7.62 mm (308) version is built for hard use and rough handling. Features ease of handling by right- or left-handed marksmen and functions under adverse weather conditions, humidity and dust. Post-type front sight; L flip-type rear sight set for 300 and 500 meters (330 and 550 yards); folding night sights are fitted with tritium lights. Telescopic, infrared or starlight sights can be fixed using special sight mounts.

SPECIFICATIONS (MODELS AR and ARM)
Ammunition: 223 REM. (5.56 mm) and 308 Win. (7.62 mm)
Finish: Black
Barrel length: 16.1" (223) and 18 1/2" (308)
Weight (empty): 8.6 lbs (AR) and 9.6 lbs. (ARM)
Length, stock folded: 27.2" (223) and 29.7" (308)
Overall length: 36 1/2" (223) and 39" (308)

**GALIL MODEL 223 AR
SEMIAUTO RIFLE**

GALIL RIFLE SYSTEM SEMIAUTOMATIC	PRICE
223 AR	$795.00
223 ARM	875.00
308 AR	849.00
308 ARM	940.00

AR —Folding stock only
ARM—Folding stock, bipod, carrying handle and wood forearm

HECKLER & KOCH
SEMIAUTOMATIC RIFLES

HK91 SEMIAUTOMATIC RIFLES
308 Caliber (7.62mm)

All HK91, 93 and 94 series semiautos feature delayed roller-locked bolt system to reduce recoil, cold hammer-forged barrels that provide maximum durability, matte black finish, choice of fixed stock of high-impact plastic or retractable metal stock, diopter sights adjustable for windage and elevation, plus ring front sight with post.

SPECIFICATIONS	A2	A3
Overall length:	40.35″	33.07″
Length of barrel:	17.71″	17.71″
Sight radius:	22.44″	22.44″
Weight w/o magazine:	9.7 lbs.	10.5 lbs.
Weight of 20-round magazine, empty:	9.88 oz.	

Price
HK91 A2 (w/20-round mag., fixed stock, muzzle cap & sling) $746.00
HK91 A3 w/retractable metal stock 879.00
Scope Mount 277.00
HK91 Scope package 1124.00

HK93 SEMIAUTOMATIC RIFLES (not shown)
223 Caliber

SPECIFICATIONS	A2	A3
Overall length:	37.0″	29.92″
Length of barrel:	16.14″	16.14″
Sight radius:	19.09″	19.09″
Weight without magazine:	7.94 lbs.	8.6 lbs.
Weight of 25-round magazine, empty:	8.84 oz.	

Price
HK93 A2 (w/25-round mag., fixed stock, muzzle cap & sling) $746.00
HK93 A3 w/retractable metal stock 879.00
Scope Mount 277.00

HK94 SEMIAUTOMATIC CARBINE
9mm

SPECIFICATIONS	A2	A3
Overall length:	34.59″	27.58″
Barrel length:	16.54″	16.54″
Weight w/o magazine:	6.43 lbs.	7.18 lbs.
Rifling:	6 groove	6 groove
Twist:	10″ R.H.	10″ R.H.

Price
Hk94 A2 (w/fixed stock $746.00
HK94 A3 w/retractable stock 879.00
Prices include 15-round magazine, barrel shroud and assault grip.

INTRATEC SEMIAUTOMATIC PISTOLS

TEC-9
$189.00

Caliber: 9mm Luger/Parabellum
Operation: Closed bolt blowback system
Barrel length: 5″
Weight: 50 oz. unloaded
Magazine capacity: 36 rounds

Weight of magazine: 22 oz. loaded
Sights: Open; fixed front, adjustable rear
Sight radius: 10″
Muzzle velocity: 1200-1400 fps
Finish: Military non-glare blue

TEC-9S (not shown)
$236.00

Caliber: 9mm Luger/Parabellum
Operation: Closed bolt blowback system
Barrel length: 12¹⁄₂″
Weight: 50 oz. unloaded
Magazine capacity: 36 rounds

Safety: Firing pin block safety
Sights: Open; fixed front, adjustable rear
Finish: Stainless steel non-glare

Also available: **TEC-9M** w/3′ barrel, blue finish, 20- round magazine. **Weight:** 44oz. Price: $174.00

IVER JOHNSON CARBINES

MINI TEC-9M (not shown)
$231.95

Caliber: 9mm Luger/Parabellum
Operation: Closed bolt blowback system
Barrel length: 3″
Weight: 44 oz. unloaded

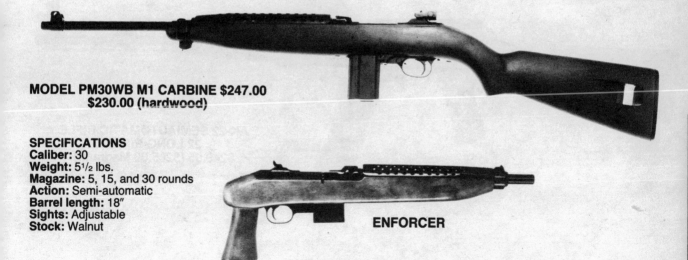

MODEL PM30WB M1 CARBINE $247.00
$230.00 (hardwood)

SPECIFICATIONS
Caliber: 30
Weight: 5¹⁄₂ lbs.
Magazine: 5, 15, and 30 rounds
Action: Semi-automatic
Barrel length: 18″
Sights: Adjustable
Stock: Walnut

ENFORCER

M.A.C. SEMIAUTOMATIC PISTOL

INGRAM M10A1S
9mm or .45 ACP
$399.00

This semiautomatic pistol offers compact firepower coupled with the same integrity as the original Military Armament Corporation's Ingram Model 10 submachine guns. Redesigned Garand-type safety combined with closed bolt operation provide a safe and dependable defensive side arm. Incredibly rugged and functional under adverse weather conditions.

SPECIFICATIONS
Operation: Closed bolt blowback system
Barrel length: 5³/₄"
Overall length: 10¹/₂"
Width: 2"
Height w/magazine: 10¹/₂" (9mm); 12¹/₂" (.45 ACP)
Weight: 6¹/₄ lbs. unloaded
Magazine weight: 1.37 lbs. (32-round mag., 9mm loaded); 2.15 lbs. (30-round mag., .45 ACP loaded)
Magazine capacity: 32 rounds (9mm); 30 rounds (.45 ACP)
Sights: Front, protected post; rear, fixed aperture 100 meters
Safety: Manually operated Garand type located in trigger guard

MITCHELL SEMIAUTOMATIC RIFLES

AK-22 SEMIAUTOMATIC RIFLE
22 LONG RIFLE
$249.95 ($265.00 Magnum)

The AK-22 semiautomatic rifle is a faithful reproduction of the original AK-47 in 22 Long Rifle. It features deluxe forend and wood buttstock, pistol grip, adjustable sights, wide magazine and built-in cleaning rod. Simple takedown.

MOSSBERG RIFLES

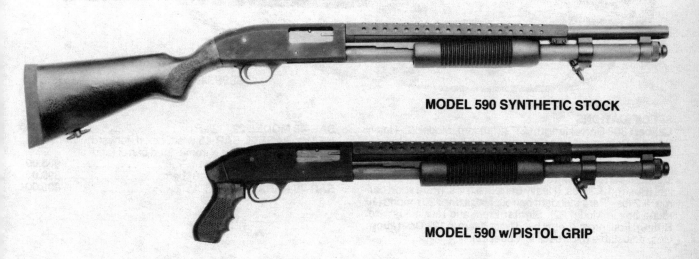

MODEL 590 SYNTHETIC STOCK

MODEL 590 w/PISTOL GRIP

MODEL 590 MILITARY 9-SHOT
$328.95

SPECIFICATIONS
Gauge: 12
Barrel length: 20″
Chamber: 2³/₄″
Finish: Blue
Sight: Bead
Choke: Cylinder Bore

Capacity: 9 shot
Features: Barrel heat shield; bayonet lug; meets MILSPEC 344E

Also available:
Model 590 w/Speed Feed **$361.95**
Model 590 Cruiser 328.95

MODEL 500 BULLPUP 6-SHOT
$394.95

SPECIFICATIONS
Gauge: 12
Barrel length: 18¹/₂″
Choke: Cylinder Bore
Sight: Rifle
Weight: 9¹/₂ lbs.
Overall length: 26¹/₂″

Features: action and trigger group enclosed and protected from exposure to elements; all models equipped w/ventilated barrel shield; rifle type sights protected within molded carrying handle; dual pistol grips; full rubber recoil pad (ready for instant shoulder firing.

Also available:
Model 500 8-Shot w/20″ barrel (28¹/₂″ overall) **$409.95**

SPRINGFIELD ARMORY

MODEL SAR-48
$899.00 (Standard)

SPECIFICATIONS
Caliber: 308 **Barrel length:** 21″ (Standard, Model 22, Heavy Barrel & Para standard barrel); 18″ (Bush & Para short barrel). **Overall length:** 43.3″ (Standard & Model 22); 40.3″ (Bush); 45.3″ (Heavy Barrel); 40.2″ (Para short barrel); 43.2″ (Para standard barrel). **Weight:** 9.5 lbs. (Standard & Model 22); 8.6 lbs. (Bush); 13.23 lbs. (Heavy Barrel); 8.3 lbs. (Para short barrel); 9.2 lbs. (Para standard barrel). **Magazine:** 20 rounds (10 round box in Model 22). **Sights:** Front and rear adjustable. **Rifling:** Four groove, right hand twist, 1 turn in 12″. **Operation:** Gas, adjustable (blowback in Model 22).

SAR-48 MODEL 22 (22 LR) $760.00
HEAVY BARREL SAR-48 w/att. bipod, forward assist cocking handle, chrome-lined barrel (and more) **905.00**
SAR-48 BUSH RIFLE w/18″ barrel **899.00**
SAR-48 PARA MODEL **899.00**

M1 GARAND STANDARD MODEL
$761.00

SPECIFICATIONS
Type: Gas-operated, semiautomatic, clip-fed. **Grade:** Standard "Issue-Grade" w/walnut stock. **Caliber:** 30M2 (30-06) and 308 (7.62mm) **Weight:** 9 lbs. 8 ozs. **Barrel length:** 24″. **Overall length:** 43½″. **Magazine capacity:** 8 rounds. **Stock dimensions:** Length of pull 13″; drop at comb 2″; drop at heel 2½″. **Sights:** Front, military square blade; rear, full click-adjustable aperture.

Also available: National Match Model, **837.00**; Ultra-Match Model, **934.00**; M1 "Tanker" Rifle, **$797.00**.

M1A STANDARD MODEL
$782.00

SPECIFICATIONS
Type: Gas-operated, semiautomatic, clip-loaded, detachable box magazine. **Caliber:** 7.62mm NATO (308 Winchester). **Weight:** 8 lbs. 15 oz. w/empty magazine. **Barrel length:** 22″ w/o flash suppressor. **Overall length:** 44½″. **Magazine capacity:** 5, 10, 20, 25 rounds. **Sights:** Military; square post; full-click adjustable aperture rear. **Sight radius:** 21¹/₁₆″. **Rifling:** 6-groove, right-hand twist; 1 turn in 11″. **Accessories:** Combination muzzle brakeflash suppressor-grenade launcher; bipod; grenade launcher-winter trigger; grenade launcher sight; bayonet; field oiling & cleaning equipment.

Also available: National Match Model **$998.00**; Super Match Model **$1125.00**; M1A-A1 Bush Assault Model **$790.00**

SPRINGFIELD ARMORY

**BERETTA BM-59 STANDARD GRADE
WITH INTEGRAL FOLDING BIPOD
Italian model $1248.00
Nigerian Model $1365.00
Alpine Paratrooper Model $1624.00**

SPECIFICATIONS

Type: Gas-operated, semiautomatic, clip-loaded, detachable box magazine. **Grade:** Standard grade with European walnut stock. **Caliber:** 7.62mm NATO (308 Win.). **Weight:** 9.5 lbs. **Barrel length:** 19.3″. **Overall length:** 43.11″. **Magazine capacity:** 20-round box type. **Rifling:** Right-hand twist, 1 turn in 11.96″. **Sights:** Military; rear aperature; front square post; also direct and indirect grenade launcher sights. **Sight radius:** 21.37″. **Accessories:** Cleaning kits; bayonets; extra magazines; scope mounts; scopes; slings. Also comes with winter trigger, grenade launcher and sights, muzzle tricompensator bipod and 20-round Beretta magazine.

Also available: BM-59 Alpine (w/folding stock) **$1435.00**

**MODEL M-21 SEMIAUTOMATIC SNIPER RIFLE
$2320.00 (w/o Accessories)**

SPECIFICATIONS

Caliber: 7.62 x 51mm NATO. **Magazine:** six 20-round magazines. **Rifling:** 1-in-10 twist standard. **Stock:** glass bedded heavy walnut w/adj. cheekpiece & rubber recoil pad. **Features and Accessories:** folding and removable bipod; knurled shoulder accepts figure-8 style op rod guide; test target supplied; adj. leather military sling; cleaning kit. **Options:** 3.5 x 10 variable power Leupold-Stevens scope and Springfield Armory Third Generation Scope Mount w/two mounting screws.

STEYR-MANNLICHER

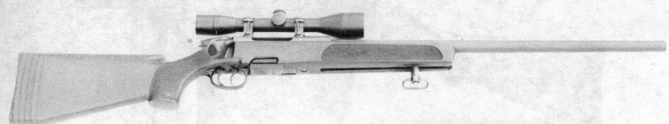

SSG-PII SNIPER RIFLE
$1156.00

The SSG-PII Sniper Rifle features 26-inch heavy match barrel without sights, functional synthetic ABS Cylolac stock.

SPECIFICATIONS
Caliber: 308 Winchester.

STEYR AUG-SA
$889.00

SPECIFICATIONS
Caliber: 223 Rem.
Barrel length: 20″
Overall length: 31″
Weight: 8¹/₂ lbs.
Stock: Synthetic, green
Sights: 1.5X scope, scope and mount form the carrying handle.
Features: Semiautomatic, gas-operated action; can be converted to suit right or left hand shooters (including ejection port). Folding vertical front grip.
Extra barrels: 16″ or 20″ $295.00
             24″ heavy barrel w/folding, adjustable
             bipod. 485.00

UZI
SEMIAUTOMATIC CARBINE

Action Arms' UZI Semiautomatic Carbine, designed by Israeli Army officer Col. Uzi Gal, incorporates modifications of his submachine gun so that it meets the requirements of U.S. Federal regulations.

In appearance the UZI Semiautomatic is virtually identical to the submachine gun, except for a longer barrel. The semiautomatic works from a closed breech with floating firing pin while the submachine gun has an open breech with fixed firing pin. The semiautomatic's 16.1-inch barrel length delivers a muzzle velocity of 1,250 to 1,500 feet per second, depending on type of ammunition used.

Price includes molded styrofoam case, 25-round magazine, carrying sling, 16.1-inch barrel, short display barrel, detailed owner's manual, sight adjustment key.   Conversion kit also available to convert carbine to accept 22LR rimfire cartridges. Kit includes Precision Breech-Block/Bolt assembly, 15-round magazine and safety-keyed barrel.

Also available: **Mini-Carbine. Barrel length: 19.75". Weight: 7.2 lbs. Overall length: 35.75". Price: $698.00.**

SPECIFICATIONS

Caliber: 9mm Parabellum, 41 A.E., or .45 ACP
Operation principle: Blowback, closed breech with floating firing pin
Magazine: Staggered box-type holding 25 or 32 rounds
Safety systems: (1.) Fire selector in position "S" (2.) Pistol grip safety
Sights: Front, "Post" type; rear, L flip type adjustable for 100m (330 ft) and 200m (660 ft)

UZI 9MM SEMIAUTOMATIC CARBINE $698.00

Stock: Folding metal stock
Weight: Empty magazine, 25 round, 200g (7.0 oz); 32 round, 220g (7.8 oz)
Length: (Metal stock folded) 620mm (24.4"); (Metal stock extended) 800mm (31.5")
Barrel length: 410mm (16.1")
Number of lands & grooves: 4; right-hand twist; 1 turn in 10"
*Approx. muzzle velocity: 380–460 m/sec (1250–1500 ft/sec)
*Maximum range: Up to 2000m (2200 yd) at 30° elevation

*Depending upon type of ammunition used. Specifications subject to change without notice

UZI SEMIAUTOMATIC PISTOL

UZI 9mm SEMIAUTOMATIC PISTOL $579.00

Like the 9mm carbine, the UZI 9mm semiautomatic pistol features the same simplicity of design, rugged reliability, perfect balance and numerous safety features. Price includes 20-round magazine, sight adjustment key, molded carrying case and detailed instruction manual. Imported by Action Arms Ltd.

SPECIFICATIONS

Operation principle: Blowback; closed breech with floating firing pin
Type of fire: Semiautomatic only
Ammo: 9mm Parabellum or 45 ACP
Safety systems: Fire selector in position "S"; grip safety
Sights: Front post-type; rear open-type, both adjustable for windage and elevation; twin white dots
Barrel length: 4.5" (115 mm)
Overall length: 9.45" (240 mm)
Rifling: 4 grooves; right-hand twist, 1 turn in 10" (254 mm)
Muzzle velocity: 1100 fps (335 m/sec)
Weight: Unloaded, 3.8 lbs. (1.73 kg)
Magazine weights: loaded, 20-round, 14.4 oz. (410 g); 25-round, 17.3 oz. (490 g); 32-round, 21.2 oz. (600 g)

VALMET
SEMIAUTOMATIC RIFLES

**VALMET M76
SEMIAUTOMATIC RIFLE**

Based on its famous assault rifle, Valmet offers this Finnish-made semiautomatic version with a choice of wooden, synthetic, or folding-steel stock.

The M76 is a lightweight infantry-based weapon in .223, .308 and 7.62 × 39 calibers. It is built to withstand rough handling, high firing loads, and all kinds of terrain and climate. It can be field-stripped without tools. The weapon is gas-operated and automatically ejects spent cartridges. The firing rate is 20 to 30 rounds per minute. External moving parts, besides the trigger and bolt, include the cocking handle and the selector lever, both on the right side. Barrel length is 16³/₄″ (also available in 20¹/₂″).

The rear leaf peep-sight has a range adjustment and, when

flipped forward, becomes a night sight with a luminous dot on either side of a V-notch. The adjustable front tunnel-guard post sight also turns to convert to a night sight with a luminous aiming dot.

The M76 is equipped with sling loops, a bayonet mount on the flash suppressor, a 15-, 20-, or 30-round magazine, and comes with a cleaning kit. An optional adapter cover, to replace the standard leaf-sight cover, is available to accept any one-inch scope.

Price:
M76 with wooden or synthetic stock $699.00
M76 with folding stock 724.00

**M78 SEMIAUTOMATIC RIFLE
$849.00**

A rugged and reliable military and police weapon, the M78 semiauto has a heavy barrel with bipod for increased stability, the Kalashnikov gas-operated mechanism, special night sight. Combat proven.

SPECIFICATIONS
Caliber: 308
Barrel length: 24¹/₈″
Overall length: 43¹/₈″
Weight: 11 lbs.
Stock: wood
Magazines: 20 round
Sights: adj. front in tunnelguard; 100 to 600 meter adj. rear sight (folding leaf w/peep); night sight

Black Powder Guns

FOR ADDRESSES AND PHONE
NUMBERS OF MANUFACTURERS AND
DISTRIBUTORS INCLUDED IN THIS
SECTION, SEE *DIRECTORY OF
MANUFACTURERS AND SUPPLIERS*

ARMSPORT

TRYON TRAILBLAZER

The only mass-produced muzzleloading back-action lock hunting and target rifle. The all-steel working parts are heat treated to proper hardness; all others decorative steel furniture is polished and bright blued to complement the select-grained European walnut stock. The chrome-lined barrel is available in 28- or 32-inch lengths, with both a folding leaf sight (windage and elevation adjustable) and a regular sight for primitive shooting.

Price (finished): $435.00 (Models 5128, 5129 & 5130)
485.00 (Engraved Model)

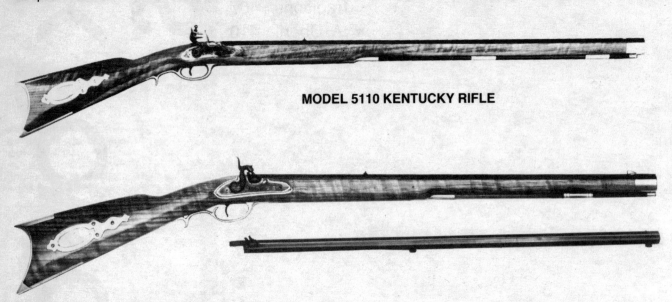

MODEL 5110 KENTUCKY RIFLE

MODEL 5115
KENTUCKY RIFLE-SHOTGUN COMBINATION

Armsport's Kentucky rifle-shotgun combination has been designed with a 28-inch grooved rifle barrel and a 28-inch 20-gauge smoothbore shotgun barrel. This model also boasts a "one-piece" select grain walnut stock, with long barrels rifled for accuracy and proof-tested for safety. All brass fittings—patch box, ferrules, butt plate—are polished to a bright finish. Kentucky rifle kits are completely inletted and pre-assembled to assure perfect wood-to-metal fitting and no missing parts.

KENTUCKY RIFLE SPECIFICATIONS

Model No. Finished	Model No. Kit	Cal.	Description	Ignition	Price (finished)
5108	5208	45	Kentucky Rifle Chr. Lined	P	$242.50
5108V		36	Kentucky Rifle	P	242.50
5109	5209	50	Kentucky Rifle Chr. Lined	P	242.50
5110	5210	45	Kentucky Rifle Chr. Lined	F	255.00
5110A	5210A	50	Kentucky Rifle Chr. Lined	F	255.00
5111		45	Deluxe Kentucky Rifle	P	300.00
5115		50/20	Kentucky Rifle & Shotgun Com. 2 Barrel Set	P	295.00
5115C		45/20	Kentucky Rifle & Shotgun Com. 2 Barrel Set	P	295.00

ARMSPORT

HAWKEN MODEL 5104 (50 Cal.)

HAWKEN MODELS 5101/5102/5103

HAWKEN RIFLE KITS WITH CHROME-LINED BARRELS

Each of these rifle-shotgun combinations is available with a 50-caliber rifle barrel and a 20-gauge shotgun barrel—two guns in one, a game shooting rifle that converts in less than 10 seconds to a shotgun in three simple steps. The smooth-bore Hawken shotgun barrels have been manufactured with the same care as the Italian trap and skeet barrels. The walnut stocks have been sanded, hand-rubbed and given a high-luster finish. All brass parts have been fitted exactly and highly polished. Rear sights are adjustable for windage and elevation. All Hawken rifles and kits are available in 45, 50, 54 and 58 calibers.

Hawken Rifles	Hawken Kits	Cal.	Description	Ignition	Price (finished)
5101	5201	45	Hawken Rifle	P	$250.00
5102	5202	50	Hawken Rifle	P	250.00
5103	5203	54	Hawken Rifle	P	250.00
5103C	5203C	58	Hawken Rifle	P	250.00
5104	5204	50	Hawken Rifle	F	275.00
5104B	5204B	54	Hawken Rifle	F	275.00

DOUBLE BARREL SHOTGUNS
(MODEL 5124 & 5125)

These hook breech 12-gauge double-barrel muzzleloading shotguns combine English tradition with modern finished wood and metal. Checkered select-grain walnut stocks with bright blued chrome-lined barrels combine with the finely en-graved lock plate to make these rugged, well-balanced shot-guns. Available also in 10 gauge.

Price (finished): $450.00 (Model 5124)
500.00 (Model 5125/10 gauge)

ARMSPORT
REPLICA REVOLVERS

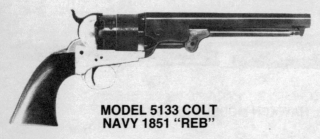

MODEL 5133 COLT
NAVY 1851 "REB"

A modern replica of a Confederate Percussion Revolver. It has a polished brass frame, a rifled blued barrel and polished walnut grips. **Price: $110.00**

MODEL 5136 COLT
NAVY 1851 STEEL

This authentic reproduction of the Colt Navy Revolver, which helped shape the history of America, features a rifled barrel, blued steel frame, engraved cylinder, polished brass trigger guard and walnut grips. **Price: $150.00**

MODEL 5120 REMINGTON
ARMY 44 CALIBER
STEEL REVOLVER

One of the most accurate cap and ball revolvers of the 1880's. Its rugged steel frame and top strap made this the favorite of all percussion cap revolvers. **Price: $180** (w/brass frame **$115.00)**

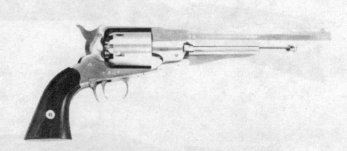

MODEL 5138 STAINLESS STEEL
REMINGTON ARMY 44 CALIBER

This stainless steel version of the 44-caliber New Remington Army Revolver is made for the shooter who seeks the best. Its stainless steel frame assures lasting good looks. **Price: $260.00**

MODEL 5139
1860 COLT ARMY

This authentic reproduction offers the same balance and ease of handling for fast shooting as the original 1860 model. **Price: $160.00**

Replica Revolvers Description	Model No. Finished	Barrel Length	Caliber	Recommended Ball Dia.
New Remington Army Stainless Steel	5138	8"	44	.451
New Remington Army	5120	8"	44	.451
1851 Navy Reb Brass	5133	7"	36	.376
1851 Navy Reb Brass	5134	7"	44	.451
1851 Navy Steel	5135	7"	36	.376
1851 Navy Steel	5136	7"	44	.451
1860 Colt Army*	5139	8"	44	.451

ARMSPORT

COLLECTOR'S PREMIUM REVOLVERS
.44 CALIBER REMINGTON, COLT ARMY & COLT NAVY

**MODEL 5152 ENGRAVED REMINGTON
OR COLT ARMY .44 CALIBER
$250.00 ($275.00 COLT ARMY)**

**MODEL 5153 ENGRAVED COLT ARMY
$275.00**

**MODEL 5154 ENGRAVED COLT NAVY
$250.00**

Also available:
Model 5138 Remington Army SS.... **$260.00** (Kit **$158.00**)
Model 5150 1860 Colt Army SS...... **265.00** (Kit **$139.00**)
Model 5133/5134 1851 Colt Navy Brass
(36 & 44 Cal.) .... **$110.00** (Kit **$99.00**)
Model 5135/5136 1851 Colt Navy Steel
(36 & 44 Cal.) .... **$150.00** (Kit **$135.00**)

CVA

SQUIRREL RIFLE
Finished: Percussion $211.95 (left hand: $223.95)
Kit: Percussion $150.95 Flintlock $153.95

Ignition: Color case-hardened and engraved lockplate; bridle, fly, screw-adjustable sear engagement; authentic V-type mainspring
Caliber: 32 percussion or flintlock
Stock: Select hardwood
Barrel: 25″ octagonal; 11/16″ across flats; hooked breech for easy take down and cleaning; rifling, one turn in 48″; 8 lands, deep grooves; blued steel
Overall length: 40³/₄″

Weight: 5 lbs. 12 oz.
Trigger: Double set (will fire set or unset)
Front sight: Dovetail, beaded blade
Rear sight: Fully adjustable, open hunting-style dovetail
Finish: Solid brass butt plate, trigger guard, wedge plates and thimbles
Accessories: Stainless steel nipple or flash hole liner; aluminum ramrod with brass tips, cleaning jag
NEW—SQUIRREL RIFLE HUNTING COMBO KIT (32 and 45 caliber percussion): **$160.95**

BLAZER II RIFLE (50 Caliber Perc.)
Finished: $95.95
Kit: $73.95

Barrel: 24¹/₂″ octagonal, 11/16″ across flats; in-line breech and nipple; deeply grooved custom rifling, one turn in 66″
Overall length: 43¹/₂″
Weight: 5 lbs. 12 oz.

Sights: Brass blade (front); fixed semi-buckhorn (rear)
Stock: Select hardwood with pistol grip
Lock: Straight-through ignition, removable; screw-adjustable sear engagement

ST. LOUIS HAWKEN RIFLE (50 Cal. Perc.) (not shown)
Finished: $189.95
Kit: $145.95

Barrel: 28″ octagonal 15/16″ across flats; hooked breech; rifling one turn in 66″, 8 lands and deep grooves
Overall length: 44″
Weight: 7 lbs. 13 oz.
Sights: Dovetail, beaded blade (front); adjustable open hunting-style dovetail (rear)

Stock: Select hardwood with beavertail cheekpiece
Triggers: Double set; fully adjustable trigger pull
Finish: Solid brass wedge plates, nose cap, ramrod thimbles, trigger guard and patch box

CVA

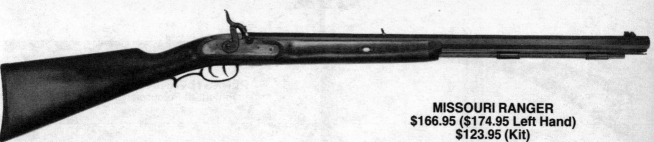

MISSOURI RANGER
$166.95 ($174.95 Left Hand)
$123.95 (Kit)

Caliber: 50 percussion
Barrel length: 28″ octagonal
Rifling: 1 turn in 66″; 8 lands, deep grooves; ¹⁵/₁₆″ across flats; hooked breech for easy takedown
Overall length: 44″
Weight: 7 lbs. 8oz.
Stock: Select hardwood

Triggers: Double set (will fire set and unset)
Sights: Brass blade in front; fixed semi-buckhorn in rear
Finish: Blackened nose cap, trigger guard, black rubber butt plate, thimbles and wedge plates
Lock: Color case hardened and engraved
Features: bridle, fly, screw-adj. sear engagement; v-type mainspring

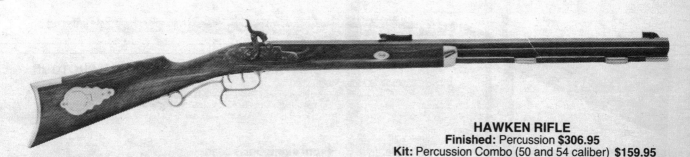

HAWKEN RIFLE
Finished: Percussion **$306.95**
Kit: Percussion Combo (50 and 54 caliber) **$159.95**

Caliber: 50 and 54 percussion or flintlock
Ignition: Color case-hardened; bridle, fly, screw adjustable sear engagement and authentic V-type mainspring; two lock screws
Barrel: 28″ octagon; rifled one turn in 66″; 1″ across the flats, barrel tenon, hooked breech
Overall length: 44″
Weight: 7 lbs. 15 oz.
Finish: Solid-brass patchbox, wedge plates, nose cap, ramrod thimbles, trigger guard and butt plate; blued steel finish

Triggers: Double set; will fire set and unset; fully adjustable for trigger pull
Sights: Beaded blade front sight; fully adjustable dovetail open hunting rear sight
Stock: Select walnut with fully formed beavertail cheekpiece
Accessories: Stainless steel nipple or flash hole liner; hardwood ramrod with brass tips and cleaning jag; kits available

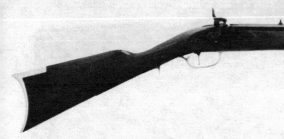

KENTUCKY RIFLE
Finished: Percussion **$217.95**
Percussion Kit $132.95
Flintlock Kit $141.95

Ignition: Engraved color case-hardened; screw adjustable sear engagement; V-type mainspring
Caliber: 45 percussion or flintlock
Barrel: 33¹/₂″, rifled, octagon
Overall length: 48″
Weight: 7 lbs. 4 oz.

Finish: Deep-luster blue, polished brass hardware
Sights: Kentucky-style front and rear
Stock: Dark, walnut tone
Accessories: Brass-tipped, hardwood ramrod, stainless steel nipple or flash hole liner

CVA

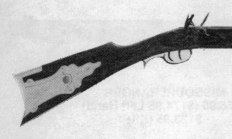

PENNSYLVANIA LONG RIFLE
Finished: Percussion $306.95

Ignition: Color case-hardened and engraved lockplate; bridle, fly, screw-adjustable sear engagement; authentic V-type mainspring
Caliber: 50 percussion or flintlock
Stock: Select walnut
Barrel: 40″ octagonal, ⁷/₈″ across flats; rifling 8 lands, deep grooves
Length: 55³/₄″ overall

Weight: 8 lbs. 3 oz.
Trigger: Double set (will fire set or unset)
Rear sight: Fixed semi-buckhorn, dovetail
Finish: Brass butt plate, patchbox, trigger guard, thimbles and nose cap
Accessories: Stainless steel nipple or flash hole liner; hardwood ramrod and brass tips

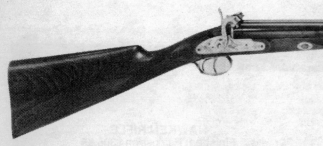

BRITTANY 12 GAUGE PERCUSSION SHOTGUN
Finished: $293.95
Kit: $223.95

Ignition: Polished steel and engraved lock plate; bridle, fly, screw-adjustable sear engagement; authentic V-type mainspring
Gauge: 12
Stock: Select hardwood, checkered (kits not checkered)
Barrel: 28″ round, double barrel, smoothbore; blued steel; hooked breech for easy take down
Length: 44¹/₄″ overall
Weight: 7 lbs. 7 oz.
Triggers: Double

Front sight: Brass bead
Finish: Polished steel wedge plates, trigger guard, triggers, tang, lock and hammers; lock, hammers, tang and trigger guard engraved
Accessories: Stainless steel nipple, wooden ramrod with brass tip

Also available: **BRITTANY II. 410 SHOTGUN. Overall length:** 38″. **Barrel length:** 24″. **Weight** 6lbs. 4oz. **Price:** $159.95 (Kit $114.95)

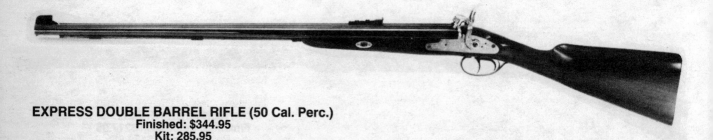

EXPRESS DOUBLE BARREL RIFLE (50 Cal. Perc.)
Finished: $344.95
Kit: 285.95

Barrels: Two laser aligned tapered 28″ round; hooked breech; rifling, 1 turn in 48″
Overall length: 44¹/₄″
Weight: 9 lbs. 3 oz.
Locks: Plate is color hardened and engraved; includes bridle, fly, screw-adjustable sear engagement
Triggers: Double, color case hardened

Sights: Fully adjustable for windage and elevation, hunting style (rear); dovetail, beaded blade (front)
Stock: Select hardwood
Finish: Polished steel wedge plates; color case hardened locks, hammers, triggers and trigger guard; engraved locks, hammers and tang

CVA

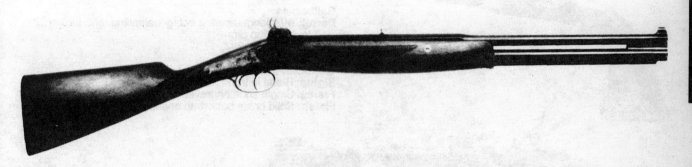

DOUBLE BARREL CARBINE
$433.95

Caliber: 50 Over/Under
Barrel length: 26″
Overall length: 41¹/₄″
Twist: 1 in 66″; 8 lands & grooves
Features: Checkered English style straight grip & beavertail forestock
Weight: 8 lbs. 8 oz.

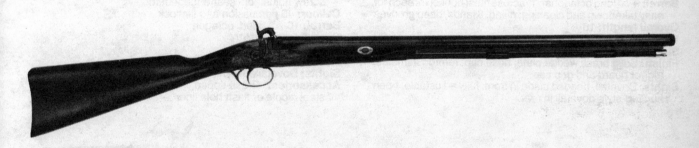

TRAPPER SHOTGUN
$216.95 ($179.95 Kit)

Gauge: 12
Barrell length: 28″ round
Stock: Select hardwood; English style straight grip
Trigger: Early style steel
Sights: Brass bead in front
Finish: Solid brass wedge plates; color-hardened lock plates, hammer, black trigger guard and tang
Features: Stainless steel nipple, wooden ramrod w/brass tip
Chokes: Interchangeable Improved, Modified and Full

CVA

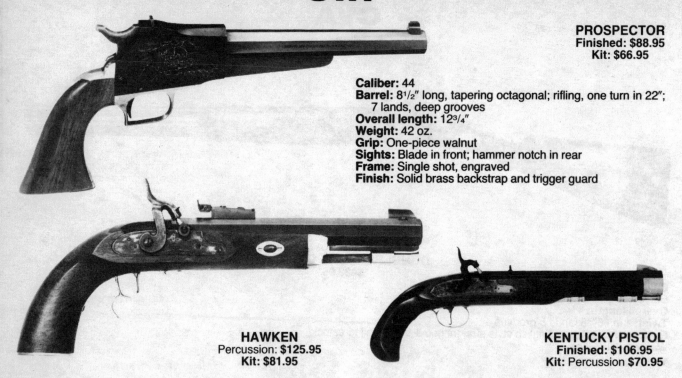

PROSPECTOR
Finished: $88.95
Kit: $66.95

Caliber: 44
Barrel: 8¹/₂″ long, tapering octagonal; rifling, one turn in 22″;
  7 lands, deep grooves
Overall length: 12³/₄″
Weight: 42 oz.
Grip: One-piece walnut
Sights: Blade in front; hammer notch in rear
Frame: Single shot, engraved
Finish: Solid brass backstrap and trigger guard

HAWKEN
Percussion: $125.95
Kit: $81.95

KENTUCKY PISTOL
Finished: $106.95
Kit: Percussion $70.95

Caliber: 50 caliber percussion or flintlock
Barrel: 9³/₄″ long octagonal; 1″ across flats; hooked breech for
  easy takedown and cleaning; rifling, 8 lands, deep grooves
Overall length: 16¹/₂″
Weight: 50 oz.
Stock: Select walnut
Finish: Solid brass wedge plate, nose cap, ramrod thimbles,
  trigger guard and grip cap
Sights: Dovetail, beaded blade in front; fully adjustable, open
  hunting-style dovetail in rear

Ignition: Engraved, color-case hardened percussion lock,
  screw adjustable sear engagement
Caliber: 45 percussion and flintlock
Barrel: 10¹/₄″, rifled, octagon
Overall length: 15¹/₄″
Weight: 40 oz.
Finish: Blued barrel, brass hardware
Sights: Dovetailed Kentucky front and rear
Accessories: Brass-tipped, hardwood ramrod; stainless
  steel nipple or flash hole liner

COLONIAL PISTOL
Finished: $82.95
Kit: Percussion $55.95

PHILADELPHIA DERRINGER
Finished: $70.95
Kit: $39.95

Ignition: Engraved, color case-hardened lock
Caliber: 45 (451 bore) percussion
Barrel: 6³/₄″, rifled, octagon
Overall length: 12³/₄″
Weight: 31 oz.
Finish: Case-hardened lock; blued barrel; brass hardware
Sights: Dovetail rear; brass blade front
Stock: Dark, walnut tone
Accessories: Steel ramrod, stainless steel nipple; kits avail-
  able for percussion and flintlock

Ignition: Color case-hardened and engraved, coil-spring
  back-action lock
Caliber: 45 percussion
Barrel: 3¹/₄″ rifled
Overall length: 7¹/₈″
Weight: 16 oz.
Finish: Brass hardware; blued barrel
Stock: Walnut toned
Accessories: Stainless steel nipple

CVA

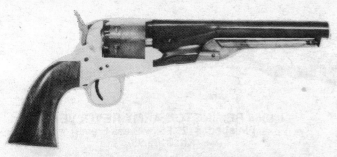

1861 COLT NAVY BRASS FRAMED REVOLVER
Finished: $105.95
Kit: $90.95

Caliber: 44
Barrel length: 7¹/₂″ rounded; creeping style
Weight: 44 oz.
Cylinder: 6-shot, engraved
Sights: Blade front; hammer notch rear
Finish: Solid brass frame, trigger guard and backstrap; blued barrel and cylinder
Grip: One-piece walnut

Also available in steel frame: **$154.95 ($129.95** Kit)

1851 COLT NAVY REVOLVER KIT
Finished: $104.95
Kit: $87.95

Caliber: 36
Barrel length: 7¹/₂″ octagonal; hinged-style loading lever
Overall length: 13″
Weight: 44 oz.
Cylinder: 6-shot, engraved
Sights: Post front; hammer notch rear
Grip: One-piece walnut
Finish: Solid brass frame, trigger guard and backtrap; blued barrel and cylinder; color case-hardened loading lever and hammer

COLT SHERIFF'S MODEL/REVOLVER
$107.95 ($92.95 Kit)

Caliber: 36
Barrel length: 5¹/₂″ (rounded w/creeping style loading lever)
Overall length: 11¹/₂″
Weight: 40¹/₂ oz.
Cylinder: 6-shot semi-fluted
Grip: One-piece walnut
Sight: Hammer notch in rear
Finish: Solid brass frame, trigger guard and backstrap

Also available Engraved Nickel Plated Model: **$210.00** (w/ matching flask)

1860 COLT ARMY REVOLVER
Finished: $152.95
Kit: $137.95

Caliber: 44
Barrel length: 8″ rounded; creeping-style loading lever
Overall length: 13″
Weight: 44 oz.
Cylinder: 6-shot, engraved and rebated
Sights: Blade front; hammer notch rear
Grip: One-piece walnut
Finish: Solid brass trigger guard; blued barrel and cylinder with color case-hardened loading lever, hammer and frame

CVA

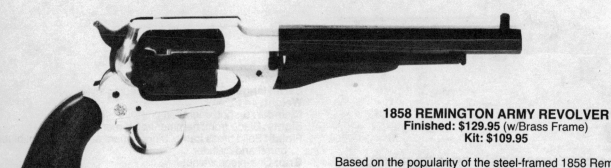

1858 REMINGTON ARMY REVOLVER
Finished: $129.95 (w/Brass Frame)
Kit: $109.95

Based on the popularity of the steel-framed 1858 Remington Army (above), CVA introduces a brass-framed addition to its revolver and revolver kit line. The same design that combines a dependable one-piece now as it was in 1858. Specifications are the same as steel model, except for solid brass frame, trigger guard and backstrap.
Also available in steel frame: **$159.95 ($139.95** Kit)

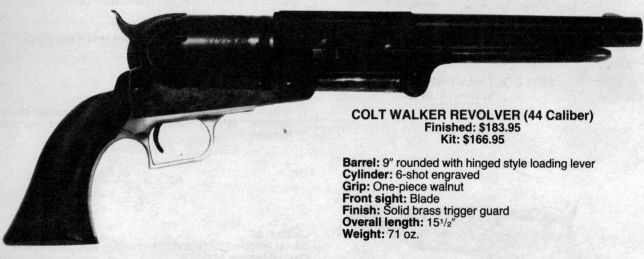

COLT WALKER REVOLVER (44 Caliber)
Finished: $183.95
Kit: $166.95

Barrel: 9″ rounded with hinged style loading lever
Cylinder: 6-shot engraved
Grip: One-piece walnut
Front sight: Blade
Finish: Solid brass trigger guard
Overall length: 15¹/₂″
Weight: 71 oz.

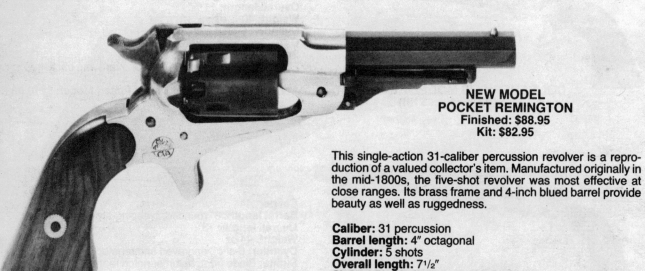

NEW MODEL POCKET REMINGTON
Finished: $88.95
Kit: $82.95

This single-action 31-caliber percussion revolver is a reproduction of a valued collector's item. Manufactured originally in the mid-1800s, the five-shot revolver was most effective at close ranges. Its brass frame and 4-inch blued barrel provide beauty as well as ruggedness.

Caliber: 31 percussion
Barrel length: 4″ octagonal
Cylinder: 5 shots
Overall length: 7¹/₂″
Sights: Post in front; groove in frame in rear
Weight: 15¹/₂ oz.
Finish: Solid brass frame

DIXIE

DIXIE NAVY REVOLVER
Plain Model $85.00
Engraved Model $97.50

This 36-caliber revolver was a favorite of the officers of the Civil War. Although called a Navy type, it is somewhat misnamed since many more of the Army personnel used it. Made in Italy; uses .376 mold or ball to fit and number 11 caps. Blued steel barrel and cylinder with brass frame.

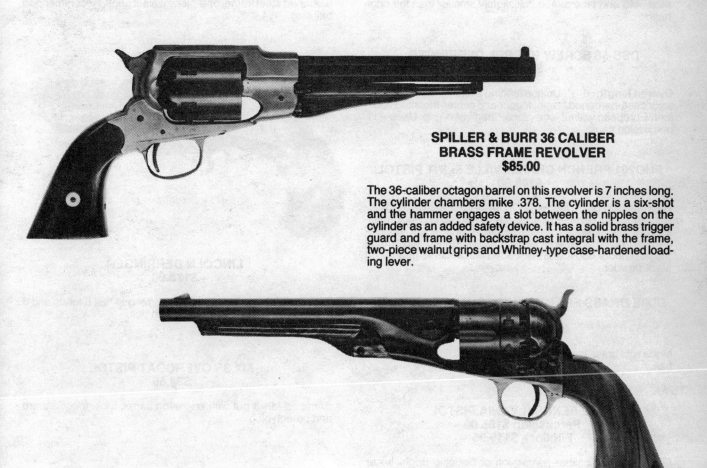

SPILLER & BURR 36 CALIBER BRASS FRAME REVOLVER
$85.00

The 36-caliber octagon barrel on this revolver is 7 inches long. The cylinder chambers mike .378. The cylinder is a six-shot and the hammer engages a slot between the nipples on the cylinder as an added safety device. It has a solid brass trigger guard and frame with backstrap cast integral with the frame, two-piece walnut grips and Whitney-type case-hardened loading lever.

"WYATT EARP" REVOLVER
$115.00

This 45-caliber revolver has a 12-inch octagon rifled barrel; cylinder is rebated. Highly polished brass frame, backstrap and trigger guard. The barrel and cylinder have a deep blue luster finish. Hammer, trigger, and loading lever are case-hardened. Walnut grips. Recommended ball size is .451.

DIXIE 1860 ARMY REVOLVER
$135.00

The Dixie 1860 Army has a half-fluted cylinder and its chamber diameter is .447. Use .451 round ball mold to fit this 8-inch barrel revolver. Cut for shoulder stock.

DIXIE

RHO200 WALKER REVOLVER
$185.00

This 4 1/2-pound, 44-caliber pistol is the largest ever made. Backstrap and guard are brass with Walker-type rounded-to-frame walnut grips; all other parts are blued. Chambers measure .445 and take a .450 ball slightly smaller than the originals.

RHO301 THIRD MODEL DRAGOON
$185.00

This engraved-cylinder, 4 1/2-pounder is a reproduction of the last model of Colt's 44 caliber "horse" revolvers. Barrel measures 7 3/8 inches, 1/8 inch shorter than the original; color case-hardened steel frame, one-piece walnut grips. Recommended ball size: .454.

DSB-58 SCREW BARREL DERRINGER
$84.00

Overall length: 6 1/2". Unique loading system; sheath trigger, color case-hardened frame, trigger and center-mounted hammer; European walnut, one-piece, "bag"-type grip. Uses #11 percussion caps.

FHO201 FRENCH CHARLEVILLE FLINT PISTOL
$140.00

Reproduction of the Model 1777 Cavalry, Revolutionary War-era pistol. Has reversed frizzen spring; forend and lock housing are all in one; case-hardened, round-faced, double-throated hammer; walnut stock; case-hardened frizzen and trigger; shoots .680 round ball loaded with about 40 grains FFg black powder.

LINCOLN DERRINGER
$173.00

This 41-caliber, 2-inch browned barrel gun has 8 lands and 8 grooves and will shoot a .400 patch ball.

DIXIE BRASS FRAMED "HIDEOUT" DERRINGER
Plain $49.95
Engraved $59.95

Made with brass frame and walnut grips and fires a .395 round ball.

DIXIE PENNSYLVANIA PISTOL
Percussion $105.00
Flintlock $119.95

Available in 44-caliber percussion or flintlock. Bright luster blued barrel measures 10 inches long; rifled, 7/8-inch octagon, takes .430 ball; barrel held in place with a steel wedge and tang screw; brass front and rear sights. The brass trigger guard, thimbles, nose cap, wedge plates and side plates are highly polished. Locks are fine quality with early styling. Plates measure 4 3/4 inches × 7/8 inch. Percussion hammer is engraved and both plates are left in the white. Flint is an excellent style lock with the gooseneck hammer having an early wide thumb piece. Stock is walnut stained and has a wide bird-head-type grip.

MX 3S OVERCOAT PISTOL
$34.50

Same as MX 3 but with engraved barrel, lock, trigger guard and breech plug.

ABILENE DERRINGER
$65.00

An all-steel version of Dixie's brass-framed derringers. The 2 1/2-inch, 41-caliber barrel is finished in a deep blue black; frame and hammer are case-hardened. Bore is rifled with 6 lands and grooves. Uses a tightly patched .395 round ball and 15 or 20 grains of FFFg powder. Walnut grips. Comes with wood presentation case.

DIXIE

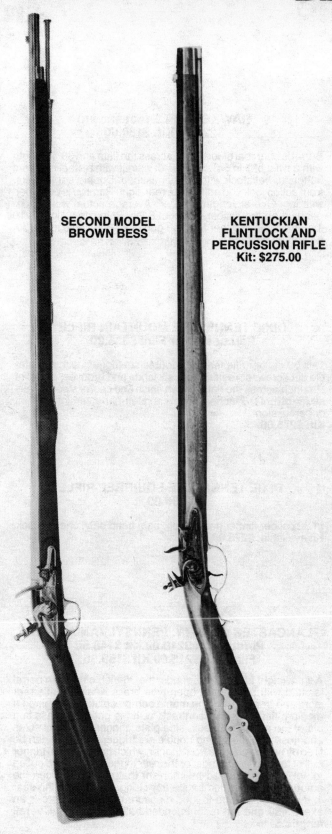

SECOND MODEL BROWN BESS

KENTUCKIAN FLINTLOCK AND PERCUSSION RIFLE Kit: $275.00

SECOND MODEL BROWN BESS MUSKET
$349.00

This 74-caliber Brown Bess has a 41³/₄-inch smoothbore barrel that takes a .715 round ball. In keeping with the traditional musket, it has brass furniture on a walnut-stained stock. The lock is marked "Tower" and has the crown with the "GR" underneath. Barrel, lock and ramrod are left bright.
Kit: $275.00

THE KENTUCKIAN FLINTLOCK AND PERCUSSION RIFLE
Flintlock $185.00
Percussion $175.00

This 45-caliber rifle has a 33¹/₂-inch blued octagon barrel that is ¹³/₁₆ inch across the flats. The bore is rifled with 6 lands and grooves of equal width and about .006 inch deep. Land-to-land diameter is .453 with groove-to-groove diameter at. 465. Ball size ranges from .445 to .448. The rifle has a brass blade front sight and a steel open rear sight. The Kentuckian is furnished with brass butt plate, trigger guard, patch box, side plate, thimbles and nose cap plus case-hardened and engraved lock plate. Highly polished and finely finished stock in European walnut. **Overall length:** 48″. **Weight:** Approx. 6¹/₄ lbs.

DIXIE DOUBLE BARREL MAGNUM MUZZLE LOADING SHOTGUN (not shown)
$299.00

A full 12-gauge, high-quality, double-barreled percussion shotgun with 30-inch browned barrels. Will take the plastic shot cups for better patterns. Bores are choked modified and full. Lock, barrel tang and trigger are case-hardened in a light gray color and are nicely engraved. Also available: **10 gauge Magnum,** double-barrel-choke cylinder bored, otherwise same specs as above: **$365.00.** In **12 gauge: $325.00.**

DIXIE

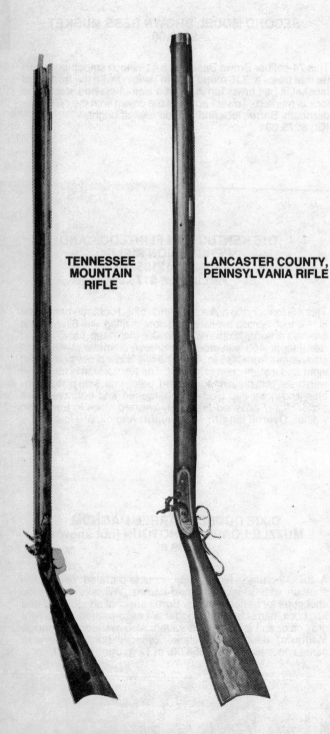

TENNESSEE MOUNTAIN RIFLE

LANCASTER COUNTY, PENNSYLVANIA RIFLE

HAWKEN RIFLE (not shown)
$225.00 Kit: $180.00

Barrel is charcoal blued, $^{15}/_{16}$" across the flats and 30" in length with a twist of 1 in 64". Stock is of walnut with a steel crescent buttplate, halfstock with brass nosecap. Double set triggers, front action lock and adjustable rear sight. Ramrod is equipped with jag. Overall length is 46$^1/_2$". Average actual weight, depending on the caliber, is about 8 lbs. Shipping weight is 10 lbs. Available in either finished gun or kit. Available in 45, 50, 54 and 58 calibers.

DIXIE TENNESSEE MOUNTAIN RIFLE
Percussion or Flint $335.00

This 50-caliber rifle features double-set triggers with adjustable set screw, bore rifled with six lands and grooves, barrel of $^{15}/_{16}$ inch across the flats, brown finish and cherry stock. **Overall length:** 41$^1/_2$ inches. Right- and left-hand versions in flint or percussion.
Kit: $275.00

DIXIE TENNESSEE SQUIRREL RIFLE
$335.00

In 32 caliber flint or percussion, right hand only, cherry stock. Kit available: **$275.00**

LANCASTER COUNTY, PENNSYLVANIA RIFLE
Percussion $210.00 Kit $148.50
Flintlock $215.00 Kit $159.95

A lightweight at just 7$^1/_2$ pounds, the 36-inch blued rifle barrel is fitted with a standard open-type brass Kentucky rifle rear sight and front blade. The maple one-piece stock is stained a medium darkness that contrasts with the polished brass butt plate, toe plate, patchbox, side plate, trigger guard, thimbles and nose cap. Featuring double-set triggers, the rifle can be fired by pulling only the front trigger, which has a normal trigger pull of four to five pounds; or the rear trigger can first be pulled to set a spring-loaded mechanism that greatly reduces the amount of pull needed for the front trigger to kick off the sear in the lock. The land-to-land measurement of the bore is an exact .450 and the recommended ball size is .445. **Overall length:** 51$^1/_2$".

DIXIE

PRO401 MISSISSIPPI RIFLE
$280.00

Commonly called the U.S. Rifle Model 1841, this Italian-made replica is rifled in a 58 caliber to use a round ball or a Minie ball; 3 grooves and regulation sights; solid brass furniture; case-hardened lock.

WINCHESTER '73 CARBINE
$495.00
ENGRAVED WINCHESTER '73 RIFLE
$550.00

This 44-40 caliber gun can use modern or black powder cartridges. **Overall length:** 39". **Barrel:** 20" round. Its full tubular magazine will hold 11 shots. The walnut forearm and buttstock complement the high-luster bluing of the all steel parts such as the frame, barrel, magazine, loading lever and butt plate.

Comes with the trap door in the butt for the cleaning rod; leaf rear sight and blade front sight. This carbine is marked "Model 1873" on the tang and caliber "44-40" on the brass carrier block.

WESSON RIFLE
$395.00

The lock work for this rifle is housed in a steel frame or receiver. Barrel is a heavy 1 1/8" × .50 caliber measuring 28" and fitted with a false muzzle. Two-piece European walnut stock is hand checkered at wrist and forearm. Barrel and underrib are finished in bright blue; receiver is case colored. Double set triggers and adjustable rear sight. Overall length is 43 1/2". Weight is 10 1/4 lbs.

BUFFALO HUNTER
$230.00

This sporterized version of Dixie's Italian-made Zouave uses a .570 ball or bullet and has the same 58-caliber rifled bore. Features walnut half-stock, checkering around the wrist, case-hardened lock, fine blued barrel and brass patchbox.

EUROARMS OF AMERICA

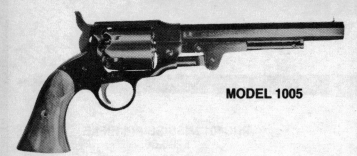

MODEL 1005

ROGERS & SPENCER ARMY REVOLVER
Model 1006 (Target)
$221.00

Caliber: 44; takes .451 round or conical lead balls; #11 percussion cap
Weight: 47 oz.
Barrel length: 7½"
Overall length: 13¾"
Finish: High-gloss blue; flared walnut grip; solid-frame design; precision-rifled barrel
Sights: Rear fully adjustable for windage and elevation; ramp front sight

ROGERS & SPENCER REVOLVER
Model 1007, London Gray
$233.00

Revolver is the same as Model 1005, except for London Gray finish, which is heat treated and buffed for rust resistance; same recommended ball size and percussion caps.

NEW MODEL ARMY REVOLVER
Model 1020
$177.00

This model is equipped with blued steel frame, brass trigger guard in 44 caliber.

Weight: 40 oz.
Barrel length: 8"
Overall length: 14¾"
Finish: Deep luster blue rifled barrel; polished walnut stock; brass trigger guard.
Model 1010: Same as Model 1020 except with 6½" barrel and in 36 caliber: $177.00

NEW MODEL ARMY
Model 1030 (Target)
$200.00

Caliber: 44
Weight: 41 oz.
Barrel: 8"; octagonal, blued, rifled
Overall length: 14¾"
Sights: Rear sight adjustable for windage and elevation; ramp front sight
Finish: Deep luster blue; rifled barrel; polished walnut stock; brass trigger guard

ROGERS & SPENCER REVOLVER
Model 1005
$205.00

Caliber: 44 Percussion; #11 percussion cap
Barrel length: 7½"
Sights: Integral rear sight notch groove in frame; brass truncated cone front sight
Overall length: 13¾"
Weight: 47 oz.
Finish: High-gloss blue; flared walnut grip; solid-frame design; precision-rifled barrel
Recommended ball diameter: .451 round or conical, pure lead

MODEL 1006

MODEL 1020

NEW MODEL ARMY ENGRAVED
Model 1040
$254.00

Classical 19th-century style scroll engraving on this 1858 Remington New Model revolver.

Caliber: 44 Percussion; #11 cap
Barrel length: 8"
Overall length: 14¾"
Weight: 41 oz.
Sights: Integral rear sight notch groove in frame; blade front sight
Recommended ball diameter: .451 round or conical, pure lead

EUROARMS OF AMERICA

NEW MODEL ARMY TARGET
Model 1045
$250.00

Caliber: 44 Percussion; #11 cap
Barrel length: 8″, precision rifled
Overall length: 14³/₄″
Weight: 41 oz.
Sights: Integral rear sight notch groove in frame; dovetailed stainless steel front sight adjustable for windage
Finish: Stainless steel; polished yellow brass trigger guard; walnut grips
Recommended ball diameter: .451 round or conical, pure lead

1851 NAVY SHERIFF

1851 NAVY
Model 1120
$158.00

Caliber: .36 percussion, #11 cap
Barrel length: 7¹/₂″, octagonal barrel, precision rifled
Overall length: 13″
Weight: 42 oz.
Finish: Blued barrel and frame; backstrap and trigger guard are polished brass; walnut grips.

REMINGTON 1858 NEW MODEL
Army Revolver Model 1046
$160.00

Caliber: 44
Barrel length: 8″
Weight: 40 oz.
Overall length: 13¹/₄″
Finish: Stainless steel with polished walnut stock; polished brass trigger guard
Model 1047: 44 Cal., 6¹/₂″ barrel, **$194.00**
Model 1048: 44 Cal., 8″ barrel, **$194.00**

1851 NAVY SHERIFF
Model 1080
$124.00

Caliber: 36 Percussion; #11 cap
Barrel length: 5″
Overall length: 11¹/₂″
Weight: 38 oz.
Sights: Rear sight is traditional V-notch groove in hammer; truncated cone front sight of brass
Finish: High-gloss blue on barrel and cylinder; backstrap frame and trigger guard polished yellow brass; walnut grips; hammer and loading lever color case-hardened
Recommended ball diameter: .375 round or conical, pure lead

1851 NAVY SHERIFF
Model 1090 (not shown)
$124.00

Same as Model 1080 except in 44 caliber, with .451 round or conical ball.

SCHNEIDER & GLASSICK
CONFEDERATE REVOLVER
36 Caliber Model 1050 $124.00
44 Caliber Model 1060 $124.00

A modern replica of a Confederate Percussion Army Revolver. Polished brass frame, rifled high-luster blued, octagonal barrel and polished walnut grips.

Weight: 40 oz.
Barrel length: 7¹/₂″
Overall length: 13″
Finish: Brass frame, backstrap and trigger guard; blued rifled barrel; case-hardened hammer and loading lever; engraved cylinder with naval battle scene

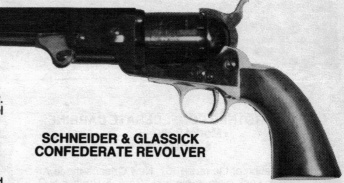

SCHNEIDER & GLASSICK
CONFEDERATE REVOLVER

EUROARMS OF AMERICA

HAWKEN RIFLE
Model 2210A
$186.00

Caliber: 50-caliber percussion
Barrel: 28″ long; blued precision rifled, octagonal
Weight: 9½–9¾ lbs., depending on density of wood
Stock: Solid one-piece walnut
Ramrod: Wooden, with brass tips threaded for cleaning jag, worm or ball puller
Sights: Target rear sight adjustable for windage and elevation; front sight dovetail cut
Triggers: Double-set triggers adjustable for hair trigger, if desired
Furniture: Polished brass mountings, barrel key

LONDON ARMORY COMPANY
3-BAND ENDFIELD RIFLED MUSKET
MODEL 2260
$427.00

Caliber: 58
Barrel length: 39″, blued and rifled
Overall length: 54″
Weight: 9½–9¾ lbs., depending on wood density
Stock: One-piece walnut; polished "bright" brass butt plate, trigger guard and nose cap; blued barrel bands
Ramrod: Steel; threaded end for accessories
Sights: Traditional Enfield folding ladder rear sight; inverted 'V' front sight

COOK & BROTHER CONFEDERATE CARBINE
Model 2300
$367.00

Classic re-creation of the rare 1861, New Orleans-made Artillery Carbine. Lock plate is marked "Cook & Brother N.O. 1861" and is stamped with a Confederate flag at rear of hammer.

Caliber: 58
Barrel length: 24″
Overall length: 40⅓″
Weight: 7½ lbs.
Sights: Adjustable dovetailed front and rear sights
Ramrod: Steel
Finish: Barrel is antique brown; butt plate, trigger guard, barrel bands, sling swivels and nose cap are polished brass; stock is walnut
Recommended ball sizes: .575 r.b., .577 Minie and .580 maxi; uses musket caps

EUROARMS OF AMERICA

LONDON ARMORY COMPANY
2-BAND RIFLE MUSKET
Model 2270
$393.00

Caliber: 58
Barrel length: 33", blued and rifled
Overall length: 49"
Weight: 8½–8¾ lbs., depending on wood density
Stock: One-piece walnut; polished "bright" brass butt plate, trigger guard and nose cap; blued barrel bands
Sights: Inverted 'V' front sight; Enfield folding ladder rear
Ramrod: Steel

LONDON ARMORY COMPANY
ENFIELD MUSKETOON
Model 2280
$367.00

Caliber: 58; Minie ball
Barrel length: 24"; round high-luster blued barrel
Overall length: 40½"
Weight: 7 to 7½ lbs., depending on density of wood
Stock: Seasoned walnut stock with sling swivels
Ramrod: Steel
Ignition: Heavy-duty percussion lock
Sights: Graduated military-leaf sight
Furniture: Brass trigger guard, nose cap and butt plate; blued barrel bands, lock plate, and swivels

SINGLE-BARRELED MAGNUM CAPE GUN
Model 2295
$310.00

Euroarms of America offers a beautifully reproduction of a classic English-styled 12-gauge single-barreled shotgun. It is a true 12 gauge with a 32-inch open choked barrel. The English-styled stock is well-proportioned, and recoil, with even relatively heavy powder charges, is moderate. The stock is of European walnut with a satin oil finish. The barrel, underrib, thimbles, nose cap, trigger guard and butt plate are finished with EOA deep, rich blue. The lock is left in the white and displays a scroll engraving, as does the bow of the trigger guard. **Overall length:** 47½". **Weight:** 7½ lbs. Uses #11 percussion caps and recommended wads are felt overpowder and cardboard overshot.

HOPKINS & ALLEN ARMS

KENTUCKY PISTOL MODEL 10
Flint $112.95
Percussion $92.95
Kit: $58.40

The Kentucky Pistol features a convertible ignition system, heavy-duty ramrod and special Hopkins & Allen breech and tang.

Caliber: 45
Barrel: Rifled, 10″ long; $^{15}/_{16}″$ wide
Overall length: $15^1/_2″$
Weight: 3 lbs.

BOOT PISTOL MODEL 13
$78.65
Kit: $60.75

The Boot Pistol comes with a sculptured walnut pistol grip and is fitted with open sights—post type front sight and open rear sight with step elevator. The H&A Boot Pistol features a rich blue-black finish and is equipped with a match trigger.

Caliber: 45
Barrel: $^{15}/_{16}″ × 6″$ octagonal
Overall length: 13″

BRUSH RIFLE MODEL 345
$207.90
Kit: $109.45

Caliber: 45 and 36
Barrel: 25″ octagon, $^{15}/_{16}″$ across flats
Weight: 7 lbs.
Stock: Selected hardwood
Sights: Notched rear; silver blade front
Features: Compact, light, quick pointing rifle; convertible ignition

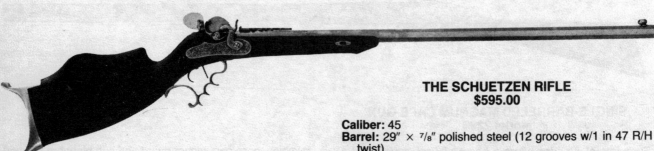

THE SCHUETZEN RIFLE
$595.00

Caliber: 45
Barrel: 29″ × $^7/_8″$ polished steel (12 grooves w/1 in 47 R/H twist)
Overall length: 44″
Weight: 10 lbs.
Sights: Aperture, tang mounted, adjusted for windage and elevation (rear)
Stock: Walnut with cheekpiece on left side

HOPKINS & ALLEN ARMS

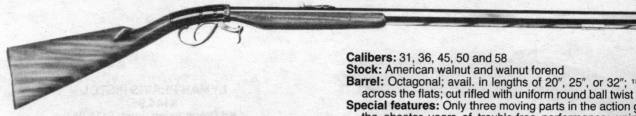

UNDERHAMMER RIFLE MODEL 32

Calibers: 31, 36, 45, 50 and 58
Stock: American walnut and walnut forend
Barrel: Octagonal; avail. in lengths of 20″, 25″, or 32″; $^{15}/_{16}$″ across the flats; cut rifled with uniform round ball twist
Special features: Only three moving parts in the action give the shooter years of trouble-free performance; uninterrupted sighting plane; target trigger; positive ignition
Four Underhammer Rifles available:
Buggy (31, 36, and 45 cal.); 20″ or 25″ barrel; weighs 6-7 lbs. **Price: $235.95**
Heritage (31, 36, 45, 50 cal.); 32″ barrel; weighs 7$^1/_2$-8 lbs. **Price: $249.15**
Deerstalker (58 cal.); 32″ barrel; weighs 9$^1/_2$ lbs. **Price: $257.35**
Target (45 cal.); 42″ barrel; weighs 11 lbs. **Price: $270.55**
Kits available **$149.35-$183.50**

PENNSYLVANIA HAWKEN RIFLE MODEL 29
$219.50
Kit $138.05

Caliber: 50
Lock mechanism: Flintlock or percussion
Barrel: 29″ long; octagonal; $^{15}/_{16}$″ across the flats; cut rifled with round ball twist
Overall length: 44″
Weight: 7$^1/_2$ lbs.
Stock: Walnut with cheekpiece and dual barrel wedges for added strength
Furniture: Brass fixtures, incl. patch box
Special feature: Convertible ignition system

IVER JOHNSON

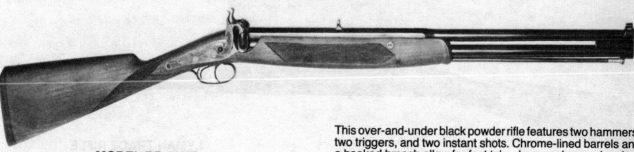

MODEL BP.50HB
$414.00

This over-and-under black powder rifle features two hammers, two triggers, and two instant shots. Chrome-lined barrels and a hooked breach allow for fast take-down and easy cleaning.

SPECIFICATIONS
Caliber: .50
Capacity: 2 rounds
Barrel length: 26″
Overall length: 41$^1/_4$″
Weight: 8$^1/_2$ lbs.
Sights: Gold-tipped front blade; folding rear adjustable for windage and elevation
Finish: Blue
Stock: Checkered walnut

LYMAN

LYMAN PLAINS PISTOL
$144.95
Kit (Percussion only): $116.95

This replica of the pistol carried by the Western pioneers of the 1830s features a pistol-sized Hawken lock with dependable coil spring and authentic rib and thimble styling. It has a richly stained walnut stock, blackened iron furniture and polished brass trigger guard and ramrod tips. Equipped with a spring-loaded trigger and a fast twist (1 in 30 inches both calibers) barrel for target accuracy. **Caliber:** 50 or 54.

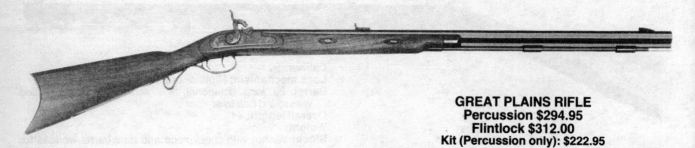

GREAT PLAINS RIFLE
Percussion $294.95
Flintlock $312.00
Kit (Percussion only): $222.95

The Great Plains Rifle has a 32-inch deep-grooved barrel and 1 in 66-inch twist to shoot patched round balls. Blued steel furniture including the thick steel wedge plates and steel toe plate; correct lock and hammer styling with coil spring dependability; and a walnut stock without a patch box. A Hawken-style trigger guard protects double-set triggers. Steel front sight and authentic buckhorn styling in an adjustable rear sight. Fixed primitive rear sight also included. **Caliber:** 50 or 54.

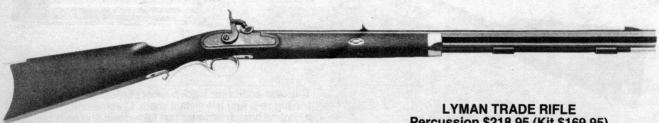

LYMAN TRADE RIFLE
Percussion $218.95 (Kit $169.95)
Flintlock $229.95 (Kit $189.95)

The Lyman Trade Rifle features a 28-inch octagonal barrel, rifled one turn at 48 inches, designed to fire both patched round balls and the popular maxistyle conical bullets. Polished brass furniture with blued finish on steel parts; walnut stock; hook breech; single spring-loaded trigger; coil-spring percussion lock; fixed steel sights; adjustable rear sight for elevation also included. Steel barrel rib and ramrod ferrule. **Caliber:** 50 or 54 percussion and flint. **Overall length:** 45″.

MICHIGAN ARMS

THE WOLVERINE

This new black powder rifle features an in-line ignition system using a standard 209 non-corrosive shotgun primer to fire the charge. One screw disassembles the barrel, breech plug and receiver for easy cleaning. The barrel is made of aircraft quality steel, and there's a choice of Michigan walnut, cherry or curly maple stock. Other features include a modern rifle trigger, positive safety, soft recoil pad, O-ring barrel seal, solid aluminum ramrod drilled and tapped for shotgun and standard black powder.

SPECIFICATIONS
Caliber: 45, 50 or 54. **Barrel length:** 26" octagonal (1" diameter, 1 turn in 66"). **Overall length:** 44". **Weight:** 7³/₄" (54 cal.). **Length of pull:** 13⁵/₈". **Sights:** Adjustable folding leaf rear and brass-bead tipped front sights, both dovetailed; receiver drilled and tapped for optional Williams peep sight. **Price: $398.00**

THE SILVERWOLF
An all Stainless Steel version of the Wolverine
Price: $595.00

THE FRIENDSHIP SPECIAL MATCH

While the design of this match rifle is the same as **Wolverine**, it features several extra components, including specially selected barrel, fully adjustable Lyman Globe front sight with inserts, Morgan adjustable recoil pad, fully adjustable trigger, special barrel lengths up to 30 inches, custom stock configuration with deep "C" pistol grip, and custom stock finish. **Price: $599.00**

NAVY ARMS REVOLVERS

LEMAT REVOLVERS

Once the official sidearm of many Confederate cavalry officers, this 9 shot .44 caliber revolver with a central single shot barrel of approx. 65 caliber gave the cavalry man 10 shots to use against the enemy. **Barrel length:** 7⅝″. **Overall length:** 14″. **Weight:** 3 lbs. 7 oz.

Cavalry Model $500.00
Navy Model 500.00
Army Model 500.00

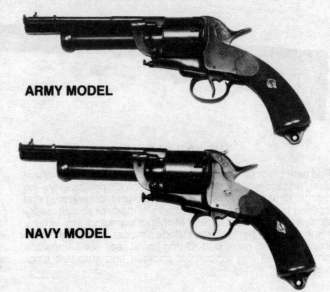

ARMY MODEL

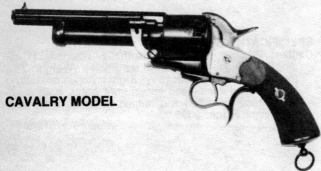

CAVALRY MODEL

NAVY MODEL

COLT WALKER 1847

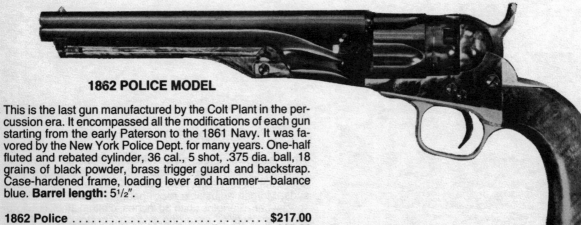

The 1847 Walker replica comes in 44 caliber with a 9-inch barrel. **Weight:** 4 lbs. 8 oz. Well suited for the collector as well as the black powder shooter. Features include: rolled cylinder scene; blued and case-hardened finish; and brass guard. Proof tested.

Colt Walter 1847 . . . . $238.00
Single Cased Set 360.00

1862 POLICE MODEL

This is the last gun manufactured by the Colt Plant in the percussion era. It encompassed all the modifications of each gun starting from the early Paterson to the 1861 Navy. It was favored by the New York Police Dept. for many years. One-half fluted and rebated cylinder, 36 cal., 5 shot, .375 dia. ball, 18 grains of black powder, brass trigger guard and backstrap. Case-hardened frame, loading lever and hammer—balance blue. **Barrel length:** 5½″.

1862 Police $217.00
Law and Order set 305.08

NAVY ARMS REVOLVERS

REB MODEL 1860

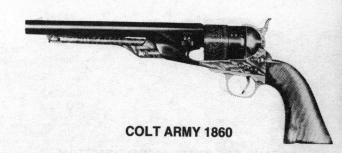

COLT ARMY 1860

A modern replica of the confederate Griswold & Gunnison percussion Army revolver. Rendered with a polished brass frame and a rifled steel barrel finished in a high-luster blue with genuine walnut grips. All Army Model 60's are completely proof-tested by the Italian government to the most exacting standards. **Calibers:** 36 and 44. **Barrel length:** 7¼". **Overall length:** 13". **Weight:** 2 lbs. 10 oz.-11 oz. **Finish:** Brass frame, backstrap and trigger guard, round barrel hinged rammer on the 44 cal. rebated cylinder.

Reb Model 1860	$121.00
Single Cased Set	233.00
Double Cased Set	359.00
Kit	85.00

These guns from the Colt line are 44 caliber and all six-shot. The cylinder was authentically roll engraved with a polished brass trigger guard and steel strap cut for shoulder stock. The frame, loading lever and hammer are finished in high-luster color case-hardening. Walnut grips. **Weight:** 2 lbs. 9 oz. **Barrel length:** 8". **Overall length:** 13⅝". **Caliber:** 44. **Finish:** Brass trigger guard, steel back strap, round barrel creeping cylinder, rebated cylinder engraved. Navy scene. Frame cut for s/stock (4 screws). Also available with full fluted cylinder and in 5½" barrel (Sheriff's model).

Army 1860	$162.00
Single Cased Set	259.00
Double Cased Set	440.00
Kit	116.50

1851 NAVY "YANK"

Originally manufactured by Colt from 1850 through 1876, this model was the most popular of the Union revolvers, mostly because it was lighter and easier to handle than the Dragoon. **Barrel length:** 7½". **Overall length:** 14". **Weight:** 2 lbs. **Rec. ball diam.:** .375 R.B.(.451 in 44 cal) **Calibers:** 36 and 44. **Capacity:** 6 shot. **Features:** Steel frame, octagonal barrel, cylinder roll-engraved with Naval battle scene, backstrap and trigger guard are polished brass.

1851 Navy "Yank"	$139.75 (Kit $97.50)
Single Cased Set	237.00
Double Cased Set	397.00

ROGERS & SPENCER NAVY REVOLVER

This revolver features a six-shot cylinder, octagonal barrel, hinged-type loading lever assembly, two-piece walnut grips, blued finish and case-hardened hammer and lever. **Caliber:** 44. **Barrel length:** 7½". **Overall length:** 13¾". **Weight:** 3 lbs.

Rogers & Spencer	$239.50

NAVY ARMS REVOLVERS

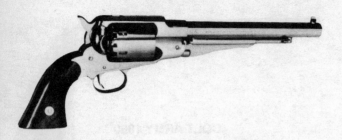

STAINLESS STEEL 1858 REMINGTON

Exactly like the standard 1858 Remington except that every part with the exception of the grips and trigger guard is manufactured from corrosion-resistant stainless steel. This gun has all the style and feel of its ancestor with all of the conveniences of stainless steel. **Caliber:** 44.

1858 Remington **$273.50**

TARGET MODEL REMINGTON REVOLVER

With its top strap and frame, the Remington Percussion Revolver is considered the magnum of Civil War revolvers and is ideally suited to the heavy 44-caliber charges. Based on the Army Model, the target gun has target sights for controlled accuracy. Ruggedly built from modern steel and proof tested.

Remington Percussion Revolver **$187.50**

REMINGTON NEW MODEL ARMY REVOLVER (not shown)

This rugged, dependable, battle-proven Civil War veteran with its top strap and rugged frame was considered the magnum of C.W. revolvers, ideally suited for the heavy 44 charges. Nickel finish in 44 cal. only. **Calibers:** 36 and 44. **Barrel length:** 8″. **Overall length:** 13 1/2″. **Weight:** 2 lbs. 9 oz.

Remington Army Revolver, blue **$166.00**
Single cased set, blue 264.00
Double cased set, blue 449.00

DELUXE 1858 REMINGTON-STYLE .44 CALIBER

Built to the exact dimensions and weight of the original Remington .44, this model features an 8″ barrel with progressive rifling, adjustable front sight for windage, all steel construction with walnut stocks and brass trigger guard. Steel is highly polished and finished in rich charcoal blue. **Barrel length:** 8″. **Overall length:** 14 1/4″. **Weight:** 2 lbs. 14 oz.

Deluxe 1858 Remington-Style .44 Cal. **$315.08**

ARMY 60 SHERIFF'S MODEL (not shown)

A shortened version of the Army Model 60 Revolver. The Sheriff's model version became popular because the shortened barrel was fast out of the leather. This is actually the original snub nose, the predecessor of the detective specials or belly guns designed for quick-draw use. A piece of traditional Americana, the Sheriff's model was adopted by many local police departments. **Calibers:** 36 and 44.

Army 60 Sheriff's Model **$121.00**
Kit 85.00

NAVY ARMS PISTOLS

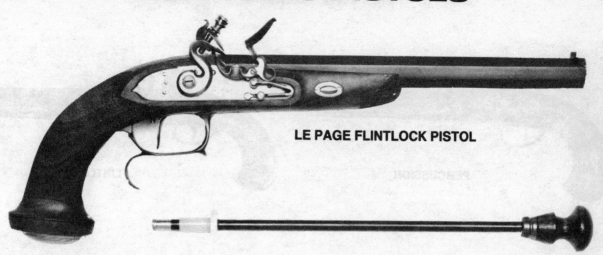

LE PAGE FLINTLOCK PISTOL

LE PAGE FLINTLOCK PISTOL
(45 Caliber)

Beautifully hand-crafted reproduction featuring hand-checkered walnut stock with hinged buttcap and carved motif of a shell at the forward portion of the stock. Single-set trigger and highly polished steel lock and furniture together with a brown finished rifled barrel make this a highly desirable target pistol. **Barrel length:** 10½″. **Overall length:** 17″. **Weight:** 2 lbs. 2 oz.

Price (rifled or smoothbore model). **$425.00**
Single Cased set. 594.00

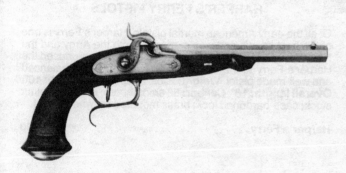

LE PAGE PERCUSSION PISTOL
(45 Caliber)

The tapered octagonal rifled barrel is in the traditional style with 7 lands and grooves. Fully adjustable single-set trigger. Engraved overall with traditional scrollwork. The European walnut stock is in the Boutet style. Spur-style trigger guard. Fully adjustable elevating rear sight. Dovetailed front sight adjustable for windage. **Barrel length:** 9″. **Overall length:** 15″. **Weight:** 2 lbs. 2 oz. **Rec. ball diameter:** 440 R.B.

Price: Percussion **$319.00**

DOUBLE CASED LE PAGE PISTOLS (not shown)
(45 Caliber)

The case is French-fitted and the accessories are the finest quality to match.

Price: Percussion **$1024.00**

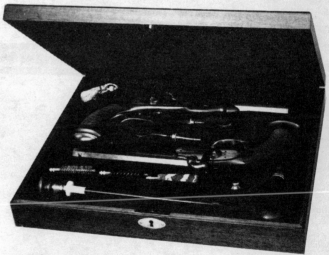

Double Cased Set
French- fitted double-cased set comprising two Le Page Pistols, turn screw, nipple key, oil bottle, cleaning brushes, leather covered flask and loading rod.

Price: Percussion **$800.00**

Single Cased Set
French-fitted single-cased set comprising one Le Page pistol, turn screw, nipple key, oil bottle, cleaning brushes, leather covered flask and loading rod.

Price: Percussion **$489.00**

NAVY ARMS PISTOLS

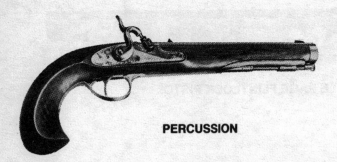

PERCUSSION

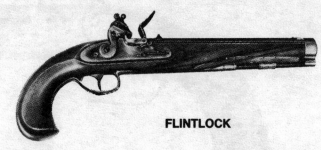

FLINTLOCK

KENTUCKY PISTOLS

The Kentucky Pistol is truly a historical American gun. It was carried during the Revolution by the Minutemen and was the sidearm of "Andy" Jackson in the Battle of New Orleans. Navy Arms Company has conducted extensive research to manufacture a pistol truly representative of its kind, with the balance and handle of the original for which it became famous.

Flint	$154.00
Single Cased Set—Flint	252.00
Percussion	139.00
Single Cased Set—Percussion	237.00
Double Cased Set, Flint	420.00
Double Cased Set, Perc.	392.00

HARPER'S FERRY PISTOLS

Of all the early American martial pistols, Harper's Ferry is one of the best known and was carried by both the Army and the Navy. Navy Arms Company has authentically reproduced the Harper's Ferry to the finest detail, providing a well-balanced and well-made pistol. **Weight:** 2 lbs. 9 oz. **Barrel length:** 10". **Overall length:** 16". **Caliber:** 58 smoothbore. **Finish:** Walnut stock; case-hardened lock; brass mounted browned barrel.

Harper's Ferry $210.00

ELGIN CUTLASS PISTOL

Part of Navy Arm's Classic Collection, this pistol represents the only combination gun (knife and pistol) ever issued by any U.S. military service. It was also the first percussion handgun officially used by the U.S. **Overall length:** 9" (12" blade). **Rec. ball diam.:** .440 R.B. **Weight:** 2 lbs.

Elgin Cutlass Pistol	$104.95
Kit	78.50

NAVY ARMS RIFLES

WHITWORTH MILITARY TARGET RIFLE

Recreation of Sir Joseph Whitworth's deadly and successful sniper and target weapon of the mid-1800s. Devised with a hexagonal bore with a pitch of 1 turn in 20 inches. Barrel is cold-forged from ordnance steel, reducing the build-up of black powder fouling. Globe front sight; open military target rifle rear sight has interchangeable blades of different heights. Walnut stock is hand-checkered. **Caliber:** 451. **Barrel length:** 36″. **Weight:** 9½ lbs.

Whitworth Military Target Rifle (incl. accessory kit) **$740.00**

PARKER-HALE 451 VOLUNTEER RIFLE

Originally designed by Irish gunmaker, William John Rigby, this relatively small-caliber rifle was issued to volunteer regiments during the 1860s. Today it is rifled by the cold-forged method, making one turn in 20 inches. Sights are adjustable: globe front and ladder-type rear with interchangeable leaves; hand-checkered walnut stock; weight 9½ lbs.

Parker-Hale 451 Volunteer Rifle (incl. accessory kit) **$700.00**
Other Parker-Hale muskets available:
2-Band Musket Model 1858
  Barrel length: 33″. **Overall length:** 48½″. **Weight:** 8½ lbs. **$485.00**
Musketoon Model 1861
  Barrel length: 24″. **Overall length:** 40¼″. **Weight:** 7½ lbs. 378.00
3-Band Musket Model 1853
  Barrel length: 39″. **Overall length:** 55″. **Weight:** 9 lbs. 500.00

SWISS FEDERAL TARGET RIFLE

An exact copy of the fine Swiss Target Rifles used in the 1880s in competition throughout Europe and the U.S. Each rifle is individually hand crafted. The rear peep sight is fully adjustable for windage and elevation. Five lever double set trigger system is adjustable down to a 4-ounce pull. Features walnut stock, color case hardened furniture, quick detachable double set triggers. **Barrel length:** 31″. **Overall length:** 49″. **Weight:** 16¼ lbs.

Swiss Federal Target Rifle **$1499.00**

ITHACA/NAVY HAWKEN RIFLE

Features a 31½″ octagonal blued barrel crowned at the muzzle with buckhorn-style rear sight, blade front sight. Color case hardened percussion lock is fitted on walnut stock. Furniture is all steel and blued (except for nose cap and escutcheons). Available in 50 and 54 cal.

Ithaca/Navy Hawken Rifle **$449.00**
Kit 359.00

NAVY ARMS RIFLES

#2 CREEDMOOR TARGET RIFLE

Features a color case hardened rolling block receiver, checkered walnut stock and forend, 30″ tapered 45/70 barrel with blue finish, hooded front sight and Creedmoor tang sight. **Barrel length: 30″. Overall length: 46″. Weight: 9 lbs.**

#2 Creedmoor Target Rifle **$595.00**

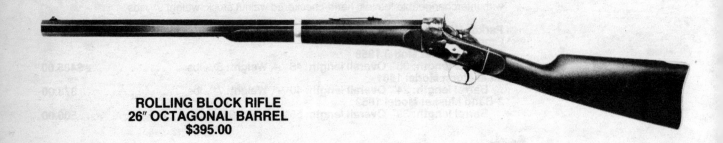

ROLLING BLOCK RIFLE
26″ OCTAGONAL BARREL
$395.00

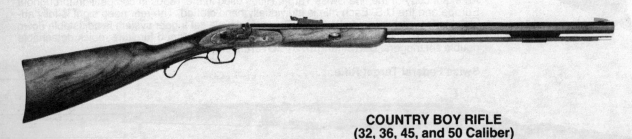

COUNTRY BOY RIFLE
(32, 36, 45, and 50 Caliber)

An authentic copy of one of the most effective percussion systems ever devised. The simple lock is trouble-free and with the nipple directly on the barrel gives fast, positive ignition. The quickest handling, fastest shooting rifle on the market today; ideal for the young beginner shooter. Features hooked breech and fully adjustable hunting sights. Simple, efficient and trustworthy. **Barrel length: 26″. Weight: 5½ lbs.**

Rifle **$250.00**
Rifle Kit **192.00**

NAVY ARMS RIFLES

1853 ENFIELD RIFLE MUSKET

The Enfield Rifle Musket marked the zenith in design and manufacture of the military percussion rifle and this perfection has been reproduced by Navy Arms Company. This and other Enfield muzzleloaders were the most coveted rifles of the Civil War, treasured by Union and Confederate troops alike for their fine quality and deadly accuracy. **Caliber:** 557. **Barrel length:** 39″. **Weight:** 9 lbs. **Overall length:** 55″. **Sights:** Fixed front; graduated rear. **Rifling:** 3 groove, cold forged. **Stock:** Seasoned walnut with solid brass furniture.

1853 Enfield Rifle Musket $479.00

1858 ENFIELD RIFLE

In the late 1850s the British Admiralty, after extensive experiments, settled on a pattern rifle with a 5-groove barrel of heavy construction, sighted to 1100 yards, designated the Naval rifle, Pattern 1858. In the recreation of this famous rifle Navy Arms has referred to the original 1858 Enfield Rifle in the Tower of London and has closely followed the specifications even to the progressive depth rifling. **Caliber:** 557. **Barrel length:** 33″. **Weight:** 8 lbs. 8 oz. **Overall length:** 48.5″. **Sights:** Fixed front; graduated rear. **Rifling:** 5-groove; cold forged. **Stock:** Seasoned walnut with solid brass furniture.

1853 Enfield Rifle $459.00

1861 ENFIELD MUSKETOON

The 1861 Enfield Musketoon is a Limited Collector's edition, individually serial numbered with certificate of authenticity. **Caliber:** 557. **Barrel length:** 24″. **Weight:** 7 lbs. 8 oz. **Overall length:** 40.25″. **Sights:** Fixed front; graduated rear. **Rifling:** 5-groove; cold forged. **Stock:** Seasoned walnut with solid brass furniture.

1861 Enfield Musketoon $338.00
Kit 239.00

1863 SPRINGFIELD RIFLE

An authentically reproduced replica of one of America's most historical firearms, the 1863 Springfield rifle features a full-size, three-band musket and precision-rifled barrel. **Caliber:** 58. **Barrel length:** 40″. **Overall length:** 56″. **Weight:** 9½ lbs. **Finish:** Walnut stock with polished metal lock and stock fittings.

1863 Springfield Rifle $467.00
Springfield Bayonet and Scabbard 40.00
Springfield kit 360.00

NAVY ARMS

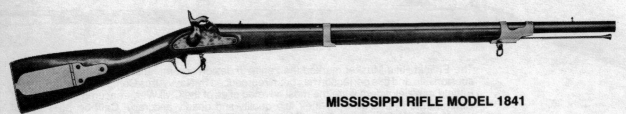

MISSISSIPPI RIFLE MODEL 1841

The historic percussion lock weapon that gained its name as a result of its performance in the hands of Jefferson Davis' Mississippi Regiment during the heroic stand at the Battle of Buena Vista. Also known as the "Yager" (a misspelling of the German Jaeger), this was the first rifle adopted by Army Ordnance to fire the traditional round ball. In 58 caliber, the Mississippi is handsomely furnished in brass, including patch box for tools and spare parts. **Weight:** 9½ lbs. **Barrel length:** 32½″. **Overall length:** 48½″. **Caliber:** 58. **Finish:** Walnut finish stock, brass mounted.

Model 1841 . . . . **$270.00**

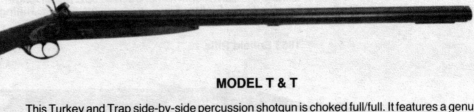

MODEL T & T

This Turkey and Trap side-by-side percussion shotgun is choked full/full. It features a genuine walnut stock with checkered wrist and oil finish, color case-hardened locks, and 28″ blued barrels. It will pattern a load of #6 shot size in excess of 85% in a 30″ circle at 30 yards and in excess of 65% at 40 yards, using 96 grains of FFg, 1¼ oz. #6 shot and 13 gauge overshot, over powder and cushion wads.

Model T & T **$385.00**

RIGBY-STYLE TARGET RIFLE

This affordable reproduction of the famed Rigby Target rifle of the 1880's features a 32″ blued barrel, target front sight with micrometer adjustment, fully adjustable vernier rear sight (adjustable up to 1000 yards), hand checkered walnut stock, color case-hardened breech plug, hammer lock plate, and escutcheons. This .451 caliber gun is cased with loading accessories, including bullet starter and sizer and special ramrod.

Rigby-Style Target Rifle **$500.00**

NAVY ARMS

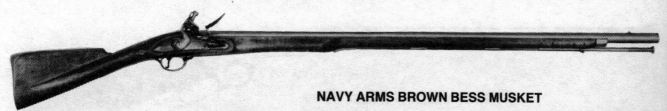

NAVY ARMS BROWN BESS MUSKET

This musket was considered to be the major arm of the American Continental Army during the American Revolution. The "Bess" was derived from Queen Elizabeth I and "Brown" came from the barrel's finish. This carefully reproduced replica carries the Colonial Williamsburg mark of authenticity and features a polished barrel and lock with brass trigger guard and butt plate. **Caliber:** 75. **Barrel length:** 42″. **Overall length:** 59″. **Weight:** 9½ lbs.

Brown Bess Musket **$525.00**

MORSE MUZZLELOADING RIFLE

Improved production techniques and modern engineering have produced this traditionally styled, muzzleloading rifle. Quality plus custom craftsmanship is evident throughout this rifle with careful attention being paid to the most minute detail. It features Navy Arms "pre-straightened" precision rifled ordnance steel barrel. 45, 50 or 58 caliber.

Morse Muzzleloading Rifle **$167.00**

KENTUCKY RIFLE—45 OR 50 CALIBER PERCUSSION

No weapon before or since has been so imbued with Americana as the Kentucky Rifle. The Kentucky was the wilderness weapon, Pennsylvania-born and universally used along the frontier. First called simply the long rifle, it was designated "the Kentucky" by gun lovers after the Civil War because Daniel Boone used it most effectively in opening up the Kentucky territory. In the hands of those who know how to use it, the Kentucky still can give many modern rifles a run for the money. **Barrel length:** 35″. Available in flint or percussion.

Kentucky Rifle Percussion **$274.00**
Flint **290.00**

NAVY ARMS

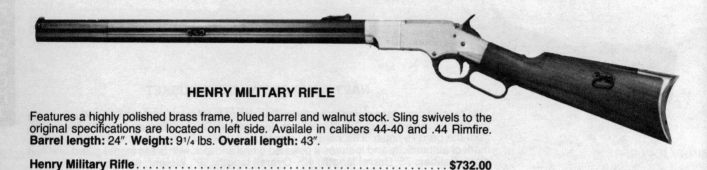

HENRY MILITARY RIFLE

Features a highly polished brass frame, blued barrel and walnut stock. Sling swivels to the original specifications are located on left side. Availale in calibers 44-40 and .44 Rimfire. **Barrel length:** 24″. **Weight:** 9¼ lbs. **Overall length:** 43″.

Henry Military Rifle **$732.00**

IRON FRAME HENRY

Same specifications as Henry Military Rifle.

Iron Frame Henry **$835.00**

HENRY TRAPPER MODEL

This short, lightweight .44/40 is ideal for the hunter. **Barrel length:** 16½″. **Overall length:** 34½″. **Weight:** 7¼ lbs.

Henry Trapper Model **$732.00**

HENRY CARBINE

The arm first utilized by the Kentucky Cavalry. Available in either original 44 rimfire caliber or in 44/40 caliber. Oil-stained American walnut stock, blued finish with brass frame. Also available in a limited deluxe edition of only 50 engraved models complete with deluxe American walnut stock, original styled engraving and silver plated frames. **Caliber:** 44 rimfire & 44/40. **Barrel length:** 23⅝″. **Overall length:** 45″.

Henry Carbine . . . . **$ 732.00**
Engraved Model **1849.00**

HENRY CARBINE ENGRAVED

This carbine version of the orginal Henry Rifle (produced between 1850 and 1866) served as a revolutionary weapon in the Civil War. Only 50 engraved units are available in .44/40 or .44 rimfire. **Barrel length:** 24″. **Overall length:** 39″. **Weight:** 8¼ lbs.

Henry Carbine Engraved **$1849.00**

SHILOH SHARPS

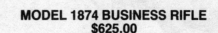

MODEL 1874 BUSINESS RIFLE
$625.00

45-70, 45-90, 45-120, 50-70, 50-90 and 50-140 calibers. 28-inch heavy-tapered round barrel, double-set triggers adjustable set, sights, blade front and sporting rear with leaf. Buttstock is straight grip rifle butt plate, forend sporting schnabel style. Receiver group and butt plate case-colored, barrel is dark blue; wood is American walnut oil-finished. **Weight:** 9 lbs. 8 oz.

MODEL 1874 MILITARY RIFLE
$800.00

45-70 and 50-70 calibers. 30-inch round barrel. Blade front and Lawrence-style sights. Military-style forend with 3 barrel bands and 1 1/4-inch swivels. Receiver group, butt plate and barrel bands case-colored. Barrel is dark blue, wood with oil finish. **Weight:** 8 lbs. 2 oz.

MODEL 1874 CARBINE
$650.00

45-70 and 45-90 calibers. 24-inch round barrel, single trigger, blade front and sporting rear sight, buttstock straight grip, steel rifle butt plate, forend sporting schnabel style. Case-colored receiver group and butt plate; barrel is dark blue; wood has oil finish. **Weight:** 8 lbs. 4 oz.

Sharps Model 1874 Rifle and Cartridge Availability Table

MODEL	40-50 1 11/16"BN	40-70 2 1/4"BN	40-90 2 5/8"BN	45-70 2 1/10"ST	45-90 2 4/10"ST	45-100 2 6/10"ST	45-110 2 7/8"ST	45-120 3 1/4"ST	50-70 1 3/4"ST	50-100 2 1/2"ST	50-140 3 1/4"ST
						CALIBER					
LONG RANGE EXPRESS	●	●	●	●	●	●	●	●		●	●
NO. 1 SPORTING RIFLE	●	●	●	●	●	●	●	●		●	●
NO. 3 SPORTING RIFLE	●	●	●	●	●			●	●	●	●
SADDLE RIFLE	●	●		●							
BUSINESS RIFLE	★	★●	★●	●	●			●	●	●	●
CARBINE	★	★●	★●	●	●		●	●	●	●	●
1874 MILITARY ●RIFLE	★	★●	★●	●					●		

● Standard
★ Available on special order. Add $75.00 to the suggested retail price for special order fee
BN = Bottleneck, ST = Straight

SHILOH SHARPS

MODEL 1874 SPORTING RIFLE NO. 1
$775.00

Calibers: 45-70, 45-90, 45-120, 50-70, 50-90 and 50-140. Features 28-inch or 30-inch tapered octagon barrel. Double-set triggers with adjustable set, blade front sight, sporting rear with elevation leaf and sporting tang sight adjustable for elevation and windage. Buttstock is pistol grip, shotgun butt, sporting forend style. Receiver group and butt plate case colored. Barrel is high finish blue-black; wood is American walnut oil finish. **Weight:** 9 lbs. 8 oz.

MODEL 1874 SPORTING RIFLE NO. 3
$675.00

45-70, 45-90, 45-120, 50-70, 50-90 and 50-140 calibers. 30-inch tapered octagon barrel, double-set triggers with adjustable set, blade front sight, sporting rear with elevation leaf and sporting tang sight adjustable for elevation and windage. Buttstock is straight grip with rifle butt plate; trigger plate is curved and checkered to match pistol grip. Forend is sporting schnabel style. Receiver group and butt plate is case colored. Barrel is high finish blue-black; wood is American walnut oil-finished. **Weight:** 9 lbs. 12 oz.

MODEL 1863 SPORTING RIFLE
$695.00

Caliber: 54; 30″ tapered octagon barrel, blade front sight, sporting rear with elevation leaf, double-set triggers with adjustable set; curved trigger plate, pistol grip buttstock with steel butt plate, forend schnable style; optional Tang sight. **Weight:** 9 lbs.
Also available: **MODEL 1863 PERCUSSION MILITARY RIFLE** $800.00
MODEL 1863 PERCUSSION CARBINE 650.00

THOMPSON/CENTER

THE PATRIOT

Features a hooked breech, double-set triggers, first-grade American walnut stock, adjustable (Patridge-type) target sights, solid brass trim, beautifully decorated and color case-hardened lock with a small dolphin-shaped hammer. **Weight:** Approximately 36 oz. Inspired by traditional gallery and dueling-type pistols, its carefully selected features retain the full flavor of antiquity, yet modern metals and manufacturing methods have been used to ensure its shooting qualities.

Patriot Pistol 36 and 45 caliber **$235.00**
Kit 180.00

THOMPSON/CENTER

COUGAR HAWKEN MODEL

This presentation series is available in 50 caliber cap lock. It features finest grade American walnut with stainless steel furniture, including hammer, lock, butt plate, triggers, trigger guard, forend cap and thimbles. A stainless steel medallion depicts a crouched cougar on right side of butt stock.

Cougar Hawken **$395.00**

THE HAWKEN
45, 50 and 54 caliber

Similar to the famous Rocky Mountain rifles made during the early 1800's, the Hawken is intended for serious shooting. Button-rifled for ultimate precision, the Hawken is available in 45, 50 or 54 caliber, flint or percussion. Featuring a hooked breech, double-set triggers, first-grade American walnut, adjustable hunting sights, solid brass trim, beautifully decorated and color case-hardened lock.

Hawken Caplock 45, 50 or 54 caliber **$315.00**
Hawken Flintlock 50 caliber. 330.00
Kit: Percussion. 220.00
     Flintlock 235.00

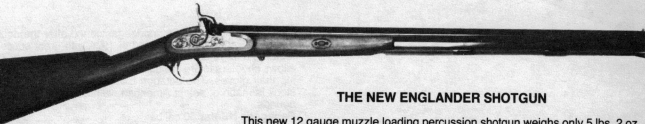

THE NEW ENGLANDER SHOTGUN

This new 12 gauge muzzle loading percussion shotgun weighs only 5 lbs. 2 oz. It features a 28-inch (improved cylinder) round barrel and is stocked with selected American black walnut.

The New Englander **$199.00**

THE NEW ENGLANDER RIFLE

Features 26″, round, .50 caliber rifle barrel (1 in 48″ twist); weighs 7 lbs. 15oz.

New Englander Rifle **$199.00**

THOMPSON/CENTER

THE RENEGADE

Available in 50, 54 or 56 caliber percussion, the Renegade was designed to provide maximum accuracy and maximum shocking power. Constructed from superior modern steel with investment cast parts fitted to an American walnut stock, the rifle features a precision-rifled (26-inch carbine-type) octagon barrel, hooked-breech system, coil spring lock, double-set triggers, adjustable hunting sights and steel trim. Weight is approx. 8 lbs.

Renegade Caplock 50 and 54 caliber and 56 caliber smoothbore (left
   or right hand) **$265.00**
Renegade Flintlock 50 caliber. 280.00
Kit: Cap Lock (left or right hand) 190.00
     Flintlock 205.00

RENEGADE HUNTER
50 Caliber

This single trigger hunter model, fashioned after the double triggered Renegade introduced in 1974 with great success, features a large bow in the shotgun style trigger guard. This allows shooters to fire the rifle in cold weather without removing their gloves. The octagon barrel measures 26" and the stock is made of select American walnut. Weight is about 8 pounds.
Renegade Hunter 50 caliber **$245.00**

THE CHEROKEE

A light percussion sporting rifle with interchangeable barrels. **Caliber:** 32, 36, or 45. **Barrel length:** 24". **Weight:** About 6 lbs. Sights are open hunting style fully adjustable for windage and elevation. Stock is American walnut with contoured cheekpiece on left-hand side.

Cherokee Caplock **$265.00**
Kit 190.00
Interchangeable barrels (w/ramrod) in 32 and 45 caliber 115.00
Kit barrels 75.00

TRADITIONS

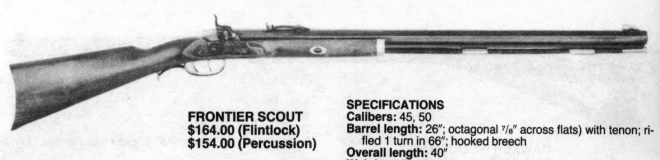

FRONTIER SCOUT
$164.00 (Flintlock)
$154.00 (Percussion)

SPECIFICATIONS
Calibers: 45, 50
Barrel length: 26"; octagonal $7/8$" across flats) with tenon; rifled 1 turn in 66"; hooked breech
Overall length: 40"
Weight: 5 lbs. 8 oz.
Length of pull: 12$1/4$"

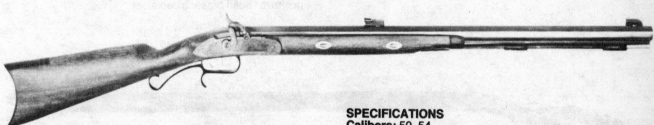

HUNTER RIFLE
$245.00 (Percussion)

SPECIFICATIONS
Calibers: 50, 54
Barrel length: 28"; octagonal (1" across flats) with 2 tenons; hooked breech, rifled 1 turn in 66"
Overall length: 44"
Weight: 8 lbs. 10 oz.
Lock: Adjustable sear engagement with fly and bridle
Stock: Walnut with contoured beavertail cheekpiece
Sights: Fully screw adjustable for windage and elevation; beaded blade front with Patridge-style open rear; both dovetailed
Furniture: Black-chromed brass with German silver wedge plates and stock ornaments

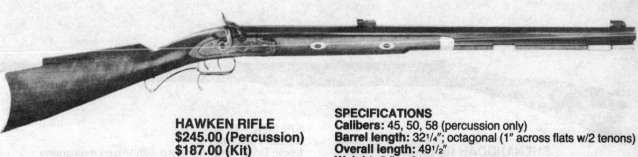

HAWKEN RIFLE
$245.00 (Percussion)
$187.00 (Kit)

SPECIFICATIONS
Calibers: 45, 50, 58 (percussion only)
Barrel length: 32$1/4$"; octagonal (1" across flats w/2 tenons)
Overall length: 49$1/2$"
Weight: 9 lbs. 2 oz.
Lock: Adjustable sear engagement with fly and bridle
Stock: Walnut, beavertail cheekpiece
Triggers: Double set (will fire set and unset)
Sights: Fully screw adjustable for windage and elevation; beaded front sight with Patridge-style open rear; both are dovetailed
Furniture: Solid brass, blued steel

TRADITIONS

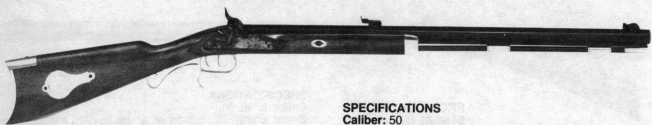

HAWKEN WOODSMAN
$214.00 (Percussion)
$174.00 (Kit)

SPECIFICATIONS
Caliber: 50
Barrel length: 24″ (octagonal); hooked breech; rifled 1 turn in 66″
Overall length: 45¼″
Weight: 8 lbs.
Triggers: Double set; will fire set or unset
Lock: Adj. sear engagement with fly and bridle
Stock: Select hardwood, walnut tone; medium gloss
Sights: Fully screw adjustable for windage and elevation; beaded balde front with patridge-style open rear
Furniture: Solid brass; blued steel

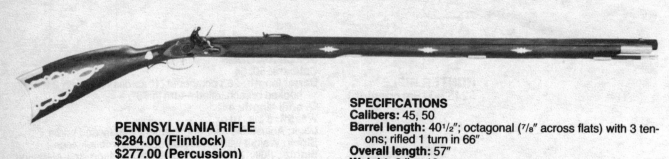

PENNSYLVANIA RIFLE
$284.00 (Flintlock)
$277.00 (Percussion)

SPECIFICATIONS
Calibers: 45, 50
Barrel length: 40½″; octagonal (⅞″ across flats) with 3 tenons; rifled 1 turn in 66″
Overall length: 57″
Weight: 9 lbs. 13 oz.
Lock: Adjustable sear engagement with fly and bridle
Stock: Select hardwood, beavertail style
Triggers: Double set (will fire set and unset)
Sights: Fully adjustable rear; brass blad front
Furniture: Solid brass, blued steel

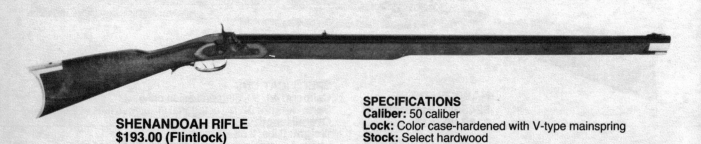

SHENANDOAH RIFLE
$193.00 (Flintlock)
$184.00 (Percussion)

SPECIFICATIONS
Caliber: 50 caliber
Lock: Color case-hardened with V-type mainspring
Stock: Select hardwood
Barrel: Octagonal (⅞″ across flats) with two tenons, 33½″ long
Triggers: Double set
Sights: Fixed rear, blade type front
Furniture: Brass buttplate, nose cap and trigger guard
Overall length: 48″
Weight: 7¼ lbs.

TRADITIONS

SINGLE BARREL FOWLER
$240.00 (Percussion)

SPECIFICATIONS
Gauge: 12
Barrel Length: 28″ or 32″ octagonal tapering to round; hooked
  breech; one barrel tenon
Overall length: 48¼″
Weight: 5 lbs. 6 oz.
Stock: Fine grained walnut, checkered at wrist
Sight: Brass bead front
Furniture: German silver wedge plate, blued trigger guard,
  tang and buttplate

TRAPPER RIFLE (w/Interchangeable Barrels)
$176.00 (Percussion)

SPECIFICATIONS
Calibers: 36, 45, and 50
Barrel length: 24″; 45 and 50 calibers rifled 1 turn in 66″; 36
  caliber rifled 1 turn in 48″; hooked breech; octagonal (⅞
  across flats)
Overall length: 40″
Weight: 5 lbs. 8 oz.
Stock: Select hardwood
Lock: Adj. sear engagement with fly and bridle
Triggers: Double set, will fire set and unset
Sights: Fully screw adjustable for windage and elevation;
  beaded blade front with patridge-style open rear
Furniture: Solid brass; blued steel
Interchangeable barrel assemblies: **$86.00**

TRAPPER PISTOL
$102.00 (Percussion)
$81.00 (Kit)

SPECIFICATIONS
Calibers: 36, 45, 50
Barrel length: 10″; octagonal (7/8″ across flats) w/tenon
Overall length: 14 ¾″
Weight: 3 lbs. 4 oz.
Stock: Select hardwood
Lock: Adj. sear engagement with fly and bridle
Triggers: Double set, will fire set and unset
Sights: Fully adjustable rear; brass blade front
Furniture: Solid brass; blued steel on assembled pistol

A. UBERTI

SPECIFICATIONS
Caliber: 44
Barrel length: 7¹/₂″ round forward of lug
Frame: Color case hardened steel
Capacity: 6 shots
Grip: One piece walnut
Overall length: 13¹/₂″
Weight: 4 lbs.
Features: Brass backstrap and trigger guard; engraved cylinder

Also available:

2nd Model Dragoon w/square cylinder bolt slot. . . **$209.00**
3rd Model Dragoon w/loading lever latch, steel
backstrap **229.00**
Texas Dragoon w/squareback trigger guard **209.00**

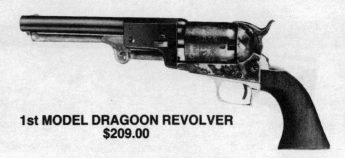

1st MODEL DRAGOON REVOLVER
$209.00

SPECIFICATIONS
Caliber: 36
Barrel length: 7¹/₂″
Overall length: 13″
Weight: 2.75 lbs.
Grip: One piece walnut
Capacity: 6 shots
Frame: Color case hardened steel

Also available:

Civil Type w/brass backstrap and trigger guard. . . .**$195.00**
Western Type w/silver plated backstrap and trigger
guard **195.00**
Fluted Cylinder Type w/steel backstrap and trigger
guard **215.00**

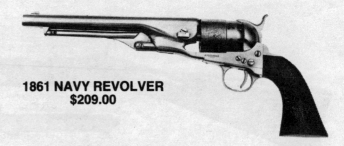

1861 NAVY REVOLVER
$209.00

1858 NEW ARMY TARGET REVOLVING CARBINE
$329.00

SPECIFICATIONS
Caliber: 44
Barrel length: 18″ octagonal tapered
Overall length: 37″
Weight: 4.63 lbs.
Sights: Vertically adjustable rear; ramp front
Frame: Blued steel
Stock: Walnut
Features: Brass trigger guard and butt plate

Also available:

1858 New Army .44 Target Revolver. **$209.00**
w/Stainless Steel **225.00**
Target Model **285.00**

SANTA FE HAWKEN RIFLE
$329.00

SPECIFICATIONS
Caliber: 54
Barrel length: 32″ octagonal
Overall length: 50″
Weight: 9¹/₂ lbs.
Stock: Walnut w/beavertail cheekpiece
Features: Brown finish; double trigger set; color case hardened lockplate; German silver wedge plates and stock turrule

Sights, Scopes & Mounts

FOR ADDRESSES AND PHONE
NUMBERS OF MANUFACTURERS AND
DISTRIBUTORS INCLUDED IN THIS
SECTION, SEE *DIRECTORY OF
MANUFACTURERS AND SUPPLIERS*

AIMPOINT SIGHTS

SERIES 2000 ELECTRONIC SIGHTS

Two versions of Aimpoint's new Series 2000 Sights. Two versions are available, Short and Long, and are offered in two finishes—black or stainless. The Short 2000 is a smaller version weighing only 5.35 ounces, with a length of 5 inches. Primarily designed for handgun users, its versatility allows for multi-use. Shooters can easily remove the sight from one firearm to another. Mounting requires standard one-inch rings and mounts. The Long 2000 is slightly larger—7¹/₄ inches overall—and weighs just over 6 ounces. The Long version can be mounted on all firearms and will work well for hunters and marksmen who use rifles and require magnification.

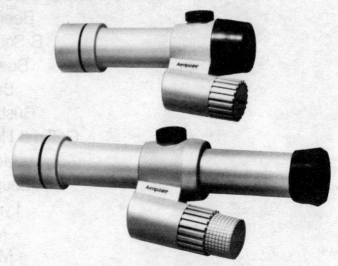

SERIES 2000 LONG AND SHORT STAINLESS STEEL

SERIES 2000 LONG AND SHORT BLACK FINISH

Series 2000 Specifications	Short	Long
Length	5"	7¹/₄"
Weight	5.35 oz.	6 oz.
Diameter	1"	1"
Magnification	None	None
Scope Attachments	None	3X
Material	Anodized Aluminum	Anodized Aluminum
Finish	Black or Stainless finish	Black or Stainless finish
Mounting	Standard 1" rings	Standard 1" rings
Positive sight adjustment	¹/₂" at 100 yards	¹/₂" at 100 yards
Lens coating	Standard	Standard
Battery types	Long cap—one piece lithium (DL ²/₃A) or two piece mercury (PX1/RM1N) Short cap—one piece lithium CR-¹/₃N, 2L76BP or DL¹/₃N	Same Same
Price: 2000 Black or Stainless	**$199.95**	**$219.95**

BAUSCH & LOMB

Since 1853 the name Bausch & Lomb has stood for superior optical performance. The repeatability—a critical factor—of Bausch & Lomb's variable and fixed power rifle-scopes enables sportsmen to enjoy optimum tracking accuracy with positive return to zero each time. The advanced design of these scopes eliminates point-of-impact shifts at high and low powers. To insure brightness, internal lens surfaces are multi-coated so light loss from reflection is minimized. Strong, durable one-piece body maintains optical alignment. All scopes are waterproof and fogproof.

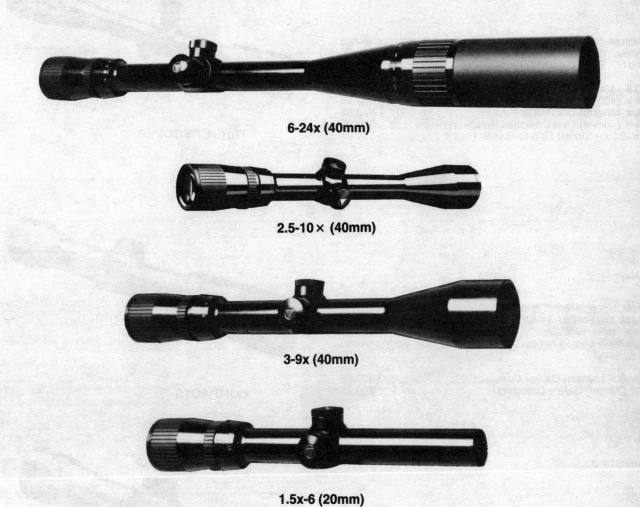

6-24x (40mm)

2.5-10× (40mm)

3-9x (40mm)

1.5x-6 (20mm)

BALVAR RIFLESCOPES

Bausch & Lomb's variable 6-24x40, 3-9x40, and 1.5-6x21 riflescopes have been redesigned, reducing their weight by 15 percent each. When set at its lowest power, the variable 1.5-6x provides a full 60-foot field at 100 yards, making it an ideal optical sight for stalking in tall timber and dense brushy areas. For maximum visibility, this scope can also zoom up to a full 6x for long range shots at big game. It weighs only 13.9 ounces and measures 11 inches in length. For benchrest competitors, long-range varmint hunters and silhouette shooters, the 6x-24x scope is sufficiently short and light. Its 40mm focusing objective lens eliminates problems with parallax regardless of distance to target. Features positive click steel windage and elevation adjustments, plus precision internal adjustments for repeatability and return to zero.

Model 64 Balvar Riflescope

6-24x40mm.	$459.95
3-9x40mm.	386.95
1.5-6x20mm.	341.95
2.5-10× 40mm.	452.95

BAUSCH & LOMB

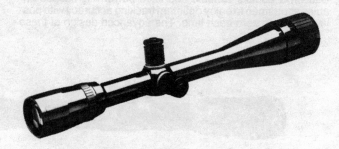

Feature crisp, repeatable 1/8 MOA click adjustments in two styles, plus hard surface multi-coated optics, sunshades (3" and 5"). Fogproof and waterproof.

36× (40mm) Dot Reticle	$579.95
36× (40mm) Fine Crosshair Reticle	579.95
24× (40mm) Dot Reticle	579.95
24× (40mm) Fine Crosshair Reticle	579.95
6×-24× (40mm) Fine Crosshair Reticle	579.95

TARGET SCOPES

Offer same features and performance as full-size Bausch & Lomb riflescopes in lightweight design. Include four times zoom ratio, resettable 1/4" MOA click adjustments, hard surface multi-coated optics, one-piece body tube. Fogproof and waterproof.

2×-8× (32mm) Balvar Compact	$339.95
4× (32mm) Balfor Compact	259.95

COMPACTS

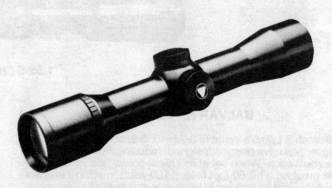

Feature one-piece body tube, resettable 1/4" MOA click adjustments, wide margin of eye relief, hard surface, multi-coated optics. Fogproof and waterproof.

4× (28mm)	$249.95
2× (20mm)	239.95

HANDGUN SCOPES

BEEMAN MOUNTS

DOUBLE ADJUSTABLE SCOPE MOUNTS

Beeman Professional Pivot Mounts. The finest scope mounts in existence for big bore. These allow scopes to be quickly and easily detached for transporting, protecting from bad weather or repairing. No tools required. Just lift mount latch, pivot scope 90° and lift out. Scope returns to zero when reattached. Built-in windage adjustment allows full use of scope's windage adjustment. Also, bases sit so low mechanical sights may be used when scope is off. **$129.50.**

Beeman Professional Dovetail Mounts. These are the finest scope mounts in existence for 22 caliber rifles. Same superb construction and built-in windage adjustment as the Pivot Mounts (above). A locking screw arrangement absolutely locks the mount into position with 11mm dovetails. No. 5085 with 25-26mm (1") rings: **$87.50.**

Double Adjustable Scope Mounts. The first mounts to have both clamp size and windage adjustment features. Using spacer bars provided, clamp size adjusts to fit grooved receivers and scope bases on all known 22 rifles (¼ to ⅝", 6mm to 15mm). Windage adjustment built into the mount center scope so that scope retains its full range of windage adjustments. These high-quality mounts are for 22 rimrife and airgun shooters who wish to mount high-performance 1" diameter scopes on their guns. No. 5084. **$26.98**

Beeman Deluxe Ring Mounts. Simpler version of 5084 without the double adjustable feature. Very sturdy and extremely solid. High tensile aviation aluminum with non-glare, honed blue-black finish. Blued steel clamping screws. No. 5081. **$23.98**

Beeman/Buehler Mounts and Bases. These bases were designed specifically for Beeman/Krico rifles. They will take any Buehler rings, however. Built-in windage adjustment. Only the medium and high rings recommended. Finest chrome moly steel, beautifully blued. Scope may be pivoted off, but this requires loosening two screws with a screwdriver. Two bases and ring heights available. No. 5094 (base-smallbore) No. 5095 (base-large-bore) No. 5096 (medium rings) No. 5097 (high rings). **$39.50** (5094 & 5095) and **$39.50** (5096 & 5097)

MODEL 68R
$298.95

MODELS 68R & 67R

These two high power scopes—with 4-12 zoom power and 3-9 zoom power, respectively—are suitable for airguns, rimfire and centerfire rifles alike. Field shooters who must make precise head shots on small game will find the higher magnifications helpful. Both models incorporate the lens bracing required to protect them from the damaging two-way snap of spring piston airguns. Other features include a speed dial (for elevation) and range focus, plus a large 40mm objective lens that provides super-bright images. **Model 67R: $289.95**

MODEL M66R
$189.95

This scope, which was designed for centerfire, 22 caliber rimfire, and adult air rifles, can zoom instantly from 2 to 7X for long range shots requiring pinpoint accuracy. It features speed dials with full saddle and range focus. There's also a special running target version—a delicate dot is set on each side of the horizontal member of a special, thin-line crosshair to provide proper leads for targets running right or left at 10 meters.

BEEMAN SCOPES

SS-1 AND SS-2 SERIES

Beeman SS-1 and SS-2 short scopes are extra compact and rugged, due largely to breakthroughs in optical engineering and computer programming of lens formulas. Less than 7 inches long, both scopes pack 11 lenses that actually gather light for bigger, brighter targets than "projected spot" targets. Scope body and built-in mounts are milled as a single unit from a solid block of hi-tensile aircraft aluminum.

SS-1 Series: $149.50
SS-2 Series: $199.50

SS-3 SERIES

Offers 1.5-4X zoom power for greater flexibility. Glare-free black matte finish is anodized into metal for deep sheen and extra toughness. Instant action dial around front of scope dials away parallax error and dials in perfect focus from 10 feet to infinity. Scope measures only 5³/₄ inches in length and weighs only 8.5 ounces.

SS-3 Series: $199.50

BLUE RIBBON AND BLUE RING SCOPES

These versatile scopes have a Range Focus Ring by which parallax error can be dialed away and perfect focus dialed in from 13 feet to infinity. Model 66R also has Speed Dials—extra large windage and elevation knobs that are especially fast and easy to use. Beeman economy scopes (Models 30A, 35R and 45R) are notable for their high lens counts.

SCOPE SPECIFICATIONS:

Model	Series	Power	Obj. Lens mm	Tube Dia. in. (mm)	Wgt. oz. (gm)	Length in. (mm)	Field of View 100 yds. (100m)	Eye Relief in. (mm)	Reticle
30A	Blue Ring	4	15	³/₄" (19)	4.5* (128)	10.2 (259)	21 (7m)	2 (50)	5 pt. TL
35R	Blue Ring	3	20	³/₄" (19)	5.2* (147)	11 (280)	25 (8.3m)	2.5 (64)	5 pt. TL
45R	Blue Ring	3-7	20	³/₄" (19)	6.3* (179)	10.8 (275)	26-12 (8.7-4m)	2.5 (64)	5 pt. TL
50R	Blue Ribbon	2.5	32	1" (25)	12.3 (350)	12 (305)	33 (11m)	3.5 (90)	5 pt. TL
54R	Blue Ribbon	4	32	1" (25)	12.3 (35)	12 (305)	29' (8.8m)	3.5 (90)	5 pt. TL
66R	Blue Ribbon	2.7	32	1" (25)	14.9 (422)	11.4 (290)	62-16 (18.9-5.3m)	3 (76)	5 pt. TL
67R	Blue Ribbon	3-9	40	1" (25)	15.2 (431)	14.4 (366)	43.5-15' (13.3-4.6m)	3 (76)	5 pt. TL
68R	Blue Ribbon	4-12	40	1" (25)	15.2 (431)	14.4 (366)	30.5'-11' (9.3-3.4m)	3 (76)	5 pt. TL
MS-1	Blue Ribbon	4	18	1" (25)	8 (227)	7.5 (191)	23' (7m)	3.5	5 pt. TL
SS-1	Blue Ribbon	2.5	16	⁷/₈" (22)	6.9* (195)	5.5 (137)	32.5 (10.8m)	3 (76)	5 pt. TL
SS-2	Blue Ribbon	3	21	1.38" (35)	13.6* (385)	6.8 (172)	34.5 (11.5m)	3.5 (90)	5 pt. TL
SS-2	Blue Ribbon	4	21	1.38" (35)	13.7 (388)	7 (182)	24.6 (8.2m)	3.5 (90)	5 pt. TL
SS-3	Blue Ribbon	1.5-4	16	⁷/₈" (22)	8.6 (241)*	5.75 (146)	44.6'-24.6' (13.6-7.5m)	3 (76)	5 pt. TL

*Includes scope mount in price and weight.   TL = Thin Line reticle.

B-SQUARE SCOPE MOUNTS

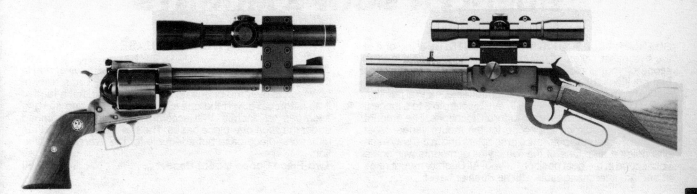

44 MAGNUM RUGER BLACKHAWK MOUNTS
$49.95 (Stainless)
$39.95 (Blue)

M-94 ANGLE EJECT SCOPE MOUNT
For Winchester 94 Angle Eject
$49.95

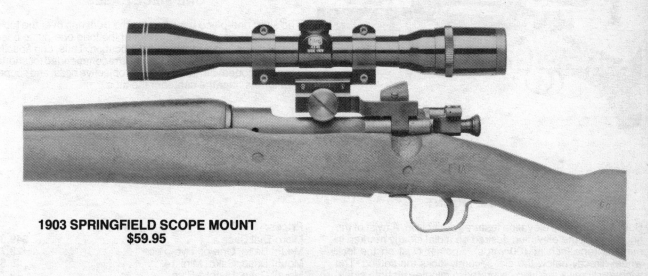

1903 SPRINGFIELD SCOPE MOUNT
$59.95

MAUSER 98

OTHER POPULAR RIFLES

ONE-PIECE BASES
$9.95

This new one-piece base fits both long and short actions. It provides better alignment than two-piece blocks for the straightest, strongest and best looking base available. It can be attached with socket screws and wrench provided. The Mauser 98 Large Ring and Small Ring bases have a notch that locates itself in the clip-lip, so there's no need to file for clip-lips or bolt handle clearance. Bases are available for Winchester 70, Savage 110, Browing A-Bolt, Remington 700, T/C Hawken, and many others.

BUEHLER SCOPE MOUNTS

BUEHLER TELESCOPIC SIGHT MOUNTS. By using one of the five basic styles of mount bases, you may position the scope of your choice in the best possible location—the one that positions the scope so that the shooter has a full field of view when his face is nestled in a comfortable, natural position against the stock. Scopes vary in eye relief from 3 to 5 inches. Sight adjustment turrets are in different locations. The amount of space available on the scope for the mount varies. Most important of all is the difference in shooters and in the way each one holds a rifle. One of the five styles of mounts will locate your scope in the best position for you. All Buehler mount rings fit and are interchangeable with all Buehler bases.

TWO-PIECE BASE

Two-piece bases locate the front ring over the receiver ring in the same place as the short one-piece base. The rear ring, however, is over the bridge on bolt-action rifles, not ahead of it as is the case with the one-piece bases. The ring spacing averages 4¹/₂ inches. Will accommodate scopes described under the *short* one-piece bases. The eye relief is shorter than either one-piece base but adequate for the average installation.

Two-Piece Scope Mount Base. **$28.50**

ONE-PIECE BASES

The short one-piece base locates the front ring over the top of the receiver ring about 1 inch aft of the long one-piece base. The rear ring is in about the same location. Thus, ring spacing averages 4 inches. The short base is recommended for shorter scopes, scopes with large and long objective bells, and scopes with turrets near the center of the tube.

MICRO DIAL MOUNT

Both windage and elevation features are built in. A twist of the fingers fixes the elevation desired on a dial clearly marked in minutes (one inch at 100 yards). Another twist on the lock wheel directly below the dial securely locks the setting. The windage screws are also calibrated in minutes on both sides. The Micro Dial is designed primarily for all scopes with internal adjustments, such as the Balvar 2¹/₂ to 8 (use Code 7 Rings for Balvar), but can be used to advantage with many other scopes. Dial also makes it possible to switch scopes between rifles. The ring spacing is 4 inches.

Prices:

Micro-Dial Base	**$49.00**
Mount Base, One or Two-piece	29.75
Mount Base, Sako, Mini-14.	45.50
Mount Base, Pistol—Blue.	29.75
Mount Base, Pistol—Stainless	37.50
Mount Base, Pistol M83, (Blue or Silver)	39.50

BUEHLER SCOPE MOUNTS

M83 BUEHLER PISTOL MOUNT
(shown on Ruger Blackhawk)

M83 PISTOL MOUNT

Installs without drilling or tapping (wrench included). Base is made of high tensile Aircraft Aluminum Alloy, anodized and dyed in black or silver to match blue or stainless steel pistols. Designed for calibers up through 357 Magnum. Use code 7 rings.

M83. . . . . $39.50

BUEHLER RINGS FOR BOTH ONE AND TWO-PIECE MOUNTS

A double split-type ring with the added beauty of a smoothly rounded "ball turret top." The steel spacer at the top of each ring is made of 16 laminations .002" thick which may be peeled off one or more at a time, thus accurately fitting all scopes up to .01" smaller in size than the normal dimension of the ring.

MOUNT RINGS

Double split rings, codes 6, 7 & 8 . . . . $38.75
Double split rings, codes 10, 11, 14, 15 . . . . 50.00
Spec. 30mm, code 30. . . . . 60.00
Engraved split rings, codes 6, 8 . . . . 95.00

BURRIS SCOPES

3X-9X FULLFIELD (illustrated)

A versatile scope for big game and varmint hunting. The most popular variable power scope because it fulfills a variety of purposes from long-range varmint shooting to shorter ranges of heavy brush shooting. A rugged, factory-sealed hunting scope with a big 14-foot field of view at 9X and a 38-foot field at 3X.

3X-9X FULLFIELD
Plex. $261.95
Post crosshair. 270.95
3"–1" dot 272.95

2X-7X FULLFIELD (not illus.)
Field of view: at 7X, 18 ft.; at 2X, 47 ft.

Plex. $247.95
Post crosshair. 256.95
3"-1" dot 258.95

1³/₄ X-5X FULLFIELD (not illus.)
Field of view: at 5X, 25ft.; at 1³/₄ X, 66 ft.

Plex. $222.95
Post crosshair. 230.95
3"–1" dot 233.95

3X-9X and 2X-7X available with Safari Finish, a Burris-developed low-luster, high-performance finish. $9.00 extra.

BURRIS SCOPES

MIKRO REVOLVER SCOPE

A scaled-down version of the big scopes, this ⅝-inch diameter tube weighs only four ounces. Designed to take the recoil of any magnum handgun. Packed with two ⅝-inch steel rings that fit standard handgun bases. Eye relief is nine inches minimum and 24 inches maximum.

Mikro Scope 2x and 3× Crosshair. $142.95

GUNSITE SCOUT SCOPE

Made for hunters who need a seven to 14-inch eye relief to mount just in front of the ejection port opening, allowing hunters to shoot with both eyes open. The 15-foot field of view and 2¾x magnification are ideal for brush guns and handgunners who use the "two-handed hold."

Gunsite Scout Scope 2 3/4x Plex XER $150.95

3X-9X FULLFIELD RAC SCOPE
WITH AUTOMATIC RANGEFINDER RETICLE

Once the crosshair has been zeroed in at 200 yards, it remains there regardless of the power setting. The range reticle automatically moves to a zero at ranges up to 500 yards as power is increased to fit the game between the stadia range wires. No need to adjust elevation knob. Bullet drop adjustment is automatic.

3X-9X Fullfield RAC . . . . $277.95 (Dot or Plex)

BURRIS SCOPES

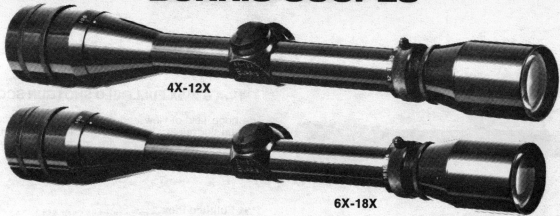

4X-12X

6X-18X

4X-12X FULLFIELD

The ideal scope for long-range varmint hunting and testing hand loads. Can also be used for big game hunting. Features crisp resolution, accurate parallax settings and a big field of view. Friction-type parallax settings from 50 yards to infinity with positive stop to prevent overturning. Fully sealed to withstand the worst field conditions and designed to deliver years of excellent service.

4X-12X FULLFIELD

Plex.	$306.95
Fine Plex.	295.95
2"–.7" Dot.	302.95

6X-18X FULLFIELD

This versatile, high magnification, variable scope can be used for hunting, testing hand loads or shooting bench rest. It features excellent optics, a precise parallax adjustment from 50 yards to infinity, accurate internal adjustments and a rugged, reliable mechanical design that will give years of dependable service. Fully sealed against moisture and dust.

6X-18X FULLFIELD

Plex.	$302.95
Fine Plex.	302.95
2"–.7" Dot	310.95
Fine Flex Silhouette	326.95

MINI 3X-9X   **MINI 2X-7X**   **2X LER**   **3X LER**

MINI 6X

MINI 4X

MINI SCOPES WITH PLEX RETICLE:

Mini 4X	$144.95
Mini 6X	156.95
Mini 3X-9X	201.95
Mini 2X-7X	195.95
Mini 4X-12X	266.95

LONG EYE RELIEF SCOPE WITH PLEX RETICLE:

1½X-4X LER	$235.95
2X LER	$144.95
3X LER	154.95
4X LER	162.95
5X LER	176.95

INTERMEDIATE EYE RELIEF SCOPE WITH PLEX RETICLE:

7X IER	$188.95
10X IER	233.95

SCOPES

BURRIS SCOPES

1¹/₂X SHOTGUN

2¹/₂X SHOTGUN

1¹/₂X & 2¹/₂X FULLFIELD SHOTGUN SCOPES

The huge field-of-view and recoil proof construction allows shotgun slug hunters to improve their accuracy. Running shots during low-light conditions are made possible with either scope.

1¹/₂x Fullfield Plex...........................$169.95
2¹/₂x Fullfield Plex............................177.95

10X, 12X & 6X–18X FULLFIELD SILHOUETTE SCOPES

These three scopes, with their precision click target type knobs and Burris Hi-Lume lenses give silhouette shooters a real edge. All new design allows fast, precise reticle adjustments, free of backlash, on both windage and elevation. Graduated knobs are easy to read and can be reset to zero once initial sighting is made. Threaded dust covers included.

10X Fullfield Fine Flex Silhouette $269.95
12X Fullfield Fine Flex Silhouette 273.95
6X–18X Fullfield Fine Flex Silhouette 336.95

10X SILHOUETTE SCOPE

12X SILHOUETTE SCOPE

6X–18X SILHOUETTE SCOPE

BURRIS RINGS, BASES AND MOUNTS

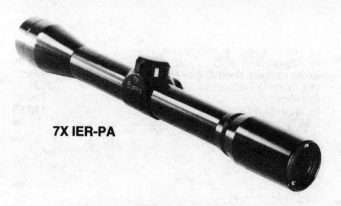

7X IER-PA

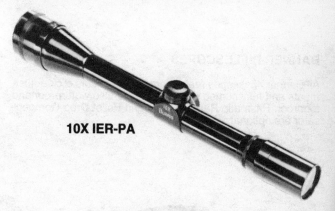

10X IER-PA

7X IER-PA
Intermediate Eye Relief
With Parallax Adjustment

This popular handgun scope has parallax settings from 25 meters to infinity. Target knobs with precision click adjustments are standard.
Price: $208.95 ($188.95 w/o p.a.)

10X IER-PA
Intermediate Eye Relief
With Parallax Adjustment

Designed for precision shooting handguns with barrels that are a minimum of 14 inches in length. Eye relief is 9 inches minimum and 14 inches maximum.
Price: $233.95 ($244.95 w/$1/2$" dot)

UNIVERSAL BASE (LU) LONG EYE RELIEF

Tough all steel bases feature a recoil stop-screw that lets the rear ring absorb the recoil generated by larger caliber handguns. They provide versatility of a universal dovetail base and magnum proof performance.

Universal Base Long Eye Relief $20.95

SILVER SAFARI BASE FOR HANDGUNS

A special nickel-chrome finish gives these bases a tough but beautiful stainless look. Features a recoil stop-screw that lets the rear ring absorb the recoil genrated by large caliber handguns.

Silver Safari Base $25.95

SUPREME BASE,
UNIVERSAL DOVETAIL
$22.95

MEDIUM EXTENSION FRONT RING,
STANDARD REAR RING,
UNIVERSAL DOVETAIL
$35.95

LONG EYE RELIEF
UNIVERSAL BASE (LU)
$20.95

TRUMOUNT BASE,
UNIVERSAL DOVETAIL
$20.95

BUSHNELL RIFLESCOPES

BANNER RIFLESCOPES

All Banner riflescopes feature precise resettable click adjustments and fully coated optics. They are also waterproof and fogproof. Prismatic Range Finder and Bullet Drop Compensator are optional.

6x-18x (40mm) Target/Varmint $215.95
4x-12x (40mm) BDC 199.95
3x-9x (38mm) Wide Angle, PRF. 145.95
16x (40mm) Target/Silhouette 194.95
6x (40mm) 129.95
4x (32mm), BDC. 110.95
2.5x (20mm) 79.95

BANNER 6X (40mm) Open Country

BANNER 4X-12X (40mm) Medium to Long Range

BANNER 4X (32mm) General-purpose w/BDC

TARGET SCOPES

These precise target riflescopes feature crisp, repeatable 1/8 MOA click adjustments in two styles, fully hard surface multi-coated optics, two sunshades (3″ and 5″), fully fogproof and waterproof.

36 × (40mm) Dot Reticle $579.95
36 × (40mm) Fine Crosshair Reticle 579.95
24 × (40mm) Dot Reticle 579.95
24 × (40mm) Fine Crosshair Reticle 579.95
6 × -24 × (40mm) Fine Crosshair Reticle 579.95

COMPACTS

Two new compact riflescopes offer the same features and performance as full-size Bausch & Lomb riflescopes in a lightweight design. Features versatile four times zoom ratio, resettable 1/4″ MOA click adjustments, fully hard surface multi-coated optics, one-piece body tube.

2 × -8 × (32mm) Balvar Compact $339.95
4 × (32mm) Balfor Compact 259.95

BUSHNELL RIFLESCOPES

BANNER 16x TARGET/SILHOUETTE RIFLESCOPE

BANNER 2.5X (20mm) Short Range

BANNER COMPACT RIFLESCOPES

Light in weight (11 ounces for the 2-8x and 8 ounces for the 4x), these scopes complement the popular lightweight rifles. They feature large 28mm objective lens for bright, sharp images, precise internal click adjustments, and a Multi-X reticle for a clearly visible aiming point.

2-8x (28mm) Banner Compact Riflescope $177.95
4x (28mm) Banner Compact Riflescope 117.95

(A) 2-8X (28mm) BANNER COMPACT RIFLESCOPE

(B) 4x (28mm) BANNER COMPACT RIFLESCOPE

BUSHNELL RIFLESCOPES

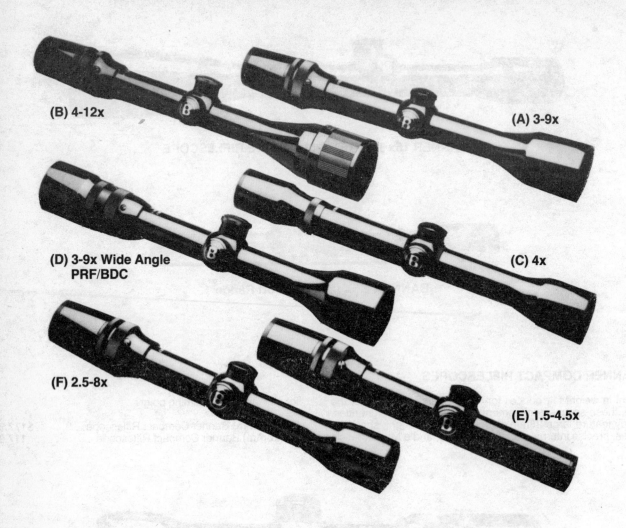

(B) 4-12x

(A) 3-9x

(D) 3-9x Wide Angle PRF/BDC

(C) 4x

(F) 2.5-8x

(E) 1.5-4.5x

SCOPECHIEF RIFLESCOPES

To maximize light transmission and image brightness, the precision ground polished lenses in the Scope Chief riflescope line are now multi-coated on all air-to-glass surfaces. Precision 1/4 M.O.A. click adjustments are standard, as is durable one-piece body tube. Scopes are hermetically sealed for full waterproof and fogproof integrity. Bullet Drop Compensator and Prismatic Range Finder included on 4-12x and 3-9x models.

3-9x40mm	$220.95
4-12x40mm PRF/BDC	269.95
3-9x40mm Wide Angle PRF/BDC	274.95
1.5-4.5x20mm	190.95
2.5-8x32mm	194.95
4x32mm	139.95

SCOPECHIEF SPECIFICATION CHART

	Variable Powers			Fixed Power
Magnification	3x-9x	2.5x-8x	1.5x-4.5x	4x
Objective Lens Aperture (mm)	40	32	20	32
Field of View at 100 yards (ft)	3x-35 9x-12.6	2.5x-45 8x-14	1.5x-73.7 4.5x-24.5	29
Weight (oz)	14.3	12.1	9.5	9.3
Length (in)	12.6	11.2	9.6	12
Eye Relief (in)	3x-3.5 9x-3.3	2.5x-3.7 8x-3.3	1.5x-3.5 4.5x-3.5	3.5
Exit Pupil (mm)	3x-13.3 9x-4.4	2.5x-12.8 8x-4	15x-13.3 4.5x-4.4	8
Relative Light Efficiency	3x-267 9x-30	2.5x-247 8x-96	1.5x-267 4.5x-30	96
MX Center CH Width at 100 yards	3x-.67 9x-.22	2.5x-.8 8x-.25	1.5x-1.3 4.5x-44	.5
Mix Distance Post Tip to Post Tip (in) at 100 yards	3x-24 9x-8	2.5x-28.8 8x-9	1.5x-48 4.5x-16	18
100 yards (in)	.5			

BUSHNELL RIFLESCOPES

VARIABLE POWER — BANNER RIFLESCOPE SPECIFICATION CHART

Magnification	Bullet Drop Compensator	Field of view at 100 yds. (ft.)	Weight (oz.)	Length (inches)	Eye distance (inches)	Entrance pupil (mm)	Exit pupil (mm)	Relative Light Efficiency	MX center CH width at 100 yds. (inches)	MX distance post tip to post tip (inches)	Graduation at 100 yds. (inches)
4x-12x 40mm	BDC	29 at 4x / 10 at 12x	15.5	13.5	3.2	40	10 at 4x / 3.3 at 12x	150 / 17	0.5 / .17	18 / 6	.75
3x-9x 40mm		35 at 3x / 12.6 at 9x	13	13	3.5	40	13.3 at 3x / 4.4 at 9x	267 / 30	.66 / .22	24 / 8	.75
3x-9x 38mm	BDC	43 at 3x WIDE ANGLE / 14.6 at 9x	14	12.1	3	38	12.7 at 3x / 4.2 at 9x	241 / 26.5	.66 / .22	24 / 8	1.0
3x-9x 32mm	BDC	39 at 3x / 13 at 9x	11	11.5	3.5	32	10.7 at 3x / 3.6 at 9x	171 / 19	.66 / .22	24 / 8	1.0
1.75x-4.5x 21mm	BDC	71 at 1.75x WIDE ANGLE / 27 at 4.5x	11.5	10.2	2.9	21	12 at 1.75x / 4.7 at 4.5x	216 / 33	1.18 / .44	45.7 / 17.8	1.5
1.5x-4x 21mm		63 at 1.5x / 28 at 4x	10.3	10.5	3.5	21	14 at 1.5x / 5 at 4x	294 / 41	1.3 / 0.5	48 / 18	1.5

FIXED POWER

Magnification	Bullet Drop Compensator	Field of view at 100 yds. (ft.)	Weight (oz.)	Length (inches)	Eye distance (inches)	Entrance pupil (mm)	Exit pupil (mm)	Relative Light Efficiency	MX center CH width at 100 yds. (inches)	MX distance post tip to post tip (inches)	Graduation at 100 yds. (inches)
10x 40mm	BDC	12	14.0	14.5	3	40	4	24	0.2	7.2	.66
6x 40mm		19.5	11.5	13.5	3	40	6.7	67	0.3	12	.75
4x 40mm	BDC	37.3 WIDE ANGLE	12	12.3	3	40	10	150	0.6	21	1.0
4x 32mm	BDC	29	10	12.0	3.5	32	8	96	0.5	18	1.0
2.5x 20mm		45	8	10.9	3.5	20	8	96	0.8	28.8	1.5

SPORTSVIEW TRUSCOPE

Lets the hunter confirm that the rifle is shooting where he is aiming in the field (where firing a shot would spook the game).

Truscope w/22 & 30 caliber arbor $47.95

SPORTVIEW RANGEFINDER

This compact hand-held unit combines a 5x modular prism system with three reticles calibrated for deer, antelope and elk. By bracketing the game within the stadia lines, the hunter has instant distance readout. The reticles are easily accessed by simply rotating the unit in the hand. The range of 25 to 125 yards covers the critical distance for bowhunters, muzzleloaders and handgun hunters. Fast focusing is achieved by an Insta-Focus system. Coated optics provide maximum light transmission., Roll down rubber eye cup ensures full field of view.

Model 14-0520 Sportview Compact Rangefinder . . $69.00

GRIFFIN & HOWE

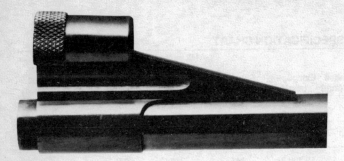

FRONT SIGHT
$275.00

The Griffin & Howe-type matted ramp front sight is hand-fitted to the barrel with a band. When fitted with a gold or ivory bead front sight and removable front sight cover, this sight gives a pleasing appearance and maximum efficiency. Available only on an installed basis.

BARREL BAND
$110.00

The forward swing swivel may be attached by a barrel band in front of the forearm or a barrel band through the forearm. Available only on an installed basis.

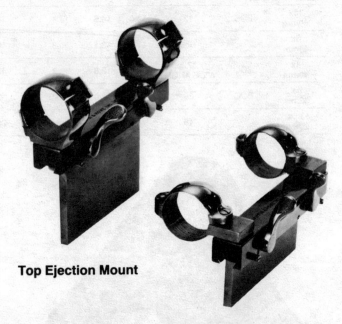

Top Ejection Mount

Standard Double-Lever Side Mount

QUARTER RIB EXPRESS SIGHT
$690.00 and up

This sight may be made with fixed standing bar and folding leaves sighted in for any range desired. All leaves are marked for distance; the surface is matted with a gold directional line extending down from a wide V. Available only on an installed basis.

TELESCOPE MOUNT

This mount has a locking cam action and is available for all models of rifles and is obtainable with 1-inch or 26mm brackets. Models are available to fit both domestic and imported telescopes. The mount holds the scope immovable in its split ring brackets. It can be mounted either low or high enough to enable use of iron sights when the telescope is mounted. It is readily detachable and, when replaced, it will always return to its original position with no scope mount adjustment necessary. Available in the following models:

Side Mount . . . . $160.00 (top ejection mount: $195.00)
Side Mount, installed 275.00
Top Mount* . . . . 330.00 and up
*Available only on an installed basis.

Standard double-lever side mount with split rings for telescopes with built-in elevation and windage adjustment; top ejection mount for rifles similar to the Winchester 94, where the fired cases extract upwards. This mount must be fitted in the off-set position; Garand mount, designed for use on the Garand military rifle, is mounted on the left side of the receiver to permit clip loading and top ejection.

JAEGER MOUNTS & ACCESSORIES

QUICK DETACHABLE SIDE MOUNT $250.00

The Jaeger mount permits removing and attaching the scope within a few seconds without the use of any coins or tools. The construction combines light weight with great rigidity. The unique clamping device locks the slide to the base securely and ensures return to zero. All mounts have windage adjustment at the rear ring.

Made for most bolt-action rifles as well as Remington 740 & 760, Savage 99, Winchester 88 and other lever-action rifles.

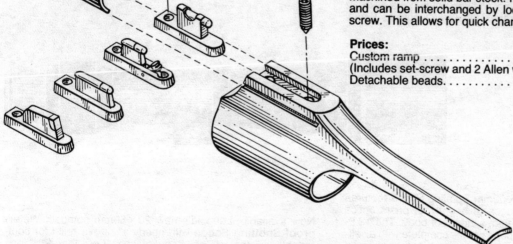

All mounts have split rings and are made in the following ring sizes and heights:

Mod. 20—1″ low
Mod. 21—1″ medium
Mod. 22—1″ high

Low rings for most scopes in low position; medium height rings for large objective scopes in low position; high rings for use of iron sights below scope.

Prices:

Complete mount w/1″ reg. rings $185.00
w/1″ front ext. ring 199.00
w/30mm reg. rings 199.00
w/30mm front ext. ring 199.00
All base sets 85.00
Rear rings 43.00
Front rings . . . . 56.00 to 64.00

CUSTOM FRONT SIGHT RAMP

Machined from solid bar stock. Front sights include a slide fit and can be interchanged by loosening a small socket set-screw. This allows for quick changes in height and style.

Prices:

Custom ramp $45.00
(Includes set-screw and 2 Allen wrenches)
Detachable beads . . . . 7.50 to 20.00

LEUPOLD RIFLE SCOPES

VARI-X II LINE
Reticles are the same apparent size throughout power range, stay centered during elevation and windage adjustments. Eyepieces are adjustable and fog-free.

Vari-X II 2x7

VARI-X II 2x7
A compact scope, no larger than the Leupold M8-4X, offering a wide range of power. It can be set at 2X for close ranges in heavy cover or zoomed to maximum power for shooting or identifying game at longer ranges. **$297.20**

Vari-X II 3x9

VARI-X II 3x9 (2 Models)
A wide selection of powers lets you choose the right combination of field of view and magnification to fit the particular conditions you are hunting at the time. Many hunters use the 3X or 4X setting most of the time, cranking up to 9X for positive identification of game or for extremely long shots. The adjustable objective eliminates parallax and permits precise focusing on any object from less than 50 yards to infinity for extra-sharp definition. **$299.95;** (with adjustable objective) **$337.40**

Vari-X II 4x12 A.O.

VARI-X II 4x12 A.O.
The ideal answer for big game and varmint hunters alike. At 12.25 inches, the 4x12 is virtually the same length as Vari-X II 3x9. **$361.45**

SPOTTING SCOPE

Leupold's Golden Ring 20 × 60mm Spotting Scope features extraordinary eye relief and crisp, bright roof prism optics housed in a lightweight, sealed, waterproof body. The 12.9-inch, 19.5-ounce Spotting Scope comes complete with a self-storing screw-on sunshade, lens caps, and a leather-trimmed green canvas case. **$419.65**

Now available: Leupold's new 20 × 50mm compact **Waterproof Spotting Scope** with nearly 1″ of eye relief for comfortable viewing with or without glasses. Less than 9¹/₂″ long and weighs only 17¹/₂″ ounces. **Price: $401.80**

LEUPOLD RIFLE SCOPES

VARIABLE POWER SCOPES
VARI-X III LINE

The Vari-X III scopes feature a power-changing system that is similar to the sophisticated lens systems in today's finest cameras. Some of the improvements include an extremely accurate internal control system and a sharp, superb-contrast sight picture. Reticles are the same apparent size throughout power range, stay centered during elevation/windage adjustments. Eyepieces are adjustable and fog-free.

VARI-X III 1.5x5

Here's a fine selection of hunting powers for ranges varying from very short to those at which big game is normally taken. The exceptional field at 1.5X lets you get on a fast-moving animal quickly. With the generous magnification at 5X, you can hunt medium and big game around the world at all but the longest ranges. **$312.25.** Also available in new matte finish. **$330.10**

Vari-X III 1.5 × 5

VARI-X III 2.5 × 8

This is an excellent range of powers for almost any kind of game, inlcuding varmints. In fact, it possibly is the best all-around variable going today. The top magnification provides plenty of resolution for practically any situation. **$352.15**

Vari-X III 2.5 × 8

VARI-X III 3.5x10

The extra power range makes these scopes the optimum choice for year-around big game and varmint hunting. The adjustable objective model, with its precise focusing at any range beyond 50 yards, also is an excellent choice for some forms of target shooting. **$368.35 ($405.90 with adjustable objective)**

Vari-X III 3.5 × 10

VARI-X III 6.5 × 20

This scope has the widest range of power settings in our variable line, with magnifications that are especially useful to hunters of all types of varmints. In addition, it can be used for any kind of big game hunting where higher magnifications are an aid. (with adjustable objective) **$436.30**

**Vari-X III 6.5 × 20
(with adjustable objective)**

LEUPOLD SCOPES

THE COMPACT SCOPE LINE

The introduction of the Leupold Compacts has coincided with the increasing popularity of the new featherweight rifles. Leupold Compact scopes give a more balanced appearance atop these new scaled-down rifles and offer generous eye relief, magnification and field of view, yet are smaller inside and out. Fog-free.

2.5X COMPACT
The 2.5X Compact is only 8½ inches long and weighs just 7.4 ounces. **$186.35**

2.5X COMPACT

4X COMPACT
& 4X RF Special

4X COMPACT
The 4X Compact is over an inch shorter than the standard 4X. The 4X RF Special is focused to 75 yards and has a Duplex reticle with finer crosshairs. **$212.85**

6X COMPACT

6X COMPACT
To make the 6X Compact, Leupold's shaved an ounce and a half and .7 inch off the standard scope of the same magnification. **$217.20**

6X COMPACT
(with adjustable objective)

6X COMPACT A.O.
The popularity of this magnification seems to be growing at the same rate as the availability of lighter or so-called "mountain" rifles. Now available with adjustable objective lens. **$254.70**

2X7 COMPACT

2X7 COMPACT
Two ounces lighter and a whole inch shorter than its full-size counterpart, this 2x7 is one of the world's most compact variable power scopes. It's the perfect hunting scope for today's trend toward smaller and lighter rifles. **$268.50**

3x9 COMPACT

3X9 COMPACT
The 3X9 Compact is a full-blown variable that's 3½ ounces lighter and 1.3 inches shorter than a standard 3x9. Also available in new flat black, matte finish. **$289.50**

3x9 COMPACT
(with adjustable objective)

3X9 COMPACT A.O.
Big scope performance in a package compatible with the growing list of scaled down and featherweight rifles. Now available with adjustable objective lens. **$327.05**

LEUPOLD SCOPES

THE TARGET SCOPE LINE

Shooters using Leupold target scopes are dominating both local and national bench rest and silhouette matches. Fog-free.

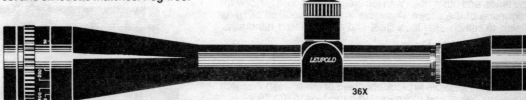

36X

36X TARGET SCOPE

A full 36 power magnification with clear, sharp resolution is possible with Leupold's 36X target scope, all in a package that is only 13.9 inches long and weighs just 15½ ounces. Adjustable objective. **$497.30**

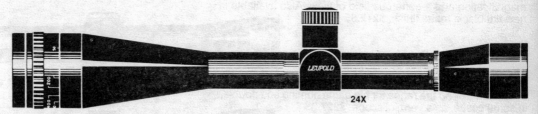

24X

24X TARGET SCOPE

The 24X is just 13.6 inches long and weighs only 14½ ounces. It is compact enough to be receiver mounted and light enough to permit transfer of significant weight from scope to rifle. Adjustable objective. **497.30**

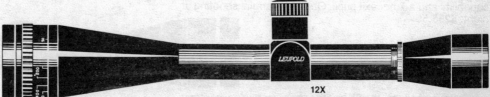

12X

12X TARGET SCOPE

The 12X target scope has the magnification and clear, sharp-contrast sight picture that target shooters need. Two types of redesigned windage/elevation adjustment knobs are included. Adjustable objective. **$374.50**

VARI-X III 6.5x20

VARI-X III 6.5x20 TARGET SCOPE

The 6.5x20 target allows a shooter to not only change magnifications quickly to match target range, but also rapidly select the windage and elevation needed for each shot, knowing he can unerringly return to a previous setting with ease. Adjustable objective. **$497.30**

LEUPOLD SCOPES

EXTENDED EYE RELIEF HANDGUN SCOPE LINE

2X EER

With an optimum eye relief of 12-24 inches, the 2X EER is an excellent choice for most handguns. It is equally favorable for carbines and other rifles with top ejection that calls for forward mounting of the scope. Available in black anodized or silver finish to match stianless steel and nickel-plated handguns. **$166.05**

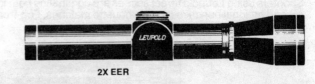
2X EER

4X EER

Only 8.4 inches long and 7.6 ounces. Optimum eye relief 12-24 inches. Avaialble in black anodized or silver finish to match stainless steeel and nickel-plated handguns. **$202.70**

4X EER

FIXED-POWER SCOPE LINE

4X

The all-time favorite is the 4X which delivers a widely used magnification and a generous field of view. Also available in new flat black, matte finish. **$212.85**

4X

6X

Gaining popularity fast among fixed power scopes is the 6X, which can extend the range for big game hunting and double, in some cases, as a varmint scope. **$227.35**

6X

6X42mm

Large 42mm objective lens features increased light gathering capability and a 7mm exit pupil. Great for varmint shooting at night. **$255.55**

8X

A true varmint scope, the 8X has the sharp resolution, contrast and accuracy that also make it effective for some types of target shooting. Adjustable objective permits precise, parallax-free focusing. **$303.05**

   Also available: **8 × 36mm**

   Features a target style dot and thinner Duplex reticle for long range use (focused at 300 yds. instead of 150). **$303.05 ($324.05** w/target style dot.)

8X

12X

Superlative optical qualities, outstanding resolution and magnification make the 12X a natural for the varmint shooter. Adjustable objective is standard for parallax-free focusing. **$307.00**

12X

LYMAN RECEIVER SIGHTS

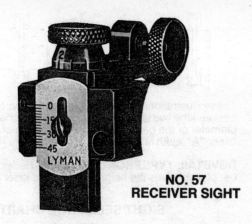

**NO. 57
RECEIVER SIGHT**

LYMAN 57 RECEIVER SIGHT

An unobtrusive micrometer receiver sight for hunting or target shooting with sporter, target or military rifle. This sight is equipped with a push-button quick release slide that makes it ideal for alternating use on a scope-equipped rifle.

Fully adjustable with audible 1/4-minute clicks for windage and elevation. Coin-slotted stayset knobs for hunting.

Slide adjustments are equipped with precision scales to aid in pre-setting sights for specific ranges or wind conditions. Slide furnished with elevation stop screw that facilitates return to "zero" if removed and reattached. Slide operates in dovetail channel.
No. 57 Receiver Sight, complete $52.95

LYMAN 66 RECEIVER SIGHT

Similar in design and construction to the No. 57 receiver sight, the Model 66 was designed specifically for autoloading, pump-action and lever-action rifles. Ideally suited for use on the Ruger 44 Carbine. Features include 1/4-minute click adjustments for windage and elevation, quick release slide, and elevation stop screw for return to "zero" if detached.

Push button release features of slide facilitate speedy removal and reattachment. Coin-slotted stayset hunting knobs only. Like the Model 57, this sight is furnished with settings scales for easy reference.
No. 66 Receiver Sight, complete $52.95

**NO. 66
RECEIVER SIGHT**

MODEL 66U RECEIVER SIGHT

Designed for use on most modern shotguns with a flat-sided, round-top receiver (only exceptions are Browning "hump-back" and Remington Model 11). Offers 1/4-minute elevation and windage adjustments. Will not fog up and is impervious to moisture.

No. 66U Receiver Sight $49.95

SERIES 17A TARGET FRONTS

Teamed with a Lyman receiver sight, these low silhouette front sights provide precise, X-ring accuracy on the range. Designed for use with dovetail slot mounting, they are supplied with seven interchangeable inserts (see descriptions below) that are locked into place with a threaded cap.

Series 17A Target Front Sight complete with inserts. $22.95

TARGET FRONT SIGHTS
SIGHT HEIGHT*

17AHB . . . .360 in.   17 AMI. . .445 in.   17AUG. . . .532 in.
*From bottom of dovetail to center of aperture.

LYMAN HUNTING FRONT SIGHTS

Despite the exceptionally sharp definition provided by a fine aperture receiver sight, an equally fine front sight is necessary for consistently accurate shooting, particularly in extreme glare and overcast in the field. Lyman ivory bead front sights are the ideal field front sights. They present a flat optical surface that's equally illuminated by bright or dull light, and they keep their "color" under all light conditions. The Lyman ivory bead front sight is the perfect teammate for your favorite Lyman receiver sight, and will give you a reliable, sharply defined, glareless aiming surface, even under the worst conditions. You can fit a ready adaptable Lyman bead front sight to your rifle in minutes.

A—WIDTH   F—WIDTH

These illustrations show the size and appearance difference between the two standard base widths. In general, the outside diameter of the barrel determines the width of the base to be used. "A" width is used with most ramps.

DOVETAIL-TYPE FRONT SIGHTS (first letter following number of sight gives the height, the second letter the width)

NO. 31 FRONT SIGHT
1/16-inch BEAD

This sight is designed to be used on ramps. Standard 3/8-inch dovetail. Ivory bead. See Sight Selection Chart.

Price: No. 31 Front Sight $7.50

NO. 3 FRONT SIGHT
1/16-inch BEAD

This sight is mounted directly in the barrel dovetail. 3/8-inch dovetail is standard. Ivory bead. See Sight Selection Chart.

Price: No. 3 Front Sight $7.50

NO. 18 SCREW-ON TYPE RAMP

The screw-on ramp is designed to be secured with a heavy 8-40 screw (it may be brazed on if desired). Screw-on ramps are ruggedly built and extremely versatile. They use A width front sights, and are available in the following heights:

18A—Low Ramp: .100-inch from top of barrel to bottom of dovetail.

18C—Medium Ramp: .250-inch from top of barrel to bottom of dovetail.

18E—High Ramp: .350-inch from top of barrel to bottom of dovetail.

No. 18 Screw-On Ramp less sight. $13.50

SIGHT SELECTION CHART

MODELS SUPPLIED 1/16" bead	Height Inches	Width Inches
31BA	.240	11/32
31CA	.290	11/32
3CF	.290	17/32
31FA	.330	11/32
3FF	.330	17/32
31GA	.345	11/32
3GF	.345	17/32
31HA	.360	11/32
3HF	.360	17/32
31JA	.390	11/32
3JF	.390	17/32
31KA	.410	11/32
3KF	.410	17/32
31MA	.445	11/32
3MF	.445	17/32
31SA	.500	11/32
3SF	.500	17/32
31VA	.560	11/32
3VF	.560	17/32

RAMP FRONT SIGHTS

18E

18A

18C

Sight Height Chart (Hunting Front Sights)

Height	.240	.290	.330	.345	.360	.390	.410	.445	.500	.560
3 17/32" Base (Ivory)		CF 3030038	FF 3030039	GF 3030040	HF 3030041	JF 3030042	KF 3030043	MF 3030044	SF 3030046	VF 3030047
3 17/32" Base (Gold)		CF 3030054	FF 3030055	GF 3030056	HF 3030057	JF 3030058	KF 3030059	MF 3030060	SF 3030062	VF 3030063
28 17/32" Base (Ivory)		CF 3281254	FF 3281255	GF 3281256	HF 3281257	JF 3281258	KF 3281259	MF 3281260	SF 3281262	VF 3281263
28 17/32" Base (Gold)		CF 3281279	FF 3281280	GF 3281281	HF 3281282	JF 3281283	KF 3281284	MF 3281285	SF 3281287	VF 3281288
31 11/32" Base (Ivory)	BA 3311366	CA 3311367	FA 3311368	GA 3311369	HA 3311370	JA 3311371	KA 3311372	MA 3311373	SA 3311375	VA 3311377
31 11/32" Base (Gold)	BA 3311407	CA 3311408	FA 3311409	GA 3311410	HA 3311411	JA 3311412	KA 3311413	MA 3311414	SA 3311416	VA 3311417
37 11/32" Base (Ivory)	BA 3371668	CA 3371669	FA 3371670	GA 3371671	HA 3371672	JA 3371673	KA 3371674	MA 3371675	SA 3371677	VA 3371678
37 11/32" Base (Gold)	BA 3371709	CA 3371710	FA 3371711	GA 3371712	HA 3371713	JA 3371714	KA 3371715	MA 3371716	SA 3371718	VA 3371719

LYMAN SIGHTS

BASES
NO. 25 BASES

Permit the installation of dovetail rear sights (such as Lyman 16 leaf sight) on rifles that do not have dovetail cut in barrel. They also supply a higher line of sight when needed. The No. 25 Base is mounted by drilling and tapping the barrel for two 6-48 screws. Screws are supplied with base.

Price: No. 25 Base $6.95

STANDARD BASES	HEIGHT FROM TOP OF BARREL TO BOTTOM OF DOVETAIL	BARREL RADIUS
25A Base (Low)	.025″	.875 or larger
25C Base (High)	.125″	.875 or larger
SPECIAL BASES		
25B Base	.125″	.875 or larger

Fits factory screw holes on Remington 740, 742, 760, 725 & replaces factory rear

LEAF SIGHTS
NO. 16 FOLDING LEAF SIGHT

Designed primarily as open rear sights with adjustable elevation, leaf sights make excellent auxiliary sights for scope-mounted rifles. They fold close to the barrel when not in use, and they can be installed and left on the rifle without interfering with scope or mount. Two lock screws hold the elevation blade adjustments firmly in place. A sight of this type could save the day if the scope becomes damaged through rough handling. Leaf sights are available in the following heights:

16A—.400″ high; elevates to .500″.
16B—.345″ high; elevates to .445″.
16C—.500″ high; elevates to .600″.

For installation on rifles without a dovetail slot, use Lyman No. 25 Base.

Price: No. 16 Folding Leaf Sight $10.95

NO. 12 SLOT BLANKS

These blanks fill the standard 3/8-inch rear barrel dovetail when a receiver sight is installed. They are also available for front sight dovetails and ramps when a scope is being used. Three lengths are available, all fit standard 3/8-inch dovetails. **Price: $3.50** (all sizes)
No. 12S (3/8″ × 5/8″ long) for standard rear barrel slots.
No. 12SS (3/8″ × 9/16″ long) for standard front sight slots and some rear slots in narrow barrels.
No. 12SF (3/8″ × 11/32″ long) has square ends and is intended for use in ramps.

SHOTGUN SIGHTS

Lyman shotgun sights are available for all shotguns. Equipped with oversized ivory beads that give perfect definition on either bright or dull days, they are easy to see under any light conditions. They quickly catch your eye on fast upland targets, and point out the lead on long passing shots. Lyman shotgun sights are available with white bead, and can be fitted to your gun in minutes.

No. 10 Front sight (press fit) for use on double-barrel, or ribbed single-barrel guns. $3.50
No. 10D Front sight (screw fit) for use on non-ribbed single-barrel guns; supplied with a wrench. 4.50
No. 11 Middle sight (press fit). This small middle sight is intended for use on double-barrel and ribbed single-barrel guns. 3.50

When you replace an open rear sight with a receiver sight, it is usually necessary to install a higher front sight to compensate for the higher plane of the new receiver sight. The table below shows the increase in front sight height that's required to compensate for a given error at 100 yards.

AMOUNT OF ADJUSTMENT NECESSARY TO CORRECT FRONT SIGHT ERROR																				
DISTANCE BETWEEN FRONT AND REAR SIGHTS	14″	15″	16″	17″	18″	19″	20″	21″	22″	23″	24″	25″	26″	27″	28″	29″	30″	31″	32″	33″	34″
1	.0038	.0041	.0044	.0047	.0050	.0053	.0055	.0058	.0061	.0064	.0066	.0069	.0072	.0074	.0077	.0080	.0082	.0085	.0088	.0091	.0093
Amount of **2**	.0078	.0083	.0089	.0094	.0100	.0105	.0111	.0116	.0122	.0127	.0133	.0138	.0144	.0149	.0155	.0160	.0156	.0171	.0177	.0182	.0188
Error **3**	.0117	.0125	.0133	.0142	.0150	.0159	.0167	.0175	.0184	.0192	.0201	.0209	.0217	.0226	.0234	.0243	.0251	.0259	.0268	.0276	.0285
100 Yards **4**	.0155	.0167	.0178	.0189	.0200	.0211	.0222	.0234	.0244	.0255	.0266	.0278	.0289	.0300	.0311	.0322	.0333	.0344	.0355	.0366	.0377
Given in **5**	.0194	.0208	.0222	.0236	.0250	.0264	.0278	.0292	.0306	.0319	.0333	.0347	.0361	.0375	.0389	.0403	.0417	.0431	.0445	.0458	.0472
Inches **6**	.0233	.0250	.0267	.0283	.0300	.0317	.0333	.0350	.0367	.0384	.0400	.0417	.0434	.0450	.0467	.0484	.0500	.0517	.0534	.0551	.0567

EXAMPLE: Suppose your rifle has a 27-inch sight radius, and shoots 4 inches high at 100 yards, with the receiver sight adjusted as low as possible. The 27-inch column shows that the correction for a 4-inch error is .0300 inch. This correction is added to the overall height of the front sight (including dovetail). Use a micrometer or similar accurate device to measure sight height. Thus, if your original sight measured .360 inch, it should be replaced with a sight .390 inch high, such as a J height sight.

MERIT SHOOTING AIDS

IRIS SHUTTER DELUX MASTER TARGET DISC WITH FLEXIBLE NEOPRENE LIGHT SHIELD

May be cut to size. Particularly adapted for use with extension, telescope height and tang sights. The 1½-inch diameter flexible neoprene light shield is permanently attached to the eye cup, which is replaceable by removing three screws. The shield is concentrically ribbed on its concave face for cutting to suitable size. It is more advantageous than a large metal disc since it protects the sighting equipment in case the disc is accidentally bumped.

The Master Target Disc may be used on all sights having clearance for a disc ⁷⁄₁₆-inch thick and ¾-inch or larger in diameter.

Merit Delux Master Disc	$60.00
Replacement Shield	8.95
Delux Replacement Shield and Steel Cup	10.00

MERIT DELUX NO. 3 SERIES DISC

Side View **Front Views**
(minimum and maximum opening)

Other size apertures are obtained by simply turning the knurled eyepiece right or left respectively to decrease or increase the opening.

Merit Delux No. 3LS **$50.00**
Outside diameter of disc ¹¹⁄₁₆″. Shank ¹¹⁄₃₂″ long.

Merit Delux No. 3A **50.00**
Outside diameter of disc ¹¹⁄₁₆″. Shank ¹⁵⁄₃₂″ long. Disc thickness ⁷⁄₃₂″.

Merit No. 4SS—Outside diameter of disc ½″. Shank ⁵⁄₁₆″ long. Disc thickness ¼″. **$40.00**
Merit No. 4LS—Outside diameter of disc ½″. Shank ¹¹⁄₃₂″ long. Disc thickness ¼″. **40.00**
Merit No. 4ELS—Outside diameter of disc ½″. Shank ½″ long. Disc thickness ¼″. **40.00**

The merit optical attachment with aperture is the answer to a shooter's problem when eyesight is impaired. It (1) concentrates and sharpens the vision by increasing the focal depth of the eye, making pistol or rifle sights stand out sharp and clear; (2) cuts out objectionable side lights; (3) helps the shooter to take the same position for each shot; (4) gives instant and easy choice of the right aperture to suit your own eye and particular conditions at time of shooting. The Delux model has swinging arm feature so that the shooter can swing the aperture from the line of vision when not shooting.

Delux Optical Attachment **$60.00**

Replacement suction cup **8.00**

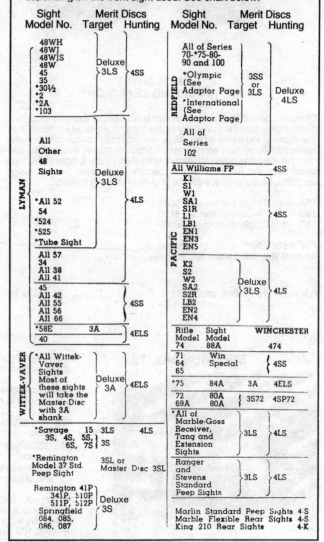

SIGHT CHART

Popular Peep Sights and the proper Merit Discs to fit them. The Merit Master Target Disc may be had with any of the No. 3 series shanks. All of the sights marked ★ will take the Master Disc depending on the front sight used. See chart below:

Sight Model No.	Merit Discs Target	Hunting
LYMAN		
48WH / 48WJ / 48WJS / 48W / 45 / 35 / *30½ / *2 / *2A / *103	Deluxe 3LS	4SS
All Other 48 Sights	Deluxe 3LS	
*All 52 / 54 / *524 / *525 / *Tube Sight		4LS
All 57 / 34 / All 38 / All 41		
45 / All 42 / All 55 / All 56 / All 66		4SS
*58E	3A	4ELS
40		
WITTEK-VAVER		
*All Wittek-Vaver Sights Most of these sights will take the Master Disc with 3A shank	Deluxe 3A	4ELS
*Savage 3S, 4S, 5S, 6S, 7S	3LS / 3S	4LS
*Remington Model 37 Std. Peep Sight	3SL or Master Disc 3SL	
Remington 41P 341P, 510P 511P, 512P Springfield 084, 085, 086, 087	Deluxe 3S	

Sight Model No.	Merit Discs Target	Hunting
REDFIELD		
All of Series 70-*75-80-90 and 100		
*Olympic (See Adaptor Page)	3SS or 3LS	Deluxe 4LS
*International (See Adaptor Page)		
All of Series 102		
All Williams FP		4SS
PACIFIC		
K1 / S1 / W1 / SA1 / S1R / L1 / LB1 / EN1 / EN3 / EN5		4SS
K2 / S2 / W2 / SA2 / S2R / LB2 / EN2 / EN4	Deluxe 3LS	4LS

Rifle Model	Sight Model	**WINCHESTER**
74	88A	474
71 / 64 / 65	Win Special	4SS
*75	84A	3A 4ELS
72 / 69A	80A / 80A	3S72 4SP72
*All of Marble-Goss Receiver, Tang and Extension Sights		3LS 4LS
Ranger and Stevens Standard Peep Sights		3LS 4LS

Marlin Standard Peep Sights	4-S
Marble Flexible Rear Sights	4-S
King 210 Rear Sights	4-K

MILLET SIGHTS™
SCOPE MOUNTS

Adjustable Rear

Fixed Rear

Front Sight

SCOPE-SITE™

Scope-Site solves two major problems that arise in effective use of telescopic sights. First, scopes are not useable for low-light, close-in shots in densely wooded areas. Second, scopes on high magnification take too much time to align on distant shots for fast, elusive game.

Scope-Site provides open patridge-style high visibility sights above the telescopic sight. The rear sights are either click-adjustable or fixed. Both types come with white outline apertures. Front post sights are blaze orange.

Scope-Site is far superior to see-through type mounts, because the telescopic sight remains close to the bore for proper cheeking on the stock comb. Scope-Site requires the rifleman to move his head only one inch to see through his open sights.

Scope-Site Ring Set Adjustable	**$69.95**
Scope-Site Ring Set Fixed	39.95
Convertible Top Cap Set Adjustable	56.95
Two-Piece Base Set	20.95

ANGLE-LOC SCOPE RINGS
(for Weaver-Type Bases)

Millett's 1″ Angle-Loc scope rings (for use with Weaver-type bases) feature positive clamping mounts for solid alignment of the base to the ring, and windage adjustment integral to the rings enabling shooters to fine-tune the scope rings to their firearms. Available in three heights and also with engravings

Angle-Loc Scope-Site Fixed (low, medium, high)	**$39.95**
Angle-Loc Scope-Site Adjustable (low, medium, high)	69.95
Angle-Loc Engraved Rings (low, medium, high)	39.95
Angle-Loc Smooth Rings (low, medium, high)	26.95
.26 mm Angle-Loc Smooth Rings (low, medium, high)	29.95
.26mm Engraved Rings (low, medium, high)	42.95

UNIVERSAL CUSTOM SCULPTURED BASES

Millett's 2-piece scope bases have outstanding features. Custom crafted style on the outside with all of the excess mass remove from the underside, makes these bases the lightest, heat treated, nickel steel bases on the market, 40% lighter.

700 Series (Two piece set)	SB70001	**$20.95**
FN Series (Two piece set)	FN00002	20.95
70 Series (Two Piece Set)	WB70003	20.95

MILLETT SIGHTS ™
Rifle Sights

COLT AR-15 (And similar models)

Riflemen will appreciate this new peep sight system for AR-15's. Fully adjustable for windage and elevation at the rear sight. No more difficult front sight adjustment. The Millett front sight is a serrated post design that provides a sharp, crisp sight picture under all lighting conditions. A real improvement over the round factory front sight. The rear peep sight blade has a large eye piece that blocks out the surrounding light and allows a sharp, crisp image to show through the cone-shaped aperture. Easy to install requiring no special tools.

Combo Peep Sight (Peep Sight Rear/Serrated Ramp Front)	AR15001	**$55.95**
Rear Only Peep Sight (.080 Dia. Aperture)	AR15002	**45.95**
Front Only Serrated Ramp	AR15003	**10.95**

RUGER MINI-14

Mini-14 owners will be elated with this new Series 100 adjustable sight system. Precision click adjustments for windage and elevation with easy return to zero. The large eye piece on the peep sight blade blocks out surrounding light to provide a sharp sight picture which greatly improves shooting accuracy. The cone-shaped aperture totally eliminates sighting error caused by reflected light. Easy to install with no special tools or gunsmithing required.

Mini-14 Rear Peep Sight (.080 Dia. Aperture)	RM14001	**$45.95**
Mini-14 Front Sight		**15.95**
Mini-14 Combo (Rear peep/post front)		**60.95**

H&K 91, 93 (And similar models)

Now H&K owners can have a traditional peep sight system, fully adjustable for windage and elevation, with precision click adjustments and an easy return to zero. The single aperture rear blade has a large eye piece that blocks out surrounding light to provide a sharp, crisp sight picture, greatly improving shooting accuracy. The cone-shaped aperture totally eliminates sighting error caused by reflected light. Easy to install with no special tools or gunsmithing required.

Rear Only Peep Sight (.080 Dia. Aperture)	HK91001	**$45.95**

RUGER 10/22 INTERCHANGEABLE COMBO

10/22 owners will love this new sight system. Highly visible and super accurate because the blaze orange and the white bar front sights contrast so well against the background. The rear sight blade provides a sharp horizontal sighting plane with a deep notch for fast sighting. The Ruger 10/22 Interchangeable Combo is sold with or without the quickchange front sight feature. Your choice of white outline or target rear blades. Interchangeable Combo includes 2 front sights white bar and blaze orange.

Ruger 10/22 Interchangeable Front Combo (White Rear/White & Orange Front)	RF00001	**$77.69**
Ruger 10/22 Interchangeable Front Combo (Target Rear/White & Orange Front)	RF00002	**77.69**
Ruger 10/22 Combo (White Rear/White Front)	RF00003	**56.69**
Ruger 10/22 Combo (White Rear/Orange Front)	RF00004	**56.69**
Ruger 10/22 Combo (Target Rear/White Front)	RF00005	**56.69**
Ruger 10/22 Combo (Target Rear/Orange Front)	RF00006	**56.69**
Interchangeable Front Sight Base Only (.157)	RF00009	**11.49**

Also fits Win. 77, 94 Carbine, & Rem. 740-760, 700 old model dovetail rear

OPEN RIFLE SIGHTS
Dovetail Rear Mount

The Series 100 Adjustable Sight System for Dovetail rear mount rifles provide a highly visible sight picture and fast, accurate sightings every time. Precision click adjustments for windage and elevation insure fine sighting. Made of heat treated steel and easy to install. Especially recommended for Marlin 336 owners. Front sights feature blaze orange and white bar enhance contrast, especially in dim light. Rear sight blade provides a sharp horizontal sighting plane with deep notch for fast sighting (choice of white outline or target rear blades). **Price: Rear Sight $47.29; Front Sight $10.49.**

FRONT SIGHT CHART

HEIGHT	MAKE & MODEL
.540	Ruger 44 Carbine, #3, 375
.540	Marlin 336, 375
.540	Winchester 94 Trapper
.540	Browning, BLR 22
.500	Winchester 77, 94 Carbine
.500	Remington 740-760, 700 Old Model with Dovetail
.500	Ruger 10/22
.460	Marlin 44, 88-89, 39 A-M
.460	Remington 121, 241, 510-513T
.460	Savage 110, 170, 99T-E-C
.430	Savage 340 Old Model, 99 Old Model
.400	Winchester 88, 70 pre 1964, 94 pre 1964, 71 pre 1964
.400	Marlin 780 22 LR, 1894-1895
.400	Browning Bar 22
.400	Savage 340
.343	Winchester 9422
.343	Use with Interchangeable Base to make .500 height

MILLETT SIGHTS™

RUGER STANDARD AUTO

The Ruger Standard Auto Combo provides a highly visible sight picture even under low light conditions. The blaze orange or white bar front sight allows the shooter to get on target fast. Great for target use or plinking. Uses Factory Front Sight on adjustable model guns when using Millett target rear only. All other installations use Millett Front Sight. Easy to intall.

Combo (White rear/White front)	RS22001	$59.79
Combo (White rear/Orange front)	RS22002	59.79
Combo (Target rear/White front)	RS22003	59.79
Combo (Target rear/Orange front)	RS22004	59.79
Rear Only (White Outline)	RS22005	47.29
Rear Only (Silhouette Target Blade)	RS22006	47.29
Front Only (White)	RS22007	13.59
Front Only (Orange)	RS22008	13.59
Front Only (Serrated Ramp)	RS22009	13.59
Front Only (Target-Adjsutable Model/White Bar)	RS22010	13.59
Front Only (Target-Adjustable Model/Orange Bar)	RS22011	13.59

INTERCHANGEABLE SIGHT BLADES

The Millett Series 100 Adjustable Sight System is the first group of completely interchangeable component gun sights. All of the sight blades will interchange so now you can have your choice and have extra blades for the differing shooting conditions.

Rear Blades Only

.312 (White Outline)	BL31201	$16.79
.312 (Target Blade)	BL31202	16.79
.312 (Target Silhouette Blade)	BL31206	16.79
.360 (White Outline)	BL36003	16.79
.360 (Target Blade)	BL36004	16.79
.360 (Target Silhouette Blade)	BL36007	16.79
.360 Narrow Notch (White Outline)	BL36008	16.79
.360 Rifle Peep Sight Blade .050 Dia. Aperture	BL00010	16.95
.360 Rifle Peep Sight Blade .080 Dia. Aperture	BL00011	16.95
.410 (White Outline)	BL41005	16.79
.410 (Target Blade)	BL41009	16.79

POCKET SIGHT ADJUSTMENT TOOL

This handy little tool prevents the bluing from being scratched and makes sight adjustment quick and easy.

Sight Adjusting Tool (Series 100 System)	SA00008	$3.10

MARKSMAN SPEED-COMBO

The Marksman Speed-Combo is State-of-the-art in sight technology. Designed specifically to meet the demands of the I.P.S.C. competition shooting. The large target rear blade is uniquely engineered to provide sharp crisp sighting under all daylight conditions. The extra deep angled rear notch provides the competitive edge for fast sight acquisition. Available with Blaze Orange or Serrated Ramp front sight.

COLT GOLD CUP

Marksman Speed-Combo (Dual-Crimp Orange Front)	GC00016	$54.59
Marksman Speed-Combo (Dual-Crimp Serrated Ramp Front)	GC00017	54.59
Marksman Speed Rear Only (Target .410 Blade)	GC00018	41.95

CUSTOM COMBAT LOW PROFILE

Marksman Speed-Combo (Dual-Crimp Orange Front)	CC00017	$59.79
Marksman Speed-Combo (Dual-Crimp Serrated Ramp Front)	CC00018	59.79
Marksman Speed Rear Only (Target .410 Blade)	CC00015	47.29

COLT GOVERNMENT AND COMMANDER (HIGH PROFILE)

Marksman Speed-Combo (Dual-Crimp Orange Front)	CA00016	$59.79
Marksman Speed-Combo (Dual-Crimp Serrated Ramp Front)	CA00017	59.79
Marksman Speed Rear Only (Target .410 Blade)	CA00018	47.29

SIG/SAUER P-220, P-225, P-226

Now Sig Pistol owners can obtain a Series-100 adjustable sight system for their guns. Precision click adjustment for windage and elevation makes it easy to zero when using different loads. The high visibility features assures fast sight acquisition when under the poorest light conditions. Made of high quality heat treated nickel steel and built to last. Extremely easy to install on P-225 and P-226. The P-220 and Browning BDA 45 require the Dual-Crimp front sight installation.

Sig P220 Combo (White Rear/Dual-Crimp White Front)	SP22001	$59.79
Sig P220 Combo (White Rear/Dual-Crimp Orange Front)	SP22002	59.79
Sig P220-25-26 Rear Only (White)	SP22003	47.29
Sig P220-25-26 Rear Only (Target)	SP22004	47.29
Sig P225-6 Combo (White Rear/Dovetail White Front)	SP22561	59.79
Sig P225-6 Combo (White Rear/Dovetail Orange Front)	SP22562	59.79
Sig P225-6 (White) Dovetail Front	SP22565	13.59
Sig P225-6 (Orange) Dovetail Front	SP22566	13.59

The Sig P220 Uses .360 Dual-Crimp Front Sight. The Sig P225-6 Uses a Dovetail Mount Front Sight

SCOPES

MILLETT SIGHTS™

SMITH & WESSON 39/59

This sight system provides fast and accurate sighting capability even under low light conditions. The unique white outline rear blade teamed up with the blaze orange or white bar front sight creates a highly visible sight picture, ideal for match or duty use.

Combo (White rear/Dual-Crimp White Front)	SW39591	$62.95
Combo (White rear/Dual-Crimp Orange Front)	SW39592	62.95
Combo (Target rear/Dual-Crimp White Front)	SW39593	62.95
Combo (Target rear/Dual-Crimp Orange Front)	SW39594	62.95
Rear Only (White outline)	SW39595	50.39
Rear Only (Target Blade)	SW39596	50.39

Requires .340 Dual-Crimp Front

SMITH & WESSON 469, 669, 659, 459, 645 AUTOPISTOL SIGHTS

Rear Sight	**$47.29**
Front Sight	13.59
Rear/Front Combination	59.79

SMITH & WESSON 400/500/600 SERIES AUTOPISTOL SIGHTS

Rear Sight	$48.29
Front Sight	13.59
Rear/Front Combination	60.95

BROWNING HI-POWER

The Series 100 Adjustable Sight System for Browning Hi-Power will provide accurate high visibility sighting for both fixed and adjustable slides with no machine modifications required to the dovetail. Most adjustable slide model Hi-Powers can use the factory front sight as shown in the photo. The fixed slide model requires a new front sight installation. We highly recommend the Dual-Crimp front sight installation on this gun.

Browning Hi-Power (Adjustable Slide Model)

Combo (White rear/Stake-On White Front)	BA00001	$59.79
Combo (White rear/Stake-On Orange Front)	BA00002	59.79
Combo (White rear/Dual-Crimp White Front)	BA00003	59.79
Combo (White rear/Dual-Crimp Orange Front)	BA00004	59.79
Rear Only (White Outline)	BA00009	47.29
Rear Only (Target Blade)	BA00010	47.29

Hi-Power Requires .340 High Front Sight.

Browning Hi-Power (Fixed Slide Model)

Combo (White rear/Stake-On White Front)	BF00001	$59.79
Combo (White rear/Stake-On Orange Front)	BF00002	59.79
Combo (White rear/Dual-Crimp White Front)	BF00003	59.79
Combo (White rear/Dual-Crimp Orange Front)	BF00004	59.79
Rear Only (White Outline)	BF00009	47.29
Rear Only (Target Blade)	BF00010	47.29

Hi-Power Requires .340 High Front Sight

MODELS CZ75/TZ75/TA90 AUTOPISTOL SIGHTS

Rear Sight (white and Target) only	$47.29

COLT 45

This Series 100 High Profile Adjustable Sight is a rugged, all-steel, precision sight which fits the standard factory dovetail with no machine modifications required. This sight provides a highly visible sight picture even under low light conditions. Blaze orange or white bar front sight, precision click adjustments for windage and elevation make the Colt 45 Auto Combo the handgunners' choice.

Combo (White rear/Stake-On White Front)	CA00001	$59.79
Combo (White rear/Stake-On Orange Front)	CA00002	59.79
Combo (White rear/Dual-Crimp White Front)	CA00003	59.79
Combo (White rear/Dual-Crimp Orange Front)	CA00004	59.79
Combo (Target rear/Stake-On White Front)	CA00005	59.79
Combo (Target rear/Stake-On Orange Front)	CA00006	59.79
Combo (Target rear/Dual-Crimp White Front)	CA00007	59.79
Combo (Target rear/Dual-Crimp Orange Front)	CA00008	59.79
Rear Only (White Outline)	CA00009	47.29
Rear Only (Target Blade)	CA00010	47.29

Colt Gov. and Com. Require .312 High Front Sight.

BERETTA ACCURIZER COMBO

This amazing new sight system not only provides a highly visible sight picture but also tunes the barrel lockup to improve your accuracy and reduce your group size by as much as 50%. The Beretta Accurizer sight system fits the 92S, 92SB, 84 and 85 models. Easy to install. Requires the drilling of one hole for installation. Your choice of rear blade styles. Front sight comes in white bar, serrated ramp or blaze orange.

Combo (White Rear/White Bar Front)	BE00001	$67.29
Combo (White Rear/Orange Bar Front)	BE00002	67.29
Combo (Target Rear/White Bar Front)	BE00003	67.29
Combo (Target Rear/Orange Bar Front)	BE00004	67.29
Rear Only (White Outline)	BE00005	47.95
Rear Only (Target Blade)	BE00006	47.95
Front Only (White Bar)	BE00007	20.95
Front Only (Orange Bar)	BE00008	20.95
Front Only (Serrated Ramp)	BE00009	20.95

Fits Models 92S, 92SB, 85, 84

MILLETT SIGHTS™
Revolver Sights

COLT REVOLVER

The Series 100 Adjustable Sight System offers today's discriminating Colt owner the finest quality replacement sight available. 12 crisp click stops for each turn of adjustment, delivers 5/8" of adjustment per click at 100 yards with a 6" barrel. Easy to install, using factory front sight. Guaranteed to give your Colt that custom look.

For Colt Python, Trooper, Diamond Back, and new Frontier single action army.

Rear Only (White Outline)	CR00001	$41.95
Rear Only (Target Blade)	CR00002	41.95
Rear Only (Silhouette)	CR00003	41.95

Colt owners will really appreciate the high visibility feature of Colt front sights. Easy to install—just drill 2 holes in the new sight and pin on. All steel. Your choice of blaze orange or white bar. Fits 4", 6" & 8" barrels only.

Colt Python (White or Orange Bar)	FB00007–8	$11.59
Trooper, Diamond Back, King Cobra, Peace-maker	FB00015–16	11.59

SMITH & WESSON

The Series 100 Adjustable Sight System for Smith & Wesson revolvers provides the sight picture and crisp click adjustments desired by the discriminating shooter. 1/2" of adjustment per click, at 100 yards on elevation, and 5/8" on windage, with a 6" barrel. Can be installed in a few minutes, using factory front sight.

K&N frames manufactured prior to 1974 did not standardize on front screw hole location, so the front hole must be drilled and counterbored on these sights.

Smith & Wesson **N** Frame
N.312—Model 25-5, all bbl., 27-3 1/2" & 5", 28-4" & 6"
N.360—Model 25, 27, 29, 57, & 629-4, 6 & 6 1/2" bbl.
N.410—Model 27, 29, 57, 629 with 8 3/8" bbl.

Smith & Wesson **K&L** Frame
K.312—Models 14, 15, 18, 48-4", & 53
K&L360—Models 16, 17, 19, 48-6", 8 3/8", 66, 686, 586

Smith & Wesson K&L-Frame		
Rear Only .312 (White Outline)	SK00001	$41.95
Rear Only .312 (Target Blade)	SK00002	41.95
Rear Only .360 (White Outline)	SK00003	41.95
Rear Only .360 (Target Blade)	SK00004	41.95
Rear Only .410 (White Outline)	SK00005	41.95
Rear Only .410 (Target Blade)	SK00006	41.95

Smith & Wesson K&N Old Style		
Rear Only .312 (White Outline)	KN00001	$41.95
Rear Only .312 (Target Blade)	KN00002	41.95
Rear Only .360 (White Outline)	KN00003	41.95
Rear Only .360 (Target Blade)	KN00004	41.95
Rear Only .410 (White Outline)	KN00005	41.95
Rear Only .410 (Target Blade)	KN00006	41.95

Smith & Wesson N-Frame		
Rear Only .312 (White Outline)	SN00001	$41.95
Rear Only .312 (Target Blade)	SN00002	41.95
Rear Only .360 (White Outline)	SN00003	41.95
Rear Only .360 (Target Blade)	SN00004	41.95
Rear Only .410 (White Outline)	SN00005	41.95
Rear Only .410 (Target Blade)	KN00006	41.95

RUGER

The high visibility white outline sight picture and precision click adjustments of the Series 100 Adjustable Sight System will greatly improve the accuracy and fast sighting capability of your Ruger. 3/4" per click at 100 yard for elevation, 5/8" per click for windage, with 6" barrel. Can be easily installed, using factory front sight or all-steel replacement front sight which is a major improvement over the factory front. Visibility is greatly increased for fast sighting. Easy to install by drilling one hole in the new front sight.

The Red Hawk all-steel replacement front sight is highly visible and easy to pickup under all lighting conditions. Very easy to install. Fits the factory replacement system.

SERIES 100 RUGER DOUBLE ACTION REVOLVER SIGHTS	
Rear Sight (fits all adjustable models)	$41.95
Front Sight (Security Six, Police Six, Speed Six)	11.59
Front Sight (Redhawk and GP-100)	13.59

SERIES 100 RUGER SINGLE ACTION REVOLVER SIGHTS	
Rear Sight (Black Hawk Standard & Super; Bisley Large Frame, Single-Six	41.95
Front Sight (Millet Replacement sights not available for Ruger single action revolvers).	

DAN WESSON

This sight is exactly what every Dan Wesson owner has been looking for. The Series 100 Adjustable Sight System provides 12 crisp click stops for each turn of adjustment, with 5/8" per click for windage, with a 6" barrel. Can be easily installed, using the factory front or new Millett high visibility front sights.

Choice of white outline or target blade.

Rear Only (White Outline)	DW00001	$41.95
Rear Only (Target Blade)	DW00002	41.95
Rear Only (White Outline) 44 Mag.	DW00003	41.95
Rear Only (Target Blade) 44 Mag.	DW00004	41.95

If you want super-fast sighting capability for your Dan Wesson, the new Millett blaze orange or white bar front is the answer. Easy to install. Fits factory quick-change system. All steel, no plastic. Available in both heights.

Dan Wesson .44 Mag & 15-2 (White Bar) (high)	FB00009	$11.59
Dan Wesson .44 Mag & 15-2 (Orange Bar) (high)	FB00010	11.59
Dan Wesson 22 Caliber (White Bar) (low)	FB00011	11.59
Dan Wesson 22 Caliber (Orange Bar) (low)	FB00012	11.59

MILLET SIGHTS™

FLUSH-MOUNT HARRIS BIPOD ADAPTER

Millett's flush-mount sling swivels have a simple-to-use adapter for the Harris bipod, that detaches quickly so the loop can then be installed in the bipod loop receptacle. Will also fit Pachmayr flush-mount bases.

Harris Bipod Adapter	SS00004	**$6.95**

FLUSH-MOUNT SLING SWIVELS

Millett's flush-mount redesigned Pachmayr sling swivels are quick detachable and beautifully styled in heat treated nickel steel. The sling swivel loop has been redesigned to guide the sling into the loop, eliminating twisitng and fraying on edges of sling. Millett flush-mount bases are much easier to install than the old Pachmayr design, with no threading and an easy to use step drill.

Flush-Mount Swivels (pair)	SS00001	**$13.95**
Loops Only	SS00002	6.95
Piloted Counterbore	SS00003	14.95

DUAL-CRIMP INSTALLATION TOOL KIT

The Dual-Crimp System is a new revolutionary way of installing front sights on autos. Now it is not necessary to heliarc or silver solder to get a good secure job. Dual-Crimp has a two-post, hollow rivet design that works very much like an aircraft rivet and withstands the heavy abuse of hardball ammo. Your choice of four styles and nine heights. Dual-Crimp is the quick and easy system for professionals. Requires a drill press.

Dual-Crimp Tool Set, Complete	DC0002	**$129.95**
Application Tool		69.95
Reverse counterbore (solid carbvide)		31.50
3/16″ Drill (solid carbide)		13.95
Drill Jig		19.95
Stake-On Tool		74.95
Service Kit		99.95

SHURSHOT RIBBED SHOTGUN SIGHTS

The greatest deterrent to shotgun accuracy is raising your head from the stock when shooting. With the Millett ShurShot, accuracy is improved by giving the shooter a reference point to align his head position on the stock. The blaze orange inserts are highly visible in low light and aids the eye in picking up the target. Late in the day deer hunters or early morning duck hunters can get on the game quickly and accurately. ShurShot works great with slugs or shot. Shooting is quick and natural. Eye instinct will automatically align and center the rib and sight bar.

ShurShot Shotgun Sight Combo (Orange) Fits Rem. 1100 & 870	SG00001	**$15.95**
ShurShot Shotgun Sight (Rear Only Orange) Fits Rem. 1100 & 870	SG00002	9.95
ShurShot Shotgun Sight (Front Only Orange)	SG00003	6.95
ShurShot Shotgun Combo (Orange)	SG00004	15.95
Other Models ShurShot Shotgun Sight (Rear Only Orange)	SG00005	9.95
Other Models ShurShot Adj. Shotgun Sight Combo (Orange)	SG00006	21.95
ShurShot Adj. Shotgun Sight (Rear Only Orange)	SG00007	15.95

GLOCK 17 REPLACEMENT SIGHT

The Innovative Glock 17 pistol, the first production pistol to use plastic for the major part of its construction, leaves many shooters looking for better, fully adjustable sights. The Millet sight, in either white outline or target black blade) retrofits the factory dovetail. The plastic factory front sight must be replaced with a Millett Dual-Crimp front (.340 height) and is available in white, orange or black serrated ramp. Rear sight is fully adjustable with positive clicks for windage and elevation. All-steel construction.

GLOCK 17 Sight

Rear Sight	47.29
Front Sight	13.59
Rear Front Combination	59.79

REDFIELD SCOPES

THE TRACKER

The Tracker series brings you a superior combination of price and value. It provides the same superb quality, precision and strength of construction found in all Redfield scopes, but at an easily affordable price. Features include the tough, one-piece tube, machined and hand-fitted internal parts, excellent optical quality and traditional Redfield styling.

TRACKER SCOPES

2x-7x Tracker Variable Power
122300 2x-7x 4 Plex $167.95

3x-9x Tracker Variable Power
123300 3x-9x 4 Plex   185.95

4x Tracker Fixed Power
135300 4x 4 Plex   125.95

Matte Finish
122308 2x-7x 4 Plex   181.95
122308 3x-9x 4 Plex   200.95
122308 4x 4 Plex   140.95

3X-9X Widefield® Accu-Trac® Variable

THE ILLUMINATOR

Every sportsman knows that dawn and dusk are the most productive times to hunt. Game use the cover of darkness for security while feeding, blending in easily with the greens, grays and browns of the outdoors during dim light conditions.

With this new Illuminator series, you can add precious minutes to morning and evening hunting. These scopes actually compensate for the low light, letting you "see" contrasts between field and game.

Optimum resolution, contrast, color correction, flatness of field, edge-to-edge sharpness and absolute fidelity are improved by the unique air-spaced, triplet objective, and the advanced 5-element erector lens system.

The Illuminators also feature a zero tolerance nylon cam follower and thrust washers to provide absolute point of impact hold through all power ranges. The one-piece tube construction is virtually indestructible, tested at 1200g acceleration forces, and fog-free through the elimination of potential leak paths.

Offered in both the Traditional and Widefield® variable power configurations, the Illuminator is also available with the Accu-Trac® feature.

Illuminator Scopes

3x-9x Traditional Variable Power
123886 3x-9x 4 Plex $398.95

3x-9x Widefield Variable Power
112886 3x-9x 4 Plex   441.95

3x-9x Widefield Accu-Trac Variable Power
112880 3x-9x 4 Plex   488.95

3x9 Widefield Matte Finish
112888   450.95

REDFIELD SCOPES

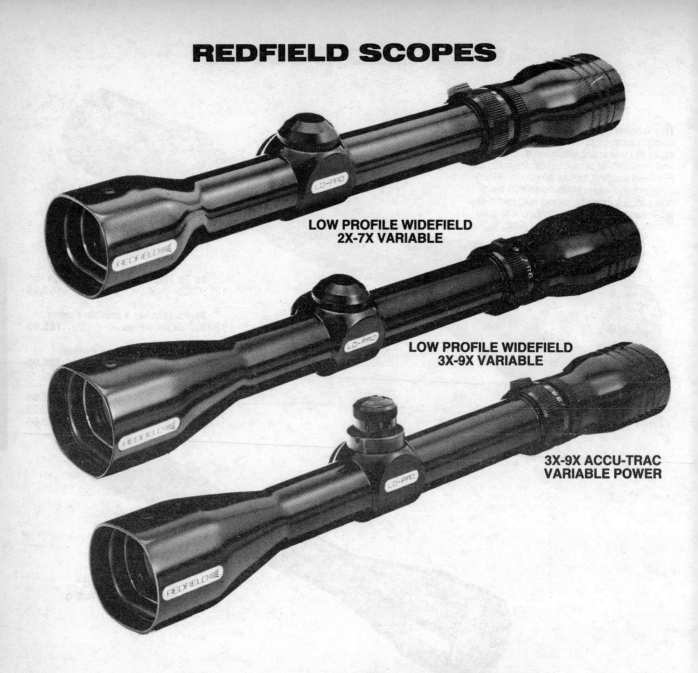

LOW PROFILE WIDEFIELD 2X-7X VARIABLE

LOW PROFILE WIDEFIELD 3X-9X VARIABLE

3X-9X ACCU-TRAC VARIABLE POWER

LOW PROFILE WIDEFIELD

In heavy cover, game may jump out of the brush 10 feet away or appear in a clearing several hundred yards off, either standing or on the move.

The Widefield®, with 25% more field of view than conventional scopes, lets you spot game quicker, stay with it and see other animals that might be missed.

The patented Low Profile design means a low mounting on the receiver, allowing you to keep your cheek tight on the stock for a more natural and accurate shooting stance, especially when swinging on running game.

The one-piece, fog-proof tube is machined with high tensile strength aluminum alloy and is anodized to a lustrous finish that's rust-free and virtually scratch-proof. Available in 7 models.

WIDEFIELD LOW PROFILE SCOPES

1³/₄x-5x Low Profile Variable Power	
113806 1³/₄x-5x 4 Plex	$284.95
2x-7x Low Profile Variable Power	
111806 2x-7x 4 Plex	$293.95
2x-7x Low Profile Accu-Trac Variable Power	
111810 2x-7x 4 Plex AT	$343.95
3x-9x Low Profile Variable Power	
112806 3x-9x 4 Plex	$324.95
3x-9x Low Profile Accu-Trac Variable Power	
112810 3x-9x 4 Plex AT	$376.95
2³/₄x Low Profile Fixed Power	
141807 2³/₄x 4 Plex	$205.95
4x Low Profile Fixed Power	
143806 4x 4 Plex	$231.95
6x Low Profile Fixed Power	
146806 6x 4 Plex	$250.95

SAKO SCOPE MOUNTS

Weighing less than 3 ounces, these new Sako scope mounts are lighter, yet stronger than ever. Tempered steel allows the paring of every last gram of unnecessary weight without sacrificing strength. Like the original mount, these rings clamp directly to the tapered dovetails on Sako rifles, thus eliminating the need for separate bases and screws. Annular grooves inside the rings preclude scope slippage even under the recoil of the heaviest calibers. Nicely streamlined and finished in a rich blue-black to complement any Sako rifle.

Price: low, medium, or high **$99.95**

SCHMIDT & BENDER RIFLE SCOPES

These fine Schmidt & Bender rifle scopes offer brightness and resolution, color fidelity, and excellent field-of-view. Each model comes with a 30-year guarantee and incorporates the essential ingredients every hunter looks for in rough hunting conditions: recoil-proof, centered reticles; dust and moisture-proof assembly (nitrogen-filled), and precise click adjustments. To guarantee that its scopes will stand up to the most severe hunting conditions, Schmidt & Bender subjects them to vibration tests exceeding the demands of the most powerful cartridges, environmental tests from $-40°$ F to $+122°$ F, and heavy rain testing. All variable scopes have 30mm center tubes; all fixed power scopes have 1″ tubes.

VARIABLE POWER SCOPE 1¼-4 × 20
$525.00

VARIABLE POWER SCOPE 1½-6 × 42
$550.00

VARIABLE POWER SCOPE 2½-10 × 56
$675.00

SCHMIDT & BENDER

FIXED POWER SCOPE 1½ × 15
(steel tube w/o mounting rail)
$365.00

FIXED POWER SCOPE 4 × 36
(steel tube w/o mounting rail)
$399.00

FIXED POWER SCOPE 6 × 42
(steel tube w/o mounting rail)
$429.00

FIXED POWER SCOPE 12 × 42
(steel tube w/o mounting rail)
$429.00

FIXED POWER SCOPE 8 × 56
(steel tube w/o mounting rail)
$499.00

SIMMONS SCOPES

SILHOUETTE AND TARGET RIFLESCOPES

MODEL 1074
6.5-20X40mm

Field of view: 17.8'-6.2'
Eye relief: 3.5-3.3 Truplex
Weight: 16.2 oz.
Length: 15"
Price: $224.75

MODEL 1075
6.5-20X40mm

Field of view: 17.8'-6.2'
Eye relief: 3.5-3.3 Dot
Weight: 16.2 oz.
Length: 15"
Price: $224.75

MODEL 1076
15X40mm

Field of view: 11.5'
Eye relief: 3.4 Truplex
Weight: 15.6 oz.
Length: 15"
Price: $181.25

MODEL 1077
15X40mm

Field of view: 11.5'
Eye relief: 3.4 Dot
Weight: 15.6 oz.
Length: 15"
Price: $181.25

MODEL 1078
24X40mm

Field of view: 6.2'
Eye relief: 3.3 Truplex
Weight: 15.6 oz.
Length: 15"
Price: $181.25

MODEL 1079
24X40mm

Field of view: 6.2'
Eye relief: 3.3 Dot
Weight: 15.6 oz.
Length: 15"
Price: $181.25

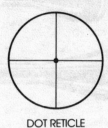

DOT RETICLE

TRUPLEX RETICLE

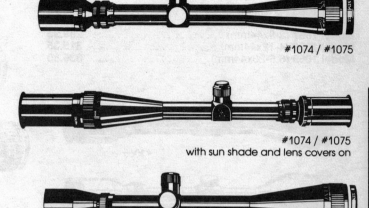

#1074 / #1075

#1074 / #1075
with sun shade and lens covers on

#1076 / #1077 / #1078 / #1079

GOLD MEDAL SERIES

RANGER MODEL 1045
3-9X44mm

Field of view: 42-14
Eye relief: 4.0-3.3
Weight: 16.2 oz./Length: 13"

Price: $337.15

MODEL 1046
4-12X44mm

Field of view: 31-11
Eye relief: 3.9-3.2
Weight: 19.1 oz./Length: 14.2"

Price: $358.85

MODEL 1050
4-X32 Compact

Field of view: 22" at 100 yds.
Eye relief: 4.8"
Weight: 9 oz.

Price: $130.50

MODEL 1054
3-9X32 Compact

Field of view: 40"-14"
Eye relief: 3.5"
Weight: 10.4 oz.

Price: $174.50

MODEL 1047
6.5-20X44mm

Field of view: 17.8-6.1
Eye relief: 3.4-3.2
Weight: 19.4 oz./Length: 15.4"

Price: $376.95

SCOPES

SIMMONS SCOPES

GOLD MEDAL PRESIDENTIAL SERIES

Features "SIMCOAT" multi-coating on all lenses . . . 360°
Wide-angle . . . 44mm Objective lens . . . Anodized high gloss
finish . . . Speed focusing . . . ¼ minute click adjustments

Model 1065 (4x44mm). **$253.75**
Model 1066 (2-7x44mm) **289.95**
Model 1067 (3-9x44mm) **289.95**
Model 1068 (4-12x44mm) **315.35**
Model 1069 (6.5-20x44mm) **336.50**

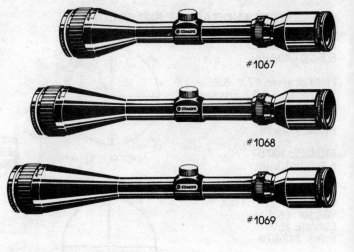

#1067

#1068

#1069

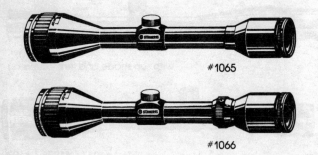

#1065

#1066

SIMMONS MODEL	X	Field of View (Feet)	Eye Relief (Inches)	Length (Inches)	Weight (Ounces)	Exit Pupil mm	Relative Brightness	Twilight Factor at High Power
#1065 4x44mm		35	3.5	13	15.5	11	121	13.3
#1066 2-7x44mm	2	55.1	3.3	12.6	16.6	22	484	
#1066 2-7x44mm	7	18.3	2.9			6.3	40	17.6
#1067 3-9x44mm	3	42	4.0	13	16.2	14.7	216	
#1067 3-9x44mm	9	14	3.3			4.9	54	19.9
#1068 4-12x44mm	4	31	3.9	14.2	19.1	11	121	
#1068 4-12x44mm	12	11	3.2			3.7	14	23
#1069 6.5-20x44mm	6.5	17.8	3.4	15.4	19.4	6.8	46	
#1069 6.5-20x44mm	20	6.1	3.2			2.2	5	30

RIFLESCOPE RINGS

Low 1" Set **Model 1401** **$8.50**
High 1" Set **Model 1403** **8.50**
1" See-Thru Set **Model 1405** **9.50**
1" Rings for 22 Grooved Receiver **Model 1406** **8.50**
1" Deluxe Rings for 22 Grooved Receiver **Model
1408** **17.50**

#1401

#1406

#1403

#1408

SIMMONS SCOPES

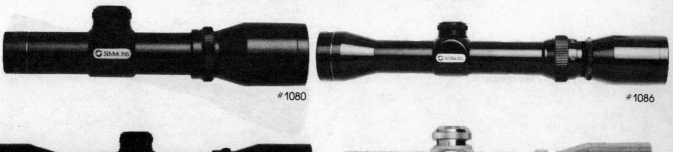

#1080

#1086

#1084

#1081

SILVER MEDAL RIFLESCOPE SERIES
QUAD VARIABLES

Model 1013 1-4x20 Quad. $104.45
Model 1015 3-12x40 Quad. 99.95
Model 1017 4-16x40 Quad. 120.35
Model 1018 6-24x40 Quad. 137.75

#1013

#1015

#1017

#1018

SILVER MEDAL PISTOLSCOPE SERIES

Fixed power, variable power and silhouette models are all available in this series in traditional blue or silver finish with multi-coated lenses and one-1/2iece tubes (to withstand shock of magnum calibers.

Model 1080 2x20 . . . . $94.25
Model 1081 10x20 Polished Alum 94.25
Model 1084 4-32 . . . . 108.75
Model 1085 4x32 w/Target Turret 145.50
Model 1086 1-3 × 32 . . . . 217.50
Model 1087 2-6 × 32 . . . . 253.75
Model 1088 4x32 Polished Alum 108.75

SCOPES

SOVEREIGN SCOPES

Waterproof/fogproof
Field of view at 100 yards: 33′ at 3x; 11′ at 9x
Eye relief: 3″
Quick sighting Mag-Plex reticle

3-9 × 40mm
$69.00

Waterproof/fogproof
Field of view at 100 yards: 33′ at 3x; 12′ at 9x
Eye relief: 3.5″
Quick sighting Mag-Plex reticle

3-9 × 32mm
$59.95

Waterproof/fogproof
Field of view at 100 yards: 28′
Eye relief: 4″
Quick sighting Mag-Plex reticle

4-32mm
$31.20

Parallax corrected at 75 yards
Field of view at 100 yards: 18′
Eye relief: 2.25″
Quick sighting Mag-Plex reticle
Mounts and lens caps

22 RIFLE SCOPE
4 × 15 mm
$11.95

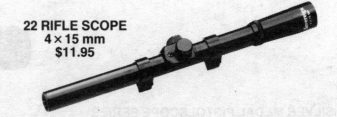

SWAROVSKI OPTIK

SPECIFICATIONS

Telescopic Sights	1.5x20	4x32	6x42	8x56	1.5-6x42	2.2-9x42	3-12x56
Magnification	1.5x	4x	6x	8x	1.5-6x	2.2-9x	3-12x
Max. effective objective dia.	20mm	32mm	42mm	56mm	42mm	42mm	56mm
Exit pupil dia.	12.7mm	8mm	7mm	7mm	14.3-7mm	14.3-4.7mm	14.3-4.7mm
Field of view at 100m	18.5m	10m	7m	5.2m	18.5-6.5m	12-4.5m	9-3.3m
Twilight effective factor (DIN 58388)	4.2	11.3	15.9	21.1	4.2-15.9	6.2-19.4	8.5-25.9
Intermediary tube dia. Steel-Standard	26mm	26mm	26mm	26mm	30mm	30mm	30mm
Objective tube dia.	26mm	38mm	48mm	62mm	48mm	48mm	62mm
Ocular tube dia.	40mm	40mm	40mm	40mm	40mm	40mm	40mm
Scope length	247mm	290mm	322mm	370mm	322mm	342mm	391mm
Weight (approx.) Steel	360g	430g	500g	660g	570g	580g	710g
Light metal with rail		370g	400g	490g	480g	470g	540g
A change of the impact point per click in mm/100m	12	7	6	4	9	6	4

AMERICAN LIGHTWEIGHT SCOPE

This new model features precision ground, coated and aligned optics sealed in a special aluminum alloy tube to withstand heavy recoil. Eye relief is 85mm and the recoiling eyepiece protects the eye. Positive click adjustments for elevation and windage change the impact point (approx. 1/4") per click at 100 yards, with parallax also set at 100 yards. Weight is only 13 ounces.

ZFM 6x42 MILITARY STYLE SNIPER SCOPE
Mounted on H&K G-3 Rifle w/ARMS G-3 Scope Base

Provides a detailed, color-true contrast image, even in adverse light conditions. Scope is corrosion resistant and durable.

SWAROVSKI OPTIK

HABICHT NOVA TELESCOPIC SIGHTS

These fine Austrian-made sights feature brilliant optics with high-quality lens coating and optimal sighting under poor light and weather conditions. The Nova ocular system with telescope recoil damping reduces the danger of injury, especially with shots aimed in an upward direction. The main tube is selectable in steel or light metal construction with a mounting rail. Because of Nova's centered reticle, the aiming mark remains in the center of the field of view regardless of corrections of the impact point.

VARIABLE POWER

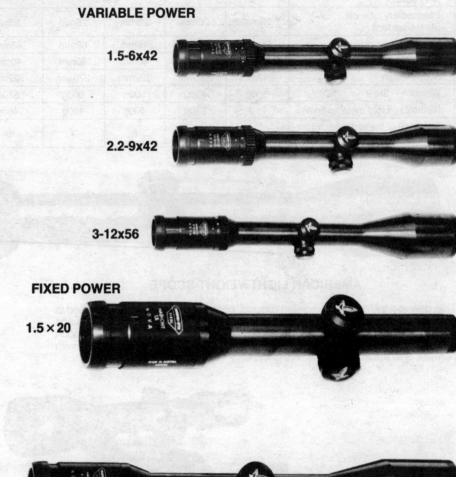

1.5-6x42

2.2-9x42

3-12x56

FIXED POWER

1.5 × 20

6 × 42

8 × 56

TASCO SCOPES

EURO-CLASS RIFLESCOPES

This new Tasco line of riflescopes features a 30mm tube providing great rigidity without undue point-of-impact change. It offers a large objective lens, fast focusing, hard anodized dull satin finsih, fully coated optics (plus Supercon-coated lenses for maximum light transmission), haze filter caps, and positive low-profile windage and elevation adjustments.

SPECIFICATIONS

**Model	Power	Objective Diameter	Finish	Reticle	Field of View @ 100 yards	Eye Relief	Tube Diam.	Scope Length	Scope Weight	Price
EU4X44	4	44mm	Dull Satin	30/30	29'	3"	30mm	12³/₈"	16 oz.	279.95
EU6X44	6	44mm	Dull Satin	30/30	20'	3"	30mm	12³/₈"	16 oz.	279.95
EU39X44	3-9	44mm	Dull Satin	30/30	37¹/₂-14'	3"	30mm	12¹/₈"	18.5 oz.	309.95
EU312X52	3-12	52mm	Dull Satin	30/30	33"-8¹/₂'	3"	30mm	12¹/₄"	18.5 oz.	329.95
EU1.56X44	1.5-6	44mm	Dull Satin	30/30	52¹/₂'-16'	3³/₄"	30mm	12"	19.6 oz.	289.95
EUIR39X44	3-9	44mm	Dull Satin	SBD	37¹/₂'-13'	3¹/₄"	30mm	12⁵/₈"	18.5 oz.	599.95

ILLUMINATED RETICLE RIFLE & PISTOL SCOPES

Specially designed for low-light conditions. Light intensity can be adjusted. Scope may also be used for normal viewing conditions. Includes illuminated cross hair reticle, fully coated optics, ¹/₄-minute positive click stops, fast focus eyepiece, nonremovable eye bell, haze filter caps.

SPECIFICATIONS

Model No.	Power	Objective Diameter (mm)	Finish	Reticle	Field of view @ 100 yards	Eye Relief	Tube Diam. (in.)	Scope Length (in.)	Scope Weight (oz.)	Price
IR1X20P	1	20mm	Black	Illuminated	24'	21"	1"	9¹/₄"	8 oz.	$299.95
IR39X40WA	3-9	40mm	Black	Illuminated	14'-38'	3"	1"	12³/₄"	14.8 oz.	304.95
IR4X40WA	4	40mm	Black	Illuminated	35'	3"	1"	12¹/₂"	14 oz.	274.95
IR4X20	4	20mm	Black	Illuminated	18'	4¹/₄"	1"	7¹/₈"	8 oz.	299.95
IR1X20WA	1	20mm	Black	Illuminated	97'	3³/₄"	1"	9⁵/₈"	12.3 oz.	304.95
IR1.5X20P	1.5	20mm	Black	Illuminated	18'	21"	1"	8⁷/₈"	8 oz.	279.95
IR4X20DS	4	20mm	Black	Illuminated	18'	3¹/₂"	1"	7¹/₈"	8 oz.	279.95
IR4X20P	4	20mm	Black	Illuminated	18'	17"-25"	1"	9³/₈"	8 oz.	279.95
IR27X32WA	2-7	32mm	Black	Illuminated	15'-57'	3"	1"	11³/₄"	14.3 oz.	304.95

TASCO SCOPES

WORLD CLASS WIDE ANGLE® RIFLESCOPE

MODEL WA13.5 × 20

This newest addition to Tasco's World Class Wide Angle line offers a wide field of view—115 feet at 1X and 31 feet at 3.5X—and quick sighting without depending on a critical view. The scope is ideal for hunting deer and dangerous game, especially in close quarters or in heavily wooded and poorly lit areas. Other features include ¹/₂-minute positive click stops, fully coated lenses (including Supercon process), nonremovable eyebell and windage/elevation screws. Length is 9³/₄", with 1" diameter tube. Weight is 10.5 ounces.

Model WA13.5X20 . . . . **$199.95**

MODEL WA39 × 40

- 25% larger field of view
- Exceptional optics
- Fully coated for maximum light transmission
- Waterproof, shockproof, fog-proof
- Non-removable eye bell
- Free haze filter lens caps
- TASCO's unique World Class Lifetime Warranty

WIDE ANGLE VARIABLE ZOOM RIFLESCOPES (ALL WATERPROOF)

MODEL NO.	DESCRIPTION	RETICLE		PRICE
WA1×20	1X (20mm)	Wide Angle	30/30	$179.95
WA13.5×20	1X-3.5X Zoom (20mm)	Wide Angle	30/30	199.95
WA2.5×32	2.5X (32mm)	Wide Angle	30/30	159.95
WA4×32	4X (32mm)	Wide Angle	30/30	149.95
WA4×40	4X (40mm)	Wide Angle	30/30	159.95
WA6×40	6X (40mm)	Wide Angle	30/30	159.95
WA1.755×20	1.75X-5X Zoom (20mm)	Wide Angle	30/30	179.95
WA27×32	2X-7X Zoom (32mm)	Wide Angle	30/30	179.95
WA39×32	3X-9X Zoom (32mm)	Wide Angle	30/30	169.95
WA39×40	3X-9X Zoom (40mm)	Wide Angle	30/30	179.95
WA39×40D	3X-9X Zoom (40mm) Dot Ret.	Wide Angle	Dot	179.95
WA13.5X20				

TASCO SCOPES

SMALL BORE/AIRGUN

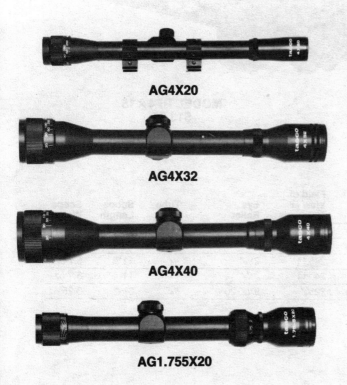

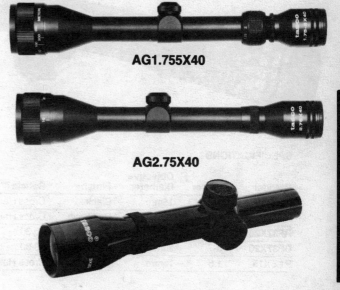

AG4X20

AG1.755X40

AG4X32

AG2.75X40

AG4X40

AG1.755X20

Air rifle shooting, both for individual sport and competition matches, has reached an all-time high in popularity. All 1-inch scopes in this category are waterproof, with an abrasive-resistant anodized finish. All include 1/4-minute positive click stops, 30/30 range-finding reticle, fully coated optics, Compu-Ring®, Tasco's exclusive competition parallax correction ring, and haze filter caps. They are also fog-proof and shock-proof—tested with more impact force than the recoil of a 458 rifle.

MODEL NO.	POWER = X OBJ. DIAM. = mm	FIELD OF VIEW AT 1000 YDS.	TUBE DIAM.	PRICE
AG4X20	4X20mm	20'	3/4'	$ 59.95
AG4X32	4X32mm	27'	1"	149.95
AGI.755X20	1.75-5X20mm	72'-24'	1"	209.95
AG1.755X40	1.75-5X40mm	48'-18'	1"	229.95
AG2.75X40	2.75X40mm	34 1/2'	1"	179.95
AG37X20	3-7X20mm	24 3/4'-11 1/2'	1"	89.95
AG4X40WA	4X40mm	34'	1"	199.95
AG6X40WA	6X40mm	20 1/4'	1"	209.95
AG27X32WA	2-7X32mm	57'-16 1/2'	1"	229.95
AG39X50	3-9X50mm	27'-9'	1"	299.95

MAG-IV® RIFLESCOPES

Tasco's new MAG-IV® scopes provide 33% more power than standard waterproof riflescopes, yet are no larger and weigh no more. MAG-IV® riflescopes give the hunter a larger high power range, without sacrificing the lower power and its field of view. They will withstand all weather conditions and altitude variances. They are also fog-proof and shock-tested with more impact force than that generated by the recoil of a .458 rifle. Each features a fully coated optical system, plus Tasco's exclusive Supercon® coating, 1/4-minute positive click stops, Opti-Centered® 30/30 range finding reticle, and haze filter caps.

MODEL NO.	DESCRIPTION	PRICE
W312X40	3X-12X Zoom (40mm)	$119.95
W416X40	4X-16X Zoom (40mm)	179.95
W624X40	6X-24X Zoom (40mm)	209.95
SW2.510X32	2.5X-10X Zoom (32mm)	149.95

TASCO SCOPES

RIMFIRE RIFLESCOPE
FOR 22's WITH 22 RING MOUNTS

MODEL RF4 × 15
$13.95

SPECIFICATIONS

**Model	Power	Objective Diameter	Finish	Reticle	Field of View @ 100 yards	Eye Relief	Tube Diam.	Scope Length	Scope Weight
RF4X15	4	15mm	Black	Cross Hair	21'	2¹/₂"	³/₄"	11"	4 oz.
RF4X20DS	4	20mm	Dull Satin	Cross Hair	20'	2¹/₂"	³/₄"	10¹/₂"	3.8 oz.
RF37X20	3-7	20mm	Black	30/30	24'-11'	2¹/₂"	³/₄"	11¹/₂"	5.7 oz.
DF37X20	3-7	20mm	Dull Finish	30/30	24'-11'	2¹/₂"	³/₄"	11¹/₂"	5.7 oz.
P1.5X15	1.5	15mm	Black	Cross Hair	22¹/₂'	9¹/₂"-20³/₄"	³/₄"	8³/₄"	3.25 oz.

MODEL TR 39 × 40 WA

TRAJECTORY-RANGE FINDING WORLD-CLASS
WIDE ANGLE® RIFLESCOPE
with Lifetime Warranty

All Tasco TR Scopes have fully coated optics, Opti-Centered®
stadia reticle, ¹/₄-minute positive click stops and haze filter
caps. All are fog-proof, shockproof, waterproof and anodized.

MODEL NO.	DESCRIPTION	RETICLE	PRICE
TR312X32	3X-12X Zoom (32mm)	30/30 RF	$149.95
TR39X40WA	3X-9X Zoom (40mm) Wide Angle	30/30 RF	199.95
TR416X40	4X-16X Zoom (40mm)	30/30 RF	239.95
TR624X40	6X-24X Zoom (40mm)	30/30 RF	249.95
IR618X40TR	6X-18X Zoom (40mm) Illuminated Reticle	30/30 RF	349.95

TASCO TS® SCOPES

For silhouette and target shooting, Tasco's TS® scopes adjust for varying long-range targets, with 1/8-minute Positrac® micrometer windage and elevation adjustments. All TS® scopes are waterproof, fog-proof, shockproof, fully Supercon-coated, and include screw-in metal lens protectors. All include two metal mirage deflection and sunshade hoods, five and eight inches in length, which can be used separately or together to eliminate image distortion resulting from excessive barrel temperatures or to shade the objective lens from direct sunlight. All include a focusing objective for precise parallax correction and extra-large 44mm objective lenses for extra brightness at high magnifications. Each scope is available in a choice of three reticle patterns: 1/2-minute dot, fine crosshair, and opti-centered 30/30 range finding.

MODEL NO.	DESCRIPTION	PRICE
TS16X44	16X (44mm)	$319.95
TS24X44	24X (44mm)	319.95
TS36X44	36X (44mm)	349.95
TS624X44	6X-24X Zoom (44mm)	399.95
TS416X44	4X-16X (44 mm)	379.95

TS Scopes available in choice of three reticle patterns: Opti-centered 15/15/ Range Finding, Fine Crosshair & 1/2-minute dot.

Standard features: Two mirage deflection and sunshine hoods (3″ and 5″)

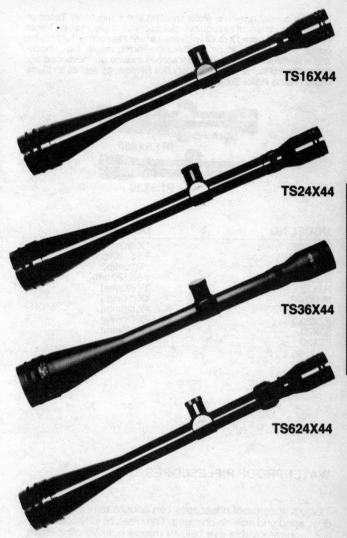

TS16X44

TS24X44

TS36X44

TS624X44

SGI.755x20
$39.95

SHOTGUN SCOPE COMBO

Tasco's shotgun scope/mount combo is designed for Remington Models 1100 and 870 shotguns. They feature fully coated optics, Opti-Centered 30/30 reticle, 1/4 minute positive click stops, non-removable eye bell, special one-piece mounting system that requires no drilling, non-removable windage and elevation screws. Other models available to fit Browning A5, Winchester Ranger, Mossberg 500 and Savage 67.

**Model	Power	Objective Diameter	Finish	Reticle	Field of View @ 100 Yards	Eye Relief	Tube Diam.	Scope Length	Scope Weight
SG1.755X20	1.75-5	20mm	Black	30/30	72'-24'	3¼″	1″	10⅝″	16.2 oz.
SG2.5X32	2.5	32mm	Black	30/30	42'	3¼″	1″	11¾″	15.7 oz.
SG13.5X20WA	1-3.5	20mm	Black	30/30	115'-31'	3½″	1″	9¾″	16.2 oz.

TASCO PISTOL SCOPES

With the current growth of pistol shooting and competition, Tasco offers an assortment of high-quality pistol scopes to keep you on target. Power range is from 1X to 4X, with deluxe features such as fully coated optics, positive click stops, 30/30 range-finding reticle, fog-, shock-, and waterproofing. Tasco's pistol scopes include our advanced and competitive pistol shooter's Battery Dot System, as well as an illuminated Reticle Pistol Scope.

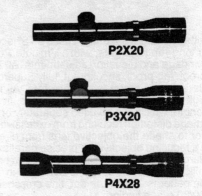

P2X20

P3X20

P4X28

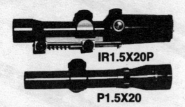

IR1.5X20P

P1.5X20

MODEL NO.	DESCRIPTION	RETICLE	PRICE
IR1X20P	1X (20mm)	Illuminated	$279.95
IR1.5X20P	1.5X (20mm)	Illuminated	259.95
P1X20	1X(20mm)	30/30	119.95
P1.5X20D	1.5X (20mm)	Dot	104.95
P3X20	3X (20mm)	30/30	104.95
IR4X20P	4X (20mm)	Illuminated	279.95
P4X28	4X (28mm)	30/30	114.95
P2X20	2X (20mm)	30/30	114.95
S3X20	3X (20mm)	30/30	114.95
P2X20	2X (20mm)	30/30	104.95

WATERPROOF RIFLESCOPES

Tasco's waterproof riflescopes can endure rain, snow, heat, dust, sand and altitude changes. They feature fully coated optics, non-removable eye bell, 1/4 minute positive click stops, Opticentered 30/30 rangefinding reticle, haze filter caps.

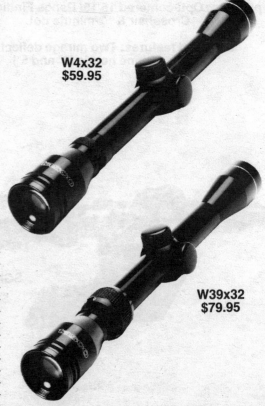

W4x32
$59.95

W39x32
$79.95

**Model	Power	Objective Diameter	Finish	Reticle	Field of View @ 100 Yards	Eye Relief	Tube Diam.	Scope Length	Scope Weight
W1.755X20	1.75-5	20mm	Black	30/30	68'-20'	3"	1"	10½"	10 oz.
W4X32	4	32mm	Black	30/30	28'	3"	1"	11¾"	9.5 oz.
W4X40	4	40mm	Black	30/30	28'	3¼"	1"	12½"	12.2 oz.
W39X32DS	3-9	32mm	Dull Satin	30/30	35'-14'	3¼"	1"	12¾"	11.2 oz.
W39X32	3-9	32mm	Black	30/30	35'-14'	3¼"	1"	12¾"	11.2 oz.
W39X40	3-9	40mm	Black	30/30	35'-14'	3¼"	1"	12⅝"	12.3 oz.
W4X32DS	4	32mm	Dull Satin	30/30	28'	3¼"	1"	11¾"	9.5 oz.
SW39X32	3-9	32mm	Black	30/30	35'-13'	3¼"	1"	11⅛"	11 oz.
SW2.510X32	2.5-10	32mm	Black	30/30	41'-10½'	3¼"	1"	11¼"	8.5 oz.
W1.755X32	1.75-5	32mm	Black	30/30	41'-10½'	3¼"	1"	11¼"	9.5 oz.
W1.755X40	1.75-5	40mm	Black	30/30	47'-18'	3¼"	1"	12⅛"	12.5 oz.
W2.5X32	2.5	32mm	Black	30/30	42'	3¼"	1"	12¼"	12.5 oz.
W2.75X40	2.75	40mm	Black	30/30	36'	3½"	1"	11⅞"	8.75 oz.

THOMPSON/CENTER SCOPES

RECOIL PROOF ELECTRA DOT RIFLE SCOPES

Designed and built to take the pounding of the heaviest Magnum loads, these scopes are subjected to a test force of 1,400 G's. All lenses and reticle house attachments are seated in neoprene and locked in place with finely threaded, double lock retaining rings. Waterproof construction, undetachable eye piece, anodized scope body and scratch-resistant finish. Electra Dot affords a clear, magnified view of the target under adverse light conditions. As the light fades, you simply switch on the battery-powered reticle. The center dot and a portion of both horizontal and vertical crosswires are instantly illuminated.

Model TC4 (No. 8610) $180.00
Model TC3/9V (No. 8620) 250.00

TC 3/9V
#8620

SCOPES

SPECIFICATIONS

No. 8610 & No. 8620	**TC 4** 4 POWER with 1" tube Standard Turrets Electra Dot Reticle	**TC 3/9V** 3 to 9 VARIABLE with 1" tube Standard Turrets Electra Dot Reticle
Power	4X	3X to 9X
Field of View	29 ft. at 100 yds.	35.3 ft. on 3X 13.2 ft. on 9X
Eye Relief	3.3"	3.3"
Relative Brightness	64	177 on 3X 19 on 9X
Main Tube Diameter	1"	1"
Overall Length	12^{15}/$_{16}$"	12^7/$_8$"
Weight	12.3 ounces	15.5 ounces
Maximum Windage and Elevation Adjustment (at 100 yds.)	40" in either direction	40" in either direction
Click Value (at 100 yds.)	^{1}/$_3$"	^{1}/$_4$"
Dot with Crosshairs Reticle (Dot coverage at 100 yds.)	2"	2"

4X SHORT TUBE RIFLE SCOPE
#8640
$185.00

TC 1.5 RP PISTOL SCOPE
#8302 1^1/$_2$ Power w/1" Tube & Target Turrets
$140.00

LOBO SCOPES (not shown)

Designed for light to medium recoil calibers, these long eye relief scopes for pistols and black powder rifles feature adjustable eye pieces, are nitrogen filled and shock proof, and include self-centering crosswire reticles. Internal adjustments are protected by removable weather caps.

Lobo 1^1/$_2$X (No. 7550) $105.00
Lobo 3X (No. 7553) 110.00

Thompson/Center Scope Mounts are available for Contender, Smith & Wesson, Ruger, Hawken/Renegade and Seneca/Cherokee $11.95

SPECIFICATIONS LOBO SCOPES

	1^1/$_2$X	3X
Power	1^1/$_2$X	3X
Reticle	Crosshair	Crosshair
Field of View	16 ft. at 100 yds.	9 ft. at 100 yds.
Eye Relief	11 to 20 inches	11 to 20 inches
Relative Brightness	127	49
Main Tube Diameter	^{7}/$_8$"	^{7}/$_8$"
Overall Length	7^1/$_4$"	9"
Weight	5 ounces	6.3 ounces
Max. Windage & Elevation Adjustment (at 100 yds.)	5.25 ft. at 100 yards	5.25 ft. at 100 yards
Click Value (at 100 yds.)	^{1}/$_3$"	^{1}/$_3$"
Center of Crosshairs (Coverage at 100 yds.)	1.574"	1.181"

WEATHERBY SUPREME SCOPES

WEATHERBY SUPREME SCOPES

As every hunter knows, one of the most difficult problems is keeping running game in the field of view of the scope. Once lost, precious seconds fade away trying to find the animal in the scope again. Too much time wasted means the ultimate frustration. No second shot. Or no shot at all. The Weatherby Wide Field helps you surmount the problem by increasing your field of view.

FEATURES:

Optical excellence—now protected with multicoated anti-glare coating. • Fog-free and waterproof construction. • Constantly self-centered reticles. • Non-magnifying reticle. • ¹/₄" adjustments. • Quick variable power change. • Unique luminous reticle. • Neoprene eyepiece. • Binocular-type speed focusing. • Rugged score tube construction. Autocom point-blank system.

4 POWER

These are fixed-power scopes for big game and varmint hunting. Bright, clear image. Multicoated lenses for maximum luminosity under adverse conditions. 32-foot field of view at 100 yards.

3 TO 9 POWER

The most desirable variable for every kind of shooting from target to long-range big game. Outstanding light-gathering power. Fast, convenient focusing adjustment.

Fixed Power: PRICES

4 × 34	$220.00
4 × 44	270.00
Variable Power:	
1.75-5 × 20	260.00
2-7 × 34	270.00
3-9 × 44	320.00

1³/₄ TO 5 POWER

A popular model for close-range hunting with large-bore rifles. Includes the Autocom system, which automatically compensates for trajectory and eliminates the need for range-finding without making elevation adjustments. Just aim and shoot!

SUPREME RIFLESCOPES SPECIFICATIONS

Item	1.75-5X20	4X34	2-7X34	4X44	3-9X44
Actual Magnification	1.7-5	4	2.1-6.83	3.9	3.15-8.98
Field of View @ 100 yards	66.6-21.4 ft.	32 ft.	59-16 ft.	32 ft.	36-13 ft.
Eye Relief (inches)	3.4	3.1	3.4	3.0	3.5
Exit Pupil dia. in mm	11.9-4	8	10-4.9	10	10-4.9
Clear Aperture of Objective	20mm	34mm	34mm	44mm	44mm
Twilight Factor	5.9-10	11.7	8.2-15.4	13.3	11.5-19.9
Tube Diameter	1"	1"	1"	1"	1"
O.D. of Objective	1"	1.610"	1.610"	2"	2"
O.D. of Ocular	1.635"	1.635"	1.635"	1.635"	1.635"
Overall Length	10.7"	11.125"	11.125"	12.5"	12.7"
Weight	11 oz.	9.6 oz.	10.4 oz.	11.6 oz.	11.6 oz.
Adjustment Graduations					
Major Divisions:	1 MOA	1 MOA	1 MOA	1 MOA	1 MOA
Minor Divisions:	1/4 MOA	1/4 MOA	1/4 MOA	1/4 MOA	1/4 MOA
Maximum Adjustment (W&E)	60"	60"	60"	60"	60"
Reticles Available	LUMIPLEX	LUMIPLEX	LUMIPLEX	LUMIPLEX	LUMIPLEX

WEAVER RINGS AND BASES

1. **DETACHABLE TOP MOUNT RINGS.** Made with split rings in $7/8''$ and 1″ diameters. The 1″ blued rings are available in standard, medium, high and extension styles. New stainless steel rings in 1″ medium also available. High Top Mount Rings and Medium Top Mount Rings (in 1″ diameter only) provide adequate barrel and iron sight clearance for scopes with adjective diameters greater than $1\,3/4''$. **$22.88** (**$34.98** for High Top Mount Rings and 1″ Medium Stainless Steel)

2. **EXTENSION DETACHABLE MOUNT RINGS.** In 1″ diameter only. Position scope $3/4''$ further forward, or backward, for improved eye relief. **$26.73**

3. **DETACHABLE SIDE MOUNTS.** Designed for Winchester 94 (except Angle Eject models) without drilling or tapping. Made with 1″ diameter split-rings and brackets. Also offered in High style for greater clearance. **$23.32** (**27.28** for 1″ Long)

4. **PIVOT MOUNT RINGS.** Change from scope to iron sights with a gentle push. Spring latch locks rings in place when scope is in sighting position. No drilling or tapping required. **$31.02**

5. **SEE-THRU MOUNT RINGS.** Attach to any bases which have square-cut cross bolt slots. Detach easily and offer built-in remounting precision. **$22.88** (**$26.73** for 1″ Extension; **$16.28** for $7/8''$)

6. **INTEGRAL 1″ SEE-THROUGH RINGS.** No drilling or tapping, and no base needed. Large aperature offers wide field of view with iron sights. **$16.28**

7. **1″ TIP-OFF MOUNTS, SPLIT RINGS.** For mounting 1″ scopes on rimfire rifles with $3/8''$ dovetailed factory-grooved receiver. No bases required. **$22.44**

8. **$7/8''$ TIP-OFF MOUNTS, SOLID RINGS.** Designed to mount $7/8''$ scopes. Also available in $3/4''$ rings to fit $3/4''$ scopes. **$19.80**

9. **BLUED MOUNT BASE SYSTEMS. $59.50**

10. **STAINLESS STEEL MOUNT BASE SYSTEMS.** Require no drilling or tapping. Simply remove rear sight and slip on barrel yoke. Base attaches easily with two screws. Includes two Detachable Mount Rings, Mount Base, barrel yoke, screws and Allen wrench. **$83.27**

11. **SCOPE MOUNT SYSTEMS.** For fast mounting on Remington 870 or 1100 shotguns with no drilling or tapping. System meshes with existing trigger plate pins. Remove pins, replace with bolts. **$59.51**

12. **MODEL 94 ANGLE EJECT BASES.** For scoping Angle Eject Winchester 94's. **$9.63**

13. **BASES. $2.31-$11.99** top mount); **$5.06-$8.47** (pivot mount); **$8.80** (side mount)

WILLIAMS TWILIGHT SCOPES

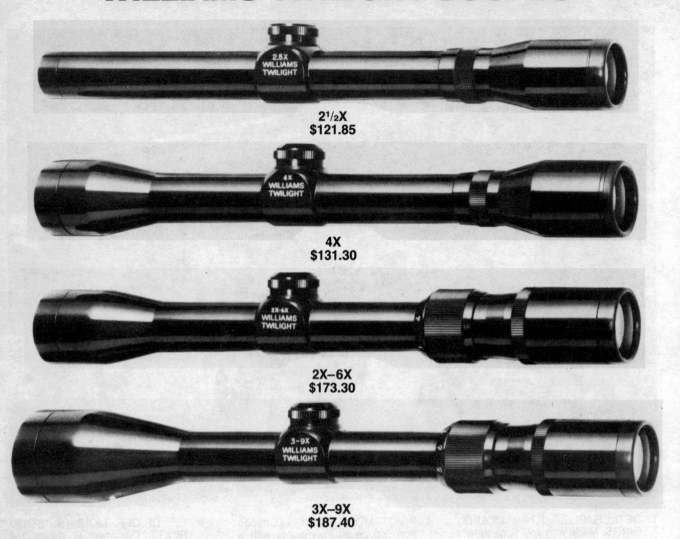

2¹/₂X
$121.85

4X
$131.30

2X–6X
$173.30

3X–9X
$187.40

The "Twilight" series of scopes was introduced to accommodate those shooters who want a high-quality scope in the medium-priced field. The "Twilight" scopes are waterproof and shockproof, have coated lenses and are nitrogen-filled. Resolution is sharp and clear. All "Twilight" scopes have a highly polished, rich, black, hard anodized finish.

There are four models available—the 2¹/₂X, the 4X, the 2X-6X, and the 3X-9X. They are available in T-N-T reticle only (which stands for "thick and thin").

		2.5X	4X	2X-6X At 2X	2X-6X At 6X	3X-9X At 3X	3X-9X At 9X
TWILIGHT SPECIFICATIONS	**OPTICAL SPECIFICATIONS**						
	Clear aperture of objective lens	20mm	32mm	32mm	Same	40mm	Same
	Clear aperture of ocular lens	32mm	32mm	32mm	Same	32mm	Same
	Exit Pupil	8mm	8mm	16mm	5.3mm	13.3mm	44.4mm
	Relative Brightness	64	64	256	28	161.2	17.6
	Field of view (degree of angle)	6°20'	5°30'	8°30'	3°10'	7°	2°20'
	Field of view at 100 yards	32"	29'	45¹/₂'	16³/₄'	36¹/₂'	12³/₄'
	Eye Relief	3.7"	3.6"	3"	3"	3.1"	2.9"
	Parallax Correction (at)	50 yds.	100 yds.	100 yds.	Same	100 yds.	Same
	Lens Construction	9	9	11	Same	11	Same
	MECHANICAL SPECIFICATIONS						
	Outside diameter of objective end	1.00"	1.525"	1.525"	Same	1.850"	1.850"
	Outside diameter of ocular end	1.455"	1.455"	1.455"	Same	1.455"	Same
	Ouside diameter of tube	1"	1"	1"	Same	1"	Same
	Internal adjustment graduation	¹/₄ min.	¹/₄" min.	¹/₄ min.	Same	¹/₄" min.	Same
	Minimum internal adjustment	75 min.	75 min.	75 min.	Same	60 min.	Same
	Finish	Glossy Hard Black Anodized					
	Length	10"	11³/₄"	11¹/₂"	11¹/₂"	12³/₄"	12³/₄"
	Weight	8¹/₂ oz.	9¹/₂ oz.	11¹/₂ oz.	Same	13¹/₂ oz.	Same

WILLIAMS SCOPE MOUNTS

Shown on Model 70A Winchester

STREAMLINE TOP MOUNT

The Williams "Streamline" top mount is a revolutionary concept in two-piece mount design. Its solid ring-base construction allows the strongest possible installation of scope to rifle.

Because the bases are the rings, there can be no movement between the rings and bases as on other two-piece mounts. By design, the "Streamline" mount eliminates the need for extension rings as the mounts can be reversed allowing for installation of virtually all 1-inch scopes.

Features:
- Available for wide assortment of factory drilled rifles
- Precision-machined and lightweight
- Solid construction
- Eliminates need for extension rings—allows use of virtually all 1" scopes
- The bases are the rings
- Hard black anodized finish

Williams "Streamline" Two-Piece Top Mount
Complete **$21.00**
Williams "Steamline" Front or Rear Base Only 10.50
Williams "Streamline" Two-Piece Top Mount with
Sub-Blocks for Hawken M/L 28.65

MODELS	Front	Rear
Remington Models 760, 740, 742, and Savage Model 170	1	2
Winchester Models 70 Standard, 670 and 770	4	3
*1917 Enfield	4	4
Remington Models 700, 721, 722, 725, Remington 700 L.H. and Remington 40X; BSA; Weatherby MK-V & Vanguard; Ruger 77ST; and S&W 1500	4	5
Savage Models 110, 111 and 112V	4	16
Winchester Models 88 and 100	6	6
Browning BAR Auto and BLR Lever	7	7
Marlin Models 336, 1894 & 1894C	8	8
Remington Model 788	9	9
Thompson/Center 45 & 50 Cal. Hawken and 54 Cal. Renegade	10**	10**
Remington 541-S. Also, Remington Models 580, 581, 582 (require drilling & tapping)	11	11
Ruger Model 44	11	12
Ruger Model 10/22	13	12
Browning Safari Bolt and Mark X	14	15
Ithaca LSA-55 and LSA-65 Bolt.	16	16
Rem. Models Four, Six, 7400 and 7600	17	18
Savage Model 99	19	20**
Winchester Model 94 Angle Eject	21	22

*With the rear receiver radiused the same diameter as the front receiver ring.

**Requires Sub-block

Shown on Thompson/Center Renegade w/Sub-blocks

WILLIAMS SIGHT CHART

AMOUNT OF ADJUSTMENT NECESSARY TO CORRECT FRONT SIGHT ERROR

DISTANCE BETWEEN FRONT AND REAR SIGHTS		14"	15"	16"	17"	18"	19"	20"	21"	22"	23"	24"	25"	26"	27"	28"	29"	30"	31"	32"	33"	34"
Amount of	1	.0038	.0041	.0044	.0047	.0050	.0053	.0055	.0058	.0061	.0064	.0066	.0069	.0072	.0074	.0077	.0080	.0082	.0085	.0088	.0091	.0093
Error	2	.0078	.0083	.0089	.0094	.0100	.0105	.0111	.0116	.0122	.0127	.0133	.0138	.0144	.0149	.0155	.0160	.0156	.0171	.0177	.0182	.0188
at	3	.0117	.0125	.0133	.0142	.0150	.0159	.0167	.0175	.0184	.0192	.0201	.0209	.0217	.0226	.0234	.0243	.0251	.0259	.0268	.0276	.0285
100 Yards	4	.0155	.0167	.0178	.0189	.0200	.0211	.0222	.0234	.0244	.0255	.0266	.0278	.0289	.0300	.0311	.0322	.0333	.0344	.0355	.0366	.0377
Given in	5	.0194	.0208	.0222	.0236	.0250	.0264	.0278	.0292	.0306	.0319	.0333	.0347	.0361	.0375	.0389	.0403	.0417	.0431	.0445	.0458	.0472
Inches	6	.0233	.0250	.0267	.0283	.0300	.0317	.0333	.0350	.0367	.0384	.0400	.0417	.0434	.0450	.0467	.0484	.0500	.0517	.0534	.0551	.0567

When you replace an open rear sight with a receiver sight, it is usually necessary to install a higher front sight, to compensate for the higher plane of the new receiver sight. The table above shows the increase in front sight height that's required to compensate for a given error at 100 yards. Suppose your rifle has a 19 inch sight radius, and shoots 6 inches high at 100 yards, with the receiver sight adjusted as low as possible. The 19 inch column shows that the correction for a 6 inch error is .0317 inch. This correction is added to the over-all height of the front sight (including dovetail). Use a micrometer or similar accurate device to measure sight height. Thus, if your original sight measured .250 inch, it should be replaced with a sight .290 inch high.

WILLIAMS

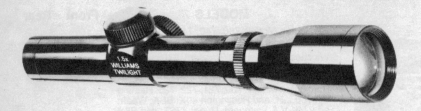

1.5X PISTOL & BOW SCOPE
$118.00

2X PISTOL & BOW SCOPE
$120.00

TWILIGHT SCOPES
FOR PISTOLS AND BOWS
WITH LONG EYE RELIEF

Built tough, compact and lightweight, the Twilight Scope was designed specifically for handgun hunters and precision target shooters. And for archers, these scopes offer the first practical scope-aiming device, including the new Wiliams bow scope mount, which opens up target and hunting possibilities never before available to the archer.

MECHANICAL SPECIFICATIONS	1.5X20	2.20
Outside Diameter of Objective End	1"	1"
Outside Diameter of Ocular End	36.5mm	36.5mm
Outside Diameter of Tube	1"	1"
Internal Adjustment Graduation	1/4"	1/4"
Minimum Internal Adjustment	170"	162"
Finish	Glossy Hard Black Anodized	
Length	209mm	216mm
Weight	6.4 oz.	6.6 oz.

OPTICAL SPECIFICATIONS	1.5X20	2X20
Clear Aperture of Objective Lens	20mm	20mm
Clear Aperture of Ocular Lens	30mm	30mm
Exit Pupil	13.3mm	10mm
Relative Brightness	177	100
Field of View (Degree of Angle)	3°4'	3°20'
Field of View at 100 Yards	19 ft.	17 1/2 ft.
Eye Relief	18"-25"	18"-25"
Parallax Correciton (at)	50 yds.	50 yds.
Lens Construction	6	6

NEW SM94/36 SIDE MOUNT ON THE 94
WINCHESTER $27.85

MOUNTING PLATES:
FOR 30-M1 CARBINE
(Attach with 8-40 fillister screws.) Use the Williams SM-740 side mount base with this mounting plate. Scope can be offset or high over bore. **Price: $11.50**

FOR SMLE NO. 1
(Attach with 8-40 fillister head mounting screws.) This mounting plate is supplied with long 8-40 fillister head screws to replace SM-70 short screws. Use the SM-70 base. Mount can be installed offset or central over bore. **Price: $7.40**

FOR M1 GARAND RIFLE
The mounting screws for this mounting plate are 8-40 × .475 fillister head. Use the Williams SM-740 (4 holes) side mount with this mounting plate. **Price: $11.50**

WILLIAMS SIGHT-THRU MOUNTS

SHOWN ON REMINGTON MODEL 742

SHOWN ON WINCHESTER MODEL 70

Features:
- One-piece construction
- Large field of view for Iron Sights right under the scope
- Available for a wide assortment of factory-drilled rifles
- All parts are precision-machined
- Lightweight
- Hard black anodized finish
- Fast, accurate sighting under all field conditions

The Williams Sight-Thru Mount provides instant use of scope above, or iron sights below. Easily installed. Uses existing holes on top of receiver. No drilling or tapping necessary. The Sight-Thru is compact and lightweight—will not alter balance of the rifle. The high tensile strength alloy will never rust. All parts are precision-machined. Completely rigid. Shockproof. The attractive streamlined appearance is further enhanced by a beautiful, hard black anodized finish. Rings are 1" in size; 7/8" sleeves available.

Williams "Sight-Thru" Mount Complete $21.00
Williams "Sight-Thru" Base and Ring 10.50

MODELS	FRONT	REAR
Winchester Models 88 and 100; Sako Finn-wolf; Ithaca 37†.	A	A
Remington Models 760, 740, 742 and Savage Model 170	A	B
Winchester Models 70 Standard, 670 and 770; Browning BBR.	D	C
Remington Models 700 R.H. and L.H., 721, 722, 725; Weatherby MK-V and Vanguard; BSA round top receivers; Ruger 77ST; Smith & Wesson Model 1500.	D	E
Savage Models 110, 111 and 112V	D	F
Browning BLR Lever Action	O	O
Browning BAR High Power Auto; Mossberg 800; Remington 541S †. Will also fit Ward's Western Field Model 72 and Mossberg Model 472 lever action.*.	G	G
Late models Marlin 336, 1894 and 1894C	H	H
FN Mauser; Browning Bolt Action; J. C. Higgins 50-51; Interarms Mark X Mauser	D	I
Savage 99 (New Style)	J	K**
Schultz & Larsen.	A	G
1917 Enfield	J	J
Ruger 10/22	L	M
Ruger 44	O	M
Ruger 77R and RS Series †	H	P
Remington Models 4, 7400, 6, and 7600 . .	R	S

*When ordering 'G' bases for Western Field Model 72 and Mossberg Model 472, please specify that 360 screws must be furnished.
**Requires Sub-block   †Drilling and Tapping Required

WILLIAMS FRONT SIGHT RISER BLOCK

This riser block adds .250 inch to the height of the dovetail. It is especially handy on such guns as the Ruger 10/22 and any other models that require a higher than normal front sight (when installing a receiver sight). This model is available in two widths—the .250 for Williams Streamlined ramps and other ramps having a 1/4-inch top width—and the .340 to work on all standard factory ramps (Winchester, Remington, Savage, etc.) having this base width. It incorporates the standard 3/8-inch dovetail.

Price. $4.15

WILLIAMS SIGHT-OVER-SCOPE

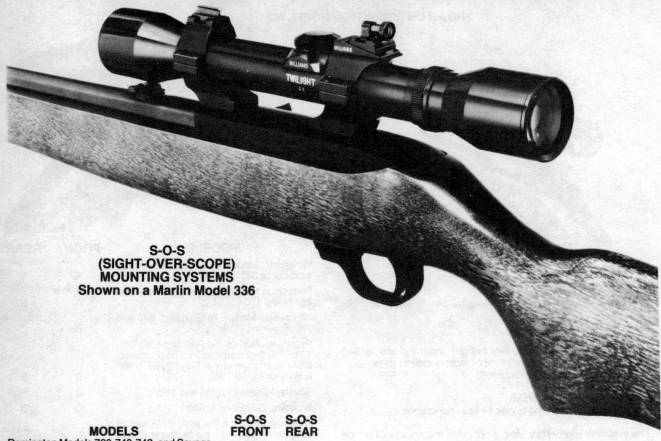

**S-O-S
(SIGHT-OVER-SCOPE)
MOUNTING SYSTEMS
Shown on a Marlin Model 336**

MODELS	S-O-S FRONT	S-O-S REAR
Remington Models 760-740-742, and Savage Model 170.	1	2
Winchester Models 70 Standard, 670 & 770	4	3
*1917 Enfield	4	4
Remington Models 700-721-722-725, L.H. and 40X; BSA; Weatherby MK-V and Vanguard; Ruger 77ST; and S&W 1500	4	5
Savage Models 110, 111 and 112V	4	16
Winchester Models 88 and 100	6	6
Browning BAR Auto and BLR Lever	7	7
Marlin Models 336, 1894 & 1894C	8	8
Remington Model 788	9	9
Thompson/Center 45 & 50 Cal. Hawken and 54 Cal. Renegade	10**	10**
Remington 541-S. Also, Remington Models 580-581-582 (require drilling & tapping)	11	11
Ruger Model 44.	11	12
Ruger Model 10/22	13	12
Browning Safari Bolt and Mark X	14	15
Ithaca LSA-55 and LSA-65 Bolt	16	16
Rem. Models Four, Six, 7400 and 7600	17	18
Savage Model 99.	19	20**
Winchester Model 94 Angle Eject	21	22**

***With the rear receiver radiused the same
diameter as the front receiver ring.
Requires sub-block

The S-O-S System (on a Ruger 10/22)
S-O-S Kit Complete for Williams Rings **$47.00**
S-O-S Streamline Set (except w/sub-block) **54.15**
S-O-S Streamline Set 10 & 10 . . . . **61.75**
S-O-S Streamline Set 19, 20, 21 & 22 . . . . **56.55**

This concept in sighting known as the S-O-S (Sight-Over-Scope) allows the scope to be mounted low and permits instant use of open sight for quick, fast action shots at close range. The compact S-O-S has both elevation and windage in the rear sight, and the front sight has additional windage.

The "Guide-Line" S-O-S ring top kit will work with all Williams mounts having the two-piece 1-inch rings. The sights are made from an aluminum alloy. They are rustproof and attractively anodized.

The S-O-S front sight is furnished with a fluorescent orange $3/32$-inch bead (white or gold is optional.) The S-O-S rear sight is furnished with the WGRS-M/L Guide Receiver Sight with the regular $3/8 \times .125$ Buckbuster long shank aperture. (Twilight or Regular apertures in the $3/8 \times .093$ and $3/8 \times .050$ are optional.) Specify the long shank aperture to fit the WGRS receiver sight.

ZEISS SCOPES

EUROPEAN Z-TYPE SCOPES

These five new scopes include the following features: mounting rails (for center tube mounting); large objective diameter and good twilight performance; metric graduation of reticle adjustment (1 click = 1cm/100m); traditional reticle types; and constant relationship between reticle and target when changing power (enabling use of reticle also for range estimation).

DIATAL-Z 4 × 32T
$450.00

DIATAL-Z 6 × 42T
$525.00

DIATAL-Z 8 × 56T
$600.00

DIAVARI-Z 1.5-6 × 42T
$730.00

DIAVARI-Z 2.5-10 × 52T
$850.00

ZEISS RIFLESCOPES

THE C-SERIES

The C-Series was designed by Zeiss specifically for the American hunter. It is based on space-age alloy tubes with integral objective and ocular bells, and an integral adjustment turret. This strong, rigid one-piece construction allows perfect lens alignment, micro-precise adjustments and structural integrity. Other features include quick focusing, a generous 3½" of eye relief, rubber armoring, T-Star multi-layer coating, and parallax setting (free at 100 yards).

10 × 36
$550.00

3-9 × 36
$725.00

6 × 32
$470.00

4x32
$425.00

4.5 × 18T
$625.00

PRODUCT SPECIFICATIONS	4×32	6×32	10×36	3-9×36		C1.5-4.5×18	
Magnification	4X	6X	10X	3X	9X	1.5X	4.5X
Objective Diameter (mm)/(inch)	1.26"	1.26"	1.42"	1.42"		15.0/0.6	18.0/0.7
Exit Pupil	0.32"	0.21"	0.14"	0.39"	0.16"	10.0	4.0
Twilight Performance	11.3	13.9	19.0	8.5	18.0	4.2	9.0
Field of View at 100 yds.	30'	20'	12'	36'	13'	72'	27'
Eye Relief	3.5"	3.5"	3.5"	3.5"	3.5"	3.5"	
Maximum Interval Adjustment (elevation and windage (MOA)	80	80	50	50		10.5' @ 100 yds.	
Click-Stop Adjustment 1 click = 1 interval (MOA)	¼	¼	¼	¼		.36" @ 100 yds.	
Length	10.6"	10.6"	12.7"	11.2"		11.8"	
Weight approx. (ounces)	11.3	11.3	14.1	15.2		13.4	
Tube Diameter	1"	1"	1"	1"		1"	
Objective Tube Diameter	1.65"	1.65"	1.89"	1.73"		1"	
Eyepiece O.D.	1.67"	1.67"	1.67"	1.67"		1.8"	

Ammunition

FOR ADDRESSES AND PHONE
NUMBERS OF MANUFACTURERS AND
DISTRIBUTORS INCLUDED IN THIS
SECTION, SEE *DIRECTORY OF
MANUFACTURERS AND SUPPLIERS*

FEDERAL AMMUNITION

HI-POWER® SHOTSHELLS

LOAD NO.	GAUGE	SHELL LENGTH (INCHES)	POWDER DRAMS EQUIV.	OUNCES SHOT	SHOT SIZES	APPROX. CASE WT. (LBS.)	RETAIL PRICE (SUGGESTED) PER BOX
HI-POWER® POWER MAGNUM LOADS — 25 rounds per box, 10 boxes per case. 250 rounds per case.							
F103	10	3½	4¼	2	BB, 2,4	44	29.51
F131	12	3	4	1⅞	BB, 2,4	39	18.47
F129	12	3	4	1⅝	2,4, 6	36	17.07
F130	12	2¾	3¾	1½	BB, 2,4,5,6	33	15.42
F165	16	2¾	3¼	1¼	2,4, 6	28	15.17
F207	20	3	3	1¼	2,4, 6, 7½	27	14.25
F205	20	2¾	2¾	1⅛	2,4, 6, 7½	25	12.64
LIGHT MAGNUM LOADS — 25 rounds per box, 20 boxes per case. 500 rounds per case.							
F138	12	2¾	4	1⅜	4, 6, 7½	61	14.42
HI-POWER® LOADS — 25 rounds per box, 20 boxes per case. 500 rounds per case.							
F127	12	2¾	3¾	1¼	BB, 2,4,5,6, 7½,8, 9	57	12.52
F164	16	2¾	3¼	1⅛	4, 6, 7½	52	12.00
F203	20	2¾	2¾	1	4,5,6, 7½,8	45	11.00
F283	28	2¾	2¼	¾	6, 7½	37	11.09
F413	410	3	Max.	11/16	4,5,6, 7½,8	30	10.30
F412	410	2½	Max.	½	6, 7½	24	8.75
MAGNUM STEEL SHOT LOADS — 25 rounds per box, 10 boxes per case. 250 rounds per case.							
W104	10	3½	Max.	1⅝	BB, 2	38	26.27
W149	12	3	Max.	1⅜	BB,1,2,4	31	18.59
W140	12	3	Max.	1¼	BB,1,2,4	32	17.10
W148	12	2¾	Max.	1¼	BB,1,2,4	28	17.10
W209	20	3	3¼	1	4, 6	22	15.00
HI-POWER® STEEL SHOT LOADS — 25 rounds per box, 20 boxes per case. 500 rounds per case.							
W147	12	2¾	3¾	1⅛	2,4, 6	54	15.67
W208	20	2¾	3	¾	4, 6	39	14.00
FIELD LOADS — 25 rounds per box, 20 boxes per case. 500 rounds per case.							
*F125	12	2¾	3¼	1¼	7½,8	56	14.00
F124	12	2¾	3¼	1¼	7½,8, 9	56	11.00
F123	12	2¾	3¼	1⅛	4, 6, 7½,8, 9	51	10.04
F162	16	2¾	2¾	1⅛	6, 7½,8	51	10.04
F202	20	2¾	2½	1	6, 7½,8	45	9.42

*Flyer Load

HI-SHOK HOLLOW POINT RIFLED SLUG LOADS — 5 rounds per box, 50 boxes per case. 250 rounds per case.

LOAD NO.	GAUGE	SHELL LENGTH (INCHES)	POWDER DRAMS EQUIV.	OUNCES SHOT	SHOT SIZES	APPROX. CASE WT. (LBS.)	RETAIL PRICE (SUGGESTED) PER BOX
F103	10	3½	Mag.	1¾	Rifled Slug	40	7.13
F130	12	2¾	Mag.	1¼	Rifled Slug	30	5.12
F127	12	2¾	Max.	1	Rifled Slug	26	4.12
F164	16	2¾	Max.	⅘	Rifled Slug	22	4.12
F203	20	2¾	Max.	¾	Rifled Slug	19	3.77
F412	410	2½	Max.	⅕	Rifled Slug	9	3.57

FEDERAL AMMUNITION

SHOTSHELLS

LOAD NO.	GAUGE	SHELL LENGTH (INCHES)	POWDER DRAMS EQUIV.	SHOT SIZES		APPROX. CASE WT. (LBS.)	RETAIL PRICE (SUGGESTED) PER BOX
HI-POWER® BUCKSHOT LOADS — 5 rounds per box, 50 boxes per case. 250 rounds per case.							
G108	10	3½	Mag.	00 Buck	18 Pellets	52	6.75
G108	10	3½	Mag.	No. 4 Buck	54 Pellets	54	6.75
F131	12	3	Mag.	000 Buck	10 Pellets	38	5.08
F131	12	3	Mag.	00 Buck	15 Pellets	39	5.08
F131	12	3	Mag.	No. 1 Buck	24 Pellets	44	5.08
F131	12	3	Mag.	No. 4 Buck	41 Pellets	40	5.08
*A131	12	3	Mag.	No. 4 Buck	41 Pellets	40	25.42
F130	12	2¾	Mag.	00 Buck	12 Pellets	33	4.47
F130	12	2¾	Mag.	No. 1 Buck	20 Pellets	38	4.47
F130	12	2¾	Mag.	No. 4 Buck	34 Pellets	35	4.47
*A130	12	2¾	Mag.	No. 4 Buck	34 Pellets	35	22.34
F207	20	3	Mag.	No. 2 Buck	18 Pellets	30	4.47
F127	12	2¾	Max.	000 Buck	8 Pellets	30	3.57
F127	12	2¾	Max.	00 Buck	9 Pellets	27	3.57
F127	12	2¾	Max.	0 Buck	12 Pellets	32	3.57
F127	12	2¾	Max.	No. 1 Buck	16 Pellets	33	3.57
F127	12	2¾	Max.	No. 4 Buck	27 Pellets	30	3.57
F164	16	2¾	Max.	No. 1 Buck	12 Pellets	26	3.57
F203	20	2¾	Max.	No. 3 Buck	20 Pellets	25	3.57

*A131 and A130 are packed 25 rounds per box — 250 rounds per case.

22 RIMFIRE CARTRIDGES

LOAD NO.	CARTRIDGES	BULLET TYPE	BULLET WEIGHT GRAINS	APPROX. CASE WT. (LBS.)	RETAIL PRICE (SUGGESTED) PER BOX
HI-POWER® 22's — 50 rounds per box, 100 boxes per case. 5000 rounds per case.					
701	22 Short	Copper Plated	29	30	2.47
706	22 Long	Copper Plated	29	32	2.67
710	22 Long Rifle	Copper Plated	40	40	2.82
712	Long Rifle	Copper Plated, Hollow Pt	38	40	3.12
716	22 Long Rifle	#12 Shot	#12 Shot	34	5.75
HI-POWER® 22's-100 PACK — 100 rounds per box, 50 boxes per case. 5000 rounds per case.					
810	22 Long Rifle	Copper Plated	40	45	5.63
812	22 Long Rifle	Copper Plated, Hollow Pt	38	45	6.24
MAGNUM 22's — 50 rounds per box, 100 boxes per case. 5000 rounds per case.					
737	22 Long Rifle	Full Metal Jacket	40	50	7.57
747	22 Long Rifle	Jacketed Hollow Pt	40	50	7.57
SPITFIRE HYPER-VELOCITY 22's — 50 rounds per Sport-Pak™. 20 packs per carton, 6 cartons per 6,000 rd. case.					
720	22 Long Rifle	Truncated Cone, Solid	36	48	3.07
722	22 Long Rifle	Truncated Cone, Hollow Pt	33	45	3.15
CHAMPION™ STANDARD VELOCITY 22's — 50 rounds per box, 100 boxes per case. 5000 rounds per case.					
711	22 Long Rifle	Lead Lubricated	40	40	2.82
CHAMPION™ STANDARD VELOCITY 22's - 100 PACK — 100 rounds per box, 50 boxes per case. 5000 rounds per case.					
811	22 Long Rifle	Lead Lubricated	40	45	5.63

FEDERAL AMMUNITION
CENTERFIRE RIFLE CARTRIDGES

LOAD NO.	CARTRIDGES	BULLET TYPE	BULLET WEIGHT GRAINS	APPROX. CASE WT. (LBS.)	RETAIL PRICE (SUGGESTED) PER BOX
222A	222 Remington	Soft Point	50	15	11.37
222B	222 Remington	Metal Case Boat Tail	55	15	11.37
22250A	22-250 Remington	Soft Point	55	22	12.44
22250C	22-250 Remington	BLITZ Hollow Point	40	21	12.92
223A	223 Rem. (5.56 mm)	Soft Point	55	15	12.44
223B	223 Rem. (5.56 mm)	Metal Case Boat Tail	55	15	12.44
223C	223 Rem. (5.56 mm)	Hollow Point Boat Tail	55	15	13.34
223D	223 Rem. (5.56 mm)	BLITZ Hollow Point	40	14	13.34
6A	6 mm Remington	Soft Point	80	27	15.54
6B	6 mm Remington	Hi-Shok Soft Point	100	28	15.54
243A	243 Winchester	Soft Point	80	25	15.54
243B	243 Winchester	Hi-Shok Soft Point	100	27	15.54
257A	257 Roberts (High Vel. - P)	Hi-Shok Soft Point	117	30	17.37
2506A	25-06 Remington	Hollow Point	90	28	16.87
2506B	25-06 Remington	Hi-Shok Soft Point	117	30	16.87
270A	270 Winchester	Hi-Shok Soft Point	130	31	16.87
270B	270 Winchester	Hi-Shok Soft Point	150	33	16.87
7A	7 mm Mauser	Hi-Shok Soft Point	175	33	17.17
7B	7 mm Mauser	Hi-Shok Soft Point	140	31	17.17
7RA	7 mm Rem. Magnum	Hi-Shok Soft Point	150	37	20.89
7RB	7 mm Rem. Magnum	Hi-Shok Soft Point	175	39	20.89
30CA	30 Carbine	Soft Point	110	16	10.84
30CB	30 Carbine	Metal Case	110	16	10.84
730A	7-30 Waters	Boat Tail Soft Point	120	25	15.67
3030A	30-30 Winchester	Hi-Shok Soft Point	150	27	13.24
3030B	30-30 Winchester	Hi-Shok Soft Point	170	28	13.24
3030C	30-30 Winchester	Hollow Point	125	25	13.24
3006A	30-06 Springfield	Hi-Shok Soft Point	150	33	16.87
3006B	30-06 Springfield	Hi-Shok Soft Point	180	35	16.87
3006C	30-06 Springfield	Soft Point	125	31	16.87
3006D	30-06 Springfield	Boat Tail Soft Point	165	34	17.59
3006H	30-06 Springfield	Hi-Shok Soft Point	220	37	16.87
300A	300 Savage	Hi-Shok Soft Point	150	30	17.04
300B	300 Savage	Hi-Shok Soft Point	180	32	17.04
300WB	300 Win. Magnum	Hi-Shok Soft Point	180	40	22.05
308A	308 Winchester	Hi-Shok Soft Point	150	31	16.87
308B	308 Winchester	Hi-Shok Soft Point	180	32	16.87
8A	8 mm Mauser	Hi-Shok Soft Point	170	32	17.37
32A	32 Win. Special	Hi-Shok Soft Point	170	29	14.12
35A	35 Remington	Hi-Shok Soft Point	200	32	15.57
•44A	44 Remington Magnum	Hollow Soft Point	240	29	12.90
4570A	45-70 Government	Hollow Soft Point	300	42	19.20

20 rounds per box, 25 boxes per case. 500 rounds per case.

•For Rifle or Pistol
All prices include the 11% excise tax and are subject to change without notice.

FEDERAL AMMUNITION

CENTERFIRE PISTOL CARTRIDGES

LOAD NO.	CARTRIDGES	BULLET TYPE	BULLET WEIGHT GRAINS	APPROX. CASE WT. (LBS.)	RETAIL PRICE (SUGGESTED) PER BOX
*25AP	25 Auto Pistol (6.35mm)	Metal Case	50	12	8.34
32AP	32 Auto Pistol (7.65mm)	Metal Case	71	18	18.85
32LA	32 S&W Long	Lead Wadcutter	98	20	18.09
32LB	32 S&W Long	Lead Round Nose	98	20	16.77
32HRA	32 H&R Magnum	Lead Semi-Wadcutter	95	25	17.25
32HRB	32 H&R Magnum	Jacketed Hollow Point	85	21	20.92
380AP	380 Auto Pistol	Metal Case	95	23	19.29
380BP	380 Auto Pistol	Jacketed Hollow Point	90	22	19.29
9AP	9 mm Luger Auto Pistol	Metal Case	123	29	23.40
9BP	9 mm Luger Auto Pistol	Jacketed Hollow Point	115	28	23.40
9CP	9 mm Luger Auto Pistol	Jacketed Soft Point	95	28	23.40
38A	38 Special (Match)	Lead Wadcutter	148	34	18.52
38B	38 Special	Lead Round Nose	158	35	17.79
38C	38 Special	Lead Semi-Wadcutter	158	35	19.12
‡38D	38 Special (High Vel + P)	Lead Round Nose	158	35	19.75
‡38E	38 Special (High Vel + P)	Jacketed Hollow Point	125	30	22.55
‡38F	38 Special (High Vel + P)	Jacketed Hollow Point	110	28	22.55
‡38G	38 Special (High Vel + P)	Lead SW Hollow Point	158	34	19.32
‡38H	38 Special (High Vel + P)	Lead Semi-Wadcutter	158	35	19.75
‡38J	38 Special (High Vel + P)	Jacketed Soft Point	125	30	22.55
357A	357 Magnum	Jacketed Soft Point	158	39	24.74
357B	357 Magnum	Jacketed Hollow Point	125	34	24.74
357C	357 Magnum	Lead Semi-Wadcutter	158	37	20.90
357D	357 Magnum	Jacketed Hollow Point	110	30	24.74
357E	357 Magnum	Jacketed Hollow Point	158	39	24.74
357G	357 Magnum	Jacketed Hollow Point	180	44	24.74
41A	41 Remington Magnum	Jacketed Hollow Point	210	54	32.54
44B	44 Remington Magnum	Jacketed Hollow Point	180	50	32.29
**A44B	44 Remington Magnum	Jacketed Hollow Point	180	50	13.34
•44C	44 Remington Magnum	Metal Case Profile	220	56	34.44
44SA	44 S & W Special	Lead SW Hollow Point	200	50	24.89
45LCA	45 Colt	Lead SW Hollow Point	225	50	25.29
45A	45 Automatic (Match)	Metal Case	230	49	25.76
45B	45 Automatic (Match)	Metal Case, S.W.C.	185	42	27.09
45C	45 Automatic	Jacketed Hollow Point	185	42	27.09

50 rounds per box, 20 boxes per case. 1000 rounds per case.

NYCLAD® CENTERFIRE PISTOL CARTRIDGES — 50 rounds per box, 20 boxes per case, 1000 rounds per case.

LOAD NO.	CARTRIDGES	BULLET TYPE	BULLET WEIGHT GRAINS	APPROX. CASE WT. (LBS.)	RETAIL PRICE (SUGGESTED) PER BOX
N38A	38 Special	Lead Wadcutter	148	34	20.25
N38B	38 Special	Lead Round Nose	158	35	19.17
N38C	38 Special	Lead Semi-Wadcutter	158	35	20.25
‡N38G	38 Special (High Vel + P)	SW Hollow Point	158	35	22.25
‡N38H	38 Special (High Vel + P)	Lead Semi-Wadcutter	158	35	22.25
N38M	38 Special	Hollow Point	125	30	22.25
‡N38N	38 Special (High Vel + P)	Hollow Point	125	30	22.25
N357C	357 Magnum	Lead Semi-Waductter	158	37	24.75
N357E	357 Magnum	SW Hollow Point	158	39	24.75

*25AP packed 25 rounds per box.
•For Rifle or Pistol   **A44B packed 20 rounds per box, 1000 rounds per case.
‡This ammunition is loaded to a higher pressure, as indicated by the " + P" marking on the case headstamp, to achieve higher velocity. Use only in firearms especially designed for this cartridge and so recommended by the manufacturer.

HORNADY AMMUNITION

RIFLE AMMUNITION

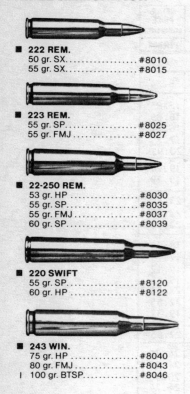

- **222 REM.**
  50 gr. SX................. #8010
  55 gr. SX................. #8015

- **223 REM.**
  55 gr. SP................. #8025
  55 gr. FMJ............... #8027

- **22-250 REM.**
  53 gr. HP................ #8030
  55 gr. SP................ #8035
  55 gr. FMJ.............. #8037
  60 gr. SP................ #8039

- **220 SWIFT**
  55 gr. SP................ #8120
  60 gr. HP................ #8122

- **243 WIN.**
  75 gr. HP................ #8040
  80 gr. FMJ.............. #8043
  I 100 gr. BTSP............ #8046

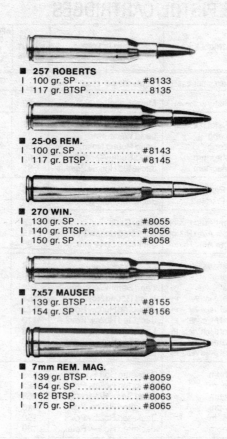

- **257 ROBERTS**
  I 100 gr. SP............. #8133
  I 117 gr. BTSP........... 8135

- **25-06 REM.**
  I 100 gr. SP............. #8143
  I 117 gr. BTSP........... #8145

- **270 WIN.**
  I 130 gr. SP............. #8055
  I 140 gr. BTSP........... #8056
  I 150 gr. SP............. #8058

- **7x57 MAUSER**
  I 139 gr. BTSP........... #8155
  I 154 gr. SP............. #8156

- **7mm REM. MAG.**
  I 139 gr. BTSP............ #8059
  I 154 gr. SP............. #8060
  I 162 BTSP............... #8063
  I 175 gr. SP............. #8065

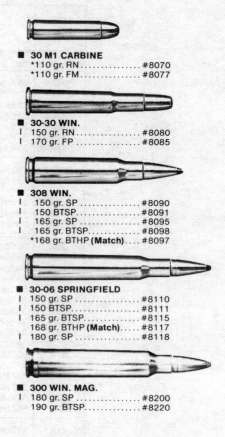

- **30 M1 CARBINE**
  *110 gr. RN.......... #8070
  *110 gr. FM.............. #8077

- **30-30 WIN.**
  I 150 gr. RN............. #8080
  I 170 gr. FP............. #8085

- **308 WIN.**
  I 150 gr. SP............. #8090
  I 150 BTSP.............. #8091
  I 165 gr. SP............. #8095
  I 165 gr. BTSP........... #8098
  *168 gr. BTHP **(Match)**.... #8097

- **30-06 SPRINGFIELD**
  I 150 gr. SP............. #8110
  I 150 BTSP.............. #8111
  I 165 gr. BTSP........... #8115
  168 gr. BTHP **(Match)**..... #8117
  I 180 gr. SP............. #8118

- **300 WIN. MAG.**
  180 gr. SP............. #8200
  190 gr. BTSP............ #8220

PISTOL AMMUNITION

- **25 AUTO**
  *50 gr. FMJ-RN .... #9000

- **380 AUTO**
  *90 gr. JHP............. #9010
  *100 gr. FMJ............. #9015

- **9MM LUGER**
  *90 gr. JHP............. #9020
  *100 gr. FMJ............. #9023
  *115 gr. JHP............. #9025
  *124 gr. FMJ-FP......... #9027
  *124 gr. RN............. #9029

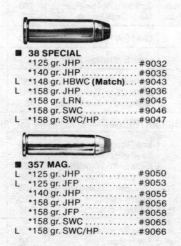

- **38 SPECIAL**
  *125 gr. JHP............. #9032
  *140 gr. JHP............. #9035
  L *148 gr. HBWC **(Match)**... #9043
  L *158 gr. JHP............. #9036
  *158 gr. LRN............. #9045
  *158 gr. SWC............. #9046
  L *158 gr. SWC/HP .... #9047

- **357 MAG.**
  L *125 gr. JHP............. #9050
  L *125 gr. JFP............. #9053
  *140 gr. JHP............. #9055
  *158 gr. JHP............. #9056
  *158 gr. JFP............. #9058
  *158 gr. SWC............. #9065
  L *158 gr. SWC/HP......... #9066

- **44 REM. MAG.**
  180 JHP...... **NEW**...... #9081
  200 gr. JHP............. #9080
  240 gr. JHP............. #9085
  L *240 gr. SWC/HP .... #9086
  240 gr. SWC............. #9087

- **45 ACP**
  185 gr. JHP.............. #9090
  200 gr. SWC .... #9110
  200 gr. FMJ-C/T **(Match)**.... #9111
  230 gr. FMJ-RN .... #9097
  230 gr. FMJ-FP .... #9098

"I" Denotes Interlock Bullet.   Packed 50 per box. All others packed 20 per box.   "L" Denotes Swaged Lead Bullet

REMINGTON CENTERFIRE AMMUNITION

The centerfire cartridges pictured below represent the most recent additions to Remington's ammunition lineup. They are being introduced in 1987 and will join the other cartridges pictured and described on the following pages.

**357 REM. MAGNUM
140-Gr. SEMI-JACKETED
HOLLOW POINT**

**45 COLT
225-Gr. LEAD
SEMI-WADCUTTER**

**45-70 GOVERNMENT
300-Gr. SEMI-JACKETED
HOLLOW POINT**

**338 WIN. MAGNUM
250-Gr. POINTED SOFT POINT**

**257 ROBERTS
100-Gr. PSP "CORE-LOKT"**

REMINGTON CENTERFIRE RIFLE CARTRIDGES

223 Remington (5.56mm)

No.	Bullet weight	Bullet style	Wt. case, lbs.
R223R1	55 gr.	Pointed Soft Point	15
R223R2	55 gr.	Hollow Point "Power-Lokt"	15
R223R3	55 gr.	Metal Case	15

20 in a box, 500 in a case.

17 Remington

No.	Bullet weight	Bullet style	Wt. case, lbs.
R17REM	25 gr.	Hollow Point "Power-Lokt"	12

20 in a box, 500 in a case.

6mm Remington

No.	Bullet weight	Bullet style	Wt. case, lbs.
R6MM1*	80 gr.	Pointed Soft Point	26
R6MM2*	80 gr.	Hollow Point "Power-Lokt"	26
R6MM4	100 gr.	Pointed Soft Point "Core-Lokt"	26

20 in a box, 500 in a case.

(*) May be used in rifles chambered for .244 Remington.

22 Hornet

No.	Bullet weight	Bullet style	Wt. case, lbs.
R22HN1	45 gr.	Pointed Soft Point	9
R22HN2	45 gr.	Hollow Point	9

50 in a box, 500 in a case.

243 Win.

No.	Bullet weight	Bullet style	Wt. case, lbs.
R243W1	80 gr.	Pointed Soft Point	49
R243W2	80 gr.	Hollow Point "Power-Lokt"	49
★R243W3	100 gr.	Pointed Soft Point "Core-Lokt"	49

20 in a box, 1,000 in a case.

222 Remington

No.	Bullet weight	Bullet style	Wt. case, lbs.
R222R1	50 gr.	Pointed Soft Point	27
R222R4	55 gr.	Metal Case	27
R222R3	50 gr.	Hollow Point "Power-Lokt"	27

20 in a box, 1,000 in a case.

25-06 Remington

No.	Bullet weight	Bullet style	Wt. case, lbs.
R25061	87 gr.	Hollow Point "Power-Lokt"	27
R25062	100 gr.	Pointed Soft Point "Core-Lokt"	27
R25063	120 gr.	Pointed Soft Point "Core-Lokt"	27

20 in a box, 500 in a case.

222 Remington Magnum

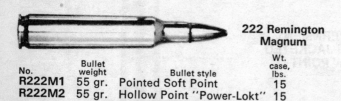

No.	Bullet weight	Bullet style	Wt. case, lbs.
R222M1	55 gr.	Pointed Soft Point	15
R222M2	55 gr.	Hollow Point "Power-Lokt"	15

20 in a box, 500 in a case.

22-250 Remington

No.	Bullet weight	Bullet style	Wt. case, lbs.
R22501	55 gr.	Pointed Soft Point	42
R22502	55 gr.	Hollow Point "Power-Lokt"	42

20 in a box, 1,000 in a case.

25-20 Win.

No.	Bullet weight	Bullet style	Wt. case, lbs.
R25202	86 gr.	Soft Point	13

50 in a box, 500 in a case.

REMINGTON CENTERFIRE RIFLE CARTRIDGES

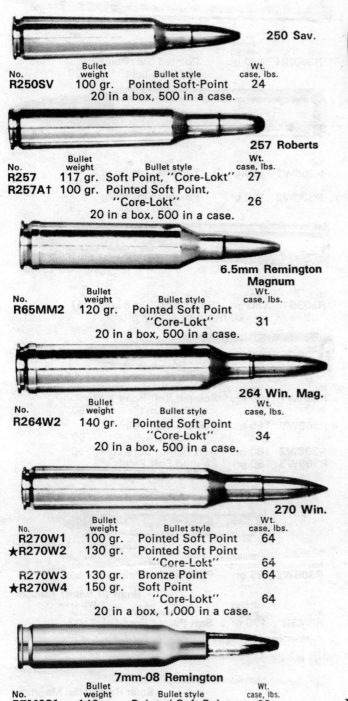

250 Sav.

No.	Bullet weight	Bullet style	Wt. case, lbs.
R250SV	100 gr.	Pointed Soft-Point	24

20 in a box, 500 in a case.

257 Roberts

No.	Bullet weight	Bullet style	Wt. case, lbs.
R257	117 gr.	Soft Point, "Core-Lokt"	27
R257A†	100 gr.	Pointed Soft Point, "Core-Lokt"	26

20 in a box, 500 in a case.

6.5mm Remington Magnum

No.	Bullet weight	Bullet style	Wt. case, lbs.
R65MM2	120 gr.	Pointed Soft Point "Core-Lokt"	31

20 in a box, 500 in a case.

264 Win. Mag.

No.	Bullet weight	Bullet style	Wt. case, lbs.
R264W2	140 gr.	Pointed Soft Point "Core-Lokt"	34

20 in a box, 500 in a case.

270 Win.

No.	Bullet weight	Bullet style	Wt. case, lbs.
R270W1	100 gr.	Pointed Soft Point	64
★R270W2	130 gr.	Pointed Soft Point "Core-Lokt"	64
R270W3	130 gr.	Bronze Point	64
★R270W4	150 gr.	Soft Point "Core-Lokt"	64

20 in a box, 1,000 in a case.

7mm-08 Remington

No.	Bullet weight	Bullet style	Wt. case, lbs.
R7M081	140 gr.	Pointed Soft Point	60

280 Remington ‡

No.	Bullet weight	Bullet style	Wt. case, lbs.
R280R3	140 gr.	Pointed Soft Point	33
R280R1	150 gr.	Pointed Soft Point "Core-Lokt"	33
R280R2	165 gr.	Soft Point "Core-Lokt"	34

20 in a box, 500 in a case.

‡ Interchangeable with 7mm "Express" Rem.   † New for 1987

7mm Remington Magnum

No.	Bullet weight	Bullet style	Wt. case, lbs.
R7MM2	150 gr.	Pointed Soft Point "Core-Lokt"	37
R7MM3	175 gr.	Pointed Soft Point "Core-Lokt"	37

20 in a box, 500 in a case.

7mm Mauser (7x57)

No.	Bullet weight	Bullet style	Wt. case, lbs.
R7MSR1	140 gr.	Pointed Soft Point	32

20 in a box, 500 in a case.

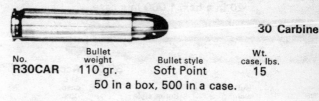

30 Carbine

No.	Bullet weight	Bullet style	Wt. case, lbs.
R30CAR	110 gr.	Soft Point	15

50 in a box, 500 in a case.

30-30 Win.

No.	Bullet weight	Bullet style	Wt. case, lbs.
★R30301	150 gr.	Soft Point "Core-Lokt"	53
★R30302	170 gr.	Soft Point "Core-Lokt"	53
R30303	170 gr.	Hollow Point "Core-Lokt"	53

20 in a box, 1,000 in a case.

REMINGTON CENTERFIRE RIFLE CARTRIDGES

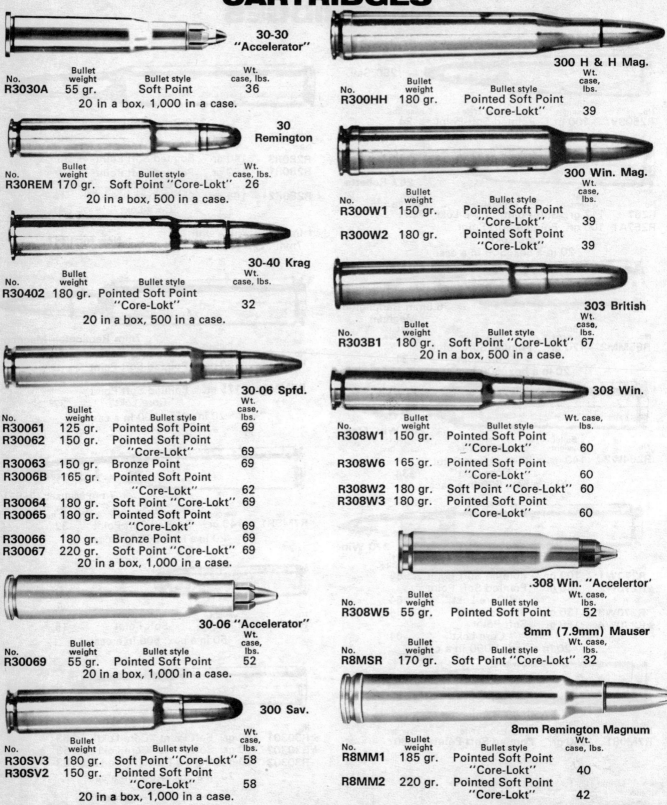

30-30 "Accelerator"

No.	Bullet weight	Bullet style	Wt. case, lbs.
R3030A	55 gr.	Soft Point	36

20 in a box, 1,000 in a case.

30 Remington

No.	Bullet weight	Bullet style	Wt. case, lbs.
R30REM	170 gr.	Soft Point "Core-Lokt"	26

20 in a box, 500 in a case.

30-40 Krag

No.	Bullet weight	Bullet style	Wt. case, lbs.
R30402	180 gr.	Pointed Soft Point "Core-Lokt"	32

20 in a box, 500 in a case.

30-06 Spfd.

No.	Bullet weight	Bullet style	Wt. case, lbs.
R30061	125 gr.	Pointed Soft Point	69
R30062	150 gr.	Pointed Soft Point "Core-Lokt"	69
R30063	150 gr.	Bronze Point	69
R3006B	165 gr.	Pointed Soft Point "Core-Lokt"	62
R30064	180 gr.	Soft Point "Core-Lokt"	69
R30065	180 gr.	Pointed Soft Point "Core-Lokt"	69
R30066	180 gr.	Bronze Point	69
R30067	220 gr.	Soft Point "Core-Lokt"	69

20 in a box, 1,000 in a case.

30-06 "Accelerator"

No.	Bullet weight	Bullet style	Wt. case, lbs.
R30069	55 gr.	Pointed Soft Point	52

20 in a box, 1,000 in a case.

300 Sav.

No.	Bullet weight	Bullet style	Wt. case, lbs.
R30SV3	180 gr.	Soft Point "Core-Lokt"	58
R30SV2	150 gr.	Pointed Soft Point "Core-Lokt"	58

20 in a box, 1,000 in a case.

300 H & H Mag.

No.	Bullet weight	Bullet style	Wt. case, lbs.
R300HH	180 gr.	Pointed Soft Point "Core-Lokt"	39

300 Win. Mag.

No.	Bullet weight	Bullet style	Wt. case, lbs.
R300W1	150 gr.	Pointed Soft Point "Core-Lokt"	39
R300W2	180 gr.	Pointed Soft Point "Core-Lokt"	39

303 British

No.	Bullet weight	Bullet style	Wt. case, lbs.
R303B1	180 gr.	Soft Point "Core-Lokt"	67

20 in a box, 500 in a case.

308 Win.

No.	Bullet weight	Bullet style	Wt. case, lbs.
R308W1	150 gr.	Pointed Soft Point "Core-Lokt"	60
R308W6	165 gr.	Pointed Soft Point "Core-Lokt"	60
R308W2	180 gr.	Soft Point "Core-Lokt"	60
R308W3	180 gr.	Pointed Soft Point "Core-Lokt"	60

.308 Win. "Accelertor'

No.	Bullet weight	Bullet style	Wt. case, lbs.
R308W5	55 gr.	Pointed Soft Point	52

8mm (7.9mm) Mauser

No.	Bullet weight	Bullet style	Wt. case, lbs.
R8MSR	170 gr.	Soft Point "Core-Lokt"	32

8mm Remington Magnum

No.	Bullet weight	Bullet style	Wt. case, lbs.
R8MM1	185 gr.	Pointed Soft Point "Core-Lokt"	40
R8MM2	220 gr.	Pointed Soft Point "Core-Lokt"	42

REMINGTON CENTERFIRE RIFLE CARTRIDGES

32 Win. Special

No.	Bullet weight	Bullet style	Wt. case, lbs.
R32WS2	170 gr.	Soft Point "Core-Lokt"	54

20 in a box, 1,000 in a case.

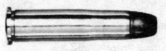

32-20 Win.

No.	Bullet weight	Bullet style	Wt. case, lbs.
R32201	100 gr.	Lead	14
R32202	100 gr.	Soft Point	14

50 in a box, 500 in a case.

338 Win. Mag.

No.	Bullet weight	Bullet style	Wt. case, lbs.
R338W1†	225 gr.	Pointed Soft Point	42
R338W2†	250 gr.	Pointed Soft Point	45

20 in a box, 500 in a case.

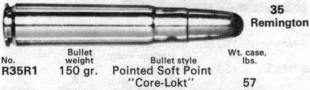

35 Remington

No.	Bullet weight	Bullet style	Wt. case, lbs.
R35R1	150 gr.	Pointed Soft Point "Core-Lokt"	57
R35R2	200 gr.	Soft Point "Core-Lokt"	57

20 in a box, 1,000 in a case.

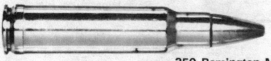

350 Remington Magnum

No.	Bullet weight	Bullet style	Wt. case, lbs.
R350M1	200 gr.	Pointed Soft Point "Core-Lokt"	40

20 in a box, 500 in a case.

375 H & H Magnum

No.	Bullet weight	Bullet style	Wt. case, lbs.
R375M1	270 gr.	Soft Point	48
R375M2	300 gr.	Metal Case	48

20 in a box, 500 in a case.

458 Win. Magnum

No.	Bullet weight	Bullet style	Wt. case, lbs.
R458W1	500 gr.	Metal Case	61
R458W2	510 gr.	Soft Point	61

20 in a box, 500 in a case.

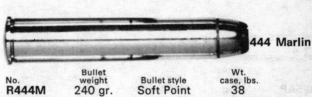

444 Marlin

No.	Bullet weight	Bullet style	Wt. case, lbs.
R444M	240 gr.	Soft Point	38
R444M2	265 gr.	Soft Point	40

20 in a box, 500 in a case.

44-40 Win.

No.	Bullet weight	Bullet style	Wt. case, lbs.
R4440W	200 gr.	Soft Point	23

50 in a box, 500 in a case.

44 Remington Magnum

No.	Bullet weight	Bullet style	Wt. case, lbs.
R44MG2	240 gr.	Soft Point	29

45-70 Government

No.	Bullet weight	Bullet style	Wt. case, lbs.
R4570G	405 gr.	Soft Point	47
R4570L†	300 gr.	Jacketed Hollow Point	45

20 in a box, 500 in a case.

REMINGTON CENTERFIRE PISTOL AND REVOLVER CARTRIDGES

22 Remington "Jet" Magnum

No.	Bullet weight	Bullet style	Wt. case, lbs.
R22JET	40 gr.	Soft Point	12

50 in a box, 500 in a case.

221 Remington "Fire Ball"

No.	Bullet weight	Bullet style	Wt. case, lbs.
R221F	50 gr.	PTd. Soft Point	12

20 in a box, 500 in a case.

25 (6.35mm) Auto. Pistol

No.	Bullet weight	Bullet style	Wt. case, lbs.
R25AP	50 gr.	Metal Case	28

50 in a box, 2,000 in a case.

32 Short Colt

No.	Bullet weight	Bullet style	Wt. case, lbs.
R32SC	80 gr.	Lead	10

50 in a box, 500 in a case.

32 Long Colt

No.	Bullet weight	Bullet style	Wt. case, lbs.
R32LC	82 gr.	Lead	10

50 in a box, 500 in a case.

32 (7.65mm) Auto. Pistol

No.	Bullet weight	Bullet style	Wt. case, lbs.
R32AP	71 gr.	Metal Case	36

50 in a box, 2,000 in a case.

32 S & W

No.	Bullet weight	Bullet style	Wt. case, lbs.
R32SW	88 gr.	Lead	41

50 in a box, 2,000 in a case.

32 S & W Long

No.	Bullet weight	Bullet style	Wt. case, lbs.
R32SWL	98 gr.	Lead	46

50 in a box, 2,000 in a case.

357 Magnum

No.	Bullet weight	Bullet style	Wt. case, lbs.
R357M7	110 gr.	Semi-Jacketed Hollow Point	63
R357M1	125 gr.	Semi-Jacketed Hollow Point	65
R357M8	125 gr.	Semi-Jacketed Soft Point	65
R357M9†	140 gr.	Semi-Jacketed Hollow Point	70
R357M2	158 gr.	Semi-Jacketed Hollow Point	75
R357M3	158 gr.	Soft Point	75
R357M4	158 gr.	Metal Point	77
R357M5	158 gr.	Lead	75
R357M6	158 gr.	Lead (Brass Case)	77

50 in a box, 2,000 in a case.

357 Remington Maximum

No.	Bullet weight	Bullet style	Wt. case, lbs.
357MX1	158 gr.	Semi-Jacketed Hollow Point	29
357MX3	180 gr.	Semi-Jacketed Hollow Point	29

20 in a box, 500 in a case.

9mm Luger Auto. Pistol

No.	Bullet weight	Bullet style	Wt. case, lbs.
R9MM1	115 gr.	Jacketed Hollow Point	54
R9MM2	124 gr.	Metal Case	56

50 in a box, 2,000 in a case.

38 S & W

No.	Bullet weight	Bullet style	Wt. case, lbs.
R38SW	146 gr.	Lead	63

50 in a box, 2,000 in a case.

(+P) Ammunition with (+P) on the case headstamp is loaded to higher pressure. Use only in firearms designated for this cartridge and so recommended by the gun manufacturer.

REMINGTON CENTERFIRE PISTOL AND REVOLVER CARTRIDGES

38 Special

No.	Bullet weight	Bullet style	Wt. case, lbs.
R38S1	95 gr.	Semi-Jacketed Hollow Point (+P)	52
R38S10	110 gr.	Semi-Jacketed Hollow Point (+P)	52
R38S2	125 gr.	Semi-Jacketed Hollow Point (+P)	65
R38S13	125 gr.	Semi-Jacketed Soft Point (+P)	65
R38S3	148 gr.	Targetmaster Lead Wadcutter, brass case	66
R38S4	158 gr.	Targetmaster Lead Round Nose	70
R38S5	158 gr.	Lead	70
R38S6	158 gr.	Lead Semi-Wadcutter	70
*R38S14	158 gr.	Lead Semi-Wadcutter (+P)	70
R38S7	158 gr.	Metal Point	70
R38S8	158 gr.	Lead (+P)	70
R38S12	158 gr.	Jacketed Hollow Point (+P)	69
R38S9	200 gr.	Lead	82

38 Short Colt

No.	Bullet weight	Bullet style	Wt. case, lbs.
R38SC	125 gr.	Lead	14

50 in a box, 500 in a case.

38 Super Auto. Colt Pistol

Adapted only for 38 Colt Super and Colt Commander Automatic Pistols.

No.	Bullet weight	Bullet style	Wt. case, lbs.
R38SUI	115 gr.	Jacketed Hollow Point (+P)	56
R38SUP	130 gr.	Metal Case (+P)	62

50 in a box, 2,000 in a case.

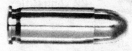

38 Auto. Colt Pistol

Adapted only for 38 Colt Sporting, Military and Pocket Model Automatic Pistols.

No.	Bullet weight	Bullet style	Wt. case, lbs.
R38ACP	130 gr.	Metal Case	62

50 in a box, 2,000 in a case.

380 Auto. Pistol

No.	Bullet weight	Bullet style	Wt. case, lbs.
R380A1	88 gr.	Jacketed Hollow Point	45
R380AP	95 gr.	Metal Case	45

50 in a box, 2,000 in a case.

41 Magnum

No.	Bullet weight	Bullet style	Wt. case, lbs.
R41MG1	210 gr.	Soft Point	52
R41MG2	210 gr.	Lead	49

50 in a box, 1,000 in a case.

44 S&W Special

No.	Bullet weight	Bullet style	Wt. case, lbs.
R44SW	246 gr.	Lead	25
R44SW1	200 gr.	Lead Semi-Wadcutter	22

50 in a box, 500 in a case.

44 Remington Magnum

No.	Bullet weight	Bullet style	Wt. case, lbs.
R44MG1	240 gr.	Lead, Gas-Check	57
R44MG4	240 gr.	Lead	57

50 in a box, 1,000 in a case.

R44MG2	240 gr.	Soft Point	29
R44MG3	240 gr.	Semi-Jacketed Hollow Point	29
R44MG5	180 gr.	Semi-Jacketed Hollow Point	29

20 in a box, 500 in a case.

45 Colt

No.	Bullet weight	Bullet style	Wt. case, lbs.
R45C	250 gr.	Lead	26
R45C1†	225 gr.	Lead Semi-Wadcutter	24

50 in a box, 500 in a case.

REMINGTON CENTERFIRE PISTOL AND REVOLVER CARTRIDGES

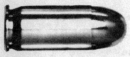

45 Auto.

No.	Bullet weight	Bullet style	Wt. case, lbs.
R45AP1	185 gr.	Targetmaster Metal Case Wadcutter	43
R45AP2	185 gr.	Jacketed Hollow Point	43
R45AP4	230 gr.	Metal Case	49

50 in a box, 1,000 in a case.

45 Auto. Rim

No.	Bullet weight	Bullet style	Wt. case, lbs.
R45AR	230 gr.	Lead	27

50 in a box, 500 in a case.

REMINGTON CENTER FIRE BLANK

.45 Auto Shot Cartridge

No.	Caliber	No. in case	Wt. case, lbs.
R32BLNK	32 S & W	5,000	37
R38SWBL	38 S & W	2,000	25
R38BLNK	38 Special	2,000	28

50 in a box.

No.	Bullet style	Wt. case, lbs.
R45AP5	650 Pellets—No. 12 Shot	18

REMINGTON RIMFIRE CARTRIDGES

"HIGH VELOCITY" CARTRIDGES with "Golden" Bullets

22 Short

No.	Bullet weight and style	Wt. case, lbs.
1022	29 gr., Lead	29
1122	27 gr., Lead, Hollow Point	28

50 in a box, 5,000 in a case.

22 Long

No.	Bullet weight and style	Wt. case, lbs.
1322	29 gr., Lead	31

50 in a box, 5,000 in a case.

22 Long Rifle

No.	Bullet weight and style	Wt. case, lbs.
1522	40 gr., Lead	40
1622	36 gr., Lead, Hollow Point	38

50 in a box, 5,000 in a case.

"TARGET" STANDARD VELOCITY CARTRIDGES

22 Short

No.	Bullet weight and style	Wt. case, lbs.
5522	29 gr., Lead	29

50 in a box, 5,000 in a case.

22 Long Rifle

No.	Bullet weight and style	Wt. case, lbs.
6122	40 gr., Lead	40

50 in a box, 5,000 in a case.

.22 Long Rifle, Target 100 pack.

No.	Bullet weight and style	Wt. case, lbs.
6100	40 gr., Lead	40

100 in a box, 5,000 in a case.

"YELLOW JACKET" CARTRIDGES Hyper-Velocity

22 Long Rifle

No.	Bullet weight and style	Wt. case, lbs.
1722	33 gr. Truncated Cone, Hollow Point	36

50 in a box, 5,000 in a case.

"VIPER" CARTRIDGES Hyper-Velocity

22 Long Rifle

No.	Bullet weight and style	Wt. case, lbs.
1922	36 gr. Truncated Cone, Solid Point, Copper Plated	38

50 in a box, 5,000 in a case.

REMINGTON SHOTGUN SHELLS

REMINGTON "EXPRESS" BUCKSHOT LOADS AND "SLUGGER" RIFLED SLUGS

	No.	Gauge	Length shell, in.	Powder equiv. drams	Shot, oz.	Size shot	Wt. case, lbs.
	SP12BK	12	2¾	3¾	. . .	000 Buck— 8 Pellets	31
	SP12BK	12	2¾	3¾	. . .	00 Buck— 9 Pellets	29
"Power Pakt"	SP12BK	12	2¾	3¾	. . .	0 Buck—12 Pellets	32
"EXPRESS"	SP12BK	12	2¾	3¾	. . .	1 Buck—16 Pellets	32
BUCKSHOT LOADS	SP12BK	12	2¾	3¾	. . .	4 Buck—27 Pellets	31
	SP16BK	16	2¾	3	. . .	1 Buck—12 Pellets	26
	SP20BK	20	2¾	2¾	. . .	3 Buck—20 Pelelts	24
"Power Pkt"	SP12SMagBK	12	2¾	4	. . .	00 Buck—12 Pellets	34
"EXPRESS"	SP12SMagBK	12	2¾	4	. . .	1 Buck—20 Pellets	34
MAGNUM	SP12HMagBK	12	3	4	. . .	000 Buck—10 Pellets	40
BUCKSHOT LOADS	SP12HMagBK	12	3	4	. . .	00 Buck—15 Pellets	40
	SP12HMagBK	12	3	4	. . .	1 Buck—24 Pellets	40
	SP12HMagBK	12	3	4	. . .	4 Buck—41 Pellets	42
"SLUGGER"	SP12RS	12	2¾	3¾	1	Rifled Slug H.P.	26
RIFLED SLUG	SP16RS	16	2¾	3	⅘	Rifled Slug H.P.	24
LOADS	SP20RS	20	2¾	2¾	⅝	Rifled Slug H.P.	19
	SP41RS	410	2½	Max.	⅕	Rifled Slug	8

Packed 5 in a box, 250 per case.

REMINGTON STEEL SHOT WATERFOWL LOADS

	No.	Gauge	Length shell, in.	Powder equiv. drams	Shot, oz.	Size shot	Wt. case, lbs.
STEEL SHOT	STL12	12	2¾	Max.	1⅛	BB, 1, 2, 4, 6	28
WATERFOWL	STL12Mag	12	3	Max.	1¼	BB, 1, 2, 4, 6	30
LOADS	STL12SMag†	12	2¾	Max.	1¼	1, 2, 4	30
	STL20HMag†	20	3	Max.	1	2, 4, 6	25
	SP12BK	12	2¾	3¾	. . .	000 Buck— 8 Pellets	31
	SP12BK	12	2¾	3¾	. . .	00 Buck— 9 Pellets	29
"Power Pakt"	SP12BK	12	2¾	3¾	. . .	0 Buck—12 Pellets	32
"EXPRESS"	SP12BK	12	2¾	3¾	. . .	1 Buck—16 Pellets	32
BUCKSHOT LOADS	SP12BK	12	2¾	3¾	. . .	4 Buck—27 Pellets	31
	SP16BK	16	2¾	3	. . .	1 Buck—12 Pellets	26
	SP20BK	20	2¾	2¾	. . .	3 Buck—20 Pelelts	24
"Power Pkt"	SP12SMagBK	12	2¾	4	. . .	00 Buck—12 Pellets	34
"EXPRESS"	SP12SMagBK	12	2¾	4	. . .	1 Buck—20 Pellets	34
MAGNUM	SP12HMagBK	12	3	4	. . .	000 Buck—10 Pellets	40
BUCKSHOT LOADS	SP12HMagBK	12	3	4	. . .	00 Buck—15 Pellets	40
	SP12HMagBK	12	3	4	. . .	1 Buck—24 Pellets	40
	SP12HMagBK	12	3	4	. . .	4 Buck—41 Pellets	42
"SLUGGER" MAGNUM	SP12SMagRS†	12	2¾	Max.	1	Rifled Slug	26
RIFLED SLUG LOADS	SP12MagRS†	12	3	Max.	1	Rifled Slug	26
"SLUGGER"	SP12RS	12	2¾	Max.	1	Rifled Slug H.P.	26
RIFLED SLUG	SP16RS	16	2¾	3	⅘	Rifled Slug H.P.	24
LOADS	SP20RS	20	2¾	2¾	⅝	Rifled Slug H.P.	19
	SP410RS	410	2½	Max.	⅕	Rifled Slug	8

Packed 5 in a box, 250 per case.

REMINGTON SHOTGUN SHELLS

REMINGTON "PREMIER" HIGHEST GRADE SHOTSHELLS WITH "COPPER-LOKT"
EXTRA HARD PLATED SHOT AND "POWER-PISTON" WADS

	No.	Gauge	Length shell, in.	Powder equiv. drams	Shot, oz.	Size shot		Wt. case, lbs.
PREMIER™	PR12S Mag.	12	2¾	Max.	1½	BB, 2, 4, 6		34
EXTENDED RANGE	PR12 Mag.	12	3	4	1⅝	4, 6		37
BUFFERED	PR12H Mag.	12	3	Max.	1⅞	BB, 2, 4		41
MAGNUM LOADS	PR20S Mag.	20	2¾	Max.	1⅛	4, 6		26
	PR20H Mag.	20	3	Max.	1¼	2, 4, 6		30
PREMIER™								
EXTRA LONG	PR12	12	2¾	3¾	1¼	2, 4, 6, 7½		29
RANGE LOADS	PR20	20	2¾	2¾	1	4, 6		24
PREMIER™								
"POWER-	PR12F	12	2¾	3¼	1⅛	7½, 8		29
PATTERN"	PR12HF	12	2¾	3¼	1¼	7½, 8		29
FIELD LOADS	PR20F	20	2¾	2½	1	7½, 8		23

25 in a box, 250 in a case.

REMINGTON "NITRO MAGNUM," "EXPRESS" AND "SHUR SHOT" SHOTSHELLS

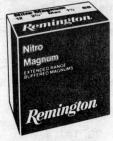  

	No.	Gauge	Length shell, in.	Powder equiv. drams	Shot, oz.	Size shot		Wt. case, lbs.
NITRO MAGNUM™	SP12SNM●	12	2¾	Max.	1½	BB, 2, 4, 5, 6		34
EXTENDED RANGE	SP12NM●	12	3	4	1⅝	2, 4, 6		35
BUFFERED	SP12HNM●	12	3	Max.	1⅞	BB, 2, 4		35
MAGNUMS	SP20SNM●	20	2¾	Max.	1⅛	4, 6, 7½		26
NEW FOR 1983	SP20HNM●	20	3	Max.	1¼	2, 4, 6, 7½		30
"EXPRESS"	SP10 Mag.	10	3½	Max.	2	BB, 2, 4		45
MAGNUM LOADS	SP16C Mag.	16	2¾	Max.	1¼	2, 4, 6		29
	SP12	12	2¾	3¾	1¼	BB, 2, 4, 5, 6, 7½, 9		58
"EXPRESS"	SP16	16	2¾	3¼	1⅛	4, 5, 6, 7½, 9		52
LONG RANGE	SP20	20	2¾	2¾	1	4, 5, 6, 7½, 9		47
LOADS	SP28	28	2¾	2¼	¾	6, 7½		36
	SP410	410	2½	Max.	½	4, 6, 7½		23
	SP4103	410	3	Max.	11⁄16	4, 5, 6, 7½, 9		31
	R12H	12	2¾	3¼	1⅛	4, 5, 6, 9		51
	R12H250CS●	12	2¾	3¼	1⅛	7½, 8		29
"SHUR SHOT"	RP12H250CS●	12	2¾	3¼	1¼	7½, 8		30
FIELD	R16H	16	2¾	2¾	1⅛	4, 6, 7½, 8, 9		51
LOADS	R20M	20	2¾	2½	1	4, 5, 6, 9		45
	R20M250CS●	20	2¾	2½	1	7½, 8		23

● Packed 250 per case.
25 in a box, 500 in a case.

REMINGTON SHOTGUN SHELLS

REMINGTON "PREMIER" TRAP & SKEET LOADS

	No.	Gauge	Length shell, in.	Power equiv. drams	Shot, oz.	Size shot	Wt. case, lbs.	Per box
REMINGTON TRAP & SKEET LOADS	RTL12L•†	12	2¾	2¾	1⅛	7½, 8, 8½, 9	27	
	RTL12M•†	12	2¾	3	1⅛	7½, 8, 8½, 9	27	
	RTL20†	20	2¾	2¼	⅞	9	41	
	SP28	28	2¾	2	¾	9	37	
	SP410	410	2½	Max.	½	9	22	
INTERNATIONAL TARGET LOADS	SP12H	12	2¾	3¼	1⅛	7½, 8	54	
	NSP12H	12	2¾	3¼	1⅛	7½, 8 (nickel)	54	

• Packed 25 in a box, 250 per case.

25 in a box, 500 in a case.

SHOTGUN SHELLS
REMINGTON "SPECIAL PURPOSE" MULTIRANGE "DUPLEX" SHOTSHELLS

REMINGTON "DUPLEX" SHOTGUN SHELL

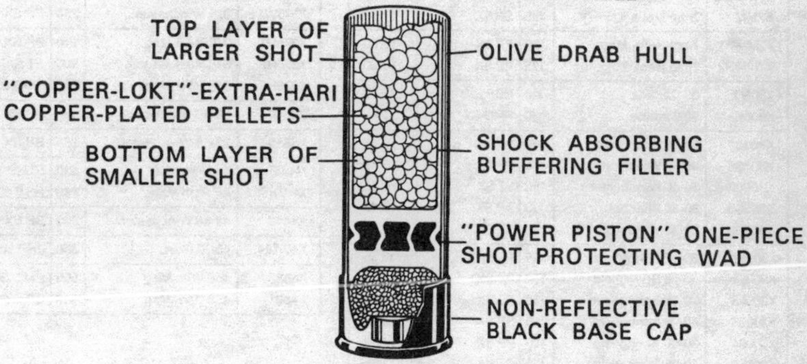

TOP LAYER OF LARGER SHOT — OLIVE DRAB HULL

"COPPER-LOKT"-EXTRA-HARD COPPER-PLATED PELLETS

BOTTOM LAYER OF SMALLER SHOT

SHOCK ABSORBING BUFFERING FILLER

"POWER PISTON" ONE-PIECE SHOT PROTECTING WAD

NON-REFLECTIVE BLACK BASE CAP

Combined large and smaller shot sizes. Available in lead or steel shot magnum loads.

Olive drab hull, non-reflective black base cap. Power-Piston wads. Shock absorbing buffering filler.

	No.	Gauge	Length shell, in.	Powder equiv. drams	Shot, oz.	Size shot	Wt. case, lbs.	Per box
MULTIRANGE DUPLEX MAGNUM COPPER PLATED LEAD SHOT†	MRP12S	12	2¾	Max.	1½	BBx4, 2x6	35	
	MRP12H	12	3	Max.	1⅞	BBx4, 2x6	41	
MULTIRANGE DUPLEX MAGNUM STEEL SHOT†	MRS12	12	2¾	Max.	1⅛	BBx2, BBx4, 2x6	29	
	MRS12H	12	3	Max.	1¼	BBx2, BBx4, 2x6	29	

10 in a box, 250 in a case.

WINCHESTER AMMUNITION

SPORTING AMMUNITION

CENTERFIRE RIFLE
(Packed 20 per box unless indicated)

Symbol No.	Cartridge	Wt. Grs.	Type of Bullet	Sug. Retail Per Box
• X218B	218 Bee	46	HP SX	$35.30
• X22H1	22 Hornet	45	SP SX	21.10
• X22H2	22 Hornet	46	HP SX	21.10
X222501	22-250 Remington	55	PSP SX	10.20
X222R	222 Remington	50	PSP SX	9.00
X222R1	222 Remington	55	FMC SX	9.00
X223RH	223 Remington	53	HP SX	10.55
X223R	223 Remington	55	PSP SX	9.85
X223R1	223 Remington	55	FMC SX	9.85
X2251	225 Winchester	55	PSP SX	12.15
X2431	243 Winchester	80	PSP SX	12.30
X2432	243 Winchester	100	PP SX	12.30
X6MMR1	6mm Remington	80	PSP SX	12.30
X6MMR2	6mm Remington	100	PP SX	12.30
X25061	25-06 Remington	90	PEP SX	15.55
X25062	25-06 Remington	120	PEP SX	15.55
• X25202	25-20 Winchester	86	SP SX	23.95
X2535	25-35 Winchester	117	SP SX	15.50
X2503	250 Savage	100	ST SX	12.45
X257P2	257 Roberts +P	100	ST SX+P	13.75
X257P3	257 Roberts +P	117	PP SX+P	13.75
X2642	264 Win. Mag.	140	PP SX	18.10
X2701	270 Winchester	100	PSP SX	13.35
X2705	270 Winchester	130	PP SX	13.35
X2703	270 Winchester	130	ST SX	13.35
X2704	270 Winchester	150	PP SX	13.35
X2841	284 Winchester	125	PP SX	17.50
X2842	284 Winchester	150	PP SX	17.50
X7MM1 New	7mm Maus. (7×57)	145	PP SX	13.60
X7MM	7mm Maus. (7×57)	175	SP SX	13.60
X7MMR1	7mm Rem. Mag.	150	PP SX	16.50
X7MMR2	7mm Rem. Mag.	175	PP SX	16.50
• X30M1	30 Carbine	110	HSP SX	21.40
• X30M2	30 Carbine	110	FMC SX	21.40
X30301	30-30 Winchester	150	HP SX	10.45
X30306	30-30 Winchester	150	PP SX	10.45
X30302	30-30 Winchester	150	ST SX	10.45
X30303	30-30 Winchester	170	PP SX	10.45
X30304	30-30 Winchester	170	ST SX	10.45
X30062	30-06 Springfield	125	PSP SX	13.35
X30061	30-06 Springfield	150	PP SX	13.35
X30063	30-06 Springfield	150	ST SX	13.35
X30065	30-06 Springfield	165	SP SX	13.35
X30064	30-06 Springfield	180	PP SX	13.35
X30066	30-06 Springfield	180	ST SX	13.35
X30067 New	30-06 Springfield	180	STBT SX	18.05
X30069	30-06 Springfield	220	PP SX	13.35
X30401	30-40 Krag	180	PP SX	14.05

CENTERFIRE RIFLE
(Continued)

Symbol No.	Cartridge	Wt. Grs.	Type of Bullet	Sug. Retail Per Box
X30WM1	300 Win. Mag.	150	PP SX	$17.50
X30WM2	300 Win. Mag.	180	PP SX	17.50
X30WM3	300 Win. Mag.	220	ST SX	17.50
X300H2	300 H&H.	180	ST SX	17.50
X3001	300 Savage	150	PP SX	13.50
X3003	300 Savage	150	ST SX	13.50
X3004	300 Savage	180	PP SX	13.50
X3032	303 Savage	190	ST SX	17.05
X303B1	303 British	180	PP SX	13.75
X3075	307 Winchester	150	PP SX	14.85
X3076	307 Winchester	180	PP SX	13.50
X3085	308 Winchester	150	PP SX	13.35
X3082	308 Winchester	150	ST SX	13.35
X3086	308 Winchester	180	PP SX	13.35
X3083	308 Winchester	180	ST SX	13.35
X32WS2	32 Win. Special	170	PP SX	11.15
X32WS3	32 Win. Special	170	ST SX	11.15
• X32201	32-20 Winchester	100	L SX	17.05
X8MM	8mm Mauser (8×57)	170	PP SX	13.75
X3381	338 Win. Mag.	200	PP SX	20.95
X35R1	35 Remington	200	PP SX	12.30
X35R3	35 Remington	200	ST SX	12.30
• X351SL2	351 Win. Self-load	180	SP SX	38.70
X3561	356 Winchester	200	PP SX	20.95
X3563	356 Winchester	250	PP SX	20.95
• X3574P	357 Mag.	158	JHP SX	19.55
• X3575P	357 Mag.	158	JSP SX	19.55
X3581	358 Winchester	200	ST SX	20.95
X375W	375 Winchester	200	PP SX	18.05
X375W1	375 Winchester	250	PP SX	18.05
X375H1	375 H&H Mag.	270	PP SX	21.80
X375H2	375 H&H Mag.	300	ST SX	21.80
X375H3	375 H&H Mag.	300	FMC SX	21.80
• X3840	38-40 Winchester	180	SP SX	28.85
X3855	38-55 Winchester	255	SP SX	16.75
X44MSTHP2	44 Rem. Mag.	210	STHP SX	11.45
X44MHSP2	44 Rem. Mag.	240	HSP SX	10.40
• X4440	44-40 Winchester	200	SP SX	26.90
X4570H	45-70 Govt.	300	JHP SX	15.95
X4580	458 Win. Mag.	500	FMC SX	42.45
X4581	458 Win. Mag.	510	SP SX	28.00

CENTERFIRE PISTOL & REVOLVER
(Packed 50 per box unless indicated)

Symbol No.	Cartridge	Wt. Grs.	Type of Bullet	Sug. Retail Per Box
X25AXP	25 Auto. (6.35mm)	45	EP SX**	14.10
X25AP	25 Auto. (6.35mm)	50	FMC SX	13.00
X30LP	30 Luger (7.65mm)	93	FMC SX	23.70
X30M1	30 Carbine	110	HSP SX	21.40
X30M2	30 Carbine	110	FMC SX	21.40
X32SWP	32 S & W	85	LRN SX	12.55
X32SWLP	32 S & W Long (Colt New Police)	98	LRN SX	13.25
X32SCP	32 Short Colt	80	LRN SX	12.50
X32LCP	32 Long Colt	82	LRN SX	13.10
X32ASHP	32 Automatic	60	STHP SX	16.45
X32AP	32 Automatic	71	FMC SX	14.90
X38SWP	38 S & W	145	LRN SX	14.00
X380ASHP	380 Automatic	85	STHP SX	16.80
X380AP	380 Automatic	95	FMC SX	15.25
X38S9HP	38 Special	110	STHP SX	19.35
X38S1P	38 Special	158	LRN SX	14.05
X38WCPSV	38 Special	158	LSWC SX	14.65
X38S2P	38 Special	158	MP SX	17.85
X38SSHP	38 Special +P	95	STHP SX+P	19.60
X38S6PH	38 Special +P	110	JHP SX+P	17.80
X38S7PH	38 Special +P	125	JHP SX+P	17.80
X38S8HP	38 Special +P	125	STHP SX+P	19.60
X38SPD	38 Special +P	158	LHP SX+P	15.25
X38WCP	38 Special +P	158	SWC SX+P	15.60
X38SMRP	38 Special Match	148	LMR(CC)M	14.65
X9LP	9mm Luger (Par)	115	FMC SX	18.50
X9MMSHP	9mm Luger (Par)	115	STHP SX	20.40
X38ASHP	38 Super Auto. +P*	125	STHP SX+P	18.75
X38A1P	38 Super Auto. +P*	130	FMC SX+P	16.15
X38A2P	38 Automatic++	130	FMC SX	16.65
X3573P	357 Magnum	110	JHP SX	19.55
X3576P	357 Magnum	125	JHP SX	19.55
X357SHP	357 Magnum	145	STHP SX	21.50
X3571P	357 Magnum**	158	L SWC SX	16.55
X3574P	357 Magnum	158	JHP SX	19.55
X3575P	357 Magnum	158	JSP SX	19.55
X41MSTHP	41 Remington Mag.	175	STHP SX	28.35
X41MP	41 Remington Mag.	210	L SWC SX	22.00
X41MJSP	41 Remington Mag.	210	JSP SX	25.75
□X41MHP2	41 Remington Mag.	210	JHP SX	10.45
□X44STHPS2	44 S & W Special	200	STHP SX	8.80
X44SP	44 S & W Special	246	L RN SX	19.70

+P = Ammunition with a (+P) on the case head stamp is loaded to higher pressure. Use only in firearms designated for this cartridge and so recommended by the gun manufacturer.

• Packed 50 Per Box

□ Packed 20 Per Box

* For use only in 38 Super Automatic Pistols.

** Lubaloy Coated

++ For all 38 Colt Automatic Pistols

CC—Clean Cutting	JSP—Jacketed Soft Point	M—Match
EP—Expanding Point	L—Lead	MP—Metal Point
FMC—Full Metal Case	LHP—Lead Hollow Point	MV—Medium Velocity
GC—Gas Check	LMR—Lead Mid-Range	OPE—Open Point Expanding
HP—Hollow Point	LRN—Lead Round Nose	Par—Parabellum
HSP—Hollow Soft Point	Mag.—Magnum	PEP—Positive Expanding Point
JHP—Jacketed Hollow Point	LSWC—Lead Semi-Wad Cutter	PP—Power-Point

PSP—Pointed Soft Point
Rem.—Remington
SL—Self-Loading
SP—Soft Point

STBT—Silvertip Boattail
STHP—Silvertip Hollow Point
SWC—Semi-Wad Cutter
SX—Super-X
Win.—Winchester

WINCHESTER AMMUNITION

CENTERFIRE PISTOL & REVOLVER (Continued)

Symbol No.	Cartridge	Wt. Grs.	Type of Bullet	Sug. Retail Per Box
□X44MSTHP2	44 Rem. Mag.	210	STHP SX	$11.45
X44MWCP	44 Rem. Mag.	240	LSWC (MV) SX	21.35
X44MP	44 Rem. Mag.	240	LSWC (GC) SX	25.30
□X44MHSP2	44 Rem. Mag.	240	HSP SX	10.40
□X45ASHP2	45 Automatic	185	STHP SX	9.10
□X45A1P2	45 Automatic	230	FMC SX	8.25
X45AWCP	45 Automatic SM	185	FMC SX	21.45
□X45CSHP2	45 Colt	225	STHP SX	8.95
□X45CP2	45 Colt	255	LRN SX	8.15
X45WM	45 Win. Mag. (Not for arms chambered for standard 45 Automatic)	230	FMC SX	24.75

CENTERFIRE BLANK CARTRIDGES

32BL2P	32 Smith & Wesson Black Powder	12.45
38BLP	38 Smith & Wesson Smokeless Powder	15.05
38SBLP	38 Special Smokeless Powder	15.10

□ Packed 20 Per Box

SHOTSHELLS—SUPER-X GAME LOADS

(Packed 25 Per Box unless indicated)

Symbol No.	Gauge	Length of Shell Inches	Pwdr. Dram Equiv.	Oz. Shot	Shot Sizes	Sug. Retail Per Box
X12	12	2¾	3¾	1¼	2,4,5,6,7½,9	9.90
X16H	16	2¾	3¼	1⅛	4,6,7½	9.50
X20	20	2¾	2¾	1	4,5,6,7½,9	8.70
X28	28	2¾	2¼	¾	6,7½	8.75
X41	410	2½	Max.	½	4,6,7½	6.90
X413	410	3	Max.	11/16	4,6,7½	8.14

DOUBLE X MAGNUM—GAME LOADS COPPERPLATED, BUFFERED SHOT

X103XC	10	3½ Mag.	4½	2¼	BB,2,4	24.90
X123XC	12	3 Mag.	4	1⅞	BB,2,4,6	14.60
◊ X123XCT **New**	12	3	4	1⅞	4, 6	6.15
X12MXC	12	3 Mag.	4	1⅝	2,4,5,6	13.50
X12XC	12	2¾ Mag.	Max.	1½	BB,2,4,5,6	12.20
◊ X12XCT **New**	12	2¾	3¾	1½	4, 6	5.10
X16XC	16	2¾	3¼	1¼	2,4,6	12.00
X203XC	20	3 Mag.	3	1¼	2,4,6	11.30
X20XC	20	2¾ Mag.	2¾	1⅛	4,6,7½	10.00

XPERT FIELD LOADS

WW12SP	12	2¾	3¼	1¼	6,7½,8	8.35
UWH12	12	2¾	3¼	1⅛	6,7½,8,9	7.60
UWL12	12	2¾	3¼	1	6,7½,8	7.25
UWH16	16	2¾	2¾	1⅛	6,7½,8	7.60
UWH20	20	2¾	2½	1	6,7½,8,9	7.15
UWL20	20	2¾	2½	⅞	6,7½,8	6.80

SUPER-X BUCKSHOT LOADS WITH BUFFERED SHOT-5 ROUND PACK

△ X12RB	12	2¾	—	—	9 Pellets—00 Buck	14.00
X12000B5	12	2¾	—	—	8 Pellets—000 Buck	2.80
X12RB5	12	2¾	—	—	9 Pellets—00 Buck	2.80
X120B5	12	2¾	—	—	12 Pellets—0 Buck	2.80
X121B5	12	2¾	—	—	16 Pellets—1 Buck	2.80
X124B5	12	2¾	—	—	27 Pellets—4 Buck	2.80
X16B5	16	2¾	—	—	12 Pellets—1 Buck	2.80
X20B5	20	2¾	—	—	20 Pellets—3 Buck	2.80

DOUBLE-X MAGNUM BUCKSHOT LOADS COPPERPLATED, BUFFERED SHOT-5 ROUND PACK

X10C4B	10	3½	—	—	54 Pellets—4 Buck	5.70
X123C000B	12	3	—	—	10 Pellets—000 Buck	4.00
X12XC3B5	12	3	—	—	15 Pellets—00 Buck	4.00
X12XC0B5	12	2¾	—	—	12 Pellets—00 Buck	3.55
X12C1B	12	2¾	—	—	20 Pellets—1 Buck	3.55
X12XCMB5	12	3	—	—	41 Pellets—4 Buck	4.00
X12XC4B5	12	2¾	—	—	34 Pellets—4 Buck	3.55

SUPER-X HOLLOW POINT RIFLED SLUG LOADS—5 ROUND PACK

X12RS15	12	2¾	Max.	1	Rifled Slug	3.25
X16RS5	16	2¾	Max.	⅘	Rifled Slug	3.25
X20RSM5	20	2¾	Max.	¾	Rifled Slug	3.00
X41RS5	410	2½	Max.	⅕	Rifled Slug	2.85

SUPER STEEL NON-TOXIC GAME LOADS

W12SD **New**	12	2¾	Max	1	2, 4	10.90
X12SSL	12	2¾	Max	1⅛	1, 2, 3, 4, 6	12.40
X20SSL	20	2¾	Max	¾	4, 6,	11.20

SUPER STEEL NON-TOXIC MAGNUM LOADS

X10SSM	10	3½	Max.	1¾	BB,2	21.05
*X12SSM **New**	12	3	Max.	1⅜	BB,1,2,3,4	—
X123SSM	12	3	Max.	1¼	BB,1,2,3,4	13.50
X12SSF	12	2¾	Max.	1¼	BB,1,2,3,4,6	13.50
X20SSM	20	3	Max.	1	2,3,4,6	11.85

SUPER-X HIGH VELOCITY—RIMFIRE CARTRIDGES

Symbol No.	Cartridge	Bullet or Shot Wt. Grs.	Type of Bullet	Cart. Per Box	Sug. Retail Per Box
X22S	22 Short, SX	29	Lead-RN**	50	1.80
X22SC	22 Short, SX Blister Card	29	Lead-RN**	50	1.94
X22LR	22 L.R., SX	40	Lead-RN**	50	1.72
X22LRC	22 L.R., SX Blister Card	40	Lead-RN**	50	1.84
X22LR1	22 L.R., SX	40	Lead-RN**	100	3.44
X22LRBP	22 L.R., SX Bulk Pack	40	Lead-RN**	250	8.16
X22LRH	22 L.R. HP, SX	37	Lead-HP**	50	1.99
X22LRHC	22 L.R. HP SX Blister Card	37	Lead-HP**	50	2.13
X22LRH1	22 L.R. HP, SX	37	Lead-HP**	100	3.98

SUPER-X 22 WINCHESTER MAGNUM CARTRIDGES

X22WMR	22 Win. Mag., SX	40	JHP	50	6.07
X22WMRC	22 Win. Mag., SX Blister Card	40	JHP	50	6.53
X22MR1	22 Win. Mag., SX	40	FMC	50	6.07

SUPER SILHOUETTE RIMFIRE CARTRIDGE

XS22LR1	22 L.R. Super Silhouette	42	Lead-TC	100	5.15

T22 STANDARD VELOCITY CARTRIDGES

XT22LR	22 L.R., T22	40	Lead-RN	50	1.72

SUPER-MATCH CARTRIDGES

SM22LR4	22 L.R., SUPER-MATCH MARK IV	40	Lead-RN	50	5.10

SUPER-MATCH cartridges are especially recommended for the highest degree of match shooting with pistols.

OTHER WINCHESTER RIMFIRE CARTRIDGES

X22LRS	22 Long Rifle, Shot	37 #12 Shot	50	4.58
22BL	22 Short Blank	Black Powder	50	2.70
WW22CBS2	22 Short C.B.	29 Lead-RN	250	10.38

*available mid-year
Loads with 7½ or 8 shot recommended for trap shooting
Black Powder
**Lubaloy Coated
◊ Packed 10 rounds Per Box.
△ Packed 25 rounds Per Box.

HP—Hollow Point
JHP-Jacketed Hollow Point
RN-Round Nose

L.R.—Long Rifle
TC-Truncated Cone
FMC-Full Metal Case

Ballistics

FOR ADDRESSES AND PHONE
NUMBERS OF MANUFACTURERS AND
DISTRIBUTORS INCLUDED IN THIS
SECTION, SEE *DIRECTORY OF
MANUFACTURERS AND SUPPLIERS*

CCI BALLISTICS

BLAZER™ CENTERFIRE AMMO

Caliber & Bullet Description	Bullet Wt. (GRS.)	No. Per Box	Velocity F.P.S. Muzzle	50 Yds.	100 Yds.	Energy Ft.-Lbs. Muzzle	50 Yds.	100 Yds.	Barrel Length	Mid-Range Trajectory 50 Yds.	100 Yds.	Use	Part Number
45 Auto FMJ+	230	50*	845	804	775	363	329	304	5"	1.6"	6.5"	P,T	3570
45 Auto JHP	200	50	975	917	860	421	372	328	5"	1.4"	5.0"	P,V,SG	3568
357 Magnum JHP	158	50	1235	1104	1015	535	428	361	4"VB	0.8"	3.5"	P,V,S	3542
357 Magnum JHP	125	50	1450	1240	1090	583	427	330	4"VB	0.6"	2.8"	P,V,SG	3532
38 Spl + P JHP	158	50	915	878	844	294	270	250	4"VB	1.4"	5.6"	P,V	3526
38 Spl + P L-SWC HP	158	50	915	878	844	294	270	250	4"VB	1.4"	5.6"	P,T,V	3523
38 Special L-RN	158	50*	755	723	692	200	183	168	4"VB	2.0"	8.3"	P,T,V	3522
38 Spl + P FMJ+	150	50	910	870	835	276	252	232	4"VB	1.4"	5.7"	P,T,V	3519
38 Special HBWC	148	50*	710	634	566	166	132	105	4"VB	2.4"	10.8"	P,T,M	3517
38 Spl + P JHP	125	50	945	898	858	248	224	204	4"VB	1.3"	5.4"	P,T,V,SG	3514
9mm Luger FMJ+	115	50*	1155	1047	971	341	280	241	4"	0.9"	3.9"	P,T,V	3509
9mm Luger JHP	115	50*	1155	1047	971	341	280	241	4"	0.9"	3.9"	P,V	3508
380 Auto FMJ+	95	50	955	865	785	190	160	130	3¾"	1.4"	5.9"	P	3505
380 Auto JHP	88	50	1000	920	870	195	164	148	3¾"	1.2"	5.1"	P	3504
25 Auto FMJ+	50	50	810	755	700	73	63	54	2"	1.8"	7.7"	P	3501
25 Auto JHP	45	50	850	760	683	72	58	46	2"	1.5"	6.3"	P	3500

22 RIMFIRE AMMO
18½" Barrel (Except WMR-20" Barrel)

Caliber & Bullet Description	Bullet Wt. (GRS.)	No. Per Box	Velocity F.P.S. Muzzle	50 Yds.	100 Yds.	Energy Ft.-Lbs. Muzzle	50 Yds.	100 Yds.	Muz. Vel. 6" BA.	Mid-Range Trajectory 100 Yds.	Use	Part Number
Noise Blank	—	100	—	—	—	—	—	—	—	—	—	0044
Mini CB Cap	29	100	727	667	610	33	28	24	706	—	P	0026
Short Target	29	100	830	752	695	44	36	31	786	6.8"	P,T	0037
Mini-Mag Short HP	27	100	1164	1013	920	81	62	50	1077	4.3"	P	0028
Mini-Mag Short	29	100	1132	1004	920	83	65	54	1065	4.1"	P	0027
CB Long	29	100	727	667	610	33	28	24	706	—	P,T,SG	0038
Mini-Mag Long	29	100	1180	1038	946	90	69	57	1031	4.1"	P,V,SG	0029
LR Competition Green Tag	40	100	1138	1046	975	116	97	84	1027	4.0"	P,T	0033
LR Standard Velocity	40	100**	1138	1046	975	116	97	84	1027	4.0"	P,T,S	0032
Mini-Mag LR HP	36	100#	1280	1126	1012	135	101	84	1089	3.5"	P,V,SG	0031
Mini-Mag LR HS	40	50=*	1255	1110	1016	140	109	92	1060	3.6"	P,V,SG	0030
Stinger LR HP	32	100	1640	1277	1132	191	115	91	1395	2.6"	P,V,SG,S	0050
Maxi-Mag WMR HP	40	50	1910	1490	1326	324	197	156	1428	1.7"	P,V,SG,S	0024
Maxi-Mag WMR HS	40	50	1910	1490	1326	324	197	156	1428	1.7"	P,V,SG,S	0023

+ TMJ™–Totally Metal Jacketed™
= *Also available in 100-round box, 200-round Plinker Pak and 275-round Belt Pak.
* Also available in 100-Pak.
\# Also available in 275-round Belt Pak.
** Also available in 200-round Plinker Pak.

Abbreviation Guide: FMJ–Full Metal Jacket; JHP–Jacketed Hollow Point; JSP–Jacketed Soft Point; HBWC–Hollow Base Wadcutter; L-SWC–Semi-Wadcutter Lead; L-RN–Round Nose Lead; HP–Hollow Point; VB–Vente Barrel. Test barrels are used to determine ballistic figures. Individual firearms may differ. These figures are approximate and are shown for reference only.
Usage Codes: P–Plinking; T–Target; V–Varmint; SG–Small Game; S–Silhouette; D–Deer; M–Match.

CCI BALLISTICS

LAWMAN™ CENTERFIRE AMMO

CALIBER & BULLET DESCRIPTION	BULLET WT. (GRS.)	NO. PER BOX	VELOCITY F.P.S. MUZZLE	50 YDS.	100 YDS.	ENERGY FT.-LBS. MUZZLE	50 YDS.	100 YDS.	BARREL LENGTH	MID-RANGE TRAJECTORY 50 YDS.	100 YDS.	PRIMARY USE	PART NUMBER
357 Magnum JHP	125	50	1450	1240	1090	583	427	330	4"VB	0.6"	2.8"	P.V.SG	3920
357 Magnum JHP	110	50	1295	1094	975	410	292	232	4"VB	0.8"	3.5"	P.V.SG	3910
38 Spl + P JHP	158	50	915	878	844	294	270	250	4"VB	1.4"	5.6"	P.T.V.S	3760
38 Spl + P JSP	158	50	915	878	844	294	270	250	4"VB	1.4"	5.6"	P.T.V.S	3759
38 Special L-RN	158	50	755	723	692	200	183	168	4"VB	2.0"	8.3"	P.T.V	3758
38 Special L-SWC	158	50	755	723	692	200	183	168	4"VB	2.0"	8.3"	P.T.V	3752
38 Spl + P FMJ+	150	50	910	870	834	276	252	232	4"VB	1.4"	5.7"	P.T.V	3750
38 Spl Match HBWC	148	50	710	634	566	166	132	105	4"VB	2.4"	10.8"	P.T.M	3748
38 Spl + P JHP	140	50	930	872	826	269	235	211	4"VB	1.3"	5.3"	P.T.V.SG	3740
38 Spl + P JSP	125	50	945	898	858	248	224	204	4"VB	1.3"	5.4"	P.T.V.SG	3725
38 Spl + P JHP	125	50	945	898	858	248	224	204	4"VB	1.3"	5.4"	P.T.V.SG	3720
38 Special JHP	110	50	1000	925	865	244	209	183	4"VB	1.2"	5.1"	P.T.V	3710
9mm Luger JSP	125	50	1100	1005	935	335	280	243	4"	1.0"	4.1"	P.V	3620
9mm Luger FMJ+	115	50	1155	1047	971	341	280	241	4"	0.9"	3.9"	P.T	3615

LAWMAN™ CENTERFIRE AMMO

CALIBER & BULLET DESCRIPTION	BULLET WT. (GRS.)	NO. PER BOX	VELOCITY F.P.S. MUZZLE	50 YDS.	100 YDS.	ENERGY FT.-LBS. MUZZLE	50 YDS.	100 YDS.	BARREL LENGTH	MID-RANGE TRAJECTORY 50 YDS.	100 YDS.	PRIMARY USE	PART NUMBER
45 Auto JHP	200	25	975	917	860	421	372	328	5"	1.4"	5.0"	P.V.SG	3965
44 Magnum JSP	240	25	1350	1186	1069	970	749	609	6.5"	0.7"	3.1"	P.T.V.SG.S,D	3974
44 Magnum JHP	200	25	1420	1210	1055	894	650	494	6.5"	0.6"	2.7"	P.T.V.SG	3972
357 Magnum JHP	158	50	1235	1104	1015	535	428	361	4"VB	0.8"	3.5"	P.V.S	3960
357 Magnum JSP	158	50	1235	1104	1015	535	428	361	4"VB	0.8"	3.5"	P.V.S	3959
357 Magnum FMJ+	150	50	1270	1191	1090	537	471	394	4"VB	0.7"	3.3"	P.V	3950
357 Magnum JHP	140	50	1380	1209	1080	591	455	363	4"VB	0.6"	3.3"	P.V.SG	3940
357 Magnum JSP	125	50	1450	1240	1090	583	427	330	4"VB	0.6"	2.8"	P.V.SG	3925

SHOTSHELL AMMO

CALIBER & BULLET DESCRIPTION	TOTAL CAPSULE WEIGHT	SIZE SHOT	MUZZLE VEL.	MUZ. VEL. 6" BA.	BOX OF 10	BOX OF 20	BOX OF 50	PART #
Mini-Mag Shotshell	—	#12		950	0039	—	—	
Maxi-Mag Shotshell	—	#11	1000		—	0025	—	
44 Magnum Shotshell	150 Grs.	#9	1000 FPS		—	—	—	3979
38 Special Shotshell	109 Grs.	#9	1000 FPS		3709	—	—	3708

Abbreviation Guide: FMJ–Full Metal Jacket; JHP–Jacketed Hollow Point; JSP–Jacketed Soft Point; HBWC–Hollow Base Wadcutter; L-SWC–Semi-Wadcutter Lead; L-RN–Round Nose Lead; HP–Hollow Point; VB–Vented Barrel. Test barrels are used to determine ballistic figures. Individual firearms may differ. These figures are approximate and are shown for reference only. Usage Codes: P-Plinking; T-Target; V-Varmint; SG-Small Game; S-Silhouette; D-Deer; M-Match. +TMJ–Totally Metal Jacketed™

FEDERAL BALLISTICS

Hi-Shok® Centerfire Rifle Ballistics (Approximate)

Federal Load No.	Caliber	Bullet Wgt. in Grains	Bullet Style	Factory Primer	Velocity In Feet Per Second						Energy In Foot/Pounds					
					Muzzle	100 yds	200 yds	300 yds	400 yds	500 yds	Muzzle	100 yds	200 yds	300 yds	400 yds	500 yds
222A	222 Remington	50	Soft Point	205	3140	2600	2120	1700	1350	1110	1095	750	500	320	200	135
222B		55	Metal Cs. Boat-T.	205	3020	2740	2480	2230	1990	1780	1115	915	750	610	485	385
22250A	22-250 Remington	55	Soft Point	210	3680	3140	2660	2220	1830	1490	1655	1200	860	605	410	270
22250C		40	Hollow Point Blitz	210	4000	3320	2720	2200	1740	1360	1420	980	660	430	265	165
223A	223 Remington	55	Soft Point	205	3240	2750	2300	1910	1550	1270	1280	920	650	445	295	195
223B		55	Metal Cs. Boat-T.	205	3240	2950	2670	2410	2170	1940	1280	1060	875	710	575	460
223C		55	Boat Tail H.P.	205	3240	2770	2340	1950	1610	1330	1280	935	670	465	315	215
223D		40	Hollow Point Blitz	205	3650	3010	2450	1950	1530	1210	1185	805	535	340	205	130
6A	6mm Remington	80	Soft Point	210	3470	3060	2690	2350	2040	1750	2140	1665	1290	980	735	540
6B		100	Hi-Shok S.P.	210	3100	2830	2570	2330	2100	1890	2135	1775	1470	1205	985	790
243A	243 Winchester	80	Soft Point	210	3350	2960	2590	2260	1950	1670	1995	1550	1195	905	675	495
243B		100	Hi-Shok S.P.	210	2960	2700	2450	2220	1990	1790	1945	1615	1330	1090	880	710
257A	257 Roberts (Hi-Vel. + P)	117	Hi-Shok S.P.	210	2780	2560	2360	2160	1970	1790	2010	1710	1445	1210	1010	835
2506A	25-'06 Remington	90	Hollow Point	210	3440	3040	2680	2340	2030	1750	2365	1850	1435	1100	825	610
2506B		117	Hi-Shok S.P.	210	2990	2730	2480	2250	2030	1830	2380	1985	1645	1350	1100	885
270A	270 Winchester	130	Hi-Shok S.P.	210	3060	2800	2560	2330	2110	1900	2700	2265	1890	1565	1285	1045
270B		150	Hi-Shok S.P.	210	2850	2500	2180	1890	1620	1390	2705	2085	1585	1185	870	640
7A	7mm Mauser	175	Hi-Shok S.P.	210	2440	2140	1860	1600	1380	1200	2315	1775	1340	1000	740	565
7B		140	Hi-Shok S.P.	210	2660	2450	2260	2070	1890	1730	2200	1865	1585	1330	1110	930
7RA	7mm Remington Magnum	150	Hi-Shok S.P.	215	3110	2830	2570	2320	2090	1870	3220	2670	2200	1790	1450	1160
7RB		175	Hi-Shok S.P.	215	2860	2650	2440	2240	2060	1880	3180	2720	2310	1960	1640	1370
*†30CA	30 Carbine	110	Soft Point	205	1990	1570	1240	1040	920	840	965	600	375	260	210	175
*†30CB		110	Metal Case	205	1990	1600	1280	1070	950	870	970	620	400	280	220	185
730A	7-30 Waters	120	Boat Tail S.P.	210	2700	2300	1930	1600	1330	1140	1940	1405	990	685	470	345
3030A	30-30 Winchester	150	Hi-Shok S.P.	210	2390	2020	1680	1400	1180	1040	1900	1355	945	650	460	355
3030B		170	Hi-Shok S.P.	210	2200	1900	1620	1380	1190	1060	1830	1355	990	720	535	425
3030C		125	Hollow Point	210	2570	2090	1660	1320	1080	960	1830	1210	770	480	320	260
3006A	30-'06 Springfield	150	Hi-Shok S.P.	210	2910	2620	2340	2080	1840	1620	2820	2280	1825	1445	1130	875
3006B		180	Hi-Shok S.P.	210	2700	2470	2250	2040	1850	1660	2915	2435	2025	1665	1360	1105
3006C		125	Soft Point	210	3140	2780	2450	2140	1850	1600	2735	2145	1660	1270	955	705
3006D		165	Boat Tail S.P.	210	2800	2610	2420	2240	2070	1910	2870	2490	2150	1840	1580	1340
3006H		220	Round Nose S.P.	210	2410	2130	1870	1630	1420	1250	2835	2215	1705	1300	985	760
New 3006J		180	Round Nose S.P.	210	2700	2350	2020	1730	1470	1250	2915	2200	1630	1190	860	620
300WB	300 Winchester Magnum	180	Hi-Shok S.P.	215	2960	2750	2540	2340	2160	1980	3500	3010	2580	2195	1860	1565
300A	300 Savage	150	Hi-Shok S.P.	210	2630	2350	2100	1850	1630	1430	2305	1845	1460	1145	885	685
300B		180	Hi-Shok S.P.	210	2350	2140	1940	1750	1570	1410	2205	1825	1495	1215	985	800
308A	308 Winchester	150	Hi-Shok S.P.	210	2820	2530	2260	2010	1770	1560	2650	2140	1705	1345	1050	810
308B		180	Hi-Shok S.P.	210	2620	2390	2180	1970	1780	1600	2745	2290	1895	1555	1270	1030
**8A	8mm Mauser	170	Hi-Shok S.P.	210	2360	1970	1620	1330	1120	1000	2100	1465	995	670	475	375
32A	32 Winchester Special	170	Hi-Shok S.P.	210	2250	1920	1630	1370	1180	1040	1910	1395	1000	710	520	410
35A	35 Remington	200	Hi-Shok S.P.	210	2080	1700	1380	1140	1000	910	1920	1280	840	575	445	370
*††357G	357 Magnum	180	Hollow S.P.	100	1550	1160	980	860	770	680	960	535	385	295	235	185
*†44A	44 Remington Magnum	240	Hollow S.P.	150	1760	1380	1090	950	860	790	1650	1015	640	485	395	330
*4570A	45-'70 Government	300	Hollow S.P.	210	1880	1650	1430	1240	1110	1010	2355	1815	1355	1015	810	680

Unless otherwise noted, ballistic specifications were derived from test barrels 24 inches in length.   †Test Barrel Length 20 Inches.   ††Test Barrel Length 18 Inches.   *Without Cartridge Carrier.
**Only for use in barrels intended for .323 inch diameter bullets. Do not use in 8mm Commission Rifles (M1888) or sporting arms of similar bore diameter. Rifle cartridges packed 20 rounds per box, 25 boxes per case. Exception: 357G packed 50 rounds per box.   Velocity figures rounded off to nearest "10." Energy figures rounded off to nearest "5."

FEDERAL BALLISTICS

Height of Trajectory
Inches above line of sight if sighted in at ⊕ yards. For sights .9″ above bore.
Trajectory figures show the height of bullet impact above or below the line of sight at the indicated yardages.
Aim low indicated amount for + figures and high for − figures. Zero ranges indicated by circled crosses.

Bullet Drop — In Inches From Bore Line					Drift — In Inches In 10 mph Crosswind					Height of Trajectory												
100 yds	200 yds	300 yds	400 yds	500 yds	100 yds	200 yds	300 yds	400 yds	500 yds	50 yds	100 yds	150 yds	200 yds	250 yds	300 yds	100 yds	150 yds	200 yds	250 yds	300 yds	400 yds	500 yds
2.0	9.2	24.3	51.6	98.2	1.7	7.3	18.3	36.4	63.1	+0.5	+0.9	⊕	−2.5	−6.9	−13.7	+2.2	+1.9	⊕	−3.8	−10.0	−32.3	−73.8
2.0	8.6	21.0	40.8	68.2	0.9	3.4	8.5	16.8	26.3	+0.5	+0.8	⊕	−2.1	−5.4	−10.8	+1.9	+1.6	⊕	−2.8	−7.7	−22.7	−45.3
1.4	6.4	16.4	33.5	61.2	1.2	5.2	12.5	24.4	42.0	+0.2	+0.5	⊕	−1.6	−4.4	−8.6	+2.3	+2.6	+1.9	⊕	−3.4	−15.8	−38.6
1.2	5.7	14.8	31.3	59.2	1.3	5.7	14.0	27.9	49.2	+0.1	+0.4	⊕	−1.4	−4.0	−8.0	+2.0	+2.4	+1.8	⊕	−3.2	−15.5	−39.3
1.8	8.4	21.5	44.4	81.8	1.4	6.1	15.0	29.4	50.8	+0.4	+0.8	⊕	−2.2	−6.0	−11.8	+1.9	+1.6	⊕	−3.3	−8.5	−26.7	−59.6
1.8	7.5	18.2	34.8	58.8	1.8	3.3	7.8	14.5	24.0	+0.3	+0.7	⊕	−1.8	−4.8	−9.1	+1.6	+1.3	⊕	−2.5	−6.4	−18.9	−38.7
1.8	8.3	21.1	43.1	78.4	1.3	5.8	14.2	27.7	47.6	+0.4	+0.8	⊕	−2.1	−5.8	−11.4	+1.8	+1.6	⊕	−3.2	−8.2	−25.7	−56.4
1.5	6.9	18.1	38.6	73.6	1.5	6.5	16.1	32.3	56.9	+0.2	+0.6	⊕	−1.8	−5.0	−10.0	+1.5	+1.3	⊕	−2.8	−7.4	−24.0	−55.1
1.6	6.9	17.0	33.4	58.3	1.0	4.1	9.9	18.8	31.6	+0.3	+0.6	⊕	−1.6	−4.5	−8.7	+2.4	+2.7	+1.9	⊕	−3.3	−14.9	−35.0
1.9	8.2	19.8	37.7	63.6	0.8	3.3	7.9	14.7	24.1	+0.4	+0.8	⊕	−1.9	−5.2	−9.9	+1.7	+1.5	⊕	−2.8	−7.0	−20.4	−41.7
1.7	7.4	18.3	36.0	63.0	1.0	4.3	10.4	19.8	33.3	+0.3	+0.7	⊕	−1.8	−4.9	−9.4	+2.6	+2.9	+2.1	⊕	−3.6	−16.2	−37.9
2.1	9.0	21.7	41.6	70.2	0.9	3.6	8.4	15.7	25.8	+0.5	+0.9	⊕	−2.2	−5.8	−11.0	+1.9	+1.6	⊕	−3.1	−7.8	−22.6	−46.3
2.4	10.1	24.0	45.4	75.8	0.8	3.3	7.7	14.3	23.4	+0.7	+1.0	⊕	−2.4	−6.4	−12.1	+2.2	+1.8	⊕	−3.4	−8.5	−24.4	−49.3
1.6	7.0	17.2	33.8	58.9	1.0	4.1	9.8	18.7	31.3	+0.3	+0.6	⊕	−1.7	−4.5	−8.8	+2.4	+2.7	+2.0	⊕	−3.4	−15.0	−35.2
2.1	8.8	21.2	40.5	68.2	0.8	3.4	8.1	15.1	24.9	+0.5	+0.8	⊕	−2.1	−5.7	−10.8	+1.9	+1.6	⊕	−3.0	−7.6	−22.3	−45.8
2.0	8.4	20.1	38.3	64.3	0.8	3.2	7.6	14.2	23.3	+0.4	+0.8	⊕	−2.0	−5.3	−10.1	+1.8	+1.5	⊕	−2.8	−7.1	−20.6	−42.0
2.3	10.3	25.5	50.6	89.2	1.2	5.3	12.8	24.5	41.3	+0.7	+1.0	⊕	−2.6	−7.1	−13.6	+2.3	+2.0	⊕	−3.8	−9.7	−29.2	−62.2
3.1	13.7	34.1	62.8	119.3	1.5	6.2	15.0	28.7	47.8	+0.4	⊕	−2.2	−6.6	−13.4	−23.0	+1.5	⊕	−3.6	−9.7	−18.6	−46.8	−92.8
2.7	10.9	26.3	50.0	81.9	1.3	3.2	8.2	15.4	23.4	+0.4	⊕	−1.5	−4.6	−9.9	−16.4	+2.4	+2.1	⊕	−3.2	−9.6	−27.3	−53.5
1.9	8.2	19.7	37.8	63.9	0.8	3.4	8.1	15.1	24.9	+0.4	+0.8	⊕	−1.9	−5.2	−9.9	+1.7	+1.5	⊕	−2.8	−7.0	−20.5	−42.1
2.2	9.5	22.5	42.5	70.8	0.7	3.1	7.2	13.3	21.7	+0.6	+0.9	⊕	−2.3	−6.0	−11.3	+2.0	+1.7	⊕	−3.2	−7.9	−22.7	−45.8
5.2	24.8	67.2	142.0	257.6	3.4	15.0	35.5	63.2	96.7	+0.9	⊕	−4.5	−13.5	−28.3	−49.9	⊕	+4.5	−13.5	−28.3	−49.9	−118.6	−228.1
5.1	24.1	64.5	135.1	244.1	3.1	13.7	32.6	58.7	90.3	+0.9	⊕	−4.3	−13.0	−26.9	−47.4	+2.9	⊕	−7.2	−19.7	−38.7	−100.4	−200.5
2.7	12.0	30.8	63.1	113.9	1.6	7.2	17.7	34.5	58.1	+0.3	⊕	−1.9	−5.8	−12.0	−21.0	+1.3	⊕	−3.2	−8.8	−17.2	−44.6	−90.7
3.4	15.4	39.9	82.3	149.8	2.0	8.5	20.9	40.1	66.1	+0.5	⊕	−2.6	−7.7	−16.0	−27.9	+1.7	⊕	−4.3	−11.6	−22.7	−59.1	−120.5
4.0	17.7	44.8	90.3	160.2	1.9	8.0	19.4	36.7	59.8	+0.6	⊕	−3.0	−8.9	−18.0	−31.1	+2.0	⊕	−4.8	−13.0	−25.1	−63.6	−126.7
3.0	14.2	38.0	81.0	148.7	2.2	10.1	25.4	49.4	81.6	+0.1	⊕	−2.0	−7.3	−15.8	−28.1	+3.2	+2.4	⊕	−5.5	−15.8	−51.7	−112.3
2.2	9.5	23.2	44.9	76.9	1.0	4.2	9.9	18.7	31.2	+0.6	+0.9	⊕	−2.3	−6.3	−12.0	+2.1	+1.8	⊕	−3.3	−8.5	−25.0	−51.8
2.5	10.8	25.9	49.4	83.2	0.9	3.7	8.8	16.5	27.1	+0.2	⊕	−1.6	−4.8	−9.7	−16.5	+2.4	+2.0	⊕	−3.7	−9.3	−27.0	−54.9
1.9	8.3	20.6	40.6	70.7	1.1	4.5	10.8	20.5	34.4	+0.4	+0.8	⊕	−2.1	−5.6	−10.7	+1.8	+1.5	⊕	−3.0	−7.7	−23.0	−48.5
2.2	9.5	22.7	42.8	71.0	0.7	2.8	6.6	12.3	19.9	+0.5	⊕	−1.1	−4.2	−8.8	−14.3	+2.1	+1.8	⊕	−3.0	−8.0	−22.9	−45.9
3.3	14.2	35.2	69.2	120.0	1.4	6.0	14.3	27.2	45.0	+0.4	⊕	−2.3	−6.8	−13.8	−23.6	+3.4	+2.8	⊕	−5.3	−13.4	−39.9	−83.1
2.6	11.7	29.7	59.9	106.8	1.5	6.4	15.7	30.4	51.2	+0.2	⊕	−1.8	−5.6	−11.5	−20.0	+2.8	+2.3	⊕	−4.5	−11.6	−35.5	−76.1
2.1	8.8	20.9	39.4	65.3	0.7	2.8	6.6	12.3	20.0	+0.5	+0.8	⊕	−2.1	−5.5	−10.4	+1.9	+1.6	⊕	−2.9	−7.3	−20.9	−41.9
2.7	11.7	28.7	55.8	96.1	1.1	4.8	11.6	21.9	36.3	+0.3	⊕	−1.8	−5.4	−11.0	−18.8	+2.7	+2.2	⊕	−4.2	−10.7	−31.5	−65.5
3.4	14.3	34.7	66.4	112.3	1.1	4.6	10.9	20.3	33.3	+0.4	⊕	−2.3	−6.7	−13.5	−22.8	+1.5	⊕	−3.6	−9.6	−18.2	−44.1	−84.2
2.3	10.1	24.8	48.0	82.4	1.0	4.4	10.4	19.7	32.7	+0.2	⊕	−1.5	−4.5	−9.3	−15.9	+2.3	+1.9	⊕	−3.6	−9.1	−26.9	−55.7
2.7	11.5	27.6	52.7	88.8	0.9	3.9	9.2	17.2	28.3	+0.2	⊕	−1.8	−5.2	−10.4	−17.7	+2.6	+2.1	⊕	−4.0	−9.9	−28.9	−58.8
3.5	21.1	42.1	87.8	161.0	2.1	9.3	22.9	43.9	71.7	+0.5	⊕	−2.7	−8.2	−17.0	−29.8	+1.8	⊕	−4.5	−12.4	−24.3	−63.8	−130.7
3.8	17.1	43.7	88.9	159.3	1.9	8.4	20.3	38.6	63.0	+0.6	⊕	−2.9	−8.6	−17.6	−30.5	+1.9	⊕	−4.7	−12.7	−24.7	−63.2	−126.9
4.6	21.5	56.9	118.9	215.6	2.7	12.0	29.0	53.3	83.3	+0.8	⊕	−3.8	−11.3	−23.5	−41.2	+2.5	⊕	−6.3	−17.1	−33.6	−87.7	−176.3
8.9	42.2	107.8	NA	NA	5.8	21.7	45.2	76.1	NA	⊕	−4.0	−14.2	−31.5	−56.8	−91.2	⊕	−8.2	−23.4	−46.8	−79.1	NA	NA
6.7	32.4	87.0	179.8	319.6	4.2	17.8	39.8	68.3	102.5	⊕	−2.7	−10.2	−23.6	−44.2	−73.3	⊕	−6.1	−18.1	−37.4	−65.1	−150.3	−282.5
4.3	21.5	57.2	112.8	NA	1.7	7.6	18.6	35.7	NA	⊕	−2.4	−8.2	−17.6	−31.4	−51.5	⊕	−4.6	−12.8	−25.4	−44.3	−95.5	NA

NOTE: These trajectory tables were calculated by computer and are given here unaltered. The computer used a standard modern scientific technique to predict trajectories from the best available data for each round. Each trajectory is expected to be reasonably representative of the behavior of the ammunition at sea level conditions, but the shooter is cautioned that trajectories differ because of variations in ammunition, rifles, and atmospheric conditions.

FEDERAL BALLISTICS

25AP 32AP 380AP 9AP 9BP 38B 38D 38C 38G 38H 38E 38F 38J 357A 357B 357D 357E 44SA 45A 45B

AUTOMATIC PISTOL BALLISTICS (Approximate)

Federal Load No.	Caliber	Bullet Style	Bullet Weight in Grains	Velocity in Feet Per Second Muzzle	50 yds.	Energy in Foot/Lbs. Muzzle	50 yds.	Mid-range Trajectory 50 yds.	Test Barrel Length
25AP	25 Auto Pistol (6.35mm)	Metal Case	50	760	730	64	59	1.8"	2"
32AP	32 Auto Pistol (7.65mm)	Metal Case	71	905	855	129	115	1.4"	4"
380AP	380 Auto Pistol	Metal Case	95	955	865	190	160	1.4"	3¾"
380BP	380 Auto Pistol	Jacketed Hollow Point	90	1000	890	200	160	1.4"	3¾"
9AP	9mm Luger Auto Pistol	Metal Case	123	1120	1030	345	290	1.0"	4"
9BP	9mm Luger Auto Pistol	Jacketed Hollow Point	115	1160	1060	345	285	0.9"	4"
9CP	9mm Luger Auto Pistol	Jacketed Soft Point	95	1350	1140	385	275	0.7"	4"
45A	45 Automatic (Match)	Metal Case	230	850	810	370	335	1.6"	5"
45B	45 Automatic (Match)	Metal Case, S.W.C.	185	775	695	247	200	2.0"	5"
45C	45 Automatic (Match)	Jacketed Hollow Point	185	950	900	370	335	1.3"	5"

REVOLVER BALLISTICS (Approximate)

Federal Load No.	Caliber	Bullet Style	Bullet Weight in Grains	Velocity in Feet Per Second Muzzle	50 yds.	Energy in Foot/Lbs. Muzzle	50 yds.	Mid-range Trajectory 50 yds.	Test Barrel Length*
32LA	32 S&W Long	Lead Wadcutter	98	780	630	130	85	2.2"	4"
32LB	32 S&W Long	Lead Round Nose	98	705	670	115	98	2.3"	4"
32HRA	32 H&R Magnum	Lead Semi-Wadcutter	95	1030	940	225	190	1.1"	4½"
32HRB	32 H&R Magnum	Jacketed Hollow Point	85	1100	1020	230	195	1.0"	4½"
38A	38 Special (Match)	Lead Wadcutter	148	710	634	166	132	2.4"	4" -V
38B	38 Special	Lead Round Nose	158	755	723	200	183	2.0"	4" -V
38C	38 Special	Lead Semi-Wadcutter	158	755	723	200	183	2.0"	4" -V
▲38D	38 Special (High Velocity + P)	Lead Round Nose	158	890	855	278	257	1.4"	4" -V
▲38E	38 Special (High Velocity + P)	Jacketed Hollow Point	125	945	898	248	224	1.3"	4" -V
▲38F	38 Special (High Velocity + P)	Jacketed Hollow Point	110	995	926	242	210	1.2"	4" -V
▲38G	38 Special (High Velocity + P)	Semi-Wadcutter Hollow Point	158	890	855	278	257	1.4"	4" -V
▲38H	38 Special (High Velocity + P)	Lead Semi-Wadcutter	158	890	855	278	257	1.4"	4" -V
▲38J	38 Special (High Velocity + P)	Jacketed Soft Point	125	945	898	248	224	1.3"	4" -V
357A	357 Magnum	Jacketed Soft Point	158	1235	1104	535	428	0.8"	4" -V
357B	357 Magnum	Jacketed Soft Point	125	1450	1240	583	427	0.6"	4" -V
357C	357 Magnum	Lead Semi-Wadcutter	158	1235	1104	535	428	0.8"	4" -V
357D	357 Magnum	Jacketed Hollow Point	110	1295	1094	410	292	0.8"	4" -V
357E	357 Magnum	Jacketed Hollow Point	158	1235	1104	535	428	0.8"	4" -V
357G	357 Magnum	Jacketed Hollow Point	180	1090	980	475	385	1.0"	4" -V
41A	41 Rem.	Jacketed Hollow Point	210	1300	1130	790	595	0.7"	4" -V
41SA	44 S&W Special	Semi-Wadcutter Hollow Point	200	900	830	360	305	1.4"	6½"-V
44A	44 Rem. Magnum	Jacketed Hollow Point	240	1180	1081	741	623	0.9"	6½"-V
44B	44 Rem. Magnum	Jacketed Hollow Point	180	1610	1365	1045	750	0.5"	6½"-V
A44B	44 Rem. Magnum	Jacketed Hollow Point	180	1610	1365	1045	750	0.5"	6½"-V
44C	44 Rem. Magnum	Metal Case Profile	220	1390	1260	945	775	0.6"	6½"-V
45LCA	45 Colt	Semi-Wadcutter Hollow Point	225	900	860	405	369	1.6"	5½"

*"V" indicates vented barrels to simulate service conditions.
▲This "+P" ammunition is loaded to a higher pressure. Use only in firearms so recommended by the manufacturer.
Pistol and revolver cartridges packed 50 rounds per box, 20 boxes per case. Exceptions: 44A and A44B packed 20 rounds per box; 25AP packed 25 rounds per box.

FEDERAL BALLISTICS

NYCLAD REVOLVER BALLISTICS-VENTED BARREL* (Approximate)

Federal Load No.	Caliber	Bullet Style	Bullet Weight In Grains	Muzzle Velocity In Feet Per Second	Muzzle Energy In Foot/Lbs.	Test Barrel Length
N38A	38 Special	Lead Wadcutter	148	710	166	4"
N38B	38 Special	Lead Round Nose	158	755	200	4"
N38C	38 Special	Lead Semi-Wadcutter	158	755	200	4"
▲N38G	38 Special (High Velocity + P)	Semi-Wadcutter Hollow Point	158	915	294	4"
▲N38H	38 Special (High Velocity + P)	Lead Semi-Wadcutter	158	890	278	4"
N38M	38 Special (Chief's Special)	Hollow Point	125	825	190	2"
▲N38N	38 Special (High Velocity + P)	Hollow Point	125	945	248	4"
N357C	357 Magnum	Lead Semi-Wadcutter	158	1235	535	4"
N357E	357 Magnum	Semi-Wadcutter Hollow Point	158	1235	535	4"

*All of the above ballistics are based on a 4 inch vented test barrel, with the exception of the Chief's Special which are derived from a 2" revolver.

▲This "+ P" ammunition is loaded to a higher pressure. Use only in firearms so recommended by the manufacturer.
Nyclad cartridges packed 50 rounds per box, 20 boxes (1,000 rounds) per case.

RIMFIRE BALLISTICS

	Federal Load Number	Cartridges Per Box	Cartridge	Bullet Type	Bullet Weight in Grains	Velocity in Feet Per Second		Energy in Foot/Lbs.		Height of Trajectory Inches above line of sight if sighted in at ⊕ yardage. Sight .9" above bore.				
						Muzzle	100 yds.	Muzzle	100 yds.	50 yds.	100 yds.	50 yds.	100 yds.	150 yds.
Spitfire™ 22s (hypervelocity copper-plated bullets):	720	50	22 Long Rifle	Trun. Cone, Solid	36	1410	1055	160	90	⊕	−5.1	+2.6	⊕	−10.2
	722	50	22 Long Rifle	Truncated Cone Hollow Point	33	1500	1075	165	85	⊕	−4.7	+2.3	⊕	− 9.3
Hi-Power® 22s (copper-plated bullets):	701	50	22 Short	Solid	29	1095	905	77	53	⊕	−8.0	+4.0	⊕	−14.7
	706	50	22 Long	Solid	29	1240	960	99	60	⊕	−6.8	+3.4	⊕	−12.8
	710	50	22 Long Rifle	Solid	40	1255	1015	140	92	⊕	−6.2	+3.1	⊕	−11.5
	810	100	22 Long Rifle	Solid	40	1255	1015	140	92	⊕	−6.2	+3.1	⊕	−11.5
	712	50	22 Long Rifle	Hollow Point	38	1280	1020	138	88	⊕	−6.1	+3.1	⊕	−11.4
	812	100	22 Long Rifle	Hollow Point	38	1280	1020	138	88	⊕	−6.1	+3.1	⊕	−11.4
	716	50	22 Long Rifle	No. 12 Shot	25	—		—		—	—	—	—	—
Lightning™ 22s (lubricated lead bullets):	510	50	22 Long Rifle	Solid	40	1255	1015	140	92					
	910	200	22 Long Rifle	Solid	40	1255	1015	140	92					
Champion™ 22s (lubricated lead bullets):	711	50	22 Long Rifle	Solid	40	1150	975	117	85					
	811	100	22 Long Rifle	Solid	40	1150	975	117	85					

Unless otherwise noted, these ballistic specifications were derived from test barrels 24 inches in length.
All specifications are nominal, individual guns may vary from test barrel figures.

Sighting in 22s:

Most small game hunting with 22s is done at short ranges. By sighting-in at 25 yards, the hunter achieves a relatively flat trajectory from close-in to 50 yards. (See example at right for load Hi-Power No. 712 long rifle cartridge with 38 grain hollow point bullet, with scope sights.)

		Height of Trajectory Inches above line of sight if sighted in at ⊕ yardage. Sight 1.5" above bore.			
	Muzzle	25 yds.	50 yds.	75 yds.	100 yds.
Velocity in Feet Per Second	1280	1195	1125	1065	1020
Energy in Foot/Lbs.	138	120	107	96	88
Trajectory	−1.5	⊕	−0.6	−3.0	−7.2
Drift (inches; 10 m.p.h. crosswind)	0	0.4	1.4	3.2	5.6

22 Win. Magnum

Get Magnum velocity, power and performance from two new rimfire cartridges. Federal's 22 Win. Magnums are loaded with either 40-grain full metal jacket or 40-grain jacketed hollow point bullets. Both deliver plenty of range and impact energy for varminting and other small game hunting.

Federal Load Number	Cartridges Per Box	Cartridge	Bullet Type	Bullet Weight in Grains	Velocity in Feet Per Second		Energy in Foot/Lbs.		Height of Trajectory Inches above line of sight if sighted in at ⊕ yardage. Sight .9" above bore.				
					Muzzle	100 yds.	Muzzle	100 yds.	50 yds.	100 yds.	50 yds.	100 yds.	150 yds.
737	50	22 Winchester Magnum	Full Metal Jacket	40	1910	1330	325	155	⊕	−2.6	+1.3	⊕	−6.1
747	50	22 Winchester Magnum	Jacketed Hollow Point	40	1910	1330	325	155	⊕	−2.6	+1.3	⊕	−6.1
757	50	22 Winchester Magnum	Jacketed Hollow Point	50	1650	1280	300	180	⊕	−3.3	+1.6	⊕	−6.9

NORMA BALLISTICS

Caliber Bullet weight Ref.	Velocity – Feet per sec.				Energy – Foot pounds				Sight at yards	Line of sights 1½ above center of bore. + indicates point of impact in inches above, − in inches below sighting point.					
	Muzzle	100 yards	200 yards	300 yards	Muzzle	100 yards	200 yards	300 yards		25 yards	50 yards	100 yards	150 yards	200 yards	300 yards
22 Hornet 45 gr/2.9 g Ref. 15601	2428	1896	1451	1135	589	360	210	129	100 150 200	−0.4 ±0 +0.6	+0.2 +1.1 +2.3	○ +1.8 +4.2	−2.6 ○ +3.7	−8.4 −4.9 ○	−33.1 −27.8 −20.5
220 Swift 50 gr/3.2 g Ref. 15701	4110	3611	3133	2681	1877	1448	1090	799	100 180 200	−0.9 −0.8 −0.8	−0.5 −0.3 −0.2	○ +0.4 +0.6	−0.2 +0.4 +0.7	−1.2 −0.4 ○	−5.9 −4.7 −4.1
222 Rem. 50 gr/3.2 g Ref. 15711	3200	2650	2170	1750	1137	780	520	340	100 180 200	−0.8 −0.5 −0.4	−0.3 +0.3 +0.5	○ +1.2 +1.6	−0.9 +0.8 +1.5	−3.2 −0.9 ○	−12.9 −9.4 −8.2
222 Rem. 50 gr/3.2 g Ref. 15712	3200	2610	2080	1630	1137	756	480	295	100 180 200	−0.7 −0.4 −0.3	−0.2 +0.5 +0.7	○ +1.4 +1.9	−1.1 +1.0 +1.7	−3.7 −1.0 ○	−15.7 −11.6 −10.1
22–250 53 gr/3.4 g Ref. 15733	3707	3192	2741	2332	1616	1198	883	639	100 180 200	−0.9 −0.7 −0.6	−0.4 −0.1 +0.1	○ +0.7 +1.0	−0.5 +0.5 +1.0	−1.9 −0.6 ○	−8.6 −6.6 −5.7
5.6x52 R 71 gr/4.6 g Ref. 15604	2790	2329	1955	1640	1226	855	603	424	100 180 200	−0.6 −0.2 ○	−0.1 +0.8 +1.1	○ +1.8 +2.4	−1.5 +1.2 +2.1	−4.8 −1.2 ○	−18.6 −13.2 −11.4
243 Win. 100 gr/6.5 g Ref. 16003	3070	2790	2540	2320	2090	1730	1430	1190	100 180 200	−0.7 −0.5 −0.4	−0.2 +0.3 +0.5	○ +1.1 +1.4	−0.9 +0.7 +1.3	−2.9 −0.7 ○	−10.6 −7.4 −6.3
6.5 Jap. 139 gr/9.0 g Ref. 16531	2362	2185	2021	1867	1722	1473	1260	1076	100 130 200	−0.6 −0.3 +0.2	−0.1 +0.4 +1.5	○ +1.0 +3.2	−2.3 −0.9 +2.4	−6.4 −4.4 ○	−20.9 −17.9 −11.3
6.5 Jap. 156 gr/10.1 g Ref. 16532	2065	1871	1692	1529	1481	1213	992	810	100 130 200	−0.3 ±0 +0.8	+0.4 +0.9 +2.5	○ +1.1 +4.3	−2.9 −1.2 +3.5	−8.5 −6.3 ○	−29.2 −26.0 −16.4
6.5 Carcano 156 gr/10.1 g Ref. 16535	2430	2208	2000	1800	2046	1689	1386	1123	100 180 200	−0.5 ±0 +0.2	+0.1 +1.2 +1.5	○ +2.2 +2.9	−1.9 +1.4 +2.4	−5.7 −1.3 ○	−20.2 −13.7 −11.7
6.5x55 139 gr/9.0 g Ref. 16551	2854	2691	2533	2370	2512	2233	1978	1732	100 180 200	−0.7 −0.6 −0.2	−0.2 +0.4 +0.5	○ +1.3 +1.7	−1.0 +0.8 +1.5	−2.3 −0.8 ○	−12.3 −8.6 −7.4
6.5x55 156 gr/10.1 g Ref. 16552	2495	2271	2062	1867	2153	1787	1473	1208	100 180 200	−0.6 ±0 +0.1	+0.2 +1.0 +1.3	○ +2.0 +2.6	−1.7 +1.3 +2.2	−5.3 −1.3 ○	−18.8 −12.7 −10.9
270 Win. 130 gr/8.4 g Ref. 16902	3140	2884	2639	2404	2847	2401	2011	1669	100 180 200	−0.8 −0.5 −0.4	−0.3 +0.2 +0.4	○ +1.0 +1.4	−0.8 +0.7 +1.3	−2.7 −0.7 ○	−10.7 −7.7 −6.6
270 Win. 150 gr/9.7 g Ref. 16903	2800	2616	2436	2262	2616	2280	1977	1705	100 180 200	−0.7 −0.3 −0.2	−0.2 +0.5 +0.7	○ +1.4 +1.8	−1.1 +0.9 +1.6	−3.6 −0.9 ○	−13.1 −9.0 −7.7
7x57 150 gr/9.7 g Ref. 17002	2755	2539	2331	2133	2530	2148	1810	1516	100 180 200	−0.7 −0.3 −0.2	−0.1 +0.6 +0.9	○ +1.5 +2.0	−1.2 +1.0 +1.7	−3.9 −1.0 ○	−14.3 −9.8 −8.4
7x57 R 150 gr/9.7 g Ref. 17005	2690	2476	2270	2077	2411	2042	1717	1437	100 180 200	−0.6 −0.2 −0.1	−0.1 +0.7 +1.0	○ +1.6 +2.1	−1.3 +1.1 +1.8	−4.2 −1.0 ○	−15.2 −10.4 −8.9
7 mm Rem. M. 150 gr/9.7 g Ref. 17021	3250	2960	2690	2440	3519	2919	2410	1983	100 180 200	−0.8 −0.6 −0.5	−0.3 +0.1 +0.3	○ +0.9 +1.2	−0.7 +0.6 +1.1	−2.4 +0.6 ○	−9.5 −6.8 −5.8
7x64 150 gr/9.7 g Ref. 17013	2890	2625	2375	2165	2779	2295	1879	1561	100 180 200	−0.7 −0.4 −0.3	−0.2 +0.4 +0.6	○ +1.2 +1.7	−1.0 +0.9 +1.5	−3.3 −0.8 ○	−12.5 −8.8 −7.5
280 Rem. 150 gr/9.7 g Ref. 17050	2900	2683	2475	2277	2802	2398	2041	1727	100 180 200	−0.7 −0.4 −0.3	−0.2 +0.4 +0.7	○ +1.2 +1.7	−1.0 +1.1 +1.5	−3.4 −0.8 ○	−12.4 −8.6 −7.4
7.5x55 Swiss 180 gr/11.6 g Ref. 17511	2650	2461	2277	2106	2807	2420	2072	1773	100 180 200	−0.6 −0.2 −0.1	−0.1 +0.7 +1.0	○ +1.6 +2.1	−1.4 +1.1 +1.8	−4.3 −1.0 ○	−15.3 −10.4 −8.9

NORMA BALLISTICS

Caliber Bullet weight Ref.	Velocity – Feet per sec.				Energy – Foot pounds				Sight at yards	Line of sights 1½ above center of bore. + indicates point of impact in inches above, – in inches below sighting point.					
	Muzzle	100 yards	200 yards	300 yards	Muzzle	100 yards	200 yards	300 yards		25 yards	50 yards	100 yards	150 yards	200 yards	300 yards
7.62 Russian 180 gr/11.6 g Ref. 17634	2575	2382	2211	2041	2650	2268	1954	1665	100 180 200	−0.6 −0.1 ±0	±0 +0.9 +1.2	O +1.7 +2.3	−1.5 +1.1 +2.0	−4.6 −1.1 O	−16.5 −11.2 −9.5
30–06 130 gr/8.4 g Ref. 17640	3205	2876	2561	2263	2966	2388	1894	1479	100 180 200	−0.8 −0.5 −0.4	−0.3 +0.2 +0.4	O +1.0 +1.4	−0.8 +0.7 +1.3	−2.7 −0.7 O	−10.8 −7.8 −6.7
30–06 150 gr/9.7 g Ref. 17643	2970	2680	2402	2141	2943	2393	1922	1527	100 180 200	−0.7 −0.4 −0.3	−0.2 +0.4 +0.6	O +1.3 +1.7	−1.0 +0.9 +1.5	−3.4 −0.9 O	−12.9 −9.1 −7.8
30–06 180 gr/11.6 g Ref. 17648	2700	2493	2297	2106	2914	2484	2109	1773	100 180 200	−0.6 −0.3 −0.1	−0.1 +0.7 +0.9	O +1.6 +2.1	−1.3 +1.0 +1.8	−4.1 −1.7 O	−14.9 −10.2 −8.7
30–06 180 gr/11.6 g Ref. 17649	2700	2513	2336	2152	2914	2524	2181	1851	100 180 200	−0.6 −0.3 −0.1	−0.1 +0.7 +0.9	O +1.5 +2.0	−1.3 +1.0 +1.8	−4.1 −1.0 O	−14.8 −10.2 −8.7
30–06 180 gr/11.6 g Ref. 17653	2700	2513	2336	2152	2914	2524	2181	1851	100 180 200	−0.6 −0.3 −0.1	−0.1 +0.7 +0.9	O +1.5 +2.0	−1.3 +1.0 +1.8	−4.1 −1.0 O	−14.8 −10.2 −8.7
30–30 Win. 150 gr/9.7 g Ref. 17630	2329	1998	1722	1486	1806	1330	988	735	100 130 200	−0.4 −0.3 +0.5	+0.2 +0.7 +2.1	O +0.9 +3.8	−2.6 −1.1 +3.3	−7.6 −5.8 O	−28.3 −25.6 −16.8
308 Win. 130 gr/8.4 g Ref. 17623	2900	2590	2300	2030	2428	1937	1527	1190	100 180 200	−0.7 −0.4 −0.2	−0.2 +0.5 +0.8	O +1.4 +1.9	−1.1 +1.0 +1.7	−3.7 −0.9 O	−14.2 −10.0 −8.6
308 Win. 150 gr/9.7 g Ref. 17624	2860	2570	2300	2050	2725	2200	1760	1400	100 180 200	−0.7 −0.3 −0.2	−0.2 +0.6 +0.8	O +1.4 +1.9	−1.2 +1.0 +1.7	−3.8 −1.0 O	−14.2 −10.0 −8.5
308 Win. 180 gr/11.6 g Ref. 17628	2610	2400	2210	2020	2725	2303	1952	1631	100 180 200	−0.6 −0.2 ±0	−0.1 +0.8 +1.1	O +1.7 +2.3	−1.4 +1.1 +1.9	−4.5 −1.1 O	−16.2 −11.0 −9.4
308 Win. 180 gr/11.6 g Ref. 17635	2610	2400	2210	2020	2725	2303	1952	1631	100 180 200	−0.6 −0.2 ±0	−0.1 +0.8 +1.1	O +1.7 +2.3	−1.4 +1.1 +1.9	−4.5 −1.1 O	−16.2 −11.0 −9.4
308 Win. 180 gr/11.6 g Ref. 17636	2610	2393	2185	1988	2725	2287	1906	1578	100 180 200	−0.6 −0.2 ±0	±0 +0.8 +1.1	O +1.7 +2.3	−1.5 +1.1 +2.0	−4.6 −1.1 O	−16.5 −11.3 −9.6
308 Norma M. 180 gr/11.6 g Ref. 17638	3020	2815	2618	2435	3646	3167	2739	2370	100 180 200	−0.8 −0.5 −0.4	−0.3 +0.2 +0.4	O +1.0 +1.3	−0.8 +0.7 +1.2	−2.6 −0.7 O	−10.1 −7.1 −6.1
7.65 Argentine 150 gr/9.7 g Ref. 17701	2789	2533	2290	2067	2591	2137	1747	1423	100 180 200	−0.7 −0.3 −0.2	−0.1 +0.6 +0.9	O +1.5 +2.0	−1.3 +1.0 +1.7	−4.1 −1.0 O	−14.8 −10.1 −8.7
303 British 150 gr/9.7 g Ref. 17712	2720	2440	2170	1930	2465	1983	1569	1241	100 180 200	−0.6 −0.2 −0.1	−0.1 +0.7 +1.0	O +1.7 +2.2	−1.4 +1.1 +1.9	−4.4 −1.1 O	−16.3 −11.3 −9.7
7.7 Jap. 130 gr/8.4 g Ref. 17721	2950	2635	2340	2065	2513	2004	1581	1231	100 180 200	−0.7 −0.4 −0.3	−0.2 +0.5 +0.7	O +1.3 +1.8	−1.1 +0.9 +1.6	−3.5 −0.9 O	−13.5 −9.5 −8.2
7.7 Jap. 180 gr/11.6 g Ref. 17722	2495	2292	2101	1922	2484	2100	1765	1477	100 130 200	−0.6 −0.4 +0.1	±0 +0.3 +1.3	O +0.6 +2.6	−1.7 −0.8 +2.2	−5.2 −3.9 O	−18.1 −16.3 −10.4
8x57 JS 196 gr/12.7 g Ref. 18003	2525	2195	1894	1627	2778	2097	1562	1152	100 130 200	−0.6 −0.4 +0.2	±0 +0.4 +1.5	O +0.7 +2.9	−1.8 −0.8 +2.5	−5.8 −4.4 O	−21.4 −19.3 −12.7
9.3x57 286 gr/18.5 g Ref. 19303	2065	1818	1595	1404	2714	2099	1616	1252	100 130 200	−0.3 ±0 +0.9	+0.4 +1.0 +2.7	O +1.1 +4.6	−3.1 −1.3 +3.8	−9.1 −6.8 O	−32.0 −28.5 −18.3
9.3x62 286 gr/18.5 g Ref. 19315	2360	2088	1815	1592	3544	2769	2092	1609	100 180 200	−0.5 +0.1 +0.3	+0.1 +1.4 +1.8	O +2.5 +3.3	−2.1 +1.6 +2.8	−6.5 −1.6 O	−23.5 −16.0 −13.7

REMINGTON BALLISTICS

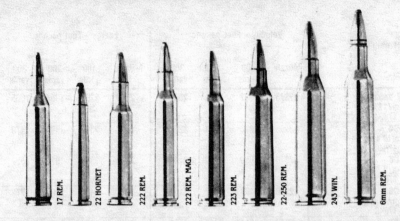

Remington Ballistics

CALIBERS	REMINGTON Order No.	BULLET Wt.-Grs.	BULLET Style	Primer No.
17 REM.	R17REM	25*	Hollow Point Power-Lokt®	7½
22 HORNET	R22HN1	45*	Pointed Soft Point	6½
	R22HN2	45	Hollow Point	6½
222 REM.	R222R1	50	Pointed Soft Point	7½
	R222R3	50*	Hollow Point Power-Lokt	7½
	R222R4	55	Metal Case	7½
222 REM. MAG.	R222M1	55*	Pointed Soft Point	7½
	R222M2	55	Hollow Point Power-Lokt	7½
223 REM.	R223R1	55	Pointed Soft Point	7½
	R223R2	55*	Hollow Point Power-Lokt	7½
	R223R3	55	Metal Case	7½
22-250 REM.	R22501	55*	Pointed Soft Point	9½
	R22502	55	Hollow Point Power-Lokt	9½
243 WIN.	R243W1	80	Pointed Soft Point	9½
	R243W2	80*	Hollow Point Power-Lokt	9½
	R243W3	100	Pointed Soft Point Core-Lokt®	9½
6mm REM.	R6MM1	80**	Pointed Soft Point	9½
	R6MM2	80**	Hollow Point Power-Lokt	9½
	R6MM4	100*	Pointed Soft Point Core-Lokt	9½
25-20 WIN.	R25202	86*	Soft Point	6½
250 SAV.	R250SV	100*	Pointed Soft Point	9½
257 ROBERTS	R257	117*	Soft Point Core-Lokt	9½
25-06 REM.	R25061	87	Hollow Point Power-Lokt	9½
	R25062	100*	Pointed Soft Point Core-Lokt	9½
	R25063	120	Pointed Soft Point Core-Lokt	9½
6.5mm REM. MAG.	R65MM2	120*	Pointed Soft Point Core-Lokt	9½M
264 WIN. MAG.	R264W2	140*	Pointed Soft Point Core-Lokt	9½M
270 WIN.	R270W1	100	Pointed Soft Point	9½
	R270W2	130*	Pointed Soft Point Core-Lokt	9½
	R270W3	130	Bronze Point	9½
	R270W4	150	Soft Point Core-Lokt	9½
7mm MAUSER (7x57)	R7MSR1	140*	Pointed Soft Point	9½
7mm-08 REM.	R7M081	140*	Pointed Soft Point	9½
280 REM.††	R280R3 ★	140	Pointed Soft Point	9½
	R280R1	150*	Pointed Soft Point Core-Lokt	9½
	R280R2	165*	Soft Point Core-Lokt	9½
7mm REM. MAG.	R7MM2	150*	Pointed Soft Point Core-Lokt	9½M
	R7MM3	175	Pointed Soft Point Core-Lokt	9½M
30 CARBINE	R30CAR	110*	Soft Point	6½
30 REM.	R30REM	170*	Soft Point Core-Lokt	9½
30-30 WIN. "ACCELERATOR"	R3030A	55*	Soft Point	9½
30-30 WIN.	R30301	150*	Soft Point Core-Lokt	9½
	R30302	170	Soft Point Core-Lokt	9½
	R30303	170	Hollow Point Core-Lokt	9½

REMINGTON BALLISTICS

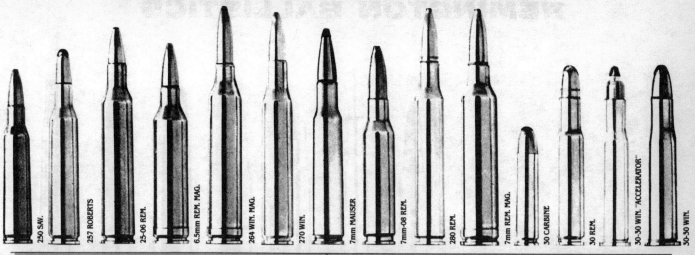

Cartridges shown (left to right): 250 SAV. · 257 ROBERTS · 25-06 REM. · 6.5mm REM. MAG. · 264 WIN. MAG. · 270 WIN. · 7mm MAUSER · 7mm-08 REM. · 280 REM. · 7mm REM. MAG. · 30 CARBINE · 30 REM. · 30-30 WIN. "ACCELERATOR" · 30-30 WIN.

TRAJECTORY†   0.0 Indicates yardage at which rifle was sighted in.

SHORT RANGE — Bullet does not rise more than one inch above line of sight from muzzle to sighting-in range.

LONG RANGE — Bullet does not rise more than three inches above line of sight from muzzle to sighting-in range.

VELOCITY FEET PER SECOND						ENERGY FOOT-POUNDS						SHORT RANGE						LONG RANGE							BARREL LENGTH
Muzzle	100	200	300	400	500	Muzzle	100	200	300	400	500	50	100	150	200	250	300	100	150	200	250	300	400	500	
4040	3284	2644	2086	1606	1235	906	599	388	242	143	85	0.1	0.5	0.0	-1.5	-4.2	-8.5	2.1	2.5	1.9	0.0	-3.4	-17.0	-44.3	24"
2690	2042	1502	1128	948	840	723	417	225	127	90	70	0.3	0.0	-2.4	-7.7	-16.9	-31.3	1.6	0.0	-4.5	-12.8	-26.4	-75.6	-163.4	
2690	2042	1502	1128	948	840	723	417	225	127	90	70	0.3	0.0	-2.4	-7.7	-16.9	-31.3	1.6	0.0	-4.5	-12.8	-26.4	-75.6	-163.4	24"
3140	2602	2123	1700	1350	1107	1094	752	500	321	202	136	0.5	0.9	0.0	-2.5	-6.9	-13.7	2.2	1.9	0.0	-3.8	-10.0	-32.3	-73.8	
3140	2635	2182	1777	1432	1172	1094	771	529	351	228	152	0.5	0.9	0.0	-2.4	-6.6	-13.1	2.1	1.8	0.0	-3.6	-9.5	-30.2	-68.1	
3020	2562	2147	1773	1451	1201	1114	801	563	384	257	176	0.6	1.0	0.0	-2.5	-7.0	-13.7	2.2	1.9	0.0	-3.8	-9.9	-31.0	-68.7	24"
3240	2748	2305	1906	1556	1272	1282	922	649	444	296	198	0.4	0.8	0.0	-2.2	-6.0	-11.8	1.9	1.6	0.0	-3.3	-8.5	-26.7	-59.5	
3240	2773	2352	1969	1627	1341	1282	939	675	473	323	220	0.4	0.8	0.0	-2.1	-5.8	-11.4	1.8	1.6	0.0	-3.2	-8.2	-25.5	-56.0	24"
3240	2747	2304	1905	1554	1270	1282	921	648	443	295	197	0.4	0.8	0.0	-2.2	-6.0	-11.8	1.9	1.6	0.0	-3.3	-8.5	-26.7	-59.6	
3240	2773	2352	1969	1627	1341	1282	939	675	473	323	220	0.4	0.8	0.0	-2.1	-5.8	-11.4	1.8	1.6	0.0	-3.2	-8.2	-25.5	-56.0	
3240	2759	2326	1933	1587	1301	1282	929	660	456	307	207	0.4	0.8	0.0	-2.1	-5.9	-11.6	1.9	1.6	0.0	-3.2	-8.4	-26.2	-57.9	24"
3680	3137	2656	2222	1832	1493	1654	1201	861	603	410	272	0.2	0.5	0.0	-1.6	-4.4	-8.7	2.3	2.6	1.9	0.0	-3.4	-15.9	-38.9	
3680	3209	2785	2400	2046	1725	1654	1257	947	703	511	363	0.2	0.5	0.0	-1.5	-4.1	-8.0	2.1	2.5	1.8	0.0	-3.1	-14.1	-33.4	24"
3350	2955	2593	2259	1951	1670	1993	1551	1194	906	676	495	0.3	0.7	0.0	-1.8	-4.9	-9.4	2.6	2.9	2.1	0.0	-3.6	-16.2	-37.9	
3350	2955	2593	2259	1951	1670	1993	1551	1194	906	676	495	0.3	0.7	0.0	-1.8	-4.9	-9.4	2.6	2.9	2.1	0.0	-3.6	-16.2	-37.9	
2960	2697	2449	2215	1993	1786	1945	1615	1332	1089	882	708	0.5	0.9	0.0	-2.2	-5.8	-11.0	1.9	1.6	0.0	-3.1	-7.8	-22.6	-46.3	24"
3470	3064	2694	2352	2036	1747	2139	1667	1289	982	736	542	0.3	0.6	0.0	-1.6	-4.5	-8.7	2.4	2.7	1.9	0.0	-3.3	-14.9	-35.0	
3470	3064	2694	2352	2036	1747	2139	1667	1289	982	736	542	0.3	0.6	0.0	-1.6	-4.5	-8.7	2.4	2.7	1.9	0.0	-3.3	-14.9	-35.0	
3100	2829	2573	2332	2104	1889	2133	1777	1470	1207	983	792	0.4	0.8	0.0	-1.9	-5.2	-9.9	1.7	1.5	0.0	-2.8	-7.0	-20.4	-41.7	24"
1460	1194	1030	931	858	797	407	272	203	165	141	121	0.0	-4.1	-14.4	-31.8	-57.3	-92.0	0.0	-8.2	-23.5	-47.0	-79.6	-175.9	-319.4	24"
2820	2504	2210	1936	1684	1461	1765	1392	1084	832	630	474		0.0	-1.6	-4.7	-9.6	-16.5	2.3	2.0	0.0	-3.7	-9.5	-28.3	-59.5	24"
2650	2291	1961	1663	1404	1199	1824	1363	999	718	512	373		0.0	-1.9	-5.8	-11.9	-20.7	2.9	2.4	0.0	-4.7	-12.0	-36.7	-79.2	24"
3440	2995	2591	2222	1884	1583	2286	1733	1297	954	686	484	0.3	0.6	0.0	-1.7	-4.8	-9.3	2.5	2.9	2.1	0.0	-3.6	-16.4	-39.1	
3230	2893	2580	2287	2014	1762	2316	1858	1478	1161	901	689	0.4	0.7	0.0	-1.9	-5.0	-9.7	1.6	1.4	0.0	-2.7	-6.9	-20.5	-42.7	
2990	2730	2484	2252	2032	1825	2382	1985	1644	1351	1100	887	0.5	0.8	0.0	-2.1	-5.6	-10.7	1.9	1.6	0.0	-3.0	-7.5	-22.0	-44.8	24"
3210	2905	2621	2353	2102	1867	2745	2248	1830	1475	1177	929	0.4	0.7	0.0	-1.8	-4.9	-9.5	2.7	3.0	2.1	0.0	-3.5	-15.5	-35.3	24"
3030	2782	2548	2326	2114	1914	2854	2406	2016	1682	1389	1139	0.5	0.8	0.0	-2.0	-5.4	-10.2	1.8	1.5	0.0	-2.9	-7.2	-20.8	-42.2	24"
3430	3021	2649	2305	1988	1699	2612	2027	1557	1179	877	641	0.3	0.6	0.0	-1.7	-4.6	-9.0	2.5	2.8	2.0	0.0	-3.4	-15.5	-36.4	
3060	2776	2510	2259	2022	1801	2702	2225	1818	1472	1180	936	0.5	0.8	0.0	-2.0	-5.5	-10.4	1.8	1.5	0.0	-2.9	-7.4	-21.6	-44.3	
3060	2802	2559	2329	2110	1904	2702	2267	1890	1565	1285	1046	0.4	0.8	0.0	-2.0	-5.3	-10.1	1.8	1.5	0.0	-2.8	-7.1	-20.6	-42.0	
2850	2504	2183	1886	1618	1385	2705	2087	1587	1185	872	639	0.7	1.0	0.0	-2.6	-7.1	-13.6	2.3	2.0	0.0	-3.8	-9.7	-29.2	-62.2	24"
2660	2435	2221	2018	1827	1648	2199	1843	1533	1266	1037	844	0.2	0.0	-1.7	-5.0	-10.0	-17.0	2.5	2.0	0.0	-3.6	-9.6	-27.7	-56.3	24"
2860	2625	2402	2189	1988	1798	2542	2142	1793	1490	1228	1005	0.6	0.9	0.0	-2.3	-6.1	-11.6	2.1	1.7	0.0	-3.2	-8.1	-23.5	-47.7	24"
3000	2758	2528	2309	2102	1905	2797	2363	1986	1657	1373	1128	0.5	0.8	0.0	-2.1	-5.5	-10.4	1.8	1.5	0.0	-2.9	-7.3	-21.1	-42.9	
2890	2624	2373	2135	1912	1705	2781	2293	1875	1518	1217	968	0.6	0.9	0.0	-2.3	-6.2	-11.8	2.1	1.7	0.0	-3.3	-8.3	-24.2	-49.7	
2820	2510	2220	1950	1701	1479	2913	2308	1805	1393	1060	801	0.2	0.0	-1.5	-4.6	-9.5	-16.4	2.3	1.9	0.0	-3.7	-9.4	-28.1	-58.8	24"
3110	2830	2568	2320	2085	1866	3320	2667	2196	1792	1448	1160	0.4	0.8	0.0	-1.9	-5.2	-9.9	1.7	1.5	0.0	-2.8	-7.0	-20.5	-42.1	
2860	2645	2440	2244	2057	1879	3178	2718	2313	1956	1644	1372	0.6	0.9	0.0	-2.3	-6.0	-11.5	2.0	1.7	0.0	-3.2	-7.9	-22.7	-45.8	24"
1990	1567	1236	1035	923	842	967	600	373	262	208	173	0.9	0.0	-4.5	-13.5	-28.3	-49.9	0.0	-4.5	-13.5	-28.3	-49.9	-118.6	-228.2	20"
2120	1822	1555	1328	1153	1036	1696	1253	913	666	502	405	0.7	0.0	-3.3	-9.7	-19.6	-33.8	2.2	0.0	-5.3	-14.1	-27.2	-69.0	-136.9	24"
3400	2693	2085	1570	1187	986	1412	886	521	301	172	119	0.4	0.8	0.0	-2.4	-6.7	-13.8	2.0		0.0	-3.8	-10.2	-35.0	-84.4	
2390	1973	1605	1303	1095	974	1902	1296	858	565	399	316	0.5	0.0	-2.7	-8.2	-17.0	-30.0	1.8	0.0	-4.6	-12.5	-24.6	-65.3	-134.9	
2200	1895	1619	1381	1191	1061	1827	1355	989	720	535	425	0.6	0.0	-3.0	-8.9	-18.0	-31.1	2.0	0.0	-4.8	-13.0	-25.1	-63.6	-126.7	
2200	1895	1619	1381	1191	1061	1827	1355	989	720	535	425	0.6	0.0	-3.0	-8.9	-18.0	-31.1	2.0	0.0	-4.8	-13.0	-25.1	-63.6	-126.7	24"

REMINGTON BALLISTICS

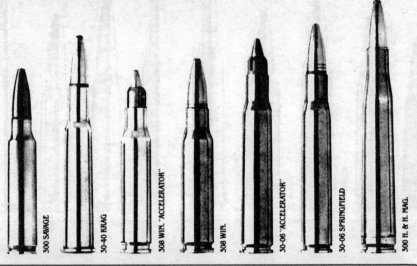

Remington Ballistics

CALIBERS	REMINGTON Order No.	BULLET Wt.-Grs.	BULLET Style	Primer No.
300 SAVAGE	R30SV3	180	Soft Point Core-Lokt	9½
	R30SV4	180*	Pointed Soft Point Core-Lokt	9½
30-40 KRAG	R30402	180*	Pointed Soft Point Core-Lokt	9½
308 WIN. "ACCELERATOR"	R308W5	55*	Pointed Soft Point	9½
308 WIN.	R308W1 ★	150*	Pointed Soft Point Core-Lokt	9½
	R308W6 ★	165	Pointed Soft Point Core-Lokt	9½
	R308W2	180	Soft Point Core-Lokt	9½
	R308W3	180	Pointed Soft Point Core-Lokt	9½
30-06 "ACCELERATOR"	R30069	55*	Pointed Soft Point	9½
30-06 SPRINGFIELD	R30061	125	Pointed Soft Point	9½
	R30062	150	Pointed Soft Point Core-Lokt	9½
	R30063	150	Bronze Point	9½
	R3006B	165*	Pointed Soft Point Core-Lokt	9½
	R30064	180	Soft Point Core-Lokt	9½
	R30065	180	Pointed Soft Point Core-Lokt	9½
	R30066	180	Bronze Point	9½
	R30067	220	Soft Point Core-Lokt	9½
300 H. & H. MAG.	R300HH	180*	Pointed Soft Point Core-Lokt	9½M
300 WIN. MAG.	R300W1	150	Pointed Soft Point Core-Lokt	9½M
	R300W2	180*	Pointed Soft Point Core-Lokt	9½M
303 BRITISH	R303B1	180*	Soft Point Core-Lokt	9½
32-20 WIN.	R32201	100	Lead	6½
	R32202	100*	Soft Point	6½
32 WIN. SPECIAL	R32WS2	170*	Soft Point Core-Lokt	9½
8mm MAUSER	R8MSR	170*	Soft Point Core-Lokt	9½
8mm REM. MAG.	R8MM1	185*	Pointed Soft Point Core-Lokt	9½M
	R8MM2	220	Pointed Soft Point Core-Lokt	9½M
35 REM.	R35R1	150	Pointed Soft Point Core-Lokt	9½
	R35R2	200*	Soft Point Core-Lokt	9½
350 REM. MAG.	R350M1	200*	Pointed Soft Point Core-Lokt	9½M
375 H. & H. MAG.	R375M1	270*	Soft Point	9½M
	R375M2	300	Metal Case	9½M
44-40 WIN.	R4440W	200*	Soft Point	2½
44 REM. MAG.	R44MG2	240	Soft Point	2½
	R44MG3	240	Semi-Jacketed Hollow Point	2½
444 MAR.	R444M	240	Soft Point	9½
	R444M2	265*	Soft Point	9½
45-70 GOVERNMENT	R4570G	405*	Soft Point	9½
458 WIN. MAG.	R458W1	500	Metal Case	9½M
	R458W2	500*	Soft Point	9½M

REMINGTON BALLISTICS

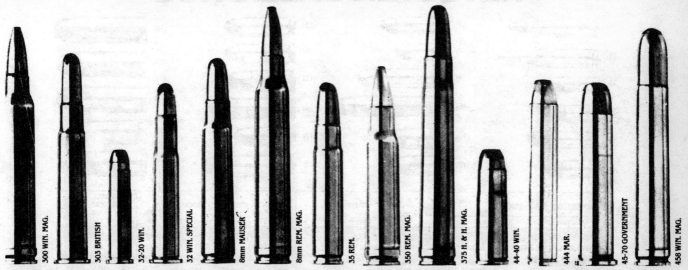

300 WIN. MAG. · 303 BRITISH · 32-20 WIN. · 32 WIN. SPECIAL · 8mm MAUSER · 8mm REM. MAG. · 35 REM. · 350 REM. MAG. · 375 H. & H. MAG. · 44-40 WIN. · 444 MAR. · 45-70 GOVERNMENT · 458 WIN. MAG.

TRAJECTORY† 0.0 indicates yardage at which rifle was sighted in.

SHORT RANGE — Bullet does not rise more than one inch above line of sight from muzzle to sighting-in range.

LONG RANGE — Bullet does not rise more than three inches above line of sight from muzzle to sighting-in range.

\	VELOCITY FEET PER SECOND						ENERGY FOOT-POUNDS						SHORT RANGE						LONG RANGE							BARREL LENGTH
	Muzzle	100 Yds.	200 Yds.	300 Yds.	400 Yds.	500 Yds.	Muzzle	100 Yds.	200 Yds.	300 Yds.	400 Yds.	500 Yds.	50 Yds.	100 Yds.	150 Yds.	200 Yds.	250 Yds.	300 Yds.	100 Yds.	150 Yds.	200 Yds.	250 Yds.	300 Yds.	400 Yds.	500 Yds.	
	2350	2025	1728	1467	1252	1098	2207	1639	1193	860	626	482	0.5	0.0	-2.6	-7.7	-15.6	-27.1	1.7	0.0	-4.2	-11.3	-21.9	-55.8	-112.0	24"
	2350	2137	1935	1745	1570	1413	2207	1825	1496	1217	985	798	0.4	0.0	-2.3	-6.7	-13.5	-22.8	1.5	0.0	-3.6	-9.6	-18.2	-44.1	-84.2	
	2430	2213	2007	1813	1632	1468	2360	1957	1610	1314	1064	861	0.4	0.0	-2.1	-6.2	-12.5	-21.1	1.4	0.0	-3.4	-8.9	-16.8	-40.9	-78.1	24"
	3770	3215	2726	2286	1888	1541	1735	1262	907	638	435	290	0.2	0.5	0.0	-1.5	-4.2	-8.2	2.2	2.5	1.8	0.0	-3.2	-15.0	-36.7	24"
	2820	2533	2263	2009	1774	1560	2648	2137	1705	1344	1048	810	0.2	0.0	-1.5	-4.5	-9.3	-15.9	2.3	1.9	0.0	-3.6	-9.1	-26.9	-55.7	24"
	2700	2440	2194	1963	1748	1551	2670	2180	1763	1411	1119	881	0.2	0.0	-1.7	-5.0	-10.1	-17.2	2.5	2.1	0.0	-3.9	-9.7	-28.5	-58.8	
	2620	2274	1955	1666	1414	1212	2743	2066	1527	1109	799	587	0.3	0.0	-2.0	-5.9	-12.1	-20.9	2.9	2.4	0.0	-4.7	-12.1	-36.9	-79.1	
	2620	2393	2178	1974	1782	1604	2743	2288	1896	1557	1269	1028	0.2	0.0	-1.8	-5.2	-10.4	-17.7	2.6	2.1	0.0	-4.0	-9.9	-28.9	-58.8	
	4080	3485	2965	2502	2083	1709	2033	1483	1074	764	530	356	0.4	1.0	0.9	0.0	-1.9	-5.0	1.8	2.1	1.5	0.0	-2.7	-12.5	-30.5	24"
	3140	2780	2447	2138	1853	1595	2736	2145	1662	1269	953	706	0.4	0.8	0.0	-2.1	-5.6	-10.7	1.8	1.5	0.0	-3.0	-7.7	-23.0	-48.5	24"
	2910	2617	2342	2083	1843	1622	2820	2281	1827	1445	1131	876	0.6	0.9	0.0	-2.3	-6.3	-12.0	2.1	1.8	0.0	-3.3	-8.5	-25.0	-51.8	
	2910	2656	2416	2189	1974	1773	2820	2349	1944	1596	1298	1047	0.6	0.9	0.0	-2.2	-6.0	-11.4	2.0	1.7	0.0	-3.2	-8.0	-23.5	-47.5	
	2800	2534	2283	2047	1825	1621	2872	2352	1909	1534	1220	963	0.7	1.0	0.0	-2.5	-6.7	-12.7	2.3	1.9	0.0	-3.6	-9.0	-26.3	-54.1	
	2700	2348	2023	1727	1466	1251	2913	2203	1635	1192	859	625	0.2	0.0	-1.8	-5.5	-11.2	-19.5	2.7	2.3	0.0	-4.4	-11.3	-34.4	-73.7	
	2700	2469	2250	2042	1846	1663	2913	2436	2023	1666	1362	1105	0.2	0.0	-1.6	-4.8	-9.7	-16.5	2.4	2.0	0.0	-3.7	-9.3	-27.0	-54.9	
	2700	2485	2280	2084	1899	1725	2913	2468	2077	1736	1441	1189	0.2	0.0	-1.6	-4.7	-9.6	-16.2	2.4	2.0	0.0	-3.6	-9.1	-26.2	-53.0	
	2410	2130	1870	1632	1422	1246	2837	2216	1708	1301	988	758	0.4	0.0	-2.3	-6.8	-13.8	-23.6	1.5	0.0	-3.7	-9.9	-19.0	-47.4	-93.1	
	2880	2640	2412	2196	1990	1798	3315	2785	2325	1927	1583	1292	0.6	0.9	0.0	-2.3	-6.0	-11.5	2.1	1.7	0.0	-3.2	-8.0	-23.3	-47.4	24"
	3290	2951	2636	2342	2068	1813	3605	2900	2314	1827	1424	1095	0.3	0.7	0.0	-1.8	-4.8	-9.3	2.6	2.9	2.1	0.0	-3.5	-15.4	-35.5	24"
	2960	2745	2540	2344	2157	1979	3501	3011	2578	2196	1859	1565	0.2	0.0	-2.1	-5.5	-10.4		1.9	1.6	0.0	-2.9	-7.3	-20.9	-41.9	
	2460	2124	1817	1542	1311	1137	2418	1803	1319	950	687	517	0.4	0.0	-2.3	-6.9	-14.1	-24.4	1.5	0.0	-3.8	-10.2	-19.8	-50.5	-101.5	24"
	1210	1021	913	834	769	712	325	231	185	154	131	113	0.0	-6.3	-20.9	-44.9	-79.3	-125.1	0.0	-11.5	-32.3	-63.8	-106.3	-230.3	-413.5	24"
	1210	1021	913	834	769	712	325	231	185	154	131	113	0.0	-6.3	-20.9	-44.9	-79.3	-125.1	0.0	-11.5	-32.3	-63.8	-106.3	-230.3	-413.5	
	2250	1921	1626	1372	1175	1044	1911	1393	998	710	521	411	0.6	0.0	-2.9	-8.6	-17.6	-30.5	1.9	0.0	-4.7	-12.7	-24.7	-63.2	-126.9	24"
	2360	1969	1622	1333	1123	997	2102	1463	993	671	476	375	0.5	0.0	-2.7	-8.2	-17.0	-29.8	1.8	0.0	-4.5	-12.4	-24.3	-63.8	-130.7	24"
	3080	2761	2464	2186	1927	1688	3896	3131	2494	1963	1525	1170	0.5	0.8	0.0	-2.1	-5.6	-10.7	1.8	1.6	0.0	-3.0	-7.6	-22.5	-46.8	24"
	2830	2581	2346	2123	1913	1716	3912	3254	2688	2201	1787	1438	0.6	1.0	0.0	-2.4	-6.4	-12.1	2.2	1.8	0.0	-3.4	-8.5	-24.7	-50.5	
	2300	1874	1506	1218	1039	934	1762	1169	755	494	359	291	0.6	0.0	-3.0	-9.2	-19.1	-33.9	2.0	0.0	-5.1	-14.1	-27.8	-74.0	-152.3	24"
	2080	1698	1376	1140	1001	911	1921	1280	841	577	445	369	0.8	0.0	-3.8	-11.3	-23.5	-41.2	2.5	0.0	-6.3	-17.1	-33.6	-87.7	-176.4	
	2710	2410	2130	1870	1631	1421	3261	2579	2014	1553	1181	897	0.2	0.0	-1.7	-5.1	-10.4	-17.9	2.6	2.1	0.0	-4.0	-10.3	-30.5	-64.0	20"
	2690	2420	2166	1928	1707	1507	4337	3510	2812	2228	1747	1361	0.2	0.0	-1.7	-5.1	-10.3	-17.6	2.5	2.1	0.0	-3.9	-10.0	-29.4	-60.7	24"
	2530	2171	1843	1551	1307	1126	4263	3139	2262	1602	1138	844	0.3	0.0	-2.2	-6.5	-13.5	-23.4	1.5	0.0	-3.6	-9.8	-19.1	-49.1	-99.5	
	1190	1006	900	822	756	699	629	449	360	300	254	217	0.0	-6.5	-21.6	-46.3	-81.8	-129.1	0.0	-11.8	-33.3	-65.5	-109.5	-237.4	-426.2	24"
	1760	1380	1114	970	878	806	1650	1015	661	501	411	346	0.0	-2.7	-10.0	-23.0	-43.0	-71.2	0.0	-5.9	-17.6	-36.3	-63.1	-145.5	-273.0	20"
	1760	1380	1114	970	878	806	1650	1015	661	501	411	346	0.0	-2.7	-10.0	-23.0	-43.0	-71.2	0.0	-5.9	-17.6	-36.3	-63.1	-145.5	-273.0	
	2350	1815	1377	1087	941	846	2942	1755	1010	630	472	381	0.6	0.0	-3.2	-9.9	-21.3	-38.5	2.1	0.0	-5.6	-15.9	-32.1	-87.8	-182.7	24"
	2120	1733	1405	1160	1012	920	2644	1768	1162	791	603	498	0.7	0.0	-3.6	-10.8	-22.5	-39.5	2.4	0.0	-6.0	-16.4	-32.2	-84.3	-170.2	
	1330	1168	1055	977	918	869	1590	1227	1001	858	758	679	0.0	-4.7	-15.8	-34.0	-60.0	-94.5	0.0	-8.7	-24.6	-48.2	-80.3	-172.4	-505.9	24"
	2040	1823	1623	1442	1237	1161	4620	3689	2924	2308	1839	1469	0.7	0.0	-3.3	-9.6	-19.2	-32.5	2.2	0.0	-5.2	-13.6	-25.8	-63.2	-121.7	24"
	2040	1770	1527	1319	1157	1046	4712	3547	2640	1970	1516	1239	0.8	0.0	-3.5	-10.3	-20.8	-35.6	2.4	0.0	-5.6	-14.9	-28.5	-71.5	-140.4	

REMINGTON PISTOL & REVOLVER BALLISTICS

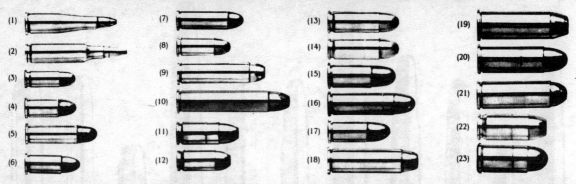

Remington Ballistics		Primer No.	Wt.· Grs.	BULLET		VELOCITY (FPS)			ENERGY (FT LB)			MID-RANGE TRAJECTORY		BARREL LENGTH
CALIBER	Order No.				Style	Muzzle	50 Yds.	100 Yds.	Muzzle	50 Yds.	100 Yds.	50 Yds.	100 Yds.	
(1) 22 REM. "JET" MAG.	R22JET	6½	40*	Soft Point		2100	1790	1510	390	285	200	0.3"	1.4"	8⅜"
(2) 221 REM. "FIRE BALL"	R221F	7½	50*	Pointed Soft Point		2650	2380	2130	780	630	505	0.2"	0.8"	10½"
(3) 25 (6.35mm) AUTO. PISTOL	R25AP	1½	50*	Metal Case		760	707	659	64	56	48	2.0"	8.7"	2"
(4) 32 S. & W.	R32SW	5½	88*	Lead		680	645	610	90	81	73	2.5"	10.5"	3"
(5) 32 S. & W. LONG	R32SWL	1½	98*	Lead		705	670	635	115	98	88	2.3"	10.5"	4"
(6) 32 SHORT COLT	R32SC	1½	80*	Lead		745	665	590	100	79	62	2.2"	9.9"	4"
(7) 32 LONG COLT	R32LC	1½	82*	Lead		755	715	675	100	93	83	2.0"	8.7"	4"
(8) 32 (7.65mm) AUTO. PISTOL	R32AP	1½	71*	Metal Case		905	855	810	129	115	97	1.4"	5.8"	4"
(9) 357 MAG. Vented Barrel	R357M7	5½	110	Semi-Jacketed H.P.		1295	1094	975	410	292	232	0.8"	3.5"	4"
	R357M1	5½	125	Semi-Jacketed H.P.		1450	1240	1090	583	427	330	0.6"	2.8"	4"
	R357M8	5½	125	Semi-Jacketed S.P.		1450	1240	1090	583	427	330	0.6"	2.8"	4"
	R357M2	5½	158	Semi-Jacketed H.P.		1235	1104	1015	535	428	361	0.8"	3.5"	4"
	R357M3	5½	158	Soft Point		1235	1104	1015	535	428	361	0.8"	3.5"	4"
	R357M4	5½	158	Metal Point		1235	1104	1015	535	428	361	0.8"	3.5"	4"
	R357M5	5½	158	Lead		1235	1104	1015	535	428	361	0.8"	3.5"	4"
	R357M6	5½	158	Lead (Brass Case)		1235	1104	1015	535	428	361	0.8"	3.5"	4"
(10) 357 REM. "MAXIMUM"**	357MX1	7½	158	Semi-Jacketed H.P.		1825	1588	1381	1168	885	669	0.4"	1.7"	10½"
	357MX3	7½	180	Semi-Jacketed H.P.		1555	1328	1154	966	705	532	0.5"	2.5"	10½"
(11) 9mm LUGER AUTO. PISTOL	R9MM1	1½	115*	Jacketed H.P.		1155	1047	971	341	280	241	0.9"	3.9"	4"
	R9MM2	1½	124	Metal Case		1110	1030	971	339	292	259	1.0"	4.1"	4"
(12) 380 AUTO. PISTOL	R380AP	1½	95	Metal Case		955	865	785	190	160	130	1.4"	5.9"	4"
	R380A1	1½	88*	Jacketed H.P.		990	920	868	191	165	146	1.2"	5.1"	4"
(13) 38 AUTO. COLT PISTOL (A)	R38ACP	1½	130*	Metal Case		1040	980	925	310	275	245	1.0"	4.7"	4½"
(14) 38 SUPER AUTO. COLT PISTOL (B)	R38SU1	1½	115*	Jacketed H.P. (+P)†		1300	1147	1041	431	336	277	0.7"	3.3"	5"
	R38SUP	1½	130	Metal Case (+P)†		1215	1099	1017	426	348	298	0.8"	3.6"	5"
(15) 38 S. & W.	R38SW	1½	146*	Lead		685	650	620	150	135	125	2.4"	10.0"	4"
(16) 38 SPECIAL Vented Barrel	R38S1	1½	95	Semi-Jacketed H.P. (+P)†		1175	1044	959	291	230	194	0.9"	3.9"	4"
	R38S10	1½	110	Semi-Jacketed H.P. (+P)†		995	926	871	242	210	185	1.2"	5.1"	4"
	R38S2	1½	125	Semi-Jacketed H.P. (+P)†		945	898	858	248	224	204	1.3"	5.4"	4"
	R38S13	1½	125	Semi-Jacketed S.P. (+P)†		945	908	875	248	229	212	1.3"	5.3"	4"
	R38S3	1½	148	"Targetmaster" Lead W.C.		710	634	566	166	132	105	2.4"	10.8"	4"
	R38S4	1½	158	"Targetmaster" Lead		755	723	692	200	183	168	2.0"	8.3"	4"
	R38S5	1½	158*	Lead (Round Nose)		755	723	692	200	183	168	2.0"	8.3"	4"
	R38S14★	1½	158	Semi-Wadcutter (+P)		890	855	823	278	257	238	1.4"	6.0"	4"
	R38S6	1½	158	Semi-Wadcutter		755	723	692	200	183	168	2.0"	8.3"	4"
	R38S7	1½	158	Metal Point		755	723	692	200	183	168	2.0"	8.3"	4"
	R38S8	1½	158	Lead (+P)†		890	855	823	278	257	238	1.4"	6.0"	4"
	R38S12	1½	158	Lead H.P. (+P)†		890	855	823	278	257	238	1.4"	6.0"	4"
	R38S9	1½	200	Lead		635	614	594	179	168	157	2.8"	11.5"	4"
(17) 38 SHORT COLT	R38SC	1½	125*	Lead		730	685	645	150	130	115	2.2"	9.4"	6"
(18) 41 REM. MAG. Vented Barrel	R41MG1	2½	210*	Soft Point		1300	1162	1062	788	630	526	0.7"	3.2"	4"
	R41MG2	2½	210	Lead		965	898	842	434	376	331	1.3"	5.4"	4"
(19) 44 REM. MAG. Vented Barrel	R44MG5	2½	180*	Semi-Jacketed H.P.		1610	1365	1175	1036	745	551	0.5"	2.3"	4"
	R44MG1	2½	240	Lead Gas Check		1350	1186	1069	971	749	608	0.7"	3.1"	4"
	R44MG2	2½	240	Soft Point		1180	1081	1010	741	623	543	0.9"	3.7"	4"
	R44MG3	2½	240	Semi-Jacketed H.P.		1180	1081	1010	741	623	543	0.9"	3.7"	4"
	R44MG4	2½	240	Lead (Med. Vel.)		1000	947	902	533	477	433	1.1"	4.8"	6½"
(20) 44 S. & W. SPECIAL	R44SW	2½	246*	Lead		755	725	695	310	285	265	2.0"	8.3"	6½"
	R44SW1★	2½	200	Semi-Wadcutter		1035	938	866	475	391	333	1.1"	4.9"	6½"
(21) 45 COLT	R45C	2½	250*	Lead		860	820	780	410	375	340	1.6"	6.6"	5½"
(22) 45 AUTO.	R45AP1	2½	185	Metal Case Wadcutter		770	707	650	244	205	174	2.0"	8.7"	5"
	R45AP2	2½	185*	Jacketed H.P.		940	890	846	363	325	294	1.3"	5.5"	5"
	R45AP4	2½	230	Metal Case		810	776	745	335	308	284	1.7"	7.2"	5"
(23) 45 AUTO. RIM	R45AR	2½	230*	Lead		810	770	730	335	305	270	1.8"	7.4"	5½"
38 S. & W.	R38SWBL	1½	– *	Blank		–	–	–	–	–	–	–	–	–
32 S. & W.	R32BLNK	5½	–	Blank		–	–	–	–	–	–	–	–	–
38 SPECIAL	R38BLNK	1½	–	Blank		–	–	–	–	–	–	–	–	–

†Ammunition with (+P) on the case headstamp is loaded to higher pressure. Use only in firearms designated for this cartridge and so recommended by the gun manufacturer.
*Illustrated (not shown in actual size). **Will not chamber in 357 Mag. or 38 Special handguns. ★New for 1986.

(A) Adapted only for .38 Colt sporting, military and pocket model automatic pistols. These pistols were discontinued after 1928.

(B) Adapted only for .38 Colt Super and Colt Commander automatic pistols. Not for use in sporting, military and pocket models.

WINCHESTER BALLISTICS
CENTERFIRE PISTOL AND REVOLVER

Cartridge	Symbol	Bullet Wt. Grs.	Type	Velocity (fps) Muzzle	Velocity (fps) 50 Yds.	Velocity (fps) 100 Yds.	Energy (ft-lbs.) Muzzle	Energy (ft-lbs.) 50 Yds.	Energy (ft-lbs.) 100 Yds.	Mid Range Traj. (in.) 50 Yds.	Mid Range Traj. (in.) 100 Yds.	Barrel Length Inches
25 Automatic (6.35mm) Expanding Point Super-X	X25AXP	45	XP**	815	729	655	66	53	42	1.8	7.7	2
25 Automatic (6.35mm) Full Metal Case Super-X	X25AP	50	FMC	760	707	659	64	56	48	2.0	8.7	2
30 Luger (7.65mm) Full Metal Case Super-X	X30LP	93	FMC	1220	1110	1040	305	255	225	0.9	3.5	4½
# 30 Carbine Hollow Soft Point Super-X	X30M1	110	HSP	1790	1601	1430	783	626	500	0.4	1.7	10
# 30 Carbine Full Metal Case Super-X	X30M2	110	FMC	1740	1552	1384	740	588	468	0.4	1.8	10
32 Smith & Wesson Lead Round Nose Super-X (Inside Lubricated)	X32SWP	85	Lead-RN	680	645	610	90	81	73	2.5	10.5	3
32 Smith & Wesson Long (Colt New Police) Lead Round Nose Super-X (Inside Lubricated)	X32SWLP	98	Lead-RN	705	670	635	115	98	88	2.3	10.5	4
32 Short Colt Lead Round Nose Super-X (Greased)	X32SCP	80	Lead-RN	745	665	590	100	79	62	2.2	9.9	4
32 Long Colt Lead Round Nose Super-X (Inside Lubricated)	X32LCP	82	Lead-RN	755	715	675	105	93	83	2.0	8.7	4
32 Automatic Silvertip Hollow Point Super-X	X32ASHP	60	STHP	970	895	835	125	107	93	1.3	5.4	4
32 Automatic Full Metal Case Super-X	X32AP	71	FMC	905	855	810	129	115	97	1.4	5.8	4
38 Smith & Wesson Lead Round Nose Super-X (Inside Lubricated)	X38SWP	145	Lead-RN	685	650	620	150	135	125	2.4	10.0	4
380 Automatic Silvertip Hollow Point Super-X	X380ASHP	85	STHP	1000	921	860	189	160	140	1.2	5.1	3¾
380 Automatic Full Metal Case Super-X	X380AP	95	FMC	955	865	785	190	160	130	1.4	5.9	3¾
38 Special Silvertip Hollow Point Super-X	X38S9HP	110	STHP	945	894	850	218	195	176	1.3	5.4	4V
38 Special Lead Round Nose Super-X (Inside Lubricated)	X38S1P	158	Lead-RN	755	723	693	200	183	168	2.0	8.3	4V
38 Special Lead Semi-Wad Cutter Super-X (Inside Lubricated)	X38WCPSV	158	Lead-SWC	755	721	689	200	182	167	2.0	8.4	4V
38 Special Metal Point Super-X (Inside Lubricated) (Lead Bearing)	X38S2P	158	Met. Pt.	755	723	693	200	183	168	2.0	8.3	4V
38 Special Silvertip Hollow Point + P Super-X	X38SSHP	95	STHP	1100	1002	932	255	212	183	1.0	4.3	4V
38 Special Jacketed Hollow Point + P Super-X	X38S6PH	110	JHP	995	926	871	242	210	185	1.2	5.1	4V
# 38 Special Jacketed Hollow Point + P Super-X	X38S7PH	125	JHP	945	898	858	248	224	204	1.3	5.4	4V
# 38 Special Silvertip Hollow Point + P Super-X	X38S8HP	125	STHP	945	898	858	248	224	204	1.3	5.4	4V
38 Special Lead Hollow Point + P Super-X (Inside Lubricated)	X38SPD	158	Lead-HP	890	855	823	278	257	238	1.4	6.0	4V
38 Special Lead Semi-Wad Cutter + P Super-X (Inside Lubricated)	X38WCP	158	Lead-SWC	890	855	823	278	257	238	1.4	6.0	4V
38 Special Match Lead Mid-Range (Clean Cutting) Mach (Inside Lubricated)	X38SMRP	148	Lead-WC	710	634	566	166	132	105	2.4	10.8	4V
9mm Luger (Parabellum) Full Metal Case Super-X	X9LP	115	FMC	1155	1047	971	341	280	241	0.9	3.9	4
9mm Luger (Parabellum) Silvertip Hollow Point Super-X	X9MMSHP	115	STHP	1225	1095	1007	383	306	259	0.8	3.6	4
* 38 Super Automatic Silvertip Hollow Point + P Super-X	X38ASHP	125	STHP	1240	1130	1050	427	354	306	0.8	3.4	5
* 38 Super Automatic Full Metal Case + P Super-X	X38A1P	130	FMC	1215	1099	1017	426	348	298	0.8	3.6	5
38 Automatic (For all 38 Automatic Pistols) Full Metal Case Super-X	X38A2P	130	FMC	1040	980	925	310	275	245	1.0	4.7	4½
# 357 Magnum Jacketed Hollow Point Super-X	X3573P	110	JHP	1295	1095	975	410	292	232	0.8	3.5	4V
# 357 Magnum Jacketed Hollow Point Super-X	X3576P	125	JHP	1450	1240	1090	583	427	330	0.6	2.8	4V
# 357 Magnum Silvertip Hollow Point Super-X	X357SHP	145	STHP	1290	1155	1060	535	428	361	0.8	3.5	4V
# 357 Magnum Lead Semi-Wad Cutter Super-X (Inside Lubricated)	X3571P	158	Lead-SWC**	1235	1104	1015	535	428	361	0.8	3.5	4V
# 357 Magnum Jacketed Hollow Point Super-X	X3574P	158	JHP	1235	1104	1015	535	428	361	0.8	3.5	4V
# 357 Magnum Jacketed Soft Point Super-X	X3575P	158	JSP	1235	1104	1015	535	428	361	0.8	3.5	4V
9mm Winchester Magnum Full Metal Case Super-X	X9MMWM	115	FMC	1475	1264	1109	555	408	314	0.6	2.7	5
# 41 Remington Magnum Silvertip Hollow Point Super-X	X41MSTHP	175	STHP	1250	1120	1029	607	488	412	0.8	3.4	4V
# 41 Remington Magnum Lead Semi-Wad Cutter Super-X	X41MP	210	Lead-SWC	965	898	842	434	376	331	1.3	5.4	4V
# 41 Remington Magnum Jacketed Soft Point Super-X	X41MJSP	210	JSP	1300	1162	1062	788	630	526	0.7	3.2	4V
# 41 Remington Magnum Jacketed Hollow Point Super-X	X41MHP	210	JHP	1300	1162	1062	788	630	526	0.7	3.2	4V
# 44 Smith & Wesson Special Silvertip Hollow Point Super-X	X44STHPS	200	STHP	900	860	822	360	328	300	1.4	5.9	6½
# 44 Smith & Wesson Special Lead Round Nose Super-X (Inside Lubricated)	X44SP	246	Lead-RN	755	725	695	310	285	265	2.0	8.3	6½
# 44 Remington Magnum Silvertip Hollow Point Super-X	X44MSTHP	210	STHP	1250	1106	1010	729	570	475	0.8	3.5	4V
# 44 Remington Magnum Lead Semi-Wad Cutter (Med. Vel.) Super-X (Inside Lubricated)	X44MWCP	240	Lead-SWC	1000	937	885	533	468	417	1.2	4.9	6½V
44 Remington Magnum Lead Semi-Wad Cutter (Gas Check) Super-X	X44MP	240	Lead-SWC	1350	1186	1069	971	749	608	0.7	3.1	4V
45 Automatic Silvertip Hollow Point Super-X	X45ASHP5	185	STHP	1000	938	888	411	362	324	1.2	4.9	5
45 Automatic Full Metal Case Super-X	X45A1P	230	FMC	810	776	745	335	308	284	1.7	7.2	5
45 Automatic Super-Match Full Metal Case Semi-Wad Cutter	X45AWCP	185	FMC-SWC	770	707	650	244	205	174	2.0	8.7	5
# 45 Colt Silvertip Hollow Point Super-X	X45CSHP	225	STHP	920	877	839	423	384	352	1.4	5.6	5½
# 45 Colt Lead Round Nose Super-X (Inside Lubricated)	X45CP	255	Lead-RN	860	820	780	420	380	345	1.5	6.1	5½
# 45 Winchester Magnum Full Metal Case Super-X (Not for Arms Chambered for Standard 45 Automatic)	X45WM	230	FMC	1400	1232	1107	1001	775	636	0.6	2.8	5

CENTERFIRE BLANK CARTRIDGES

Cartridge	Symbol	Type
32 Smith & Wesson Black Powder	32BL2P	Black Powder
38 Smith & Wesson Smokeless Powder	38BLP	Smokeless Powder
38 Special Smokeless Powder	38SBLP	Smokeless Powder

FMC-Full Metal Case • JHP-Jacketed Hollow Point • JSP-Jacketed Soft Point.
LHP-Lubaloy Hollow Point • RN-Round Nose
Met. Pt.-Metal Point • XP-Expanding Point • WC-Wad Cutter • SWC-Semi Wad Cutter
STHP-Silvertip Hollow Point • HP-Hollow Point
L-Lubaloy   ** Wax Coated
HSP - Hollow Soft Point

+ P Ammunition with (+ P) on the case head stamp is loaded to higher pressure. Use only in firearms designated for this cartridge and so recommended by the gun manufacturer.
V-Data is based on velocity obtained from 4' vented test barrels for revolver cartridges (38 Special, 357 Magnum, 41 Rem. Mag. and 44 Rem. Mag.)
*For use only in 38 Super Automatic Pistols.
Acceptable for use in rifles also.

Specifications are nominal. Test barrels are used to determine ballistics figures. Individual firearms may differ from test barrel statistics. Specifications subject to change without notice.

WINCHESTER BALLISTICS
CENTERFIRE RIFLE

Cartridge	Symbol	Game Selector Guide	Bullet Wt. Grs.	Type	Barrel Length Inches	Muzzle	100	200	300	400	500
218 Bee Super-X	X218B	V	46	HP	24	2760	2102	1550	1155	961	850
22 Hornet Super-X	X22H1	V	45	SP	24	2690	2042	1502	1128	948	840
22 Hornet Super-X	X22H2	V	46	HP	24	2690	2042	1502	1128	948	841
22-250 Remington Super-X	X222501	V	55	PSP	24	3680	3137	2656	2222	1832	1493
222 Remington Super-X	X222R	V	50	PSP	24	3140	2602	2123	1700	1350	1107
222 Remington Super-X	X222R1	V	55	FMC	24	3020	2675	2355	2057	1783	1537
223 Remington Super-X	X223RH	V	53	HP	24	3330	2882	2477	2106	1770	1475
223 Remington Super-X	X223R	V	55	PSP	24	3240	2747	2304	1905	1554	1270
223 Remington Super-X	X223R1	V	55	FMC	24	3240	2877	2543	2232	1943	1679
225 Winchester Super-X	X2251	V	55	PSP	24	3570	3066	2616	2208	1838	1514
243 Winchester Super-X	X2431	V	80	PSP	24	3350	2955	2593	2259	1951	1670
243 Winchester Super-X	X2432	D,O/P	100	PP	24	2960	2697	2449	2215	1993	1786
6mm Remington Super-X	X6MMR1	V	80	PSP	24	3470	3064	2694	2352	2036	1747
6mm Remington Super-X	X6MMR2	D,O/P	100	PP	24	3100	2829	2573	2332	2104	1889
25-06 Remington Super-X	X25061	V	90	PEP	24	3440	3043	2680	2344	2034	1749
25-06 Remington Super-X	X25062	D,O/P	120	PEP	24	2990	2730	2484	2252	2032	1825
# 25-20 Winchester Super-X	X25202	V	86	SP	24	1460	1194	1030	931	858	798
25-35 Winchester Super-X	X2535	D	117	SP	24	2230	1866	1545	1282	1097	984
† 250 Savage Super-X	X2501	V	87	PSP	24	3030	2673	2342	2036	1755	1504
250 Savage Super-X	X2503	D,O/P	100	ST	24	2820	2467	2140	1839	1569	1339
† # 256 Winchester Mag. Super-X	X2561P	V	60	HP	24	2760	2097	1542	1149	957	846
257 Roberts + P Super-X	X257P2	D,O/P	100	ST	24	3000	2633	2295	1982	1697	1447
257 Roberts + P Super-X	X257P3	D,O/P	117	PP	24	2780	2411	2071	1761	1488	1263
† 264 Winchester Mag. Super-X	X2641	V	100	PSP	24	3320	2926	2565	2231	1923	1644
264 Winchester Mag. Super-X	X2642	D,O/P	140	PP	24	3030	2782	2548	2326	2114	1914
270 Winchester Super-X	X2701	V	100	PSP	24	3430	3021	2649	2305	1988	1699
270 Winchester Super-X	X2705	D,O/P	130	PP	24	3060	2802	2559	2329	2110	1904
270 Winchester Super-X	X2703	D,O/P	130	ST	24	3060	2776	2510	2259	2022	1801
270 Winchester Super-X	X2704	D,M	150	PP	24	2850	2585	2336	2100	1879	1673
284 Winchester Super-X	X2841	D,O/P	125	PP	24	3140	2829	2538	2265	2010	1772
284 Winchester Super-X	X2842	D,O/P,M	150	PP	24	2860	2595	2344	2108	1886	1680
7mm Mauser (7 × 57) Super-X	X7MM1	D	175	SP	24	2440	2137	1857	1603	1382	1204
7mm Remington Mag. Super-X	X7MMR1	D,O/P,M	150	PP	24	3110	2830	2568	2320	2085	1866
7mm Remington Mag. Super-X	X7MMR2	D,O/P,M	175	PP	24	2860	2645	2440	2244	2057	1879
# 30 Carbine Super-X	X30M1	V	110	HSP	20	1990	1567	1236	1035	923	842
# 30 Carbine Super-X	X30M2	V	110	FMC	20	1990	1596	1278	1070	952	870
30-30 Winchester Super-X	X30301	D	150	HP	24	2390	2018	1684	1398	1177	1036
30-30 Winchester Super-X	X30306	D	150	PP	24	2390	2018	1684	1398	1177	1036
30-30 Winchester Super-X	X30302	D	150	ST	24	2390	2018	1684	1398	1177	1036
30-30 Winchester Super-X	X30303	D	170	PP	24	2200	1895	1619	1381	1191	1061
30-30 Winchester Super-X	X30304	D	170	ST	24	2200	1895	1619	1381	1191	1061
30-06 Springfield Super-X	X30062	V	125	PSP	24	3140	2780	2447	2138	1853	1595
30-06 Springfield Super-X	X30061	D,O/P	150	PP	24	2920	2580	2265	1972	1704	1466
30-06 Springfield Super-X	X30063	D,O/P	150	ST	24	2910	2617	2342	2083	1843	1622
30-06 Springfield Super-X	X30065	D,O/P,M	165	SP	24	2800	2573	2357	2151	1956	1772
30-06 Springfield Super-X	X30064	D,O/P,M,L	180	PP	24	2700	2348	2023	1727	1466	1251
30-06 Springfield Super-X	X30066	D,O/P,M,L	180	ST	24	2700	2469	2250	2042	1846	1663
30-06 Springfield Super-X	X30069	M,L	220	ST	24	2410	2192	1985	1791	1611	1448
30-40 Krag Super-X	X30401	D	180	PP	24	2430	2099	1795	1525	1298	1128

TRAJECTORY Inches above (+) or below (−) line of sight. 0 = yardage at which rifle is sighted in.

Specifications are nominal. Test barrels are used to determine ballistics figures. Individual firearms may differ from these test barrels statistics. Specifications subject to change without notice.

#Acceptable for use in pistols and revolvers also. †These items will be obsolete subject to existing inventories.
HSP-Hollow Soft Point, PEP-Positive Expanding Point, PSP-Pointed Soft Point, PP-Power-Point®, FMC-Full Metal Case, SP-Soft Point, HP-Hollow Point, ST-Silvertip®, JHP-Jacketed Hollow Point, STHP-Silvertip Hollow Point

GAME SELECTOR CODE

V = Varmint	D = Deer	M = Medium Game (i.e. Elk)	L = Large Game (i.e. Moose)	O/P = Open or Plains shooting (i.e. Antelope, Deer)

XL = Extra Large Game (i.e. Kodiak Bear)

WINCHESTER BALLISTICS
CENTERFIRE RIFLE

Energy In Foot-Pounds (ft.-lbs.)						Trajectory, Short Range						Trajectory, Long Range						
Muzzle	100	200	300	400	500	50	100	150 (Yards)	200	250	300	100	150	200	250 (Yards)	300	400	500
778	451	245	136	94	74	0.3	0	-2.3	-7.2	-15.8	-29.4	1.5	0	-4.2	-12.0	-24.8	-71.4	-155.6
723	417	225	127	90	70	0.3	0	-2.4	-7.7	-16.9	-31.3	1.6	0	-4.5	-12.8	-26.4	-75.6	-163.4
739	426	230	130	92	72	0.3	0	-2.4	-7.7	-16.9	-31.3	1.6	0	-4.5	-12.8	-26.4	-75.5	-163.3
1654	1201	861	603	410	272	0.2	0.5	0	-1.6	-4.4	-8.7	2.3	2.6	1.9	0	-3.4	-15.9	-38.9
1094	752	500	321	202	136	0.5	0.9	0	-2.5	-6.9	-13.7	2.2	1.9	0	-3.8	-10.0	-32.3	-73.8
1114	874	677	517	388	288	0.5	0.9	0	-2.2	-6.1	-11.7	2.0	1.7	0	-3.3	-8.3	-24.9	-52.5
1305	978	722	522	369	256	0.3	0.7	0	-1.9	-5.3	-10.3	1.7	1.4	0	-2.9	-7.4	-22.7	-49.1
1282	921	648	443	295	197	0.4	0.8	0	-2.2	-6.0	-11.8	1.9	1.6	0	-3.3	-8.5	-26.7	-59.6
1282	1011	790	608	461	344	0.4	0.7	0	-1.9	-5.1	-9.9	1.7	1.4	0	-2.8	-7.1	-21.2	-44.6
1556	1148	836	595	412	280	0.2	0.6	0	-1.7	-4.6	-9.0	2.4	2.8	2.0	0	-3.5	-16.3	-39.5
1993	1551	1194	906	676	495	0.3	0.7	0	-1.8	-4.9	-9.4	2.6	2.9	2.1	0	-3.6	-16.2	-37.9
1945	1615	1332	1089	882	708	0.5	0.9	0	-2.2	-5.8	-11.0	1.9	1.6	0	-3.1	-7.8	-22.6	-46.3
2139	1667	1289	982	736	542	0.3	0.6	0	-1.6	-4.5	-8.7	2.4	2.7	1.9	0	-3.3	-14.9	-35.0
2133	1777	1470	1207	983	792	0.4	0.8	0	-1.9	-5.2	-9.9	1.7	1.5	0	-2.8	-7.0	-20.4	-41.7
2364	1850	1435	1098	827	611	0.3	0.6	0	-1.7	-4.5	-8.8	2.4	2.7	2.0	0	-3.4	-15.0	-35.2
2382	1985	1644	1351	1100	887	0.5	0.8	0	-2.1	-5.6	-10.7	1.9	1.6	0	-3.0	-7.5	-22.0	-44.8
407	272	203	165	141	122	0	-4.1	-14.4	-31.8	-57.3	-92.0	0	-8.2	-23.5	-47.0	-79.6	-175.9	-319.4
1292	904	620	427	313	252	0.6	0	-3.1	-9.2	-19.0	-33.1	2.1	0	-5.1	-13.8	-27.0	-70.1	-142.0
1773	1380	1059	801	595	437	0.5	0.9	0	-2.3	-6.1	-11.8	2.0	1.7	0	-3.3	-8.4	-25.2	-53.4
1765	1351	1017	751	547	398	0.2	0	-1.6	-4.9	-10.0	-17.4	2.4	2.0	0	-3.9	-10.1	-30.5	-65.2
1015	586	317	176	122	95	0.3	0	-2.3	-7.3	-15.9	-29.6	1.5	0	-4.2	-12.1	-25.0	-72.1	-157.2
1998	1539	1169	872	639	465	0.5	0.9	0	-2.4	-4.9	-12.3	2.9	3.0	1.6	0	-6.4	-23.2	-51.2
2009	1511	1115	806	576	415	0.8	1.1	0	-2.9	-7.8	-15.1	2.6	2.2	0	-4.2	-10.8	-33.0	-70.0
2447	1901	1461	1105	821	600	0.3	0.7	0	-1.8	-5.0	-9.7	2.7	3.0	2.2	0	-3.7	-16.6	-38.9
2854	2406	2018	1682	1389	1139	0.5	0.8	0	-2.0	-5.4	-10.2	1.8	1.5	0	-2.9	-7.2	-20.8	-42.2
2612	2027	1557	1179	877	641	0.3	0.6	0	-1.7	-4.6	-9.0	2.5	2.8	2.0	0	-3.4	-15.5	-36.4
2702	2267	1890	1565	1285	1046	0.4	0.8	0	-2.0	-5.3	-10.1	1.8	1.5	0	-2.8	-7.1	-20.6	-42.0
2702	2225	1818	1472	1180	936	0.5	0.8	0	-2.0	-5.5	-10.4	1.8	1.5	0	-2.9	-7.4	-21.6	-44.3
2705	2226	1817	1468	1175	932	0.6	1.0	0	-2.4	-6.4	-12.2	2.2	1.8	0	-3.4	-8.6	-25.0	-51.4
2736	2221	1788	1424	1121	871	0.4	0.8	0	-2.0	-6.4	-10.1	1.7	1.5	0	-2.8	-7.2	-21.1	-43.7
2724	2243	1830	1480	1185	940	0.6	1.0	0	-2.4	-6.3	-12.1	2.1	1.8	0	-3.4	-8.5	-24.8	-51.0
2313	1774	1340	998	742	563	0.4	0	-2.3	-6.8	-13.8	-23.7	1.5	0	-3.7	-10.0	-19.1	-48.1	-95.4
3221	2667	2196	1792	1448	1160	0.4	0.8	0	-1.9	-5.2	-9.9	1.7	1.5	0	-2.8	-7.0	-20.5	-42.1
3178	2718	2313	1956	1644	1372	0.6	0.9	0	-2.3	-6.0	-11.3	2.0	1.7	0	-3.2	-7.9	-22.7	-45.8
967	600	373	262	208	173	0.9	0	-4.5	-13.5	-28.3	-49.9	0	-4.5	-13.5	-28.3	-49.9	-118.6	-228.2
967	622	399	280	221	185	0.9	0	-4.3	-13.0	-26.9	-47.4	2.9	0	-7.2	-19.7	-38.7	-100.4	-200.5
1902	1356	944	651	461	357	0.5	0	-2.6	-7.7	-16.0	-27.9	1.7	0	-4.3	-11.6	-22.7	-59.1	-120.5
1902	1356	944	651	461	357	0.5	0	-2.6	-7.7	-16.0	-27.9	1.7	0	-4.3	-11.6	-22.7	-59.1	-120.5
1902	1356	944	651	461	357	0.5	0	-2.6	-7.7	-16.0	-27.9	1.7	0	-4.3	-11.6	-22.7	-59.1	-120.5
1827	1355	989	720	535	425	0.6	0	-3.0	-8.9	-18.0	-31.1	2.0	0	-4.8	-13.0	-25.1	-63.6	-126.7
1827	1355	989	720	535	425	0.6	0	-3.0	-8.9	-18.0	-31.1	2.0	0	-4.8	-13.0	-25.1	-63.6	-126.7
2736	2145	1662	1269	953	706	0.4	0.8	0	-2.1	-5.6	-10.7	1.8	1.5	0	-3.0	-7.7	-23.0	-48.5
2839	2217	1708	1295	967	716	0.6	1.0	0	-2.4	-6.6	-12.7	2.2	1.8	0	-3.5	-9.0	-27.0	-57.1
2820	2281	1827	1445	1131	876	0.6	0.9	0	-2.3	-6.3	-12.0	2.1	1.8	0	-3.3	-8.5	-25.0	-51.8
2873	2426	2036	1696	1402	1151	0.7	1.0	0	-2.5	-6.5	-12.2	2.2	1.9	0	-3.6	-8.4	-24.4	-49.6
2913	2003	1635	1192	859	625	0.2	0	-1.8	-5.5	-11.2	-19.5	2.7	2.3	0	-4.4	-11.3	-34.4	-73.7
2913	2436	2023	1666	1362	1105	0.2	0	-1.6	-4.8	-9.7	-16.5	2.4	2.0	0	-3.7	-9.3	-27.0	-54.9
2837	2347	1924	1567	1268	1024	0.4	0	-2.2	-6.4	-12.7	-21.6	1.5	0	-3.5	-9.1	-17.2	-41.8	-79.9
2360	1761	1288	929	673	508	0.4	0	-2.4	-7.1	-14.5	-25.0	1.6	0	-3.9	-10.5	-20.3	-51.7	-103.9

WINCHESTER BALLISTICS
CENTERFIRE RIFLE

Cartridge	Symbol	Game Selector Guide	Wt. Grs.	Bullet Type	Barrel Length Inches	Muzzle	100	200	300	400	500
							\multicolumn{5}{}{Velocity In Feet Per Second (fps)}				
300 Winchester Mag. Super-X	X30WM1	D,O/P	150	PP	24	3290	2951	2636	2342	2068	1813
300 Winchester Mag. Super-X	X30WM2	O/P,M,L	180	PP	24	2960	2745	2540	2344	2157	1979
300 Winchester Mag. Super-X	X30WM3	M,L,XL	220	ST	24	2680	2448	2228	2020	1823	1640
300 H. & H. Magnum Super-X	X300H2	O/P,M,L	180	ST	24	2880	2640	2412	2196	1991	1798
300 Savage Super-X	X3001	D,O/P	150	PP	24	2630	2311	2015	1743	1500	1295
300 Savage Super-X	X3003	D,O/P	150	ST	24	2630	2354	2095	1853	1631	1434
300 Savage Super-X	X3004	D	180	PP	24	2350	2025	1728	1467	1252	1098
303 Savage Super-X	X3032	D	190	ST	24	1890	1612	1372	1183	1055	970
303 British Super-X	X303B1	D	180	PP	24	2460	2233	2018	1816	1629	1459
307 Winchester Super-X	X3075	D	150	PP	24	2760	2321	1924	1575	1289	1091
† 307 Winchester Super-X	X3076	D,M	180	PP	24	2510	2179	1874	1599	1362	1177
† 308 Winchester Super-X	X3087	V	125	PSP	24	3050	2697	2370	2067	1788	1537
308 Winchester Super-X	X3085	D,O/P	150	PP	24	2820	2488	2179	1893	1633	1405
308 Winchester Super-X	X3082	D,O/P	150	ST	24	2820	2533	2263	2009	1774	1560
308 Winchester Super-X	X3086	D,O/P,M	180	PP	24	2620	2274	1955	1666	1414	1212
308 Winchester Super-X	X3083	D,O/P,M	180	ST	24	2620	2393	2178	1974	1782	1604
32 Win. Special Super-X	X32WS2	D	170	PP	24	2250	1870	1537	1267	1082	971
32 Win. Special Super-X	X32WS3	D	170	ST	24	2250	1870	1537	1267	1082	971
# 32-20 Winchester Super-X	X32202	V	100	SP	24	1210	1021	913	834	769	712
# 32-20 Winchester Super-X	X32201	V	100	Lead	24	1210	1021	913	834	769	712
8mm Mauser (8 × 57) Super-X	X8MM	D	170	PP	24	2360	1969	1622	1333	1123	997
338 Winchester Mag. Super-X	X3381	D,O/P,M	200	PP	24	2960	2658	2375	2110	1862	1635
338 Winchester Mag. Super-X	X3383	M,L,XL	225	SP	24	2780	2572	2374	2184	2003	1832
348 Winchester Super-X	X3482	D,M	200	ST	24	2520	2215	1931	1672	1443	1253
35 Remington Super-X	X35R1	D	200	PP	24	2020	1646	1335	1114	985	901
35 Remington Super-X	X35R3	D	200	ST	24	2020	1646	1335	1114	985	901
351 Winchester S.L. Super-X	X351SL2	D	180	SP	20	1850	1556	1310	1128	1012	933
356 Winchester Super-X	X3561	D,M	200	PP	24	2460	2114	1797	1517	1284	1113
† 356 Winchester Super-X	X3563	M,L	250	PP	24	2160	1911	1682	1476	1299	1158
357 Magnum Super-X	X3574P	V,D	158	JHP	20	1810	1408	1125	972	877	803
357 Magnum Super-X	X3575P	V,D	158	JSP	20	1830	1427	1138	980	883	809
358 Winchester 8.8mm Super-X	X3581	D,M	200	ST	24	2490	2171	1876	1610	1379	1194
375 Winchester Super-X	X375W	D,M	200	PP	24	2200	1841	1526	1268	1089	980
375 Winchester Super-X	X375W1	D,M	250	PP	24	1900	1647	1424	1239	1103	1011
375 H. & H. Magnum Super-X	X375H1	M,L,XL	270	PP	24	2690	2420	2166	1928	1707	1507
375 H. & H. Magnum Super-X	X375H2	M,L,XL	300	ST	24	2530	2268	2022	1793	1583	1397
375 H. & H. Magnum Super-X	X375H3	XL	300	FMC	24	2530	2171	1843	1551	1307	1126
# 38-40 Winchester Super-X	X3840	D	180	SP	24	1160	999	901	827	764	710
38-55 Winchester Super-X	X3855	D	255	SP	24	1320	1190	1091	1018	963	917
# 44 Remington Magnum Super-X	X44MSTHP	V,D	210	STHP	20	1580	1198	993	879	795	725
# 44 Remington Magnum Super-X	X44MHSP5	D	240	HSP	20	1760	1362	1094	953	861	789
# 44-40 Winchester Super-X	X4440	D	200	SP	24	1190	1006	900	822	756	699
45-70 Government Super-X	X4570H	D,M	300	JHP	24	1880	1650	1425	1235	1105	1010
458 Winchester Mag. Super-X	X4580	XL	500	FMC	24	2040	1823	1623	1442	1287	1161
458 Winchester Mag. Super-X	X4581	L,XL	510	SP	24	2040	1770	1527	1319	1157	1046

WINCHESTER BALLISTICS
CENTERFIRE RIFLE

Energy In Foot-Pounds (ft.-lbs.)						Trajectory, Short Range						Trajectory, Long Range						
Muzzle	100	200	300	400	500	50	100	150 Yards	200	250	300	100	150	200 Yards	250	300	400	500
3605	2900	2314	1827	1424	1095	0.3	0.7	0	-1.8	-4.8	-9.3	2.6	2.9	2.1	0	-3.5	-15.4	-35.5
3501	3011	2578	2196	1859	1565	0.5	0.8	0	-2.1	-5.5	-10.4	1.9	1.6	0	-2.9	-7.3	-20.9	-41.9
3508	2927	2424	1993	1623	1314	0.2	0	-1.7	-4.9	-9.9	-16.9	2.5	2.0	0	-3.8	-9.5	-27.5	-56.1
3315	2785	2325	1927	1584	1292	0.6	0.9	0	-2.3	-6.0	-11.5	2.1	1.7	0	-3.2	-8.0	-23.3	-47.4
2303	1779	1352	1012	749	558	0.3	0	-1.9	-5.7	-11.6	-19.9	2.8	2.3	0	-4.5	-11.5	-34.4	-73.0
2303	1845	1462	1143	886	685	0.3	0	-1.8	-5.4	-11.0	-18.8	2.7	2.2	0	-4.2	-10.7	-31.5	-65.5
2207	1639	1193	860	626	482	0.5	0	-2.6	-7.7	-15.6	-27.1	1.7	0	-4.2	-11.3	-21.9	-55.8	-112.0
1507	1096	794	591	469	397	1.0	0	-4.3	-12.6	-25.5	-43.7	2.9	0	-6.8	-18.3	-35.1	-88.2	-172.5
2418	1993	1627	1318	1060	851	0.3	0	-2.1	-6.1	-12.2	-20.8	1.4	0	-3.3	-8.8	-16.6	-40.4	-77.4
2538	1795	1233	826	554	397	0.2	0	-1.9	-5.6	-11.8	-20.8	1.2	0	-3.2	-8.7	-17.1	-44.9	-92.2
2519	1898	1404	1022	742	554	0.3	0	-2.2	-6.5	-13.3	-22.9	1.5	0	-3.6	-9.6	-18.6	-47.1	-93.7
2582	2019	1559	1186	887	656	0.5	0.8	0	-2.2	-6.0	-11.5	2.0	1.7	0	-3.2	-8.2	-24.6	-51.9
2648	2061	1581	1193	888	657	0.2	0	-1.6	-4.8	-9.8	-16.9	2.4	2.0	0	-3.8	-9.8	-29.3	-62.0
2648	2137	1705	1344	1048	810	0.2	0	-1.5	-4.5	-9.3	-15.9	2.3	1.9	0	-3.6	-9.1	-26.9	-55.7
2743	2066	1527	1109	799	587	0.3	0	-2.0	-5.9	-12.1	-20.9	2.9	2.4	0	-4.7	-12.1	-36.9	-79.1
2743	2288	1896	1557	1269	1028	0.2	0	-1.8	-5.2	-10.4	-17.7	2.6	2.1	0	-4.0	-9.9	-28.9	-58.8
1911	1320	892	606	442	356	0.6	0	-3.1	-9.2	-19.0	-33.2	2.0	0	-5.1	-13.8	-27.1	-70.9	-144.3
1911	1320	892	606	442	356	0.6	0	-3.1	-9.2	-19.0	-33.2	2.0	0	-5.1	-13.8	-27.1	-70.9	-144.3
325	231	185	154	131	113	0	-6.3	-20.9	-44.9	-79.3	-125.1	0	-11.5	-32.3	-63.6	-106.3	-230.3	-413.3
325	231	185	154	131	113	0	-6.3	-20.9	-44.9	-79.3	-125.1	0	-11.5	-32.3	-63.6	-106.3	-230.3	-413.3
2102	1463	993	671	476	375	0.5	0	-2.7	-8.2	-17.0	-29.8	1.8	0	-4.5	-12.4	-24.3	-63.8	-130.7
3890	3137	2505	1977	1539	1187	0.5	0.9	0	-2.3	-6.1	-11.6	2.0	1.7	0	-3.2	-8.2	-24.3	-50.4
3862	3306	2816	2384	2005	1677	1.2	1.3	0	-2.7	-7.1	-12.9	2.7	2.1	0	-3.6	-9.4	-25.0	-49.9
2820	2178	1656	1241	925	697	0.3	0	-2.1	-6.2	-12.7	-21.9	1.4	0	-3.4	-9.2	-17.7	-44.4	-87.9
1812	1203	791	551	431	360	0.9	0	-4.1	-12.1	-25.1	-43.9	2.7	0	-6.7	-18.3	-35.8	-92.8	-185.5
1812	1203	791	551	431	360	0.9	0	-4.1	-12.1	-25.1	-43.9	2.7	0	-6.7	-18.3	-35.8	-92.8	-185.5
1368	968	686	508	409	348	0	-2.1	-7.8	-17.8	-32.9	-53.9	0	-4.7	-13.6	-27.6	-47.5	-108.8	-203.9
2688	1985	1434	1022	732	550	0.4	0	-2.3	-7.0	-14.3	-24.7	1.6	0	-3.8	-10.4	-20.1	-51.2	-102.3
2591	2028	1571	1210	937	745	0.6	0	-3.0	-8.7	-17.4	-30.0	2.0	0	-4.7	-12.4	-23.7	-58.4	-112.9
1150	696	444	332	270	226	0	-2.5	-9.4	-21.6	-40.2	-65.8	0	-5.6	-16.6	-33.9	-58.3	-131.0	-240.5
1175	715	454	337	274	229	0	-2.4	-9.1	-21.0	-39.2	-64.3	0	-5.5	-16.2	-33.1	-57.0	-128.3	-235.8
2753	2093	1563	1151	844	633	0.4	0		-6.5	-13.3	-23.0	1.5	0	-3.6	-9.7	-18.6	-47.2	-94.1
2150	1506	1034	714	527	427	0.6	0	-3.2	-9.5	-19.5	-33.8	2.1	0	-5.2	-14.1	-27.4	-70.1	-138.1
2005	1506	1126	852	676	568	0.9	0	-4.1	-12.0	-24.0	-40.9	2.7	0	-6.5	-17.2	-32.7	-80.6	-154.1
4337	3510	2812	2228	1747	1361	0.2	0	-1.7	-5.1	-10.3	-17.6	2.5	2.1	0	-3.9	-10.0	-29.4	-60.7
4263	3426	2723	2141	1669	1300	0.3	0	-2.0	-5.9	-11.9	-20.3	2.9	2.4	0	-4.5	-11.5	-33.8	-70.1
4263	3139	2262	1602	1138	844	0.3	0	-2.2	-6.5	-13.5	-23.4	1.5	0	-3.6	-9.8	-19.1	-49.1	-99.5
538	399	324	273	233	201	0	-6.7	-22.2	-47.3	-83.2	-130.8	0	-12.1	-33.9	-66.4	-110.6	-238.3	-425.6
987	802	674	587	525	476	0	-4.7	-15.4	-32.7	-57.2	-89.3	0	-8.4	-23.4	-45.6	-75.2	-158.8	-277.4
1164	670	460	361	295	245	0	-3.7	-13.3	-29.8	-54.2	-87.3	0	-7.7	-22.4	-44.9	-76.1	-168.0	-305.8
1650	988	638	484	395	332	0	-2.7	-10.2	-23.6	-44.2	-73.3	0	-6.1	-18.1	-37.4	-65.1	-150.3	-282.5
629	449	360	300	254	217	0	-6.5	-21.6	-46.3	-81.8	-129.1	0	-11.8	-33.3	-65.5	-109.5	-237.4	-426.2
2355	1815	1355	1015	810	680	0	-2.4	-8.2	-17.6	-31.4	-51.5	0	-4.6	-12.8	-25.4	-44.3	-95.5	—
4620	3689	2924	2308	1839	1496	0.7	0	-3.3	-9.6	-19.2	-32.5	2.2	0	-5.2	-13.6	-25.8	-63.2	-121.7
4712	3547	2640	1970	1516	1239	0.8	0	-3.5	-10.3	-20.8	-35.6	2.4	0	-5.6	-14.9	-28.5	-71.5	-140.4

CONVERSION FACTORS

Common inch calibers converted to metric

.25 inch = 6.35mm
.256 inch = 6.5mm
.270 inch = 6.858mm
.280 inch = 7.11mm
.297 inch = 7.54mm
.300 inch = 7.62mm
.301 inch = 7.62mm
.303 inch = 7.696mm
.308 inch = 7.82mm
.311 inch = 7.899mm
.312 inch = 7.925mm
.380 inch = 9.65mm
.400 inch = 10.16mm
.402 inch = 10.21mm
.450 inch = 11.43mm
.455 inch = 11.557mm
.500 inch = 12.7mm
.550 inch = 13.97mm
.577 inch = 14.65mm
.600 inch = 15.24mm
.661 inch = 16.79mm

Pressure

1 kg per sq cm = 14.223 lb per sq inch
1 kg per sq cm = 0.0063493 tons per sq inch
1 kg per sq cm = 0.968 Atmospheres
1 Atmosphere = 14.7 lb. per sq inch
1 Atmosphere = 0.00655 tons per sq inch

1 ton per sq inch = 152.0 Atmospheres
1 lb per sq inch = 0.0680 Atmospheres
1 Atmosphere = 1.03 kg per sq cm
1 lb per sq inch = 0.070309 kg per sq cm
1 ton per sq inch = 157.49 kg per sq cm

Energy

1 m.kg = 7.2331 foot lb
1 foot lb = 0.13825 m.kg

Velocity

1 meter per second = 3.2809 feet per second
1 foot   per second = 0.30479 meters per second

Weight

1 gram = 15.432 grains
1 grain = 0.0648 grams
1 oz   = 28.349 grams

Linear

1 meter = 1.0936 yards
1 meter = 3.2808 feet
1 yard = 0.91438 meters
1 foot = 0.30479 meters
1 inch = 25.4mm
$1/4$ inch = 6.35mm
$1/2$ inch = 12.7mm
$3/4$ inch = 19.05mm
$1/8$ inch = 3.175mm
$3/8$ inch = 9.525mm
$5/8$ inch = 15.875mm
$7/8$ inch = 22.225mm
$1/16$ inch = 1.5875mm
$3/16$ inch = 4.7625mm
$5/16$ inch = 7.9375mm
$7/16$ inch = 11.1125mm
$9/16$ inch = 14.2875mm
$11/16$ inch = 17.4625mm
$13/16$ inch = 20.6375mm
$15/16$ inch = 23.8125mm

Reloading

FOR ADDRESSES AND PHONE
NUMBERS OF MANUFACTURERS AND
DISTRIBUTORS INCLUDED IN THIS
SECTION, SEE *DIRECTORY OF
MANUFACTURERS AND SUPPLIERS*

HORNADY RIFLE BULLETS

"I" denotes interlock bullets.

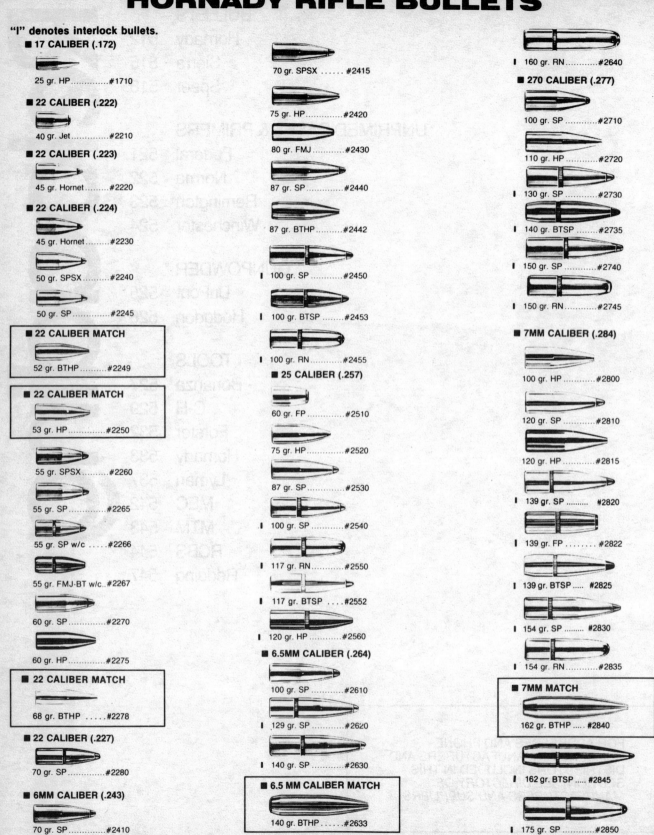

■ 17 CALIBER (.172)

25 gr. HP............#1710

■ 22 CALIBER (.222)

40 gr. Jet............#2210

■ 22 CALIBER (.223)

45 gr. Hornet........#2220

■ 22 CALIBER (.224)

45 gr. Hornet........#2230

50 gr. SPSX..........#2240

50 gr. SP.............#2245

■ 22 CALIBER MATCH

52 gr. BTHP.........#2249

■ 22 CALIBER MATCH

53 gr. HP.............#2250

55 gr. SPSX.........#2260

55 gr. SP.............#2265

55 gr. SP w/c .....#2266

55 gr. FMJ-BT w/c..#2267

60 gr. SP.............#2270

60 gr. HP.............#2275

■ 22 CALIBER MATCH

68 gr. BTHP .....#2278

■ 22 CALIBER (.227)

70 gr. SP.............#2280

■ 6MM CALIBER (.243)

70 gr. SP.............#2410

---

70 gr. SPSX ...... #2415

75 gr. HP.............#2420

80 gr. FMJ...........#2430

87 gr. SP ....#2440

87 gr. BTHP.........#2442

I 100 gr. SP ....#2450

I 100 gr. BTSP ....#2453

I 100 gr. RN ....#2455

■ 25 CALIBER (.257)

60 gr. FP ....#2510

75 gr. HP ....#2520

87 gr. SP ....#2530

I 100 gr. SP ....#2540

I 117 gr. RN ....#2550

I 117 gr. BTSP ....#2552

I 120 gr. HP ....#2560

■ 6.5MM CALIBER (.264)

100 gr. SP ....#2610

I 129 gr. SP ....#2620

I 140 gr. SP ....#2630

■ 6.5 MM CALIBER MATCH

140 gr. BTHP......#2633

I 160 gr. RN..........#2640

■ 270 CALIBER (.277)

100 gr. SP ....#2710

110 gr. HP ....#2720

I 130 gr. SP ....#2730

I 140 gr. BTSP ....#2735

I 150 gr. SP ....#2740

I 150 gr. RN ....#2745

■ 7MM CALIBER (.284)

100 gr. HP ....#2800

120 gr. SP ....#2810

120 gr. HP ....#2815

I 139 gr. SP .... #2820

I 139 gr. FP .... #2822

I 139 gr. BTSP ..... #2825

I 154 gr. SP .... #2830

I 154 gr. RN ....#2835

■ 7MM MATCH

162 gr. BTHP ..... #2840

I 162 gr. BTSP ..... #2845

I 175 gr. SP ....#2850

HORNADY PISTOL BULLETS

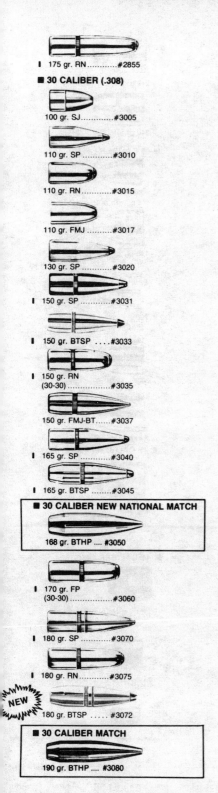

175 gr. RN	#2855	

■ 30 CALIBER (.308)

- 100 gr. SJ .... #3005
- 110 gr. SP .... #3010
- 110 gr. RN .... #3015
- 110 gr. FMJ .... #3017
- 130 gr. SP .... #3020
- 150 gr. SP .... #3031
- 150 gr. BTSP .... #3033
- 150 gr. RN (30-30) .... #3035
- 150 gr. FMJ-BT ..... #3037
- 165 gr. SP .... #3040
- 165 gr. BTSP .... #3045

■ 30 CALIBER NEW NATIONAL MATCH

- 168 gr. BTHP .... #3050

- 170 gr. FP (30-30) .... #3060
- 180 gr. SP .... #3070
- 180 gr. RN .... #3075

NEW
- 180 gr. BTSP ..... #3072

■ 30 CALIBER MATCH

- 190 gr. BTHP .... #3080

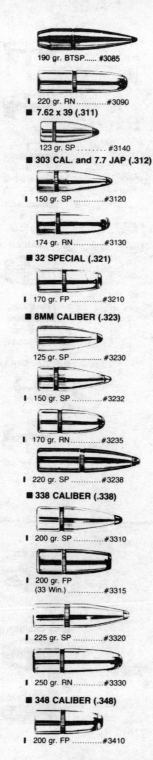

- 190 gr. BTSP ...... #3085
- 220 gr. RN .... #3090

■ 7.62 x 39 (.311)

- 123 gr. SP .... #3140

■ 303 CAL. and 7.7 JAP (.312)

- 150 gr. SP .... #3120
- 174 gr. RN .... #3130

■ 32 SPECIAL (.321)

- 170 gr. FP .... #3210

■ 8MM CALIBER (.323)

- 125 gr. SP .... #3230
- 150 gr. SP .... #3232
- 170 gr. RN .... #3235
- 220 gr. SP .... #3238

■ 338 CALIBER (.338)

- 200 gr. SP .... #3310
- 200 gr. FP (33 Win.) .... #3315
- 225 gr. SP .... #3320
- 250 gr. RN .... #3330

■ 348 CALIBER (.348)

- 200 gr. FP .... #3410

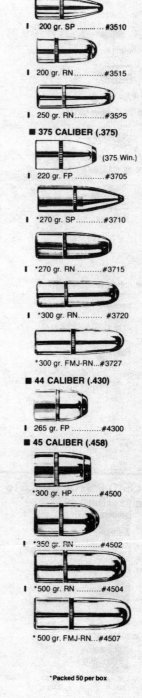

■ 35 CALIBER (.358)

- 200 gr. SP .... #3510
- 200 gr. RN .... #3515
- 250 gr. RN .... #3525

■ 375 CALIBER (.375)

(375 Win.)
- 220 gr. FP .... #3705
- *270 gr. SP .... #3710
- *270 gr. RN .... #3715
- *300 gr. RN............ #3720
- *300 gr. FMJ-RN...#3727

■ 44 CALIBER (.430)

- 265 gr. FP .... #4300

■ 45 CALIBER (.458)

- *300 gr. HP............#4500
- *350 gr. RN ....#4502
- *500 gr. RN ....#4504
- *500 gr. FMJ-RN...#4507

*Packed 50 per box

LEGEND

BBWC—Bevel Base Wadcutter	HBWC—Hollow Base Wadcutter	SWC—Semi-Wadcutter
BT—Boat Tail	HP—Hollow Point	SX—Super Explosive
DEWC—Double End Wadcutter	RN—Round Nose	JTC—Jacketed Truncated Cone
FMJ—Full Metal Jacket	SJ—Short Jacket	SIL—Silhouette
FP—Flat Point	SP—Spire Point	

HORNADY RIFLE BULLETS

■ 25 CALIBER (.251)

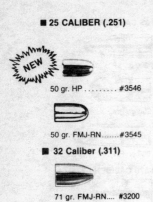

50 gr. HP .... #3546

50 gr. FMJ-RN ......#3545

■ 32 Caliber (.311)

71 gr. FMJ-RN.... #3200

■ 32 CALIBER (.312)

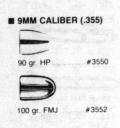

85 gr. JHP .... #3025

■ 9MM CALIBER (.355)

90 gr. HP .... #3550

100 gr. FMJ ......#3552

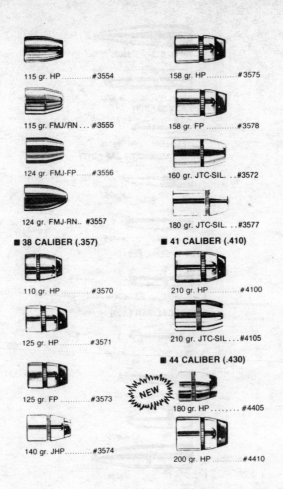

115 gr. HP .... #3554

115 gr. FMJ/RN ... #3555

124 gr. FMJ-FP ...#3556

124 gr. FMJ-RN.. #3557

■ 38 CALIBER (.357)

110 gr. HP .... #3570

125 gr. HP .... #3571

125 gr. FP .... #3573

140 gr. JHP.......... #3574

158 gr. HP........... #3575

158 gr. FP .... #3578

160 gr. JTC-SIL. ...#3572

180 gr. JTC-SIL. ..#3577

■ 41 CALIBER (.410)

210 gr. HP ....#4100

210 gr. JTC-SIL ...#4105

■ 44 CALIBER (.430)

180 gr. HP ...,.... #4405

200 gr. HP ....#4410

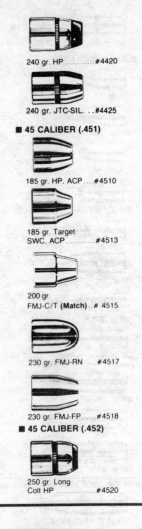

240 gr. HP .... #4420

240 gr. JTC-SIL. ..#4425

■ 45 CALIBER (.451)

185 gr. HP. ACP ... #4510

185 gr. Target
SWC. ACP..........#4513

200 gr.
FMJ-C/T (Match) . # 4515

230 gr. FMJ-RN ....#4517

230 gr. FMJ-FP ....#4518

■ 45 CALIBER (.452)

250 gr. Long
Colt HP ....#4520

LEAD PISTOL BULLETS

■ 32 CALIBER (.314)

90 gr.   #3250
SWC .... • #1000

■ 32 Caliber (.312)

90 gr.   #3252
HBWC .... *#1002

■ 9MM (.355)

124 gr.   #3567
LRN ....#1005

■ 38 CALIBER (.358)

148 gr.   #3580
BBWC ....*#1010

38 cal. (.358)

148 gr.   #3582
HBWC............ • #1020

38 cal. (.358)

148 gr.   (Bulk only)
DEWC............ • #1030

38 cal. (.358)

158 gr. RN ...... #3586
                  • #1050

38 cal. (.358)

                  #3588
158 gr. SWC ... • #1040

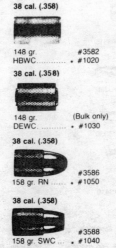

38 cal. (.358)

                  #3589
158 gr. SWC/HP *#1042

■ 44 CALIBER (.430)

240 gr. SWC .... #4430
                      • #1110

240 gr. SWC/HP   #4431
                  *#1111

■ 45 CALIBER (.452)

                  #4526
200 gr. SWC .... • #1210

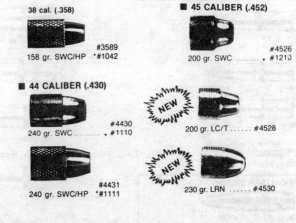

200 gr. LC/T ......#4528

230 gr. LRN ......#4530

500 Per Box except 44 cal. (400 per box) — *Bulk Price Per 1000
Bulk lead bullets must be ordered in increments of carton quantities per bullet,
5000 bullets per carton except 44 caliber is 4000 per carton.

SIERRA BULLETS

RIFLE

.22 Caliber Hornet
(.223/5.66MM Diameter)

40 gr. Hornet
Varminter #1100

45 gr. Hornet
Varminter #1110

.22 Caliber Hornet
(.224/5.69MM Diameter)

40 gr. Hornet
Varminter #1200

45 gr. Hornet
Varminter #1210

.22 Caliber
(.224/5.69MM Diameter)
High Velocity

40 gr. HP
Varminter #1385

45 gr. SMP
Varminter #1300

45 gr. SPT
Varminter #1310

50 gr. SMP
Varminter #1320

50 gr. SPT
Varminter #1330

50 gr. Blitz
Varminter #1340

52 gr. HPBT
MatchKing #1410

53 gr. HP
MatchKing #1400

55 gr. Blitz
Varminter #1345

55 gr. SMP
Varminter #1350

55 gr. FMJBT
GameKing #1355

55 gr. SPT
Varminter #1360

55 gr. HPBT
GameKing #1390

55 gr. SBT
GameKing #1365

60 gr. HP
Varminter #1375

63 gr. SMP
Varminter #1370

69 gr. HPBT
MatchKing #1380

6MM .243 Caliber
(2.43/6.17MM Diameter)

60 gr. HP
Varminter #1500

70 gr. HPBT
MatchKing #1505

75 gr. HP
Varminter #1510

85 gr. SPT
Varminter #1520

85 gr. HPBT
GameKing #1530

90 gr. FMJBT
GameKing #1535

100 gr. SPT
Pro-Hunter #1540

100 gr. SMP
Pro-Hunter #1550

100 gr. SBT
GameKing #1560

.25 Caliber
(.257/6.53MM Diameter)

75 gr. HP
Varminter #1600

87 gr. SPT
Varminter #1610

90 gr. HPBT
GameKing #1615

100 gr. SPT
Pro-Hunter #1620

100 gr. SBT
GameKing #1625

117 gr. SBT
GameKing #1630

117 gr. SPT
Pro-Hunter #1640

120 gr. HPBT
GameKing #1650

6.5MM .264 Caliber
(.264/6.71MM Diameter)

85 gr. HP
Varminter #1700

100 gr. HP
Varminter #1710

120 gr. SPT
Pro-Hunter #1720

140 gr. SBT
GameKing #1730

140 gr. HPBT
MatchKing #1740

.270 Caliber
(.277/7.04MM Diameter)

90 gr. HP
Varminter #1800

110 gr. SPT
Pro-Hunter #1810

130 gr. SBT
GameKing #1820

130 gr. SPT
Pro-Hunter #1830

140 gr. SBT
GameKing #1845

140 gr. HPBT
GameKing #1835

150 gr. SBT
GameKing #1840

150 gr. RN
Pro-Hunter #1850

7MM .284 Caliber
(.284/7.21MM Diameter)

120 gr. SPT
Pro-Hunter #1900

140 gr. SBT
GameKing #1905

140 gr. SPT
Pro-Hunter #1910

NEW 150 gr. SBT
GameKing #1913

150 gr. HPBT
MatchKing #1915

160 gr. SBT
GameKing #1920

168 gr. HPBT
MatchKing #1930

170 gr. RN
Pro-Hunter #1950

175 gr. SBT
GameKing #1940

SIERRA BULLETS

.30 (30-30) Caliber
(.308/7.82MM Diameter)

125 gr. HP
Pro-Hunter #2020

150 gr. FN
Pro-Hunter #2000

170 gr. FN
Pro-Hunter #2010

.30 Caliber 7.62MM
(.308/7.82MM Diameter)

110 gr. RN
Pro-Hunter #2100

110 gr. FMJ
Pro-Hunter #2105

110 gr. HP
Varminter #2110

125 gr. SPT
Pro-Hunter #2120

150 gr. FMJBT
GameKing #2115

150 gr. SPT
Pro-Hunter #2130

150 gr. SBT
GameKing #2125

150 gr. HPBT
MatchKing #2190

150 gr. RN
Pro-Hunter #2135

165 gr. SBT
GameKing #2145

165 gr. HPBT
GameKing #2140

168 gr. HPBT
MatchKing #2200

180 gr. SPT
Pro-Hunter #2150

180 gr. SBT
GameKing #2160

*180 gr. HPBT
MatchKing #2220

* New & Improved. The angle of boat tail has been increased to allow more bearing surface, providing substantial improvement in bullet accuracy. Now one of the most accurate in the Sierra line.

180 gr. RN
Pro-Hunter #2170

190 gr. HPBT
MatchKing #2210

200 gr. SBT
GameKing #2165

200 gr. HPBT
MatchKing #2230

220 gr. HPBT
MatchKing #2240

220 gr. RN
Pro-Hunter #2180

.303 Caliber 7.7MM
(.311/7.90MM Diameter)

150 gr. SPT
Pro-Hunter #2300

180 gr. SPT
Pro-Hunter #2310

8MM
(.323/8.20MM Diameter)

150 gr. SPT
Pro-Hunter #2400

175 gr. SPT
Pro-Hunter #2410

220 gr. SBT
GameKing #2420

.338 Caliber
(.338/8.59MM Diameter)

250 gr. SBT
GameKing #2600

.35 Caliber
(.358/9.09MM Diameter)

200 gr. RN
Pro-Hunter #2800

.375 Caliber
(.375/9.53MM Diameter)

NEW 200 gr. FN
Pro-Hunter #2900
POWER JACKET

300 gr. SBT
GameKing #3000

.45 Caliber (45-70)
(.458/11.63MM Diameter)

300 gr. HP
Pro-Hunter #8900

SIERRA BULLETS

HANDGUN

.25 Caliber
(.251/6.38MM Diameter)

50 gr. FMJ
SportsMaster #8000

.32 Caliber 7.65MM
(.312/7.92MM Diameter)

71 gr. FMJ
Tournament Master #8010

.32 Mag. .312/7.92MM Diameter

NEW 90 gr. JHC
Sports Master #8030
POWER JACKET

9MM .355 Caliber
(.355/9.02MM Diameter)

90 gr. JHP
Sports Master #8100
POWER JACKET

95 gr. FMJ
Tournament Master #8105

115 gr. JHP
Sports Master #8110
POWER JACKET

115 gr. FMJ
Tournament Master #8115

125 gr. FMJ
Tournament Master #8120

130 gr. FMJ
Tournament Master #8345

.38 Caliber
(.357/9.07MM Diameter)

110 gr. JHC Blitz
Sports Master #8300

125 gr. JSP
Sports Master #8310

125 gr. JHC
Sports Master #8320
POWER JACKET

140 gr. JHC
Sports Master #8325
POWER JACKET

158 gr. JHC
Sports Master #8360
POWER JACKET

158 gr. JSP
Sports Master #8340

170 gr. JHC
Sports Master #8365
POWER JACKET

170 gr. FMJ Match
Tournament Master #8350

180 gr. FJP Match
Tournament Master #8370

.41 Caliber
(.410/10.41MM Diameter)

170 gr. JHC
Sports Master #8500
POWER JACKET

210 gr. JHC
Sports Master #8520
POWER JACKET

220 gr. FPJ Match
Tournament Master #8530

.44 Magnum
(.4295/10.91MM Diameter)

180 gr. JHC
Sports Master #8600
POWER JACKET

210 gr. JHC
Sports Master #8620
POWER JACKET

220 gr. FPJ Match
Tournament Master #8605

240 gr. JHC
Sports Master #8610
POWER JACKET

250 gr. FPJ Match
Tournament Master #8615

.45 Caliber
(.4515/11.47MM Diameter)

185 gr. JHP
Sports Master #8800
POWER JACKET

185 gr. FPJ Match
Tournament Master #8810

200 gr. FPJ Match
Tournament Master #8825

230 gr. FMJ Match
Tournament Master #8815

240 gr. JHC
Sports Master #8820
POWER JACKET

NEW Single Shot Pistol Bullets

NEW
7MM .284 Dia. 130 gr. SPT
Pro-Hunter #7250

NEW
7MM .243 Dia. 80 gr. SPT
Pro-Hunter #7150

NEW
30 Cal. .308 Dia. 135 gr. SPT
Pro-Hunter #7350

Abbreviations:

SBT—Spitzer Boat Tail	JHP—Jacketed	JSP—Jacketed	RN—Round Nose	SMP—Semi-Pointed
SPT—Spitzer	Hollow Point	Soft Point	FMJ—Full Metal Jacket	FPH—Full Profile Jacket
HP—Hollow Point	JHC—Jacketed	FN—Flat Nose	HPBT—Hollow Point	FMJBT—Full Metal Jacket
	Hollow Cavity		Boat Tail	Boat Tail

SPEER BULLETS

HANDGUN BULLETS

CALIBER & TYPE	25 FMJ+	9mm HP	9mm FMJ+	9mm HP	9mm FMJ+	9mm HP	9mm FMJ+	9mm SP	38 HP	38 SP	38 HP	38 HP	38 HP	38 FMJ+
WEIGHT (GRS.)	50	88	95	100	115	115	124	125	110	125	125	140	146	150
DIAMETER	.251"	.355"	.355"	.355"	.355"	.355"	.355"	.355"	.357"	.357"	.357"	.357"	.357"	.357"
USE	P	P,V	P	P,V	P,T,V	P,V	P,T,V	P,V	P,V	P,V	P,V	P,V	P,V	P,T,V
PART NUMBER	3982	4000	4001	3983	3995*	3996	4004	4005	4007	4011	4013	4203	4205	4207

	38 HP	38 SP	38 SP	38 FMJ+ Sil.	38 FMJ+ Sil.	41 HP	41 SP	44 Mag. HP	44 HP	44 SP	44 Mag. HP	44 Mag. SP	44 FMJ+ Sil.	45 HP
	158	158	160	180	200	200	220	200	225	240	240	240	240	200
	.357"	.357"	.357"	.357"	.357"	.410"	.410"	.429"	.429"	.429"	.429"	.429"	.429"	.451"
	P,V,S	P,V,S	P,V,S	P,S	P,S	P,V,SG,S	P,V,S,D	P,V,SG,S	P,V,SG,S,D	P,V,SG,S,D	P,V,SG,S,D	P,V,SG,S,D	P,V,S	P,V,SG
	4211	4217	4223	4229*	4231*	4405	4417	4425	4435	4447	4453	4457	4459*	4477

	45 Mag. HP	45 FMJ+	45 HP	32 HB WC	9mm Round Nose	38 BB WC	38 HB WC	38 SWC	38 SWC HP	38 Round Nose	44 SWC	45 SWC	45 Round Nose	45 SWC
	225	230	260	98	125	148	148	158	158	158	240	200	230	250
	.451"	.451"	.451"	.314"	.356"	.358"	.358"	.358"	.358"	.358"	.430"	.452"	.452"	.452"
	P,V,SG,S	P,T,S	P,V,S,D	P,T,M	P,T	P,T	P,T,M	P,T,V,SG	P,T,V,SG	P,T	P,T,V,SG,D	P,T,M	P,T	P,T,V,SG,D
	4479	4480*	4481	4600**	4601*	4605*	4617*	4623*	4627*	4647*	4660*	4677*	4690*	4683*

PLASTIC SHOT CAPSULES

CALIBER	38	44
NO. PER BOX	50	50
PART NUMBER	8780	8782

PLASTIC INDOOR AMMO

	BULLETS	CASES
NO. PER BOX	50	50
38 CAL.	8510	8515
44 CAL.	8520	8525
45 CAL.	8530	See Note

Abbreviation Guide: HP–Hollow Point; FMJ–Full Metal Jacket; SP–Soft Point; Sil.–Silhouette; WC–Wadcutter; SWC–Semi-Wadcutter; HB–Hollow Base; BB–Bevel Base.

Usage Codes: P–Plinking; T–Target; V–Varmint; SG–Small Game; S–Silhouette; D–Deer; M–Match.

+ TMJ™ = Totally Metal Jacketed™
* Also available in 500-bullet Bulk-Pak.
** Available in bulk quantities only.

NOTE: Shown are 44 bullet and 44 case. 45 bullet is used with regular brass case.

LEAD BALLS

WT. (GRS)	64	80	120	128	133	138	141	144	177	182	224	230	278
DIAMETER	.350"	.375"	.433"	.440"	.445"	.451"	.454"	.457"	.490"	.495"	.530"	.535"	.570"
PART #	5110	5113	5127	5129	5131	5133	5135	5137	5139	5140	5142	5150	5180
GUN TYPE	Some 36 Pistols & Rifles	36 Sheriffs Revolver / 36 Leech & Rigdon Revolver / 36 Navy Revolver	45 Hawken / 45 Kentucky / 45 Percussion Pistols	45 Thompson Center Rifle / Seneca / Hawken	45 Kentucky (F&P) / 45 Mountain / 45 Yorkshire / 45 Michigan Carbine / 45 Morse Navy / 45 Springfield / 45 Huntsman	44 Revolvers / 44 Percussion Revolving Carb. / 44 Ballister Revolver	44 Percussion Revolving Carb.	Ruger New Old Army	50 Thompson Center Hawken	50 Douglas / 50 Sharon / 50 Morse Navy	54 Thompson Center Renegade	54 Douglas / 54 Sharon / 54 Mountain	58 Morse Navy / 58 Harpers Ferry Pistol

SPEER BULLETS

*HOT COR

BULLET CALIBER AND TYPE	22 Spire Soft Point	22 Spitzer Soft Point	22 Spire Soft Point	22 Spitzer Soft Point	22 Spitzer Soft Point	22 Hollow Point	22 Full Metal Jacket	22 Spitzer Soft Point	22 Spitzer S.P. w/ Cannelure	22 Semi-Spitzer Soft Point	6mm Hollow Point	6mm Spitzer Soft Point*	6mm Spitzer Soft Point B.T.	6mm Full Metal Jacket
DIAMETER	.223″	.223″	.224″	.224″	.224″	.224″	.224″	.224″	.224″	.224″	.243″	.243″	.243″	.243″
WEIGHT (GRS.)	40	45	40	45	50	52	55	55	55	70	75	80	85	90
USE	V	V	V	V	V	V,M	V	V	V	BG	V	V	V,BG	V
PART NUMBER	1005	1011	1017	1023	1029	1035	1045	1047	1049	1053	1205	1211	1213	1215

CAL. & TYPE	270 Spitzer Soft Point B.T.	270 Spitzer Soft Point*	7mm Hollow Point	7mm Spitzer Soft Point*	7mm Spitzer Soft Point B.T.	7mm Spitzer Soft Point B.T.	7mm Spitzer Soft Point*	7mm Match B.T.	7mm Spitzer Soft Point B.T.	7mm Spitzer Soft Point*	7mm Mag-Tip Soft Point*	7mm Mag-Tip Soft Point*	30 Round Soft Point Plinker®	30 Hollow Point	30 Round Soft Point*
DIA.	.277″	.277″	.284″	.284″	.284″	.284″	.284″	.284″	.284″	.284″	.284″	.284″	.308″	.308″	.308″
WT.	150	150	115	130	130	145	145	145	160	160	160	175	100	110	110
USE	BG	BG	V	V,BG	V,BG	BG	BG	M	BG	BG	BG	BG	V	V	V
PART #	1604	1605	1617	1623	1624	1628	1629 +	1631 +	1634	1635 +	1637	1641	1805	1835	1845

CAL. & TYPE	30 Mag-Tip Soft Point*	30 Match B.T.	30 Spitzer Soft Point*	303 Spitzer Soft Point*	303 Round Soft Point*	32 Flat Soft Point*	8mm Spitzer Soft Point*	8mm Semi-Spitzer Soft Point*	8mm Spitzer Soft Point*	338 Spitzer Soft Point*	338 Semi-Spitzer Soft Point*	35 Flat Soft Point*	35 Flat Soft Point*	35 Spitzer Soft Point*	9.3mm Semi-Spitzer Soft Point*
DIA.	.308″	.308″	.308″	.311″	.311″	.321″	.323″	.323″	.323″	.338″	.338″	.358″	.358″	.358″	.366″
WT.	180	190	200	150	180	170	150	170	200	200	275	180	220	250	270
USE	BG	M	BG	BG	BG	BG	BG	BG	BG	BG	BG	BG	BG	BG	BG
PART #	2059	2080	2211	2217	2223	2259	2277	2283	2285	2405	2411	2435	2439	2453	2459

V–Varmint; BG–Big Game; M–Match.
+ Also available in 500 bullet Bulk-Pak.

SPEER BULLETS

6mm Spitzer Soft Point*	6mm Spitzer Soft Point B.T.	6mm Round Soft Point*	6mm Spitzer Soft Point*	25 Spitzer Soft Point*	25 Spitzer Soft Point*	25 Hollow Point	25 Spitzer Soft Point*	25 Spitzer Soft Point B.T.	25 Spitzer Soft Point*	6.5mm Spitzer Soft Point*	6.5mm Spitzer Soft Point*	270 Hollow Point	270 Spitzer Soft Point*	270 Spitzer Soft Point*	270 Spitzer Soft Point*
.243″	.243″	.243″	.243″	.257″	.257″	.257″	.257″	.257″	.257″	.263″	.263″	.277″	.277″	.277″	.277″
90	100	105	105	87	100	100	100	120	120	120	140	100	100	130	130
V,BG	V,BG	BG	BG	V	V,BG	V	V,BG	BG	BG	V,BG	BG	V	V	BG	BG
1217	1220	1223	1229	1241	1405	1407	1408	1410	1411	1435	1441	1447	1453	1458	1459

30 Spire Soft Point*	30 Hollow Point	30 Flat Soft Point*	30 Flat Soft Point*	30 Round Soft Point*	30 Spitzer Soft Point B.T.	30 Spitzer Soft Point*	30 Mag-Tip Soft Point*	30 Round Soft Point*	30 Spitzer Soft Point*	30 Spitzer Soft Point B.T.	30 Match B.T.	30 Flat Soft Point*	30 Round Soft Point*	30 Spitzer Soft Point*	30 Spitzer Soft Point B.T.
.308″	.308″	.308″	.308″	.308″	.308″	.308″	.308″	.308″	.308″	.308″	.308″	.308″	.308″	.308″	.308″
110	130	130	150	150	150	150	150	165	165	165	168	170	180	180	180
V	V	V,BG	BG	BG	BG	BG	BG	BG	BG	BG	M	BG	BG	BG	BG
1855	2005	2007	2011	2017	2022	2023	2025	2029	2034	2035	2040+	2041	2047	2052	2053

375 Semi-Spitzer Soft Point*	45 Flat Soft Point
.375″	.458″
235	400
BG	BG
2471	2479

GRAND SLAM

BULLET CALIBER AND TYPE	270 G.S. Soft Point*	270 G.S. Soft Point*	7mm G.S. Soft Point*	7mm G.S. Soft Point*	30 G.S. Soft Point*	30 G.S. Soft Point*	338 G.S. Soft Point*	375 G.S. Soft Point*
DIAMETER	.277″	.277″	.284″	.284″	.308″	.308″	.338″	.375″
WEIGHT (GRS.)	130	150	160	175	165	180	250	285
USE	BG	BG	BG	BG	BG	BG	BG	BG
PART NUMBER	1465	1608	1638	1643	2038	2063	2408	2473

FEDERAL PRIMERS

PRIMERS Non-corrosive/Non-Mercuric

ITEM NUMBER	DESCRIPTION	NOMINAL DIAMETER IN INCHES	COLOR CODING	PACKAGED	WEIGHT PER CASE	SUGGESTED RETAIL PRICE Per 1000
100	Small Pistol	.175	Green		4.8 lbs.	17.05
150	Large Pistol	.210	Green		6.1	17.05
155	Large Magnum Pistol	.210	Blue		6.7	20.45
200	Small Rifle & Mag. Pistol	.175	Red	100 per Box	4.9	17.05
205	Small Rifle	.175	Purple	10 Boxes per ctn.,	4.9	17.05
210	Large Rifle	.210	Red	5 ctn. per Case	6.5	17.05
215	Large Magnum Rifle	.210	Purple	of 5000	6.5	20.45
205M	Small Rifle Match	.175	Purple		4.9	25.20
210M	Large Rifle Match	.210	Red		6.5	25.20
209	Shotshell (12, 16 & 20 ga.)	.243	—		16.7	30.30
410	Shotshell (.410 & 28 ga.)	.243	—		16.7	30.30

FEDERAL UNPRIMED CASES

UNPRIMED BRASS PISTOL CASES

ITEM NUMBER	DESCRIPTION	RECOMMENDED FEDERAL PRIMER NUMBER FOR HAND LOADS	PACKAGED	APPR. WEIGHT PER CASE	SUGGESTED RETAIL PRICE PER BOX
380UP	380 Auto	100		8.4 lbs.	7.50
9UP	9mm Luger Auto	200		10.0	11.15
38UP	38 Special	100		10.6	7.85
357UP	357 Magnum	200	50 per Box,	12.4	8.65
357MXUP	357 Maximum	200	20 Boxes	18.0	11.00
41UP	41 Rem. Magnum	150 or 155	per Case of	18.6	11.70
44UP	44 Rem. Magnum	150 or 155	1000 Rounds	18.6	11.70
45UP	45 Auto	150		14.1	11.15
45LCAUP	45 Colt	150		19.6	11.70

UNPRIMED BRASS RIFLE CASES

ITEM NUMBER	DESCRIPTION	RECOMMENDED FEDERAL PRIMER NUMBER FOR HAND LOADS	PACKAGED	APPR. WEIGHT PER CASE	SUGGESTED RETAIL PRICE PER BOX
222UP	22 Remington	200 or 205		18.2 lbs.	5.35
22250UP	22-250 Remington	210		29.4	7.60
223UP	223 Remington	200 or 205		18.3	6.55
243UP	243 Winchester	210		30.4	7.60
2506UP	25-06 Remington	210	20 per Box,	34.0	8.00
270UP	270 Winchester	210	50 Boxes	34.2	8.00
7RUP	7mm Rem. Magnum	215	per Case of	40.5	10.00
3030UP	30-30 Winchester	210	1000 Rounds	26.0	6.90
30006UP	30-30 Springfield	210		34.4	8.00
300WUP	300 Win. Magnum	215		42.0	10.00
308UP	308 Winchester	210		31.0	7.60
4570UP	45-70 Government	210		16.1	7.40

UNPRIMED NICKEL PLATED MATCH RIFLE CASES

ITEM NUMBER	DESCRIPTION	RECOMMENDED FEDERAL PRIMER NUMBER FOR HAND LOADS	PACKAGED	APPR. WEIGHT PER CASE	SUGGESTED RETAIL PRICE PER BOX
222MUP	222 Remington Match	205M	20 per Box, 50 Boxes per Case of 1000 Rounds	18.5 lbs.	6.50
308MUP	308 Winchester Match	210M		30.6	8.80

NORMA UNPRIMED CASES

NORMA CENTERFIRE UNPRIMED BRASS RIFLE CASES—Popular Calibers
20 Rounds Per Box, 50 Boxes Per Case, 1000 Rounds Per Case

Stock Number	Caliber	Suggested Retail Price Per Box		Stock Number	Caliber	Suggested Retail Price Per Box
25601	22 Hornet	15.00		27201	7mm Rem. Magnum	11.77
25711	222 Rem.	6.50		27623	308 Win.	8.60
25731	22-250 Rem.	8.60		27640	30-06 Spfld.	8.77
26001	243 Win.	8.60		27630	30-30 Win.	7.95
26901	270 Win.	8.77		27666	300 Win. Magnum	11.77
				27637	308 Norma Magnum	12.38

NORMA CENTERFIRE UNPRIMED BRASS RIFLE CASES—Specialty Calibers
20 Rounds Per Box, 50 Boxes per Case, 1000 Rounds Per Case

Stock Number	Caliber	Price		Stock Number	Caliber	Price
25701	220 Swift	10.07		27511	7.5 × 55 Swiss	10.40
26531	6.5 × 50 Japanese	10.07		27634	7.62 × 54R Russian	10.40
26535	6.5 × 52 Carcano	10.07		27701	7.65 × 53 Argentine	10.07
26551	6.5 × 55 Swedish	10.07		27111	303 British	10.40
27012	7 × 64 Brenneke	10.40		27721	7.7 × 58 Japanese	10.40

NORMA CENTERFIRE UNPRIMED BRASS PISTOL CASES—Boxes
50 Rounds Per Box, 40 Boxes Per Case, 2000 Rounds Per Case

Stock Number	Caliber	Price		Stock Number	Caliber	Price
29021	9mm Luger	12.25		29101	357 Magnum	10.55
29110	38 Special	9.33		21001	10mm Auto	16.25
				21101	44 Magnum	16.25

REMINGTON CASES & PRIMERS

Remington brass cases with 5% more brass for extra strength in head section—annealed neck section for longer reloading life—primer pocket dimension controlled to .0005 inch to assure precise primer fit—heavier bridge and sidewalls—formed and machined to exacting tolerances for consistent powder capacity—choice of seventy-one center fire rifle, pistol and revolver cases—

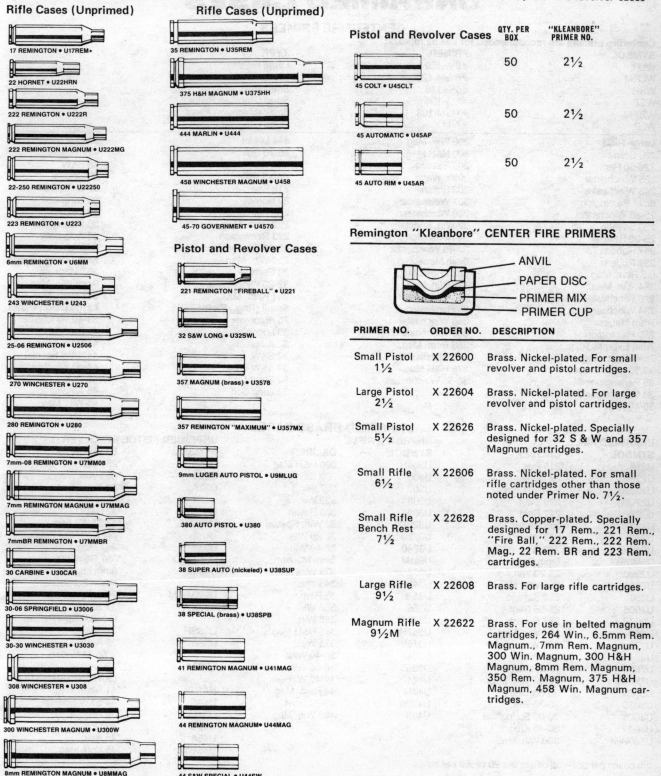

Rifle Cases (Unprimed)

- 17 REMINGTON • U17REM∗
- 22 HORNET • U22HRN
- 222 REMINGTON • U222R
- 222 REMINGTON MAGNUM • U222MG
- 22-250 REMINGTON • U22250
- 223 REMINGTON • U223
- 6mm REMINGTON • U6MM
- 243 WINCHESTER • U243
- 25-06 REMINGTON • U2506
- 270 WINCHESTER • U270
- 280 REMINGTON • U280
- 7mm-08 REMINGTON • U7MM08
- 7mm REMINGTON MAGNUM • U7MMAG
- 7mmBR REMINGTON • U7MMBR
- 30 CARBINE • U30CAR
- 30-06 SPRINGFIELD • U3006
- 30-30 WINCHESTER • U3030
- 308 WINCHESTER • U308
- 300 WINCHESTER MAGNUM • U300W
- 8mm REMINGTON MAGNUM • U8MMAG

Rifle Cases (Unprimed)

- 35 REMINGTON • U35REM
- 375 H&H MAGNUM • U375HH
- 444 MARLIN • U444
- 458 WINCHESTER MAGNUM • U458
- 45-70 GOVERNMENT • U4570

Pistol and Revolver Cases

- 221 REMINGTON "FIREBALL" • U221
- 32 S&W LONG • U32SWL
- 357 MAGNUM (brass) • U3578
- 357 REMINGTON "MAXIMUM" • U357MX
- 9mm LUGER AUTO PISTOL • U9MLUG
- 380 AUTO PISTOL • U380
- 38 SUPER AUTO (nickeled) • U38SUP
- 38 SPECIAL (brass) • U38SPB
- 41 REMINGTON MAGNUM • U41MAG
- 44 REMINGTON MAGNUM • U44MAG
- 44 S&W SPECIAL • U44SW

Pistol and Revolver Cases

	QTY. PER BOX	"KLEANBORE" PRIMER NO.
45 COLT • U45CLT	50	2½
45 AUTOMATIC • U45AP	50	2½
45 AUTO RIM • U45AR	50	2½

Remington "Kleanbore" CENTER FIRE PRIMERS

- ANVIL
- PAPER DISC
- PRIMER MIX
- PRIMER CUP

PRIMER NO.	ORDER NO.	DESCRIPTION
Small Pistol 1½	X 22600	Brass. Nickel-plated. For small revolver and pistol cartridges.
Large Pistol 2½	X 22604	Brass. Nickel-plated. For large revolver and pistol cartridges.
Small Pistol 5½	X 22626	Brass. Nickel-plated. Specially designed for 32 S & W and 357 Magnum cartridges.
Small Rifle 6½	X 22606	Brass. Nickel-plated. For small rifle cartridges other than those noted under Primer No. 7½.
Small Rifle Bench Rest 7½	X 22628	Brass. Copper-plated. Specially designed for 17 Rem., 221 Rem., "Fire Ball," 222 Rem., 222 Rem. Mag., 22 Rem. BR and 223 Rem. cartridges.
Large Rifle 9½	X 22608	Brass. For large rifle cartridges.
Magnum Rifle 9½M	X 22622	Brass. For use in belted magnum cartridges, 264 Win., 6.5mm Rem. Magnum., 7mm Rem. Magnum, 300 Win. Magnum, 300 H&H Magnum, 8mm Rem. Magnum, 350 Rem. Magnum, 375 H&H Magnum, 458 Win. Magnum cartridges.

∗ Designed for Remington No. 7½ primer only. Substitutions not recommended. U number is unprimed.

WINCHESTER PRIMERS & UNPRIMED CASES

CENTERFIRE PRIMERS

Centerfire primers are recommended for use as follows:

SYMBOL	PRIMER	TYPE
WLR	#8½-120	Large Rifle
WLRM	#8½M-120	Large Rifle Magnum
WSR	#6½-116	Small Rifle
WSP	#1½-108	Small (Regular) Pistol
WSPM	#1½M-108	Small (Magnum) Pistol
WLP	#7-111	Large (Regular Pistol)

Large Rifle
220 Swift
22-250 Rem.
225 Winchester
243 Winchester
6mm Remington
25-35 Winchester
250 Savage
25-06 Rem.
257 Roberts
257 Roberts + P
6.5 Rem. Mag.
264 Win. Mag.
270 Winchester
284 Winchester
7mm Mauser
280 Remington
7mm Express Rem.
7mm Rem. Mag.
30-30 Winchester
30 Remington
30-06 Springfield
30-40 Krag

300 Win. Mag.
300 H&H Mag.
300 Savage
303 Savage
303 British
307 Winchester
308 Winchester
32 Win. Special
32 Remington
32-40 Winchester
8mm Mauser
8mm Rem. Mag.
338 Win. Mag.
348 Winchester
35 Remington
356 Winchester
358 Winchester
350 Rem. Mag.
375 Winchester
375 H&H Mag.
38-55 Winchester

444 Marlin
45-70 Gov.
458 Win. Mag.
Small Rifle
218 Bee
22 Hornet
222 Remington
222 Rem. Mag.
223 Remington
25-20 Winchester
256 Win. Mag.
30 Carbine
32-20 Winchester
357 Rem. Max.
Small (Reg.) Pistol
25 Automatic
30 Luger
32 Automatic
32 S&W
32 S&W Long
32 Short Colt
32 Long Colt

32 Colt New Police
9mm Luger
38 S&W
38 Special
38 Short Colt
38 Long Colt
38 Colt New Police
38 Super-Auto
38 Automatic
380 Automatic
Small (Mag.) Pistol
357 Magnum
9mm Win. Mag.
357 Rem. Max.
Large (Reg.) Pistol
38-40 Winchester
41 Rem. Mag.
44 Rem. Mag.
44 S&W Special
44-40 Winchester
45 Colt
45 Automatic
45 Win. Mag.

UNPRIMED BRASS CASES

UNPRIMED RIFLE SYMBOL	CALIBER	UNPRIMED RIFLE SYMBOL	CALIBER	UNPRIMED PISTOL/REVOLVER SYMBOL	CALIBER
U218	*218 Bee	U300H	300 H&H Mag.	U25A	*25 Auto.
U22H	*22 Hornet	U300	300 Savage	U256	*256 Win. Mag.
U22250	22-250 Rem.	U307	307 Win.	U32A	*32 Auto.
U22OS	220 Swift	U308	308 Win.		(7.65mm Browning)
U222R	222 Rem.	U303	303 British	U32SW	*32 S&W
U223R	223 Rem.	U32W	32 Win. Special	U32SWL	*32 S&W Long
U225	225 Win.	U3220	*32-20 Win.		(32 Colt New Police)
U243	243 Win.	U3240	32-40 Win.	U357	*357 Mag.
U6MMR	6mm Rem.	U8MM	8mm Mauser	U357MAX	*357 Rem. Max.
U2520	25-20 Win.	U338	338 Win. Mag.	U9MM	*9mm Luger
U256	*256 Win. Mag.	U348	348 Win.		(9mm Parabellum)
U250	250 Savage	U35R	35 Rem.	U9MMWM	*9mm Win. Mag.
U2506	25-06 Rem.	U356	356 Win.	U38SW	*38 S&W
U257P	257 Roberts + P	U358	358 Win.		(38 Colt New Police)
U264	264 Win. Mag.	U357H	375 H&H Mag.	U38SP	*38 Special
U270	270 Win.	U375W	375 Win.	U38A	*38 Auto
U284	284 Win.	U3840	38-40 Win.		(and 38 Super)
U7MM	7mm Mauser	U3855	*38-55 Win.	U380A	*380 Auto
U7MAG.	7mm Rem. Mag.	U4440	*44-40 Win.		(9mm Short-9mm Corto)
U30C	*30 Carbine	U44M	*44 Rem. Mag.	U41	*41 Rem. Mag.
U3030	30-30 Win.	U4570	*45-70 Govt.	U44S	*44 S&W Special
U3006	30-06 Springfield	U458	458 Win. Mag.	U44M	*44 Rem. Mag.
U3040	30-40 Krag			U45C	*45 Colt
U300WM	300 Win. Mag.			U45A	*45 Auto
				U45WM	*45 Win. Mag.

*50 cases per box—all others are 20 cases per box.

DU PONT SMOKELESS POWDERS

SHOTSHELL POWDER

Hi-Skor 700-X Double-Base Shotshell Powder. Specifically designed for today's 12-gauge components. Developed to give optimum ballistics at minimum charge weight (means more reloads per pound of powder). 700-X is dense, easy to load, clean to handle, and loads uniformly.

PB Shotshell Powder. Produces exceptional 20- and 28-gauge skeet reloads; preferred by many in 12-gauge target loads, it gives 3-dram equivalent velocity at relatively low chamber pressures.

Hi-Skor 800-X Shotshell Powder. An excellent powder for 12-gauge field loads and 20- and 28-gauge loads.

SR-4756 Powder. Great all-around powder for target and field loads.

SR-7625 Powder. A fast growing "favorite" for reloading target as well as light and heavy field loads in 4 gauges. Excellent velocity-chamber pressure.

IMR-4227 Powder. Can be used effectively for reloading .410-gauge shotshell ammunition.

RIFLE POWDER

IMR-3031 Rifle Powder. Specifically recommended for medium-capacity cartridges.

IMR-4064 Rifle Powder. Has exceptionally uniform burning qualities when used in medium- and large-capacity cartridges.

IMR-4198. Made the Remington 222 cartridge famous. Developed for small- and medium-capacity cartridges.

IMR-4227 Rifle Powder. Fastest burning of the IMR Series. Specifically designed for the 22 Hornet class of cartridges.

SR-4759. Brought back by shooter demand. Available for cast bullet loads.

IMR-4320. Recommended for high-velocity cartridges.

IMR-4350 Rifle Powder. Gives unusually uniform results when loaded in Magnum cartridges. Slowest burning powder of the IMR series.

IMR-4831. Produced as a canister-grade handloading powder. Packaged in 1 lb. canister, 8 lb. caddy and 20 lb. kegs.

IMR-4895 Rifle Powder. The time-tested standard for caliber 30 military ammunition; slightly faster than IMR-4320. Loads uniformly in all powder measures. One of the country's favorite powders.

IMR-7828 Rifle Powder. The slowest-burning DuPont IMR cannister powder, intended for large capacity and magnum-type cases with heavy bullets.

PISTOL POWDER

PB Powder. Another powder for reloading a wide variety of centerfire handgun ammunition.

IMR-4227 Powder. Can be used effectively for reloading "Magnum" handgun ammunition.

"Hi-Skor" 700-X Powder. The same qualities that make it a superior powder contribute to its exellent performance in all the popular handguns.

SR-7625 Powder. For reloading a wide variety of centerfire handgun ammunition.

SR-4756, IMR-3031 and IMR-4198. Three more powders in a good selection—all clean burning and with uniform performance.

HODGDON SMOKELESS POWDER

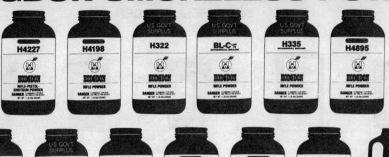

RIFLE POWDER

H4227 AND H4198
$14.50/lb.

H4227 is the fastest burning of the IMR series. Well adapted to Hornet, light bullets in 222 and all bullets in 357 and 44 Magnum pistols. Cuts leading with lead bullets. H4198 was developed especially for small and medium capacity cartridges.

H322
$14.50/lb.

A new extruded bench rest powder which has proved to be capable of producing fine accuracy in the 22 and 308 bench rest guns. This powder fills the gap between H4198 and BL-C(2). Performs best in small to medium capacity cases.

SPHERICAL BL-C®, Lot No. 2
$14.50/lb.

A highly popular favorite of the bench rest shooters. Best performance is in the 222, and in other cases smaller than 30/06.

SHOTGUN AND
PISTOL POWDER

HP38
$13.25/lb.

A fast pistol powder for most pistol loading. Especially recommended for mid-range 38 specials.

TRAP 100
$11.95/lb.

Trap 100 is a spherical trap and light field load powder, also excellent for target loads in centerfire pistols. Mild recoil.

SPHERICAL H335®
$11.50/lb.

Similar to BL-C(2), H335 is popular for its performance in medium capacity cases, especially in 222 and 308 Winchester.

H4895®
$14.50/lb.

4895 may well be considered the most versatile of all propellants. It gives desirable performance in almost all cases from 222 Rem. to 458 Win. Reduced loads, to as low as 3/5 of maximum, still give target accuracy.

SPHERICAL H380®
$14.50/lb.

This number fills a gap between 4320 and 4350. It is excellent in 22/250, 220 Swift, the 6mm's, 257 and 30/06.

#25 DATA MANUAL (544 pp.)
$14.95

HS-6 and HS-7
$12.95/lb.

HS-6 and HS-7 for Magnum field loads are unsurpassed, since they do not pack in the measure. They deliver uniform charges and are dense to allow sufficient wad column for best patterns.

H110
$13.25/lb.

A spherical powder made especially for the 30 M1 carbine. H110 also does very well in 357, 44 Spec., 44 Mag. or .410 ga. shotshell. Magnum primers are recommended for consistent ignition.

SPHERICAL H414®
$7.99/lb.

A new development in spherical powder. In many popular medium to medium-large calibers, pressure velocity relationship is better.

SPHERICAL H870®
$7.25/lb.

Very slow burning rate adaptable to overbore capacity Magnum cases such as 257, 264, 270 and 300 Mags with heavy bullets.

H4350
$14.50/lb.

This powder gives superb accuracy at optimum velocity for many large capacity metallic rifle cartridges.

H4831®
$14.50/lb.

The most popular of all powders. Outstanding performance with medium and heavy bullets in the 6mm's, 25/06, 270 and Magnum calibers.

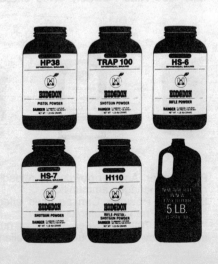

BONANZA RELOADING TOOLS

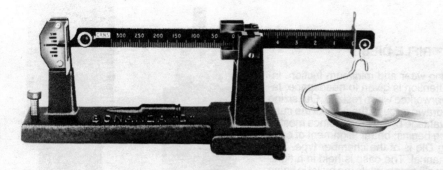

POWDER AND BULLET SCALE
MODEL "D"™ $44.00

330-grain capacity, tempered stainless steel right-hand poise, diamond-polished agate "V" bearings, non-glare white markings. Die cast aluminum base, strengthened beam at pivot points, powder pan for right or left pouring. Easy to read pointer and reference point. Guaranteed accurate to $\frac{1}{10}$ grain; sensitivity guaranteed to $\frac{1}{20}$ grain.

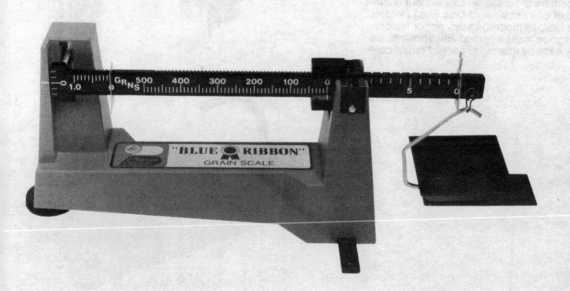

BLUE RIBBON GRAIN SCALE

511-grain capacity for ease of weighing powder. "Blue Ribbon" scales have three poises for better accuracy and convenience. White markings on non-glare enhance reading with less eye strain. Comparator scale and resting point locator lie in the same plane, which eliminates errors in reading due to parallax. Base has three point suspension, eliminating rocking. Guaranteed accurate to $\frac{1}{10}$ grain. Sensitivity to $\frac{1}{20}$ grain.

"Blue Ribbon"™ Magnetic Dampened Grain Scale $59.90

BONANZA RELOADING TOOLS

CO-AX® BENCH REST® RIFLE DIES

Bench Rest Rifle Dies are glass hard for long wear and minimum friction. Interiors are polished mirror smooth. Special attention is given to headspace, tapers and diameters so that brass will not be overworked when resized. Our sizing die has an elevated expander button which is drawn through the neck of the case at the moment of the greatest mechanical advantage of the press. Since most of the case neck is still in the die when expanding begins, better alignment of case and neck is obtained. **Bench Rest® Seating Die** is of the chamber type. The bullet is held in alignment in a close-fitting channel. The case is held in a tight-fitting chamber. Both bullet and case are held in alignment while the bullet is being seated. Cross-bolt lock ring included at no charge.

Bench Rest® Die Set	$46.50
Full Length Sizer	19.90
Bench Rest Seating Die	29.00

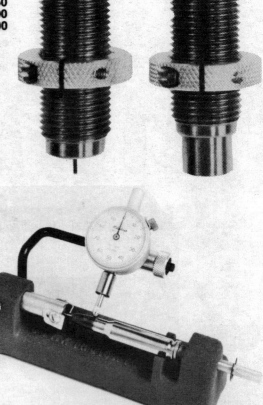

PRIMER SEATER

The Bonanza Primer Seater is designed so that primers are seated Co-Axially (primer in line with primer pocket). Mechanical leverage allows primers to be seated fully without crushing. With the addition of one extra set of Disc Shell Holders and one extra Primer Unit, all modern cases, rim or rimless, from 222 up to 458 Magnum, can be primed. Shell holders are easily adjusted to any case by rotating to contact rim or cannelure of the case.

Primer Seater	$45.00
Primer Tube	3.25

CO-AX® INDICATOR

Bullets will not leave a rifle barrel at a uniform angle unless they are started uniformly. The Co-Ax Indicator provides a reading of how closely the axis of the bullet corresponds to the axis of the cartridge case. The Indicator features a spring-loaded plunger to hold cartridges against a recessed, adjustable rod while the cartridge is supported in a "V" block. To operate, simply rotate the cartridge with the fingers; the degree of misalignment is transferred to an indicator which measures in one-thousandths.

Price	$39.00

C-H RELOADING ACCESSORIES

NO. 725 POWDER and BULLET SCALE

Chrome-plated, brass beam. Graduated in 10 gr., 1 gr. and 1/10th gr. increments. Convenient pouring spout on pan. Leveling screw on base. All metal construction. 360 gr. capacity.

Price...................................... $35.95

NO. 301 CASE TRIMMER

This design features a unique clamp to lock case holder in position. Ensures perfect uniformity from 22 through 45 caliber whether rifle or pistol cases. Complete including hardened case holder.

No. 301 Case Trimmer $21.95
Extra case holders (hardened & hand-lapped)....... 3.50

UNIVERSAL SHELL HOLDERS

Up to now, shell holders came in one piece—you needed as many shell holders as the calibers you wished to reload. With the C-H Universal Shell Holder all the reloader needs is the Shell Holder ram.

No. 408 Universal "C" or "H" Shell
   Holder Head $4.00
No. 407 Universal "H" Shell Holder
   Ram 5.25
No. 412 Universal "C" Shell Holder
   Ram 10.50

CARTRIDGE RACK TRAY

Holds 60 cartridges. Comes in black, white or red. It is handy for the reloader who works up cases for different loads, etc. Holes, which are $15/16$" deep, are not large enough for 45/70 or 348 but holds all sizes up to 375 H&H.

No. 403 Cartridge Rack Tray $1.65

POWDER MEASURE

The steel drum is designed so the handle can be placed on either the right or left side, and the charge can be dropped on either the up or down stroke. Or reverse for use with micrometer either front or back. Base threads are $7/8$-inch $\times$ 14. The rifle micrometer adjusts precisely and permits up to 100 grains of 4831. The pistol micrometer permits up to 12 grains of Bullseye. A baffle plate is supplied with the optional 10-inch production hopper.

No. 502 Powder Measure (specify Rifle or Pistol)... $44.95
No. 502-1 Stand $7/8$" thread 6.95
No. 502-2 Micrometer (specify Rifle or Pistol)....... 13.95
No. 592-3 10" Production Hopper (with baffle)....... 6.50

UNIVERSAL PRIMING ARM

Accommodates all standard rifle and pistol primers. Made of fine metal—not a stamping—for extra strength and dimensional stability. Packaged in clear acetate tube. No. 414 Universal "C" Priming Arm $6.95

BULLET PULLER

C-H Bullet Puller features positive die-locking action, removes the bullet easily without any damage to housing or bullet. The detachable handle is constructed of $3/8$" stock and adjusts to any position. The hex nut for crescent wrench adjustment locks the die into firm position. Extra long internal thread for extra locking leeway.

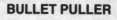
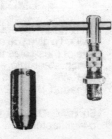

No. 402 with Collet $10.50
No. 402-1 Extra Collet......... 3.25

C-H RELOADING ACCESSORIES

ZINC BASE SWAGE DIE

- Maximum Energy
- 100% expansion, every time
- Zinc Base coats the bore with every shot
- Actually cleans the bore as you shoot
- No leading, even using maximum loads
- Perfect gas seal
- Use with any standard loading press
- Simple to use—one stroke of the handle and tap the finished bullet out.
- The perfect lubricating qualities of zinc combined with the perfect expansion

of pure lead produce outstanding, accurate bullets and will appreciably increase bore life.

No. 105-Z Zinc Base Swage Dies, 38/357 SWC
Shipping weight, 1 lb. $29.95
No. 105 Z1 Nose Punch, SWC, caliber 38/357 . . . . 4.00
38/357 caliber Zinc Base Washer, per 1000 (shipping weight per M, 1 lb.). 23.20

308 WINCHESTER AND 223 REMINGTON TAPER CRIMP DIE

- No longer necessary to have perfect trimmed cases
- Use as a separate die to form a perfect taper crimp each time
- Eliminates time-consuming trimming
- Produces Match Grade ammo
- Perfect feeding in semiauto rifles
- Load your ammo just like the factory does

Taper Crimp Die
Shipping weight 1 lb. $17.00

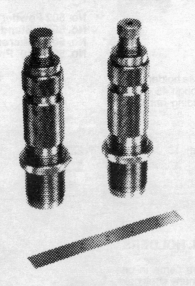

50 CALIBER BMG LOADING DIES

With **50 BMG Priming Accessories** the priming post and the shell holder can be used as is with any Hollywood tool. With the addition of the shell holder die, the priming can be accomplished with any existing loading tool with ⅞-inch top threads. The shell holder die screws into the top of the tool and the threaded shell holder is screwed into this. By adding the priming post you have a complete separate priming system.

Priming Post complete $11.95
Shell Holder Die 9.95
Shell Holder with lock ring 17.95

BMG DIE SET

C-H offers a die set for loading 50 caliber BMG. To give you an idea of the massive size of these dies they are shown with a 6-inch steel rule alongside a standard 308 Win. die and cartridge. They are threaded 1½ × 12.

50 BMG Die set (full-length sizer and crimp seater) $275.00

DEBURRING/CHAMFERING TOOL

Standard size: Bevels both the inside and outside of the case mouth for easy bullet insertion. Hardened for long life. Extra sharp cutters. Fits 17 to 45 calibers.
Magnum size: For those who load 45 caliber and over, a Magnum Deburring Tool is available from C-H. Fits all cases from 45 to 60 caliber.

Standard Deburring Tool . . . . $ 8.95
Magnum Deburring Tool 14.95

C-H RELOADING TOOLS

MODEL 444 "H" PRESS

Offers 4-station versatility—two, three or four-piece die sets may be used. New casting design offers increased strength, and there is sufficient room for the longest magnum cases.

Model 444 4-Station "H" Press (includes 4 rams, 4 shell-holders, primer arm, and primer catcher **$158.00**
Same model but with one standard caliber die set 176.00

DIE BOX

Protect your dies from dust and damage with a C-H 3-compartment plastic Die Box. High-impact plastic will not break. Easy to label and stack.

No. 700 Die Box **$1.50**

³/₄ JACKETED PISTOL BULLET SWAGING DIES

- Any bullet weight from 110 gr. to 250 gr. with same set of dies
- Can be used in any good $^7/_8"$ × 14 loading tool
- Absolutely no leading
- Complete—no extras to buy
- Increased velocity
- Solid nose or hollow point (hollow point $2.50 extra)
- Available in 38/357, 41 S & W, 44 Mag. and 45 Colt calibers

Price: **$44.45**

BULLET SWAGING DIE EJECTOR

A helpful accessory for use with the new C-H jacketed bullet swaging dies. The ejector attaches easily to the swaging die body with one screw. Can be used with either the core seating die or the swage die. Ejects the seated core or finished bullet with ease. No more tapping the top of the die.

Price **$24.65**

CANNELURE TOOL

- Solid steel
- Will work on all sizes of bullets, from 17 to 45
- Completely adjustable for depth and height
- One set will process thousands of bullets
- Necessary for rolling in grooves on bullets prior to crimping
- Hardened cutting wheel, precision-machined throughout

Price: **$34.95**

FORSTER RELOADING TOOLS

CASE TRIMMER

The Forster Case Trimmer trims all cases from 17 cal. to 458 Winchester. Its shell holder is a Brown & Sharpe type collet, which closes on the case rim without pulling the case back, thus insuring uniform case length (even when there is variation in rim diameter).

Case Trimmer (less collet and pilot) $37.50
Case Trimmer Pilot 1.98
Case Trimmer Collet 6.00

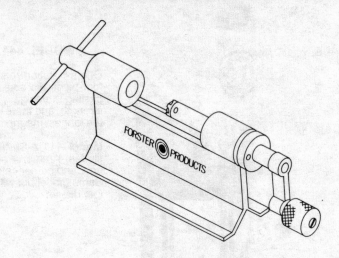

OUTSIDE NECK TURNER
(Shown on Forster Case Trimmer)

The Outside Neck Turner consists of a cutter head which carries an adjustable circular carbide cutter. The tool will turn any diameter between .170 and .375. The short pilot used in case trimming is replaced with an extra long, hardened and ground pilot of the desired caliber. As the wall of the neck passes progressively between the pilot and the cutter, the neck wall of the case is reduced to a uniform thickness. The rate of feed is controlled by rotating the feeder cam; a mechanical stop controls the length of the cut. Outside Neck Turners are available for following caliber sizes: 17, 224, 243, 257, 277, 263, 284, 308, 311, 323, 333, 338, 358 and 375.

Outside Neck Turner (complete w/one pilot) $27.00

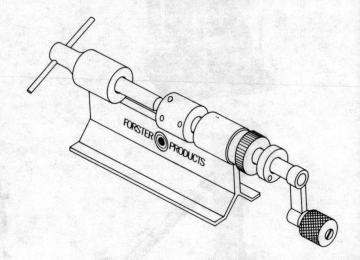

POWER CASE TRIMMER

Can be used with any standard drill press. Case length is controlled by the stop on drill press spindle. A line-up bar aligns the trimmer and drill press spindle. The threaded lever for opening and closing the Brown & Sharpe collet can be removed easily. The cutter shaft is made with a 1/4" shank and has four staggered cutting edges for chatterless trimming of cases.

Power Case Trimmer (less collet and pilot) $37.50

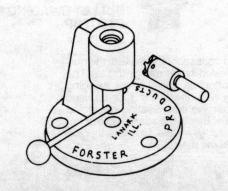

HORNADY

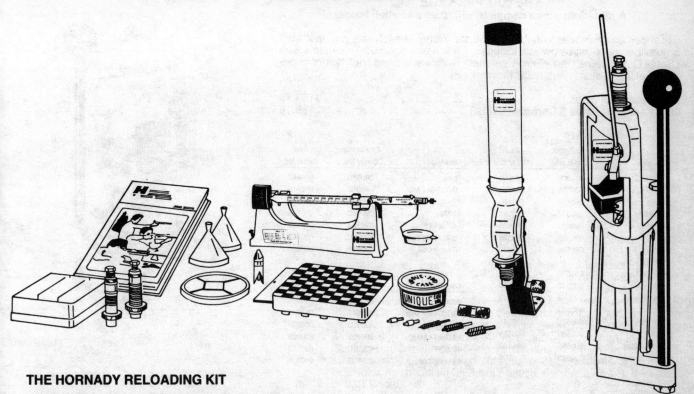

THE HORNADY RELOADING KIT

The Hornady Reloading Kit is ideal for any reloader who wants to start from scratch with a complete outfit. It includes your choice of a basic 00-7 or PRO-Jector press, completely equipped with: Set of Dies • Primer catcher • Removable shell holder • Positive Priming System • Automatic Primer Feed.

Plus, all these bench accessories: Deluxe powder measure • Magnetic scale • 2 static-resistant powder funnels • Primer turning plate • Universal reloading block • Unique case lube.

In addition, we include these case care accessories: Chamfering and deburring tool • Large and small primer pocket

cleaners • 3 case neck brushes and accessory handle. Also, a copy of the Hornady Handbook. The Hornady Kit provides substantial savings over all these items if purchased separately.

00-7 Kit (20 lbs.)	**$333.85**
00-7 Kit Series II Carbide (20 lbs.) . .	359.50
PRO-Jector Kit (29 lbs.)	435.00
PRO-Jector Kit Series II Carbide (29 lbs.)	458.40

Hornady Reloading Kits are available in these calibers . . .

Cartridge	Pro-Jector Order No.	00-7 Order No.	Cartridge	Pro-Jector Order No.	00-7 Order No.	Carbide Pro-Jector Order No.	Carbide 00-7 Order No.
222 Rem.	090500	080500	308 Win.	090550	080550	—	—
223 Rem.	090505	080505	30/06	090560	080555	—	—
22/250	090510	080510	300 Win. Mag.	090565	080560	—	—
6MM Rem.	090515	080515	30 M1 Carb.	090570	080800	—	—
243 Win.	090520	080520	9MM Luger	090575	080805	090910	080910
25/06	090525	080525	38-357-357 Max.	090580	080810	090915	080915
6.5 × 55	—	080565	375 Win.	090585	080840	—	—
270 Win.	090530	080530	41 Mag.	090590	080845	090920	080920
7 × 57			44 Spl./44 Mag.	090595	080820	090925	080925
(7MM Mau.)	090535	080535	45 ACP	090600	080825	090930	080930
7MM Rem. Mag.	090540	080540	45 Long Colt	090605	080830	090935	080935
7MM/08	090545	080543	444 Marlin	—	080835	—	—
30/30 Win.	090555	080545					

HORNADY

THE 00-7 PACKAGE
A reloading press complete with dies and shell holder

Expanded and improved to include Automatic Primer Feed. It sets you up to load any caliber in the list below and includes: Choice of a basic 00-7 complete with • Set of Durachrome Dies • Primer catcher • Removable head shell holder • Positive Priming System • Automatic Primer Feed.

00-7 Package (13 lbs.) **$163.75**
00-7 Package Series II Carbide (13 lbs.) **189.15**

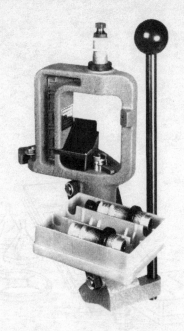

Cartridge	Pro-Jector Order No.	00-7 Order No.
222 Rem.	090500	080500
223 Rem.	090505	080505
22/250	090510	080510
6mm Rem.	090515	080515
243 Win.	090520	080520
25/06	090525	080525
270 Win.	090530	080530
6.5×55		080565
7mm Mauser	090535	080535
7mm Rem.	090540	080540
7mm/08	090545	080543
308	090550	
30/30 Win.	090555	080545
30-06	090560	080555
300 Win. Mag.	090565	080560
30 M1 Carbine	090570	080800

Cartridge	Pro-Jector Order No.	00-7 Order No.
9mm	090575	080805
38-357-357 Max.	090580	080810
375 Win.	090585	080840
41 Mag.	09059C	080845
44 Spl./44 Mag.	090595	080820
45 ACP (A11)	090600	080825
45 Long Colt	090605	080830

Cartridge	Pro-Jector Carbide	00-7 Carbide
9mm	090910	080910
38-357-357 Max.	090915	080915
41 Mag.	090920	080920
44 Spl./44 Mag.	090925	080925
45 ACP	090930	080930
45 Long Colt	090935	080935

THE HANDLOADER'S ACCESSORY PACK I

Here's everything you need in one money-saving pack. It includes: • Deluxe powder measure • Magnetic scale • 2, non-static powder funnels • Universal reloading tray • Primer turning plate • Unique case lube • Chambering and deburring tool • 3 case neck brushes • Large and small primer pocket cleaner • Accessory handle. Plus one copy of the Hornady Handbook of Cartridge Reloading.

Handloader's Accessory Pack I No. 030300 . . . . **$172.50**

HORNADY

DIE REFERENCE CHART

2-DIE SETS (Rifle)

CARTRIDGE	Die Group	Primer Punch Size	Shell Holder	Trimmer Pilot	Bullet Puller Collet
17 Rem. [.172]	I*	Small	16	Order Pilot & Cutter as one unit for all 17 cal.	1
17/222 [.172]	IV*	Small	16		1
17/223 [.172]	IV*	Small	16		1
218 Bee [.224]	III	Small	7	1	2
219 Zipper [.224]	IV	Large	2	1	2
221 Rem. [.224]	I	Small	16	1	2
222 Rem. [.224]	I*	Small	16	1	2
222 Rem. Mag. [.224]	I*	Small	16	1	2
22 Hornet [.224]	I	Small	3	1	2
22 K-Hornet [.224]	IV	Small	3	1	2
22 RCFM-Jet [.224]	IV	Small	6	1	2
22 PPC [.224]	Sil & BR Dies	Small	6	1	2
5.6 x 50 Mag. [.24]	IV	Small	16	1	2
5.6 x 52R [.227]	IV	Large	2	1	2
5.6 x 57 [.224]	IV	•Large	1	1	2
223 Rem. [.224]	I*	Small	16	1	2
22/250 [.224]	I*	Large	1	1	2
220 Swift [.224]	I*	Large	4	1	2
22 Sav. HP [.227]	IV	Large	2	1	2
224 Wby. [.224]	IV*	Large	17	1	2
225 Win. [.224]	III	Large	4	1	2
240 Wby. [.243]	III	Large	1	3	3
243 Win. [.243]	I*	Large	1	3	3
244/6MM [.243]	I*	Large	1	3	3
6MM Int. [.243]	IV	Large	1	3	3
6MM/223 [.243]	Sil & BR Dies*	Small	16	3	3
6MM/PPC [.243]	Sil & BR Dies	Small	6	3	3
6MM/284 [.243]	IV	Large	1	3	3
6 x 47 Rem. [.243]	Sil & BR Dies	Small	16	3	3
250 Sav. [.257]	III	Large	1	4	4
25/06 [.257]	I*	Large	1	4	4
257 Rbts. [.257]	I*	Large	1	4	4
25/20 Win. [.257]	IV	Small	7	4	4
25/35 Win. [.257]	III	Large	2	4	4
256 Win. [.257]	IV	Small	6	4	4
257 Wby. [.257]	III	Large	5	4	4
25 Rem. [.257]	IV	Large	12	4	4
25/284 [.257]	IV*	Large	1	4	4
6.5 x 55 [.264]	I*	Large	19	5	4
6.5/06 [.264]	IV*	Large	1	5	4
6.5MM TCU	Sil & BR Dies	Small	16	5	4
6.5 Rem. Mag. [.264]	IV*	Large	5	5	4
6.5 Mann. [.264]	IV	Large	20	5	4
6.5 Carc. [.264]	IV	Large	21	5	4
6.5 Jap. [.264]	IV	Large	34	5	4
6.5 x 57 [.264]	IV	Large	1	5	4
6.5 x 68 [.264]	IV	Large	30	5	4
264 Win. Mag. [.264]	I	Large	5	5	4
270 Win. [.270]	I*	Large	1	6	5
270 Wby. [.270]	IV	Large	5	6	5
7 x 30 Waters	iii	Large	2	7	6
7 x 57 (7MM Mau.)	I*	Large	1	7	6
7MM/08 [.284]	I*	Large	1	7	6
7MM Rem. Mag. [.284]	I*	Large	5	7	6
7MM Rem. BR [.284]	Sil & BR Dies	Large	1	7	6
7MM TCU [.284]	Sil & BR Dies*	Large	16	7	6
7MM Merrill [.284]	Sil & BR Dies	Large	4	7	6
7 x 65R [.284]	IV	Large	13	7	6
7MM Wby. [.284]	III*	Large	5	7	6
7 x 64 [.284]	I*	Large	1	7	6
7MM/223 Ingram [.284]	Sil & BR Dies*	Small	16	7	6
7 x 47 Helm [.284]	Sil & BR Dies*	Small	16	7	6
7 x 61 S & H [.284]	IV*	Large	35	7	6
7MM Exp./ 280 [.284]	I*	Large	1	7	6
284 Win. [.284]	III*	Large	1	7	6
7.35 Carc. [.300]	IV*	Large	21	8	7
30/30 Win. [.308]	I*	Large	2	9	7
300 Sav. [.308]	I	Large	1	9	7
30 Luger [.308]	III	Large	8	9	7
30 Merrill [.308]	Sil & BR Dies	Large	4	9	7

2-DIE SETS (Rifle)

CARTRIDGE	Die Group	Primer Punch Size	Shell Holder	Trimmer Pilot	Bullet Puller Collet
30 Herrett [.308]	Sil & BR Dies*	Large	2	9	7
303 Sav. [.308]	IV	Large	33	9	7
308 Win. [.308]	I*	Large	1	9	7
30/40 Krag [.308]	III	Large	11	9	7
30/06 [.308]	I*	Large	1	9	7
300 H & H [.308]	IV	Large	5	9	7
300 Win. Mag. [.308]	I	Large	5	9	7
300 Wby. [.308]	III*	Large	5	9	7
308 Norma Mag. [.308]	IV*	Large	5	9	7
7.62 Russ. [.308]	I	Large	23	9	7
7.5 Swiss [.308]	III	Large	30	9	7
7.7 Jap. [.312]	III	Large	1	10	7
303 Brit. [.312]	I	Large	11	10	7
7.65 Belg. [.312]	III	Large	24	10	7
32/20 Win. [.310]	III	Small	7	10	7
32 Win. Spl. [.321]	III	Large	2	11	8
8MM Mau. [.323]	I*	Large	1	11	8
8MM/06 [.323]	IV*	Large	1	11	8
8MM Rem. Mag. [.323]	III	Large	5	11	8
8 x 60S [.323]	IV	Large	1	11	8
8 x 68S [.323]	IV	Large	30	11	8
8.15 x 46R [.337]	IV	Large	2	11	8
338 Win. Mag. [.338]	I	Large	5	13	8
33 Win. [.338]	IV	Large	14	13	8
340 Wby. [.338]	IV	Large	5	13	8
348 Win. [.348]	IV	Large	25	14	9
35 Rem. [.358]	I*	Large	26	15	9
35 Whelen [.358]	IV	Large	1	15	9
357 B & D [.358]	Sil & BR Dies	Large	30	15	9
350 Rem. Mag. [.358]	IV*	Large	5	15	9
357 Herrett [.357]	Sil & BR Dies*	Large	2	15	9
358 Win. [.358]	III	Large	1	15	9
358 N. Mag. [.358]	IV	Large	5	15	9
375 H & H [.375]	III	Large	5	16	9
378 Wby. [.375]	IV	Large	14	16	9
9.3 x 74R [.366]	IV	Large	13	15	9
9.3 x 57 [.366]	IV	Large	1	15	9
9.3 x 62 [.366]	IV	Large	1	15	9
10.3 x 60 [.415]	IV	Small	25	17	12
460 Wby. [.458]	IV	Large	14	19	13

3-DIE SETS

CARTRIDGE	Die Group	Primer Punch Size	Shell Holder	Trimmer Pilot	Bullet Puller Collet
25 ACP [.251]	II	Small	37	4	4
30 M1 Carb. [.308]	II	Small	22	9	7
32 ACP [.311]	II	Small	22	10	7
32 S&W Long/H&R Mag. [.312]	II	Small	36	10	7
32 S&W Short [.312]	IV	Small	36	10	7
9MM Luger [.355]	II	Small	8	15	9
380 Auto [.355]	II	Small	16	15	9
38 Super Auto [.357]	IV	Small	8	15	9
38 S&W [.357]	IV	Small	28	15	9
38-357-357 Max. [.357]	II	Small	6	15	9
375 Win. [.375]	II	Large	2	16	9
38/40 Win. [.400]	IV	Large	9	16	11
41 Mag. [.410]	II	Small	29	17	11
44 Spl./44 Mag. [.430]	II	Large	30	18	12
44 Auto Mag. [.430]	Sil & BR Dies	Large	1	18	12
44/40 Win. [.429]	IV	Large	9	18	12
444 Marlin [.430]	II	Large	27	18	12
45 Auto Rim [.451]	IV	Large	31	19	13
45 ACP [.451]	II	Large	1	19	13
45 Win. Mag. [.451]	Sil & BR Dies	Large	1	19	13
45 Long Colt [.451]	II	Large	32	19	13
45/70 Govt. [.458]	II	Large	14	19	13
458 Win. [.458]	II	Large	5	19	13

*Neck size die available.

[Bullet Diameter]

RELOADING 535

HORNADY

105 SHOTSHELL RELOADER

- All the features of expensive reloaders without sacrificing quality.
- Crimps shells perfectly. Floating crimp starter automatically aligns with original crimp folds. Final crimp die is fully adjustable.
- Seats wad easily with built-in wad guide.
- Eliminates guesswork . . . all operations end up positive stop.

105 Shotshell Reloader (complete with charge bushings) **$116.55**
105 Die Set (for quick-change conversion to different gauge) **37.05**
105 Magnum Conversion Set (converts 2³/₄″ dies to load 3″ shells
    of same gauge, or vice versa **12.00**
105 Crimp Starter (8-point crimp starter standard equipment with
    loader and with Die Sets) **3.00**
Extra Charge Bushings. **2.00**

PRO-JECTOR PROGRESSIVE (includes standard set of dies)

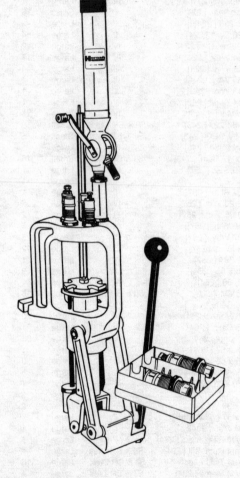

- Just place case in shell plate, start bullet, pull lever and drop powder. Automatic rotation of shell plate prepares next round.
- Fast inexpensive changeover requires only shell plate and set of standard ⁷/₈ × 14 threaded dies.
- Primes automatically.
- Power-Pac Linkage assures high-volume production even when full-length sizing.
- Uses standard powder measures and dies

Price **$335.00**
Extra Shell Plates **25.00**

00-7 PRESS

- "Power-Pac" linkage multiplies lever-to-arm power.
- Frame of press angled 30° to one side, making the "O" area of press totally accessible.
- More mounting area for rock-solid attachment to bench.
- Special strontium-alloy frame provides greater stress, resistance. Won't spring under high pressures needed for full-length resizing.

00-7 Press (does not include dies or shell holder) **$124.50**
00-7 Automatic Primer Feed (complete with large and small primer
    tubes) **14.95**

LYMAN RELOADING ACCESSORIES

TURBO TUMBLERS

Lyman's Turbo Tumblers process cases twice as fast as old style tumblers. Their unique design allows the media to swirl around totally immersed cases in a high-speed, agitated motion that cleans and polishes interior and exterior surfaces simultaneously; it also allows inspection of cases without stopping the polishing operation. The Turbo 3200 cleans and polishes up to 1,000 .38 Special cartridge cases. The Turbo 1200 can handle the equivalent of over 300 .38 Specials or 100 .30/06 cartridges. The Turbo 600 cleans half the Model 1200 capacity.

Price: Turbo 600 (7 lbs.)   110V **$107.95**   220V **$115.00**
Turbo 1200 (10 lbs.)   110V **$139.95**   220V 145.00
Turbo 3200 (13 lbs.)   110V **$209.95**   220V 210.00

Turbo™ Tumber Capacities

Model	Lyman Media	Number of .38 Special Cases	Nominal Capacity*
600	1 lb.	175	3 Pints
1200	2 lbs.	350	4 Quarts
3200	5 lbs.	1000	2.2 Gallons

*Refer to product instructions for suggested operating procedures and weight guidelines for best results.

TURBO SIFTER & MEDIA

Lyman's Turbo Sifter allows easy separation of cleaned and polished cases from the Turbo Tumbler media. Its diameter of 14″ allows the sifter to fit the mouth of most household buckets. Open grate bottom allows media to pass into recepticle while stopping the bases. **Price: $7.95**

Turbo Media produces a "factory finish" and eliminates abrasive and wax films. **Price: $3.95** (1 lb. can); **$6.95** (2 lb. box); **$19.95** (10 lb. box).

LYMAN RELOADING TOOLS

UNIVERSAL DRILL PRESS CASE TRIMMER

Intended for competitive shooters, varmint hunters, and other sportsmen who use large amounts of reloaded ammunition, this new drill press case trimmer consists of the Universal® Chuck Head, a cutter shaft adapted for use in a drill press, and two quick-change cutter heads. Its two major advantages are speed and accuracy. An experienced operator can trim several hundred cases in an hour, and each will be trimmed to a precise length.

Price: **$39.95**

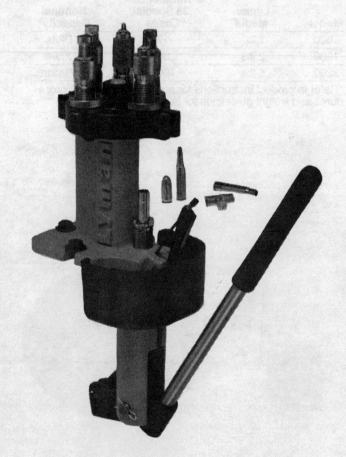

T-MAG TURRET RELOADING PRESS

With the T-Mag you can mount up to six different reloading dies on our turret. This means you can have all your dies set up, precisely mounted, locked in and ready to reload at all times. The T-Mag works with all $^7/_8 \times 14$ dies. The T-Mag turret with its quick-disconnect release system is held in rock-solid alignment by a $^3/_4$-inch steel stud.

Our T-Mag Set includes the T-Mag Press, plus the tools needed to turn out top quality reloads for your rifle or handgun:
• T-Mag Press
• Primer Catcher
• Universal Primer Arm
• Ram
• Detachable Shell Holder
• Complete Set of standard AA Dies (state caliber)

T-Mag Set (21 lbs.). **$169.95**
T-Mag Rifle Set (21 lbs.) 159.95
T-Mag Set only w/Priming Arm & Catcher 129.95

LYMAN BULLET SIZING EQUIPMENT

MAG 20 ELECTRIC FURNACE

The MAG 20 is a new furnace offering several advantages to cast bullet enthusiasts. It features a steel crucible of 20-pound capacity and incorporates a proven bottom-pour valve system and a fully adjustable mould guide. The improved design of the MAG 20 makes it equally convenient to use the bottom-pour valve, or a ladle. A new heating coil design reduces the likelihood of pour spout "freeze" Heat is controlled from "Off" to nominally 825° F by a calibrated thermostat which automatically increases temperature output when alloy is added to the crucible. A pre-heat shelf for moulds is attached to the back of the crucible. Availalbe for 100 V and 200 V systems.

Price: 110 V **$199.95**
220 V **200.00**

UNIVERSAL TRIMMER WITH NINE PILOT MULTI-PACK

This trimmer with patented chuck head accepts all metallic rifle or pistol cases, regardless of rim thickness. To change calibers, simply change the case head pilot. Other features include coarse and fine cutter adjustments, an oil-impregnated bronze bearing, and a rugged cast base to assure precision alignment and years of service.

Trimmer less pilot **$54.95**
Extra pilot (state caliber) 2.95
Replacement cutter head (2-pack) 8.50
Trimmer Multi-Pack (includes 9 pilots: 22, 24, 27, 28/7mm, 30, 9mm, 35, 44 and 45A 59.95

Deburring Tool
Lyman's deburring tool can be used for chamfering or deburring of cases up to 45 caliber. For precise bullet seating, use the pointed end of the tool to bevel the inside of new or trimmed cases. To remove burrs left by trimming, place the other end of the deburring tool over the mouth of the case and twist. The tool's centering pin will keep the case aligned **$10.95**

Mould Handles
These large hardwood handles are available in three sizes—single-, double- and four-cavity.
Single-cavity handles (for small block, black powder and specialty moulds; 12 oz.) **$17.95**
Double-cavity handles (for two-cavity and large-block single-cavity moulds; 12 oz.) 17.95
Four-cavity handles (1 lb.) 20.95

Rifle Moulds
All Lyman rifle moulds are available in double cavity only, except those moulds where the size of the bullet necessitates a single cavity (12 oz.) **$39.95**

Hollow-Point Bullet Moulds
Hollow-point moulds are cut in single-cavity blocks only and require single-cavity handles (9 oz.) **$39.95**

Shotgun Slug Moulds
Available in 12 or 20 gauge; do not require rifling. Moulds are single cavity only, cut on the larger double-cavity block and require double-cavity handles (14 oz.) **$39.95**

Lead Casting Dipper
Dipper with cast-iron head. Spout is shaped for easy, accurate pouring that prevents air pockets in the finished bullet **$8.95**

Inertia Bullet Puller
Quickly and easily removes bullets from cartridges . . **$23.95**

Gas Checks
Gas checks are gilding metal caps which fit to the base of cast bullets. These caps protect the bullet base from the burning effect of hot powder gases and permit higher velocities. Easily seated during the bullet sizing operation. Only Lyman gas checks should be used with Lyman cast bullets.

22 through 35 caliber (per 1000) **$18.95**
375 through 45 caliber (per 1000) 19.95

Lead Pot
Cast-iron pot allows bullet caster to any source of heat. Pot capacity is 8 pounds of alloy. Flat bottom prevents tipping. **$9.95**

LYMAN RELOADING TOOLS

ACCULINE TRIMMER

Lyman's new AccuTrimmer can be used for all rifle and pistol cases from 22 to 458 Winchester Magnum. Standard shell-holders are used to position the case, and the trimmer incorporates standard Lyman cutter heads and pilots. Mounting options include bolting to a bench, C-clamp or vise.

Acculine Trimmer **$29.95**
   with 9-pilot multi-pak 34.95

ACCULINE POWDER MEASURE

The new Pistol AccuMeasure uses changeable brass rotors pre-drilled to drop precise charges of ball and flake pistol propellants (the tool is not intended for use with long grain IMR-type powders). Most of the rotors are drilled with two cavities for maximum accuracy and consistency. The brass operating handle, which can be shifted for left or right hand operation, can be removed. The Pistol AccuMeasure can be mounted on all turret and single station presses; it can also be hand held with no loss of accuracy.

Pistol AccuMeasure **$19.95**
   with 3-rotor starter kit 24.95

LYMAN RELOADING TOOLS
FOR RIFLE OR PISTOL CARTRIDGES

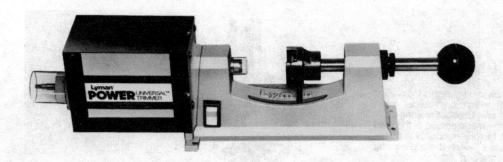

POWERED CASE TRIMMER

The new Lyman Power Trimmer is powered by a fan-cooled electric motor designed to withstand the severe demands of case trimming. The unit, which features the Universal™ Chuckhead, allows cases to be positioned for trimming or removed with fingertip ease. The Power Trimmer package includes Nine Pilot Multi-Pack. In addition to two cutter heads, a pair of wire end brushes for cleaning primer pockets are included. Other features include safety guards, on-off rocker switch, heavy cast base with receptacles for nine pilots, and bolt holes for mounting on a work bench. Available for 110 V or 220 V systems.

Prices: 110 V Model $179.95
220 V Model 180.00

UNIVERSAL PRESS ACCESSORIES

Primer Catcher: Made of heavy-duty plastic, this unit locks securely to press, yet is easily removed when emptying primers **$4.50**

Detachable Shell Holder: Precision machined and hardened to ensure perfect case fit. Used with the "Orange Crusher," O-Mag, T-Mag or Special-T and all popular presses. **$5.50**

LYMAN "ORANGE CRUSHER"

The only press for rifle or pistol cartridges that offers the advantage of powerful compound leverage combined with a true magnum press opening. A unique handle design transfers power easily where you want it—to the center of the ram. A 4½-inch press opening accommodates even the largest cartridges. Full set includes Primer Catcher, Primer Arm, Shell Holder, AA-Standard Dies or Multi-Delux Dies.
Weight: 18 lbs. **$134.95**
Press only w/Primer Arm and Catcher. 99.95

Universal Priming Arm: Seats all sizes and types of primers. Supplied with two priming sleeves (large and small), two flat priming punches (large and small), and two round priming punches (large and small). **$7.95**

Auto-primer Feed: Eliminates handling of primer with oily fingers, speeds loading. Supplied with two tubes (large and small). Specify press when ordering. **$15.50**

MEC RELOADING

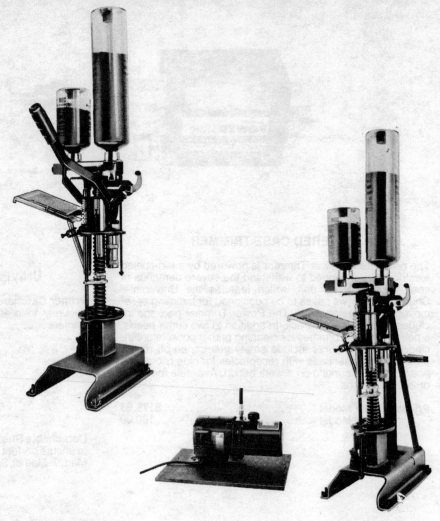

GRABBER 76

The Grabber grabs and squeezes the shell to dimensions well within commercial tolerances for new shells. Grabber resizing completely reforms the metal portion of the fired shotgun shell to factory standards in **all** respects. (Low brass 2³/₄-inch shells.) Resizing is done as an integral part of the reloading sequence and without undue agitation that might affect the uniformity of the charges. The measure assembly has been designed for strength and safety. Large capacity shot container holds 17+ pounds.

Features automatic primer feed, grabber resizing, exclusive charge bar window, flip-type measure, exclusive primer seating. 12, 16, 20, 28 or .410 gauge fitted in durable chrome.

Price (complete) **$371.89**

600 JR. MARK 5

The 600 Jr. Mark 5 shell holder positions each shell securely at each station without a transfer die; the cam action crimp dies insure that each shell is returned to original condition. Positioning wads is quick and easy. The one-piece Spindex crimp starter swivels to align itself correctly with original shell creases; charge bar window allows easy check on powder bushing. Can load 8-10 boxes per hour. Press is adjustable for 3″ shells and is available in 10, 12, 16, 20, 28 gauge and .410 bore.

Price (complete) **$137.53**
Die Sets . . . . **$52.29** ea.

HUSTLER 76

The Grabber with its revolutionary resize chamber, combined with the MEC hydraulic system, becomes the Hustler. It gives you your own miniature reloading factory, but one that resizes to under industry standards for minimum chamber. The motor operates on regular 120-volt household current and the pump supplies instant, constant pressure. The entire downstroke and upstroke functions are utilized and synchronized to allow continuous action. Every stroke of the cylinder piston is positive and performs all operations at six reloading stations. Every downstroke of the reloader produces one finished shell.

Reloader less pump and hose . . . **$476.08**
Price (complete) **$998.95**

MTM

CASE-GARD PISTOL AMMO WALLET
CASE-GARD 6, 12 AND 18

MTM offers 3 different models of varying capacity. All share common design features:
- Textured finish looks like leather, and provides good gripping surface, even when wet.
- Snap-lok latch protects contents from damage, even if unit is dropped.
- Integral hinge.
- Contents are protected from dust and moisture.
- Each round is carried securely in its own individual rattle-proof recess.
- Available in dark brown.

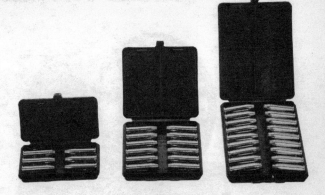

Capacity	380 Auto & 9mm	38 & 357 Mag	41 Mag	44 Mag	45 Auto
6 Round		W6-38/$2.83		W6-44/$2.83	
12 Round	W12-9/$3.05	W12-38/$3.05		W12-44/$3.05	W12-45/$3.05
18 Round	18-9/$3.60	18-38/$3.60	18-41/$3.60	18-44/$3.60	18-45/$3.60

CASE-GARD AMMO WALLET
FOR 22's

Special **Case-Gard Ammo Wallet** carrier holds 30 rounds, 22 Longs or 22 Mags . . . a convenient way to carry ammo to the range or field. Design features are:
- Leather-like finish available in dark brown.
- Snap-lok latch protects case against inadvertent opening, even if dropped.
- Each round is carried securely in its own recess.
- Virtually indestructible hinge.

30-22M $3.54

MTM HANDLOADER'S LOG

Space is provided for 1,000 entries covering date, range, group size or score, components, and conditions. Book is heavy-duty vinyl, reinforced 3-ring binder.

HL-74 . . . . $10.95
HL-50 extra pages 5.59

CASE-GARD 100 AMMO CARRIER
FOR SKEET AND TRAP

The **MTM™ Case-Gard®** 100-round shotshell case carries 100 rounds in 2 trays; or 50 rounds plus 2 boxes of factory ammo; or 50 rounds plus sandwiches and insulated liquid container; or 50 round with room left for fired hulls. Features include:
- Stainless steel pin.
- Center-balanced handles facilitate carrying and can be padlocked for security.
- High-impact material supports 300 pounds, and will not warp, split, expand or contract.
- Dustproof and rainproof.
- Each shotshell case is supplied with two 50-round trays.
- Available in textured black.

S100-12 (12 gauge) $13.99
S100-20 (20 gauge) 13.99

FUNNELS

MTM Benchrest Funnel Set is designed specifically for the bench-rest shooter. One fits 222 and 243 cases only; the other 7mm and 308 cases. Both can be used with pharmaceutical vials popular with bench-rest competitors for storage of pre-weighed charges. Funnel design prevents their rolling off the bench.

MTM Universal Funnel fits all calibers from 222 to 45.
UF-1 . . . . $1.88
Patented MTM Adapt 5-in-1 Funnel Kit includes funnel, adapters for 17 Rem., 222 Rem. and 30 through 45. Long drop tube facilitates loading of maximum charges: 222 to 45.
AF-5 . . . . $3.67

RCBS RELOADING TOOLS

SIDEWINDER CASE TUMBLER

This RCBS case tumbler cleans cases inside and out and was designed exclusively for handloaders. Instead of just vibrating, the tilted easy-access drum rotates for fast, thorough cleaning. Its built-in timer adjusts for automatic shut-offs from five minutes to 12 hours. A perforated cap doubles as a screen to separate either liquid or dry RCBS cleaning medium from cleaned cases. Capacity is up to 300 38 Special cases or 150 30-06 cases. Available in 120 or 240 volt models. An 8-ounce bottle of Liquid Case Cleaner is included.

Sidewinder Case Tumber
120 V **$177.90**
240 V **187.90**

AUTOMATIC PRIMING TOOL

Precision-engineered to provide fast, accurate and uniform seating of primers in one simple step. Single-stage leverage system is so sensitive it enables you actually to "feel" the primer being seated to the bottom of the primer pocket. This priming tool permits you to check visually each primer pocket before seating the primer, thus eliminating wasted motion or slowing down the reloading process.

Primers are released one at a time through the RCBS automatic primer feed, eliminating contamination caused by handling primers with oily fingers. Both primer rod assemblies furnished with this tool will handle all large and small American-made Boxer-type rifle and pistol primers.

Economy Features: If you already have RCBS automatic primer feed tubes and RCBS shell holders, they will fit this RCBS Priming Tool, thus eliminating the need to buy extras.

Berdan Primer Rod Assemblies: Optional Berdan Primer Rod Assemblies are available in three sizes and are interchangeable with the American Boxer-type Primer Rod Assemblies, furnished with the Priming Tool.

Priming Tool (less shell holder). **$54.50**

UNIVERSAL PRIMER ARM

RCBS primer arms are designed for fast, accurate seating of all primers. Interchangeable primer plugs and sleeves eliminate necessity of having to buy a completely new primer arm for each primer size. Primer plugs and sleeves furnished for large and small primers. Body cast of rust-resistant zinc alloy. The Universal Primer Arm is designed for use with RCBS Rock Chucker and J.R. as well as most "C" type presses.

Universal Primer Arm **$8.40**
Plug and Sleeve **2.40**

AUTOMATIC PRIMER FEED

Stop misfires—greasy hands never need to touch primers. Automatically drops primers one at a time into the primer plug and sleeve of the primer arm. Adjustable primer stop pin eliminates jamming found in other automatic primer feeds. Easily mounted on RCBS and most "C" type presses. The primer tubes for large and small primers are completely interchangeable with the body.

**Automatic Primer
Feed** **$17.50**

PRIMER POCKET SWAGER

For fast, precision removal of primer pocket crimp from military cases. Leaves primer pocket perfectly rounded and with correct dimensions for seating of American Boxer-type primers. Will not leave oval-shaped primer pocket that reaming produces. Swager Head Assemblies furnished for large and small primer pockets—no need to buy a complete unit for each primer size. For use with all presses with standard $7/8$-inch $\times$ 14 top thread, except RCBS "A-3" Press. The RCBS "A-2" Press requires the optional Case Stripper Washer.

Pocket Swager **$20.00**

PRIMER TRAY

For fast, easy handling of primers and loading automatic primer feed tubes, place primers in this tray, shake tray horizontally, and primers will automatically position themselves anvil side up. Sturdy plastic case.

Primer Tray **$2.40**

PRIMER POCKET BRUSH

A slight twist of this tool thoroughly cleans residue out of primer pockets. Interchangeable stainless steel brushes for large and small primer pockets attach easily to accessory handle.

Primer Pocket Brush **$10.50**

RCBS RELOADING TOOLS

RELOADER SPECIAL-3

This RCBS Reloader Special-3 Press is the ideal setup to get started reloading your own rifle and pistol ammo—from 12 gauge shotshells and the largest Magnums down to 22 Hornets. This press develops ample leverage and pressure to perform all reloading tasks including: (1) resizing cases their full length; (2) forming cases from one caliber into another; (3) making bullets. Rugged Block "O" Frame, designed by RCBS, prevents press from springing out of alignment—even under tons of pressure. Frame is offset 30° for unobstructed front access, and is made of 48,000 psi aluminum alloy. Compound leverage system allows you to swage bullets, full-length resize cases, form 30-06 cases into other calibers. Counter-balanced handle prevents accidental drop. Extra-long ram-bearing surface minimizes wobble and side play. Standard 7/8-inch-14 thread accepts all popular dies and reloading accessories.

Reloader Special (less
   dies) . . . . $ 89.50
Reloader Special-3 Combo,
   Rifle 111.00
Reloader Special-3 Combo,
   Pistol 114.00

ROCK CHUCKER "COMBO"

The Rock Chucker Press, with patented RCBS compound leverage system, delivers up to 200% more leverage than most presses for heavy-duty reloading of even the largest rifle and pistol cases. Rugged, Block "O" Frame prevents press from springing out of alignment even under the most strenuous operations. It case-forms as easily as most presses full-length size; it full-length sizes and makes bullets with equal ease. Shell holders snap into sturdy, all-purpose shell holder ram. Non-slip handle with convenient grip. Operates on downstroke for increased leverage. Standard 7/8-inch × 14 thread.

Rock Chucker Press (less
   dies) $129.00
Rock Chucker Combo, Rifle . . 157.00
Rock Chucker Combo,
   Pistol 160.00
Combos include interchangeable primer plugs and sleeves for seating large and small rifle and pistol primers, shell holder, and primer catcher.

RCBS RELOADING TOOLS

MODEL 5-0-5

This 511-grain capacity scale has a three-poise system with widely spaced, deep beam notches to keep them in place. Two smaller poises on right side adjust from 0.1 to 10 grains, larger one on left side adjusts in full 10-grain steps. The first scale to use magnetic dampening to eliminate beam oscillation, the 5-0-5 also has a sturdy die-cast base with large leveling legs for stability. Self-aligning agate bearings support the hardened steel beam pivots for a guaranteed sensitivity to 0.1 grains.

Model 5-0-5	09071	1½ lbs.	$58.00

MODEL 5-10

The model number has changed but this is the same scale that reloaders have been using for years. Weighs powder, bullets or complete cartridges up to 510 grains instantly and accurately thanks to a micrometer poise, an approach-to-weight indicator system, large easy-to-read graduations, magnetic dampening, agate bearings and an anti-tip pan. Guaranteed to 0.1 grain sensitivity. Also available in metric readings.

Model 5-10 Scale	09070	2 lbs.	$79.00
Model 5-10 Metric Scale	09072	2 lbs.	91.00

Scale Cover
A smart investment to protect the model 5-0-5 or 5-10 scale when not in use. Soft, vinyl dust cover folds easily to stow away, or has loop for hanging up.

Scale Cover	09075	⅛ lb.	$4.80

MODEL 10-10

Up to 1010 Grain Capacity
Normal capacity is 510 grains, which can be increased, without loss in sensitivity, by attaching the included extra weight.

Features include micrometer poise for quick, precise weighing, special approach-to-weight indicator, easy-to-read graduations, magnetic dampener, agate bearings, anti-tip pan, and dust-proof lid snaps on to cover scale for storage. Sensitivity is guaranteed to 0.1 grains.

Model 10-10 Scale	09073	3 lbs.	$92.50

ROTARY CASE TRIMMER-2

Much like a miniature lathe, this Precisioneer® tool is the ideal way to trim stretched cases, shorten a quantity of them to the same exact length, or correct slightly uneven case mouths. This improved model has been redesigned for absolute case length control. Adjustments have been simplified and refined for near-perfect precision in trimming fired cases.

Case is locked into trimmer collet, the cutting blade is adjusted to desired case length, the handle is turned a few times, and it's done. You then bevel and deburr the trimmed case, and it's ready to reload.

The interchangeable collets are available for all popular calibers (17 to 45) and are designed to lock cases securely for accurate trimming. Special trimmer pilots come in 20 sizes to fit 17 to 45 caliber cases. Each is Precisioneered®, and locks into the cutter with set screw. This type of lock ensures perfect case alignment, both vertically and horizontally.

The cutting assembly features a lock ring so that any quantity of cases can be trimmed to the exact same length with a single adjustment. Cutter blades are made of hardened steel for prolonged service life. Case trimmer also has sockets for holding extra collets and pilots and holes for screwing base to bench.
Rotary Case Trimmer-2 .... **$49.50**

CASE TRIMMER PILOT $2.60			
PART NO.	PILOT CAL.	PART NO.	PILOT CAL.
09377	17	09387	33
09378	22	09388	34
09379	24	09389	35
09380	25	09390	36
09381	26	09391	37
09382	27	09392	40
09383	28	09393	41
09384	30	09394	44
09385	31	09395	45
09386	32	09396	.45-R

This tool is used to: (1) trim to standard length those cases which have stretched after repeated firings; (2) trim a quantity of cases to the same length for uniform bullet seating; (3) correct uneven case mouths.

CASE TRIMMER COLLET $6.50			
PART NO.	COLLET NO.	PART NO.	COLLET NO.
09371	1	09373	3
09372	2	09374	4

REDDING RELOADING TOOLS

MATCH GRADE POWDER MEASURE MODEL 3BR

Designed for the most demanding reloaders—bench rest, silhouette and varmint shooters. The Model 3BR is unmatched for its precision and repeatability. Its special features include a powder baffle and zero backlash micrometer.

No. 3BR with Universal or Pistol Metering Chamber . . . . **$ 98.00**
No. 3 BRK includes both metering chambers **124.95**
No. 3-30 Benchrest metering chambers (fit only 3BR) **28.50**

MASTER POWDER MEASURE MODEL 3

Universal- or pistol-metering chambers interchange in seconds. Measures charges from 1/2 to 100 grains. Unit is fitted with lock ring for fast dump with large "clear" plastic reservoir. "See-thru" drop tube accepts all calibers from 22 to 600. Precision-fitted rotating drum is critically honed to prevent powder escape. Knife-edged powder chamber shears coarse-grained powders with ease, ensuring accurate charges.

No. 3 Master Powder Measure (specify Universal- or Pistol-Metering chamber) **$79.95**
No. 3K Kit Form, includes both Universal and Pistol chambers **98.00**
No. 3-12 Universal or Pistol chamber **19.95**

POWDER TRICKLER MODEL 5

Brings underweight charges up to accurate reading, adding powder to scale pan a granule or two at a time by rotating knob. Speeds weighing of each charge. Solid steel, low center of gravity. "Companion" height to all reloading scales; weighs a full pound.

No. 5 Powder Trickler **$13.95**

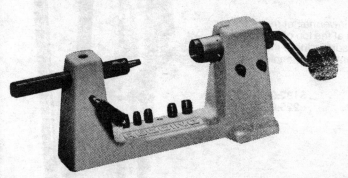

MASTER CASE TRIMMER
MODEL 1400

This unit features a universal collet that accepts all rifle and pistol cases. The frame is solid cast iron with storage holes in the base for extra pilots. Both coarse and fine adjustments are provided for case length.

The case-neck cleaning brush and primer pocket cleaners attached to the frame of this tool make it a very handy addition to the reloading bench. Trimmer comes complete with:
- New speed cutter shaft
- Two pilots (22 and 30 cal.)
- Universal collet
- Two neck cleaning brushes (22 thru 30 cal.)
- Two primer pocket cleaners (large and small)

No. 1400 Master Case Trimmer complete **$59.95**
No. 1500 Pilots **2.50**

STANDARD POWDER AND BULLET SCALE MODEL RS-1

For the beginner or veteran reloader. Only two counterpoises need to be moved to obtain the full capacity range of 1/10 grain to 380 grains. Clearly graduated with white numerals and lines on a black background. Total capacity of this scale is 380 grains. An over-and-under plate graduate in 10th grains allows checking of variations in powder charges or bullets without further adjustments.

Model No. RS-1 . . . . **$44.00**

REDDING RELOADING TOOLS

MODEL 721
"THE BOSS" PRESS

This "O" type reloading press features a rigid cast iron frame whose 36° offset provides the best visibility and access of comparable presses. Its "Smart" primer arm moves in and out of position automatically with ram travel. The priming arm is positioned at the bottom of ram travel for lowest leverage and best feel. Model 721 accepts all standard $^7/_8$-14 threaded dies and universal shell holders.

Model 721 "The Boss" $84.95

ULTRAMAG
MODEL 700

Unlike other reloading presses that connect the linkage to the lower half of the press, the Ultramag's compound leverage system is connected at the top of the press frame. This allows the reloader to develop tons of pressure without the usual concern about press frame deflection. Huge frame opening will handle 50 × 3$^1/_4$-inch Sharps with ease.

No. 700 Press, complete $192.00
No. 700K Kit, includes shell holder and one set of dies 225.00

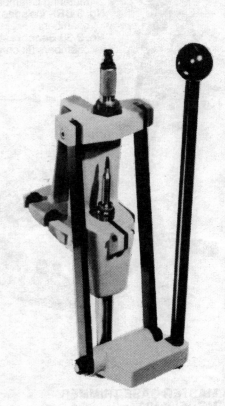

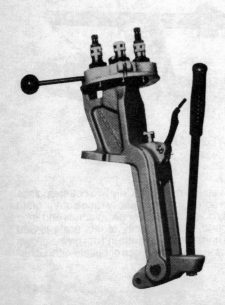

TURRET RELOADING PRESS
MODEL 25

Extremely rugged, ideal for production reloading. No need to move shell, just rotate turret head to positive alignment. Ram accepts any standard snap-in shell holder. Includes primer arm for seating both small and large primers.

No. 25 Press, complete $219.95
No. 25K Kit, includes press, shell holder, and one set of dies 253.00
No. 25T Extra Turret (6 Station). 50.00
No. 19T Automatic Primer Feeder 16.00

Reference

THE SHOOTER'S BOOKSHELF

An up-to-date listing of book titles, old and new, of interest to shooters and gun enthusiasts. Most of these books can be found at your local library, bookstore, or gun shop. If not available, contact the publisher. Names and addresses of leading publishers in the field are listed at the end of this section.

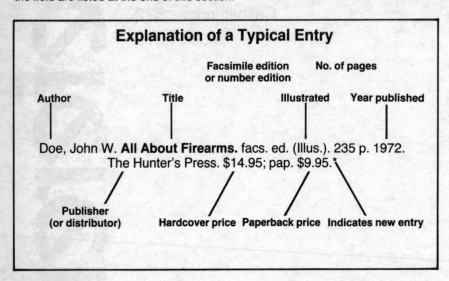

Explanation of a Typical Entry

Author — Title — Facsimile edition or number edition — Illustrated — No. of pages — Year published

Doe, John W. **All About Firearms.** facs. ed. (Illus.). 235 p. 1972. The Hunter's Press. $14.95; pap. $9.95.*

Publisher (or distributor) — Hardcover price — Paperback price — Indicates new entry

AIR GUNS
Churchill, Bob & Davies, Granville. **Modern Airweapon Shooting,** (Illus.), 1981. David & Charles. $18.95.
Walter, John. **The Airgun Book.** 1981. Stackpole. $21.95.

AMMUNITION
Brown, Ronald. **Homemade Guns & Homemade Ammo.** 191 p. 1986. Loompanics. pap. text ed. $14.95.*
Donnelly, John J. **Handloader's Manual of Cartridge Conversions.** (Illus.). 1056 p. 1987. Stoeger Pub. Co. pap. $24.95; spiral bound $29.95; hardcover $34.95.
Evaluation of Police Handgun Ammunition. (Law Enforcement Series) 1986. Gordon Press. $79.95 (lib. bdg.).*
Geary, Don. **The Reloader's Bible: The Complete Guide to Making Ammunition at Home.** (Illus.) 256 p. 1986. Prentice-Hall. $17.95.*
Goad, K.J. & Halsey, D. H. **Ammunition, Grenades & Mines.** 1982. Pergamon Press. $35.00; pap. $17.50.
Hogg, Ian V. **Jane's Directory of Military Small Arms Ammunition.** (Illus.). 160 p. 1985. Jane's Pub. Inc. $24.95.
Hoyem, George A. **History and Development of Small Arms Ammunition: Cartridge Value Guide to Vols. One and Two.** (Illus.). 16 p. 1982. pap. Armory Pubns. $4.00.
Long, Duncan. **Combat Ammunition: Everything You Need to Know.** (Illus.) 136 p. 1986. Palladin Pr. text. ed. $19.95.*
Matunas, Edward. **American Ammunition and Ballistics.** (Illus.). 1979. Winchester Press. $15.95.
Nonte, George C., Jr. **Handloading for Handgunners.** (Illus.). 288 p. pap. DBI Books. $9.95.
Parkerson, Codman. **A Brief History of Bullet Moulds.** Pioneer Press. $1.75.
Sears & Roebuck 1910 **Ammunition Catalog** (Illus.). pap. Sand Pond $2.00.
Stegen, Arthur E. **Biathlon.** (Illus.). 144 p. National Rifle Assn. $30.00.
Steindler, R. A. **Reloader's Guide.** 3rd ed. (Illus.). 1975. softbound. Stoeger. $9.95.
Trzoniec, Stanley W. **Handloader's Guide.** (Illus.). 256 p. pap. 1985. Stoeger. $11.95.
Withers, John. **Precision Handloading.** (Illus.). 224 p. 1985. Stoeger Pub. Co. pap. $11.95.

ARCHERY (see also Bow and Arrow)
Ascham, Roger. **Toxophilus, The Schole of Shootinge,** 2 bks. 1969. Repr. of 1545 ed. Walter J. Johnson, Inc. $25.00.

—**Toxophilius, 1545.** Arber, Edward ed. 1971 Repr. of 1895 ed. Scholarly Press. $29.00.
Athletic Institute, ed. **Archery: A Sport for Everyone.** (Illus.). 96 p. 1984. Athletic Inst. pap. $6.95.
Barrett, Jean. **Archery.** 3rd ed. 1980. Scott, Foresman & Co. $6.95.
Bear, Fred. **Archer's Bible.** (Illus.). 1980. pap. Doubleday, $4.50.
Bilson, Frank. **Crossbows.** (Illus.). 1982. Hippocrene Books, $14.95.
Bow & Arrow Magazine Staff, ed. **Archery Equipment Illustrated.** (Illus.). 256 p. (Orig.). 1984. pap. DBI. $10.95.
Burke, Edmund H. **History of Archery.** 1971. Repr. of 1957. Greenwood Press, $15.75.
Combs, Roger. **Archers Digest,** 4th ed. (Illus.) 256 p. 1986. DBI. pap. $12.95.*
Elliott Cheri, ed. **Archer's Digest,** 3rd ed. 288 p. 1982 pap. DBI Books. $11.95.
Gillelan. G. Howard. **Complete Book of the Bow and Arrow.** rev. ed. 1981. Stackpole Books. $11.95.
Glogan, Joseph. **Sportsman's Book of U.S. Records.** (Illus.). 1980. pap. text ed. NY Outdoor Guide. $4.95.
Henderson, Al. **Understanding Winning Archery.** Helgeland, G., ed. (Illus.). 114 p. 1983. Target Comm. pap. $8.95.
Johnson, Dewayne J. & Oliver, Robert A. **Archery.** 1980. pap. American Press. $2.95.
Klann, Margaret L. **Target Archery.** 1970. pap. Addison-W. $7.95.
Latham, J. D. ed. **Saracen Archery.** (Illus.). Albert Saifer, pub. $35.00.
Laubin, Reginald & Laubin, Gladys. **American Indian Archery.** (Illus.). 1980. University of Oklahoma Press. $18.95.
McKinney, Wayne C. **Archery.** 4th ed. 1980. pap. William C. Brown Co. Write for information.
Markham, Gervase. **The Art of Archerie.** facs. ed. 1968. Repr. of 1634 ed. George Shumway Publisher. $15.00.
Mosley, Walter M. **An Essay on Archery.** 1976. Charles River Books. $17.50.
Neade, William. **The Double Armed Man.** facs. ed. (Illus.). 1971. George Shumway Publisher. $10.00.
Odums, R.I. & Allen, D.G. **Career Guide to Officiating Archery & Riflery.** Tessman, Rita, ed. (Illus.) 150 p. 1986. Guideposts Pub. Dists. $12.95.*
Paterson, W. F. **Encyclopedia of Archery.** (Illus.) 240 p. 1985. St. Martin. $14.95.
Pszczola, Lorraine. **Archery.** 2nd ed. (Illus.). 1976. pap. Holt, Rinehart & Winston. $3.95.

Stamp, Don. **Challenge of Archery.** 2nd ed. (Illus.). 1980. Transatlantic Arts, Inc. $16.95.
—**Field Archery.** (Illus.). 1980. Transatlantic Arts, Inc. $15.95.
Wood, Sir William. **The Bowman's Glory of Archery Revived.** Repr. of 1969 ed. Ridgeway Books. $15.00.

ARMS AND ARMOR (see also Firearms)
Albion, Robert G. **Introduction to Military History.** (Illus.). 1971. Repr. of 1929 ed. AMS Press. $29.00.
American Machines & Foundry Co. **Silencers: Patterns & Principles, Vol. 2.** (Illus.). 1972. pap. Paladin Enterprises. $12.95.
Beckett, Brian. **Weapons of Tomorrow.** 160 p. 1983. Plenum Pub. $14.95.
Bivens, John. **Art of the Fire-Lock, Twentieth Century: Being a Discourse Upon the Present and Past Practices of Stocking and Mounting the Sporting Fire-Lock Rifle Gun.** 1982. Shumway. $40.00.
Blair, Claude. **Arms, Armour & Base Metalwork.** (Illus.). 532 p. 1985. Sotheby Pubns. text ed. $45.00.
Collier, Basil. **Arms and the Men: The Arms Trade and Governments.** (Illus.). 1980. (Pub. by Hamish Hamilton England). David & Charles. $37.00.
Constant, James N. **Fundamentals of Strategic Weapons.** 940 p. 1981. Sijthoff & Nordoff. $140.00.
Curtis, Anthony. **The Lyle Offical Arms & Armour Review.** 416 p. 1983. Apollo. $24.95.
—**Lyle Official Arms & Armour Review** (Illus.). 415 p. 1982. Apollo. $24.95.
Daniel, Larry J. & Gunter, Riley W. **Confederate Cannon Foundries.** Pioneer Press. ed. Pioneer Press. $17.95.
Diagram Group. **Weapons** (Illus.). 1980. St. Martin's Press. $24.00.
Dunnigan, James F. **How to Make War: A Comprehensive Guide to Modern Warfare.** (Illus.). 416 p. 1981. Morrow $14.50.
Dupuy, Trevor N. **The Evolution of Weapons & Warfare.** (Illus.). 360 p. 1984. Repr. of 1980 ed. Hero Bks. text ed. $19.95.
Ezell, Edward C. **Small Arms Today: Latest Reports on the World's Weapons & Ammunition.** 256 p. (Orig.). 1984. pap. Stackpole. $16.95.
Fadala, Sam. **Black Powder Handgun.** 288 p. 1981. DBI. pap. $11.95.*
Foss, Christopher F., ed. **Jane's Armour & Artillery 1984–85.** (Illus.). 950 p. 1984. Jane's Pub. Inc. $125.00.
—**Jane's Armour & Artillery, 1985–1986.** 6th ed. (Jane's Yearbooks) 900 p. 1985. Jane's Pub. Inc. $125.00.*
—**Jane's Armour & Artillery, 1986–1987,** 7th ed. (Jane's Yearbooks) 930 p. 1986. Jane's Pub. Inc. $137.50.*
Frost, H. Gordon. **Blades and Barrels: Six Centuries of Combination Weapons.** Walloon Press. $16.95. deluxe ed. $25.00; presentation ed. $50.00.
Funcken, Lilane & Funcken, Fred. **Arms & Uniforms: The Second World War,** vols. I, III & IV. 120 p. 1984. P-H. $17.95 (ea.).
Gambordella, Ted. **Weapons of the Street.** (Illus.). 80 p. (Orig.). 1984. pap. Paladin Pr. $8.00.
Gordon, Don E. **Electronic Warfare: Element of Strategy & Multiplier of Combat Power.** (Illus.). 200 p. 1982. Pergamon Press. $17.50.
Gruzanski, C. V. **Spike and Chain.** Wehman Brothers, Inc. $7.50.
Guthman, William, ed. **Guns and Other Arms.** (Illus.). 1980. pap. Mayflower books. $7.95.
Hamilton, T. M. **Firearms on the Frontier: Guns at Fort Michilimackinac 1715–1781.** Armour, David A., ed. (Illus.). 1976. pap. Mackinac Island State Part Commission. $3.00.
Hart, Harold H. **Weapons & Armor: A Pictorial Archive of Woodcuts & Engravings.** 1983. Peter Smith. $14.50.
Hogg, Ian, ed. **Jane's Infantry Weapons 1986–1987,** (Illus.). 950 p. Jane's Pub. Inc. $136.00.
Hoy, M. **Exotic Weapons: An Access Book: 200 Different Weapons Described & Analyzed with Dealer Listings for All.** 1986. Gordon Pr. $90.00 (lib. bdg.).

Hoyem, George A. **History & Development of Small Arms Ammunition, Vol. 2: Ammunition: Centerfire, Primitive & Martial Long Arms.** 1982. Armory Pubns. $34.50.

Johnson, Thomas M. **Collecting the Edged Weapons of the Third Reich.** 4 vols. Bradach, Wilfred, tr. (Illus.). T. M. Johnson. Vol. 1: $18.50; pap. $10.00. Vol. 2: $18.50. Vol. 3; $20.00; Vol. 4: $25.00.

Johnson, Thomas M. & Bradach, Wilfrid. **Third Reich Edged Weapons Accoutrements.** (Illus.). 1978. pap. T. M. Johnson $10.00.

Journal of the Arms and Armour Society. Vol. 1. (Illus.). 1970. George Shumway Publisher. $12.00.

Kemp, Anthony & Haythornthwaite, Philip. **Weapons & Equipment Series,** 3 vols. 525 p. 1982. Sterling. $50.00.

Klare, Michael T. **American Arms Supermarket.** (Illus.). 336 p. 1985. pap. U. of Texas Pr. $10.95.

Kozan, S. **Manufacture of Armour and Helmets in Sixteenth Century Japan.** Albert Saifer, Publisher. $35.00.

Laking, Guy F. **A Record of European Armour and Arms Through Seven Centuries.** 5 vols. (Illus.). Repr. AMS Press. set $295.00.

McAulay, John D. **Carbines of the Civil War, 1861–1865.** 1981. Pioneer Press. $7.95.

Macksey, Kenneth. **Technology in War:** The Impact on Science of Weapon Development & Modern Battles. (Illus.) 224 p. 1986. Arco. $19.95.*

Marchant-Smith, David J. & Haslem, P. R. **Small Arms & Cannons.** (Brassey's Battlefield Weapons System & Technology: Vol. 5) 160 p. 1982. Pergamon. $26.00.

Matunas, Edward. **Handbook of Metallic Cartridge Reloading.** (Illus.) 272 p. 1981. New Century. $12.95.

Mowbray, E. Andrew, ed. **Arms-Armor: From the Atelier of Ernst Schmidt, Munich.** (Illus.). 1967. Mowbray Co. $15.00.

Moyer, Frank, A. **Special Forces Foreign Weapons Handbook.** (Illus.). 1970. Paladin Enerprises. (OP).

National Army Museum, London. **War & Weapons.** (Illus.). 48 p. (Gr. 5–up) 1982. Watts $9.80.

North, Anthony. **Islamic Arms.** (Illus.) 48 p. 1986. Stemmer Hse. $9.95.*

Owen, J. I. ed. **Brassey's Infantry Weapons of the World.** (Illus.). 2nd ed. 1979. Pergamon Press. $61.00.

—**Infantry Weapons of the Armies of Africa, the Orient and Latin America.** 1980. pap. Pergamon Press. $24.00.

—**Infantry Weapons of the NATO Armies.** 2nd ed. 1980. pap. Pergamon Press. $24.00.

—**Infantry Weapons of the Warsaw Pact Armies.** 2nd ed. 1980. Pergamon Press. $24.00.

Peterson, Harold L. **The American Sword. 1775–1945.** (Illus.). 1977. Riling, Ray, Arms Books. $25.00.

Pierre, Andrew, J. **The Global Politics of Arms Sales.** 1981. Princeton University Press. $20.00; pap. $5.95.

Pretty, Ronald T., ed. **Jane's Weapon Systems 1986–1987.** 17th ed. (Illus.) 1060 p. Jane's Pub. Inc. $145.00.*

Rossner-Owen, Davais. **Vietnam Weapons Handbook.** (Illus.) 128 p. 1986. Sterling. pap. $6.95.*

Royal United Service Institute for Defense Studies, ed. **International Weapon Developments: A Survey of Current Developments in Weapons Systems,** 4th ed. (Illus.). 1980. pap. Pergamon Press. $14.25.

Schuyler-Hartley-Graham Military Furnishers. **Illustrated Catalog Arms and Military Goods.** facs. ed. (Illus.). 1864. Flayderman, N. & Co. $9.50.

Seaton, Lionel. **The International Arms Review,** Vol. I. (Illus.). 1977. Jolex. $6.95.

Seaton, Lionel tr. **The International Arms Review,** Vol. II. (Illus.). 1979. Jolex. $6.95.

Smith, W. H. **Small Arms of the World: A Basic Manual of Small Arms,** 12 ed. 1042 p. 1983. Stackpole, $59.95.

Snodgrass, A. M. **Arms and Armour of the Greeks.** (Illus.). 1967. Cornell University Press. $25.00.

Suenega, M. **Pictorial History of Ancient Japanese Weapons, Armour & Artifacts.** (Illus.). 100 p. 1983. pap. Saifer. $12.95.

Traister, John. **Learn Gunsmithing: The Troubleshooting Method.** (Illus.). 1980. Winchester Press. $16.95.

Truby, J. David. **Quiet Killers, Vol. 1.** (Illus.). 1972. pap. Paladin Enterprises. $8.00.

—**Quiet Killers II: Silencer Update** (Illus.). 1979. pap. Paladin Enterprises. $8.00.

Warry, John. **Warfare in the Classical World: An Illustrated Encyclopedia of Weapons, Warriors and Warfare in the Ancient Civilizations of Greece and Rome.** 1981. St. Martin. $19.95.

Wintringham, Thomas H. **Story of Weapons and Tactics.** facs. ed. 1943. Arno Press. $16.00.

Wright, James & Rossi, Peter. **Under the Gun: Weapons, Crime & Violence in America.** 360 p. 1983. Aldine Pub. $24.95.

Zaloga, Stephen J. & Grandsen, James. **The Eastern Front.** 96 p. 1983. Squad Sig. Pubns $7.95.

ARTILLERY

Bidwell, Shefford, ed. **Brassey's Artillery of the World.** 2nd rev. ed. 1981. Pergamon Press. $49.50.

Bourne, William. **The Arte of Shooting in Great Ordnaunce.** 1969. Repr. of 1587 ed. W. J. Johnson. $13.00.

Foss, Christopher. **Artillery of the World.** 3rd rev. ed. (Illus.). 1981. Scribner's. $17.50.

Foss, Christopher F., ed. **Jane's Armour & Artillery 1984–85.** (Illus.). 950 p. 1984. Jane's Pub. Inc. $125.00.

—**Jane's Armour & Artillery 1985–86.** 6th ed. (Illus.). 900 p. 1985. Jane's Pub. Inc. $125.00.

Hogg, Ian & Gander, Terry. **Artillery.** 1982. State Mutual Book & Periodical Service. $60.00.

Hughes, B. P. **Open Fire:** Artillery Tactics from Malborough to Wellington. 240 p. 1983. Hippocrene Books. $22.50.

Macchiavelli, Niccolo. **The Arte of Warre (Certain Wales of the Orderying of Souldiours).** Whitehorne, P., tr. 1969. Repr. of 1562 ed. W. J. Johnson. $42.00.

Manucy, Albert. **Artillery through the Ages:** A Short Illus. History of Cannon Emphasizing Types Used in America. (Illus.) 96 p. 1985. Govt. Ptg. Off. pap. $2.75.*

Richardson, Doug. **Naval Armament.** (Illus.). 160 p. 1982. Jane's Pub. Inc. $19.95.

Rogers, H. C. **A History of Artillery.** (Illus.). 1977. Citadel Press. $4.95.

Simienowicz, Casimir. **The Great Art of Artillery.** 1976. Charles River Books. $20.00.

BALLISTICS

Farrar, C. L. & Leeming, D. W. **Military Ballistics: A Basic Manual.** 225 p. 1983. Pergamon Press. $27.00.

Krier, Herman & Summerfield, Martin, eds. **Interior Ballistics of Guns.** 385 p. 1979. AIAA. $69.00.

Laible, Roy C. **Ballistic Materials & Penetration Mechanics.** 1980. Elsevier. $70.00

Mann, Franklin W. **The Bullet's Flight to Target From Powder: The Ballistics of Small Arms.** 391 p. 1980. Wolfe Pub. Co. Repr. text ed. $22.50.

Mannes, Philip. **Tables of Bullet Performance.** Wolfe, Dave, ed. 407 p. (Orig.) 1980. pap. text ed. Wolfe Pub. Co. $17.50.

Matunas, Edward. **American Ammunition and Ballistics.** (Illus.). 1979. Winchester Press. $18.95.

Wilber, Charles G. **Ballistic Science for the Law Enforcement Officer.** (Illus.). 1977. C. C. Thomas. $30.75.

—**Forensic Biology for the Law Enforcement Officer.** (Illus.). 1974. C. C. Thomas. $25.75.

Williams, M. **Practical Handgun Ballistics.** 1980. C. C. Thomas. $17.50.

Wolfe, Dave, ed. **The Art of Bullet Casting.** (Illus.). 258 p. pap. 1981. Wolfe Pub. Co. pap. $12.95.

—**Propellant Profiles.** (Illus.) 158 p. 1982. Wolfe Pub. Co. pap. text ed. $12.95.

BIRD DOGS

Brenneman, Al. **Al Brenneman Trains Bird Dogs.** (Illus.). 80 p. 1983. Strode. $16.45.

Falk, John R. **The Complete Guide to Bird Dog Training.** 1976. Winchester Press. $14.95.

BLACK POWDER GUNS (see also Firearms)

Bridges, Toby. **Advanced Muzzleloader's Guide.** (Illus.). 256 p. 1985. pap. Stoeger. $11.95.

Elliot, Brook. **Complete Smoothbore Hunter.** (Illus.) 240 p. 1986. New Century. $16.95.*

Fadala, Sam. **The Black Powder Handgun.** 1981. pap. DBI Book. $9.95.

—**Gun Digest Black Powder Loading Manual.** (Illus.). 224 p. 1982. pap. DBI Books. $9.95.

Lewis, Jack. **Black Powder Gun Digest,** 3rd ed. 256 p. 1982. pap. DBI Books $10.95.

Nonte, George C. Jr., **Black Powder Guide.** (Illus.). 256 p. pap. Stoeger Pub. Co. $9.95.

Warner, Ken, ed. **Handloader's Digest Bullet & Powder Update.** 128 p. 1980. pap. DBI Books. $5.95.

BOW AND ARROW (see also Archery)

Adams, Chuck. **Bowhunter's Digest.** 2nd ed. pap. 1981. DBI Books. $9.95.

—**Complete Book of Bowhunting.** (Illus.). 1978. New Century. $16.95.

Bear, Fred. **The Archer's Bible,** rev. ed. (Illus.). 1980. Doubleday. pap. $5.95.

Bowring, Dave. **Bowhunting for Whitetails: Your Best Methods for Taking North America's Favorite Deer.** (Illus.). 320 p. 1985. Stackpole. $24.95.

Elliot, Cheri, ed. **Digest Book of Bowhunting.** 96 p. DBI. pap. $3.95.

Helgeland, G. **Archery World's Complete Guide to Bow Hunting.** 1975. P-H. pap. $5.95.

James, M. R. **Bowhunting for Whitetail and Mule Deer.** rev. ed. 224 p. 1976. pap. Jolex. $6.95.

Kinton, Tony. **The Beginning Bowhunter.** (Illus.). 128 p. 1985. ICS Books. pap. $9.95.

Schuyler, Keith C. **Bowhunting for Big Game.** 224 p. 1977. pap. Stackpole, $7.95.

Smythe, John. **Bow Versus Gun.** 1974. Repr. of 1590 ed. text ed. British Book Center (OP).

Thayer, Dixon. **Bow Hunting Basics: Fundamentals for Successful Hunting.** (Illus.). 32 p. 1985. Blue Sky. pap. $2.95.

CARTRIDGES

Anderson, Robert S. **Metallic Cartridge Reloading.** (Illus.) 320 p. 1982. DBI. pap. $13.95.

Bartlett, W. A. & Gallatin, D. B. **B and G Cartridge Manual,** Pioneer Press. $2.00.

Datig, Fred A. **Cartridges for Collectors,** 3 vols. Borden. $8.95 ea.

Donnelly, John J. **Handloader's Manual of Cartridge Conversions.** (Illus.) 1056 p. 1987. Stoeger Pub. Co. pap. $24.95; spiral bound $29.95; hardcover $34.95.*

Harvey, Clay. **Popular Sporting Rifle Cartridges.** 320 p., 1984. pap. DBI. $12.95.

Hogg, Ian V. **The Cartridge Guide. The Small Arms Ammunition Identification Manual.** (Illus.). 160 p. 1982. Stackpole. $21.95.

Keith, Elmer. **Sixgun Cartridges & Loads.** 1985. Repr. of 1936 ed. Gun Room. $19.95.

Matthews, Charles. **Shoot Better With Centerfire Rifle Cartridges-Ballistics Tables.** (Illus.). 560 p. 1984. Matthews Inc. pap. $16.45.

Nonte, George. **The Home Guide to Cartridge Conversions.** rev. ed. Gun Room Press. rev. ed. $19.95.

Suydam, Charles R. **American Cartridge.** Borden. $10.95.

Thomas, Gough. **Shotguns and Cartridges for Game and Clays.** 3rd ed. (Illus.). 1976. Transatlantic Arts, Inc. $25.00.

Treadwell. **Cartridges, Regulation and Experimental.** Pioneer Press. $2.00.

COLLECTING (see Firearms—Collectors and Collecting)

COLT REVOLVERS

Bady, Donald B. **Colt Automatic Pistols,** rev. ed. 1973. Borden. $16.50.

Cochran, Keith. **Colt Peacemaker Ready-Reference Handbook.** (Illus.) 76 p. 1985. Cochran Pub. pap. $12.95.*

The Colt Point Forty-Five Auto Pistol. 1986. Gordon Pr. $79.95.*

The Colt .45 Exotic Weapons System. (Illus.). 88 p. 1984. Paladin Pr. pap. $12.00.

Graham, Ron, et al. **A Study of the Colt Single Action Army Revolver.** (Illus.) 523 p. 1985. Repr. of 1976 ed. Kopec Pubns. $69.95.*

Moore, C. Kenneth. **Colt Revolvers & the U.S. Navy 1865–1888.** (Illus.) 144 p. 1986. Dorrance. $29.95.*

Shumaker, P. L. **Colt's Variations of the Old Model Pocket Pistol.** 1957. Borden. $8.95.

Whittington, Robert D. III. **The Colt Whitneyville-Walker Pistol.** (Illus.). 96 p. 1984. Brownlee Books. $20.00.

CROSSBOWS

Payne-Gallwey, Ralph. **Cross-Bow, Medieval and Modern.** Saifer, Albert, Pub. $55.00.

Wilbur, C. Martin. **History of the Crossbow.** (Illus.). Repr. of 1936 ed. pap. Shorey. $2.95.

DECOYS (see also Duck Shooting)

Barber, Joel. **Wild Fowl Decoys.** (Illus.). pap. Dover. $6.95.

—**Wild Fowl Decoys.** (Illus.). Peter Smith. $13.50.

Berkey, Barry R., et al. **Pioneer Decoy Carvers: A Biography of Lemuel and Stephen Ward.** (Illus.). 1977. Tidewater. $17.50.

Bridenhagen, Keith. **Decoy Pattern Book.** (Illus.). 224 p. (Orig.). 1984. pap. Sterling. $9.95.

—**Realistic Decoys.** 224 p. 1985. Stoeger Pub. Co. pap. $14.95.*

Bridenhagen, Keith & Spielman, Patrick. **Realistic Decoys: Carving, Texturing, Painting & Finishing.** (Illus.). 224 p. (Orig.). 1984. Stoeger Pub. Co. pap. $14.95.

Buckwalter, Harold R. **Susquehanna River Decoys.** (Illus.). 1978. Schiffer. $12.95.

Burk, Bruce. **Game Bird Carving.** 2nd ed. (Illus.). 304 p. 1982. Winchester Press. $24.95.

Carpenter, Pearl E. **The Duck Book One & Two:** Basics for Painting Wood-Carved Ducks & Birds. (Illus.) 1984. Shades Mother Nature wkbk. $12.75.*

Chapell, Carl & Sullivan, Clark. **Wildlife Woodcarvers:** A Complete How-to-do-it Book for Carving & Painting Wildfowl. (Illus.) 216 p. 1986. Stackppole. $39.95.*

Connett, Eugene. **Duck Decoys.** 1980. Durrell. $12.50.

Coykendall, Rolf, Jr. **Duck Decoys and How to Rig Them.** (Illus.). 128 p. 1983. New Century. $21.95.

Delph, John and Delph, Shirley. **Factory Decoys of Mason Stevens.** (Illus.). Schiffer. $35.00.

Earnest, Adele. **The Art of the Decoy: American Bird Carvings.** (Illus.). 1982. pap. Schiffer. $14.95.

Frank, Chas. W., Jr. **Wetland Heritage: The Louisiana Duck Decoy.** 192 p. 1985. Pelican. $49.95.

Johnsgard, Paul A. ed. **The Bird Decoy: An American Art Form.** (Illus.). 1976. University of Nebraska Press. $17.95.

Luckey, Carl F. **Collecting Antique American Bird Decoys: An Identification and Value Guide.** (Illus.). 208 p. 1983. pap. Books Americana. $14.95.

—**Collecting Antique American Bird Decoys: Identification, & Value Guide.** (Illus.). 208 p. 1983. pap. Bks. Americana. $14.95.

Mackey, William F., Jr. & Colio, Quinton. **American Bird Decoys.** (Illus.). 1979. Repr. of 1965 ed. Schiffer. $19.95.

Murphy, Charles F. **Working Plans for Working Decoys.** (Illus.). 1979. Winchester Press. $21.95.

Parmalee, Paul W. & Loomis, Forrest D. **Decoys and Decoy Carvers of Illinois.** 1969. pap. Northern Illinois University Press. $25.00.

Reiger, George. **Floaters & Stick-Ups.** 208 p. 1986. Godine. $40.00.*

Schroeder, Roger. **How To Carve Wildfowl: Nine North American Masters Reveal the Carving and Painting Techniques That Win Them International Blue Ribbons.** 256 p. 1984. Stackpole. $34.95.

Shourds, Harry V. & Hillman, Anthony. **Carving Duck Decoys.** 1981. pap. Dover. $4.95.

Spielman, Patrick. **Making Wood Decoys.** 1982. Sterling. $16.95; lib. bdg. $18.95; pap. $8.95.

Starr, George R., Jr. **How to Make Working Decoys.** (Illus.). 1978. Winchester Press. $21.95.

Veasey, William. **Head Patterns.** (Illus.). 58 p. 1983. pap. Schiffer. $14.95.

—**Miniature Decoy Patterns.** (Illus.). 58 p. 1983. pap. $14.95.

Veasey, William & Hull, Cary S. **Waterfowl Carving: Blue Ribbon Techniques.** (Illus.). 1982. Schiffer. $35.00.

Walsh, Clune, Jr. & Jackson, Lowell G., eds. **Waterfowl Decoys of Michigan and the Lake St. Clair Region.** (Illus.). 175 p. 1983. Gale. $40.00.

DEER HUNTING (see also Hunting)

Adams, Chuck. **Complete Guide to Bowhunting Deer.** 256 p. 1984. pap. DBI. $10.95.

Bauer, Erwin. A. **Digest Book of Deer Hunting.** pap. DBI Books. $2.95.

Chalmers, Patrick R. **Deer-Stalking.** 256 p. 1985. State Mutual Bks. $60.00.*

Conway, Bryant W. **Successful Hints on Hunting White Tail Deer.** 2nd ed. 1967. pap. Claitors. $1.98.

Dalrymple, Bryon W. **The Complete Book of Deer Hunting.** 256 p. pap. Stoeger. $8.95.

—**Deer Hunting with Dalrymple: A Lifetime of Lore on The Whitetail and Mule Deer.** 256 p. 1983. pap. Arco. $7.95.

Darner, Kirt. **How To Find Giant Bucks.** (Illus.). 283 p. 1984. Walsworth's $20.00.

Deer Hunter's Guide. (Illus.). 160 p. Nat'l Rifle Assn. $4.95.

Elman, Robert, ed. **All About Deer Hunting in America.** 1976. New Century. $16.95.

Fadala, Sam. **Successful Deer Hunting.** 288 p. 1983. pap. DBI Books. $10.95.

Guide to Deer Hunting in the Catskill Mountains. pap. Outdoor Pubns. $1.75.

Hayes, Tom. **How to Hunt the White Tail Deer.** A. S. Barnes, rev. ed. pap. $6.95.

Horner, Kent. **Art & Science of Whitetail Hunting:** How to Interpret the Facts & Find the Deer. (Illus.) 192 p. 1986. Stackpole. pap. $11.95.*

Laycock, George. **Deer Hunter's Bible.** rev. ed. (Illus.). 1971. pap. Doubleday. $3.95.

Sell, Francis E. **Art of Successful Deer Hunting.** 1980. pap. Willow Creek. $5.95.

Sisley, Nick. **Deer Hunting Across North America.** (Illus.). 1975. Freshet Press. $12.95.

Smith, Richard P. **Deer Hunting.** rev. ed. (Illus.). 1981. pap. Stackpole Books. $9.95.

Tillett, Paul. **Doe Day: The Antlerless Deer Controversy in New Jersey.** 1963. pap. Rutgers University Press. $5.95.

Wegner, Robert. **Deer & Deer Hunting:** The Serious Hunter's Guide. 324 p. 1984. Stackpole. $24.95.

Weiss, John. **The Whitetail Deer Hunter's Handbook.** (Illus.). 1979. pap. Winchester Press. $11.95.

Whitehead, Kenneth. **Hunting and Stalking Deer Throughout the Ages.** (Illus.). 1980. David & Charles. $45.00.

—**Hunting & Stalking Deer Throughout the World.** (Illus.). 300 p. 1982. St. Martin. $19.95.

Wooters, John. **Hunting Trophy Deer.** rev. ed. (Illus.). 265 p. 1983. pap. New Century. $12.95.

Zumbo, Jim & Elman, Robert. **All-American Deer Hunter's Guide.** (Illus.). 320 p. 1983. New Century. $29.95.

DUCK & GEESE SHOOTING (see also Decoys)

Adams, Chuck. **The Digest Book of Duck and Goose Hunting.** (Illus.). pap. DBI Books. $3.95.

Cadieux, Charles L. **Goose Hunting.** 208 p. pap. 1984. Stoeger Pub. Co. $9.95.

Hinman, Bob. **The Duck Hunter's Handbook.** (Illus.). 1976. softbound. Stoeger. $9.95.

—**The Duck Hunter's Handbook,** rev. ed. 288 p. 1985. New Century. $15.95.

Jordan, James M. & Alcorn, George T., eds. **The Wildfowler's Heritage.** (Illus.). 120 p. 1984. JCP Corp. Va. $46.50.

Kramer, Theodore F. **Fifty Years of Duck Hunting.** 1985. Carlton. $7.50.

MacQuarrie, Gordon. **The Last Stories of the Old Duck Hunters.** (Illus.). 204 p. 1985. Willow Creek. $15.00.

—**Stories of the Old Duck Hunters & Other Drivel.** repr. of 1967 ed. Willow Creek. $15.00.

Milner, Robert. **Retriever Training for the Duck Hunter.** (Illus.) 150 p. 1985. Repr. of 1983 ed. Junction Press. $18.95.*

Romashko, Sandra D. **Wild Ducks and Geese of North America.** (Illus.). 1978. pap. Windward Publishing. $2.95.

Smith, Steve. **Hunting Ducks & Geese: Hard Facts, Good Bets and Serious Advice From a Duck Hunter You Can Trust.** 160 p. 1984. Stackpole. $14.95.

FALCONRY (see also Fowling)

Ap Evans, Humphrey. **Falconry.** (Illus.). 1974. Arco. $15.00.

Beebe, Frank L. **A Falconry Manual.** (Illus.). 128 p. 1983. pap. Hancock House. $12.95.

Berners, Juliana. **The Book of Hawking, Hunting and Blasing of Arms.** 1969. Repr. of 1486 ed. W. J. Johnson. $42.00.

Bert, Edmund. **An Approved Treatise of Hawkes and Hawking Divided into Three Bookes.** 1968. Repr. of 1619 ed. W. J. Johnson. $16.00.

Burton, Richard F. **Falconry in the Valley of the Indus.** 1971. Falcon Head Press. $50.00.

Fisher, Charles H. **Falconry Reminiscences.** 1972. Falcon Head Press. $15.00; deluxe ed. $25.00.

Ford, Emma. **Falconry in News and Field.** (Illus.). 1982. Branford. $32.50.

Fox, David G. **Garden of Eagles: The Life & Times of a Falconer.** (Illus.). 216 p. 1984. Merrimack Pub. Cir. $16.95.

Frederick II of Hohenstaufen. **The Art of Falconry.** Wood, Casey A. & Fyfe, F. Marjorie, eds. (Illus.). 1943. Stanford University Press. $39.50.

Freeman, Gage E. & Salvin, Francis H. **Falconry: Its Claims, History and Practice.** 1972. Falcon Head Press. $12.50; deluxe ed. $25.00.

Gryndall, William. **Hawking, Hunting, Fouling and Fishing;** Newly Corrected by W. Gryndall Faulkener. 1972. Repr. of 1596 ed. Walter J. Johnson, Inc. $13.00.

Harting, J. E. **Hints on the Management of Hawks and Practical Falconry.** 1982. (Pub. by Saiga). State Mutual Book & Periodical Service. $50.00.

Harting, James E. **Bibliotheca Accipitraria, a Catalogue of Books Ancient and Modern Relating to Falconry.** 1977. Repr. of 1963 ed. Oak Knoll Books. $45.00.

Jameson, Everett W., Jr. **The Hawking of Japan, the History and Development of Japanese Falconry.** (Illus.). Repr. of 1962 ed. Jameson & Peeters. $24.50.

Jameson, E. W. Jr. & Peeters, Hans J. **Introduction to Hawking.** 2nd ed. (Illus.). 1977. pap. E. W. Jameson, Jr. $8.85.

Lascelles, Gerald. **Art of Falconry.** (Illus.). Saifer. $12.50.

Latham, Simon. **Lathams Falconry, 2 pts.** 1977. Repr. of 1615 ed. Walter J. Johnson, Inc. $32.50.

Madden, D. H. **Chapter of Medieval History.** 1969. Repr. of 1924 ed. Kennikat. $15.00.

Mellor, J. E. **Falconry Notes by Mellor.** 1972. Falcon Head Press. $8.50.

Mitchell, E. B. **Art & Practice of Falconry.** (Illus.). 303 p. Saifer. $15.00.

Oswald, Allan. **The History & Practice of Falconry.** 128 p. 1981. State Mutual Book Svce. $25.00.

Phillott, D. C. & Harcourt, E. S., trs. from Persian Urdu. **Falconry—Two Treatises.** 1968. text ed. Falcon Head Press. $30.00.

Rowley, Sam R. **Discovering Falconry: A Comprehensive Guide to Contemporary Falconry.** (Illus.). 160 p. 1985. New Dawn. pap. $11.95.

Samson, Jack. **Modern Falconry: Your Illustrated Guide To The Art & Sport of Hunting With North American Hawks.** 160 p.

Schlegel, H. & Verster De Wulverhorst, J. A. **The World of Falconry.** 1980. Vendome Press. $60.00.

Schlegel, H. & Wulverhorst, A. H. **Traite De Fauconnerie: Treatise of Falconry.** Hanlon, Thomas, tr. (Illus.). 1973. Chasse Pubns. $32.50.

FIREARMS (see also Arms and Armor, Pistols, Revolvers, Rifles, Shotguns)

Ackley, Parker O. **Home Gun Care and Repair.** (Illus.). 1974. pap. Stackpole Books. $6.95.

Akehurst, Richard. **Game Guns & Rifles:** From Percussion to Hammerless Ejector in Britain. (Illus.) 192 p. 1985. Sterling. $19.95.*

Anderson, Robert S. **Metallic Cartridge Reloading.** (Illus.). 1982. pap. DBI Books. $10.95.

Askins, Charles. **Askins on Pistols and Revolvers.** Bryant, Ted & Askins, Bill. eds., 1980. National Rifle Association, $25.00; pap. $8.95.

Automatic and Concealable Firearms: Design Book, 3 vols. 1986. Gordon Pr. $299.00 (lib. bdg.).

Barwick, Humphrey. **Concerning the Force and Effect of Manuall Weapons of Fire.** 1974. Repr. of 1594 ed. W. J. Johnson. $8.00.

Bell, Bob. **Scopes & Mounts: Gun Digest Book.** 224 p. 1983. pap. DBI Books. $9.95.

Berger, Robert J. **Know Your Broomhandle Mausers.** (Illus.). 96 p. 1985. Blacksmith Corp. pap. $6.95.

Bodio, Stephen. **Good Guns.** 128 p. 1986. N. Lyons Bks. $14.95.*

Bridges, Toby. **Advanced Muzzleloader's Guide.** 256 p. 1985. Stoeger Pub. Co. pap. $11.95.

Browne, Bellmore H. **Guns and Gunning.** (Illus.). Repr. of 1908 ed. pap. Shorey. $4.95.

The Browning Hi-Power Exotic Weapons System. (Illus.). 72 p. 1985. Paladin Pr. pap. $12.00.

Cameron, Frank & Campione, Frank. **Micro Guns.** (Illus.). 48 p. 1982. Mosaic Press, OH. $24.00.

Chant, Chris. **Armed Forces of the United Kingdom.** (Illus.). 1980. David & Charles. $14.95.

Clede, Bill. **Police Handgun Manual: How To Get Street-Smart Survival Habits.** (Illus.). 128 p. Stackpole. $11.95.

Combs, Roger. **Holsters and Other Gun Leather: Gun Digest Book.** 256 p. 1983. pap. DBI Books. $9.95.

The Compleat Gunner: Sixteen Seventy-Two. 250 p. 1983. Saifer. $17.50.

Cromwell, Giles. **The Virginia Manufactory of Arms.** 1975. University Press of Virginia. $20.00.

Davis, John E. **Introduction to Tool Marks, Firearms and the Striagraph.** (Illus.). 1958. C. C. Thomas. $24.50.

Daw, George. **Gun Patents 1864.** 1982. Saifer. $15.00.

Edsall, James. **Volcanic Firearms and Their Successors.** Pioneer Press. $2.50.

Educational Research Council of America. **Firearms Examiner.** Ferris, Theodore N. & Marchak, John P., eds. (Illus.). 1977. Changing Times Education Service. $2.25.

Erickson, Wayne R. & Pate, Charles E. **The Broomhandle Pistol: 1896–1936.** 300 p. E&P Enter. $49.95.

Ezell, Edward C. **Handguns of the World.** (Illus.). 1981. Stackpole Books, $39.95.

—**Small Arms Today: Latest Reports on the World's Weapons & Ammunition.** 256 p. (Orig.). 1984. pap. Stackpole. $16.95.

Fadala, Sam. **The Complete Shooter.** (Illus.). 480 p. (Orig.). 1984. pap. DBI. $15.95.

Farnum, John. **The Street Smart Gun Book.** Police Bookshelf. pap. $11.95.*

Flores, Eliezer, ed. **How To Make Disposable Silencers, Vol. II.** (Illus.). 120 p. 1985. J.O. Flores. pap. $12.00.

Gambordella, Ted. **Weapons of the Street.** (Illus.). 80 p. 1984. Paladin Pr. pap. $8.00.

George, John N. **English Pistols and Revolvers.** Albert Saifer, Pub. $20.00.

Grennell, Dean A. **ABC's of Reloading.** 2nd ed. (Illus.). 1980. pap. DBI Books. $9.95.

—**Gun Digest Book of 9MM Handguns.** (Illus.) 256 p. 1986. DBI. pap. $12.95.*

Hamilton, T. M. **Early Indian Trade Guns: 1625–1775.** (Contributions of the Museum of the Great Plains Ser.: No. 3). (Illus.). 1968. pap. Museum of the Great Plains Pubns. Dept. $4.00.

Hatcher. **The Book of the Garand.** Gun Room Press. $15.00.

Hatcher, et al. **Firearms Investigation, Identification and Evidence.** 1977. Repr. Stackpole Books. $26.95.

Hatcher, Julian S. **Hatcher's Notebook.** rev. ed. (Illus.). 1962. Stackpole Books. $19.95.

Hoffschmidt, Edward J. **Know Your Gun, incl. Know Your .45 Auto Pistols; Know Your Walther P. .38 Pistols; Know Your Walther P. P. and P. P. K. Pistols; Know Your M1 Garand Rifles; Know Your Mauser Broomhandle Pistol; Know Your Anti-Tank Rifle.** 1976. Borden pap. $5.95. ea.

Hogg, Brig., fwrd. by **The Compleat Gunner.** (Illus.). 1976. Repr. Charles River Books. $10.50.

Hogg, Ian V. **Guns and How They Work.** (Illus.). 1979. Everest House. $16.95.

Home Workshop Silencers 1. 1980. pap. Paladin Enterprises. $12.00.

Howe, Walter J. **Professional Gunsmithing.** (Illus.). 1946. Stackpole Books. $24.95.

Huebner, Siegfried. **Silencers for Hand Firearms.** Schreier, Konrad & Lund, Peter C., eds. 1976. pap. Paladin Enterprises. $11.95.

Huntington, R. T. **Hall's Breechloaders: John H. Hall's Invention and Development of a Breechloading Rifle with Precision-Made Interchangeable Parts, and Its Introduction Into the United States Service.** (Illus.). 1972. pap. George Shumway Publisher. $20.00.

Jackson & Whitelaw. **European Hand Firearms.** 1978. Albert Saifer, Pub. $22.50.

James, Garry, ed. **Guns for Home Defense.** (Illus.). 1975. pap. Petersen Publishing. $3.95.

Kelly, Palo. **An American Tradition: Handguns.** (Illus.). 250 p. 1986. Tarantula Press. pap. $9.95.*

Kennedy, Monty. **Checkering and Carving of Gunstocks.** rev. ed. (Illus.). 1952. Stackpole Books. $27.95.

King, Peter. **The Shooting Field: One Hundred Fifty Years with Holland & Holland.** (Illus.). 176 p. 1985. Blacksmith. $39.95.

Larson, E. Dixon. **Remington Tips.** Pioneer Press. $4.95.

Lauber, George. **How to Build Your Own Flintlock Rifle or Pistol.** Seaton. Lionel tr. from Ger. (Illus.). 1976. pap. Jolex. $6.95.

—**How To Build Your Own Percussion Rifle or Pistol.** Seaton, Lionel, tr. from Ger. (Illus.).1976. pap. Jolex. $6.95.

—**How To Build Your Own Wheellock Rifle or Pistol.** Seaton, Lionel, tr. from Ger. (Illus.). 1976. pap. Jolex. $6.95.

Lenk, Torsten. **Flintlock: Its Origin and Development.** Albert Saifer, Pub. $45.00.

Lewis, Jack. **Law Enforcement Handgun Digest.** 3rd ed. 1980. pap. DBI Books. $9.95.

—**Black Powder Gun Digest.** 3rd ed. 256 p. pap. 1982. DBI. $10.95.

—**Gun Digest Book of Modern Gun Values,** 5th ed. (Illus.). 432 p. 1985. DBI. pap. $14.95.

Lindsay, Merrill. **Twenty Great American Guns.** (Illus.). 1976. Repr. pap. Arma Press. $1.75.

Miller, Martin. **Collector's Illustrated Guide to Firearms.** (Illus.). 1978. Mayflower Books. $24.95.

Murtz, Harold A., ed. **Gun Digest Book of Exploded Firearms Drawings.** 2nd ed. 1982. pap. DBI Books. $12.95.

—**Guns Illustrated.** 1987. (Illus.) 320 p. 1986. DBI. pap. $14.95.*

Myatt, F. **An Illustrated Guide to Rifles and Automatic Weapons.** (Illus.). 1981. Arco. $9.95.

National Muzzle Loading Rifle Association. **Muzzle Blasts: Early Years Plus Vol. I and II 1939–41.** 1974. pap. George Shumway Publisher. $18.00.

Nonte, George C., Jr. **Handgun Competition.** (Illus.). 1978. Winchester Press. $16.95.

—**Home Guide to Muzzle Loaders.** (Illus.). 1982. pap. Stackpole Books. $14.95.

Nonte, George C., Jr. **Combat Handguns.** Jurras, Lee F., ed. (Illus.). 1980. Stackpole Books. $19.95.

Norton (R. W.) Art Gallery. **E. C. Prudhomme: Master Gun Engraver.** (Illus.). 1973. pap. Norton Art Gallery. $3.00.

NRA Gun Collectors Guide. 336 p. Nat'l Rifle Assn. $4.50.

Olson, John. **Olson's Encyclopedia of Small Arms.** (Illus.). 1985. New Century. $22.95.

Pollard, Hugh B. **The History of Firearms.** 1974. Burt Franklin, Pub. $29.50; pap. $8.95.

Price, Robert M. **Firearms Self-Defense: An Introductory Guide.** (Illus.). 1981. Paladin Enterprises. $19.95.

Rees, Clair. **Sportsman's Handgunning Bible.** (Illus.). 336 p. 1985. New Century. $22.95.

Reese, Michael, II. **Nineteen Hundred Luger—U.S. Test Trials.** 2nd rev. ed. Pioneer Press, ed. (Illus.). Pioneer Press. $4.95.

Reilly, Robert M. **United States Military Small Arms, 1816–1865.** 1983. Gun Room. $35.00.

Rifles & Automatic Weapons. (Illus.) 1983. Arco. $9.95.

Riling, Ray. **Guns and Shooting: A Bibliography.** (Illus.). 1981. Ray Riling. $75.00.

Riviere, Bill. **The Gunner's Bible.** rev. ed. 1973. pap. Doubleday. $3.95.

The Ruger Exotic Weapons System. (Illus.). 96 p. (Orig.). 1984. pap. Paladin Pr. $12.00.

Ryan, J. W. **Guns, Mortars and Rockets. Vol. 2.** (Illus.). 1982. Pergamon Press. $40.00; pap. $16.00.

Shelsby, Earl, ed. **NRA Gunsmithing Guide:** Updated rev. ed. (Illus.). 336 p. (Orig.). 1980. pap. Nat'l Rifle Assn. $11.95.

Shooter's Bible, 1987. No. 78. 1986. Stoeger Pub. Co. pap. $13.95.

Shooter's Bible 1988. Vol. 79. 576 p. 1987. Stoeger Pub. Co. pap. $14.95.*

Smythe, John & Barwick, Humphrey. **Bow vs. Gun.** 1976. Repr. Charles River Books. $15.00.

Steindler, R. A. **Reloader's Guide.** (Illus.). 3rd ed. 1975. softbound. Stoeger. $9.95.

—**Steindler's New Firearms Dictionary.** (Illus.). 320 p. 1985. Stackpole. $24.95.

Steiner, Bradley. **The Death Dealer's Manual.** (Illus.). 120 p. 1982. pap. Paladin Press. $10.00.

Stockbridge, V. D. **Digest of U.S. Patents Relating to Breech-loading & Magazine Small Arms, 1836–1873.** (Illus.). 1963. N. Flayderman & Co. $12.50.

Sybertz, Gustav. **Technical Dictionary for Weaponry.** (Ger.-Eng.). 1969. pap. French & European Pubns. Inc. $120.00.

Taylor, Chuck. **The Combat Shotgun & Submachine Gun: A Special Weapons Analysis.** 176 p. 1985. Paladin Pr. pap. $14.95.

Thielen, Thomas W. **The Complete Guide to Gun Shows.** 1980. pap. Loompanics Unlimited. $6.95.

Thomas, Donald G. **Silencer Patents, Vol. III: European Patents 1901–1978.** (Illus.). 1978. Paladin Enterprises. $15.00.

—**Complete Book of Thompson Patents.** 1985. Gun Room. pap. $15.95.

Traister, John E. **How To Buy and Sell Used Guns.** (Illus.). 1982. softbound. Stoeger. $10.95.

—**Gunsmithing at Home.** (Illus.). 256 p. pap. (Orig.). 1985. Stoeger. $11.95.

—**Professional Care & Finishing of Gun Stocks.** (Illus.). 208 p. 1985. TAB Bks. $21.95; pap. $15.95.

Trzoniec, Stanley. **Handloader's Guide.** 256 p. 1985. Stoeger Pub. Co. pap. $11.95.

Van Rensselaer, S. **American Firearms.** (Illus.). 1948. pap. Century House. $10.00.

Waite, Malden & Ernst, Bernard. **Trapdoor Springfield.** 1985. Gun Room. $29.95.

Warner, Ken, ed. **Handloader's Digest.** 10th ed. 1984. DBI Books. $12.95.

—**Gun Digest, 1987.** 41st ed. (Illus.). 480 p. 1986. DBI. pap. $16.95.

West, Bill. **Winchester, Cartridges, and History.** (Illus.). B. West. $29.00.

—**Winchester Encyclopedia.** (Illus.). B. West. $15.00.

—**Winchester Lever-Action Handbook.** (Illus.). B. West. $25.00.

—**The Winchester Single Shot.** (Illus.). B. West. $15.00.

Weston, Paul B. **The New Handbook of Handgunning.** (Illus.). 1980. C. C. Thomas $12.95.

Williams, John J. **Survival Guns and Ammo: Raw Meat.** (Illus.). 1979. pap. Consumertronics. $19.00.

Williams, Mason. **The Law Enforcement Book of Weapons, Ammunition & Training Procedures: Handguns, Rifles and Shotguns.** (Illus.). 1977. C. C. Thomas. $35.75.

Wirnsberger, Gerhard. **Standard Directory of Proof Marks.** Steindler, R. A. tr. from Ger. (Illus.). 1976. pap. Jolex. $5.95.

Withers, John. **Precision Handloading.** 224 p. 1985. Stoeger Pub. Co. pap. $11.95.

Wood, J. B. **Gun Digest Book of Firearm Assembly-Disassembly: Law Enforcement Weapons, Pt. VI** (Illus.). 1981. pap. DBI Books. $12.95.

—**Gun Digest Book of Gun Care, Cleaning & Refinishing. Book I: Handguns.** (Illus.). 192 p. 1984. pap. DBI. $8.95.

—**Gun Digest Book of Gun Care, Cleaning & Refinishing. Book 2: Long Guns.** (Illus.). 192 p. (Orig.) 1984. pap. DBI. $8.95.

FIREARMS—CATALOGS

Barnes, Frank L. **Cartridges of the World,** 5th ed. (Illus.). 416 p. 1985. DBI. pap. $15.95.

Catalogue of Rim Fire and Center Fire Pistol, Rifle & Military Cartridges, U.S. Cartridge Co. 1881. 116 p. 1984. Rolling Block. pap. $8.00.

E. Remington & Son's Sporting Arms & Ammunition, 1887, Revised Price List. 36 p. 1984. Rolling Block. pap. $5.00.

Hogg, Ian V. **Jane's Infantry Weapons 1985–85.** 11th ed. (Illus.). 975 p. 1985. Jane's Pub. Inc. $125.00.

Murtz, Harold, ed. **Guns Illustrated 1986.** 18th ed. (Illus.). 320 p. 1985. DBI. pap. $13.95.

The Official Price Guide to Antique & Modern Firearms. 5th & 6th eds. 1985. Hse of Collectibles. $10.95 (5th ed.) & $11.95 (6th ed.).

Remington Gun Catalog 1877. Pioneer Press. $1.50.

Sears & Roebuck c1910 Ammunition Catalog. (Illus.). pap. Sand Pond. $2.00.

Tarassuk, Leonid, ed. **Antique European and American Firearms at the Hermitage Museum.** (Illus., Eng. & Rus.). 1985. Arma Press. ltd. ed. $40.00.

Tinkham, Sandra S., ed. **Catalog of Tools, Hardware, Firearms, and Vehicles.** 1979. Somerset House. pap. incl. color microfiche. $260.00.

United States Cartridge Co.-Lowell, Mass. 1891 Catalog. (Illus.). Sand Pond. $2.50.

Wahl, Paul. **Gun Trader's Guide,** 12th ed. 464 p. 1986. Stoeger Pub. Co. pap. $13.95.*

West, Bill. **Remington Arms Catalogues, 1877–1899.** 1st ed. (Illus.). 1971. B. West. $8.00.

Winchester Shotshell Catalog 1897. (Illus.). pap. Sand Pond. $1.50.

FIREARMS—COLLECTORS AND COLLECTING

Chapel, Charles E. **The Gun Collector's Handbook of Values.** 14th ed. (Illus.). 523 p. 1983. Putnam Pub. Group. $19.95.

—**Gun Collector's Handbook of Values.** 1984. Putnam Pub. Gp. pap. $11.95.

Dicarpegna, N. **Firearms in the Princes Odescalchi Collection in Rome.** (Illus.). 1976. Repr. of 1969 ed. Arma Press. $20.00.

Dixie Gun Works Antique Arms Catalog. Pioneer Press. $1.50.

Flayerman, Norm. **Flayerman's Guide to Antique American Firearms and Their Values.** 2nd ed. (Illus.). 1980. pap. DBI Books. $15.95.

Frith, James & Andrews, Ronald. **Antique Pistols Collection 1400–1860.** Saifer. $25.00.

Gusler, Wallace B. & Lavin, James D. **Decorated Firearms 1540–1870, from the Collection of Clay P. Bedford.** 1977. University Press of Virginia. $25.00.

Madaus, H. Michael. **The Warner Collector's Guide to American Long Arms.** 1981. pap. Warner Books. $9.95.

The Official Price Guide to Antique and Modern Firearms. 5th ed. 1985. House of Collectibles. $10.95.

The Official Price Guide to Collector Handguns. pap. House of Collectibles. $11.95.

Quertermous, Russel & Quertermous, Steve. **Modern Guns, Identification and Values.** 4th ed. 1980. pap. Wallace-Homestead. $11.95.

Serven, James. **Rare and Valuable Antique Arms.** 1976. Pioneer Press. $4.95.

Shumaker, P. L. **Colt's Variations of the Old Model Pocket Pistol.** 1957. Borden. $8.95.

Traister, John E. **How To Buy and Sell Used Guns.** (Illus.). 1982. softbound. Stoeger. $10.95.

Wahl, Paul. **Gun Trader's Guide.** 12th ed. (Illus.). softbound. Stoeger. $13.95.

Wilson, R. L. **Colt—Christie's Rare and Historic Firearms Auction Catalogue.** (Illus.). 1981. Arma Press. $25.00.

FIREARMS—HISTORY

Anderson, Jervis. **Guns in American Life.** 128 p. 1984. Random. $12.95.

Ayalon, David. **Gunpowder and Firearms in the Mamluk Kingdom: A Challenge to Midaeval Society.** 2nd ed. 1978. Biblio Distrubition Centre. $22.50.

Barnes, Duncan. **History of Winchester Firearms 1866–1980.** 5th ed. rev. (Illus.). 256 p. New Century. $16.95.

Blanch, H. J. A. **A Century of Guns: A Sketch of the Leading Types of Sporting and Military Small Arms.** (Illus.). 1977. Repr. of 1909 ed. Charles River Books. $25.00.

Brown, M. L. **Firearms in Colonial America: The Impact of History and Technology 1492–1792.** 1980. Smithsonian Institution Press. $45.00.

Buchele, W. & Shumway, G. **Recreating the American Long Rifle.** Orig. Title: **Recreating the Kentucky Rifle.** (Illus.). 1973. pap. George Shumway Publisher. $16.00.

Cooper, Jeff. **Fireworks: A Gunsite Anthology.** 1981. Janus Press. $19.95.

Fuller, Claude E. **Breech-Loader in the Service 1816–1917.** (Illus.). 1965. Flayderman, N. & Co. $14.50.

Fuller, Claude E. & Stewart, Richard D. **Firearms of the Confederacy.** 1977. Reprint of 1944 ed. Quarterman. $25.00.

Garavaglia, Louis A & Worman, Charles G. **Firearms of the American West, 1803–1865.** (Illus.). 1983. U of NM Press. $35.00.

Gusler, Wallace B. & Lavin, James D. **Decorated Firearms, 1540–1870 from the Collection of Clay P. Bedford.** 1977. (Colonial Williamburg Foundation). University Press of Virginia. $25.00.

Hackley, F. W. et al. **History of Modern U.S. Military Small Arms Ammunition: Vol. 2, 1940–1945.** Gun Room Press. $25.00.

Hamilton, T. M. ed. **Indian Trade Guns.** 1983. Pioneer Press. $10.95.

Helmer, William J. **The Gun That Made the Twenties Roar.** Gun Room Press. $16.95.

Hetrick, Calvin. **The Bedford County Rifle and Its Makers.** (Illus.). 1975. pap. George Shumway Publisher. (OP).

Holme, N. & Kirby, E. L. **Medal Rolls: Twenty-Third Foot Royal Welch Fusiliers, Napoleonic Period.** 1979. S. J. Durst. $39.00.

Hutslar, Donald A. **Gunsmiths of Ohio: 18th and 19th Centuries.** Vol. j. (Illus.). casebound. George Shumway Publisher. $35.00.

Jackson, Melvin H. & De Beer, Charles. **Eighteenth Century Gunfounding.** (Illus.). 1974. Smithsonian Institution Press. $19.95.

Kennet, Lee & Anderson, James L. **The Gun in America: The Origins of a National Dilemma.** (Illus., Orig). 1975. Greenwood Press. $22.50; pap. $3.95.

Lindsay, Merrill. **The New England Gun: The First 200 Years.** (Illus.). 1976. Arma Press. $20.00. pap. $12.50.

Nonte, George C., Jr. **Black Powder Guide.** 2nd ed. (Illus.). pap. Stoeger. $9.95.

North & North. **Simeon North: First Official Pistol Maker of the United States.** Repr. Gun Room Press. $9.95.

Peterson, Harold. **Historical Treasury of American Guns.** Benjamin Co. pap. $2.95.

Pollard, Hugh B. **History of Firearms.** (Illus.). 1974. B. Franklin. $29.50; pap. $8.95.

Reese, Michael II. **Nineteen-hundred Luger-U.S. Test Trials.** 2nd rev. ed. (Illus.). pap. Pioneer Press. $4.95.

Rosebush, Waldo E. **American Firearms and the Changing Frontier.** 1962. pap. Eastern Washington State Historical Society. $3.00.

Rywell, Martin. **American Antique Pistols.** Pioneer Press. $2.00.

—**Confederate Guns.** Pioneer Press. $2.00.

Schreier, Konrad F., Jr. **Remington Rolling Block Firearms.** (Illus.). pap. Pioneer Press. $3.95.

Sellers, Frank M. **Sharps Firearms.** (Illus.). 1982. Sellers Pubns. $39.95.

Shelton, Lawrence P. **California Gunsmiths.** (Illus.). 302 p. 1977. casebound. George Shumway Publisher. $29.95.

Tonso, William R. **Gun & Society: The Social and Existential Roots of the American Attachment to Firearms.** 1982. U Press of America. pap. $14.25 lib bdg. $26.50.

West, Bill. **Marlin and Ballard, Arms and History, 1861–1978.** (Illus.). 1978. B. West. $29.00.

—**Savage Stevens, Arms and History, 1849–1971.** (Illus.). 1971. B. West. $29.00.

FIREARMS—IDENTIFICATION

Anti-Tank Rifle. (Illus.). 12 p. 1983. pap. Ide House. $2.95.

Baer, Larry L. **The Parker Gun.** Gun Room. $29.95.

Brophy, Williams S. **The Krag Rifle.** Gun Room. $29.95.

—**L.C. Smith Shotguns.** Gun Room. $29.95.

Garton, George. **Colt's SAA Post-War Models.** Gun Room. $21.95.

Madaus, H. Michael. **The Warner Collector's Guide to American Long Arms.** 1981. pap. Warner Books. $9.95.

Matthews, J. Howard. **Firearms Identification: Original Photographs and Other Illustrations of Hand Guns, Vol. 2.** 1973. Repr. of 1962 ed. C. C. Thomas. $56.75.

—**Firearms Identification Original Photographs and Other Illustrations of Hand Guns, Data on Rifling Characteristics of Hand Guns & Rifles, Vol. 3.** Wilimovsky, Allan E., ed. (Illus.). 1973. C. C. Thomas. $88.00.

—**Firearms Identification: The Laboratory Examination of Small Arms, Rifling Characteristics in Hand Guns, and Notes on Automatic Pistols, Vol. 1.** 1973. Repr. of 1962 ed. C. C. Thomas. $56.75.

Nelson, Thomas B. & Lockhaven, Hans B. **The World's Submachine Guns: Developments from 1915 to 1963.** Vol. I rev. ed. 1980. TBN Ent. $29.95.

Ruth, Larry. **M-1 Carbine.** pap. Gun Room. $17.95.

Small Arms Training: Sten Machine Carbine, Vol. I. 1983. pap. Ide House $2.95.

Wilber, Charles G. **Ballistic Science for the Law Enforcement Officer.** (Illus.). 1977. C. C. Thomas. $30.75.

FIREARMS—INDUSTRY AND TRADE

Farley, Philip J., et al. **Arms Across the Sea.** 1978. Brookings Institution. $10.95; pap. $4.95.

Grancsay, Stephen V. & Lindsay, Merrill. **Illustrated British Firearms Patents 1718–1853.** limited ed. (Illus.). Arma Press. $75.00.

Hartzler, Daniel D. **Arms Makers of Maryland.** 1975. George Shumway Publisher. $35.00.

Kirkland, Turner. **Southern Derringers of the Mississippi Valley.** Pioneer Press. $2.00.

Noel-Baker, Phillip. **The Private Manufacture of Armaments.** 1971. pap. Dover. $6.00.

Russell, Carl P. **Guns on the Early Frontiers: A History of Firearms from Colonial Times through the Years of the Western Fur Trade.** 1980. University of Nebraska Press. $27.95. pap. $10.95.

Russell, Nick. **The Gun Shop Manual.** 180 p. 1986. TTR Pub. pap. $15.95.*

Stockholm International Peace Research Institute (SIPRI). **The Arms Trade Registers.** 1975. MIT Press. $18.00.

West, Bill. **Browning Arms and History, 1842–1973.** (Illus.). 1972. B. West. $29.00.

FIREARMS—LAWS AND REGULATIONS

Cook, Phillip J. & Lambert, Richard D., eds. **Gun Control.** 1981. American Academy of Political and Social Science. $7.50. pap. $6.00.

Cruit, Ronald L. **Intruder in Your Home: How to Defend Yourself Legally with a Firearm.** 288 p. 1983. Stein & Day. $17.95.

Garrison, William L. **Women's Views on Guns & Self-Defense.** 114 p. (Orig.). 1983. pap. Second Amend. $5.50.

Gun Control. 1976. pap. American Enterprise Institute for Public Policy Research. $3.75.

Halbrook, Stephen P. **That Every Man Be Armed: An Evolution of a Constitutional Right.** 240 p. 1984. U of N Mex. pap. $19.95.

Kates, Don B., ed. **Firearms & Violence: Issues of Public Policy.** 475 p. 1983. pap. Pacific Inst. Pub. $12.95.

Kennet, Lee & Anderson, James L. **The Gun in America.** (Illus.). text ed. pap. Greenwood Press. $22.50; pap. $3.95.

Krema, Vaclav. **Identification and Registration of Firearms.** (Illus.). 1971. C. C. Thomas. $19.75.

Kruschke, Earl R. **The Right To Keep and Bear Arms.** 230 p. 1985. C.C. Thomas. $24.50.

Kukla, Robert J. **Gun Control: A Written Record of Efforts to Eliminate the Private Possession of Firearms in America.** Orig. Title: Other Side of Gun Control. 1973. pap. Stackpole Books. $4.95.

Lester, David. **Gun Control: Issues & Answers.** 144 p. 1983. pap. C. C. Thomas. $14.75.

Lindell, James. W. **Handgun Retention System.** 1982. pap. Calibre Press. $12.50.

The Right To Keep & Bear Arms: A Presentation of Both Sides. 1986. Gordon Pr. $79.95 (lib. bdg.).*

Shields, Pete. **Guns Don't Die—People Do: The Pros, the Cons, the Facts.** 1981. pap. Arbor House. $5.95.

Siegel, Mark A. et al. **Gun Control: Restricting Rights or Protecting People?** 88 p. 1985. Instruct. Aids Tx. pap. $14.95.

Whisker, James B. **The Citizen Soldier and U.S. Military Policy.** 1979. North River Press. $7.50; pap. $4.50.

FOWLING (see also Decoys, Duck & Geese Shooting, Falconry)

Bauer, Erwin A. **Duck Hunter's Bible.** pap. Doubleday. $3.95.

Begbie, Eric. **Modern Waterfowling.** (Illus.). 190 p. 1980. Saiga. $14.95.

Bell, Bob. **Hunting the Long Tailed Bird.** (Illus.). 1975. Freshet Press. $14.95.

Dalrymple, Byron W. **Bird Hunting with Dalrymple:** The Rewards of Shotgunning Across North America. (Illus.) 288 p. 1987. Stackpole. $29.95.*

Dickey, Charley. **Quail Hunting.** (Illus.). 1975. softbound. Stoeger. $3.95.

Elliot, Charles. **Turkey Hunting With Charlie Elliot.** 288 p. Arco. $14.95; pap. $8.95.

Gryndall, William. **Hawking, Hunting, Fowling and Fishing; Newly Corrected by W. Gryndall Faulkner.** 1972. Repr. of 1596 ed. W. J. Johnson. $13.00.

Harbour, Dave. **Hunting the American Wild Turkey.** 258 p. 1974. Stackpole. $14.95.

Johnson, A. E. **Shooting Woodpigeon.** (Illus.). 126 p. 1980. Longwood Pub. Gp. $14.95.

Norman, Geoffrey. **The Orvis Book of Upland Bird Shooting.** 160 p. 1985. New Century. $14.95.

Smith, Steve. **Hunting Ducks & Geese: Hard Facts, Good Bets and Serious Advice From a Duck Hunter You Can Trust.** 160 p. 1984. Stackpole. $14.95.

Williams, Lovett E., Jr. **The Book of the Wild Turkey.** 1981. Winchester Press. $19.95.

Zutz, Don. **Modern Waterfowl Guns & Gunning.** 288 p. 1985. Stoeger Pub. Co. pap. $11.95.

GAME AND GAME BIRDS (see also Duck & Geese Hunting, Fowling, Hunting)

Beasom, Sam L. & Roberson, Sheila F., eds. **Game Harvest Management.** (Illus.). 300 p. 1985. CK Wildlife Res. $20.00; pap. $15.00.

Billmeyer, Patricia. **The Encyclopedia of Wild Game and Fish Cleaning and Cooking.** Yeshaby Pubs. $3.95.

Blair, Gerry. **Predator Caller's Companion.** 1981. Winchester Press. $15.95.

Candy, Robert. **Getting The Most From Your Game & Fish.** (Illus.). 278 p. (Orig.). 1984. pap. A. C. Hood Pub. $12.95.

Grooms, Steve. **Modern Pheasant Hunting.** (Illus.). 224 p. 1984. pap. Stackpole. $8.95.

Hagerbaumer, David. **Selected American Game Birds.** 1972. Caxton. $30.00.

Harbour, Dave. **Advanced Wild Turkey Hunting & World Records.** (Illus.). 264 p. 1983. New Century. $19.95.

—**Hunting the American Wild Turkey.** (illus.) 258 p. 1974. Stackpole. $14.95.

McDaniel, John M. **Spring Turkey Hunting:** The Serious Hunter's Guide. (Illus.) 224 p. 1986. Stackpole. $21.95.*

McKelvie, Colin. **A Future for Game?** (Illus.) 240 p. 1985. Allen & Unwin. $15.95.*

Marchington, John **The Natural History of Game.** (Illus.) 256 p. 1984. Longwood Publ. Gp. $25.00.

Nesbitt, W. H., ed. **Eighteenth Boone & Crockett Big Game Awards, 1980–82.** (Illus.). 250 p. 1983. Boone & Crockett. $19.50.

Nesbitt, W. H. & Wright, Phillip L., eds. **Records at North American Big Game.** 8th ed. 412 p. 1981, Boone & Crockett. $195.00.

Oldham, J. **The West of England Flying Tumbler.** 1981. State Mutual Book & Periodical Service, Ltd. $25.00.

Robbins, Charles T., ed. **Wildlife Feeding and Nutrition.** 1983. Academic Press. $31.50.

Scott, Peter. **A Coloured Key to the Wildfowl of the World.** rev. ed. (Illus.) 1972. Heinman. $11.50.

Sherwood, Morgan. **Big Game in Alaska.** 1981. Yale University Press. $27.50.

Smith, Guy N. **Gamekeeping & Shooting for Amateurs.** 3rd ed. (Illus.). 160 p. 1983. Triplegate. $15.50.

GAME AND GAME BIRDS—NORTH AMERICA

Elman, Robert and Peper, George. **Hunting America's Game Animals and Birds.** (Illus.). 1980. Winchester Press. $15.95.

Foster. **New England Grouse Shooting.** 1983. Willow Creek. $45.00.

Johnsgard, Paul A. **North American Game Birds of Upland and Shoreline.** (Illus.). pap. University of Nebraska Press. $7.95.

Leopold, A. Starker, et al. **North American Game Birds and Mammals.** (Illus.). 224 p. 1981. Scribner. $19.95.

Leopold, A. Starker & Gutierrez, Ralph J. **North American Game Birds and Mammals.** (Illus.). 208 p. 1984. pap. Scribner. $14.95.

Nesbitt, W. H. & Wright, Phillip L., eds. **Records of North American Big Game.** 8th ed. 1981. Boone & Crockett Club. $29.50.

Phillips, John C. **American Game Mammals and Birds: A Catalog of Books, Sports, Natural History and Conservation. 1582–1925.** 1978. Repr. of 1930 ed. Arno Press. $37.00.

Sanderson, Glen C., ed. **Management of Migratory Shore & Upland Game Birds in North America.** 1980. pap. University of Nebraska Press. $10.95.

Tinsley, Russell, ed. **All About Small-Game Hunting in America.** 1976. Winchester Press. $14.95.

Walsh, Harry M. **The Outlaw Gunner.** 1971. Cornell Maritime Press. $12.50.

Walsh, Roy. **Gunning the Chesapeake.** 1960. Cornell Maritime. $10.00

GAME COOKERY (see also Outdoor Cookery)

Angier, Bradford. **Home Cookbook of Wild Meat and Game.** (Illus.). 1982. pap. Stackpole Books. $9.95.

Barbour, Judy. **Elegant Elk: Delicious Deer.** 3rd ed. (Illus.). 196 p. 1983 reprint of 1978 ed. Peters Studio. $12.95.

Bashline, Sylvia. **Sylvia Bashline's Savory Game Cookbook.** 224 p. 1983. Stackpole. $13.95.

Beard, James. **Fowl & Game Bird Cookery.** 1983. Peter Smith. $11.75.

Billmeyer, Patricia. **The Encyclopedia of Wild Game and Fish Cleaning and Cooking.** pap. Yesnaby Pubs. $3.95.

Bryant, Jim. **The Wild Game & Fish Cookbook.** (Illus.). 224 p. 1983. Little. $14.95.

Cameron, Angus & Jones, Judith. **The L. L. Bean Game & Fish Cookbook.** 1983. Random. $19.95.

Canino, Thomas L. **Mountain Man Cookbook: Venison & Other Recipes.** 85 p. 1985. TLC Enterprises. pap. $7.95.

Chicken and Game Hen Menus. 1983. Silver. $15.95.

Cone, Joan. **Fish and Game Cooking.** 1981. pap. EPM Publications. $7.95.

Del Guidice, Paula J. **Microwave Game & Fish Cookbook.** (Illus.) 160 p. 1985. Stackpole. pap. $12.95.*

D'Ermo. Dominique. **Dominique's Famous Fish, Game & Meat Recipes.** 1981. pap. Acropolis. $8.95.

Duffala, Sharon L. **Rocky Mountain Cache: Western Wild Game Cookbook.** (Illus.). 72 p. 1982. pap. Pruett. $5.95.

Fadala, Sam. **Complete Guide to Game Care & Cookery.** 288 p. DBI. pap. $12.95.*

Goolsby, Sam. **Great Southern Wild Game Cookbook.** 193 p. 1980. Pelican. $13.95.

Gorton, Audrey A. **Venison Book: How to Dress, Cut Up and Cook Your Deer.** 1957. pap. Greene. $4.95.

Gray, Rebecca & Reeve, Cintra. **Gray's Wild Game Cookbook: A Menu Cookbook.** (Illus.). 220 p. 1983. Grays Sporting. $25.00.

Hibler, Jane. **Fair Game: A Hunter's Cookbook.** Lawrence, Betsy, ed. 1983. pap. Chalmers. $5.95.

Humphreys, Angela. **Game Cookery.** (Illus.) 144 p. 1986. David & Charles. $19.95.*

Jaxson, Jay. **Wild Country All Game & Fish Recipes.** (Illus.). 81 p. 1982. pap. Jackson G. B. $7.95.

Johnson, L. W., ed. **Wild Game Cookbook: A Remington Sportsmen's Library Bk.** pap. Benjamin Co. $3.95.

Knight, Jacqueline E. **The Hunter's Game Cookbook.** (Illus.). 1978. Winchester Press. $12.95.

Lamagna, Joseph. **Wild Game Cookbook for Beginner and Expert.** J. Lamagna. $6.95.

Mabbutt, Bill & Mabbutt, Anita: **North American Wild Game Cookbook.** 216 p. 1982. NC Book Exp. $9.95.

Mabbutt, Bill, et al. **North American Game Fish Cookbook.** 192 p. 1983. NC Bk. pap. $9.95.

Macliquham, Frances. **Complete Fish & Game Cookery of North America.** (Illus.). 304 p. 1983. Winchester Press. $29.95.

Marsh, Judy and Dyer, Carole, eds. **The Maine Way—A Collection of Maine Fish and Game Recipes.** (Illus.). 1978. DeLorme Pub. $3.95.

Michigan United Conservation Clubs. **The Wildlife Chef.** new ed. 1977. pap. Mich United Conserv. $3.95.

Oakland, Ann. **Buffalo at Steak.** 32 p. 1983. pap. One Percent. $3.95.

Orcutt, Georgia and Taylor, Sandra, eds. **Poultry and Game Birds.** 1982. pap. Yankee Books. $8.95.

Pederson, Rolf A. **Rolf's Collection of Wild Game Recipes:** Vol. I: Upland Game Birds. 174 p. 1982. pap. Rolf's Gallery. $9.95.

—**Waterfowl,** Vol. II. 1983. pap. Rolf's Gallery. $9.95.

Perkins, Roni. **Game in Season: The Orvis Cookbook.** (Illus.) 224 p. 1986. New Century. $19.95.*

Rojas-Lombardi, Felipe. **Game Cookery.** (Illus.). 1973. Livingston, dura. $2.95.

—**Game Cookery.** (Illus.). 1973. plastic bdg. Harrowood Books. $2.95.

Rywell, Martin. **Wild Game Cook Book.** 1952. pap. Buck Hill. $4.95.

Sagstetter, Brad. **The Venison Handbook.** (Illus.). 80 p. 1981. Larksdale. $6.95.

Smith, Capt. James A. **Dress 'Em Out.** 256 p. pap. (Orig.). Stoeger. $12.95.

Smith, John A. **Wild Game Cookbook.** 64 p. 1986. Dover. pap. $4.95.*

Steindler, Geraldine. **Game Cookbook.** New Revised Edition. 1985. softbound. Stoeger. $12.95.

Turkey, **Duck & Goose Menus.** 1985. (Pub. by Time-Life) Silver. $15.94.

Upland Game Birds, Vol. I. (Illus.). 174 p. pap. Rolf's Gallery. $9.95.

Wary, Carol. **Wild Game Cookery: The Hunter's Home Companion.** (Illus.). 1984. pap. (Orig.). Countryman. $8.95.

Willard, John. **Game Is Good Eating.** 4th rev. ed. (Illus.). 111 p. repr. of 1954 ed. J.A. Willard. $6.95.

Wongrey, Jan. **Southern Wildfowl and Wildgame Cookbook.** 1976. Sandlapper Store. $5.95.

Zumbo, Jim & Zumbo, Lois. **The Venison Cookbook.** (Illus.) 208 p. 1986. P-H. $17.45.*

GUNPOWDER (see Black Powder Guns, Ammunition)

GUNS (see Firearms, Pistols, Revolvers, Rifles, Shotguns)

GUNSMITHING

Angier, R. H. **Firearms Blueing and Browning.** 1936. Stackpole Books. $12.95.

Bailey, De Witt and Nic, Douglas A. **English Gunmakers: The Birmingham and Provincial Guntrade in the 18th and 19th Century.** (Illus.). 1978. Arco. $18.95.

Bish, Tommy L. **Home Gunsmithing Digest,** 3rd ed. 256 p. 1984. pap. DBI. $10.95.

Demeritt, Dwight B., Jr. **Maine Made Guns and Their Makers.** (Illus.). Maine State Museum Pubns. $22.00.

Dunlap, Roy F. **Gunsmithing.** 1963. Stackpole Books. $24.95.

Hartzler, Daniel D. **Arms Makers of Maryland.** (Illus.). 1977. George Shumway Publisher. $35.00.

Howe, J. V. **Modern Gunsmith.** (Illus.). 1983. Outlet Book. $14.98.

Howe, Walter J. **Professional Gunsmithing.** (Illus.). 1946. Stackpole Books. $24.95.

Hutslar, Donald A. **Gunsmiths of Ohio: 18th and 19th Centuries.** Vol. 1. (Illus.). 1973. George Shumway Publisher. $35.00.

Mitchell, Jack. **Gun Digest Book of Pistolsmithing.** 1980. pap. DBI Books. $9.95.

—**Gun Digest Book of Riflesmithing.** 256 p. 1982. pap. DBI Books. $11.95.

Newell, A. Donald. **Gunstock Finishing and Care.** (Illus.). 1949. Stackpole Books. $22.95.

Norton Art Gallery. **Artistry in Arms: The Art of Gunsmithing and Gun Engraving.** (Illus.). 1971. pap. Norton Art Gallery. $2.50.

NRA Gunsmithing Guide. 336 p. Natl Rifle Assn. $9.95.

Sellers, Frank M. **American Gunsmiths: A Source Book.** 1983. Gun Room. $39.95.

Shelsby, Earl, ed. **NRA Gunsmithing Guide: Updated.** rev. ed. (Illus.) 336 p. 1980. pap. Natl. Rifle Assn. $11.95.

Shelton, Lawrence P. **California Gunsmiths.** (Illus.). 1977. George Shumway Publisher. $29.65.

Stelle & Harrison. **The Gunsmith's Manual: A Complete Handbook for the American Gunsmith.** (Illus.). Repr. of 1883 ed. Gun Room Press. $12.95.

Traister, John. **Modern Gunsmithing.** (Illus.). 1981. Stackpole Books. $24.95.

—**First Book of Gunsmithing.** (Illus.). 1981. Stackpole Books. $18.95.

—**Gun Digest Book of Gunsmithing Tools and Their Uses.** 1980. pap. DBI Books. $8.95.

—**Gunsmithing at Home.** (Illus.). 256 p. pap. (Orig.). Stoeger. $11.95.

Walker, Ralph. **Shotgun Gunsmithing: Gun Digest Book.** 256 p. 1983. pap. DBI. $9.95.

Wood, J. B. **Gunsmithing: Tricks of the Trade.** (Illus.). 1982. pap. DBI Books. $11.95.

HAWKEN RIFLES

Baird, John D. **Fifteen Years in the Hawken Lode.** (Illus.). Gun Room Press. $17.95.

—**Hawken Rifles. The Mountain Man's Choice.** Gun Room Press. $17.95.

HUNTING (see also Bird Dogs, Decoys, Deer Hunting, Duck & Geese Shooting, Fowling, Hunting Dogs)

Acerrano, Anthony J. **The Practical Hunter's Handbook.** (Illus.). 1978. pap. Winchester Press. $9.95.

Anderson, Luther A. **Hunting the Woodlands for Small and Big Game.** (Illus.). 1980. A. S. Barnes. $12.00.

Bashline, L. James. ed. **The Eastern Trail.** 1972. Freshet Press. $8.95.

Begbie, Eric. **Sportsman's Companion.** 266 p. 1981. Saiga. $14.95.

Bell, Bob. **Digest Book of Upland Game Hunting.** 96 p. pap. DBI. $2.95.

Berners, Juliana. **The Book of Hawking, Hunting and Blasing of Arms.** 1969. Repr. of 1486 ed. W. J. Johnson. $42.00.

Bland, Dwain. **Turkey Hunter's Digest.** (Illus.) 256 p. 1986. DBI. pap. $12.95.*

Bourjaily, Vance. **Country Matters: Collected Reports from the Fields and Streams of Iowa and Other Places.** 1973. Dial Press. $8.95.

Brister, Bob. **Shotgunning: The Art and the Science.** 1976. Winchester Press. $15.95.

Burnham, Murry & Tinsley, Russell. **Murry Burnham's Hunting Secrets.** (Illus.). 244 p. 1983. New Century. $17.95.

Cadieux, Charles L. **Goose Hunting.** 208 p. 1983. Stoeger. $9.95.

Camp, Doug. **Turkey Hunting: Spring & Fall.** (Illus.). 176 p. 1983. pap. Outdoor Skills. $12.95.

Capossela, Jim. **How to Turn Your Fishing-Hunting Experiences Into Cash: Twenty-Five Ways to Earn Cash from Your Hobbies.** 1982. pap. Northeast Sportsmans. $3.50.

Douglas, James. **The Sporting Gun.** (Illus.). 240 p. 1983. David & Charles. $23.50.

Elliott, William. **Carolina Sports by Land and Water: Incidents of Devil-Fishing. Wild-Cat, Deer and Bear Hunting.** (Illus.). 1978. Repr. of 1859 ed. Attic Press. $10.00.

Elman, Robert. **The Hunter's Field Guide to the Game Birds and Animals of North America.** 1982. Knopf. $12.95.

—**One Thousand One Hunting Tips.** rev. ed. 1983. pap. New Century. $14.95.

Fears, J. Wayne. **Successful Turkey Hunting.** 92 p. 1984. Target Comm. pap. $4.95.

Fergus, Charles, et al. **Rabbit Hunting.** 1985. Allegheny. pap. $7.95.*

Field & Stream. **Field and Stream Reader.** facs. ed. 1946. Arno. $19.50.

Fischl, Josef & Rue, Leonard Lee, III. **After Your Deer is Down.** 1981. pap. Winchester Press. $9.95.

Geer, Galen. **Meat On The Table: Modern Small-Game Hunting.** (Illus.). 216 p. 1985. Paladin Pr. $14.95.

Gilsvik, Bob. **The Guide to Good Cheap Hunting.** (Illus.). 1979. Stein & Day. pap. $5.95.

Grinnell, George B. & Sheldon, Charles, eds. **Hunting and Conservation.** 1970. Repr. of 1925 ed. Arno. $25.00.

Gryndall, William. **Hawking, Hunting, Fouling and Fishing: Newly Corrected by W. Gryndall Faulkener.** 1972. Repr. of 1596 ed. W. J. Johnson. $13.00.

Hagel, Bob. **Game Loads and Practical Ballistics for the American Hunter.** (Illus.). 1978. Knopf. $13.95.

—**Guns, Loads & Hunting Tips.** Wolfe, Dave, ed. (Illus.) 536 p. 1986. Wolfe Pub. Co. $19.50.*

Hammond, Samuel H. **Wild Northern Scenes or Sporting Adventures with Rifle and Rod.** (Illus.). 1979. Repr. of 1857 ed. Harbor Hill Books. $12.50.

Harbour, Dave. **Advanced Wild Turkey Hunting & World Records.** (Illus.). 264 p. 1983. New Century. $19.95.

Henckel, Mark. **Hunter's Guide to Montana.** (Illus.). 224 p. 1985. Falcon Pr. MT. pap. $8.95.

Hill, Gene. **A Hunter's Fireside Book: Tales of Dogs, Ducks, Birds and Guns.** (Illus.). 1972. Winchester Press. $12.95.

—**Mostly Tailfeathers.** 1975. Winchester Press. $12.95.

Hill, Gene & Smith, Steve. **Outdoor Yarns & Outright Lies.** 168 p. 1983. Stackpole. $12.95.

Humphreys, John. **The Do-It-Yourself Game Shoot.** (Illus.). 144 p. 1983. David & Charles. $18.95.

James, David & Stephens, Wilson, eds. **In Praise of Hunting.** (Illus.). 1961. Devin-Adair Co. $10.00.

Janes, Edward C. **Ringneck! Pheasants and Pheasant Hunting.** (Illus.). 1975. Crown. $8.95.

Johnson, et al. **Outdoor Tips.** pap. Benjamin Co. $2.95.

Knap, Jerome J. **Digest Book of Hunting Tips.** pap. DBI Books. $2.95.

Laycock, George. **Shotgunner's Bible.** (Illus.). 1969. pap. Doubleday. $3.95.

Lindner, Kurt. **The Second Hunting Book of Wolfgang Birkner.** (Illus.). 1976. Ltd. ed. Arma Press. $175.00.

Liu, Allan J. **The American Sporting Collector's Handbook.** (Illus.). pap. Stoeger. $5.95.

McClane, A. J., ed. **McClane's Great Fishing & Hunting Lodges of North America.** 176 p. 1984. HR&W. $29.95.

McIntyre, Thomas. **Days Afield: Journeys & Discoveries in Hunting and Fishing.** 192 p. 1984. Dutton. $14.95.

Madden, D. H. **Chapter of Mediaeval History.** 1969. Repr. of 1924 ed. Kennikat Press. $15.00.

Madden, Dodgson H. **Diary of Master William Silence: A Study of Shakespeare and Elizabethan Sport.** 1970. Repr. of 1897. ed. Haskell Booksellers. $51.95.

Merrill, William K. **Hunter's Bible.** (Illus.). 1968. Doubleday. $4.50.

Merrill, Wm. & Rees, Clair. **Hunter's Bible,** rev. ed. (Illus.) 192 p. 1986. Doubleday. pap. $6.95.*

Meyer, Jerry. **Bear Hunting.** 224 p. 1983. Stackpole. $14.95.

NRA Guidebook for Hunters. 144 p. Nat'l Rifle Assn. $5.00.

Painter, Doug. **Hunting & Firearms Safety Primer.** 128 p. 1986. N. Lyons Bks. pap. $8.95.*

Pyle, Wilf E. **Hunting Predators for Hides & Profit.** 224 p. Stoeger Pub. Co. pap. $11.95.

Schwenk, Sigrid, et al. eds. **Multum et Multa: Beitraege zur Literatur, Geschichte und Kultur der Jagd.** (Illus.). 1971. De Gruyter. $75.00.

Shelsby, Earl & Gilford, James eds. **Basic Hunter's Guide,** rev. ed. (Illus.). 280 p. 1982. pap. Nat'l Rifle Assn. $14.95.

Shooter's Bible 1987. (Illus.). 576 p. 1986. Stoeger Pub. Co. $13.95.

Shooter's Bible 1988. (Illus.). 576 p. 1987. Stoeger Pub. Co. pap. $14.95.*

Smith, James A. **Dress 'Em Out.** (Illus.). 1982. pap. Stoeger. $11.95.

Stehsel, Donald. L. **Hunting the California Black Bear.** (Illus.). pap. Donald Stehsel. $7.00.

Strong, Norman. **The Art of Hunting.** (Illus.). 160 p. 1984. Cy De Cosse. $16.95.

Walrod, Dennis. **More Than a Trophy.** (Illus.). 256 p. 1983. pap. Stackpole. $12.95.

—**Grouse Hunter's Guide.** 192 p. 1985. Stackpole. $16.95.

Washburn, O. A. **General Red.** (Illus.). Jenkins. $5.50.

Waterman, C. F. **The Hunter's World.** (Illus.). 250 p. 1983. reprint of 1973 ed. New Century. $29.95.

Whelen, Townsend. **The Hunting Rifle.** 464 p. 1984. Repr. of 1924 ed. Wolfe Pub. Co. $39.00.

Whisker, James B. **The Right to Hunt.** 1981. North River Press. $8.95.

Wolfe, Ed. **Elk Hunting in the Northern Rockies.** 164 p. 1984. pap. Stoneydale Pr. Pub. $8.95.

Young, Ralph. W. **Grizzlies Don't Come Easy.** (Illus.). 1981. Winchester Press. $15.95.

—**My Lost Wilderness.** (Illus.). 196 p. 1984. New Century. $15.95.

Zern, Ed. **Fishing & Hunting From A to Zern.** 288 p. 1985. New Century. $14.95.

Zumbo, Jim. **Hunting America's Mule Deer.** 1981. Winchester Press. $14.95.

Zutz, Don. **Handloading for Hunters.** 1977. pap. Winchester Press. $9.95.

HUNTING—DICTIONARIES

Burnand, Tony. **Dictionnaire de la Chasse.** 250 p. (Fr.) 1970. pap. French & European Pubns. $7.50.

Frevert, W. **Woerterbuch der Jaegerei.** 4th ed. (Ger.) 1975. French & European Pubns. Inc. $12.00.

Kehrein, Franz. **Woerterbuch der Weldmannssprache.** (Ger.) 1969. French & European Pubns. Inc. $36.00.

Kirchoff, Anne. **Woerterbuch der Jagel. (Ger., Eng. & Fr. Dictionary of Hunting.)** 1976. French & European Pubns. Inc. $27.50.

Sisley, Nick. **All about Varmint Hunting.** (Illus.). 1982. pap. Stone Wall Press. $8.95.

Wisconsin Hunting Encyclopedia. 1976. pap. Wisconsin Sportsman. $2.95.

HUNTING—HISTORY

Greene, Robert. **The Third and Last Part of Conny-Catching.** 1923. Arden Library. $12.50.

Harding, Robert S. ed. **Omnivorous Primates: Gathering and Hunting in Human Evolution.** Teleki, Geza P. (Illus.). 1981. Columbia University Press. $45.00.

Petersen, Eugene T. **Hunters' Heritage: A History of Hunting in Michigan.** Lowe, Kenneth S. ed. (Illus.). 1979. Michigan United Conservation Clubs. $4.65.

Rick, John W. **Prehistoric Hunters of the High Andes.** (Studies in Archaeology Ser.). 1980. Academic Press. $27.50.

Speth, John D. **Bison Kills and Bone Counts: Decision Making by Ancient Hunters.** 272 p. 1983. pap. U of Chicago. $9.00.

Spiess, Arthur E. **Reindeer and Caribou Hunters: An Archaeological Study.** (Studies in Archaeology Ser.). 1979. Academic Press. $30.00.

HUNTING—AFRICA

Capstick, Peter H. **Death in the Long Grass.** (Illus.). 1978. St. Martin's Press. $11.95.

—**Death in the Dark Continent.** (Illus.). 320 p. 1983. St. Martin. $14.95.

Cloudsley-Thompson, J. L. **Animal Twilight, Man and Game in Eastern Africa.** (Illus.). 1967. Dufour Editions, Inc. $12.00.

Findlay, Frederick R. N. & Croonwright-Schreiner, S. C. **Big Game Shooting and Travel in Southeast Africa: Account of Shooting Trips in the Cheringoma and Gorongoza Divisions of Portuguese South-East Africa and in Zululand.** Repr. of 1903 ed. Arno $40.25.

Gilmore, Parker. **Days and Nights by the Desert.** Repr. of 1888 ed. Arno. $20.50.

Hemingway, Ernest. **Green Hills of Africa.** 1935. Scribner's. $17.50. pap. $5.95.

Holub, Emil. **Seven Years in South Africa.** 2 vols. 1881. Set. Scholarly Press. $45.00.

—**Seven Years in South Africa: Travels, Researches and Hunting Adventures Between the Diamond Field and the Zambesi, 1827–79.** 2 vols. 1971. Repr. of 1881 ed. Johnson Reprint Corp. $57.00.

MacQueen, Peter. **In Wildest Africa.** 1909. Scholarly Press. $29.00.

Selous, Frederick. **Hunter's Wanderings in Africa.** 526 p. 1986. repr. of 1920 ed. Wolfe Pub. Co. $47.00.*

Stigand, Chauncey H. **Hunting the Elephant in Africa.** (Illus.) 400 p. 1985. St. Martin. $14.95.*

Wynne-Jones, Aubrey. **Hunting: On Safari in East and Southern Africa.** (Illus.). 1982. International Scholarly Book Service. $29.95.

HUNTING—ALASKA

Keim, Charles J. **Alaska Game Trails with a Master Guide.** pap. Alaska Northwest. $6.95.

Waugh, Hal & Keim, Charles J. **Fair Chase with Alaskan Guide.** (Illus.). 1972. pap. Alaska Northwest. $3.95.

HUNTING—GREAT BRITAIN

Edward of Norwich. **Master of Game: Oldest English Book on Hunting.** Baillie-Grohman. William A. & Baillie-Grohman, F. eds. (Illus.). Repr. of 1909 ed. AMS Press. $45.00.

Jeffries, Richard. **The Gamekeeper at Home and the Amateur Poacher.** 1978. pap. Oxford University Press. $5.95.

Thomas, William B. **Hunting England: A Survey of the Sport and of its Chief Grounds.** 1978. Repr. of 1936 ed. R. West. $30.00.

Watson, J. N. **British and Irish Hunts and Huntsmen: Vols. I & II.** (Illus.). 1981. David & Charles. Set. $50.00 ea; set $85.00.

HUNTING—NORTH AMERICA

Dalrymple, Byron W. **Bird Hunting with Dalrymple:** The Rewards of Shotgunning Across North America. (Illus.) 288 p. 1987. Stackpole. $29.95.*

Leopold, Luna. B., ed. **Round River: From the Journals of Aldo Leopold.** (Illus.). 1972. pap. Oxford University Press. $3.95.

HUNTING—U.S.

Abbott, Henry. **Birch Bark Books of Henry Abbott: Sporting Adventures and Nature Observations in the Adirondacks in the Early 1900s.** Illus., Repr. of 1914 & 1932 eds.). 1980. Harbor Hill Books. $19.95.

Baily's Hunting Directory. 1978–79. (Illus.). 1978. J. A. Allen. $36.00.

Barsness, John. **Hunting the Great Plains.** 164 p. 1979. pap. Mountain Press. $6.95.

Cadbury, Warder, intro by. **Journal of a Hunting Excursion to Louis Lake, 1851.** (Illus.). 1961. Syracuse University Press. $8.95.

Catsis, John R., ed. **Hunter's Handbook:** Western Edition. 526 p. 1986. Sabio Pub. pap. $12.95.*

Cory, Charles B. **Hunting and Fishing in Florida, Including a Key to the Water Birds.** 1970. Repr. of 1896 ed. Arno. $14.00.

Elman, Robert, ed. **All About Deer Hunting in America** 1976. New Century. $16.95.

Hirsch, Bob. **Outdoors in Arizona: A Guide to Fishing & Hunting.** 192 p. 1986. Arizona Highway. pap. $12.95.*

Huggler, Tom. **Hunt Michigan: How to, Where to, When to.** (Illus.). 1985. Mich. United Conserv. pap. $12.95.

Lang, Varley. **Follow the Water.** (Illus.). 1961. John F. Blair. $6.95.

Lowenstein, Bill. **Hunting in Michigan: The Early 80's.** Arnold, David A., ed. 1981. pap. Michigan Natural Resources Michigan. $6.95.

Mitchell, John G. **The Hunt.** 1980. Knopf. $11.95.

—**The Hunt.** 1981. pap. Penguin. $4.95.

Murray, William H. **Adventures in the Wilderness.** Verner, William K., ed. (Illus.). 1970. Repr. Syracuse University Press. $10.50.

Roosevelt, Theodore. **Hunting Trips of a Ranchman.** Repr. of 1885 ed. Irvington, $17.50.

—**Outdoor Pastimes of an American Hunter.** 1970. Repr. of 1905 ed. Arno Press. $24.00.

—**Ranch Life and the Hunting-Trail.** 1985. Repr. of 1901 ed. Hippocrene. pap. $8.95.

—**Ranch Life.** 210 p. 1983 pap. University of Nebraska. $8.95.

—**Theodore Roosevelt's America.** Wiley, Farida, ed. (Illus.). 1955. Devin-Adair Co. $10.00.

—**Wilderness Hunter.** 1970. Repr. of 1900 ed. Irvington, $16.00.

Sandoz, Mari. **The Buffalo-Hunters: The Story of the Hide Men.** 1978. pap. University of Nebraska Press. $6.50.

Tillett, Paul. **Doe Day: The Antlerless Deer Controversy in New Jersey.** 1963. Rutgers University Press. pap. $5.95.

Tome, Philip. **Pioneer Life or Thirty Years a Hunter: Being Scenes and Adventures in the Life of Philip Tome.** (Illus.). 1971. Repr. of 1854 ed. Arno Press. $15.00.

Wootters, John. **A Guide to Hunting in Texas.** 1979. pap. Pacesetter Press. $5.95.

Zumbo, Jim. **Hunt Elk.** 256 p. 1985. New Century. $17.95.

HUNTING DOGS (see also Bird Dogs)
Bernard, Art. **Dog Days.** 1969. Caxton. $5.95.

Duffey, David M. **Hunting Dog Know-How** (Illus.). 1972. Winchester Press. pap. $8.95.

Falk, John R. **The Practical Hunter's Dog Book.** (Illus.). 1984. pap. New Century. $11.95.

Goodall, Charles. **How to Train Your Own Gun Dog.** (Illus.). 1978. Howell Book House, Inc. $10.95.

Hartley, Oliver. **Hunting Dogs.** pap. A. R. Harding Pub. $3.00.

Irving, Joe. **Training Spaniels.** (Illus.). 1980. David & Charles. $16.95.

Knap, Jerome. **Digest Book of Hunting Dogs.** 96 p. DBI. pap. $3.95.*

Lent, Patricia A. **Sport with Terriers.** (Illus.). 1973. Arner Publications, $9.95.

Long, Paul. **Training Pointing Dogs.** 1985. N. Lyons Books. pap. $8.95.

Maxwell, C. Bede. **The New German Shorthaired Pointer.** 4th ed. Howell Book House. $14.95.

Pata, Jan L., **Pointer Champions: 1889-1980.** (Illus.). 1981. pap. Pata Pubns. $19.95.

Roebuck, Kenneth C. **Gun-Dog Training Spaniels and Retrievers.** 1982. Stackpole. $12.95.

—**Gun-Dog Training Pointing Dogs.** 192 p. 1983. Stackpole. $12.95.

Salmon, H. M. **Gazehounds and Coursing.** (Illus.). 1977. North Star Press. $18.50.

Smith, Guy N. **Sporting and Working Dogs.** 1981. (Pub. by Saiga). State Mutual Book and Periodical Service. $40.00.

Tarrant, Bill. **Best Way to Train Your Gun Dog: The Dalmar Smith Method.** 1977. David McKay Co. $10.95.

Wehle, Robert G. **Wing and Shot.** 1964. Country Press NY. $12.00.

Whitney, Leon F. & Underwood, Acil B. **Coon Hunter's Handbook.** Hart, Ernest, ed. (Illus.). 1952. Holt, Rinehart & Winston. $5.95.

Wolters, Richard A. **Gun Dog. Revolutionary Rapid Training Method.** (Illus.). 1961. Dutton. $12.50.

—**Water Dog.** (Illus.) 1964. Dutton. $12.95.

HUNTING STORIES
Hill, Gene. **Hill Country: Stories About Hunting and Fishing and Dogs and Such.** (Illus.). 198. Dutton. $13.50.

McManus, Patrick. **They Shoot Canoes, Don't They?** 1981. Holt, Rinehart & Winston. $10.95.

MacQuarrie, Gordon. **Stories of the Old Duck Hunters.** 1979. pap. Willow Creek Press. $5.95.

—**More Stories of the Old Duck Hunters.** 1983. Willow Creek. $15.00.

—**Stories of the Old Duck Hunters & Other Drivel.** 228 p. 1985. repr. of 1967 ed. Willow Creek. $15.00.

Sassoon, Siegfried. **Memoirs of a Fox-Hunting Man.** 320 p. 1960. pap. Faber & Faber. $6.95.

HUNTING WITH BOW AND ARROW (see Bow and Arrow)

KNIVES
Berner, Douglas C. **Survival Knife Reference Guide.** (Illus.). 207 p. 1986. Bee Tree. pap. $12.95.*

Blade Magazine Staff. **American Blades 1986.** Am. Blade Bk. Svce. $11.95.*

Brewster, Melvyn & Hoyem, George. **Remington Bullet Knives.** (Illus.). 60 p. 1985. Armory Pubns. (price on request).

Combs, Roger & Lewis, Jack, ed. **Gun Digest Book of Knives,** 2d ed. 288 p. 1982. DBI. $10.95.

Erhardt, Roy & Ferrell, J. **Encyclopedia of Pocket Knives: Book One and Book Two Price Guide.** rev. ed. (Illus.). 1977. Heart of America Press. $6.95.

Goins, John E. **Pocketknives—Markings, Manufacturers & Dealers.** 2d ed. 280 p. 1982. pap. Knife World. $8.95.

Hardin, Albert N., Jr. & Hedden, Robert W. **Light but Efficient: A Study of the M1880 Hunting and M1890 Intrenching Knives and Scabbards.** (Illus.). 1973. Albert N. Hardin. $7.95.

Hughes, B. R. **Modern Hand-Made Knives.** Pioneer Press. $9.95.

Latham, Sid. **Knifecraft.** Stackpole Books. $24.95.

—**Knives and Knifemakers.** (Illus.). 1974. pap. Macmillan. $7.95.

Levine, Bernard R. **The Knife Identification & Value Guide.** (Illus.). 184 p. 1981. Knife World. $7.95.

—**Levine's Guide to Knife Values.** (Illus.). 480 p. 1985. DBI. pap. $19.95.

Loveless, R. W. **Contemporary Knifemaking.** 1986. Am Blade Bk. Svce. $18.95.*

McCreight, Tim. **Custom Knifemaking: 10 Projects from a Master Craftsman.** (Illus.). 234 p. 1985. Stackpole. pap. $14.95.

Nielsen, James R. **Knives and the Law.** 60 p. 1981. pap. Knife World. $4.95.

Parker, James F. **The Official Price Guide to Collector Knives.** 7th ed. 728 p. 1985. Hse of Collectibles. $10.95.

—**The Official Price Guide to Collector Knives.** 8th ed. 1985. Hse of Collectibles. $11.95.

Peterson, Harold L. **American Knives.** 1980. Gun Room. $17.95.

Sanchez, John. **Blade Master: Advanced Survival Skills for the Knife Fighter.** (Illus.). 96 p. 1982. pap. Paladin Press. $8.00.

Stephens, Frederick J. **Fighting Knives.** (Illus.). 144 p. 1985. Arco. pap. $11.95.

Tappan, Mel. ed. **A Guide to Handmade Knives and the Official Directory of the Knifemaker's Guild.** (Illus.). 1977. Janus Press. $9.95.

—**Knives 1986,** 6th ed. (Illus.) 256 p. 1985. DBI. pap. $11.95.

Warner, Ken. **Practical Book of Knives.** (Illus.). 1976. softbound. Stoeger. $9.95.

Warner, Ken, ed. **Knives Eighty Six,** 6th ed. 256 p. 1985. pap. DBI. $11.95.

NATURAL HISTORY—OUTDOOR BOOKS
Barrus, Clara, ed. **The Heart of Burrough's Journals.** 1979. Repr. of 1928 ed. Arden Lib. $30.00.

Bedichek, Roy. **Adventures with a Texas Naturalist.** (Illus.). 1961. pap. University of Texas Press. $8.95.

Errington, Paul L. **The Red Gods Call.** (Illus.). 1973. Iowa State University Press. $6.95.

Fuller, Raymond T. **Now That We Have to Walk: Exploring the Out-of-Doors.** facsimile ed. Repr. of 1943 ed. Arno Press. $17.00.

Godfrey, Michael A. **A Sierra Club Naturalist's Guide to the Piedmont of Eastern North America.** (Illus.). 432 p. 1980. pap. Sierra. $9.95.

Jefferies, Richard. **Old House at Coate.** 1948. Arno Press. $16.00.

Kieran, John F. **Nature Notes.** facs. ed. 1941. Arno Press. $14.50.

Leopold, Aldo. **Sand County Almanac: With Other Essays on Conservation from Round River.** (Illus.). 1966. Oxford University Press. $15.95.

—**Sand County Almanac Illustrated.** new ed. 1977. Tamarack Press. $25.00.

Olson, Sigurd F. **Listening Point.** (Illus.). 1958. Knopf. $13.45.

—**Sigurd Olson's Wilderness Days.** (Illus.). 1972. Knopf. $22.95.

Pearson, Haydn S. **Sea Flavor.** facs. ed. 1948. Arno Press. $15.00.

Rowlands, John J. **Cache Lake County.** (Illus.). 1959. W. W. Norton & Co. $12.95.

Sharp, Dallas L. **Face of the Fields.** facs. ed. 1911. Arno Press. $15.00.

—**Sanctuary! Sanctuary!** facs. ed. 1926. Arno Press. $10.00.

Sharp, William. **Where the Forest Murmurs.** 1906. Arno Press. $19.50.

Shepard, Odell. **Harvest of a Quiet Eye: A Book of Digressions.** facs. ed. Repr. of 1927 ed. Arno Press. $19.50.

Wiley, Farida, ed. **John Burroughs' America.** (Illus.). Devin-Adair Co. $10.50; pap. $5.25.

ORDNANCE (see also Ballistics)
Colby, C. B. **Civil War Weapons: Small Arms and Artillery of the Blue and Gray.** (Illus.). 1962. Coward, McCann & Geoghegan. $5.29.

Derby, Harry L. **The Hand Cannons of Imperial Japan.** Reidy, John and Welge, Albert, eds., 1981. Derby Publishing Co. $37.95.

Lewis, Ernest A. **The Fremont Cannon: High Up and Far Back.** 1981. Arthur H. Clark. $32.50.

Marchant-Smith, D. J. & Haslem, P. R. **Small Arms and Cannons.** 1982. Pergamon Press. $26.00; pap. $13.00.

Norton, Robert. **The Gunner, Shewing the Whole Practise of Artillerie.** 1973. Repr. of 1628 ed. W. J. Johnson. $40.00.

Office of Strategic Service. **OSS Sabotage and Demolition Manual.** (Illus.). 1973. pap. Paladin Enterprises. $12.95.

Simon, Leslie E. **Secret Weapons of the Third Reich: German Research in World War II.** (Illus.). 1970. Paladin Enterprises. pap. $8.95.

Tomlinson, Howard. **Guns and Government: The Ordnance Office Under the Later Stuarts.** 1979. Humanities Press. $42.50.

ORIENTATION
Burton, Maurice. **The Sixth Sense of Animals.** (Illus.). 192 p. 1973. Taplinger. $7.95.

Disley, John. **Orienteering.** (Illus.). rev. 2nd ed. 1979. Stackpole Books. pap. $8.95.

Henley, B. M. **Orienteering.** (Illus.). 1976. Charles River Books. $6.95.

Kals, W. S. **Land Navigation Handbook: The Sierra Club Guide to Map & Compass.** (Illus.). 288 p. 1983. pap. Sierra. $8.95.

Lynn, R. **Attention, Arousal & The Orientation Reaction.** 1966. ed. pap. Pergamon. $10.25.

Ratliff, Donald E. **Map Compass and Campfire.** (Illus.). 1970. Binford & Mort Pubs. pap. $2.50.

Vassilevsky, B. **Where is the North?** 1977. pap. Imported Pubns. $3.95.

Watson, J. D. **Orienteering.** (Illus.). 1975. Charles River Books, pap. $2.50.

OUTDOOR COOKERY (see also Game Cookery)
Anderson, Beverly M. & Hamilton, Donna M. **The New High Altitude Cookbook.** (Illus.). 1980. Random House. $14.95.

Angier, Bradford & Taylor, Zack. **Camping-on-the-Go Cookery.** (Illus.). 160 p. 1983. pap. Stackpole. $9.95.

Antell, Steven. **Backpacker's Recipe Book.** (Illus.). 1980. pap. Pruett. $5.50.

Banks, James E. **Alfred Packer's Wilderness Cookbook.** (Illus.). 1969. Filter Press. $7.00. pap. $1.50.

Barker, Harriett. **The One-Burner Gourmet.** rev. ed. 1981. pap. Contemporary Books. $8.95.

Beardsley, Richard. **Trail and Camp Cooking with the Chinese Wok.** (Illus.). 1982. pap. Pruett. $2.95.

Bock, Richard. **Camper Cookery.** 1977. pap. Lorenz Press. $5.95.

Brent, Carol D., ed. **Barbecue: The Fine Art of Charcoal, Gas and Hibachi Outdoor Cooking.** (Illus.). 1971. Doubleday. (OP).

Bunnelle, Hasse. **Food for Knapsackers: And Other Trail Travelers.** 1971. pap. Sierra Club Books. $4.95.

Bunnelle, Hasse & Sarvis, Shirley. **Cooking for Camp and Trail.** 1972. pap. Sierra Club. $4.95.

Drew, Edwin P. **The Complete Light-Pack Camping and Trail-Food Cookbook.** 1977. pap. McGraw-Hill. $3.95.

Farm Journal's Food Editors. **Farm Journal's Picnic and Barbecue Cookbook.** Ward, Patricia, ed. (Illus.). 1982. Farm Journal. $13.95.

Fears, J. Wayne. **Backcountry Cooking.** (Illus.). 1980. East Woods Press. $11.95; pap. $7.95.

Fleming, June. **The Well-Fed Backpacker.** (Illus.). 1981, pap. Random House. $3.95.

Heffron, Lauren. **Cycle Food: A Guide to Satisfying Your Inner Tube.** (Illus.). 96 p. 1983. pap. Ten Speed Press. $4.95.

Hemingway, Joan & Maricich, Connie. **The Picnic Gourmet.** (Illus.). 1978. pap. Random House. $7.95.

Holm, Don. **Old-Fashioned Dutch Oven Cookbook.** 1969. pap. Caxton Printers. $5.95.

Hughes, Stella. **Chuck Wagon Cookin'.** 1974. pap. University of Arizona Press. $8.50.

Kahn, Frederick E., ed. **Outdoor Cooking.** (Illus.) 144 p. 1984. Nautilus Books. pap. $4.95.

Kinmont, Vikki, & Axcell, Claudia. **Simple Foods for the Pack.** (Illus.). 1976. pap. Sierra Club Books. $5.95.

Krenzel, Kathleen & Heckendorf, Robyn. **The Sporting Life Gourmet.** (Illus.). 74 p. 1980. R. Louis Pub. $9.95.

Lund, Duane R. **Camp Cooking . . . Made Easy and Kind of Fun.** Adventure Publications. 1978. $4.45.

McElfresh, Beth. **Chuck Wagon Cookbook.** pap. Swallow Press. 72 p. 1960. $4.95.

McHugh, Gretchen. **The Hungry Hiker's Book of Good Cooking.** (Illus.). 1982. Alfred A. Knopf. $17.50. pap. $7.95.

Macmillan, Diane D. **The Portable Feast.** (Illus.). 1973. 101 Productions. pap. $4.95.

Maurer, Stephen G. **The Bannock Book: Food for the Outdoors.** (Illus.) 64 p. 1986. Heritage Assn. pap. $6.95.*

Mendenhall, Ruth D. **Backpack Cookery.** (Illus.). 1974. pap. La Siesta. $1.95.

Miller, Dorcas S. **The Healthy Trail Food Book.** rev. ed. (Illus.). 1980. pap. East Woods Press. $3.95.

Nagy, Jean. **Brown Bagging It: A Guide to Fresh Food Cooking in the Wilderness.** 1976 pap. Marty-Nagy Bookworks. $2.50.

Outdoor Cooking. (Illus.). 176 p. 1983. Time Life. $14.95.

Picnic and Outdoor Menus. 1984. Silver. $15.94.

Prater, Yvonne & Mendenhall, Ruth D. **Gorp, Glop and Glue Stew: Favorite Foods from 165 Outdoor Experts.** (Illus.). 1981. pap. Mountaineers. $6.95.

Raup, Lucy G. **Camper's Cookbook.** 1967. pap. C. E. Tuttle. $3.75.

Roden, Claudia. **Picnic.** 1981. State Mutual Book & Periodical Service. $40.00.

Schultz, Philip S. **Cooking with Fire and Smoke.** 273 p. 1986. S&S. $17.95.

Tarr, Yvonne Y. **The Complete Outdoor Cookbook.** (Illus.). 1973. Times Books. $8.95.

Thomas, Dian. **Roughing It Easy: A Unique Ideabook on Camping and Cooking.** (Illus.). 1974. pap. Brigham Young University Press. $8.95. pap. $6.95.

Wilder, James A. **Pine-Tree Jim's Jack-Knife Cookery: A Classic of Outdoor Lore.** 1982. pap. Siemens Communication Graphics. $7.95.

Wood, Jane. **Elegant Fare from the Weber Kettle.** (Illus.). 1977. Western Publishing. $6.95.

Woodall's Campsite Cookbook. Woodall. pap. $4.95.

Woodruff, Leroy L. **Cooking the Dutch Oven Way.** (Illus.). 1980. pap. ICS Books. $6.95.

OUTDOOR LIFE

Acerrano, Anthony. **The Outdoorsman's Emergency Manual.** 1976. 352 p. softbound. Stoeger. $9.95.

Anderson, Steve. **The Orienteering Book.** (Illus.). 1980. pap. Anderson World. $3.95.

Angier, Bradford. **Backcountry Basics.** 352 p. Stackpole. $19.95.

—**How to Live in the Woods on Pennies a Day.** (Illus.). 1971. pap. Stackpole Books. $7.95.

—**How to Stay Alive in the Woods.** Orig. Title: **Living off the Country.** 1962. pap. Macmillan. $2.95.

—**The Master Backwoodsman.** 1979. pap. Fawcett Book Group. $4.95.

—**The Master Backwoodsman.** 1978. Stackpole Books. $10.95.

Brown, Vinson. **Reading the Outdoors at Night.** (Illus.). 1982. pap. Stackpole Books. $9.95.

Crawford, John S. **Wolves, Bears and Bighorns: Wilderness Observations and Experiences of a Professional Outdoorsman.** (Illus.). 1981. Alaska Northwest. $19.95; pap. $12.95.

Eastman, P. F. **Advanced First Aid for All Outdoors.** 1976. pap. Cornell Maritime Press. $6.00.

Fear, Gene. **Fundamentals of Outdoor Enjoyment.** (Illus.). 1976. pap. Survival Ed. Assoc. $5.00.

Green, Paul. **The Outdoor Leadership Handbook.** 42 p. 1982. pap. Survival Ed. Assoc. (write for info).

Grow, Laurence. **The Old House Book of Outdoor Living Places.** (Illus.). 1981. Warner Books. $15.00; pap. $8.95.

Hamper, Stanley R. **Wilderness Survival.** 3rd ed. 1975. Repr. of 1963 ed. Peddlers Wagon. $1.79.

Hanley, Wayne. **A Life Outdoors: A Curmudgeon Looks at the Natural World.** (Illus.). 1980. Stephen Greene Press. pap. $5.95.

Hickin, Norman. **Beachcombing for Beginners.** 1976. pap. Wilshire Book Co. $2.00.

Johnson, et al. **Outdoor Tips: A Remington Sportsman's Library Book.** pap. Benjamin Co. $2.95.

Kodet, E. Russell & Angier, Bradford. **Being Your Own Wilderness Doctor.** (Illus.). 1975. Stackpole Books. $7.95.

Lund, Duane R. Nature's **Bounty for Your Table.** 1982. Adventure Pubns. $6.95.

Maughan, Jackie J. & Collins, Kathryn. **The Outdoor Women's Guide to Sports, Fitness & Nutrition.** (Illus.). 288 p. 1983. Stackpole. $15.95.

Merrill, W. K. **The Survival Handbook.** (Illus.). 1972. Winchester Press. $12.95.

Olsen, Larry D. **Outdoor Survival Skills.** rev. ed. 1973. Brigham Young University Press. $7.95.

Olson, Sigurd F. **Olson's Wilderness Days.** (Illus.) 1972. Knopf. $22.95.

Outdoor Living Skills Instructor's Manual. 1979. pap. American Camping Association. $5.00.

Owings, Loren C., ed. **Environmental Values, 1860–1972: A Guide to Information Sources.** 1976. Gale Research Co. $40.00.

Patmore, J. Allan. **Land and Leisure in England and Wales.** 1971. Fairleigh Dickinson. $27.50.

Paul, Don, ed. **Great Livin' in Grubby Times.** (Illus.) 140 p. 1986. Pathfinder HL. pap. $12.95.*

—**Green Beret's Guide to Outdoor Survival.** (Illus.) 134 p. 1986. Pathfinder HL. pap. $12.95.*

Platten, David. **The Outdoor Survival Handbook.** David & Charles. $6.95.

Rae, William E., ed. **A Treasury of Outdoor Life.** (Illus.). 520 p. 1983. Stackpole. $24.95.

Rafferty, Milton D. **The Ozarks Outdoors:** A Guide for Fishermen, Hunters & Tourists. (Illus.) 408 p. 1985. U of Okla. Press. $24.95.*

Rawick, George P. **From Sundown to Sunup.** 1972. pap. Greenwood Press. $15.00; pap. $4.45.

Risk, Paul H. **Outdoor Safety and Survival.** 300 p. 1983. Wiley. $15.95; pap. text ed. $11.00.

Roberts, Harry. **Keeping Warm and Dry.** (Illus.). 1982. pap. Stone Wall Press. $7.95.

Rutstrum, Calvin. **New Way of the Wilderness.** (Illus.). 1966. pap. Macmillan. $2.95.

—**Once Upon a Wilderness.** (Illus.). 1973. Macmillan. $10.95.

Scharff, Robert. **Projects for Outdoor Living.** 1981. Reston. $7.95.

Shepherd, Laurie. **A Dreamer's Log Cabin: A Woman's Walden.** (Illus.). 1981. Dembner Books. $8.95.

Stackpole. ed. **Taking Care of Outdoor Gear.** (Illus.). 326 p. 1983. pap. Stackpole. $9.95.

Thomas, Martha. **Guide to Outdoor Careers.** 272 p. 1983. pap. Stackpole. $9.95.

Van De Smissen, Betty, et al. **Leader's Guide to Nature-Oriented Activities.** 3rd ed. (Illus.). 1977. pap. Iowa State University Press. $7.95.

Wood, Dave. **Wisconsin Life Trip.** 1982. Adventure Pubns. $4.95.

Wurman, Richard S. et al. **The Nature of Recreation: A Handbook in Honor of Frederick Law Olmstead.** 1972. pap. MIT Press. $5.95.

PISTOL SHOOTING

Duncan, Mark. **On Target with Mark Duncan:** An Illustrated Pocket Guide to Handgun Accuracy. (Illus.) 52 p. 1984. Duncan Gun. pap. $4.95.

Given, T. **Survival Shooting: Handguns & Shotguns.** 1986. Gordon Pr. $79.95 (lib. bdg.).*

Mason, James D. **Combat Handgun Shooting.** (Illus.) 286 p. 1980. C. C. Thomas. $28.50.

Taylor, C. **The Complete Book of Combat Handgunning.** 1986. Gordon Press. $79.905 (lib. bdg.).*

PISTOLS

American Historical Founcation Staff, ed. **M1911A1 Automatic Pistol:Proud American Legend.** (Illus.) 1985. Am. Hist. Found. pap. $8.95.*

Askins, Charles. **Askins on Pistols and Revolvers.** Bryant, Ted & Askins, Bill, eds. 1980. National Rifle Association. $25.00; pap. $8.95.

Blackmore, Howard L. **English Pistols.** (Illus.) 64 p. 1985. Sterling. $12.95.*

Catalogue of Rim Fire & Center Fire Pistol, Rifle & Military Cartridges, U.S. Cartridge Company, 1881. 116 p. 1984. Rolling Block. pap. $8.00.

Cormack, A. G. **Famous Pistols and Hand Guns.** (Illus.). 160 p. 1983. pap. Arco. $9.95.

Datig, Fred A. **Luger Pistol.** rev. ed. Borden, $12.50.

Dixon, Norman. **Georgian Pistols: The Art and Craft of the Flintlock Pistol, 1715–1840.** 1972. George Shumway Publisher. $22.50.

Dyke, S. E. **Thoughts on the American Flintlock Pistol.** (Illus.). 1974. George Shumway Publisher. $6.50.

Erickson, Wayne & Pate, Charles E. **The Broomhandle Pistol, 1896 to 1936.** 300 p. 1985. E&P Enter. $49.95.

Grennel, Dean, ed. **Pistol and Revolver Digest.** 3rd ed. (Illus.). 1982. pap. DBI Books. $9.95.

Grennell, Dean. **Autoloading Pistols: Gun Digest Book.** 288 p. 1983. pap. DBI. $10.95.

Hoffschmidt, E. J. **Know Your Forty-Five Caliber Auto Pistols.** (Illus.). 1973. pap. Blacksmith Corp. $5.95.

—**Know Your Walther PP and PPK Pistols.** (Illus.). 1975. pap. Blacksmith Corp. $5.95.

—**Know Your Walther P. 38 Pistols.** (Illus.). pap. 1974. Blacksmith Corp. $5.95.

Horlacher, R., ed. **The Famous Automatic Pistols of Europe.** Seaton, L. & Steindler, R. A. trs. from Ger. (Illus.). 1976. pap. Jolex. $6.95.

Kirkland, Turner. **Southern Derringers of the Mississippi Valley.** Pioneer Press. $2.00.

Klay, Frank. **The Sammuel E. Dyke Collection of Kentucky Pistols.** 1980. Gun Room Press. $2.00.

Landskron, Jerry. **Remington Rolling Block Pistols.** (Illus.). 1981. Rolling Block Press. $34.95; deluxe ed. $39.95.

Long, Duncan. **Assault Pistols, Rifle & Submachine Guns.** 1986. Gordon Pr. $79.95 (lib. bdg.).*

Mitchell, Jack. **The Gun Digest of Pistolsmithing.** 1980. pap. DBI Books. $9.95.

Myatt, F. **An Illustrated Guide to Pistols and Revolvers.** 1981. Arco. $8.95.

Nonte, George C. Jr. **Pistol Guide.** (Illus.). 1980. Stoeger. $10.95.

—**Pistol Guide.** (Illus.) 280 p. Stoeger Pub. Co. pap. $10.95.

Nonte, George C., Jr. **Combat Handguns.** Jurras, Lee F. ed. (Illus.). 1980. Stackpole. $19.95.

—**Pistolsmithing.** (Illus.). 1974. Stackpole. $19.95.

North & North. **Simeon North: First Official Pistol Maker of the United States.** Repr. Gun Room Press. $9.95.

The Parabellum Automatic Pistol. 1986. Gordon Pr. $79.95 (lib. bdg.).*

Pistols & Revolvers. (Illus.). Arco. $9.95.

Reese. Michael. **Collector's Guide to Luger Values.** 1972. pap. Pelican. $1.95.

Reese, Michael, II. **Luger Tips.** 1976. Pioneer Press. $6.95.

The Ruger Pistol Exotic Weapon System. 1986. Gordon Pr. $79.95 (lib. bdg.).*

Seaton, Lionel, tr. **Famous Auto Pistols and Revolvers, Vol. II.** (Illus.). 1971. Jolex. $6.95.

Van Der Mark, Kist & Van Der Sloot, Puype. **Dutch Muskets and Pistols.** (Illus.). 1974. George Shumway Publisher. $25.00.

Wallack, L. R. **American Pistol and Revolver Design and Performance.** 1978. Winchester Press. $16.95.

Walter, John. **The Pistol Book.** 176 p. 1984. Arco. $19.95.

Weeks, John & Hogg, Ian. **Pistols of the World.** rev. ed. 306 p. 1982. DBI. $12.95.

Whittington, Robert D. **German Pistols and Holsters, 1943–45: Military-Police-NSDAP.** (Illus.). Gun Room Press. $15.00.

Whittington, Robert D. III. **The Colt Whitneyville-Walker Pistol.** 96 p. 1984. Brownlee Books. $20.00.

Wilkinson, F. J. **Flintlock Pistols.** (Illus.). 1976. pap. Hippocrene Books, $2.95.

Williams, Mason. **The Sporting Use of the Handgun.** (Illus.). 1979. C. C. Thomas. $14.75.
Wood, J. B. **Gun Digest Book of Firearms Assembly-Disassembly. Pt. 1: Automatic Pistols.** (Illus.). 1979. pap. DBI Books. $9.95.
—**Beretta Automatic Pistols: The Collector's & Shooter's Comprehensive Guide.** (Illus.). 192 p. 1985. Stackpole. $19.95.

RELOADING
Anderson, Robert S., ed. **Reloading for Shotgunners.** 1981. pap. DBI Books. $8.95.
Donnelly, John J. **Handloader's Manual of Cartridge Conversions.** (Illus.) 1056 p. 1987. Stoeger Pub. Co. pap. $24.95; spiral bound $29.95; hardcover $34.95.*
Matunas, Edward. **Handbook of Metallic Cartridge Reloading.** (Illus.). 1981. Winchester Press. $15.95.
Steindler, R. A. **Reloader's Guide.** 3rd ed. (Illus.). 1975. softbound. Stoeger, $9.95.

REVOLVERS (see also Colt Revolvers)
Askins, Charles. **Askins on Pistols and Revolvers.** Bryant, Ted & Askins, Bill, eds. 1980. National Rifle Association. $25.00; pap. $8.95.
Carmichael, Jim. **The Women's Guide to Handguns.** 190 p. Stoeger Pub. Co. $8.95.
Dougan, John C. **Know Your Ruger Single Action Revolvers: 1953–1963.** Amber, John T., ed. 1981. Blacksmith Corp. $35.00.
Hogg, Ian V. **Revolvers.** (Illus.). 1984. Stackpole. $12.95.
Lewis, Jack. **Gun Digest Book of Single-Action Revolvers.** (Illus.). 1982. pap. DBI Books. $9.95.
Munnell, J. C. **A Blacksmith Guide to Ruger Revolvers.** (Illus.). 56 p. 1982. pap. Blacksmith Corp. $7.50.
Myatt, F. **An Illustrated Guide to Pistols & Revolvers.** 160 p. 1981. Arco. (Illus.). 1980. Stoeger. $8.95.
Nonte, George C. Jr. **Revolver Guide.** (Illus.). 1980. Stoeger. $10.95.
Pistols & Revolvers. (Illus.) 1981. Arco. $9.95.
Report of Board on Tests of Revolvers and Automatic Pistols. 1907. (Illus.). Sand Pond. $3.50.
Ross, H. W. **A Blacksmith Guide to Ruger Flattops & Super Blackhawks.** (Illus.). 96 p. 1982. pap. Blacksmith Corp. $9.95.
Seaton, Lionel, tr. **Famous Auto Pistols and Revolvers, Vol. II.** (Illus.). 1979. Jolex. $6.95.
Williams, Mason. **The Sporting Use of the Handgun.** (Illus.). 1979. C. C. Thomas. $14.75.
Wood, J. B. **Gun Digest Book of Firearms Assembly-Disassembly: Part II: Revolvers.** 320 p. 1979. pap. DBI. $10.95.

RIFLES (see also Firearms, Hawken Rifles, Sharps Rifles, Winchester Rifles)
Bridges, Toby. **Custom Muzzleloading Rifles:** An Illustrated Guide to Building or Buying a Handcrafted Muzzleloader. (Illus.) 224 p. 1986. Stackpole. pap. $16.95.*
Buchele, William and Shumway, George. **Recreating the American Longrifle.** Orig. Title: Recreating the Kentucky Rifle. (Illus.). 1973. pap. George Shumway Publisher. $16.00.
Clayton, Joseph D. **The Ruger Number One Rifle.** (Illus.). 212 p. 1982. Blacksmith Corp. $39.95.
Colvin & Viall. **The Manufacture of Model 1903 Springfield Service Rifle.** 392 p. 1984. repr. of 1917 ed. Wolfe Pub. Co. $19.50.
Davis, Henry. **A Forgotten Heritage: The Story of the Early American Rifle.** 1976. Repr. of 1941 ed. Gun Room Press. $9.95.
DeHaas, Frank. **Bolt Action Rifle.** rev. ed. 448 p. 1984. DBI. pap. $14.95.
—**Single Shot's Gunsmithing Idea Book.** (Illus.) 176 p. 1983. TAB Bks. $13.50.
Ezell, Edw. C. **The Great Rifle Controversy: Search for The Ultimate Infantry Weapon From World War II Through Vietnam & Beyond.** 352 p. 1984. Stackpole. $29.95.
Fremantle, J. F. **The Book of the Rifle.** (Illus.). 576 p. 1985. repr. of 1901 ed. Wolfe Pub. Co. $54.00.
Grant James J. **More Single Shot Rifles.** (Illus.). Gun Room Press. $25.00.
—**Single-Shot Rifles.** Gun Room Press. $25.00.
—**Still More Single Shot Rifles.** 1979. Pioneer Press. $17.50.

Grissom, Ken. **Buckskins & Black Powder: A Mountain Man's Guide to Muzzle Loading.** (Illus.). 224 p. New Century. $15.95.
Hanson. **The Plains Rifle.** Gun Room Press. $15.00.
Hoffschmidt, E. J. **Know Your M-1 Garand Rifles.** 1976. pap. Blacksmith Corp. $5.95.
Hoyem, George. **The History & Development of Small Arms: British Sporting Rifle,** vol. 3. 236 p. 1985. Armory Pubns. $39.50.
Huddleston, Joe D. **Colonial Riflemen in the American Revolution.** (Illus.). 1978. George Shumway Publisher. $18.00.
Keith, Elmer. **Big Game Rifles & Cartridges.** 176 p. 1985. repr. of 1936 ed. Gun Room. $19.95.
—**Big Game Rifles & Cartridges.** (Illus.). 176 p. 1984. Deluxe ed. Wolfe Pub. Co. $30.00.
Kindig, Joe, Jr. **Thoughts on the Kentucky Rifle in Its Golden Age.** annotated 2nd ed. (Illus.). 1982. George Shumway Publisher. $75.00.
Kirton, Jonathan G. **British Falling Block Breechloading Rifles From 1865.** (Illus.). 250 p. 1985. Armory Pubns. $39.95.
Klinger, Bernd., ed. **Rifle Shooting As a Sport.** 1981. A. S. Barnes. $15.00.
Lewis, Jack. **The Hunting Rifle: A Gun Digest Book.** 356 p. 1983. pap. DBI. $10.95.
McAulay, John D. **Carbines of the Civil War, 1861–1865.** 1981. Pioneer Press. $7.95.
Mallory, Franklin B. & Olson, Ludwig. **The Krag Rifle Story.** 1980. Springfield Research Service. $20.00.
Matthews, Charles W. **Shoot Better With Centerfire Rifle Cartridges-Ballistic Tables.** (Illus.). 560 p. 1984. Matthews Inc. pap. $16.45.
Myatt, F. **An Illustrated Guide to Rifles and Automatic Weapons.** (Illus.). 1981. Arco. $8.95.
O'Connor, Jack, **The Rifle Book.** 3rd ed. (Illus.). 1978. Knopf. $13.95; pap. $10.95.
Otteson, Stuart. **The Bolt Action.** 2 vols. rev. ed. 1983. Winchester Press. $14.95.
—**The Bolt Action.** (Illus.). 304 p. 1984. pap. Wolfe Pub. Co. $14.95
—**Benchrest Actions & Triggers.** Wolfe, Dave, ed. 61 p. 1983. Wolfe Pub. Co. pap. $8.50.
Page, Warren. **The Accurate Rifle.** (Illus.). 1975. softbound. Stoeger. $8.95.
Rifles & Automatic Weapons. (Illus.) 1983. Arco. $9.95.
Rywell, Martin. **American Antique Rifles.** Pioneer Press. $2.00.
Shelsby, Earl, ed. **NRA Gunsmithing Guide.** Updated rev. ed. (Illus.). 336 p. (Orig.). 1980. pap. Nat'l Rifle Assn. $11.95.
Shumway, George. **Pennsylvania Longrifles of Note.** (Illus.). 1977. pap. George Shumway Publisher. $7.50.
—**Rifles of Colonial America.** 2 vols. incl. Vol. 1; Vol. 2. (Illus.). 1980. casebound. George Shumway Publisher. ea. $49.50.
Steindler, R. A. **Rifle Guide.** 1978. softbound. Stoeger. $9.95.
Taylor, C. **African Rifles and Cartridges.** Gun Room Press. $16.95.
—**The Fighting Rifles.** 1986. Gordon Pr. $79.95 (lib. bdg.).*
U.S. Rifle Caliber .30 Model 1903. Pioneer Press. $2.00.
U.S. Rifle Model 1866 Springfield. Pioneer Press. $0.75.
U.S. Rifle Model 1870 Remington. Pioneer Press. $0.75.
Whelen, Townsend. **The Hunting Rifle.** 464 p. 1984. Repr. of 1924 ed. Wolfe Pub. Co. $39.00.
Womack, Lester. **The Commercial Mauser Ninety Eight Sporting Rifle.** Angevine, Jay B., Jr., ed. (Illus.). 1981. Womack Assoc. $20.00.
Wood, J. B. **Gun Digest Book of Firearms Assembly/Disassembly. Pt. III: Rimfire Rifles.** (Illus.). 1980. pap. DBI Books. $8.95.
—**Gun Digest Book of Firearms Assembly/Disassembly. Part IV: Centerfire Rifles.** (Illus.). 1979. pap. $12.95.
Workman, William E. **Know Your Ruger 10-22 Carbine.** (Illus.) 96 p. 1986. Blacksmith Corp. pap. $9.95.*

SHARPS RIFLES
Manual of Arms for the Sharps Rifle. Pioneer Press. $1.50.
Rywell, Martin. **Sharps Rifle: The Gun That Shaped American Destiny.** Pioneer Press. $5.00.

SHOOTING (see also Firearms, Trap & Skeet Shooting)
Berger, Robert J. **Know Your Broomhandle Mauser.** (Illus.) 96 p. 1985. Blacksmith Corp. pap. $6.95.*

Brister, Bob. **Shotgunning: The Art and the Science.** (Illus.). 1976. Winchester Press. $15.95.
Crossman, Jim. **Olympic Shooting.** (Illus.). 144 p. Natl Rifle Assn. $12.95.
Day, J. Wentworth. **The Modern Shooter.** 1976. Repr. of 1952 ed. Charles River Books. $15.00.
Farrow, W. M. **How I Became a Crack Shot With Hints to Beginners.** (Illus.). 204 p. Wolfe Pub. Co. $16.50.
Gates, Elgin. **Gun Digest Book of Metallic Silhouette Shooting.** 1979. pap. DBI Books. $7.95.
Humphreys, John. **Learning To Shoot.** (Illus.). 192 p. 1985. David & Charles. $16.95.
Jarrett, William S., ed. **Shooter's Bible 1987.** No. 78. (Illus.). 576 p. 1986. Stoeger Pub. Co. $13.95.
—**Shooter's Bible 1988.** 79th ed. (Illus.). 576 p. 1987. Stoeger Pub. Co. pap. $14.95.
King, Peter. **The Shooting Field: 150 Years With Holland & Holland.** (Illus.). 176 p. 1985. Blacksmith. $39.95.
Klinger, Bernd, ed. **Rifle Shooting as a Sport.** (Illus.). 186 p. 1981. A. S. Barnes. $15.00.
Lind, Ernie. **Complete Book of Trick and Fancy Shooting.** (Illus.). 1977. pap. Citadel Press. $3.95.
McGivern, Ed. **Fast and Fancy Revolver Shooting.** New Century. $14.95.
Marchington, John. **Shooting: A Complete Guide for Beginners.** (Illus.). 1982. pap. Faber & Faber. $6.95.
Merkley, Jay P. **Marksmanship with Rifles: A Basic Guide.** (Illus.). pap. American Press. $2.95.
Rees, Clair. **Be An Expert Shot: With Rifle, Handgun, or Shotgun.** (Illus.). 192 p. 1984. New Century. $19.95.
Reynolds, Mike & Barnes, Mike. **Shooting Made Easy.** (Illus.) 144 p. 1986. Longwood Pub. Gp. $17.95.*
Riling, Ray. **Guns and Shooting: A Bibliography.** (Illus.). 1981. Ray Riling. $75.00.
Ruffer, J. E. **Good Shooting.** (Illus.). 1980. David & Charles. $22.50.
Set Your Sights: A Guide to Handgun Basics. (Illus.). 1982. Outdoor Empire. $1.95.
Sherrod, Blackie. **Blackie Sherrod . . . Scattershooting.** 1975. Strode. $6.95.
Weston, Paul B. **Combat Shooting for Police.** 2nd ed. (Illus.). 1978. C. C. Thomas. $12.75.
Willock, Colin. **The ABC of Shooting.** (Illus.). 353 p. 1975. Andre Deutsch. $18.95.
—**Duck Shooting.** (Illus.). 144 p. 1981. Andre Deutsch. $14.95.
Yochem, Barbara. **Barbara Yochem's Inner Shooting.** 1981. By By Productions. $6.95; pap. $3.95.

SHOTGUNS
Anderson, Robert S., ed. **Reloading for Shotgunners.** (Illus.). 224 p. 1981. pap. DBI Books. $9.95.
Bowlen, Bruce. **The Orvis Wing Shooting Handbook.** 96 p. 1985. N. Lyons Bks. pap. $8.95.*
Brockway, William R. **Recreating the Double Barrel Muzzleloading Shotgun.** (Illus.). 1985. Shumway. $27.50; pap. $20.00.
Burch, Monte. **Shotgunner's Guide.** (Illus.). 1980. Winchester Press. $15.95.
Grozik, Richard S. **Game Gun.** (Illus.) 160 p. 1986. Willow Creek. $39.00.*
Hastings, Macdonald. **The Shotgun: A Social History.** 1981. David & Charles. $29.95.
Hinman, Bob. **The Golden Age of Shotgunning,** 2nd ed. Wolfe, Dave, ed. (Illus.). 175 p. Wolfe Pub. Co. $17.95.
Johnson, Peter H. **Parker, America's First Shotgun.** (Illus.). 272 p. Stackpole. $17.95.
Laycock, George. **Shotgunner's Bible.** (Illus.). 1969. pap. Doubleday. $3.95.
Lewis, Jack & Mitchell, Jack. **Shotgun Digest.** 2nd ed. 1980. pap. DBI Books. $9.95.
McIntosh, Michael. **The Best Shotguns Ever Made in America: Seven Vintage Doubles to Shoot and to Treasure.** 1981. Scribner's. $17.95.
Marshall-Ball, Robin. **The Sporting Shotgun.** 1981. Saiga. $14.95.
O'Connor, Jack. **The Shotgun Book,** 2nd ed. rev. (Illus.). 1978. Knopf. pap. $9.95.
Robinson, Roger H. **The Police Shotgun Manual.** (Illus.). 1973. C. C. Thomas. $14.75.
Skillen, Charles R. **Combat Shotgun Training.** (Illus.). 1982. C. C. Thomas. $26.75.
Swearengen, Thomas F. **World's Fighting Shotguns.** 1978. TBN Ent. $29.95.
Thomas, Gough. **Shotguns and Cartridges for Game and Clays.** 3rd ed. (Illus.). 1976. Transatlantic Arts, Inc. $25.00.

Wallack, L. R. **American Shotgun Design and Performance.** 1977. Winchester Press. $16.95.

Zutz, Don. **The Double Shotgun,** rev. ed. 304 p. (Illus.). 1985. New Century. $19.95.

SURVIVAL (see also Outdoor Life)

Angier, Bradford. **How to Stay Alive in the Woods.** Orig. Title: **Living Off the Country.** 1962. pap. Macmillan. $2.95.

Benson, Ragnar. **Live Off the Land in The City and Country.** (Illus.). 1981. Paladin Enterprises. $16.95.

Canadian Government. **Never Say Die: The Canadian Air Force Survival Manual.** (Illus.). 208 p. 1979. Paladin Pr. pap. $8.00.

Clayton, Bruce D. **Life After Doomsday: A Survivalist Guide to Nuclear War and Other Disasters.** (Illus.). 1981. pap. Dial Press. $8.95.

Dennis, Lawrence. **Operational Thinking for Survival.** 1969. R. Myles. $5.95.

Dept. of the Air Force. **Survival: Air Force Manual 64–5.** (Illus.). 1976. pap. Paladin Enterprises. $8.00.

Fear, Daniel E., ed. **Surviving the Unexpected: A Curriculum Guide for Wilderness Survival and Survival from Natural and Man Made Disasters.** (Illus.). rev. ed. 1974. Survival Education Association. $5.00.

Fear, Eugene H. **Surviving the Unexpected Wilderness Emergency.** 6th ed. (Illus.). 1979. pap. Survival Education Association. $5.00.

Freeman, Daniel B. **Speaking of Survival.** (Illus.). pap. Oxford University Press. $5.95.

Merill, Bill. **The Survival Handbook.** 1974. pap. Arco Books. $2.50.

Olsen, Larry D. **Outdoor Survival Skills.** 4th rev. ed. 1973. Brigham Young University Press. $7.95.

—**Outdoor Survival Skills.** 1984. pap. Pocket Books. $3.95.

Read, Piers Paul. **Alive: The Story of the Andes Survivors.** (Illus.). 1974. pap. Harper & Row. $12.50.

Survival Improvised Weapons. 1986. Gordon Press. $79.95 (lib. bdg.).*

Thygerson, Alton L. **Disaster Survival Handbook.** (Illus.). 1979. pap. Brigham Young University Press. $7.95.

Wiseman, John. **Survive Safely Anywhere:** The SAS Survival Manual. (Illus.) 1986. Crown. $24.95.*

TAXIDERMY

Farnham, Albert B. **Home Taxidermy for Pleasure and Profit.** (Illus.). pap. A. R. Harding Publishing. $3.00.

Grantz, Gerald J. **Home Book of Taxidermy and Tanning.** (Illus.). 1985. Stackpole. pap. $8.95.

Harrison, James M. **Bird Taxidermy.** (Illus.). 1977. David & Charles. $12.50.

Haynes, Michael D. **Haynes on Air Brush Taxidermy.** (Illus.). 1979. Arco. $12.50.

McFall, Waddy F. **Taxidermy Step by Step.** (Illus.). 1975. Winchester Press. $12.95.

Metcalf, John C. **Taxidermy: A Computer Manual.** (Illus.). 166 p. 1981. pap. Biblio Dist. $15.00.

Moyer, John W. **Practical Taxidermy.** 2nd ed. 1979. Wiley. $15.95.

Pray, Leon L. **Taxidermy.** (Illus.). 1943. Macmillan. $9.95.

Smith, Capt. James A. **Dress 'Em Out, Vol. 1.** (Illus.). 1982. softbound. Stoeger. $11.95.

Tinsley, Russell. **Taxidermy Guide.** 2nd ed. (Illus.). 1977. softbound. Stoeger. $9.95.

TRAP AND SKEET SHOOTING

Blatt, Art. **Gun Digest Book of Trap & Skeet Shooting.** 256 p. 1984. pap. DBI. $10.95.

Campbell, Robert, ed. **Trapshooting with D. Lee Braun and the Remington Pros.** pap. Benjamin Co. $5.95.

—**Skeet Shooting with D. Lee Braun:** A Remington Sportsman's Library Book. Benjamin Co. $4.95.

Cradock, Chris. **Manual of Clayshooting.** (Illus.) 192 p. 1986. David & Charles. $29.95.*

National Skeet Shooting Association Record Annual. 320 p. Natl. Skeet Shoot. Assn. $7.00.

Skeet Shooting Review (monthly). 56 p. Natl Skeet Shoot. Assn. $17.00 (annual subs.).

TRAPPING

Bateman, J. E. **Trapping: A Practical Guide.** (Illus.). 1979. Stackpole Books. $14.95.

Bateman, James A. **Animal Traps and Trapping.** (Illus.). 1971. Stackpole Books. $12.95.

Clawson, George. **Trapping and Tracking.** (Illus.). 1977. Winchester Press. $13.95.

Errington, Paul L. **Muskrats and Marsh Management.** (Illus.). 1978. University of Nebraska Press. $13.50; pap. $3.25.

Geary, Steven. **Fur Trapping in North America.** (Illus.). 384 p. 1985. Stackpole. $44.95.

Gertsell, Richard. **The Steel Trap in North America.** (Illus.). 384 p. 1985. Stackpole. $44.95.

Get Set To Trap. (Illus.). 1982. Outdoor Empire. $1.95.

Gilsvik, Bob. **The Modern Trapline: Methods and Materials.** 1980. Chilton Book Co. $12.50.

Harding, A. R. **Deadfalls and Snares.** (Illus.). pap. A. R. Harding Publishing. $3.00.

—**Fox Trapping.** (Illus.). pap. A. R. Harding Publishing. $3.00.

—**Mink Trapping.** (Illus.). pap. A. R. Harding Publishing. $3.00.

—**Trappers' Handbook.** 1975. pap. A. R. Harding Publishing. $1.50.

—**Trapping as a Profession.** 1975. pap. A. R. Harding Publishing. $1.50.

—**Wolf & Coyote Trapping.** (Illus.) 252 p. A. R. Harding Pub. pap. $3.50.*

Jamison, Rick. **Trapper's Handbook.** 224 p. 1983. pap. DBI. $10.95.

Kreps, E. **Science of Trappings.** (Illus.). pap. A. R. Harding Publishing. $3.00.

Lindsey, Neil M. **Tales of A Wilderness Trapper.** 1973. pap. A. R. Harding Publishing. $1.50.

Lynch, V. E. **Trails to Successful Trapping.** pap. A. R. Harding Publishing. $3.00.

McCracken, Harold & Van Cleve, Harry. **Trapping.** (Illus.). 1974. A. S. Barnes. $8.95.

Mascall, Leonard. **A Booke of Fishing with Hooke and Line.** 1973. Repr. of 1590 ed. Walter J. Johnson. $9.50.

Montgomery, David. **Mountain Man Crafts & Skills.** (Illus.). 1981. Horizon Utah. $9.95.

Musgrove, Bill & Blair, Gerry. **Fur Trapping.** (Illus.). 1984. New Century. $13.95.

Russell, Andy. **Trails of a Wilderness Wanderer.** 1975. Knopf. $10.95.

Sandoz, Mari. **The Beaver Men: Spearheads of Empire.** (Illus.). 1978. pap. University of Nebraska Press. $5.95.

Simms, Jeptha R. **Trappers of New York.** 1980. Repr. of 1871 ed. Harbor Hill Books. $15.00.

Smith, Guy N. **Ferreting and Trapping for Amateur Game Keepers.** 1981. (Pub. by Saiga). State Mutual Book & Periodical Service. $25.00.

The Trapper's Companion. (Illus.). pap. A. R. Harding Publishing. $2.00.

Walters, Keith. **The Book of the Free Trapper.** 1981. Pioneer Press. $7.95.

Woodcock, E. N. **Fifty Years a Hunter and Trapper.** pap. A. R. Harding Publishing. $3.00.

WINCHESTER RIFLES

Fadala, Sam. **Winchester's 30-30, Model 94:** The Rifle America Loves. (Illus.) 224 p. 1986. Stackpole. $24.95.*

Madis, George. **The Winchester Model Twelve.** (Illus.). 1982. Art & Ref. $14.95.

—**The Winchester Book.** 3rd ed. (Illus.). 1979. Art & Reference House. $39.50.

—**The Winchester Handbook.** 1981. Art & Reference House. $19.50.

Stadt, Ronald W. **Winchester Shotguns & Shotshells.** (Illus.). 200 p. 1984. Armory Pubns. $30.00.

Twesten, Gary. **Winchester 1894 Carbine: A 90-Year History of the Variations of the Winchester Carbine 1894–1984.** (Illus.). 1984. G. Twesten. $20.00; pap. $10.00.

—**Winchester Model 1892 Carbine.** 1985. G. Tuesten. Pap. $10.00.*

West, Bill. **Winchester Encyclopedia.** (Illus.). B. West. $15.00.

—**Winchester Lever-Action Handbook.** (Illus.). B. West. $25.00.

—**Winchester Single Shot.** (Illus.). B. West. $15.00.

—**Winchesters, Cartridges and History.** (Illus.). B. West. $29.00.

Winchester—Complete Volume I: All Early Winchester Arms 1849–1919. (Illus.) 1981. B. West. $36.00

Winchester—Complete Volume II: All Winchester Arms 1920–1982. 1981. B. West. $36.00.

Names and Addresses of Leading Gun Book Publishers

ARCO PUBLISHING INC.
(see Prentice-Hall Inc.)

ARMORY PUBLICATIONS
P.O. Box 44372
Tacoma, Washington 98444

BLACKSMITH CORP.
P.O. Box 424
Southport, Ct. 06490

DAVID & CHARLES INC.
P.O. Box 57
Pomfret, Vermont 05053

DBI BOOKS, INC.
4092 Commercial Avenue
Northbrook, Illinois 60062

DENLINGER'S PUBLISHERS LTD.
P.O. Box 76
Fairfax, Virginia 22030

E & P ENTERPRISES
P.O. Box 2116
San Antonio, Texas 78297-2116

GUN ROOM PRESS
127 Raritan Avenue
Highland Park, N.J. 08904

HOUSE OF COLLECTIBLES
1904 Premier Row
Orlando, Florida 32809

JANE'S PUBLISHING INC.
c/o International Thomson Organisation Inc.
135 W. 50 Street
New York, N.Y. 10020

ALFRED A. KNOPF, INC.
201 E. 50 Street
New York, N.Y. 10022

LONGWOOD PUBLISHING GROUP INC.
51 Washington Street
Dover, New Hampshire 03820

NATIONAL RIFLE ASSOCIATION
1600 Rhode Island Avenue NW
Washington, D.C. 20036

NEW CENTURY PUBLICATIONS, INC.
220 Old New Brunswick Road
Piscataway, N.J. 08854
(also handles titles published under Winchester
Press imprint)

PALADIN PRESS
P.O. Box 1307
Boulder, Colorado 80306

PRENTICE-HALL
Englewood Cliffs, N.J. 07632

ROLLING BLOCK PRESS
P.O. Box 5357
Buena Park, California 90622

ALBERT SAIFER, PUBLISHERS
P.O. Box 239
West Orange, N.J. 07052

SAIGA PUBLISHING CO. LTD.
(see under Longwood Pub. Group Inc.)

GEORGE SHUMWAY PUBLISHERS
RD 7, P.O. Box 388B
York, Pennsylvania 17402

STACKPOLE BOOKS
P.O. Box 1831
Harrisburg, Pennsylvania 17105

STEIN & DAY
Scarborough House
Briarcliff Manor, N.Y. 10510

STERLING PUBLISHING CO., INC.
2 Park Avenue
New York, N.Y. 10016

STOEGER PUBLISHING COMPANY
55 Ruta Court
South Hackensack, N.J. 07606

TAB BOOKS INC.
Blue Ridge Summit
Pennsylvania 17214

TARGET COMMUNICATIONS CORP.
7626 West Donges Bay Road
P.O. Box 188
Mequon, Wisconsin 53092

WILLOW CREEK PRESS
Div. of Wisconsin Sportsman
P.O. Box 2266
Oshkosh, Wisconsin 54903

WOLFE PUBLISHING COMPANY, INC.
P.O. Box 3030
Prescott, Arizona 86302

Directory of Manufacturers
and Suppliers

Action Arms, Ltd. (UZI, Samson ammunition, Galil paramilitary)
P.O. Box 9573
Philadelphia, Pennsylvania 19124
(215) 744-0100

Aimpoint (sights, mounts)
203 Eldin Street, Suite 302
Herndon, Virginia 22070
(703) 471-6828

Alpha Arms, Inc. (rifles)
12923 Valley Branch
Dallas, Texas 75234
(214) 243-8124

American Arms (Diarm and AYA shotguns)
715 E. Armour Road
N. Kansas City, Missouri 64116
(816) 474-3161

American Derringer Corp. (handguns)
127 North Lacy Drive
Waco, Texas 76705
(817) 799-9111

American Industries (Calico paramilitary)
8700 Brook Park Road
Cleveland, Ohio 44129-6899
(216) 398-8300

Anschutz (rifles)
Available through Precision Sales International

Armes de Chasse (Mauser handguns, Bernardelli, Perugini-Visini, Gamba and Merkel shotguns)
P.O. Box 827
Chadds Ford, Pennsylvania 19317
(215) 388-1146

Armsport, Inc. (shotguns, black powder)
3590 NW 49th Street
Miami, Florida 33142
(305) 635-7850

Astra (handguns)
Available through Interarms

Auto-Ordnance Corp. (paramilitary)
West Hurley, N.Y. 12491
(914) 679-7225

AYA (Shotguns)
Available through American Arms

B & B Sales (Valmet paramilitary)
12521-3 Oxnard Street
North Hollywood, California 91606
(818) 985-2939

Barrett Firearms Mfg. Co., Inc. (paramilitary)
Route 1, Box 645
Murfreesboro, Tennessee 37130
(615) 896-2938

Bausch & Lomb (scopes)
See Bushnell (Division of)

Beeman Precision Arms, Inc. (imported handguns, rifles, scopes)
3440 Airway Drive
Santa Rosa, California 95401
(707) 578-7900

Benelli (shotguns)
Available through Heckler & Koch

Benson Firearms (Uberti black powder, rifles, revolvers)
P.O. Box 30137
Seattle, Washington 98103
(206) 361-2595

Beretta U.S.A. Corp. (handguns, shotguns, paramilitary)
17601 Indian Head Highway
Accokeek, Maryland 20607
(301) 283-2191

Bernardelli (handguns, rifles, paramilitary, shotguns)
Available through Springfield Armory, Inc., Armes de Chasse, and Quality Arms

Bersa (handguns)
Available through Outdoor Sports Headquarters

Birchwood Casey (gun care products)
7900 Fuller Road
Eden Prairie, Minnesota 55344
(612) 937-7933

Bonanza (reloading tools)
See Forster Products

Brno (handguns, rifles)
Available through Saki International

Browning (handguns, rifles, shotguns)
Route One
Morgan, Utah 84050
(801) 987-2711

BSA Guns Ltd.
P.O. Box 532277
Grand Prairie, Texas 75053
(214) 264-0000

B-Square Company (scope mounts)
P.O. Box 11281
Fort Worth, Texas 76109
(817) 923-0964

Maynard P. Buehler, Inc. (mounts)
17 Orinda Highway
Orinda, California 94563
(415) 254-3201

Burris Company, Inc. (scopes, sights, mounts)
311 East Eighth Street
Greeley, Colorado 80634
(303) 356-1670

Bushnell (scopes)
Division of Bausch & Lomb
2828 East Foothill Boulevard
Pasadena, California 91107
(818) 577-1500

CCI (ammunition, primers)
Available through Omark Industries, Inc.

C-H Tool & Die Corp. (reloading)
P.O. Box L
Owen, Wisconsin 54460
(715) 229-2146

CVA (black powder guns)
5988 Peachtree Corners East
Norcross, Georgia 30071
(404) 449-4687

Charter Arms Corp. (handguns, rifles)
430 Sniffens Lane
Stratford, Connecticut 06497
(203) 377-8080

Churchill (shotguns)
Available through Kassnar Imports

Colt Industries Firearms Division (handguns, rifles, paramilitary)
150 Huyshope Avenue, Box 1868
Hartford, Connecticut 06102
(203) 236-6311

Concorde (rifles, paramilitary)
Available through Kassnar Imports

Coonan Arms, Inc. (handguns)
830 Hampden Ave.
St. Paul, Minnesota 55114
(612) 328-6795

Dakota (handguns)
Available through E.M.F. Co., Inc.

Charles Daly (shotguns)
Available through Outdoor Sports Headquarters Inc.

Davis Industries (handguns)
13748 Arapahoe Place
Chino, California 91710
(714) 591-4727

Defense Systems International (M.A.C. paramilitary)
Dallas Road
Powder Springs, Georgia 30073
(404) 422-5731

Des Moines Imports (Gorosabel shotguns)
21 Glenview Drive
Des Moines, Iowa 50312

Detonics Firearms Industries (handguns)
13456 Southeast 27th Place
Bellevue, Washington 98005
(206) 747-2100

Diarm (shotguns)
Available through American Arms

Dixie Gun Works (black powder guns)
Reelfoot Avenue, P.O. Box 130
Union City, Tennessee 38261
(901) 885-0561

E.I. Du Pont de Nemours & Co., Inc. (gunpowder)
Explosives Department
1007 Market Street
Wilmington, Delaware 19898
(302) 774-1000

Dynamit Nobel of America, Inc. (Rottweil shotguns, GECO and RWS ammunition)
105 Stonehurst Court
Northvale, New Jersey 07647
(201) 767-1660

E.M.F. Company, Inc. (Dakota handguns, rifles, paramilitary, black powder)
1900 East Warner Avenue
Santa Ana, California 92705
(714) 261-6611

Euroarms of America Inc. (black powder guns)
1501 Lenoir Drive, P.O. Box 3277
Winchester, Virginia 22601
(703) 662-1863

Excam (Targa and Tanarmi pistols, shotguns)
4480 E. 11th Avenue
Hialeah, Florida 33013
(305) 681-4661-2

Exel Arms of America, Inc. (shotguns, Lanber shotguns)
14 Main Street, P.O. Box 566
Gardner, Massachusetts 01440
(617) 632-5008

Fabrique Nationale (paramilitary)
Available through Gun South Inc.

Federal Cartridge Corporation (ammunition, primers, cases)
2700 Foshay Tower
Minneapolis, Minnesota 55402
(612) 333-8255

Ferlib (shotguns)
Available through W. L. Moore & Co.

FFV Norma, Inc. (Norma ammunition, gunpowder, reloading cases)
300 South Jefferson, Suite 300
Springfield, Missouri 65806
(417) 865-9314

FIE Corporation (pistols, black powder guns, Franchi shotguns)
P.O. Box 4866
Hialeah, Florida 33014
(305) 685-5966

Forster Products (Bonanza and Forster reloading)
82 East Lanark Avenue
Lanark, Illinois 61046
(815) 493-6360

Franchi (shotguns, paramilitary)
Available through FIE Corp.

Freedom Arms (handguns)
One Freedom Lane, P.O. Box 1776
Freedom, Wyoming 83120
(307) 883-2468

Galil (paramilitary)
Available through Action Arms, Ltd.

Gamba (shotguns)
Available through Armes de Chasse

Garbi (shotguns)
Available through W. L. Moore & Co.

Gorosabel (shotguns)
Available through Des Moines Imports

Griffin & Howe, Inc. (sights, mounts)
36 W. 44th Street
New York, New York 10036
(212) 921-0980

Gun South Inc. (Aug, Fabrique Nationale, Steyr, Steyr Mannlicher rifles, paramilitary)
P.O. Box 129
Trussville, Alabama 35173
(205) 655-8299

Hammerli (handguns)
Available through Osborne's

Hatfield Rifle Works (black powder rifles and shotguns)
2028 Frederick Avenue
St. Joseph, Missouri 64506
(816) 233-9106

Heckler & Koch (handguns, rifles, paramilitary)
14601 Lee Road
Chantilly, Virginia 22021
(703) 631-2800

Hege Siber (black powder)
Available through Navy Arms

Hercules, Inc. (gunpowder)
910 Market Street
Wilmington, Delaware 19894
(302) 594-5000

Heym (rifles, shotguns)
Available through Paul Jaeger, Inc.

Hodgdon Powder Co., Inc. (gunpowder)
6231 Robinson, P.O. Box 2932
Shawnee Mission, Kansas 66202
(913) 362-9455

Hopkins & Allen Arms (black powder guns)
3 Ethel Avenue, P.O. Box 217
Hawthorne, New Jersey 07507
(201) 427-1165

Hoppe's Gun Care Products
Penguin Industries, Inc.
Coatesville, Pennsylvania 19320
(215) 384-6000

Hornady Manufacturing Company (reloading, ammunition)
P.O. Box 1848
Grand Island, Nebraska 68802-1848
(308) 382-1390

Interarms (handguns, shotguns and rifles, including Astra and Virginian, Bernardelli, Rossi, Star, Walther)
10 Prince Street
Alexandria, Virginia 22313
(703) 548-1400

International Sporting Goods (Laurona shotguns)
919 Imperial Avenue, P.O. Box 496
Calexico, California 92231
(619) 357-4005

Intratec U.S.A. Inc. (paramilitary)
11990 S.W. 128th Street
Miami, Florida 33186
(305) 232-1821

Iver Johnson (handguns, rifles, paramilitary)
2202 Redmond Road
Jacksonville, Arkansas 72076
(501) 982-9491

Paul Jaeger, Inc. (Heym rifles, shotguns, Schmidt & Bender scopes, mounts)
P.O. Box 449
1 Madison Ave.
Grand Junction, Tennessee 38039
(901) 764-6909

K.D.F. Inc. (Mauser rifles)
2485 Highway North
Seguin, Texas 78155
(512) 379-8141

Kassnar Imports (Churchill shotguns, Omega shotguns)
P.O. Box 6097
Harrisburg, Pennsylvania 17112
(717) 652-6101

Kimber (rifles, scopes)
9039 S.E. Jannsen Road
Clackamas, Oregon 97015
(503) 656-1704

Kleen Bore Inc. (gun care products)
20 Ladd Avenue
Northampton, Massachusetts 01060
(413) 586-7240

Krico (rifles)
Available through Beeman Precision Arms

Krieghoff International Inc. (shotguns, Shotguns of Ulm)
P.O. Box 549
Ottsville, Pennsylvania 18942
(215) 847-5173 (telex: 140914 DK USA)

Lanber Arms of America, Inc. (shotguns)
Available through Exel Arms

L.A.R. Manufacturing, Inc. (Grizzly handguns)
4133 West Farm Road
West Jordan, Utah 84084
(307) 883-2468

Lebeau-Courally (shotguns)
Available through W. L. Moore & Co.

Leupold & Stevens, Inc. (scopes, mounts, Nosler bullets)
P.O. Box 688
Beaverton, Oregon 97075
(503) 646-9171

Llama (handguns)
Available through Stoeger Industries

London Guns (sights, mounts)
1528 20th Street
Santa Monica, California 90404
(213) 828-8486

Lyman Products Corp. (black powder guns, sights, gun care products, scopes, reloading tools)
Route 147
Middlefield, Connecticut 06455
(203) 349-3421

M.A.C. (paramilitary)
See Defense Systems International

MEC, Inc. (reloading tools)
Mayville Engineering Company, Inc.
P.O. Box 267
Mayville, Wisconsin 53050
(414) 387-4500

MTM Molded Products Co. (reloading tools)
5680 Webster Street
Dayton, Ohio 45414
(513) 890-7461

Magnum Research Inc. (paramilitary, Galil)
7271 Commerce Circle West
Minneapolis, Minnesota 55432
(612) 574-1868

Marlin Firearms Company (rifles, shotguns)
100 Kenna Drive
North Haven, Connecticut 06473
(203) 239-5621

Mauser (handguns, rifles, shotguns)
Available through Armes de Chasse (hangduns) and
K.D.F. (rifles, shotguns)

Merit Gunsight Company (sights, optical aids)
P.O. Box 995
Sequim, Washington 98382
(206) 683-6127

Merkel (shotguns)
Available through Armes de Chasse

Michigan Arms Corp. (rifles)
363 Elmwood
Troy, Michigan 48082
(313) 583-1518

Millett Sights (sights and mounts)
16131 Gothard Street
Huntington Beach, California 92647
(714) 847-5245

Mitchell Arms (paramilitary)
19007 South Reyes Avenue
Compton, California 90221
(213) 603-0465

William L. Moore & Co. (Garbi, Ferlib, Lebeau-Courally, and Piotti shotguns)
31360 Via Colinas, No. 109
Westlake Village, California 91361
(818) 889-4160

O.F. Mossberg & Sons, Inc. (rifles, shotguns)
7 Grasso Avenue
North Haven, Connecticut 06473
(203) 288-6491

Navy Arms Company, Inc. (handguns, Lugers, shotguns, black powder guns, replicas)
689 Bergen Boulevard
Ridgefield, New Jersey 07657
(201) 945-2500

Norma (ammunition, gunpowder, reloading cases)
Available through FFV Norma, Inc.

North American Arms (handguns)
1800 North 300 West
P.O. Box 707
Spanish Fork, Utah 84660
(801) 798-9893

Olin/Winchester (ammunition, primers, cases, imported shotguns)
East Alton, Illinois 62024
(618) 258-2000

Omark Industries, Inc. (CCI ammunition, Outers gun care products, RCBS reloading tools, Speer bullets, Weaver mount rings)
Box 856
Lewiston, Idaho 83501
(208) 746-2351

Omega (shotguns)
Available through Kassnar Imports

Osborne's (Hammerli handguns)
P.O. Box 408
Cheboygan, Wisconsin 49721
(616) 625-9626

Outdoor Sports Headquarters, Inc. (Bersa handguns, Charles Daly shotguns)
P.O. Box 1327
967 Watertower Lane
Dayton, Ohio 45401
(513) 865-5855

Outers (gun care products)
See Omark Industries

Parker Hale (rifles)
Available through Precision Sports

Penguin Industries, Inc. (Hoppe's gun care products)
Airport Industrial Mall
Coatesville, Pennsylvania 19320
(215) 384-6000

Perazzi (shotguns)
206 South George Street
Rome, New York 13440
(315) 337-8566

Perugini-Visini (shotguns)
Available through Armes de Chasse

Piotti (shotguns)
Available through Kassnar Imports

Precision Sales International (Anschutz pistols, rifles)
P.O. Box 1776
Westfield, Massachusetts 01086
(413) 562-5055

Precision Sports (Parker-Hale rifles)
P.O. Box 5588, Kellogg Road
Cortland, New York 13045-5588
(607) 756-2851

Quality Arms (Bernardelli shotguns)
P.O. Box 19477
Houston, Texas 77224
(713) 870-8377

RCBS, Inc. (reloading tools)
See Omark Industries, Inc.

Redding-Hunter, Inc. (reloading tools)
114 Starr Road
Cortland, New York 13045
(607) 753-3331

Redfield (sights, scopes)
5800 East Jewell Avenue
Denver, Colorado 80224
(303) 757-6411

Remington Arms Company, Inc. (rifles, shotguns, ammunition, primers)
939 Barnum Avenue
Bridgeport, Connecticut 06601
(203) 333-1112

Rossi (handguns, rifles, shotguns)
Available through Interarms

Rottweil (shotguns)
Available through Dynamit Nobel of America, Inc.

Ruger (handguns, rifles, shotguns, black powder guns)
See Sturm, Ruger & Company, Inc.

RWS (ammunition)
Available through Dynamit Nobel

Saki International (Brno handguns, rifles)
19800 Center Ridge Road
P.O. Box 16189
Rocky River, Ohio 44116
(216) 331-3533

Sako (rifles, actions, scope mounts)
Available through Stoeger Industries

Sauer (rifles)
Available through Sigarms, Inc.

Savage Arms (rifles, shotguns, Stevens & Fox)
Springdale Road
Westfield, Massachusetts 01085
(413) 562-2361

Schmidt and Bender (scopes)
Available through Paul Jaeger, Inc.

C. Sharps Arms Co., Inc. (black powder rifles)
P.O. Box 885
Big Timber, Montana 59011
(406) 932-4353

Shotguns of Ulm (shotguns)Available through
Krieghoff International

Sierra Bullets (bullets)
10537 S. Painter Avenue
Santa Fe Springs, California, 90670
(213) 941-0251

Sigarms Inc. (Sig-Sauer handguns, Sauer rifles)
8330 Old Courthouse Road, Suite 885
Tyson's Corner, Virginia 22180
(703) 893-1940

Sig-Sauer (handguns)
Available through Sigarms Inc.

Simmons Outdoor Corp.
14205 SW 119th Ave.
Miami, Florida 33186
(305) 252-0477

Smith & Wesson (handguns)
2100 Roosevelt Avenue
Springfield, Massachusetts 01101
(413) 781-8300

Southern Gun Distributors (Sovereign rifles, shotguns, scopes)
13490 N.W. 45th Avenue
Opa-Locke (Miami), Florida 33054-0025
1-800-327-8500

Sovereign (rifles, shotguns, scopes)
Available through Southern Gun Distributors

Speer (bullets)
See Omark Industries, Inc.

Springfield Armory (rifles, paramilitary, Bernardelli handguns, rifles, shotguns, paramilitary)
420 West Main Street
Geneseo, Illinois 61254
(309) 944-5138

Star (handguns)
Available through Interarms

Stevens (rifles, shotguns)
Available through Savage Arms

Steyr (handguns, paramilitary)
Available through Gun South Inc.

Steyr Mannlicher (rifles, paramilitary)
Available through Gun South Inc.

Stoeger Industries (Llama handguns, shotguns, Sako rifles, scope mounts, actions)
55 Ruta Court
South Hackensack, New Jersey 07606
(201) 440-2700

Sturm, Ruger and Company, Inc. (Ruger handguns, black powder guns, rifles, shotguns)
Lacey Place
Southport, Connecticut 06490
(203) 259-7843

Swarovski Optik (scopes)
1 Kenney Drive
Cranston, Rhode Island 02920
(401) 463-6400

Tanarmi and Targa (pistols)
Available through Southern Gun Distributors

Tasco (scopes)
7600 N.W. 26th Street
Miami, Florida 33122
(305) 591-3670

Taurus International, Inc. (Taurus handguns)
4563 Southwest 71st Street
Miami, Florida 33155
(305) 662-2529

Thompson/Center Arms (handguns, black powder guns, paramilitary)
Farmington Road, P.O. Box 2426
Rochester, New Hampshire 03867
(603) 332-2333

Tikka (rifles, shotguns)
SF-41160
Tikkakoshi, Finland

Traditions, Inc. (black powder)
Saybrook Road
Haddam, Connecticut 06438
(203) 345-8561

Uberti & Company (black powder rifles, revolvers)
Available through Benson Firearms

U.S. Repeating Arms Co. (Winchester rifles, shotguns)
275 Winchester Avenue
New Haven, Connecticut 06504
(203) 789-5000

UZI (paramilitary)
Available through Action Arms Ltd.

Valmet, Inc. (rifles, shotguns, paramilitary)
7 Westchester Plaza
Elmsford, New York 10523
(914) 347-4440

Ventura Imports (shotguns)
P.O. Box 2782
Seal Beach, California 90740
(213) 596-5372

Walther (handguns)
Available through Interarms

Weatherby, Inc. (rifles, shotguns, scopes, ammunition)
2781 Firestone Boulevard
South Gate, California 90280
(213) 569-7186

Weaver Arms (rifles)
115 North Market Place
Escondido, California 92025
(800) 227-4896

Weaver (mount rings)
See Omark Industries

Dan Wesson Arms, Inc. (handguns)
293 Main Street
Monson, Massachusetts 01057
(413) 267-4081

Whitworth (rifles)
Available through Interarms

Williams Gun Sight Co. (sights, scopes, mounts)
7389 Lapeer Road
Davison, Michigan 48423
(313) 653-2131

Winchester (ammunition, primers, cases, imported shotguns)
See Olin/Winchester

Winchester (domestic rifles, shotguns)
See U.S. Repeating Arms Co.

Winslow Arms Co. (rifles)
P.O. Box 783
Camden, South Carolina 29020
(803) 432-2938

Zeiss Optical, Inc. (scopes)
P.O. Box 2010
Petersburg, Virginia 23804
(800) 446-1807

Angelo Zoli (shotguns)
1200 Aerowood Drive #47
Mississauga, Ontario L4W 257
Canada

GUNFINDER

To help you find the model of your choice, the following list includes each gun found in the catalog section of **Shooter's Bible 1988**. A supplemental listing of **Discontinued Models** and the **Caliberfinder** follow immediately after this section.

BLACK POWDER GUNS

MUSKETS AND RIFLES

Armsport
Tryon Trailblazer	368
Hawken Model 5101-5104	369

CVA
Squirrel	372
Blazer II	372
St. Louis Hawken	372
Missouri Ranger	373
Hawken	373
Kentucky	373
Pennsylvania Long	374
Express Double Barrel	374
Double Barrel Carbine	375

Dixie
Second Model Brown Bess	381
Kentuckian Flintlock/Perc.	381
Hawken	382
Tennessee Mountain	382
Tennessee Squirrel	382
Lancaster Co., Pennsylvania	382
Mississippi Rifle	383
Winchester '73 Carbine	383
Wesson	383
Buffalo Hunter	383

Euroarms
Hawken	386
London Armory Company	386
Cook & Brother Confederate Carbine	386
London Armory Company (two-band)	387
London Armory Company Enfield Musketoon	387

Hopkins & Allen
Brush Rifle Model 345	388
Scheutzen	388
Underhammer Model 32	389
Pennsylvania Hawken Model 29	389

Lyman
Great Plains	390
Trade	390

Michigan Arms
Wolverine	391
Silverwolf	391
Friendship Special Match	391

Navy Arms
Whitworth Military Target	397
Parker-Hale 451 Volunteer	397
Swiss Federal Target	397
Ithaca/Navy Hawken	397
#2 Creedmoor Target	398
Rolling Block	398
Country Boy	398
1853 Enfield	399
1858 Enfield	399
1861 Enfield Musketoon	399
1863 Springfield	399
Mississippi Model 1841	400
Rigby-Style Target	400
Brown Bess Musket	401
Morse Muzzleloading	401
Kentucky	401
Henry Military	402
Iron Frame Henry	402
Henry Trapper	402
Henry Carbine	402
Henry Carbine Engraved	402

Shiloh Sharps
Model 1874 Business	403
Model 1874 Military	403
Model 1874 Carbine	403
Model 1874 Sporting #1	404
Model 1874 Sporting #3	404
Model 1863 Sporting	404

Thompson/Center
Cougar Hawken	405
Hawken	405
New Englander	405
Renegade	406
Renegade Hunter	406
Cherokee	406

Traditions
Frontier Scout	407
Hunter	407
Hawken	407
Hawken Woodsman	408
Pennsylvania	408
Shenandoah	408
Single Barrel Fowler	409
Trapper	409

A. Uberti
1858 New Army Target Revolving Carbine	410
Santa Fe Hawken	410

PISTOLS

CVA
Prospector	376
Hawken	376
Kentucky	376
Colonial	376
Philadelphia Derringer	376

Dixie
Screw Barrel Derringer	380
French Charleville Flint	380
"Hideout" Derringer	380
Lincoln Derringer	380
Pennsylvania	380
Overcoat Pistol	380
Abilene Derringer	380

Hopkins & Allen
Model 10	388
Boot Pistol	388

Lyman
Plains Pistol	390

Navy Arms
LePage Flintlock	395
LePage Percussion	395
LePage Double Cased Set	395
Kentucky	396
Harper's Ferry	396
Elgin Cutlass	396

Thompson/Center
Patriot	404

Traditions
Trapper	409

REVOLVERS

Armsport
Models 5133/5136/5138/5120/5139	370
Models 5152/5153/5154	371

CVA
1861 Colt Navy	377
1851 Colt Navy	377
Colt Sheriff's Model	377
1858 Remington Army	377
1860 Colt Army	377
1858 Remington Army	378
Colt Walker	378
Pocket Remington	378

Dixie
1860 Army	379
Navy Revolver	379
Spiller & Burr	379
Wyatt Earp	379
Walker	380
Third Model Dragoon	380

Euroarms
Rogers & Spencer	384
Rogers & Spencer Army	384
Rogers & Spencer Model 1007	384
New Model Army	384
New Model Army Model 1034	384
New Model Army Engraved	384
New Model Army Target	385
Remington 1858 Model 1046	385
1851 Navy Sheriff	385
1851 Navy Sheriff Model 1090	385
1851 Navy	385
Schneider & Glassick Confederate	385

Navy Arms
Lemat	392
Colt Walker 1847	392
1862 Police	392
Reb Model 1860	393
Colt Army 1860	393
1851 Navy Yank	393
Rogers & Spencer Navy	393
Stainless Steel 1858 Remington	393
Target Model Remington	394
Deluxe 1858 Remington-Style	394
Remington New Model Army	394
Army 60 Sheriff's	394

A. Uberti
1st, 2nd & 3rd Model Dragoons	410
1861 Navy	410

SHOTGUNS

Armsport
Models 5124 & 5125	369

CVA
Brittany 12 Ga. Percussion	374
Trapper	375

Dixie
Double Barrel Magnum	381

Euroarms
Magnum Cape Gun	387

Navy Arms
Model T&T	400

Thompson/Center
New Englander	405

DOUBLE RIFLE

Iver Johnson
Model BP.50HB	389

RIFLE/SHOTGUN COMBINATION

Armsport
Models 5110, 5115	368

HANDGUNS

PISTOLS

Action Arms
Models AT-84 & AT-84P	92

American Derringer
Model 1	92
Model 3	93
Model 4	93
Model 6	93
Model 11	92
Semmerling LM-4	94

DISCONTINUED MODELS

The following models, all of which appeared in the 1987 edition of Shooter's Bible, have been discontinued by their manufacturers and/or distributors and do not appear in this year's edition.

BLACK POWDER

CVA
Frontier Rifle
1861 Colt Navy Revolver
Dixie
Sharps Military Carbine
Euroarms
Double Barrel Percussion Shotgun
Navy Arms
Moore & Patrick English Flint & Percussion
Pistol
Left Hand Hawken
Morse/Navy Single Barrel Percussion 12 Ga.
Shotgun
Thompson/Center
Seneca Rifle
Traditions
Kentucky Scout Rifle

HANDGUNS

Advantage Arms
Model 422
Bersa
Model 224
Browning
22 Challenger III Sporter
Charter Arms
Model 40
Colt
Trooper MKV
Commando Special D Frame (DA)

Detonics
Pocket 9 (9mm Para)
Heckler & Koch
Model P9S (9mm Auto)
Interarms
Virginian Revolvers
L.A.R.
Mark II Grizzly Win. Mag.
Stoeger
Llama Omni (45 & 9mm DA Auto)
North American
Model 450 Magnum Express (SA Revolver)
Rossi
Model M84 Revolver
Model 841 Revolver
Model 941 Revolver
Ruger
Redhawk DA (357 Mag.)
Smith & Wesson
Model 38 Chief's Special Airweight
Model 12 (38 Military & Police Airweight)

RIFLES

Anschutz
Model 1403DL (Left) Target
Model 1433D 22H Sporter
Beretta
Models 500/501/502 Bolt Action
Browning
Model 1886 (Grade I & High Grade)
BSA
Model CF2 Stutzen/Hunting
Model CFT Target

DuBiel Arms
Classic Model
Heckler & Koch
Models 630/770/940
Models SL7/SL6
K.D.F./Voere
Model 2005 Semiautomatic
Kimber
Model 84 Cascade
Mark X
Viscount Model
Maunz
Model 77 Service Match
Model 87 20th Century Match
Model 67 Assault Sniper
Savage/Stevens
Model 35
Thompson/Center
Aristocrat Model
Tikka
Model M07 Shotgun-Rifle

SHOTGUNS

Armsport
Over/Under Single Trigger Skeet
Hammerless Side-by-Side
Wild Boar Slug
Folding Single & Over/Under
Beretta
Model A302 Multi-Choke
Model A302 Slug
Bernardelli
Italia & Italia Extra

Browning
Superposed Continental
Superposed Pigeon, Pointer, Diana & Midas
Grades

Charles Daly
Over/Under Presentation Grade
Over/Under Diamond 3″

Churchill
Windsor Side-by-Side Grade II

Exel
Models 301, 302 (Series 300 Over/Under)

Franchi
Diamond Over/Under

Ithaca
Single Barrel Trap (Dollar Grade & 5E Grade)
Model 37 (M & P Featherlight, Field Grade,
Ultralite and English Ultralite Pumps)

Model 51A Turkey Gun, Waterfowler,
Supreme Trap and Supreme Skeet
Mag-10 (Standard, Deluxe, Supreme and
Roadblocker Models)

Krieghoff
Model ULM-S Over/Under Sidelock Skeet
(Standard and Bavaria)
Model ULM-T Over/Under Sidelock Live Trap
(Standard and Bavaria)

Mauser
Over/Under Model Contest & Contest Trap
Sidelock Side-by-Side Model Bristol

Mossberg
Model 712 Camo Speedfeed
Model 500 Hi-Rib Trap

Olin/Winchester
Grand European Trap Standard & Skeet Gun
Special Edition Grand European
Featherweight

Model 23 Pigeon Grade Side-by-Side &
Limited Edition

Remington
Model 870 Wingmaster Field Gun (Left Hand
Model)
Sportsman 12 Ga. Pump & Autoloader

Rottweil
Model 650 Field
Adjustable American Trap Combo

Valmet
Lightweight Field Grade

Weatherby
Orion Over/Under IMC Field Grade & IMC
Trap Grade

Angelo Zoli
Model HK2000 Semiautomatic

CALIBERFINDER

How to use this guide: To find a 22LR handgun, look under that heading below. You'll find several models of that description, including Beretta Model 21. Turn next to the **Gunfinder** section and locate the heading for **Beretta** (pistols, in this case). Beretta's **Model 21**, as indicated, appears on p. 98.

BLACK POWDER

HANDGUNS

31

CVA Pocket Remington

32

Dixie Tennessee Squirrel

36

Armsport Model 5133/5135
CVA 1851 & 1861 Colt Navy Revolvers/Sheriff's Model/
Dixie Navy Revolver/Spiller & Burr Revolver
Euroarms 1851 Navy & Navy Sheriff/Schneider & Glassick
Navy Arms 1862 Police Revolver/Reb Model 1860/Army 60 Sheriff's Moder/"Yank" Revolver/1851 Navy Yank/Remington New Model Army
Thompson/Center Patriot
Traditions Trapper
A. Uberti 1861 Navy

41

Dixie Abilene & Lincoln Derringers

44

Armsport Models 5138/5120/5134/5136/5139/5152/5135/5136
CVA Prospector/1861 Colt Navy/1860 Colt Army Revolvers/Colt Walker
Dixie Walker Revolver/Pennsylvania Pistol/Third Model Dragoon
Euroarms Rogers & Spencer Models 1005 & 1006/New Model Army (and Target)/Remington 1858 New Model/1851 Navy Sheriff/Schneider & Glassick
Hopkins & Allen Model 10/Yank Revolver
Navy Arms Colt Walker 1847/Reb Model 1860 Revolver/Colt Army 1860 Revolver/Rogers & Spencer Navy Revolver/Target Model Remington Revolver/Army 60 Sheriff's Model/Stainless Steel 1858 Remington/Remington New Model Army/LeMat Revolvers/1851 Navy Yank Revolver/LePage Dueling Pistol
A. Uberti 1st Model Dragoon

45

CVA Kentucky/Colonial/Philadelphia Derringer
Dixie "Wyatt Earp" Revolver
Hopkins & Allen Boot Pistol Model 13
Navy Arms LePage Perc. & Flint Pistols/Moore & Patrick English Pistols/Double Cased LePage Pistols
Thompson/Center Patriot Pistol
Traditions Trapper

50

CVA Hawken
Lyman Plains Pistol
Traditions Trapper

54

Lyman Plains Pistol

58

Navy Arms Harper's Ferry Pistols

RIFLES

32

CVA Squirrel
Navy Arms Country Boy
Thompson/Center Cherokee

36

Armsport Model 5108
Hopkins & Allen Brush Rifle/Model 32
Navy Arms Mule Ear Mountaineers Squirrel Rifle/Country Boy
Thompson/Center Seneca
Traditions Trapper

44

Navy Arms Henry Carbine

44-40

Dixie Winchester '73 Carbine
Navy Arms Henry Carbine/Henry Trapper

45

Armsport Models 5108/5110/5111/5101
CVA Kentucky/Frontier (kit)
Dixie Kentuckian (Rifle & Carbine) Hawken
Hopkins & Allen Brush Rifle/Schuetzen/Model 32
Michigan Arms Wolverine/Silverwolf
Navy Arms Morse Muzzleloading Rifle/Kentucky/Country Boy/Mule Ear Mountaineer's Squirrel Rifle
Thompson/Center Seneca/Cougar/Hawken/Cherokee/Hawken
Traditions Frontier Scout/Hawken/Pennsylvania/Kentucky Scout/Trapper

451

Navy Arms Rigby-Style Target Rifle/Whitworth Military Target/Parker-Hale 451 Volunteer

50

Armsport Models 5109/5110A/5102/5104
CVA Frontier/Blazer II/St. Louis Hawken/Pennsylvania Long Rifle, Missouri Ranger/Hawken/Express Double Rifle & Carbine
Dixie Hawken/Tennessee Mountain/Wesson
Euroarms Model 2210A Hawken
Hopkins & Allen Model 32/29
Iver Johnson Model BP .50HB
Lyman Great Plains/Trade Rifle
Michigan Arms Wolverine/Silverwolf
Navy Arms Morse Muzzleloading Rifle/Kentucky/Ithaca-Navy Hawken/Country Boy
Thompson/Center Renegade/Cougar Hawken/Hawken/New Englander
Traditions Frontier Scout/Hunter/Hawken/Pennsylvania/Kentucky Scout/Shenandoah/Trapper

54

Armsport Model 5103/5204B
CVA Hawken
Dixie Hawken
Lyman Great Plains/Trade Rifle
Michigan Arms Wolverine/Silverwolf
Navy Arms Ithaca-Navy Hawken
Shiloh Sharps Model 1863/Military Carbine
Thomspon/Center Renegade/Hawken/Sharps Model 1863
A. Uberti Santa Fe Hawken

58

Dixie Buffalo Hunter/Hawken
Euroarms Model 2260 London Armory Company Enfield Rifled Musket/Models 2270 and 2280 London Armory Company Enfield Rifled Muskets/Model 2300 Cook & Brother Confederate Carbine
Hopkins & Allen Model 32
Navy Arms Morse Muzzleloading Rifle/1863 Springfield/Mississippi Model 1841
Traditions Hawken Perc. Rifle

74

Dixie Second Model Brown Bess Musket

75

Navy Arms Brown Bess Musket

557

Navy Arms 1853 Enfield Rifle Musket/1858 Enfield/1861 Enfield Musketoon

SHOTGUNS (Black Powder)

Armsport Models 5115/5124/5125
CVA 12-Gauge Percussion/Trapper
Dixie Double Barrel Magnum 12-Gauge
Euroarms Model 2290 12-Gauge/Model 2295 Magnum Cape
Iver Johnson Model BP .50HB
Navy Arms Morse Single Barrel 12-Gauge/Classic 12-Gauge Side-by-Side/Hunter/Fowler
Thompson/Center New Englander

HANDGUNS

22LR

American Derringer Model 1, Model 7
Astra Constable
Beeman FAS 602, Korth, Unique 69 Target, Deluxe Metallic Silhouette
Beretta Model 21
Berbardelli Model 80, 100
Bersa Model 224 DA
Browning Buck Mark 22
Charter Arms Pathfinder
Dakota Model 1873, Dakota Target
Davis Model D-22
F.I.E. Arminius, Titan II
Freedom Arms FA-S, FA-BG, FA-L
Hammerli Models 150, 152, 208, 215

CALIBERFINDER

Iver Johnson Pocket, Trailsman
Llama Automatic (Small Frame)
Navy Arms Luger Automatic
North American Arms Mini-Revolvers
Rossi Model 511
Ruger New Model Single-Six, Mark II
Sako Olympic Triace
Smith & Wesson Models 422, 41, 34, 63, 17
Tanarmie Model TA 76
Targa Model GT22T
Thompson/Center Contender
A. Uberti DA Automatics (Models PP, P-38, TPH, GSP Match, GSP Jr., U.I.T.-BV
Ruger New Model Single-Six

22 Rimfire Magnum
American Derringer Model 1
Smith & Wesson Models 650/651
Dan Wesson 22 Rimfire Magnum

22 Short
Beeman FAS 601, Unique 2000-U
Beretta Model 950
Hammerli Model 232
North American Arms Mini Revolvers

22 Hornet
American Derringer Model 1
MAO Maximum

22 Win. Mag.
Charter Arms Pathfinder
Dakota Model 1873
Davis Model D-22
A. Uberti 1873 Stallion
Dan Wesson 22 Mag.

22 WMR
F.I.E. Arminius
Freedom Arms FA-S, FA-L, FA-BG, FA-LRCYL
North American Arms Mini-Revolvers
Ruger New Model Single-Six
Thompson/Center Contender

25 Colt
Beretta Model 950
Davis Model D-22
F.I.E. Titan, Model A27BW
Iver Johnson Pocket
Targa Model GT25S

221 Fireball
Kimber Predator

222 Rem
Thompson/Center Contender

223 Rem
Kimber Predator
Remington Model XP-100
Thompson/Center Contender

223 Rem Comm. Auto
American Derringer Model 1
Thompson/Center Contender

30 Luger
American Derringer Model 1

30 Carbine
Ruger Model BN-31 Blackhawk SA

30-30 Win
American Derringer Model 1
Thompson/Center Contender

32 Mag
American Derringer Model 1, Model 7
Dan Wesson 32 Mag. Six-Shot

32 Auto
Davis Models D-22, P-32
F.I.E. Titan II, Super Titan II

32 H&R
Charter Arms Police Bulldog, Police Undercover
Ruger New Model Single-Six SSM
Thompson/Center Contender

32 S&W Long
American Derringer Model 7
Charter Arms Undercover
F.I.E. Armenius
Sako Olympic Triace
Smith & Wesson Model 31
Taurus Model 73
Walther GSP-C

35 Remington
Remington Model XP-100
Thompson/Center Contender

357 Mag
American Derringer Model 1
Astra 357 mag.
Beeman Korth
Charter Arms Bulldog Tracker
Colt King Cobra, Python, Peacekeeper
Coonan Arms Model B
Dakota Target, Bisley, 1875 Outlaw. Model 1873
F.I.E. Arminius
L.A.R. Grizzly Mark I
Llama Super Comanche V, Comanche III
Magnum Research Desert Eagle
Ruger Speed-Six, GP-100, Service Six, New Model Bisley Blackhawk, Blackhawk SA
Smith & Wesson Models 19, 65, 13, 586, 27
Taurus Models 65, 66
Thompson/Center Contender
A. Uberti 1875 Remington Army Outlaw
Dan Wesson 357 Mag, 357 Super Mag.

357 Maximum
American Derringer Model 1

358 Win
MAO Maximum

38 Special
American Derringer Models 1, 7, 11, 3
Charter Arms Police Undercover, Undercover, Off-Duty
Colt Combat Commander
F.I.E. Derringer D-86, Titan Tiger, Arminius
Rossi Models 68, M951, M88, 851
Ruger Speed-Six, Service Six
Smith & Wesson Models 649, 10, 64, 15, 67, 66, 19, 65, 13
Tanarmi Model TA385B Derringer
Taurus Models 86, 80, 82, 83, 66, 85
A. Uberti 1873 Cattleman Quick Draw
Dan Wesson 38 Special Revolvers

380 Auto
American Derringer Model 1, 7
Astra Constable
Beretta Models 85BB, 84BB, 86
Bernardelli Model 80
Bersa Model 383
Browning Model BDA-380
Colt Government Model, Mustang
F.I.E. Titan II, Super Titan II
Iver Johnson Pony
Llama Automatic Small Frame
Sig Sauer Model 230
Targa Model GT380XE
Walther Models PPK/S American

38 Super
American Derringer Model 1
Sig Sauer Model 220

38 S&W
American Derringer Model 7
Smith & Wesson Models 52, 36, 60, 38, 49

41 Action Express
Action Arms Models AT-84, AT-84P

41 Mag
American Derringer Model 1
Ruger Redhawk, New Model Bisley Blackhawk, Blackhawk SA
Smith & Wesson Models 57, 657
Thompson/Center Contender
Dan Wesson 41 Mag. Revolvers

.410
American Derringer Models 1, 4, 6

9mm Luger
American Derringer Model 1
Colt Combat Commander
Smith & Wesson Models 459, 439, 469, 639, 659, 669

9mm Para
Astra Model A-90
Beretta Model SB-92F
Brno Model CZ75
Browning 9mm Hi-Power
F.I.E. Model TZ75
Mauser Luger
Iver Johnson DA 9mm Auto
Llama Automatics, Model M-82
Sig Sauer Models 220, 225, 226, P210
Springfield Armory Models 1911-A1 Standard, Star BKM & BM, Model 30M
Steyr Model GB
Tanarmi Model BTA90B
Taurus Models PT 92, PT 99
Walther Models P-38, P-88DA, P-5 DA

10mm
Colt Delta Elite

44 Magnum
American Derringer Model 1
Astra Model 44
Llama Super Comanche IV
Magnum Research Desert Eagle
Ruger Redhawk, New Model Bisley Blackhawk, Blackhawk SA
Smith & Wesson Model 29
Thompson/Center Contender
Dan Wesson 44 Mag. Revolvers

CALIBERFINDER

44 Special
American Derringer Models 1, 7
Charter Arms Bulldog

44-40
American Derringer Model 1
Dakota Models 1873, 1875 Outlaw, Bisley
A. Uberti 1873 Cattleman Quick Draw, 1875 Remington Army Outlaw

45 Auto
American Derringer Model 1
Astra Model A-90
Colt Combat Commander, Lightweight Commander, Gold Cup National Match, MKIV Series 80, Officer's ACP
Detonics Combat Master, Servicemaster II, Scoremaster, Janus Scoremaster
L.A.R. Grizzly
Llama Automatic Large Frame
Sig Sauer Model 220
Smith & Wesson Model 645
Springfield Armory Model 1911-A1 Standard, Star Model PD

45 Colt
American Derringer Models 1, 4, 6
Astra Model 45
Dakota Target, Model 1873, 1875 Outlaw, Bisley
Ruger New Model Bisley Blackhawk, Blackhawk SA
Smith & Wesson Model 25
A. Uberti 1873 Cattleman Quick Draw, 1875 Remington Army
Dan Wesson 45 Colt DA

45 Win. Mag.
American Derringer Model 1
L.A.R. Grizzly Mark I

RIFLES

CENTERFIRE BOLT ACTION RIFLES

Standard Calibers

17 Rem
Kimber Model 84
Perugini-Visini Single Shot Eagle
Sako Fiberclass/Hunter/Deluxe

22 Hornet
Beeman/Krico Models 400/420

222 Rem.
Alpha Arms Custom
Beeman/Krico Models 600/700/640 Super Sniper
Brno Model ZKK600/601/602
Churchill Regent/Highlander
K.D.F./Voere Titan Menor
Kimber Model 84
Perugini-Visini Single Shot Eagle
Sako Varmint/Fiberclass/Hunter/Deluxe
Sauer S-90
Steyr-Mannlicher Model SL
Tikka Model M55
Winslow Varmint

223 Rem.
Alpha Arms Custom/Grand Slam
Heckler & Koch Models 630/SL6
K.D.F./Voere Titan Menor
Kimber Model 84
Mark X Miniature 1500
Remington Models 700/7
Sako Fiberclass/Hunter/Varminter/Deluxe
Savage Model 1110E/11oV
Steyre-Mannlicher Model SL
Tikka Model M55
Weatherby Vanguard VGL/Fiberguard
Winchester Models 70 XTR Featherweight/Sporter Varmint/Lightweight Carbine
Winslow Varmint

22-250
Alpha Arms Custom/Grand Slam/Alaskan
Browning Short Action A-Bolt
Mark X Amiercan Field Series
Mossberg Model 1500
Parker-Hale Models M81/1000/1200/2100/1100
Perugini-Visini Single Shot Eagle
Remington Model 700
Ruger Models M-77RL/M-77RSI International/M-77V Varmint/M-77R
Sako Mannlicher-Style/Deluxe/Varminter/Carbine/Hunter/Fiberclass
Sauer Model S-90
Savage Model 110V
Steyr-Mannlicher Model L
Tikka Model M55
Weatherby Vanguard VGS/Lazermark/Euromark
Winchester Model 70 XTR Featherweight/Lightweight

243 Win.
Browning Short Action A-Bolt
Colt Sauer Short Action
Heym Models SR20/55BF/22S
K.D.F./Voere Titan
Mark X American Field Series
Mauser Models 66/77
Mossberg Model 1700LS
Parker-Hale Models M81/1000/1200/M87/1100/2100
Remington Models 700/7/4/7400/78
Ruger Models M-77RL/RS/RSI/M-77v Varmint
Sako Carbine/Varminter/Fiberclass/Hunter
Sauer Models 200/S-90 Jr.
Savage Models 110E/99C/11oK
Steyr-Mannlicher Models L/SSG Marksman/Match UIT/Luxus
Tikka Model M55
Weatherby Vanguard VGS/VGL
Winchester Models 70 XTR Featherweight/Sporter/Lightweight Carbine/Varmint/Ranger Youth
Winslow Basic/Grade Crown

6mm Rem
Parker-Hale Models M81/1000/1100/1200/2100
Remington Models 4/7/7400
Ruger Models M-77V Varmint
Steyr-Mannlicher Model L

25-06
Alpha Arms Custom/Grand Slam/Alaskan
Browning A-Bolt Action
Colt Sauer Sporting Rifles
K.D.F./Voere Model K-15/Voere Titan
Ruger Models M-77V Varmint/77RS
Sako Fiberclass/Hunter/Carbine

(Sauer Model 200)
Sauer Model 200
Steyr-Mannlicher Model M
Tikka Model M65
Weatherby Vanguard VGS
Winchester Models 70 XTR Featherweight/Sporter
Winslow Basic/Grade Crown

270 Win.
Beeman/Krico Models 600/700
Browning A-BoltAction
Churchill Regent/Highlander
Colt Sauer Sporting Rifle
Heym Model SR20
K.D.F./Voere Model K-15 Titan
Kimber Big Game
Mauser Models 66/77
Mossberg Models 1500/1700
Parker-Hale Models M81/1000/1100/1200/2100
Perugini-Visini Boxlock Express/Single Shot Eagle
Remington Models 4/78/700/740
Sako Carbine/Fiberclass/Hunter
Sauer Models 200/S-90 Stutzen
Savage Models 110CL/110E/110K
Steyr-Mannlicher Model M
Tikka Model M65
Weatherby Models Mark V Fibermark/Euromark/Vanguard VGS/VGL
Winchester Models 70 XTR Featherweight/Winlite/Ranger
Winslow Basic/Grade Crown

280 Rem.
Kimber Big Game
Remington Model 4
Windlow Basic/Grade Crown

308 Win.
Beeman/Krico Models 600/700/650 Super Sniper
Heym Models SR20/55BF
K.D.F./Voere Model K-15/Titan
Mauser Models 66/77/83
Mossberg Model 1500
Parker-Hale Models M81/1000/1100/1200/2100/M87
Remington Models 4/7/77/83
Ruger Models M-77RS/77RL/77RSI/77V Varmint
Sako Carbine/Varminter/Fiberclass/Hunter
Sauer S-90 Jr.
Savage Model 99-C
Steyr-Mannlicher Model L/SSG Marksman/Match UIT
Tikka Models M55/M65
Weatherby Vanguard VGL
Winchester Model 70 XTR Featherweight (short)
Winslow Basic/Grade Crown

30-06
Beeman/Krico Models 600/700
Browning A-Bolt Action
Churchill Regent/Highlander
Colt Sauer Sporting Rifle
Heym Models SR20/55BF
K.D.F./Voere Titan
Kimber Big Game
Mark X American Field Series
Mauser Model 66
Mossberg Models 1500/1700LS
Parker-Hale Model M81 Classic
Perugini-Visini Single Shot Eagle
Remington Models 4/78/700/7400
Ruger Models M-77RS/77RL
Sako Carbine/Fiberclass/Hunter

CALIBERFINDER

Sauer Models 200/S-90 Stutzen
Savage Models 100CL/110E/110K
Steyr-Mannlicher Model M
Tikka Model M65
Weatherby Mark V Fibermark/
Euromark/Vanguard VGS/VGL
Winchester Models 70 XTR Featherweight/
Winlite/Sporter/
Lightweight Carbine/Ranger
Winslow Basic/Grade Crown

MAGNUM CALIBERS

7mm Rem. Mag.

Browning A-Bolt Action
Churchill Regent/Highlander
Colt Sauer Sporting Rifle
Heym Model SR20
K.D.F./Voere Titan
Kimber Big Game
Mark X American Field Series
Parker-Hale Model M81 Classic
Perugini-Visini Boxlock
Express/Over-Under/Sidelock
Remington Model 700
Ruger Model M-77RS/77RL
Sako Fiberclass/Hunter/Carbine/Deluxe
Sauer Model S-90 Magnum
Savage Model 110E
Steyr Mannlicher Models S/T
Tikka Model M65
Weatherby Mark V Fibermark/Euromark/
Vanguard VGL
Winchester Model 70 XTR Sporter/Winlite
Standard/Ranger
Winslow Basic/Grade Crown

300 Win. Mag.

Browning A-Bolt Action
Colt Sauer Sporting Rifle
Heym Model SR20
K.D.F./Voere Titan
Kimber Big Game
Parker-Hale Model M81 Classic/M87
Perugini-Visini Single Shot Eagle
Ruger Model M-77RS/77R
Sako Safari Grade, Fiberclass, Hunter
Steyr Mannlicher Model S/T Magnum/Luxus
Tikka Model M65
Weatherby Mark V Fibermark, Euromark,
Vanguard VGS
Whitworth/Mark X American Field Series
Winchester Model 70 XTR Sporter Magnum
Winslow Basic, Grade Crown

338 Win. Mag.

Browning A-Bolt Action
Kimber Big Game
Perugini-Visini Boxlock Express/Sidelock
Ruger Model M-77RS, 77R, 77RL
Sako Safari Grade, Hunter, Carbine, Deluxe All,
Fiberclass
Savage Model 110K
Steyr Mannlicher Model S/T
Tikka Model M65
Winchester Model 70 Winlite
Winslow Basic, Grade Crown

375 H&H

Heym Model SR20 & 88 Safari
K.D.F. Model K-15/Voere Titan
Kimber Big Game
Parker-hale Model M81 African
Perugini-Visini Boxlock Express/Double Rifle
Express

Sako Safari Grade, Carbine, Fiberclass/Hunter
Saver S-90 Magnum
Steyr Mannlicher Model S/T
Winchester Model 70 XTR Super Express
(Standard)
Winslow Basic, Grade Crown

.411 KDF

K.D.F./Voere Dangerous Game Rifle

458 Win. Mag.

Colt Sauer Safari
Heym Model 88 Safari
Perugini-Visini Boxlock Express/Sidelock/Double
Rifle Express
Ruger Model M-77RS Tropical
Sauer S-90 Safari
Whitworth/Mark X Express
Winchester Model 70 XTR Super Express
(Standard)
Winslow Basic, Grade Crown

CENTERFIRE LEVER ACTION

222 Rem./223 Rem.

Browning Model 81 BLR

22-250

Browning Model 81 BLR & 1885

257 Roberts

Browning Model 81 BLR

243 Win.

Browning Model 81 BLR
Ruger Model No. 1 International

270

Browning Model 1885
Ruger Model No. 1 International

307 Win.

Winchester Model 94

30-30 Win.

Marlin Models 336CS, 336TS, 30AS
Winchester Model 94 Standard, XTR, Trapper,
Ranger

30-06

Browning Model 1885
Ruger Model No. 1 International

348 Win.

Browning Model 71

38 Special

Marlin Model 1894S
Rossi Puma
A. Uberti 1866 Sporting/1873 Carbine

356 Win.

Marlin Model 336ER
Winchester Model 94

357 Win.

Winchester Model 94

357 Mag.

Browning Model 92
Marlin Model 1894CS
Rossi Puma

358 Win.

Browning Model 81 BLR

375 Win.

Marlin Model 336CS

44 Special

Marlin Model 1894S

44 Rem. Mag.

Browning Model 92
Marlin Model 1894S
Winchester Model 94 Standard

444 Marlin

Marlin Model 444SS

45-70 Government

Browning Model 1885
Marlin Model 1895SS

7mm Rem. Mag.

Browning Models 1885/81 BLR

SLIDE ACTION

6m Rem.

Remington Models 6, 7600

243 Win.

Remington Models 6, 7600

270 Win.

Remington Models 6, 7600

30-06 & 30-06 Accelerator

Remington Models 6, 7600

30-08 Springfield

Remington Model 76

SINGLE SHOT

222 Rem.

Remington Model 40-XB
Savage Model 340

243 Win.

Remington Model 40-XB
Ruger No. 1 Light Sporter
T/C Hunger/Contender/781

22-250 Rem.

Remington Model 40-XB
Ruger No. 1 Standard & Special Varminter
T/C Hunter

6mm Rem.

Remington Model 40-XB
Ruger No. 1 International

270 Win.

Ruger No. 1 Light Sporter & Standard

30-30 Win.

Mossberg Model 479
Savage Model 340

30-06

Remington Model 40-XB
Ruger No. 1 Light Sporter & Standard
T/C Hunter

CALIBERFINDER

INDEX